STUDIES IN THE HISTORY OF MUSIC . 2
LEWIS LOCKWOOD AND CHRISTOPH WOLFF
GENERAL EDITORS

MUSIC IN RENAISSANCE FERRARA, 1400–1505.

THE CREATION OF A MUSICAL CENTER IN THE FIFTEENTH CENTURY

LEWIS LOCKWOOD

HARVARD UNIVERSITY PRESS
CAMBRIDGE, MASSACHUSETTS
1984

Library of Congress Cataloging in Publication Data
Lockwood, Lewis.
Music in Renaissance Ferrara 1400–1505.
Includes index.
1. Music – Italy – Ferrara – 15th century – History and
criticism.   I. Title.
ML290.8.F45L6   1984b   780'.945'45   84-4671
ISBN 0-674-59131-3

Published in the United Kingdom by Oxford University Press 1984
Published in the United States by Harvard University Press 1984

Printed in Great Britain
10   9   8   7   6   5   4   3   2   1

To Nino Pirrotta

Preface

THE project from which this book derives began as an attempt to enlarge our knowledge of one of the more prominent Italian local settings for the career and work of Josquin Desprez. In 1968, after a period of participation in work aimed at developing purely systematic and computer-aided procedures for analysis of Josquin's music, I turned back to my more deeply rooted interest in studying the music of the fifteenth and sixteenth centuries in its authentic historical contexts. Attracted at first by the problem of the origins of Josquin's Mass for Duke Ercole I d'Este – the celebrated *Missa 'Hercules Dux Ferrarie'* – and by some important new documents on Josquin and Ferrara that had then been recently discovered by the eminent Josquin scholar, Professor Helmuth Osthoff, I decided to try to open up the field encompassed by Ferrara as a musical center, through close documentary research on its role as a seat of musical life and patronage in this period. In early planning for this project I felt a sense of returning to a new vein in the rich lode of Italian historical and musical source-materials in which I had previously worked on other topics, ranging from the music of the Counter-Reformation to music at the Friulian town of Cividale. For wise and generous advice at this stage I was and am grateful to Professor Nino Pirrotta, then at Harvard. What I owe to him, well beyond the dedication of this book and this brief tribute, is more than I can hope to repay.

Although Josquin continued to loom large in research for this project – as he does in this book – and although new documents about Josquin and the Ferrarese court actually came to light during my very first days of work in the Archivio di Stato in Modena – inevitably the topic broadened as I continued my work at Modena and elsewhere in Italy. I found, as no doubt others have before me, how vast are the archival materials for a truly documentary study of any phase of life at the Ferrarese court; and that the surviving music manuscripts and, especially, the archival documentation, including payment records, contemporary chronicles, and letters from, to, and about musicians and patrons, made up a vast mosaic that took time and patience to form into a larger and intelligible pattern. The result, as presented in this book and in articles published earlier, constitutes the first extended and detailed documentary study of Ferrara as a musical center in the fifteenth century – its first and possibly its greatest period of cultural growth. I found too that the topic spills over the normally accepted boundaries of the discipline of music history, and that it contributes directly to what we may call the core history of the development of Ferrara, as well as to its place in the Italian Renaissance altogether. My close colleagues in this enterprise are therefore not only my fellow music historians working on comparable projects – Frank D'Accone (Florence), William Prizer (Mantua), Allan Atlas (Naples), and Richard Sherr (Rome), to mention only a few – but also those specialists in other historical fields who are at work on Ferrara or its many cultural developments. Above all here I must mention Werner Gundersheimer and Charles Rosenberg, from both of whom I have gained much valuable insight. Among other scholars to whom I owe equal debts are Maestro Adriano Franceschini, who provided me with generous help based on his unrivalled knowledge of Ferrarese notarial records; also Dr Luciano Chiappini, Vincent Ilardi, and Dr Luciano Capra, the latter in his capacity as Director of the Biblioteca Comunale Ariostea in Ferrara. And I owe special personal debts to Dr Adriano Cavicchi, whose love for his native Ferrara and knowledge of its past and present were of great help to me.

For aiding my work in the vast repository of documents housed in the Archivio di Stato in Modena, I am especially indebted to its former director, Dr Filippo Valenti, and to his successor, Dr Angelo Spaggiari. I remember with particular pleasure the careful and painstaking attention given to my early search for documents by Signor Lodi of the staff of the archive. At the Biblioteca Estense, comparable aid was extended by its staff, above all by Dr Selmi and Dottoressa Alessandra Chiarelli.

A project as broad as this relies, too, on the help and advice of many friends and colleagues. I include among the latter a number of former graduate students, especially those who were members of several graduate seminars on topics that grew out of this project, which I gave at Princeton University and more recently at Harvard. Besides the colleagues already named, I am grateful for assistance of various kinds to others, including Alberto Gallo, Jeremy Noble, Herbert Kellman, Keith Polk, and Isabelle Cazeaux. Among former graduate students who have subsequently done important work of their own on topics related to this one, I must mention especially Christopher Reynolds and Michael Long. Another former graduate student, Jessie Ann Owens, is now undertaking the formidable task of carrying forward basic documentary research on Ferrarese music and musicians into the mid-sixteenth century; her work will thus form a potential bridge between the period covered by this project and the highly valuable work carried out some years earlier by Anthony Newcomb for his important book *The Madrigal at Ferrara, 1579–1597*.

I am greatly indebted to the staff of Oxford University Press for their assistance in the publication of this book, and wish to thank Dr David Butchart for his painstaking and exemplary editorial work.

I am grateful too for the fellowship and travel support that were needed for this project, provided by the American Council of Learned Societies, the National Endowment for the Humanities, the American Philosophical Society, and the John Simon Guggenheim Memorial Foundation. The directors and staff of the Harvard Research Center at the Villa I Tatti made me a welcome guest during my year of residence in Florence in 1973–4. Finally, I am grateful above all to my wife, Doris Lockwood, whose work as a psychologist with families and children in Italy may have helped balance my work with aspects of their cultural history, while we were living in Italy for extended periods during the years from 1968 to 1974. To her, and to my children, Alison and Daniel, I am indebted in more ways than I can possibly express.

L. L.

Cambridge, Massachusetts

Contents

∾

Preface   vii
List of Illustrations   xiv
List of Tables   xvi
List of Music Examples   xvii
Archival References   xix
Music Manuscripts   xx

Introduction   1

PART ONE

MUSIC AT FERRARA IN THE EARLY FIFTEENTH CENTURY

1. Ferrara and the Trecento Background   7
2. Ferrara under Niccolò III d'Este (1393–1429)   11
      Music in the Earlier Years of Niccolò III (1400–29)   16
      Music at the Cathedral: Bartolomeo da Bologna (1405–27)   17

THE PERIOD OF LEONELLO D'ESTE (1429–50)

3. Ferrara in the 1430s   28
      The Council of Ferrara (1438)   30
4. Feragut and Dufay   34
5. Leonello's Rule, 1441–50; the Court Chapel   41
6. Singers and Repertoires   46
      The Manuscript Mod B   51
7. Secular Music   64
      Groups of Secular Musicians   67
      Court Dance under Leonello   70
8. Cathedral Music   74
      Ugolino di Orvieto: Scholastic and Humanistic Views of Music   77

BORSO D'ESTE AND FERRARESE COURT CULTURE (1450–71)

9. Borso as Ruler   86
   Borso as Patron of Art and Literature; Music in the Frescoes
   of the Palazzo Schifanoia   89

10. Pietrobono and the Improvisatory Tradition   95
    Court Musicians under Borso   95

11. A Secular Manuscript of the Borso Period: the Porto MS and
    Rinaldo Maria d'Este   109

PART TWO

MUSIC AT FERRARA UNDER ERCOLE I D'ESTE (1471–1505)

12. Ercole as Private and Public Figure   121

13. Recruitment of Musicians in the 1470s   130

14. Organization and Functions of the Court Musicians   135
    The *Cappella di Cantori*   135
    The Instrumentalists   139
    Music in Daily Life   146

15. Size and Structure of Ercole's *Cappella di Cantori*   149
    National Groups   151
    Rank and Hierarchy in the Chapel   154

16. Some Representative Singers of Ercole's Chapel   160
    Johannes Brebis   160
    Magister Nicolò d'Olanda   161
    Cornelio di Lorenzo of Antwerp   161
    Jachetto de Marvilla   166
    Johannes Martini   167

17. Social and Economic Status of the Musicians   173
    Inducements to Singers   174
    Salaries and Status   177

18. Benefices   185
    Benefices and the Strategy of Recruitment: the Case of don
    Philippo de Primis   193

19. The Last Years of Ercole's Patronage (1497–1505)   196
    Josquin Desprez at Ferrara (1503–4)   202
    Jacob Obrecht (1504–5)   207

PART THREE

FERRARESE MUSICAL REPERTOIRES AND STYLES IN THE
LATE FIFTEENTH CENTURY

20. The Production of Music Manuscripts under Ercole I   213
21. The Principal Repertoires in Ercole's Earlier Years (1471–82)   228
22. Masses by Martini and Other Composers   233
23. Josquin's *Missa 'Hercules Dux Ferrarie'*   241
24. The Psalms, Hymns, and Other Vespers Music by Martini
    and Brebis   250
25. The Motet at Ferrara   258
26. Secular Music at the Court: Chanson and Instrumental Music   266
    The Casanatense Chansonnier   269
    Martini's Secular Music   272
27. Music for Court Festivities and Theater   278
    Music for Public Festivals, Jousts, and Special Events   279
    Music for the *Intermedi* of Secular Drama   280
    Music for Religious Spectacles   284

    Epilogue   288

APPENDICES

 I. Sources in the Archivio di Stato, Modena   292
 II. Documents   296
III. A Précis of Papal Letters to Duke Ercole I and Duke Alfonso I
    d'Este on Provisions for the Singers of the Ferrarese Court,
    1487–1506   302
IV. A Chronology of the Correspondence between Duke Ercole I d'Este
    and Ferrarese Ambassadors at Rome and elsewhere, on Benefices   304
 V. A Chronological List of Musicians Active at Ferrara, 1377–1505   314

    Bibliography   329
    Index   345

Illustrations

1. Pisanello, Portrait of Leonello d'Este (Bergamo, Accademia Carrara)

2. Pisanello, Portrait medal of Leonello d'Este (Washington, DC, National Gallery of Art, Kress Collection)

3. Ferrara, Courtyard of Palazzo Ducale (now Palazzo Municipio), Portal of the former ducal chapel of S. Maria di Corte

4. (*a* and *b*) Cornell University Library, *Ordo* of Ferrara Cathedral, with strips of musical notation

5. (*a*) Ferrara, Palazzo Schifanoia, Sala dei Mesi, April
   (*b*) Ferrara, Palazzo Schifanoia, Sala dei Mesi, April (detail)

6. Lorenzo Costa or Ercole de' Roberti, *Concerto* (London, National Gallery. Reproduced by courtesy of the Trustees, The National Gallery, London)

7. (*a*) Portrait bust of Duke Ercole I d'Este (Crown copyright, Victoria and Albert Museum)
   (*b*) Guido Mazzoni, Sculptured figure of Duke Ercole I d'Este as Joseph of Arimathea (Ferrara, Chiesa del Gesù)
   (*c*) Dosso Dossi, Portrait of Duke Ercole I d'Este (Modena, Galleria Estense. Photo: Alinari)

8. Modena, Archivio di Stato, Portion of *Frammenti musicali* [Mod E] (Busnois, *Missa 'L'homme armé'*)

9. Modena, Biblioteca Estense, MS Alpha M. 1, 11–12 [Mod C₁ and C₂] (Portion of the psalm 'Eripe me' by Johannes Martini)

10. Modena, Biblioteca Estense, MS Alpha M. 1, 13 [Mod D], fols. 1ᵛ–2 (Portion of *Missa 'Orsus'* by Johannes Martini)

11. Rome, Biblioteca Casanatense, MS 2856, fol. 1ᵛ (Philippon, 'Tant fort', Superius and part of Contratenor)

12. (*a*) Josquin Desprez, *Missa 'Hercules Dux Ferrarie'*, Tenor: Kyrie, Gloria, Credo (from O. Petrucci, publisher, *Missarum Josquin Liber Secundus*, Venice, 1505)
    (*b*) Josquin Desprez, *Missa 'Hercules Dux Ferrarie'*, Superius: Kyrie and beginning of Gloria

13. Modena, Archivio di Stato, Documents of musicians in the period of Duke Ercole I d'Este
    (*a*) Draft of Duke Ercole's letter, 10 December 1471, to Bishop Hermann of Constance (Appendix II, doc. 1)
    (*b*) Letter of Duke Galeazzo Maria Sforza of Milan, 24 July 1475, to Duke Ercole, on singers defecting from the Milanese chapel

(*c*) Letter of Pope Innocent VIII, 2 June 1487, to Duke Ercole, on Indult for the Duke's singers

(*d*) Letter of Pope Alexander VI, 11 May 1493, to Duke Ercole, on Indult for singers of the Duke's chapel

(*e*) Letter of Girolamo da Sestola ('il Coglia'), 14 August 1502, to Duke Ercole, on Josquin Desprez

14. Map of the diocese of Ferrara and its churches (eighteenth century) (Harvard University Library, Map Collection)

Tables

1. Court Trumpeters under Ercole I d'Este in 1484   140

2. Some Principal Events at the Ferrarese Court in 1476   147

3. The Singers of the Ferrarese Court Chapel under Ercole I d'Este
   Grouped by National Origin   150

4. Musicians' Salaries under Borso d'Este, 1456   178

5. Musicians' Salaries in 1476   180

6. Salaries of Some Military Men and of Musicians, 1488–91   183

7. Extant Polyphonic Music Manuscripts from Ferrara, Datable
   between c.1479 and 1505 (Period of Ercole I d'Este)   217

8. Music Manuscripts in Two Late Fifteenth-Century Inventories
   of Estense Libraries   218

9. Some Further Payment Records for Ferrarese Polyphonic MSS   223

10. Masses by Johannes Martini   233

11. Contents of the MSS Mod C_1 and Mod C_2 251

12. Composers Represented in the MS Casanatense 2856   272

13. Johannes Martini, 'La Martinella'; Segmentation   275

14. Josquin Desprez, 'Ile Fantazies de Joskin'; Segmentation   276

Music Examples

◇◆◇

1. Bartolomeo da Bologna, 'Arte psalentes', mm. 1–36 (transcribed by Ursula Günther, 'Das Manuskript Modena, Biblioteca Estense, Alpha M. 5, 24', 26 f.).   21

2. Bartolomeo da Bologna, 'Que pena maior', mm. 1–8 (transcribed by G. Reaney, *Early Fifteenth-Century Music*, Corpus Mensurabilis Musicae, xi/5, pp. 47 ff.)   23

3. Guillaume Dufay, 'C'est bien raison', mm. 1–33 (from H. Besseler, ed., *Guillaume Dufay, Opera Omnia*, Corpus Mensurabilis Musicae, i/6, pp. 31 f.)   37

4. (*a*) Cornell University Library, MS Rare BX C36 0635, *Ordo Manualis*, p. 70.   75
    (*b*) Ibid., p. 167.   75

5. (*a*) Johannes Martini, *Missa 'Io ne tengo quanto te'*, MS Mod D, fols. 25ᵛ–40; opening Tenor segments of principal movements and proposed reconstruction of first part of melody.   236
    (*b*) Ibid.; opening Tenor segments of secondary movements, and proposed reconstruction of later part of melody.   237

6. Josquin Desprez, *Missa 'Hercules Dux Ferrarie'*, basic form of subject (from O. Petrucci, publisher, *Missarum Josquin, Liber Secundus*, 1505; reprinted in A. Smijers, ed., *Josquin Desprez, Werken. Missen*, Deel ii).   244

7. Josquin Desprez, *Missa 'La sol fa re mi'* and *Missa 'Faisant regretz'*, subjects (from A. Smijers, ed., *Josquin Desprez, Werken. Missen*, Deel i and iii).   245

8. Josquin Desprez, *Missa 'Hercules Dux Ferrarie'*, Kyrie I (after *Josquin Desprez, Werken. Missen*, Deel ii).   246

9. Josquin Desprez, *Missa 'Hercules Dux Ferrarie'*, Gloria, mm. 1–4, with plainsong intonation (cf. *Liber Usualis*, p. 88).   248

10. (*a*) Johannes Brebis, 'Deus tuorum militum', stanza 1.   252
    (*b*) Johannes Martini, 'Deus tuorum militum', stanza 2.   253

11. Johannes Martini, *Magnificat Tertii Toni*, I.   256

12. Johannes Martini, 'Salve Regina', mm. 1–13 (from Munich, Bayerische Staatsbibliothek, MS 3154, fols. 89–93).   259

13. Josquin Desprez, 'Miserere mei, Deus', mm. 1–24 (after E. E. Lowinsky, ed., *The Medici Codex of 1518*, iv, 270–96).   263

14. Rome, Biblioteca Casanatense, MS 2856, examples of adjustment of range.   270

15. Johannes Martini, 'La Martinella', mm. 1–40 (from E. G. Evans, ed., *Johannes Martini, Secular Pieces*, pp. 47 f.).   274

16. Josquin Desprez, 'Ile fantazies de Joskin', mm. 1–22 (from *Josquin
    Desprez, Werken. Wereldlijke Werken*, Deel ii).   276

17. 'G. L.' (= Giorgio Luppato?) (ascribed), 'O triumphale diamante', Italian
    secular composition in honor of Duke Ercole I d'Este, mm. 1–20
    (from Paris, Bibliothèque Nationale, MS Res. Vm[7] 676, fols. 76[v]–77).   283

Archival References

⟨∿⟩

AN	Archivio Notarile
ASF	Ferrara, Archivio di Stato
ASM	Modena, Archivio di Stato
ARo	Ambasciatori, Roma
ASE	Archivio Segreto Estense
CTPE	Carteggio tra Principi Estensi
LASP	Libri di Amministrazione dei Singoli Principi
LCD	Libri Camerali Diversi
ASMN, AG	Mantua, Archivio di Stato, Archivio Gonzaga
B.	Busta
BE	Modena, Biblioteca Estense

The abbreviation LM is used throughout this book for the standard Ferrarese monetary unit of the period, the *Lira marchesana*.

Music Manuscripts

⟨∿∿⟩

Aosta   Aosta, Biblioteca del Seminario Maggiore, MS A¹D19

Berlin 78.C.28   Berlin, Staatliche Museen der Stiftung Preussischer Kultur-besitz, Kupferstichkabinett, MS 78.C.28 (*olim* Hamilton 451)

Bologna 2216   Bologna, Biblioteca Universitaria, MS 2216

Bologna Q 15   Bologna, Civico Museo Bibliografico Musicale, MS Q 15 (*olim* 37)

Bologna Q 16   Bologna, Civico Museo Bibliografico Musicale, MS Q 16 (*olim* 109)

Brussels 9126   Brussels, Bibliothèque Royale, MS 9126

Casanatense 2856   Rome, Biblioteca Casanatense, MS 2856

Chigiana 234   Vatican City, Biblioteca Apostolica Vaticana, MS Chigi C. VIII. 234

Dijon 517   Dijon, Bibliothèque Municipale, MS 517

Escorial IV.a.24   Escorial, Real Monasterio de San Lorenzo del Escorial, Biblioteca y Archivo de Musica, MS IV.a.24

Escorial V.III.24   Escorial, Real Monasterio de San Lorenzo del Escorial, Biblioteca y Archivo de Musica, MS V.III.24

Fayrfax   London, British Library, Additional MS 5465 ('Fayrfax Manuscript')

Florence 27   Florence, Biblioteca Nazionale Centrale, MS Panciatichi 27

Florence 112bis   Florence, Biblioteca Nazionale Centrale, MS Magliabechi XIX.112bis

Florence 229   Florence, Biblioteca Nazionale Centrale, MS Banco Rari 229 (*olim* Magliabechi XIX.59)

Florence 2439   Florence, Biblioteca del Conservatorio di Musica 'Luigi Cherubini', MS Basevi 2439

Jena 3   Jena, Universitätsbibliothek, MS 3

London-Paris-Modena   London, British Library, Additional MS 19583 (portion of a single Altus partbook from an original set of five); Paris, Bibliothèque Nationale, MS fr. nouv. acq. 4599 (another portion of Altus partbook); Modena, Biblioteca Estense, MS Alpha F. 2. 29 (combines fragments of Tenor and Bass partbooks)

Milan 2267   Milan, Archivio della Veneranda Fabbrica del Duomo, Sezione Musicale, Librone 3 (*olim* 2267)

Milan 2268   Milan, Archivio della Veneranda Fabbrica del Duomo, Sezione Musicale, Librone 2 (*olim* 2268)

Milan 2269   Milan, Archivio della Veneranda Fabbrica del Duomo, Sezione Musicale, Librone 1 (*olim* 2269)

Mod A   Modena, Biblioteca Estense, MS Alpha M.5.24 (Lat. 568)

Mod B   Modena, Biblioteca Estense, MS Alpha X.1.11 (Lat. 471)

Mod C$_1$ Modena, Biblioteca Estense, MS Alpha M.1.11 (Lat. 454)

Mod C$_2$ Modena, Biblioteca Estense, MS Alpha M.1.12 (Lat. 455)

Mod D   Modena, Biblioteca Estense, MS Alpha M.1.13 (Lat. 456)

Mod E   Modena, Archivio di Stato, Frammenti Musicali (3 folios)

Mod F   Modena, Biblioteca Estense, MS Alpha M.1.2 (Lat. 457)

Montecassino 871   Montecassino, Biblioteca dell'Abbazia, MS 871

Munich 3154   Munich, Bayerische Staatsbibliothek, Musiksammlung, Musica MS 3154 ('Chorbuch des Nikolaus Leopold')

Oxford 213   Oxford, Bodleian Library, MS Canonici Miscellaneous 213

Perugia 431   Perugia, Biblioteca Comunale Augusta, MS 431 (G 20)

Porto 714   Oporto, Biblioteca pública municipal, MS 714

St. Gall 463   St. Gall, Stiftsbibliothek, Mus. MS 463

Segovia   Segovia, Catedral, MS s.s.

Seville-Paris   Seville, Biblioteca Columbina, MS 5.I.43; and Paris, Bibliothèque Nationale, nouvelle acq. fr. MS 4379 (Part I)

Sistina 15   Vatican City, Biblioteca Apostolica Vaticana, MS Cappella Sistina 15

Sistina 35   Vatican City, Biblioteca Apostolica Vaticana, MS Cappella Sistina 35

Sistina 42   Vatican City, Biblioteca Apostolica Vaticana, MS Cappella Sistina 42

Sistina 51   Vatican City, Biblioteca Apostolica Vaticana, MS Cappella Sistina 51

Spataro   Bologna, Archivio Musicale di San Petronio, MS A.XXIX (copied by Giovanni Spataro)

Trent 87   Trent, Castello del Buonconsiglio, MS 87

Trent 90   Trent, Castello del Buonconsiglio, MS 90

Trent 92   Trent, Castello del Buonconsiglio, MS 92

Vatican 1411   Vatican City, Biblioteca Apostolica Vaticana, MS Urb. lat. 1411

Verona 757   Verona, Biblioteca Capitolare, MS 757
Verona 759   Verona, Biblioteca Capitolare, MS 759
Vienna 4809   Vienna, Nationalbibliothek, MS 4809

Introduction

⟨◦ෲ◦⟩

IN a memorable passage in *The Idea of History*, R. C. Collingwood dealt with the problem of interpreting a period of history as an age of greatness or as an age of decline.

> At the present day, we are constantly presented with a view of history as consisting . . . of good and bad periods, the bad periods being divided into the primitive and the decadent, according as they come before or after the good ones. This distinction between periods of primitiveness, periods of greatness, and periods of decadence, is not and never can be historically true. It tells us much about the historians who study the facts, but nothing about the facts they study. . . . Every period of which we have competent knowledge (and by competent knowledge I mean insight into its thought, not mere acquaintance with its remains) appears in the perspective of time as an age of brilliance: the brilliance being the light of our own historical insight.[1]

Against this we may set the following excerpt from a widely-read general reference book on music, written a generation ago:

> During the fifteenth century, Italian musical development declined, at least so far as we know. Only recently have some traces of musical activity come to light. . . . Northern composers such as Dufay, Obrecht, Isaac, and Josquin travelled to the south, and features of harmony and balance found in their works have frequently, though with doubtful authenticity, been ascribed to 'sunny Italy'. While art music declined, popular music seems to have flourished, and it is this field that, towards the end of the fifteenth century, gave Italian music new life, in the *frottola* and *canti carnascialeschi*.[2]

The point at issue in the dictionary excerpt is not its factual reliability (though most of it now seems misleading or wrong), but its use of the term 'decline' to characterize the condition of music in fifteenth-century Italy. If we accept a familiar premise of traditional music history, that 'music' means 'art music', and that the central defining feature of a musical culture is the individual composer and his completed works, then the general tenor of this account seems justified. For it is true that, with the disappearance of the last representatives of the Trecento tradition, around 1425, no significant Italian composers of polyphony rose to inherit their roles and maintain a direct line of continuity from composer to composer in Italian fifteenth-century polyphony.

---

[1] *The Idea of History*, p. 327 f.
[2] *The Harvard Dictionary of Music*, 2nd edn., p. 429.

But the familiar premise is thin and insubstantial. To strengthen it, we must extend our view of the formative factors that went into the musical culture of the Quattrocento. And in doing so we must include under the broad heading of 'music' not only the greater mensural polyphonic genres of religious and secular music that were dominated by foreign composers, but also the co-existing traditions of plainsong and of improvisatory or simply-notated two-part polyphony that survived for centuries in Italy and elsewhere in Europe. We must include not only the courtly polyphonic chanson but also the improvisational singing of contemporary strophic poetry in Italian using narrative and formulaic melodic strains. We can, in fact, now trace a virtually continuous tradition of the singing of Italian verse both at popular levels and in occasional settings by foreign and Italian composers (among the former Dufay is the most famous), along with improvisational performance by native Italian poet-musicians, such as Giustinian.[3] Singer-performers receive acclaim in the mid-fifteenth century at numerous Italian centers, and they range from the *cantimpanche* and *cantastorie*, who sang of mythical lovers and warriors, to the more sophisticated self-accompanied recitations of lutenist-singers such as Pietrobono of Ferrara, of whom we shall see much more in a later chapter. It is perfectly true that foreign composers dominate the sources of mensural polyphony that were compiled in Italy throughout the century. But that is exactly what we should expect in view of their pro-ductivity, their talents, and their traveling careers, which brought many of these musicians to Italy for shorter visits or for long periods of residence and activity.

To see the Quattrocento as a potential 'age of brilliance', we must try to make imaginative use of every type of evidence by which we can reconstruct the nature of the unwritten tradition – as Nino Pirrotta has emphasized over and again – and understand the role of different kinds of music-making within the social framework of the period. To do this we will first have to concede that a musical culture, even one so integral to our Western composer-oriented tradition – was in fact a richly complex and highly developed one, even if it did not depend entirely on notational systems and on the works and repertoires made possible by these systems. We need, in short, to develop a larger vision of the Quattrocento as a pluralistic musical culture.

Adopting this perspective for at least the middle decades of the century – roughly between 1420 and the first efforts to fix the frottola literature as a notated body of music – may in fact help us understand better not only the Quattrocento but the Trecento as well. Italian music from the time of Marchettus of Padua to the time of Landini was not the result of a broad musical movement that spread over the peninsula. It grew from the concen-tration of musical and poetic talents in a limited number of important centers

---

[3] See Pirrotta, 'Ricercare e variazoni su "O rosa bella" '; repr. in Pirrotta, *Music and Culture in Italy from the Middle Ages to the Baroque.*

– primarily in Florence, secondarily and sporadically in a few of the northern courts, from Milan to Padua. But the Trecento tradition neither depended on, nor was able to foster, a long-range didactic tradition of mensural composition that could produce schools of skilled Italian singers and composers far into the fifteenth century. The turbulent political developments of the first decades of the fifteenth century contributed to the breakdown of the conditions that had nourished musical life in the Trecento, evidently built on the base of a fragile patronage system that could not maintain continuity into the next century. Further study of the disjunction between these two periods in Italy would have to take into consideration their cultural diversity and the particular histories of individual city-states – above all, Florence – as well as the changes in the social roles of Italian musicians as a professional group – their training, skills, repertoires, and means of livelihood.

It does appear that, around 1430, a new phase of Italian musical life began based on new initiatives. Patronage grew and cultural competition became intensified, in part as a result of the return of the papacy to Italy under Martin V and the re-establishment of the Pope as a secular ruler who could fully compete with the larger states of Italy for every form of cultural advantage and political gain. In consequence the musical scene became more ramified and more diversified. The courts sought higher status by acquiring artistic and intellectual talent; no doubt in part to cover their inherent political, economic, and military weakness by emulating the celebrated French and Burgundian courts in cultural matters, in part to round out their broad patronage of literature and the visual arts. It was inevitable that the ruling families, whether newly installed or resurgent dynasties, sought to furnish themselves with the professional singers who could form a princely 'chapel' – a *cappella di cantori* – and thus undertake the extensive recruitment of non-Italian singers that became endemic in the second half of the century.

The aim of this book is to trace the development of one of these centers – Ferrara, in its first and greatest period – as a matrix for music in all its forms. The story is not one of continuous growth from simple to complex, from cell to organism – but rather one of changing taste, response, and initiative on the part of the successive Este rulers who held the levers of cultural as well as political power in this small oligarchy. In a sense the story is a microcosm of the larger development of music in the period as a whole. It moves from faint beginnings under Niccolò III d'Este to the first international chapel of singers founded by Leonello in the 1440s; to the emphasis on courtly improvisatory singing and instrumentalists under Borso; and, in the last three decades of the century, to the assimilation of international musical traditions under Ercole I d'Este. The larger process of musical acculturation at Ferrara is not completed within the period to which this book is limited; but the later patronage of the children of Ercole, and the entire development of Ferrarese musical life in later periods, grows from this soil. The story is also one that aims to explore the role of music in the cultural life of the period, and a primary assumption is that the main protagonists with whom we shall be concerned – the patrons, on the one hand, the musicians on the other – are best seen as members of a mutually beneficial system. They bend towards one another in recognition of their interdependence.

PART ONE

MUSIC AT FERRARA IN THE EARLY FIFTEENTH CENTURY

༄

1

Ferrara and the Trecento Background

WE begin on barren ground. Ferrara, which became in the fifteenth and sixteenth centuries a musical center of continental importance, played no significant role in the rise of polyphony in Italy during the fourteenth century. Although reliable information on the musicians, patrons, and social foundations of musical life in Trecento Italy is still scarce, we can identify at least some of the conditions that fostered the growth of music in other states and cities of the time. Against this background it seems clear that Ferrara in the Trecento was incapable of sustaining a higher level of musical life, not only when compared to Florence but in more relevant contrast to the court-centered patronage of Padua and Verona.

Ferrara, unlike Florence, had as yet no strong civic tradition of political and artistic purpose, no concept of the revival of the glories of antiquity in the work of its statesmen, poets, and artists. It had no important and wealthy guilds that could generate a lively civic lay culture through group competition. Its middle and upper classes had not — and would never have — the range of international contacts developed by the great Florentine bankers and merchants, whose extended networks of finance, trade, and communication were expanding their direct knowledge of the art and products of northern Europe and were giving them the means to finance their increasingly opulent domestic life at home. In a still feudal and primarily agrarian state like Ferrara, before its increasing urbanization in the later fifteenth century, none of these elements was strong enough to produce the functional or recreational matrix in which the sophisticated practice of polyphonic music could have flourished. The firm political grip of the Este family was never seriously challenged by rival families after the thirteenth century, and the local landowning bourgeoisie probably found it convenient to leave the defense and government of the state in the capable hands of this ambitious and ruthless dynasty, who also set whatever local standard there was in cultural matters.

The one potential seat of cultural life was the court, and here the preserva-tion of the feudal mentality and the politically expedient promotion of chival-ric myth displaced any strong development of vernacular poetry in the forms then suitable to musical expression. Throughout the Trecento no records show the presence at the Este court of musicians associated with polyphonic practice, or even of instrumentalists hired on more than a casual basis.[1] No Ferrarese manuscripts of polyphony are known from this period, and although the sources surviving from other centers contain a number of pieces dedicated to patrons by means of acrostic or symbolic texts, they reveal none for the Estensi. Composers did, on the other hand, address such pieces to contem-porary patrons who cannot be said to have differed from the Estensi in basic outlook, such as the Visconti of Milan, the Scaligeri of Verona, and the Carrara of Padua.[2] That the Estensi were simply not then interested in the literary and artistic endeavors that would have included secular music, is also suggested by other evidence, including some that is connected with Petrarch.[3]

Admitttedly, the lack of documentation for musicians at the court in the Trecento might simply reflect a general absence of detailed evidence on court life for this period. While the fourteenth century's records at Ferrara are sparse and unrevealing, the fifteenth century confronts us with a flood of documentation preserved in an enormous number of payment registers and other types of historical sources, all of which only begin to be maintained in the 1420s and 1430s. These eventually grew in numbers as the record-keeping bureaucracy multiplied and assumed greater local importance. Still, it is likely that if any of the central musical figures of the Florentine or northern Italian sectors of Trecento polyphony had been in close touch with Ferrarese patrons,

---

[1] The only isolated exception is a single instrumentalist named Enzellino *piffaro*, who was in the service of Niccolò II d'Este in 1377, and whose son was given an investiture in 1394 (docu-ments in ASM, Camera Ducale, Investiture, Pergamene, dated 6 October 1377 and 30 July 1394).

[2] On the dedicatory pieces for the Visconti see Thibault, 'Emblems et devises des Visconti dans les œuvres musicales du Trecento'; on those for the Carrara see Petrobelli, 'Some Dates for Bartolino da Padova'; on Trecento musicians at Verona, a recent conspectus is offered by Paganuzzi, 'Medioevo e Rinascimento'. Despite Paganuzzi's view (p. 52) that the marriage of Niccolò II d'Este to Verde della Scala led to increased musical activity at Ferrara, spurred by her presence (she is presumed by some scholars to be addressed in the madrigal 'De soto 'l *Verde*', in the Rossi codex), there is no evidence to support this assertion.

[3] Wilkins, *Petrarch's Later Years*, p. 165. Petrobelli, ' "Un leggiadretto velo" ed altre cose petrarchesche', suggests a plausible personal connection between Petrarch and Jacopo da Bologna at Verona between 1348 and 1352. On Petrarch's will see Mommsen, *Petrarch's Testament*, pp. 82 f.

In 1369, writing from his hilltop stronghold near Padua, the ageing poet and humanist urged a younger member of the household, Ugo d'Este, son of Nicolò II, to stick to his studies and put aside his worldly pursuits of hawking and hunting, if he wanted to be remembered by posterity. The advice was probably ignored, however, and Ugo certainly counts as a typical member of the family of that time. In the following year, 1370, Petrarch bequeathed his lute to a certain Magister Tommaso Bombasi of Ferrara, urging him to play it 'not for the vainglory of this world, but in praise of God everlasting'. But we know from other sources that this Tommaso was not then active in his home city, and that his fame as an actor, musician, and organizer of festivities had taken him to the more fertile ground of Venice.

such contacts would have emerged through historical or textual evidence. Taking the situation as the evidence presents it, we are forced to conclude that in this period, even more than in literature or in the pictorial arts, Ferrarese musical culture remained, as Gundersheimer has put it, 'qualitatively insignificant and quantitatively trivial'.[4]

At the same time, we must also take note of recent and important revisions of traditional views of Trecento musical life and activities, chiefly advanced by Nino Pirrotta.[5] Pirrotta's viewpoint rejects a formerly prevailing concept of Trecento music as being formed exclusively or even primarily by its polyphonic manifestations. Instead, he seeks to place the limited and quite special traditions of notated polyphony within a larger social and aesthetic framework in which the normal mode of existence of music was that of an oral, improvisatory tradition, both secular and sacred. Among ecclesiastics of this and other regions, in their churches, monasteries, and religious houses, we may assume the occasional singing of simple elaborations of plainsong in the *cantus planus binatim* that have recently been found in a certain number of written manuscripts but which were probably more often produced as improvisation.[6] Indeed, in at least one Ferrarese religious house, that of the Carmelites of San Paolo, a more complex practice may have been developed, since a set of regulations of 1357 explicitly warns against the singing of 'motets', and 'other lascivious music'.[7] But this appears to have been exceptional. On the secular side, we should also assume that the court at Ferrara was exposed in a normal degree to itinerant performers and singers of secular melody, to improvisational singing of verse, and even to some occasional polyphony – but all of this is undocumented.

As suggested earlier, a more specific inhibiting factor was political; or rather, political and cultural in equal parts. From the thirteenth century on, under Azzo VI (the first of the Estensi to gain political control at Ferrara, in 1208) troubadours from Provence migrating to Italy had been particularly welcome at this court. Some of them had left songs in honor of members of the newly established dynasty, and were commemorated in a handsome manuscript of troubadour poetry (but no music) that was written at Ferrara by court scribes.[8] The Este family's enduring ambition to portray themselves as

---

[4] Gundersheimer, *Ferrara: the Style of a Renaissance Despotism*, p. 60.

[5] See especially his 'Novelty and Renewal in Italy: 1300–1600', and his 'Ars Nova e Stil Novo', both repr. in his *Music and Culture*.

[6] See Gallo, '*Cantus planus binatim*; polifonia primitiva in fonti tardive'.

[7] Kallenberg, *Fontes Liturgiae Carmelitanae*, p. 32. Kallenberg quotes at length from the Carmelite *Constitutiones* promulgated during a general chapter of the Order held in Ferrara in 1357 (of course its statutes reflect much more than local considerations). It includes this passage: 'Nullus in choro aliud vel aliter cantare presumat quam quod communis usus ordinis approbat et elegit. Sed neque motetos neque upaturam vel aliquem cantum magis ad lasciviam quam ad devocionem provocantem aliquis decantare audeat sub pena gravioris culpe per unam diem transgresssoribus infligenda'.

[8] On the troubadour tradition, see Carducci, 'La coltura estense', pp. 10–19. On the troubadour MS see Rajna, 'Ricordi di codici francesi degli Estensi nel secolo XV'.

descendants of French royalty, and to glorify their mythic origins through literary means, was reflected in the cultivation of stanzaic narratives that celebrate French chivalric heroes and ultimately led to the great Ferrarese epic poems by Boiardo and Ariosto. But in the Trecento this chivalric myth had no means of connecting with the newer Italian lyric poetry and its music, as found especially at Florence. In so far as stanzas of praise and glorification were developed and sung, they could make do with simple musical formulas, sung by a solo singer with his lute; and this is exactly the pattern that persisted far into the fifteenth century as courtly entertainment. Accordingly, if we combine the improvisational and cultural hypotheses, we can accept that the courtly circles in fourteenth-century Ferrara did not lack music – which was surely present in various forms – but rather lacked the amalgam of aesthetic, linguistic, and cultural interests that was giving rise elsewhere to Italian poetic-polyphonic forms and repertoires – the caccia, madrigal, and ballata.

Outside the court there was no other major local base. The religious confraternities had some music of their own, but neither there nor at the cathedral, until the early fifteenth century, was there any figure of distinction in musical matters. Before the 1390s there was no university at Ferrara at all, thus no seat of interest in the speculative side of music and its scholastic and theoretical traditions, to which students and citizens could gravitate. Local society, from peasants to city burghers and lords, was exposed to music in a superficial and casual sense, ranging from popular tunes to dance music and perhaps to the occasional appearance of wandering singers and players – but all of this represents nothing more than was typical of musical life in any other urban center in the region, and it gives no hint of later growth.

2

Ferrara under Niccolò III d'Este

(1393–1429)

 ❧❧❧

HISTORIANS agree that the short reign of Alberto d'Este, from 1388 to 1393, began a transformation of Ferrarese civic and court life that continued through the fifteenth century, gradually reshaping Ferrara from a backward feudal stronghold into a culturally rich and well-endowed Renaissance city. For the local public the most visible sign of change under Alberto was the formal establishment of the university, for which a papal charter was issued in March 1393. For the court and its members a comparable event was the appointment of the humanist Donato degli Albanzani, first as chancellor and later as tutor to Alberto's legitimated heir, the future Niccolò III. Donato had been a friend of Petrarch's and translator of Petrarch and Boccaccio. As politician and teacher, later as *referendarius* under Niccolò III, he brought to the court a firmer contact with the rising currents of professional humanism than it had known before.[1] The credit for Niccolò's being even modestly receptive to intellectual matters belonged to Donato, and it was Donato who was primarily responsible for the growth of the court library in these years. The increase in the library is the only available index of court literacy, and its development suggests a growing awareness in court circles of a wider range of cultural interests. Donato paved the way for the more influential scholars that were to follow him as tutors of Niccolò's sons – Toscanelli, Aurispa, and especially Guarino Veronese.

Until 1402 Niccolò ruled under a regency; thereafter, in his own right. As twelfth Marquis in the Este line he could draw on a long-established family tradition for his sense of historical position, and his career as ruler was long and colorful, but streaked with cruelty and inconsistency. He managed foreign policy with a shrewdness and caution that were sharply at odds with his domestic life. He became notorious in his time when in 1425 he murdered both his young wife, Parisina Malatesta, and his eldest son, Ugo d'Este, after

---

[1] On Donato at Ferrara see Novati, 'Donato degli Albanzani alla corte Estense'; Donato had evidently settled in Ferrara between 1377 and 1381. Of future significance too was the fact that Alberto obtained a papal agreement, in 1392, that agricultural lands in the *contado*, which had been largely owned by churches and monasteries, and distributed to the secular clergy under contracts, should not be restored to their original owners when the contracts ended but would come under marchional control; see Lazzari, 'Il Signor di Ferrara ai tempi del concilio del 1438–39: Niccolò III d'Este', 676.

discovering their love affair.[2] Yet Niccolò himself made adultery a lifelong career. The same pattern marked his treatment of a long-trusted associate, Giacomo Zilioli, and his son Zilio. Giacomo had been a member of Niccolò's inner circle and had held court posts with distinction when, in 1434, he was suddenly stripped of his titles and property and thrown into prison along with his son.[3] Although some historians have accepted the accusation of political plot and threat of betrayal which the local chroniclers recorded, that shrewd contemporary, Aeneas Sylvius Piccolomini (later Pope Pius II), was probably closer to the truth when he said that Niccolò ruined the Zilioli because Giacomo doubted the legitimacy of Niccolò's plan to have himself succeeded by his natural sons, Leonello and Borso, and not by any legal male heir that might issue from his marriage in 1431 to Rizzarda da Saluzzo.[4] The point is important because Leonello and Borso, in that order, did become Niccolò's successors, whereas Ercole (the legitimate male heir) later rose to power as a result of Borso's death and he was bitterly opposed by a son of Leonello's. The unparalleled solidity of Este rule in these centuries is characteristic of the dynasty as a whole, not of its individual members at any one moment; having little or no need to band together to prevent outside enemies from seizing power, the family members typically vented their rage on one another. And family competition, both with living rivals and with previous ruling members, is one of the basic themes that underlies the rivalry in patronage and the differences in artistic and musical achievements that emerge across generations. It is also one of the basic themes of this book.

For most of his political career, Niccolò devoted himself to mediating in disputes between other warring states, while steering clear of any military adventures that could threaten his small territory. His role as peacemaker was celebrated in poems and epitaphs, and is even mentioned in the best-known musical composition then written as a tribute to him – Dufay's ballade, 'C'est bien raison'.[5] These diplomatic initiatives went hand in hand with Niccolò's efforts to extend and consolidate the state itself. Ferrara and its *contado* had been the traditional nucleus, held by the Estensi as a papal vicariate, and in the late thirteenth century they had added the neighboring cities and lands of Modena and Reggio, as Imperial investitures. Niccolò took steps to gain other territories as well.[6]

---

[2] On the episode Ugo-Parisina see, most recently, Gundersheimer, *Ferrara*, pp. 77–9, which cites earlier literature, to which can be added the account in Gardner, *Dukes and Poets at Ferrara*, pp. 35–9. For a remarkable and imaginative treatment of major events in the life of Niccolò III, see Ezra Pound, *The Cantos of Ezra Pound (1–95)*, (New York, 1956), Canto xxiv.

[3] See Lorch, introduction to *Zilioli Ferrariensis Comediola Michaelida*, pp. 11–39. This is a Latin play written by Zilio Zilioli while in prison.

[4] See ibid., p. 39. For Aeneas Sylvius Piccolomini's opinion, see his *De Viris Aetate Sua Claris*, cited by Lazzari, 'Il Signor di Ferrara', 700, n. 1.

[5] On the epitaphs for Niccolò see Capra, 'Gli epitaphi per Niccolò III d'Este'. It is noteworthy that although several of these epitaphs mention Niccolò's prowess as a ruler and peacemaker, not one of them makes any reference to his interest in the arts or letters.

[6] In Niccolò's early years Parma and Reggio were overrun by Ottobuono Terzi. Parma was recovered by Niccolò, but was then ceded to Milan in exchange for dominion over Reggio; see

Yet not only political motives but personal curiosity must have motivated his two unusually long journeys abroad, in consecutive years. In 1413 he went to the Holy Land, and in 1414 to France. These journeys deserve some attention, as they may well have been the only culturally productive events of his rule that came from his own initiative. We are informed about the trip to Jerusalem and the Holy Sepulchre by a contemporary diarist who went along. We know that he took thirty days to travel from Ferrara to Jerusalem, mainly by sea, and exactly four months for the entire trip. Niccolò took with him a retinue of fifty-four persons and along the way he admired such sights as the antiquities of Pola in Istria, and the gardens of Corfu.[7] His journey to France, though less exotic, not only established a close political tie with the French crown but also reinforced those affinities to French culture and tradition that had long been felt in Ferrarese court life. Since Ferrarese connections with France are particularly important for this study, we can linger over some of the details of this journey, which has been wrongly interpreted by some historians as merely a pilgrimage to the shrine of Saint Antoine de Vienne in the Dauphiné, to which in fact Niccolò made two journeys. We have a close account of the 1414 trip in a contemporary chronicle.[8]

First, destinations and travel time: the trip was announced as a pilgrimage to Saint Antoine de Vienne, but its real destination was Paris and the French court.[9] Again the entire trip lasted some four months (from 5 June to 12 October 1414). Niccolò went by stages to Genoa, where he remained for eight days; then up the coast to Nice and into Provence (Aix, Avignon, Orange), reaching Saint Antoine on 21 July. After only one day there he proceeded to Lyons and then to Paris, where he remained for sixteen days, departing for home on 28 August via Savoy and the pass of Mont Cenis. The stay in Paris was by far the most important phase of the journey, and if the opinion of Simeoni is right, Niccolò was carrying out not only his own political ends but those of Pope John XXIII as well. No less important was the opportunity to see Paris and Notre Dame, mingle with the French nobility, and witness the opulence of a royal court. Niccolò visited the castles of the Dukes of Orleans and Bourbon and was well received by King Charles VI. For 23 August the chronicler reports his meeting with the Dauphin and other French nobles:

the documents in Muratori, ed., *Rerum Italicarum Scriptores . . .*, xx/2, Appendice, Nos. III, IV, V. In the 1430s Niccolò extended Estense control in the Romagna by obtaining further territorial concessions from Eugene IV; see Lazzari, 'Il Signor di Ferrara', and Chiappini, *Gli Estensi*, p. 97.

[7] An eye-witness account of the trip by Luchino da Campo was published by Ghinassi in *Collezione di opere inedite e rare*. Another is found in Muratori, ed., *Rerum Italicarum Scriptores . . .*, xx/2, Appendice, Doc. I, from the chronicle by Paolo da Legnago. A precedent for a trip of this sort was the journey to Jerusalem made by Pandolfo Malatesta in 1399, celebrated by a motet in Mod A; see Günther, 'Das Manuskript Modena, Bibl. Estense, Alpha M. 5, 24', 17–67, especially 35.

[8] The text is in Muratori, ed., *Rerum Italicarum Scriptores . . .*, xx/2, App., Doc. II, pp. 53–7.

[9] Simeoni in ibid., xx/2, App., Doc. II, p. 53, n. 1.

. . . the Marquis Niccolò with his gentlemen, dined with M. Aquitaine, the King's eldest son and M. de Guienne, and the Duke of Odalphim . . . the Duke of Bavaria served dishes at the table, and so did the Duke of Richemont and the Count of Vendome and other lords, and there was excellent playing of harp, viol, flute, and lute [*cithara*]. This Lord [the Dauphin] was young, about nineteen years old, tall, well dressed, wearing a chain around his neck worth about fifty thousand ducats and more . . . he had a rather harsh voice . . . .[10]

The French court was already one of the most important musical establishments of Europe, rivalled only by Burgundy and by the papacy at Avignon. Music at the court of Charles VI (ruled 1380–1422) followed patterns derived from his predecessor, Charles V (1364–80). Of Charles V and his sense of music in daily life, a chronicler gives a classic description that could fit many late medieval lords: 'for spiritual consolation he turned to the sweet sounds of the organ and to songs in praise of God'. He maintained a *souveraine chapelle*, and had well-paid minstrels and singers to entertain him after meals. Charles VI kept up the same forces, amid growing sophistication in the court's uses of poetry and music. In 1401 at his court was founded the *Cours amoureux* as a pastime of courtiers; in that year his chapel numbered nineteen chaplains and clerks, and remained at this large size throughout the rest of the century.[11] The chapel of Burgundy was about the same size (twenty-three in 1396, twenty-one in 1450). Epitomizing a general sense of the ideals of government, of education, and of personal culture, was Nicolas of Oresme's translation into French, with commentary, of Aristotle's *Politics*, made in the 1370s at the request of Charles V. For the French nobility, the Aristotelian praise of music in the *Politics* must have strongly reinforced the view that learning to perform and, in some degree, to understand music, was not a useless pastime but could be seen as a valuable personal attainment.[12] And it may be significant for the Italian gentry of the early fifteenth century who were seeking to emulate French manners and to establish themselves as French allies and vassals, that in 1436 Niccolò's library contained an item described in the inventory as 'Libro uno chiamado Politica, in francexe . . .'.[13]

This official visit to France bore diplomatic results some years later. In 1420, when Niccolò negotiated with Filippo Maria Visconti over Parma and Reggio Emilia, his interests were represented by Artaldo, Abbot of Saint Antoine de Vienne, as papal legate; in 1425 this same Artaldo mediated a formal alliance between Ferrara and the French crown, in which Niccolò

---

[10] Ibid., p. 55.

[11] Pirro, *La Musique à Paris sous le regne de Charles VI (1380–1422)*, *passim*. For these figures on the number of singers in the French royal and earlier Burgundian ducal chapels I am indebted to Wright, 'Voices and Instruments in the Art and Music of Northern France in the Fifteenth Century, a Conspectus', pp. 643–9.

[12] A complete critical edition of the translation was published by Menut, *Transactions of the American Philosophical Society*.

[13] The item in the Estense library inventory of 1436 is No. 244; see Cappelli, 'La Biblioteca Estense nella prima metà del secolo XV', 28. Menut, op. cit., p. 34, reports eighteen extant early copies of Oresme's translation of the *Politics*, all of which were made for important French patrons.

agreed to furnish aid to France against its enemies (more likely, the reverse
was really intended, but perhaps Ferrarese aid in the event of a French invasion of Italy was dimly foreseen).[14] In January 1431 a symbolic step was
taken to formalize this relationship: the new king, Charles VII, gave Niccolò
the right to quarter his arms with those of France and to add the three fleur-
de-lis to the Estense white eagle.[15] This formal acceptance of an alliance with
France that inevitably meant external vassallage, was to culminate in Ferrarese
support of French interests both before and during the French invasions of
1494. Later Estense rulers, especially Ercole I and Alfonso I, maintained close
relations with the French court, and the bond eventually became even more
direct when Ercole II married Princess Renée in 1529.

The French influence was more than political, as we have seen. In the court
library large numbers of French MSS mingled with Latin and Italian volumes.
More than in other Italian centers, the surge of interest in classical literature
only partially displaced a rooted attachment to French chivalric poetry and
narratives. Thus, the first extant library inventory, of 1436, shows a total of
279 volumes, of which fifty-three were in French, mainly courtly romances.[16]
As Fava points out, many of the Latin MSS in the collection bore the arms or
motto of Niccolò III, showing that they were compiled between about 1400
and the date of the inventory.[17] But it is likely that the classics were gradually
superimposed upon a chivalric base. Few of the French MSS have arms or
other indications of ownership; for Fava this shows they were 'compiled outside of Ferrara or before the period of Niccolò III'. We may now suggest that
some may have been brought back from France in 1414, while others would
have been obtained there by later agents or brought in as a by-product of
Niccolò's diplomatic connections, perhaps via the Dauphiné. Niccolò's imitation of French ways is even visible in the names of at least five of his children
– Ginevra, Rinaldo, Isotta, Gurone, and Meliaduse – as many writers have
noted; and the most conspicuous evidence of his sense of French as a high
vernacular language is the beautifully copied and illuminated French Bible
that was made for him between 1431 and 1436.[18]

Yet all this scarcely suffices to show that Niccolò was a 'famous protector
of learning in Italy', as Bertoni would have it.[19] He remained an earthy,
shrewd, and capable leader, whose spending for books simply formed part of
normal competition for status with his rivals. At the same time, it enabled
him to give his sons, especially Leonello, not only the training they needed to

---

[14] As noted by Simeoni in Muratori, ed., *Rerum Italicarum Scriptores . . .*, xx/2, p. 53, n. 10.

[15] See Cittadella, *Notizie relative a Ferrara per la maggior parte inedite*, I, 1, p. 24; Lazzari, 'Il
Signor di Ferrara', 697.

[16] The full inventory is published by Cappelli in the article cited in note 13. That portion of the
inventory containing books in French had been published earlier by Rajna, 'Ricordi di codici
francesi'.

[17] Fava, *La Biblioteca Estense nel suo sviluppo storico*, pp. 9–10.

[18] Biblioteca Vaticana MS Barberini lat. 613, illuminated by Belbello da Pavia.

[19] Bertoni, *La Biblioteca Estense e la coltura ferrarese ai tempi del Duca Ercole I*, p. 6.

become effective rulers in a changing era, but also wider horizons. We can accept the view of Niccolò as a protector of learning only on the premise that he did not personally possess it, but we can also credit him with having laid a foundation on which his sons could build.

Music in the Earlier Years of Niccolò III (1400–29)

Evidence of musical activity in these years is sparse at the court but some-what more plentiful at the cathedral. Although some scholars have attributed musical interests to Parisina, who was apparently a good manager of house-hold affairs before her abrupt demise in 1425, the evidence for this is negligible.[20] The records for these years do show the purchase of a few manu-scripts for private devotion – a Psalter and a small Office of the Madonna, in 1422 – but these are commonplace items. There is no indication of music being copied, or of the compiling of teaching materials for music, or even of the purchase of instruments.[21]

If there was anything approaching a staff of household or court musicians in Niccolò's earlier years, above all between 1410 and 1430, it amounted to a few instrumentalists and trumpeters at most. In 1401 Niccolò had a *piffaro* in his employ named Filippo da Padova, who was hired to teach his instrument to a certain Ser Pellegrino; this suggests at least very modest attempts to obtain performers.[22] By 1416 he may have engaged two more, since three musicians, of unspecified abilities, were returned to Niccolò by Giacomo II of Naples. Again, documents of 1424 show that three *piffari* (perhaps the same as those of 1416) and two trumpeters were sent to Schiavonia.[23] All of this may suggest that the three-man group of *piffari*, perhaps forming an early shawm band of the type later known as an *Alta*, was already in use at the court well before 1430; but the evidence is admittedly fragmentary.[24] Over the decade 1420–30 there are a few more isolated references. In July 1424 a certain Leonardo dal Chitarino was put on salary, and was the first Ferrarese musician to be explicitly called a lutenist (perhaps a lutenist-singer).[25] He would thus have been an early model for the great Pietrobono, soon to begin

---

[20] Gandini, 'Saggio degli usi e delle costumanze della corte di Ferrara al tempo di Niccolò III (1393–1442)', 153.

[21] Ibid., 152.

[22] Cittadella, *Notizie*, II, 2, p. 710. Marix, *Histoire de la musique et des musiciens de la cour de Bourgogne*, p. 56, n. 7, quotes the chronicle of Monstrelet (II, 69–71) as a source for the claim that in 1410 Niccolò III was escorted by three pairs of minstrels and six trumpets, and that he had a chapel of singers which he had inherited from his predecessor. I had accepted this claim in the *Dufay Quincentenary Conference Proceedings*, p. 16, n. 20. But a closer reading of the text of Monstrelet makes it absolutely clear that the singers he refers to are those of the newly elected Pope, Alexander V, not of Niccolò III: see below, p. 20. The figures given for the number of minstrels and trumpets accompanying Niccolò may well be exaggerated.

[23] ASM, ASE, Inventario, vol. 41.

[24] For a recent survey of what is known about the sizes of shawm bands of the period see Polk, 'Ensemble Performance in Dufay's Time'.

[25] ASM, ASE, Inventario, vol. 41, fol. 27ᵛ.

his auspicious career. In the same month we have a sign of Niccolò's interest in obtaining a good performer from abroad (characteristically, from France, where he now had good contacts): a *piffaro* named Giovanni d'Avignon was taken into service, given the same salary as another *piffaro*, and also a house and court stable privileges; word was passed that he was to be well treated because he had been sought in France for two years.[26] In 1426 a handsome gift of wind instruments arrived from Duke Philip the Good of Burgundy.[27] And this gift, which may have spurred Niccolò to take on players for these instruments, was then followed in 1428 by the arrival of the Burgundian *trompette de guerre* Hennequin Coppetrippe, who stayed with Niccolò until 1433, and who was the only Burgundian player to come into Ferrarese service in these years.[28] Probably a French-speaking trumpeter could serve Niccolò in other ways than as musician; trumpeters, as heralds, were often employed as emissaries, as political agents, and as spies. Before the 1430s, as we have seen earlier, there is neither a court singer nor any sign of interest in sung polyphony. Nor did Niccolò exchange musicians with other Italian regimes, despite his zealous pursuit of friendly relations with other states.

Music at the Cathedral: Bartolomeo da Bologna (1405–27)

Yet if Niccolò wished to embellish festive occasions, or add a musician of caliber to his retinue, he could turn to the cathedral. There the main figure was fra Bartolomeo da Bologna, the only musician of well-defined polyphonic talents who was in continuous residence in the city at this time, and a member of the cathedral chapter.

The massive Gothic cathedral, dedicated to St. George, already three centuries old when Niccolò ruled, was administered by its chapter under the nominal supervision of the Bishop (Ferrara had no Archbishop before the eighteenth century). Its magnificent façade, with scenes of the Last Judgement carved above the great portal, dominated one end of the center of the city, with the Castello Vecchio (1385) dominating the other. The Duomo was not only the center of religious life in the city: a covered portico of shops along its southern flank (called 'strazarie'), still in existence, served to focus its social and economic life as well. Work on the campanile was only begun in these years; it was started in 1412 on the basis of designs by Leone Battista Alberti.[29]

Thanks to documents recently published by Adriano Cavicchi, we can now

---

[26] ASM, ASE, Inventario, vol. 41, fol. 26ᵛ.

[27] On the wind instruments see Marix, *Histoire*, pp. 42, 105 (with text of the ducal order for the manufacture of these 'quatre grans instrumens de menestrels [trumpets] quatre douchaines et quatre fleustes'. These three groups of four instruments constitute the largest single acquisition of instruments by the court during the century, so far as is known.

[28] Marix, *Histoire*, especially pp. 24, 56 f., 93 f., 109-12.

[29] On the cathedral, still the best published works are those of Guarini, *Compendio historico dell' origine . . . delle chiese di Ferrara*, and Scalabrini, *Memorie storiche delle chiese di Ferrara*. For a concise account and more recent bibliographical references see the *Dictionaire d'histoire et de géographie ecclesiastique*, vol. 4, pp. 1180 f.

be certain that the beginning of the local career of Bartolomeo da Bologna at the cathedral virtually coincided with Niccolò's own independent rule. We find Bartolomeo mentioned as early as 1405, in a list of those present at the baptism of a son of Niccolò's, evidently Ugo d'Este.[30] By 1407, if not earlier, Bartolomeo was prior of the monastery of San Niccolò of Ferrara, then a Benedictine house. At about the same time, he had also become a mansionary of the cathedral, no doubt to render official his role as organist. But this double role became a casualty of those efforts at reform that were being made at Rome by one of the current claimants to the papal throne, Gregory XII. In 1410 Gregory issued a bull prohibiting individuals from amassing too many benefices, with the result that Bartolomeo was nominally deprived of his prebend; but he continued to serve as organist and also, in effect, as mansionary.[31] He remained in this post at the cathedral, as its leading musical practitioner, until 1427, to judge from the documents compiled by Scalabrini in the eighteenth century and published by Cavicchi (documents are lacking for the year 1414 and are sparse for 1415–16). The last of these that explicitly names him dates from 5 January 1427 in connection with a special ceremony for distinguished diplomatic visitors.[32] Thereafter, the post of organist is held by a certain Gioacchino Cancellieri.

In tracing what we can of Bartolomeo's career, through a small body of cathedral documents and an even smaller though suggestive sheaf of compositions, we are forced to make a rather sharp division between the everyday functions he fulfilled as organist and those special occasions of essentially private patronage that must have evoked the more complex style of his works. To trace these occasions we need to realize that extraordinary events were overtaking the papacy in these years.

From 1378, when it began, the great schism of the church had brought into confrontation two claimants to the papacy, one at Avignon and one at Rome, each the focus of a complex alliance of cardinals, bishops, and secular lords. After more than thirty years of political and administrative turmoil and confusion on a European scale, the Council of Pisa, assembled in 1409, attempted to resolve the problem by deposing both the Avignonese and Roman Popes and electing a new one, Alexander V (Pietro Filargo, Archbishop of Milan).[33] But as the claimants already in office denounced the entire procedure, there were now three contestants for the throne instead of two. During the seven

---

[30] Cavicchi, 'Sacro e profano; documenti e note su Bartolomeo da Bologna e gli organisti della cattedrale di Ferrara nel primo Quattrocento'; also Cavicchi's addendum in *RIM*, xi (1976), 178–81.

[31] See the documents in Cavicchi, 'Sacro e profano', 49, quoting Scalabrini, *Notizie storiche del . . . capitolo della S. Chiesa di Ferrara*, in Ferrara, Bibl. Comunale Ariostea MS C1. I, 125, fol. 310.

[32] Cavicchi, 'Sacro e profano', first document under 1427.

[33] For a concise description of the basic developments in this complex situation, from the mid-fourteenth century to about 1420, see Hay, *Europe in the Fourteenth and Fifteenth Centuries*, pp. 279–91. On the election of Alexander V see Valois, *La France et la grande schisme d'Occident*, vol. iv, pp. 103–106.

years (1409 until 1415) in which this situation persisted, the most recently instituted papacy, which consisted only of Alexander V and his successor John XXIII, claimed the allegiance of several north Italian lords, including Niccolò III. In November 1414 the Council of Constance was convoked, largely for the purpose of restoring stability by securing international agreement on a single solution. In 1415 John XXIII was forced to abdicate, the papal see was declared vacant by the Council, and eventually, after further difficulties had been resolved, the Council elected the new Pope, Martin V (Oddo Colonna), who ruled until 1430.[34]

For rulers of those smaller Italian states that were legally papal dependencies, these turbulent times called for delicate footwork. When there were still only two Popes, Alberto d'Este had recognized the Roman line. He had thus gained the privilege for the Studio and other favors in the 1390s from Boniface IX (ruled at Rome 1389–1404). Similarly, the young Niccolò, during his regency and just beyond, had at first followed the line of least resistance by accepting the Roman not the Avignonese obedience, up until the crisis of 1409. But at Pisa, Niccolò joined with the forces that hoped to find a new solution, led by the powerful Cardinal Baldassare Cossa, who was legate at Bologna and for practical purposes lord of the city. Niccolò not only supported the election of Alexander V, in June 1409, but made a public show of his allegiance to him when Alexander settled at Bologna in January 1410. Unable to move to Rome, Alexander remained at Bologna for three months, establishing there as much of the papal court as his influence permitted, and holding ceremonies. Among them was the bestowal of the Golden Rose on Niccolò III on 2 March 1410.[35] Alexander did not last much longer. On 3 May he died at Bologna, and was succeeded by the man who had installed him, Cardinal Cossa, who took the name of John XXIII. Niccolò was a faithful vassal to him as well, and further signs of benevolence towards Ferrara followed: in December 1410 John XXIII named Uguccione Contrari, lord of a powerful Ferrarese family, Captain-General of the Church. In March 1411 Niccolò accompanied Pope John on his departure from Bologna, and in February 1414 John made a solemn entry into Ferrara, where he remained for a week. All this anticipated Niccolò's trip to France the following summer and the opening of the Council at Constance in the autumn.[36]

It is with these circumstances, almost all outside Ferrara, that we can connect at least one composition by Bartolomeo da Bologna. Seven works altogether, each for three voices, are at present known and attributed to him, and all are found in MSS of Italian provenance that principally preserve

---

[34] On the Council of Constance see the chronicle of Ulrich von Richental, publ. as *Das Konzil zu Konstanz*.

[35] On these events, see Malvezzi, 'Alessandro V, papa, a Bologna', esp. 52. Of value as well is the contemporary chronicle of Monstrelet, published as *La Chronique d'Enguerran de Monstrelet . . . 1400–44*, pp. 66–74. See note 22 above.

[36] On John XXIII at Ferrara see *Diario ferrarese dall' anno 1409 sino al 1502 di autori incerti*, p. 14.

works by French and other non-Italian musicians: two in Mod A, four others in Oxford 213.[37] Mod A is certainly the earlier of the two, by about twenty years; the consensus of current specialized study of the MS is that its most likely place of origin is Bologna, and the date of its older fascicles is likely to be 1410/1411, in close connection with the residence there of the successive Popes of the Pisan line, Alexander V and John XXIII. This hypothesis was advanced in 1946 by Pirrotta, and subsequent scholarship, both summarized and further developed by Günther in 1972, has tended only to confirm it.[38] That the MS contains in its older fascicles a cross-section of polyphonic music from southern French and north Italian centers of the period – Avignon, Genoa, Milan, Padua, and Bologna, as Günther puts it – is entirely explicable in the light of what is known about the travels and retinues of several of the protagonists in the struggles for the papacy, including Benedict XIII, the Avignon Pope, and Alexander V.[39] A probable key figure in the assembling of the MS even in its early stages, as well as the undoubted compiler of its later fascicles, was the Italian composer Matteo de Perugia. Matteo was active at the Duomo of Milan from 1402 to 1407 and again from 1414 to 1416, but between these years, probably from 1407 to 1410, he was in the service of the same Pietro Filargo, then Archbishop of Milan, and followed him to Pavia. The chronicle of Monstrelet, mentioned earlier (cf. n. 22 above), reports that when Filargo became Alexander V he had a corps of musicians in his service and that they were inherited after his death by John XXIII. Monstrelet further records that at the festivities in Bologna for the election of John XXIII, on 17 May 1410, 'the singers . . . and also the canons of the Cardinals and of several [lords] of Italy, all rode before the Pope and sang motets and virelais . . . '.[40] As Pirrotta suggested, this occasion readily suits the second of two works by Bartolomeo in the MS, his ballade 'Arte psalentes', (Mod A, No. 73, published by Günther in complete transcription), the text of which refers to a group of singers in the presence of 'the great Pontiff' (*summo pontifice coram*). Since this piece is found in close proximity in the MS to another

---

[37] On Mod A see Pirrotta, 'Il codice estense lat. 568 e la musica francese in Italia al principio del '400', and Günther, 'Das Manuskript Modena'. On Oxford 213 the basic inventory is that of G. Reaney, 'The Manuscript Oxford, Bodleian Library, Canonici Misc. 213; and, most recently, there is the excellent study by Schoop, *Entstehung und Verwendung der Handschrift Oxford, Bodleian Library Canonici MS misc. 213*. Schoop is able to show (pp. 118–121) that the dated works in the MS (which bear dates with a number of diverse meanings, including date of composition, of performance, of copying) supply a repertoire composed between about 1421 and at latest 1436, with the bulk of the MS copied in the 1430s. The only other MS with works by Bartolomeo is the Codex Reina, ascribed to the area of Venice; see the inventory by von Fischer in 'The Manuscript Paris, Bibliothèque Nationale Nouv. acq. Frc. 6771 (Codex Reina = PR)'.

[38] Means of dating Mod A and localizing its provenance include, besides its contents and datable works, its handwriting, notation, style of decoration of initials, and external evidence about composers.

[39] On the travels of Benedict XIII and other related evidence see Günther, 'Das Manuskript Modena', 42.

[40] 'Et sy avoit chantres, par especial les chantres de la chapelle de son precedesseur, et aussi les chanoines de Cardinals et plusieurs d'Ytalie, que tous chevauchoient devant le pape et chantoient motetz et virelaiz, moult haut . . .'(*La Chronique*, p. 71).

piece for the papal chapel – the ballade 'Veri alme pastoris', by Corrado da Pistoia, with which it also has other features in common – it appears likely that both works are indeed products of an occasion that must have brought together not only these two musicians but several from other Italian centers. Bartolomeo, as we know, came not from Bologna but from nearby Ferrara; Corrado, apparently, came from Florence.[41] The varied contents of the earlier layers of the MS evidently embody a repertoire reflecting the assemblage of musicians in the service of the many ecclesiastical and secular lords who were brought to Bologna for the occasion. Monstrelet, if he is not exaggerating, reports that at the coronation of John XXIII there were twenty-four cardinals, two patriarchs, three archbishops, and twenty-seven abbots, besides other churchmen 'in great numbers'. Among the forty-four nobles, he particularly mentions Niccolò III and Carla Malatesta of Rimini; but he also reports on a Florentine delegation of almost 300 mounted visitors, including eighteen noblemen and six trumpeters, along with 'ten men playing musical instruments'.[42]

If the two works by Bartolomeo da Bologna in Mod A are representative of his style of composition of about 1410, we may regard him as an exceptionally resourceful master of current three-part polyphonic writing. In 'Arte psalentes', the upper line, apparently the only text-bearing voice, is well shaped in its larger phrase structure, combining shifts of rhythmic detail with remarkable clarity in general melodic direction; syncopated segments contrast with well-directed sequential passages in a line that moves effectively towards a local goal:

Ex. 1. B. da Bologna, 'Arte psalentes', mm. 1–36

---

[41] On notational features in common between the pieces by Corrado and by Bartolomeo see Günther, op. cit., p. 29.

[42] Monstrelet, *La Chronique*, p. 73.

In his other piece in the same MS, 'Que pena maior', we find skillful use of integration of intervallic material in the Tenor, in which the opening descending fourth is utilized in successive phrases, yet in each case with a new rhythmic form, all underpinning another well-planned upper line:

Ex. 2. B. da Bologna, 'Que pena maior', mm. 1–8

Perhaps of later vintage but equally resourceful are the pieces by him in the MS Oxford 213, recently shown by Schoop to have originated in the Veneto in the late 1420s and early 1430s. Bartolomeo's pieces are found all together in the tenth fascicle of the MS. This segment appears to contain a nest of works devoted mainly to him and including another, otherwise unknown musician from Ferrara (though very likely not active there) named 'Dominicus de Ferraria', along with some pieces by Dufay.[43] Here Bartolomeo is represented by two sets of secular and sacred compositions that have been found to be closely related as pairs: (1) his three-voice virelai, 'Vince con lena', followed by his own 'Et in terra' that draws on the virelai for its musical

[43] On the tenth fascicle of Oxford 213 see Reaney's inventory in 'The Manuscript Oxford' and his article, 'The Italian Contribution to the Manuscript Oxford, Bodleian Library, Canonici Misc. 213'. Of great value is the discussion by Schoop, op. cit., p. 43, who shows that the four works by Bartolomeo in this fascicle (the two pairs Nos. 315, 317, and 319, 320) are all in the same dark ink; while Nos. 316 (by Dominicus de Ferraria) and 318 (by Dufay) are in a lighter ink as well as being located at the lower parts of the leaves they occupy, below other works already entered. This tends to undermine the view advanced by Cavicchi, 'Sacro e profano', 55, that all these works constitute a Ferrarese fascicle, and that they might have been copied from a hypothetical original stemming from Ferrara.

material; (2) following this, his 'Morir desio', which is similarly related to a 'Patrem' by Bartolomeo that stands just before it in the MS.

These Mass movements by Bartolomeo have been recognized as being among the earliest known examples of Mass Ordinary settings based on the polyphonic content of secular models, indeed on any outside polyphonic compositions; they belong to the earliest chronological layer of the procedure of 'imitation' of polyphonic models (traditionally called 'parody' through a historical error of the nineteenth century, long perpetuated), that would develop by the end of the fifteenth century into a principal means of composition for the cyclic Mass.[44] In these early works by Bartolomeo the means of adaptation is much closer to transcription than to elaboration, but there are a few incidental touches of development of material from the model, especially in the Gloria based on 'Vince con lena'; these in a small way anticipate the subtleties of a much later phase of Mass composition.

A context for these works is thus far dimly visible in a few other single Gloria and Credo settings: three of them are by Antonius Zachara da Teramo, which are entered virtually consecutively in the MS Bologna Q 15 (Nos. 56, 58, 59).[45] Here we find two Glorias and one Credo, all based on secular antecedents, evidently written somewhat later than those of Bartolomeo, to judge from the degree of elaboration of their material, though possibly a more subtle approach coincided with a simpler one. That such works could have been composed as early as about 1410 is suggested by the most recently discovered composition by Zachara, the incomplete 'Patrem' preserved on flyleaves in Cividale, Museo Archeologico, MS LXIII and XCVIII, attributed to 'Magister A[ntonius] D[ictus] Z[achara]'. Other elements in these fragmentary remnants of a once large codex show us that the MS must have originated in Cividale, and it seems quite likely that it represents a short-lived phase of local polyphonic activity that arose in connection with the Council that met there in 1409 under Gregory XII, intended in opposition to that of Pisa.[46] Although we are unable to link Bartolomeo circumstantially with musicians in the curial circles of Gregory XII, we have good reason to connect him with the Bolognese periods of Alexander V and John XXIII, and thus to the contemporary musicians represented in Mod A.

If we now turn back to Bartolomeo's role as organist and to the documentation supplied by Cavicchi and Peverada on the uses of singers and organists at the cathedral of Ferrara in these years (to 1429), a better perspective may emerge.[47] Although these documents report a steady series of pay-

[44] On the procedures in the Gloria based on 'Vince con lena', see von Fischer, 'Kontrafakturen und Parodie in italienischer Werke des Trecento und frühen Quattrocento'.

[45] Pirrotta, 'Zachara Musicus'; repr. in *Music and Culture*.

[46] On these Cividale leaves see Pirrotta, ibid., 161, n. 22. The Council at Cividale lasted from 6 June to early September, coinciding with the Council at Pisa; see Valois, *La France*, iv, pp. 112 f.

[47] Cavicchi, 'Sacro e profano'; additional documents on musicians at the cathedral are published in Peverada, 'Vita musicale alla cattedrale di Ferrara nel Quattrocento; note e documenti'.

ments to participants in cathedral functions over these years, they record nothing unusual, as they mainly refer to normal liturgical events of general and local character. The general events are the major festivals of the liturgical cycle, for which the payments recorded here were probably for additional participants in the celebrating forces: Christmas, Epiphany, Easter, Corpus Christi, Ascension, etc. Among the major local events was the festival of St. George (24 April, mentioned in these records for the years 1411, 1413, 1417, 1423).[48] In 1424 we find payments for singing on the festival of St. Maurelius, a Ferrarese bishop and martyr who became a virtual co-patron of the city. It is in fact surprising to find no records in 1419 referring to special provisions for this saint, since in that year a series of celebrations for him included the exhumation and reburial of his relics.[49] The records also show participation by cathedral forces in certain events of state: the baptism of Ugo d'Este; processions celebrating Niccolò's victory over the Terzi at Parma (1409); and processions before, during, and after Niccolò's trip to the Holy Land (1413).[50] A number of these payments are made to Bartolomeo da Bologna as organist, but many are to unspecified 'cantori' and a few are to 'mansionari' (perhaps largely identical groups).

Not one of the records in these years stipulates the use of polyphonic music, and only a few of the documents may even be open to this inference. For the most part, we may well assume that what was sung on these events was the normal plainsong of the liturgy in its local forms; perhaps, on certain occasions, that simpler level of two-voice note-against-note polyphony which seems to have spread through northern Italy, as well as elsewhere, for processional or special uses, and as an adornment to certain favored, mainly metrical texts. But there is no evidence that this type of polyphonic practice was in any way prominent at Ferrara, whatever its popularity elsewhere.[51] The three-voice compositions attributed to Bartolomeo give us ample reason to believe that as organist he could have excelled in improvisation as well as in written polyphony, but the cathedral records mention no use of music on such levels of complexity even for major festivals.

Singers capable of vocal display comparable to that of Venice and Padua (to judge from the music of Ciconia) were rare in Ferrara, and all of them

---

[48] From liturgical manuals and chronicles of the period it is unequivocally clear that in Ferrara the festival of Saint George, the patron of the city, fell on 24 April. It was annually celebrated with these events: on the vigil (23 April) the city's guilds made an offering of various kinds of cloth which served as prizes for the races that were run on the following day. On 24 April there were horseback races in the morning, and in the afternoon foot races were run by young men and by young women, along with a race of donkeys. See Zambotti, *Diario*, pp. 6 (1476), 33 (1477), 47 (1478), 64 (1479), and further entries for this date for ensuing years. Also Caleffini, *Diario*, p. 60 (1476), and other references throughout.

[49] On these events see *Diario ferrarese*, pp. 15–16.

[50] Cavicchi, op. cit., 54 remarks that no documents of 1419 are included, perhaps owing to the absence of *Libri di Sagrestia* for that year; but on p. 59 he says that the year 1419 is documented by Scalabrini yet lacks any references to music. I agree with the latter statement.

[51] On this level of polyphony, spread widely through many parts of Europe, see, for its Italian sources of the 14th century, Martinez, *Die Musik des frühen Trecento*.

were visitors. Thus in late June or early July 1413 a 'certain Teutonic singer' was present; and in 1425 'some singers from Forlì' performed, as did, in 1427, 'a certain French singer from Padua'.[52] This man, at least, can be identified, since in that year we know that at Padua Cathedral a Giovanni da Francia *tenorista* was employed.[53] In the later 1420s we can assume that more clerical and para-clerical groups participated in the service; the documents of 1427 and 1429 speak for the first time of the combining on a single occasion of four groups: the 'mansionari', the 'cantori', the 'cappellani', and the 'clerici'; elsewhere, the same documents speak of 'pueri'. We can take for granted the existence of a cathedral school, but know little of its size or quality. Virtually coinciding with the last reference to Bartolomeo da Bologna, in 1426, is a note mentioning the appointment of a don Iohannes de Aranda as 'pulsator organorum ad instructionem clericorum'.[54] This suggests that there was now somewhat greater formalization in the teaching of music to the clerics.

Yet despite the local and regional importance of the cathedral as an institution, it seems clear that in the quality and importance of its musical and didactic functions, its roles and reputation were modest at best. This is still clearer if we compare it with the cathedral of Milan, a much more recent and much larger structure. The Milan Duomo was still under construction in 1394 when the first organ for it was commissioned and Antonio Monti da Prato was hired as organist.[55] His initial salary was thirty florins annually, but as little as a year later this was raised to fifty florins. Moreover, this Milanese post, comparable to that held by Bartolomeo at Ferrara, existed alongside the main musical position of singer and teacher, for which the *Fabbrica* in 1402 hired 'mastro Matteo da Perugia' at a salary of forty-eight florins; his main duties were to sing at Mass and Vespers, 'honoring the choir with sweet melodies'; he also had to teach music, exclusively at the Duomo and nowhere else in the city, 'to all who wish to learn', as well as gratis to three boys who would be selected by the authorities. Apart from interruptions in his service that were undoubtedly connected to the career of Archbishop Filargo (Alexander V), Matteo held this post until 1418, when he was succeeded by Ambrogio da Pessano, a priest who had in fact held the position during Matteo's absence from 1414 to 1418.[56] Although the post of Cantor in this, as any other cathedral, was an ancient title, one of the four traditional and principal 'dignities' of the medieval cathedral hierarchy, it seems clear that in hiring a musician of the caliber of Matteo, the Milanese authorities had in mind the installation of a professional musician of some attainment, not simply the filling of a traditional canonical role. Moreover,

[52] Cavicchi, op. cit., 59, item 5; 61, items 5 and 7.
[53] Casimiri, 'Musica e musicisti nella cattedrale di Padova nei secoli XIV, XV, XVI', 6.
[54] Communication from Maestro Adriano Francheschini.
[55] C. Sartori, 'Matteo da Perugia e Bertrand Feragut, i due primi maestri di cappella del Duomo di Milano', 12, which corrects the date 1395 given in earlier studies.
[56] Ibid., 20 ff.

this post and that of organist were always to be kept separate, as would also of course be true in San Marco in Venice and in other churches of comparable importance. At Ferrara during this period we can find no evidence of such differentiation of roles, and no other musician serving the cathedral alongside Bartolomeo.

In all, the situation in Ferrara was closer to that of Padua, to which it was comparable too in being an episcopal not an archiepiscopal diocese. In Padua Cathedral between 1409 and 1491, the post of *magister scolarum et cantor* was successively filled by as many as twenty-five musicians, many of them staying for as little as one year before moving on.[57] It is true that, from the late 1420s onward, new forces enter Ferrarese religious life, spurred by the energetic Bishop Giovanni Tavelli. But we must distinguish between the cathedral as the central focus of civic worship, and its role as an institutional base for the careers of musicians and for the cultivation of polyphony. Despite some efforts to improve the teaching of music and the traditions of its organ playing; despite the rebuilding of its organ in 1465 and the commissioning of Cosimo Tura to paint its magnificent organ shutters – none the less, the cathedral was undistinguished for its purely musical or didactic achievements. It remained a backward dependency of the court, where the Estensi centered their musical ambitions.[58]

[57] Casimiri, 'Musica e musicisti', 1–19.

[58] I hold to this view of the cathedral despite the additional and very valuable documentation supplied by Enrico Peverada in the article mentioned in note 47. From documents copied by Scalabrini in the 18th century, Peverada produces evidence that, as early as 1431 and until 1438, some singers in the service of Niccolò III (perhaps Niccolò Tedesco, or others unknown from archival documentary sources) performed in the cathedral on special occasions, and that his *piffari* also played there – at least once during the Offertory of the Mass (Peverada, 'Vita musicale', 5).

3

Ferrara in the 1430s

IN the 1430s Niccolò continued to wield local power, to father bastards, and to live as feudal lords had always lived. But the new shaping forces at the court, and in the seats of power in Italy, were centered in the rising influence of the forms of thought associated with humanism and the new learning. At Ferrara this was especially visible in the education and growing maturity of Niccolò's son and chosen heir, Leonello d'Este, who was to become one of the most remarkable ruling figures in the first half of the fifteenth century. By now, a familiar commonplace of local history is that Leonello's training under Guarino of Verona launched the humanistic movement at Ferrara, and that the impact of these teachings on him marks an example of the success of humanism as a program for the training of the aristocracy.

There is truth to the story. From 1429, when Guarino set up as teacher at Ferrara, he embarked on the realization of a didactic program emphasizing the classical languages, grammar, rhetoric, and moral philosophy.[1] Leonello was an apt pupil. He gained real mastery of Latin and considerable familiarity with a number of the classics of ancient history, drama, and rhetoric that were then available. The chronicler Johannes Ferrariensis certainly intended to flatter when he spoke of Leonello as 'a man of immense rarity, by the consensus of his time', but what he said was probably true.[2] There were certainly other Italian nobles in this period who commanded ancient languages and literature to some degree (though not nearly as many as believed by popular historians) but there were very few who matched Leonello. He gave Latin orations at affairs of state; wrote verse in both Latin and Italian; helped collect manuscripts of the classics; and even took an interest in certain text-critical problems in ancient writings.[3] Pride among

[1] On Guarino at Ferrara see the influential article by Garin, 'Guarino Veronese e la cultura a Ferrara', revised from an earlier version and issued in his *Ritratti di umanisti*, pp. 69-106; on the education of Leonello see Pardi, *Leonello d'Este*, pp. 28-33, and Woodward, *Studies in Education during the Age of the Renaissance*, pp. 32-47.

[2] J. Ferrariensis, *Excerpta ex Annalium Libris*, p. 30.

[3] See Decembrio, *De Politia Litteraria*, Bk. I, cap. 10, in *Politeia Litterarie Angeli Decembrii Mediolanensis*, for the claim that Leonello was the first to demonstrate that correspondence between Paul and Seneca was spurious; cf. Gardner, *Dukes and Poets*, p. 51; Gundersheimer, *Ferrara*, p. 98.

local chroniclers might account for some of the idealization of Leonello, and this became endemic later, when the rise of Borso brought a different set of personal standards to the court, somewhat displacing the central role of the professional humanists in Leonello's regime. This pride may also explain the tendency of Guarino's disciples, above all Carbone, to regard the advent of Guarino as forming the true birth of Ferrarese culture after dark ages in the past.[4] We can now see that such a view is lop-sided; the library inventory of 1436 alone should make this clear, since it is a practical impossibility that its large collection of classical Latin texts could have been assembled over the mere seven years between Guarino's arrival and the date of the inventory.[5] Yet we can be confident that Leonello not only made use of this library, but that he took an exceptionally keen interest in what he found there.

An extended portrait of Guarino's influence at Leonello's court is found in the *De Politia Litteraria* by the Milanese humanist Angelo Camillo Decembrio.[6] Its dialogues purport to convey the actual content of discussions on learned subjects by Leonello, Guarino, and a group of Ferrarese courtiers. The scene is set in Leonello's apartments in the Corte Vecchia, in the court gardens, or at the new country seat at Belriguardo. Whatever the degree of embellishment in Decembrio's scenario, the emphasis on critical appraisal of the classics, intermingled with tireless pedantry about grammatical matters, fits in well with what we know the young Leonello studied under Guarino: Virgil, Cicero, Caesar, Plutarch, and other classics. Vernacular writers, as Gardner noted, are said by Leonello to be 'those books which sometimes on winter nights we explain to our wives and children'.[7]

To the new intellectual climate there were other important contributors, among whom we should distinguish occasional visitors from long-term residents. The latter include Giovanni Aurispa, who arrived in 1427 as tutor to Niccolò's second son Meliaduse; Paolo Toscanelli, who was tutor to Borso beginning in 1431; and two famous physicians, Ugo Benzi and Michele Savonarola, both of whom became residents and taught at the university when it reopened in the 1440s. Meliaduse d'Este's friendship with Leone Battista Alberti led the latter to dedicate a comedy to Leonello in 1436 (the *Filodossio*); Alberti returned to Ferrara on at least two more occasions during the next six years. Patronage of artists began impressively with commissions to Jacopo Bellini and Pisanello to paint portaits of Leonello (cf. fig. 1) and, probably, Ginevra d'Este; and continued with Pisanello's extraordinary

---

[4] The classic statement of this view is in Lodovico Carbone's funeral oration for Guarino (d. 1460), cited by Garin, 'Guarino Veronese', p. 81.

[5] In the later 15th century, when the production of elaborate manuscripts had become much more nearly a small-scale industry at court, a year or more to produce a manuscript was not unusual.

[6] On the manuscript and printed versions of Decembrio's tract, see Gundersheimer, *Ferrara*, p. 104, n. 24; also Gardner, *Dukes and Poets*, pp. 46–9. The book was dedicated to Pope Pius II, but only because Leonello had died in 1450.

[7] Decembrio, op. cit., I, p. 6; and Gardner, op. cit., p. 48.

medal portraits of Leonello (cf. fig. 2). More publicly visible were festivities, which increased in frequency as political events, above all the marriages of three of Niccolò's children, prompted him to spend on displays of opulence. In September 1433 the Emperor Sigismund visited and remained for more than a week. And, probably in 1435, a *mascherata* was performed at court that featured a variety of mythological characters, including an Apollo with sun rays, a drunken Bacchus, Aesculapius, and Mars.[8] This may have been staged to celebrate the marriage of Leonello and Margherita Gonzaga, which brought on considerable festivities at carnival time.

As heir apparent, Leonello also took part in Niccolò's increasingly broader political initiatives in the 1430s, which spread across northern Italy from Saluzzo to Mantua. In 1431 Niccolò's third marriage, to Rizzarda da Saluzzo, opened a connection with that small state on the borders of France, and coincided with the official quartering of Estensi arms with the French crown. On the Italian front Niccolò continued to act as peacemaker, as he had done since the late 1420s. In 1433 he mediated the signing of a peace treaty at Ferrara between the Visconti and a Venetian-Florentine league. He did so again in 1435, and in that year Leonello's marriage began the long kinship between the Estensi and the Gonzaga, besides assuring Mantuan support on Leonello's eventual succession, which Niccolò had made official as early as 1433.[9]

The Council of Ferrara (1438)

As papal vassal for Ferrara, Niccolò could not avoid a degree of involvement in the continuing struggle of the papacy to re-establish its seat in Rome and its supremacy in the Western church. From the beginning of his reign, in 1431, Eugenius IV (Gabriele Condulmero of Venice) struggled to reaffirm his power in the face of opposition, above all that of the Council of Basle, which continued to meet in defiance of Eugenius and claimed authority in the affairs of Western Christendom. Basle even sought to bring Greek church leaders to a forthcoming ecumenical Council aimed at nothing less than the reunion of the Western and Eastern churches. To subvert this, Eugenius determined to assemble his own Council, to be held at an Italian center to which he could easily call high-ranking ecclesiastics of his own obedience, chiefly Italian but, if all went well, from countries as distant as Spain and Scotland.[10] For various reasons he chose Ferrara.

---

[8] Mentioned by Pardi, *Leonello d'Este*, p. 36, as taking place in 1444, in connection with Niccolò's acquisition of Lugo; but this occurred in 1436.

[9] Ibid., p. 45. Similar purposes were served in 1434 and 1437 by the marriages of Niccolò's daughters Ginevra and Lucia to Sigismondo Pandolfo Malatesta (*Diario ferrarese*, p. 20), and to Carlo di Francesco Gonzaga (*Diario ferrarese*, p. 21), respectively.

[10] On Eugenius and the Council of Ferrara-Florence see especially Gill, *The Council of Florence*; basic documentation on the Council is in course of publication by Hofmann, ed., *Acta Camerae Apostolicae . . . de Concilio Florentino*.

By June 1436 Niccolò was visiting Eugenius in nearby Bologna, to negotiate the terms on which Ferrara would become the seat of the Council. What Eugenius mainly needed was money to finance the entire gigantic venture, and Niccolò was willing to make a fair-sized contribution by purchasing from Eugenius three castle-towns in the Romagna for 14,000 ducats.[11] The choice of Ferrara was strategic and convenient for papal purposes. To the Greeks the city was said to be 'pleasing', perhaps owing to earlier contacts between Greek leaders and Ferrarese humanists, especially Guarino, who had travelled in the Near East. Eugenius's complex negotiations for the Council developed on all fronts throughout 1437, and to this increased contact between the papal curia and Niccolò III we can probably ascribe the visit of Guillaume Dufay to Ferrara in May 1437.

In January 1438 the Council formally opened. It continued to meet throughout that year, transferring to Florence in January 1439. Since the Council as a cultural and political event has been neglected by most Ferrarese historians, it will be useful to reconsider briefly its scope and size.

At its first session, on 8 January 1438 in the cathedral of Ferrara (before the arrival of the Pope and the Greek leaders) there were no fewer than five archbishops, twenty-seven bishops and thirteen abbots. By the fifth session, on 11 February (and still before the arrival of the Greeks), besides the Pope and his entourage, there were seventy-five Latin prelates, including five cardinals, four archbishops, twenty-seven bishops, and nine bishops-elect, twelve abbots and generals of Regular Orders, along with other curial officials. At the fifth session too was a delegation from Savoy, which had been asked to act as intermediary between this Council and that of Basle.[12] If we assume an average attendance at the sessions of the Council of about 100 Western delegates, and calculate for each an average of ten retainers (for the Pope this would, of course, be far too low a figure), we can assume that there were about 1,000 visitors on the Western side alone.[12] To this were joined not less than 700 Greeks, including the Patriarch of the Eastern Church, the Emperor of Byzantium, and high dignitaries from widespread areas of Eastern Europe. Although the contractual arrangements with the curia had called for the fixing of local prices for the Council delegates and the avoidance of any

---

[11] Gill, p. 92. The date of Niccolò's visit is from Muratori, ed., *Rerum Italicarum Scriptores* . . ., xxxiii, pt. 1, *Historia de Bologna*, p. 47. Gill, p. 93, gives the date incorrectly as 1437, which would place it a month after Dufay's visit. In the Papal Bull selecting Ferrara, the city was described as 'locum quidem gratum Graecis . . .' ; Ferrara offered Eugenius a city that was well governed, at peace (as Florence then was not), had the legal status of a papal vicariate, and was able to house and feed a large number of visitors.

[12] See Hofmann, 'Die Konzilsarbeit in Ferrara', esp. 127 ff. (on fifth session).

[13] On Ferrara at the period of the Council see Hofmann (art. cited in n. 12) and *Acta Camerae Apostolicae*, iii, *passim*. Gundersheimer, *Ferrara*, p. 205, cites earlier specialized research by the economic historian Sitta who proposed an estimated population of Ferrara at 100,000 persons at the end of the 15th century. Gundersheimer thinks this much too large, preferring a figure of about 30,000.

special tax that would cause hardship to the local populace, Niccolò was later accused, perhaps justly, of profiting handsomely from the Council through the imposition of such a tax.[14] If he did, he partially made up for it by the generous way in which he treated his visitors. A carpeted footbridge was built from the cathedral loggia to the Palazzo della Ragione where the Pope was housed, to facilitate his movements to and from the meetings.[15] Special accommodations were also found for the Patriarch and the Emperor. Opportunities arose for the display of local talents. Guarino acted as translator between Latins and Greeks both at Ferrara and at Florence; and Leonello offered a Latin oration on the arrival of the Pope. That Leonello actually took part in the Council, as claimed by Pardi, is doubtful.[16]

The importance of the Council for doctrinal discussions and political developments has inevitably obscured its importance as a cultural event. Throughout 1438, especially in the early months of the year, when it met more frequently, there must have been numerous opportunities for intellectual and social interchange. Its Western delegates formed a massive cross-section of the highest church dignitaries of the time, though at first with certain countries, notably Spain, France, and England, thinly represented. Even if not all of them had the breadth of interests of an Ambrogio Traversari, who played a key role in the Council, they represented precisely the circles in which, as Nino Pirrotta has convincingly argued, sacred polyphony at this period was primarily cultivated.[17] Many of these dignitaries combined intellectual backgrounds with political experience, and they undoubtedly presented the local ruling family with a vivid image of the potential relationship between personal culture, including taste in the arts, and political success.

Not only Council delegates but emissaries and agents from distant principalities were present, though for shorter periods, since many lay rulers were anxious to keep in close touch with current developments at both Basle and Ferrara. Besides the diplomatic delegation from Savoy in February, there was one from Burgundy in November. Throughout much of the year, Florentine representatives were also in Ferrara ready to negotiate for the removal of the Council to Florence if conditions for transfer became ripe.[18] The principal

---

[14] That Niccolò made money from the Council is specifically charged by the Greek delegate Sylvester Syropoulos, in his Diaries kept during the Council; see Laurent, ed., *Les 'Memoires' du . . . Sylvestre Syropoulos, sur le Concile de Florence, 1438–39*, pp. 246 f. Syropoulos claims that Niccolò doubled the usual customs fees charged at Ferrara, and that local merchants doubled their prices; he also gives a figure, perhaps inflated, of 5,000 foreigners in Ferrara during the Council. The same charge against Niccolò is made by Pius II in his *Commentaries*, Book II, p. 180.

[15] Hofmann, 'Die Konzilsarbeit', 124 f.

[16] Pardi, *Leonello d'Este*, p. 37.

[17] Pirrotta, 'Music and Cultural Tendencies', 130 ff; repr. in *Music and Culture*.

[18] D'Accone, 'The Singers of San Giovanni in Florence during the Fifteenth Century', 309 f.

'citizen' of Florence, Cosimo de' Medici, and his brother Lorenzo, were in Ferrara for this purpose for extended periods; they managed to co-ordinate this plan with the improvement of the musical forces at their own cathedral, and even secured several singers in Ferrara for service at Florence.[19]

[19] Ibid., 310.

4

Feragut and Dufay

BETWEEN 1430 and 1440 the gradual increase in musical resources doubtless owed something to the new humanistic interests of Leonello and the members of his generation. But it probably owed even more to the development of the Ferrarese court as a whole, as it became more worldly and politically more ambitious. The desire for improved cultural visibility that made the court attractive to musicians is linked in turn to the higher political and hierarchical status achieved by the formal alliance of the Estensi with the French court in 1431, a status reinforced by the city's role as seat of the Council in 1438. Although it might be expected that the emulation of greater courts and the increased festivities of the 1430s would bring about the hiring of musicians on a more regular basis than in the past, it appears that Niccolò did little about this in the first half of the decade, but then added musicians in minimal numbers to the court salary rolls during the four years from 1435 to 1438, as the plans for the Council began to mature and especially after Leonello's marriage in 1435.

The level of patronage directly traceable to Niccolò is represented by at most two surviving dedicatory compositions. One of them is by Dufay (the ballade 'C'est bien raison') and is directly addressed to Niccolò. The other, which may or may not have been intended for him but is in any case by a composer of some stature, who was at various times associated with the court, is the motet 'Francorum nobilitati' by Bertrand Feragut.[1]

That the Feragut motet is connected with Niccolò was first suggested by Pirro. Although it mentions no name other than the composer's own, its text alludes to a 'prince' who is united with the French nobility and who is praised conventionally as guardian of his flock and protector of his people against evil:

[Part 1]
Francorum nobilitati te tua bonitas associavit, princeps, cissuras malorum muniens, scelera puniendo et praeveniendo deinceps, custos vere ovilis, cadentisque populi tua industria vigil destruendo malitiam et diabolica confundens, optime pugil.[2]

---

[1] Feragut's motet is found in two contemporary manuscripts: Oxford, Canonici 213, fols. 11ᵛ–12; and Bologna, Biblioteca Universitaria, MS 2216, No. 41. It was published in transcription by Charles Van den Borren from the Oxford manuscript, in *Polyphonia Sacra*, pp. 257–61.

[2] In translation (Part 1): 'Prince, your excellence united you to the nobility of the French; guarding against the thrusts of evil, punishing and overcoming the wicked, true guardian of the flock, by your diligence preventing the fall of your people, destroying the wicked and confounding the diabolical, noblest of warriors'. See A. Pirro, *Histoire*, p. 65.

In the second part the text turns to the revelation of 'divine secrets' which 'shine forth like the sun' (*quae ut sol splendent*); the author then hopes for the prince's longevity and hopes that 'B[ertrand] Feragut' will be 'united with him', that is, join his service. Since the text seems potentially suitable to an ecclesiastical patron, typically a bishop, Van den Borren suggested that it might have been written for a French churchman who had been raised to the nobility. Possibly too, like another Feragut motet for Vicenza, it may first have been written for one patron and then adapted for another.[3] Its comparison with the sun's rays may fit Niccolò, as the sun appears as a prominent symbol on the frontispiece of the magnificently illuminated French Bible made for him between 1431 and 1436.[4] More directly relevant is that on 1 January 1431 King Charles VII of France issued the royal breve that gave Niccolò the right to quarter the Este arms with the French by adding to the Este eagle the three gold lilies on a blue field.[5]

Feragut may have been in Ferrara as early as about 1420–5, to judge from a papal document recently discovered by Alejandro Planchart. This document, in the Register of Supplications for 1427–8, mentions a 'Bertrandus Ferraguti' who was then a monk of the monastery of San Michele de Medicina, in Bologna, but had formerly been a member of the Augustinian order of 'eremitani' and had then lived in Ferrara.[6] Since we know that Feragut had been *maestro di cappella* at the Duomo of Milan in the years 1425–30, this earlier residence in Ferrara must have taken place before 1425.[7] On the other hand, we can be quite sure that Feragut was in Ferrara in 1431, when the quartering of arms was granted, thanks to a document preserved by Scalabrini which not only mentions him 'and other singers of the lord Marquis' but indicates that they were paid to sing in the cathedral on 19 August 1431 (*pro collacione cantori domine Bertrandi et aliorum cantorum domini Marchionis qui cantaverunt in coro die dominico . . .* [paid] *s. III d. II.*).[8] That this 'Bertrandus' is Feragut seems beyond question, as we know of

---

[3] See Gallo and Mantese, *Ricerche sulle origini della cappella musicale del Duomo di Vicenza*, pp. 20–3, on the motet 'Excelsa civitas Vincencia', which Feragut had written for the installation of a local bishop in 1409 and which was used again in 1433 for the ceremonies honoring his successor.

[4] I am greatly indebted to Dr Edith Kirsch for having drawn my attention to this illustration. On its frontispiece a central dividing space between the two columns of text shows a five-line musical staff containing (not in this order) the Gothic letters 'g' and 'k', two black notes (*longae*) and a small figure of a sackbut. This pattern of notes and symbols is exactly repeated on the remainder of the staff. Whether it has any symbolic meaning beyond the decorative has yet to be determined.

[5] To the references cited earlier for this important event see also Muratori, *Delle antichità estensi ed italiane*, p. 165; Frizzi, *Memorie per la storia di Ferrara*, p. 69. This remained the Este standard until 1452, when Borso's acquisition of the dukedom of Modena from Emperor Frederick III caused the addition of the imperial two-headed eagle. The papal keys symbolizing the ducal status of Ferrara were not added until 1471.

[6] For information on this document I am indebted to Professor Planchart.

[7] Sartori, 'Matteo de Perugia e Bertrand Feragut'; and Fano, *La cappella musicale del Duomo di Milano*, pt. 1, p. 19.

[8] Ferrara, Biblioteca Comunale Ariostea, MS C1. I, 456, fol. 35ᵛ.

no other musician by this name at this period, and the date fits well with Feragut's date of departure from the Milan Duomo in May 1430, a year and three months before his appearance in Ferrarese records. His service under Niccolò may perhaps have been more lasting than the presently available documentation shows, since we find that in 1438 he is mentioned once more in Ferrara, now among the singers who were hired by the Florentines for service at their cathedral. Thereafter he seems to have found his way back to southern France, for in 1449 he is listed as in the service of René d'Anjou, ex-King of Naples, then at Aix.[9]

Dufay's ballade for Niccolò, richer in content than the Feragut motet, opens the relationship between Dufay and the Estense court, a relationship that is to remain important for Ferrara long after Dufay's return to permanent residence in Cambrai as early as 1439.[10] The remarkable number of Dufay's works preserved in Ferrarese musical MSS of the Leonello period and right down to the period of Ercole, makes this clear beyond doubt. This ballade was published in complete form by Besseler from its only surviving source, the MS Oxford 213, and its allusion to Niccolò as ruler of Ferrara is explicit and unequivocal.[11] Although I had earlier ascribed this handsome work to 1437, when Dufay paid his only recorded visit to the Ferrarese court, I am now inclinced to agree with David Fallows that a more likely date is 1433, which would bring its date of composition into agreement with 'May 1436', the last date for any work entered into the Oxford manuscript.[12] The first stanza of this four-stanza text, each ending with an identical refrain, runs as follows:

> C'est bien raison de devoir essaucier
> Et honnourer tous princes de renom,
> Especial ceux qui font aprecier
> Pour leur vertus, sens et discretion.
> Pour ce voldray faire relacion
> D'un tres noble, digne de tout honneur,
> D'origine si bien que de raison.
> Bien est doté peuple d'un tel seigneur.

In its subsequent stanzas the text refers to Niccolò's alleged connection to the French royal line (*Du sanc reiaul de France tesmoignier/Puis vrayement as generacion*), a long-time myth of the Este family; to his abilities as peacemaker in Italy between warring states (*Italie soiant en grant dangier/Con de guerre et de division/Par son moyen a faitte pacefier*); and to several of his

---

[9] On these phases of Feragut's career see Gallo and Mantese, *Ricerche sulle origini*, pp. 20–2; also Sartori, *loc. cit.*; and D'Accone, 'The Singers of San Giovanni', 311 f.

[10] See Wright, 'Dufay in Cambrai; Discoveries and Revisions'.

[11] The only surviving source of the ballade is Oxford, Canonici MS 213, No. 116; see Reaney, 'The Manuscript Oxford', 92. It is available in transcription in Dufay, *Opera omnia*, vi (Rome, 1964), pp. 31–2.

[12] See Fallows, *Dufay*, p. 40.

Ex. 3. G. Dufay, 'C'est bien raison', mm. 1–33

supposed virtues as ruling figure (*Saige, discret, eloquent et entier/Large, courtois, gracieux, bel et bon*). At the very end it comes to its climax by naming Niccolò as ruler of Ferrara, with his proper title:

> Prince, je voeil manifester son nom:
> Il est marquis et souverain recteur
> De Ferare, Nicholas l'appell'on.
> Bien est doté peuple d'un tel siegneur.

On the basis of its reference to Niccolò as peacemaker, Besseler had assigned the ballade to 1433, when on 26 April he mediated a treaty of peace between the Visconti and a Florentine-Venetian league. Yet it is not really certain that this is the peacemaking action referred to; Niccolò's endeavors helped to achieve such treaties on three occasions, in 1428, 1433, and 1441. This three-fold success is even recorded on a monument later erected in his honor in Ferrara.[13] Yet the date 1428 seems to be too early, since the reference to the French royal line and his allegiance probably points to 1431 as an earliest possible date; 1441, on the other hand, is too late, in view of the dates of the Oxford manuscript. So 1433 seems likeliest at present. We must remember, however, that a court payment of 6 May 1437 reports the sum of twenty ducats paid to 'Guielmo de fait, cantadore nella capella del Papa', the reasons not being specified.[14] It may have been for musical services rendered earlier, or as a donation to maintain goodwill (just as Niccolò's distant grandson, Alfonso I d'Este, was later to pay a handsome sum to Jean Mouton).[15]

The payment of 1437 enables us, in any case, to feel sure of a direct personal connection between Dufay and the Ferrarese court in the late 1430s, and this in turn can help to build a circumstantial case for the attribution of still another Dufay piece, namely the celebrated 'Seigneur Leon', which

---

[13] See Lazzari, 'Il signor di Ferrara', 696; and Capra, 'Gli epitaphi per Niccolò III d'Este'.

[14] This payment was first reported by Valdrighi, 'Cappelle, concerti e musiche di casa d'Este dal secolo XV al XVIII', 437, who gave the recipient's name as 'Ginelino da fare'. But the correct reading was supplied by Besseler, with the help of Modenese archivists, in his 'Neue Dokumente zum Leben und Schaffen Dufay', 166.

[15] See Lockwood, 'Jean Mouton and Jean Michel: New Evidence on French Music and Musicians, 1505–1520', 212 f.

Fallows has recently proposed as being intended for Leonello d'Este.[16] This breaks with the earlier view, proposed by Plamenac and accepted by Besseler, that the text of 'Seigneur Leon' refers to a churchman who is being given an honor by the 'church militant', as the poem states.[17] They had agreed that the piece could be seen as a tribute to Leonard of Chios, Archbishop of Mitylene, who lived in Italy from 1444 on. Fallows' suggestion is striking and suggestive, and although I had earlier accepted the Leonard of Chios hypothesis, I am now inclined to agree that it might indeed be for Leonello. Ferrara was, after all, a papal fief, and its ruler, whether Marquis or Duke (after 1471), was in effect a papal vassal. In that sense the textual allusion to the recipient having been given a 'noble sword' by the church may reflect the bestowal of the territory upon Leonello. Whether it refers to 1441, however, the year of Leonello's ascent to power, is an open question. Leonello was formally recognized by his father as his legitimate successor as early as 1429, as shown by Pardi.[18] We might also observe that Leonello is portrayed as a lion (*Leone, Leonello*) by Pisanello, in one of the portrait medals made for his wedding to Maria d'Aragona in 1444, and is even shown there as a singing lion (see fig. 2).

Conflicting evidence – biographical on the one side, textual on the other – has clouded understanding of Dufay's early years in Italy, but recent findings suggest that his presence in Italy was probably continuous during the 1420s and down to 1433, when he interrupted his papal service with a prolonged stay in Savoy and Burgundy. That he had been in Italy as early as 1420, or even 1419, is inferred by Besseler from his wedding motet for Cleofe Malatesta; that his university studies in canon law took place not in the North but in Bologna has recently been shown by Craig Wright, while Planchart has argued that the most plausible years for this university attendance were 1424–28. Immediately thereafter he would have joined the service of Eugenius IV, remaining a papal singer until 1433. Planchart has also found persuasive reasons for associating other early Dufay works with patrons and institutions in Italy: e.g. the *Missa 'Sancti Iacobi'*, long thought to be for the church of St. Jacques de la Boucherie in Paris, seems more plausibly connected with the important church of San Giacomo Maggiore in Bologna.[19] The emergent picture of an extended period of residence by Dufay in Bologna, both as student and as member of the papal establishment, which resided in Bologna for long periods of time, offers suggestive possiblities of contact with Ferrara. This is not merely owing to the obvious proximity and ease of access of the two cities, but to the contacts between Niccolò and the papal establishment that increased, as we have seen, in the 1430s. At best, however, such further contacts between the younger Dufay and Ferrara remain speculative;

---

[16] See Fallows, *Dufay*, p. 63.
[17] Plamenac, 'An Unknown Composition by Dufay?'.
[18] Pardi, *Leonello d'Este*, p. 45.
[19] Planchart, 'Guillaume Dufay's Masses: a View of the Manuscript Traditions', pp. 28–33.

but his later contacts with the court, on the other hand, continue through the period of Leonello's rule, despite Dufay's return to Cambrai, and are well substantiated. They help to explain why major Ferrarese musical sources of the Leonello period are exceptionally well endowed with both sacred and secular music by Dufay.

5

Leonello's Rule, 1441–50;
the Court Chapel

MOST historians have portrayed Leonello as primarily a learned prince with some political ability. But the record of his rule suggests that these elements in him were equally balanced. By December 1441, when Niccolò III died at Milan, Leonello was a mature man of thirty-four, who had survived the death of his first wife, Margherita Gonzaga, and who, in that year, had already governed the state for six months in Niccolò's absence. Once in power as Marquis, he continued Niccolò's policies of maintaining neutrality in the long struggle between Milan and Venice, while forging strong alliances. An early diplomatic move was to remarry advantageously, and in 1441 Alfonso d'Aragona's seizure of power in the long-contested Kingdom of Naples gave him the chance. Ten months after Alfonso's victory, Leonello's representatives were in Naples to sign a contract for his marriage to one of the King's illegitimate daughters, Maria d'Aragona. Her arrival at Ferrara in May 1444 set off another round of festivities. It also forged a kinship with Naples that would later be resumed by Ercole's marriage to Maria's niece, Eleonora d'Aragona; and it opened diplomatic channels in a variety of cultural sectors, including music.[1] That Leonello had a grandiose political imagination is clear from an extraordinary plan, drawn up by him and by Borso, to extend Alfonso's power by urging him to take over Milan: he would thus become 'King of Italy', with Leonello as his chief ally. The plan was obviously designed to give Ferrara permanent protection from Venetian dreams of aggrandizement.[2] Nothing came of it, of course; but it reveals with perfect clarity the sense of outer instability that hung over the Este regime.

In 1445 Leonello sent his younger brothers, Ercole and Sigismondo, permanently to Naples to be raised there. The practice of sending younger male family members to other courts for military education was common enough. In this case it was also intended, no doubt, to remove from immediate view

---

[1] On the marriage see Pardi, *Leonello d'Este*, pp. 53 f.

[2] Pardi, pp. 96–100. Of particular interest for Neapolitan history at this time is Borso's extended description of the city of Naples, written in 1444–5, and Leonello's secret advice to Alfonso d'Aragona; all published by Foucard, 'Fonti di storia napoletana nell'Archivio di Stato di Modena; descrizione della città di Napoli e statistica del Regno nel 1444'; and his 'Proposte e documenti'.

any possible threats to the established line of succession.[3] Relations with other smaller dynasties were also improved in the 1440s by the marriages of several of Leonello's sisters, to lords of Urbino, Segni, Camerino, and Correggio.[4] And while Borso remained a trusted ally and counselor, ecclesiastical appointments were found for Leonello's two other brothers, Meliaduse at Pomposa and Gurone at Nonantola.

In civic affairs Leonello was an effective ruler. He was severe when necessary but far less violent than Niccolò had been, perhaps less prudent in financial matters, and lacking in Niccolò's earthy and popular touch. While making some improvements in the local economy, Leonello spent the court's substance for cultural ends. In 1442 he reopened the university, and gradually added to its faculty of arts the ageing Guarino, the Greek scholar Teodoro Gaza, the poet Basinio da Parma, and Francesco Accolti as Rector. He strengthened the faculties of law and medicine as well, and within his lifetime saw the international reputation of the Studio established, with students in attendance from England, France, Germany, Hungary, and Greece.[5]

In a more familiar vein, Leonello's regime brought further additions to the court library and the dedication to him of numerous works, including poetry, more copies and more translations of the classics.[6] We know of at least six copyists who were commissioned by the court to produce manuscripts, chiefly classical texts but a few in French and in Italian. The chief scribe was Biagio Bosoni of Cremona, who began at the court as early as 1435 and from whom a number of attributed manuscripts survive.[7] The more frequent copying of texts implies the establishment of locally centered teams for producing finished manuscripts, often handsomely illuminated; Leonello's short reign also marks the beginning of the great local traditions in miniature painting. In this sector the main figure of Leonello's period is Giorgio de Alamagna, who labored for eight years on a large Breviary for Leonello, now lost.[8] This

---

[3] Ercole was then fourteen years of age, Sigismondo twelve. Leonello also sent one of his own bastards, Francesco d'Este, to the court of Burgundy in 1444 (aged fifteen) where he was raised as a close companion to the Count of Charolais, the future Charles the Bold. Francesco remained attached to the Burgundian court throughout his life. That the portrait of an Este prince by Roger van der Weyden was actually of Francesco, and was made in Burgundy, not in Ferrara, was brilliantly demonstrated by Kantorowicz, 'The Este Portrait by Roger van der Weyden'; cf. Panofsky, *Early Netherlandish Painting*, pp. 272 and 273.   [4] Pardi, p. 79.

[5] On Leonello as ruler see Gundersheimer, *Ferrara*, pp. 99–103, 120–6, who accepts the favorable views of Johannes Ferrariensis and the later diarist of the *Diario ferrarese*. For evidence of sumptuary laws under Leonello that forbade female citizens to spend more than a fixed percentage of their dowries and denied any use of silk for clothes, with similar measures, see Pardi, p. 53, and Cittadella, *Notizie*, pp. 289 ff. on repressive decrees.

[6] Bertoni, *La Biblioteca Estense*, pp. 8 ff; Fava, *La Biblioteca Estense*, pp. 23–40.

[7] Fava, p. 26; Bertoni on Bosoni in 'Un copista del marchese Leonello d'Este (Biagio Bosoni da Cremona)'.

[8] Hermann, 'Zur Geschichte der Miniaturmalerei zum Hofe der Este in Ferrara', 15–23 (on miniaturists under Leonello).

represents a change in status of copyists and miniaturists from Niccolò's time; now, at least one principal specialist in each craft is employed on a regular basis as court functionary, whereas Niccolò had evidently hired them (chiefly miniaturists from Tuscany) on occasional terms. The process of book production in all its phases became the special responsibility of a court workshop and not a casual activity governed by change and opportunity.

The same increased formalization appears to some extent in court patronage of studio painters, though with greater difficulty owing to their varied wanderings and commissions. Leonello went to considerable trouble to secure works by leading masters, and some painters came to stay for short periods.[9] On a most lasting basis, after his accession, he secured the steady services of Pisanello, who had passed through the city as early as 1431; he had sent Leonello a portrait of Julius Caesar in 1435, and was in Ferrara in 1438 during the Council.[10] From the end of 1442 until 1448, Pisanello was regularly employed at court, and from these central years of Leonello's rule we have six commemorative portrait medals of Leonello by him, besides others for prominent local figures (cf. fig. 2).[11] We also find payments to Pisanello for paintings, including one for Belriguardo that earned him the considerable sum of fifty gold ducats.[12] The special status of Pisanello is in turn celebrated by local poets; and now began the vogue of making portrait medals for individual citizens of importance, in addition to the ruling circles. As a means of honoring individuals, its combination of portrayal, symbolic allusions, and aspiration to classical ideals is thoroughly typical for the period of Leonello.[13]

In all probability the organization of Leonello's daily life was different not only from that of his father but from that of many princes of his time. Although his patronage of the arts competes with that of many less literary-minded fellow patrons, his serious cultivation of books sets him apart from most of his peers in the Italian *signorie*, and more nearly rivals the accomplishments of the learned Florentine statesmen of the time. His interests reflect preoccupation with a specifically courtly, highly private aristocratic mode of life, showing little if any concern with visible displays of person, retinue, or pomp to impress the public. Many of his letters are sent from Belriguardo, where he must have spent much time, aloof from the more visible role of

---

[9] Venturi, 'I primordi del Rinascimento artistico a Ferrara', 608 ff.; also the summary by Gruyer, *L'Art ferrarais à l'époque de Princes d'Este*, pp. 34–46, and Gundersheimer, *Ferrara*, pp. 236–9.

[10] Hill, *Pisanello*, p. 59.

[11] On Pisanello's medals of prominent Ferraresi other than Este family members see, conveniently, Chiarelli's listing in *L'opera completa del Pisanello*, p. 110, and preceding inventory of works; and Hill, *A Corpus of Italian Medals of the Italian Renaissance before Cellini*.

[12] This may be compared with the twenty gold ducats paid twice to Dufay, in 1437 and 1443, and the same amount paid to Roger van der Weyden in 1450 (perhaps for the portrait of Francesco d'Este).

[13] On the symbolic aspects of Pisanello's portrait medals see Hill, *Pisanello*, pp. 142–50. Fig. 2 shows Pisanello's representation of Leonello as a lion ('Leoncello') singing mensurally-notated music.

public ruler in the city.[14] Decembrio's depiction of Leonello as devoting himself regularly to conversation with his small learned circle, pursuing private literary, artistic, and contemplative interests, may not be unduly idealized, despite its neglect of his practical obligations.

Leonello's religiosity was characteristically different in its forms of expression from that of Niccolò. Rather than make distant pilgrimages in fulfillment of vows for political purposes, Leonello put his piety to work in local projects, especially poor-relief, hospital construction, and the improvement of local ecclesiastical institutions. He built a court chapel for his own use, within the grounds of the residential palazzo.[15] All his biographers took note of this private chapel as a special achievement, not only because it was unprecedented but because it led to Leonello's recruitment of musicians from great distances. A valuable description is again given by Johannes Ferrariensis, in whose chronology of events the foundation of this chapel follows directly after the funeral of Niccolò and the accession of Leonello to power. It is indicative of the importance of piety to the ruling figure that the chronicler takes the founding of the chapel as direct evidence of Leonello's earliest efforts to symbolize the authority of his new status:

Quibus peractis, quo aliquo praeclaro facinore enitesceret (erat enim admodum gloriae cupidus) nomenque maiestatis suae ubivis celebrandum diffunderet, ampliandae religionis atque cultus gratia, miram infra suarum aedium limites capellam construxit ac more regio honorifice ac sumptuosissime paramentis, libris, iocalibus auro caelatis eam decoravit. Cantores ex Gallis accersiri iussit; quorum suavissimo concentu divinae laudes mirifice iugiter celebrabantur. Aderat Princeps et sacris misteriis indesinenter astabat; voluptatis gratia non pudebat divinas gratias concinere; in organis ludere scientem summopere habere curavit.[16]

These things done [i.e. the funeral of Niccolò III], in order that the fame of his deeds should shine forth clearly (he was then rather desirous of fame) and the glory of his name would be known everywhere, thanks to his furthering of religion and of worship, within his palace he built a chapel and in the royal manner he embellished it most honorably and sumptuously with furnishings, books, and gold reliefs. He ordered singers to be brought from France, who celebrated the divine service marvelously with

---

[14] Pardi, p. 85, notes that Leonello was also often at Consandolo, another country villa. That these sojourns were not only planned to escape from plague can be shown by comparing the dates for which the chroniclers report heavy incidence of plague during his lifetime; the most serious outbreak appears to have been in 1438, during the Council.

[15] The chapel was located in the 'palazzo ducale di Piazza', as the chroniclers called it; that is, not the Castello Vecchio but the palazzo nearer to the central square, almost opposite the cathedral. From Caleffini, *Croniche*, i, p. 270, n. 1, we learn that later, in 1482, it was called the 'cappella vecchia' and had been on the street level of the palazzo grounds. Zambotti, *Diario ferrarese dall'anno 1476 sino al 1504*, p. 5, reports that by 1476 Ercole had created his own *cappella di corte* as part of his reconstruction of the palazzo and surroundings, and that to do this he had torn down some rooms that had been near the kitchens. The basic structure of the second chapel, as later rebuilt in the period of Alfonso II, is still intact (see fig. 3).

[16] J. Ferrariensis, *Excerpta ex Annalium Libris*, p. 32. The passage was plagiarized by Sardi in his *Libro delle historie ferraresi*, p. 151, who added a comparative remark on Ercole's later chapel.

very sweet harmony. The Prince was in attendance and took part faithfully in the celebration of the holy mysteries; out of sheer pleasure he was not ashamed to take part in the singing of the divine thanks. He took the trouble to know how to play the organ extremely well.

The chapel was probably constructed early in Leonello's rule, certainly within his first three years of taking power. An inventory of 1444, discussed by Pardi, shows us what its furnishings then were: a cross of gilded silver, a gold rose (gift of Eugenius IV), an altar-piece with a crowned Virgin; two crosses of silver; a thurible, and pairs of candlesticks and silver chalices.[17] The chapel represents a new departure in the domestic scheme of the Este court. It justifies the acquisition of religious art objects, service books, an organ, and musicians to carry out its functions. It also reflects a degree of political consciousness, for although the chronicler refers to the chapel as being decorated and furnished 'in the royal manner' (*more regio*), which might be interpreted broadly, or as an imitation of the French court, it seems more likely that it hints at distant emulation of the court of Naples, with which Leonello was just then striving to form an alliance. Shortly after the conquest of Naples in 1442, Alfonso d'Aragona had built three votive chapels to mark his victorious entry into the city, all of them apparently separate small buildings.[18] As late as 1906 the remains of one of these Neapolitan chapels were still visible, and permitted description of the original structure as a small church of one nave, with a simple façade, pilastered ceiling, the walls decorated entirely with frescoes, and the whole dedicated to Santa Maria della Pace.[19] From the description of Leonello's furnishings for his chapel we see that it was equally modest in size (one pair of candlesticks sufficed for it) and, like its Neapolitan counterpart, it was dedicated to the Virgin and had a Marian altar-piece. That Leonello saw to the installation of an organ, which he was able to play himself, further suggests small size and private function. This, too, brings Naples to mind, for in 1449 he sent a wooden organ made by Constantino Tantino of Modena as a special gift to King Alfonso.[20] In the establishment of the chapel we may readily discern the mixture of personal religious feeling and of public display of religiosity at which the chronicler hints; to these he adds Leonello's recruitment of musicians and thus alludes to his active interest in music.

---

[17] Pardi, p. 53, n. 1.   [18] Hersey, *The Aragonese Arch at Naples, 1443–1475*, p. 13.

[19] See Bernich, 'Statue e frammenti architettonici della prima epoca aragonese', 8.

[20] Pardi, p. 199, n. 1 reprints the text of the letter (20 July 1449) sending the organ to Alfonso the Magnanimous.

6

Singers and Repertoires

THAT Leonello's musical literacy has not been adequately recognized undoubtedly results from the domination of contemporary humanists in the
writing of his biography, and of modern historians working primarily from
the humanistic traditions. Decembrio's idealized account has something to
say on painting, but on music no more than a few fleeting and casual
references; he allows, characteristically, that in a well-appointed library there
should be, as ornaments to its basic contents, such items as a horoscope, a
terrestrial globe, and a lute for occasional relaxation.[1] Guarino admitted
music as a recreational diversion for scholars bent normally on serious application to their books, but in his educational system it played a much smaller
role than in the rival teachings of Vittorino da Feltre at Mantua.[2] It is in just
these terms that Leonello justifies his turning to music in a letter to Guarino
apparently written during his student years: 'occasionally as I turn away from
books, I then give myself over to singing and lute-playing for the relaxation
of the spirit and as a pastime . . .'.[3]

But as early as 1433 there is evidence that Leonello had more intensive
musical interests than we have yet found for any of the Estensi. In that year
we find two 'libri de canto' copied by scribes of the court, one of them
expressly indicated as being made for Leonello.[4] In October 1435 a local
cartolaro supplies three quinterns of parchment 'for messer Leonello . . . to
write a pair of rules of singing' (i.e. treatises on music).[5] By 1437, documents
confirm that he could play the lute; in 1441 occurs the earliest of all references
to Pietrobono, later the most famous lutenist and lutenist-singer of his time,
here called 'familiar' of Leonello.[6] Music and poetry went together for

---

[1] *De Politia Litterarie*, i, p. 3: 'Intra bibliothecam insuper horoscopium aut sphaeram cos-
micam citharaque habere non dedecet; si ea quandoque delecteris, quae nisi cum volumus nihil
instrepsit . . .'.

[2] See Woodward, *Studies in Education*, pp. 10–25, on Vittorino; pp. 26–47, on Guarino. On
Vittorino's Carthusian disciple Johannes Gallicus as music theorist and critic, see Schrade,
'Renaissance: the Historical Conception of an Epoch', pp. 25 f.; and Lowinsky, 'Music of the
Renaissance as Viewed by Renaissance Musicians', pp. 134 ff.

[3] Pardi, *Leonello d'Este*, p. 33: 'interdum me ad libros revoco, porro cantui et fidibus laxandi
animi gratia temporis quicquam concedo' (from Leonello's letter in Milan, Bibl. Ambrosiana MS
C. 145 *sup.*).

[4] For the text of this document see my paper, 'Dufay and Ferrara', p. 24, Doc. 1.

[5] Ibid., p. 24, Doc. 2.

[6] The document is quoted in full in my paper, 'Pietrobono and the Instrumental Tradition at
Ferrara', 118, n. 11.

Leonello, as we should expect; in 1437 we find the copying of 'una vacheta de cantione et soneti del Illustrissimo Signore', that is, poems by Leonello.[7]

Although we have no salary rolls from the 1430s, the *Registri de' Mandati* for these years show that some musicians were hired at the court.[8] In the absence of salary rolls, their absolute status and numbers cannot be determined, but what evidence we have points to a norm of two or three trumpeters, two or three *piffari*, and for the first time, a regularly employed court 'singer'. This individual, known simply as 'Niccolò Tedesco', appears for the first time in 1436, and he remains at court for many years thereafter; he was still in service as late as 1466.[9] He is to be distinguished from two other singers, who happen to have the same name; one is Niccolò de Beccariis, called 'cantore' in a document of 1436; the other is Niccolò Philippo de Olanda, present at court from 1447 until as late as 1481. Niccolò Tedesco, evidently from Basle, was greatly admired as both *cantor* and *pulsator* (apparently as lutenist).[10] In 1436 and 1441 he was sent to Basle to procure other secular musicians, especially *piffari*, and in 1441 he was the first musician in the history of the court to be put into the regular salary rolls (the *Bolletta de' Salariati*) at a handsome wage of 300 *Lire marchesane* per year. As *pulsator* he probably accompanied his own singing, and his presence at the court in 1437 makes even more plausible the performance of Dufay's 'C'est bien raison' in that year. In 1441 he is also given six months free rent of a house in the city, as a gift from Leonello.[11] That he was a secular musician, a court performer, probably specializing in secular music or at least not hired for use in sacred music, is strongly suggested by the groupings of musicians we find in the later records. When Leonello hires chapel singers in the 1440s, the name of Niccolò Tedesco never appears among them.

Despite the more intensive musical activity that we can take for granted in

---

[7] ASM, *Mandati*, 1436–8 (under the year 1437), fol. 126.

[8] The earliest preserved registers of the *Bolletta de' Salariati* in the ASM begin only with the year 1456, and thereafter, for the entire 15th century, are sadly incomplete. The *Mandati*, despite gaps, begin in 1422 and are well preserved for the 15th century. The *Memoriali* began to be kept in 1438 but the first preserved register among them is from 1447; missing thereafter are those for 1451, 1465, 1480, and 1483.

[9] Hamm and Scott, 'A Study and Inventory of the MS Modena, Biblioteca Estense Alpha X. 1. 11', 114, cite 'various documents' in the ASM as evidence that Niccolò Tedesco is first mentioned in Ferrara in 1441. But I have found him there as early as 1436; a *Mandato* dated 18 November 1436 confirms that 'Niccolò todescho va adesso ad Basilea . . . incontinente ricevuta questa faritige dare et donare ducati venticinque doro ad spese de quilla camera . . .', ASM, *Mandati*, 1436–8, fol. 72. In 1437 and 1441 he is called 'cantor et pulsator eccellentissimo'; in 1438 and 1439 we have no record of him but also no reason to suppose him absent, since the records are not in series but record isolated payments.

[10] Niccolò Tedesco is called in one document 'Niccolò de Basilea'. He made at least these journeys on behalf of Leonello: in 1436 to Basle (see n. 9); in August 1441 to 'Alemania' to bring back 'pifferi' (*Mandati*, 1441–2, fol. 40); and again in November 1441 (ibid., fol. 133').

[11] ASM, *Mandati*, 1441–2, fol. 141'. Leonello bestowed similar gifts of houses, though for undetermined periods, on Gerard Leay, a singer of his chapel, and on the *piffaro* Corrado de Alemagna, both in 1441; see Pardi, *Leonello d'Este*, p. 198.

connection with the Council at Ferrara in 1438, it appears that the recruitment of singers from France and Flanders begins only in 1443, that is, one to two years after Leonello's accession and in coincidence with the first stages of construction of his court chapel. It also coincides, perhaps significantly, with Leonello's payment to Dufay in the same year, 1443, through a bank in Bruges; it is at least imaginable that Dufay might not only have aided Leonello's musical purposes by sending compositions but might also have helped to recruit musicians for him. What we find corroborates firmly the account given by the chronicler, though again the documentation for chapel singers comes not from salary rolls but from *Mandati* and *Guardaroba* accounts containing isolated payments; these records are not designed to show in full the numbers of functionaries in any branch of the court.[12] Still, what we have makes it possible to form a fairly clear picture of the growth of Leonello's musical forces over the eight years from 1443 to 1450.

In 1443 we find four singers; by 1445 there are as many as nine, and by the last three years of Leonello's rule the figure has grown to ten, including a regular organist; this is exclusive of other musicians at the court who are transitory and do not appear to be associated with the *cappella di corte*. In 1443, only one singer is actually called a *tenorista*, but when their identities and designations are sorted out, it appears that in that year there probably were two tenors and two singers of undesignated range (perhaps one bass, one soprano). The pair of tenors was maintained in 1445 and there were added two 'chierici', almost certainly with high voices; they are probably the boys who were assigned to live with the well-known singer Johannes Fede when he arrived in July 1445.[13] The extension of voice-ranges, together with the slowly increasing membership, corresponds well to the increasing acquisition of three- and four-part polyphony that is codified for the chapel in the MS Mod B.

Where did they come from? In 1445 the chapel singer Gerard Leay was sent to Burgundy 'on business of the Marquis Leonello', and in 1446 the singer Giovanni Filiberto (Jean Filibert) was sent to France explicitly to bring back singers for Leonello.[14] From the Low Countries was Ugolino Madoeten

---

[12] Both the *Mandati* and *Memoriali* are essentially compilations of individual payments, organized chronologically but not sub-organized by class or type of payment. For a superficial survey of Estense court registers, nevertheless the only one available, see Sitta, 'Saggio sulle istituzioni finanziarie del ducato estense', 89–254, especially 196–206.

[13] For the full texts of the documents on Fede at Ferrara see my 'Dufay and Ferrara', p. 24, Documents 3a, b, c. For further on Fede see *Die Musik in Geschichte und Gegenwart*, iv, cols. 1–2. I am not sure that the Fede listed as a *contratenorista* in the chapel of St. Peter's in 1466 could not be identical to our Fede; the argument given by Rehm (*ivi*) is based solely on the tendency of the chapel of St. Peter's to function as a preparatory stage for the Papal Chapel, but this was far from being a binding condition. At any rate, it is likely that the Fede who was in Rome in 1446 is the same man who is found in the French royal chapel in 1473–4. If Johannes Fede was about twenty-five years old in 1445, he would not have been more than fifty-five in 1475; thus it is not impossible that there was only one 15th-century musician by this name.

[14] ASM, *Mandati*, 1445–6, fols. 64ᵛ, 227. Fol. 64ᵛ: payment of 23 April 1445 to 'Gerardo Leay cantore prefati domini libras septuaginta unam soldi sedecim denari undecim marchesane

of Brabant; from Burgundy, this same Jean Filibert.[15] In 1447 a *tenorista* was brought to the court from Florence; from this and other documents published by D'Accone it seems clear that Leonello was in competition for singers with the newly established chapel of the Baptistry of San Giovanni in Florence, and that there was also considerable interplay with the Papal Chapel in the frequent comings and goings of singers. Yet the central point is that the nine years of Leonello's rule show the creation and maintenance of one of the very few active household chapels in Italy in which polyphonic music was utilized for daily liturgical purposes. It is perhaps the only courtly chapel of its type north of Florence at this time. It is wholly distinct from the foundation for the training of clerics and singers that Bishop Tavelli was seeking to establish at the cathedral during the early 1440s, emulating the cathedral schools that Pope Eugenius had recently founded at Florence, Verona, Padua, and Treviso.[16] In the absence of any really reliable information on the size, composition, or financing of Leonello's general court organization, we are at a loss to know how this group of musicians fitted into the larger framework of the court, but it seems reasonably likely that a regular staff of ten singers formed a sizeable fraction of the establishment.

Leonello provided for his singers with benefices, and continued to help them with housing as well. Documents found by Adriano Franceschini show that in October 1448 both the English singer called 'Johannes, presbiter Londini', named as a 'singer of the Marquis', took a loan on a house in the Contrada San Michele in Ferrara; and on the same date the singer 'Ugolinus filius quondam Symonis Brabant cantor' did the same. Further, the London priest is noted in the document as holder of the benefice of the chapel of Saint James the Apostle in Ferrara Cathedral, while Ugolino is named as rector of the cathedral chapel of Santa Maria a Nive. In the same year, the singer

pro expensis facto ad partes Burgundie de anno presente pro negociis prefati domini . . .'; fol. 227: '. . . domini Johanni Filiberti cantore cappellano domini florenos vigintiquinque auri pro conducendo ex partibus france cantores pro prefati domino nostro . . .'.

[15] As the lists in Appendix V show, the personnel of Leonello's chapel was only partly the same over the years from 1443 to 1450; several singers came and went, while a few remained in service. Gerard Leay, *tenorista*, is found in 1443, 1444, and 1445; in 1446 he was granted free housing (see n. 11 above), but thereafter he may have left the chapel for other forms of local activity. We are sure of the continuous presence of these singers: Giovanni dal Monte and Ugolino de Brabant (1443–1450). Some of the singers were evidently recruited in France, but Fede came directly from the Papal Chapel; and in 1448 the singer Giovanni Gobert transferred to the Papal Chapel after a short stay in Leonello's service. In at least one case the local status of singers from the north was not only parallel to that of the foreign university students at Ferrara but coincided with it. In 1444 the university rolls show that a doctorate in arts was conferred on 'Giovanni f. q. Ghilmare de Groninghen cantore'. This initiates the close connection between musicians and students that is to grow in the later 15th century. We may note that this Giovanni from Groningen foreshadows the later presence of Rudolph Agricola, also from that city, who functioned both as student and as organist at Ercole I's chapel.

[16] See D'Accone, 'The Singers of San Giovanni', 308; D'Alessi, *La cappella musicale del Duomo di Treviso*, p. 42; Spagnolo, *Le scuole accolitali in Verona*, p. 14. Eugenius's provisions for these foundations were made in the following chronological order: Florence, 23 March 1436; Treviso, 20 June 1438; Padua, 26 September 1438; Verona, 15 July 1440.

'Nicolaus Philippus de Olandia capelanus et cantor domini Marchionis' received the canonry of San Donnino de Monticulo in the diocese of Parma.[17]

That the size and prominence of the *cappella di corte* indeed impressed Leonello's contemporaries is clear above all from a rhymed chronicle written in 1462 by a local citizen, Ugo Caleffini, later the author of a prose chronicle of the period of Ercole I. Caleffini was a minor bureaucrat, not a teacher or humanist, and his portrait of Leonello is accordingly quite different from that of Johannes Ferrariensis, who taught canon law in the university. In Caleffini's awkward and naïve but revealing narrative, the primary feature of Leonello's patronage is not literature or even the visual arts, but music and especially the music of his *cappella di corte*. He first praises Leonello's own abilities in 'singing or playing', then stresses the large number of singers with whom he filled his chapel, as well as the organists who came to play in it; finally, Leonello's regular participation in the performance of Mass and Vespers, at times in the presence of the public:

> Se lui se metea in canto o sonare,
> Piacer ne prendea chi l'ascoltava
> Tuta zente se havea a maraviare.
> . . .
> Quanto li piaceva li vespri con le Messe!
> . . .
> Tanti cantadori questo signore havia
> Tuta soa capella ni era pino;
> E sempre organiti li venia
> Canti e suoni a l'officio divino
> Questa era notabele signoria
> Tanta zente era a oldire a capo chino
> Per devotione tuto stava rimesso;
> Parea che li anzoli fossoli da presso.[18]

(If he began to sing or to play, all who listened were pleased; everyone stayed to marvel at it; how he enjoyed Vespers with Masses! This lord had so many singers that his chapel was quite full of them, and organists were always coming there, to sing and play in the divine offices. This was a most notable lord. So many people came to hear, with heads bowed, for devotion, and everyone stood meekly; it seemed as if the angels were nearby.)

To this formally established staff we can add the smaller group of court musicians who are outside the chapel, that is, the instrumentalists and the singer-player Niccolò Tedesco, along with a few transient figures whose status at the court is difficult to ascertain from the few extant documents. Of

---

[17] Franceschini's sources for these documents are ASF, AN, Not. G. Loiani, matr. 78, pacco 2, prot. 1448 (doc. of 14 October 1448 on 'Iohannes cantor . . . presbiter Londini') and same source and date for document on Ugolino de Brabant. On Nicolaus Philippus de Olandia, the source is ASF, AN, Not. G. Meleghini, matr. 72, pacco 1, prot. 1448, col. 35ᵛ (16 August 1448).

[18] Caleffini, *Chronica de la illustrissima et excellentissima casa d'Este*, ed. Cappelli in 'Notizie di Ugo Caleffini . . . con la sua cronaca in rima de casa d'Este', 288–9.

these the most striking are surely the two English musicians, both named 'Johannes', who turn up in 1448; one of them also in 1449 and 1450. We will return to them shortly in connection with the repertoires of the Leonello period.

There is also some evidence of music-making beyond the plainsong level at the cathedral during these years, no doubt stimulated through the presence in its hierarchy of Ugolino di Orvieto, whose well-known and important work as music theorist was combined with some efforts in composition. But it seems clear enough that the cathedral inevitably lagged behind the court, and especially the court chapel, as a center for musicians actively concerned with polyphony.[19] Of musical life in the other religious establishments of the city, including the confraternities, we know very little. For the Carmelite monastery of San Paolo we have later evidence of the installation of a splendid organ (1459); yet although inferences have been made from the later possession of music by this institution, there is no concrete evidence to support the view that in the Leonello period it was a vital musical center.[20] Most instructive with regard to the scope and character of music available to the musicians of Leonello's chapel are the surviving repertoires of sacred music from this period at Ferrara, of which the only virtually complete source is the great manuscript of the Biblioteca Estense, MS Alpha X. 1. 11 (Mod B).

The Manuscript Mod B

To build and decorate a chapel, furnish it with devotional objects and an organ, and recruit a staff of *cappellani cantori*, did not complete the patron's obligation. He had also to furnish it with its own service books for the performance of the liturgy, in this case especially for Mass and Vespers. Although local *scriptoria* could presumably have produced the plainsong choirbooks typical of the period, Leonello acquired at least some of them elsewhere. In March 1447 we find payment for the binding in Ferrara of 'three Antiphoners written in Florence'. Apparently the unbound gatherings were notated and decorated in Florence but the binding was done locally, perhaps to insure that bindings were suitable and bore the owner's arms, as

[19] A study of the *scuole primarie* of the Duomo is being undertaken by Maestro Adriano Franceschini and will surely illuminate many aspects of the cathedral's history that are now obscure. The judgement offered here reflects the belief that Italian cathedrals of this time, even the largest and financially best supported of them, were only in very few and rare instances primary centers of polyphony, and that in this period they took part in the development of polyphonic practice in Italy largely to the extent that they fostered teaching institutions for the clergy (occasionally also on a civic basis, as in Verona) and were able to teach *canto figurato* as well as *canto plano*.

[20] I am obliged here to dissent from the views expressed by my colleague Adriano Cavicchi, who has described San Paolo as a musical center of substantial importance in the 15th century, but so far on the basis of evidence that to me remains inconclusive; see his 'Sacro e profano', esp. 64 f., and n. 39; also his contribution to the collective volume entitled *Ferrara*, vol. i, ed. Renzi, p. 325.

happened with other court MSS. The chapel must also have needed at least a Missal and a Gradual or Kyriale, but the fragmentary records available disclose no such payment. For its supply of Masses we do, however, find a revealing entry under the date 8 June 1447: on this day the chapel singer Giovanni Filiberto was reimbursed two ducats he had paid to 'two Frenchmen who had given the Marquis a book containing six new Masses'.[21] These may well be polyphonic settings of the Ordinary rather than plainsong Ordinaries, since the reference to 'new Masses' makes plainsong unlikely. In the next year, 1448, we find a payment 'per legadura de uno libro da chanto grande in charta de capreto per uxo del prefato nostro signore . . .'.[22] It is likely that this 'large book of music for the use of our lord' (i.e. Leonello) is the massive and significant polyphonic collection of Vespers music preserved in the Biblioteca Estense in Modena, known as Mod B.

This central source of polyphonic music of the first half of the fifteenth century has been discussed by scholars for more than a century, but its true provenance and even its exact contents have been known just over a decade. A complete inventory and a valuable study of the manuscript was published in 1972 by Charles Hamm and Ann Besser Scott; what follows supplements and somewhat revises their conclusions.[23]

Mod B is a substantial manuscript, containing in its final form 131 settings of Latin texts by continental and English composers, chiefly motets but also hymns, Magnificats, antiphons and other liturgical compositions. The very large motet sections project Mod B into the mainstream of the sacred and commemorative polyphony of its time. From a place in the original index at which the scribe indicated the beginning of the first motet section ('Hic incipiunt motteti') to the end of the MS as it stands, the original layer included not less than eighteen motets by Dufay and his continental peers, and an impressive fifty-two by English composers. We can follow the MS in arranging the total contents of Layer I by national groups; see p. 53. The MS gains still greater importance by virtue of its unique preservation of as many as fifty-four compositions, including eleven each by Dufay and Dunstable. Further, forty-eight works by Dufay make up more than a third of the entire contents and, as Hamm and Scott observe, almost two-thirds of all the works by continental composers that it contains. These distributions suggest that, by means not readily inferable from the historical documentation alone, the chapel under Leonello was able to acquire large numbers of

---

[21] ASM, *Guardaroba, Creditori e Debitori 'G'*, 1447, fol. 29; the full text is given in my 'Dufay and Ferrara', p. 25, Doc. 4 (the three Antiphoners). For the book of Masses see ASM, *Mandati*, 1447, fol. 75ᵛ: 'Vos factores generales dari faciatis domino Johani Filiberti cantori cappellano domini florenos duos auri donandos duobus francigenis qui dederunt prefato domino nostro librum unum cantus sex missarum novarum . . . Ludovicus Casella scriptis, viii Juni 1447'. Also in my 'Dufay and Ferrara', p. 25, Doc. 5.

[22] 'Dufay and Ferrara', p. 25, Doc. 6. The date of this payment is 17 December 1448; what is paid for is the binding in parchment of a large book of music for the 'use of our lord', i.e. Leonello; the cost of binding is 0.10.0.   [23] Hamm and Scott, 'A Study and Inventory'.

Continental		English	
Dufay	48 or 49	Dunstable	31
Binchois	12 or 13	Power	8
Benoit	3	Forest	4
Fede	2	Plummer	4
Grossin	1	Stone	2
		Benet	2
	circa 67	Pyamour	1
		Sandley	1
			53

works by Dufay and by the most prominent English composers of the period. How it did do so is open to speculation; yet the incremental structure of the manuscript itself may offer both clues and suggestions for further lines of investigation.

The scribe of Layer I of the MS set it up in the following sections:

LAYER I

Section 1 (fols. 1–20): Twenty-four Hymns for Vespers, almost all by Dufay, with liturgical assignments indicated in the MS. They form a cycle from Advent to All Saints, followed by six hymns for festivals of the Common.

Section 2 (fols. 21ᵛ–29): Four settings of liturgical texts, of which the first two are longer (Binchois's 'Te deum', and 'In exitu'), the next two shorter (two 'Benedicamus' settings by Dufay).

Section 3 (fols. 31ᵛ–43): Seven Magnificats, in Tones I, II (two), III, VI, VIII (two); to which two more were added as part of Layer II.

Section 4 (fols. 51–74): On these leaves the original scribe filled in a series of ten Antiphons and two Offertory settings, from Benoit's 'Virgo Maria' (fol. 51) to the anonymous 'Felix namque' (fol. 56), followed by eighteen 'motteti' (thus in index). A major difference between the antiphon settings and the motets in this section is not their text-types (although characteristically the motets embrace a wider range, including occasional pieces for secular events) but that the motets are longer pieces that include works for a larger number of voices, whereas the antiphons are short works for three voices, each covering a single folio side. At later stages, works were added before and after this section on then empty leaves.

Section 5 (fols. 81–136): Fifty-two motets by English composers. It is significant that this section falls entirely under Layer I and has no additions by later hands. The central figure is Dunstable, followed at a distance by Power, then by six lesser contemporaries. In this section almost all the works are longer pieces, each covering a complete opening and occasionally two openings; only a few short works are fitted on to single sides.

In its original form the manuscript was a substantial collection of its type, carefully written by its original scribe as regards music, text, and attributions; adorned with a single handsome red-and-blue calligraphic initial for its first composition and with less ornate but well-made smaller initials for the works that followed. Hamm and Scott infer from the regularity of this main hand throughout the manuscript that the copying of Layer I was done over a relatively short period of time. Whatever that period may have been, it sufficed for the bulk of the contents and for the equally well-compiled thematic index (an unusual feature for its time) that was made by the same hand. The index prefaced the entire MS, contained attributions in addition to those in the main body of the volume, and is partially preserved in the present state of the manuscript.

Hamm and Scott have provided initially persuasive evidence to show that the manuscript originated in Ferrara, some time during the years 1440–50, that is, during the period of Leonello's rule, and for his chapel. Four elements underlie their argument. First, the MS shows no sign that it was ever anywhere else than in the Estense library. Moreover, it must have been in the court library in the early 1470s, since Layer IV contains a work that could not have been written earlier than 1471. Second, one of the two watermarks in the MS is also found in archival registers of the Estense court that date from the Leonello period.[24] Third, the earliest layer includes three pieces by a certain Benoit, and a singer by this name was hired by Leonello for the chapel in 1448.[25] Fourth, Hamm and Scott believe that the calligraphic initials in Mod B resemble those of a number of illuminated choirbooks and other manuscripts made for the court in the mid-fifteenth century.[26] Though none of these arguments is conclusive, they form, when taken together, a substantial basis for Ferrarese provenance, at least so far as can be inferred from the evidence about Leonello's chapel known up until now. In fact, further evidence will tend to confirm this view more strongly, as we will see in connection with Layers II and III.

LAYER II

Four compositions entered at three places in the MS left blank by the scribe when copying Layer I: an anonymous hymn to St. Anthony of Padua entered on folios 29^v–30 just after the original Section 2; two Magnificats entered after those of Layer I (Section 3); and the Dufay motet 'Moribus et genere' (fols. 74^v–76) entered at the end of the section of motets by continental composers. Layer II was copied by the same scribe as Layer I but after the composition of the index.

[24] The watermarks in the source are given by Hamm and Scott, 104. The first, a three-petalled flower with two buds on its stem, is equivalent to Briquet No. 6306 (see Briquet, *Les Filigranes*); the second, a three-peaked crown, does not appear in Briquet but is found in Ferrarese court registers of the 1440s; see Hamm and Scott, p. 113. Since the court in the 15th century obtained most of its paper from Venice or through local *cartolai* who acquired it from mills in Italy, the watermarks are indeed strong evidence of Ferrarese provenance, but are not in themselves conclusive.   [25] The text of the document in 'Dufay and Ferrara', p. 22, n. 46. [26] Ibid., p. 22, n. 47, in which I raised doubts about the tendency to assert connections between calligraphic initials in Mod B and those of other Ferrarese MSS of this period. The general similarities in these types of initials are so great and so widespread that no local provenance seems to me to be demonstrable in the present state of knowledge.

LAYER III

This layer consists in all of Dufay's hymn 'Proles de celo' (fols. 20ᵛ–21), plus six consecutive antiphon settings, four by Dufay and two by Fede (the only works of this latter composer). The antiphons were added by a second hand on folios 48ᵛ–50, that is, just before the original Section 4. Although Hamm and Scott reported no evidence that would link Johannes Fede with Ferrara, I have found documents that definitely place him there, as a chapel singer, from July 1445 to April 1446, a ten-month stay that immediately follows his departure from papal service (1443–5) and precedes his entry into the French royal chapel (1449–50). The Ferrarese documents on Fede are quite explicit: on 14 July 1445 he is put into the salary rolls as *cantor capellanus*; in November of that year two choir boys are lodged with him to learn singing; and on 5 April 1446 his payments are canceled.[27] So 1445 or 1446 is the earliest likely date for the copying of Layer III of the MS; and a plausible date for its termination up to this point would certainly be 1450, when Leonello's death caused the chapel to disband.

We can complete this outline of the contents of the MS with a brief account of the three remaining layers, following Hamm and Scott's nomenclature:

LAYER IV

A single motet by Johannes Brebis for Ercole I d'Este, 'Hercules omni memorandus aevo', was entered at the end of the continental motet section. This piece cannot have been written earlier than the very end of 1471 or, more likely, the summer of 1472 (as will be seen later). I follow Hamm and Scott in calling the hand that entered this piece Hand E.

LAYER V

Another piece (Hand C), an anonymous fauxbourdon setting of 'Collaudemus venerantes' from the hymn 'Tibi Christi splendor', was fitted in on folios 12ᵛ–13 below a Dufay humn.

LAYER VI

Three more anonymous hymns, later added by Hand B; one on folios 11ᵛ–12, in the hymn section, and the other two on fols. 78ᵛ–79 and 79ᵛ–80.

If we now look at the manuscript in its original formation (Layer I) we find that its five well-spaced sections bear different relationships to the central contemporary sources of polyphony emanating from Italian centers, especially the MSS Bologna Q 15 and Aosta. The corpus of hymns in Section 1, all but one by Dufay, shows the assimilation into local use of a recently-composed hymn cycle that was rapidly and widely gaining favor in Italian chapels of the time that were open to polyphony. The Dufay cycle is virtually complete in Mod B and in Bologna Q 15, where nineteen Dufay hymns are intermingled with three settings by Johannes de Lymburgia (who apparently had a hand in the compilation of Q 15) and one by Feragut, which complete the cycle. The

---

[27] Ibid., p. 24 f. (Doc. 3a, b, c).

56 *Singers and Repertoires*

same cycle was copied much later into the papal MS, Sistina 15, but not before the very end of the fifteenth century. Other hymn cycles are found in MSS from Naples and Verona that were made between two and four decades after the completion of the original layer of Mod B.[28]

The very small Section 2 of Mod B also relates closely to Q 15 and to the MSS Florence 112bis and Trent 90; the Magnificats of Section 3 display an especially strong connection to Florence 112bis. In that source, a manuscript partially similar to Mod B (containing Hymns, Antiphons, and Magnificats) but not strictly arranged by composition type, three of the Magnificats of Section 3 of Mod B are found consecutively (Florence 112bis, fols. 13–21).[29]

The extensive sections of motets in Mod B present difficult problems of provenance and transmission. In the continental motet section (fols. 46ᵛ–74) we find that at least two Dufay motets for specific occasions are *unica*, although they were certainly not written for Ferrara. One is Dufay's 'Magnanime gentis', composed in connection with a treaty of 1438 between the cities of Berne and Fribourg; the other is his 'Salve flos tusce gentis', undoubtedly for a Florentine occasion and very likely written in 1435 or 1436.[30] Equally, as many as eight Binchois works in Mod B are known from no other source. In both cases we must infer a massive loss of source material, but we may also speculate, on the best information available, on the possible sources of so much musical material by outside composers. For the entire section of motets by continental composers we may hypothesize five main lines of transmission, not all of them mutually exclusive:

1. *Dufay.* In view of Dufay's documented visit to Ferrara in 1437 and of Leonello's payment to him in Bruges in 1443, it seems highly likely that Dufay had more than an incidental relationship to Leonello and his chapel. During his years as a member of the papal entourage, works of his could easily have been transmitted either personally or by other papal singers, the latter possibility being more likely in 1438. Thereafter, when Dufay had returned to Cambrai, letters and payments show that he kept up contacts with several of his former Italian patrons, including those at Ferrara and Florence, and that he found ways to send his music over continental distances by means of intermediaries.[31]

2. *Florence.* Eugenius IV was often in residence in Florence as well as in Bologna, especially after the transfer of his Council to Florence in January

---

[28] On the Dufay hymn cycle and other cycles of 15th-century hymns see Kanazawa, 'Polyphonic Music for Vespers in the 15th Century', and Ward, 'The Polyphonic Office Hymn and the Liturgy of 15th-Century Italy'.

[29] For the contents of Florence 112bis see Becherini, *Catalogo dei manoscritti musicali della Biblioteca Nazionale di Firenze*, pp. 47 f. Becherini's listing requires correction, however, in that the order of her Nos. 13 and 15 must be reversed, leaving No. 14 intact.

[30] On 'Salve flos, Tuscae' see Besseler, *Bourdon und Fauxbourdon*, pp. 171 ff.; on 'Magnanime gentis' see Besseler, 'Neue Dokumente zum Leben und Schaffen Dufay', 167–70.

[31] For a fuller discussion of Dufay's relationship to Italian patrons after his return to Cambrai in 1439 see my 'Dufay and Ferrara'.

1439. Guarinian humanism spurred interchange between Ferrara and Florence on intellectual matters, and there was other commerce as well. A plausible link for music is through the singer Benoit; he is known in Ferrarese registers as 'Benedetto di Giovanni dito Benoit' and in Florence as 'Benotto di Giovanni'; this is undoubtedly the same man. We find him hired in Ferrara by Florentine representatives in 1438, and evidently he spent the next ten years in Florence. He briefly emerged again in Ferrara in 1448 and then disappeared.[32] He could well have brought back music to Ferrara that had circulated in Florence during his years there. This seems plausible since Benoit has as many as three attributed works in Mod B, the first a hymn and the other two antiphons, all evidently part of Layer I.

3. *The Papal Court under Eugenius IV.* Between about 1431, when Niccolò's diplomacy and Leonello's training encouraged greater cultural efforts, and 1438, when the Council began, Eugenius was principally in residence at Florence and Bologna. Then, the entire papal court and its singers were in residence in Ferrara from January 1438 to January 1439. Interchange between Eugenius and the Estensi extends, in fact, from the beginning of his reign until his death in 1447. Accordingly, the possibility exists that Mod B may in part reflect the repertoires familiar to the Papal Chapel of the late 1430s.

4. *Burgundy.* The presence of so many works by Binchois in the MS suggests some contact with Burgundian sources. This is strengthened by the inclusion of works for saints who can be linked to Burgundy, and of a motet for the birth of a son to Philip the Good in 1430.[33] Connections between the two courts go back, of course, to the 1420s, when Philip had sent the wind instruments to Niccolò III and transferred a trumpeter to his service; but in the 1430s a plausible opportunity for the transmission of music is afforded by the Burgundian delegation to the Council of Ferrara in 1438. We may also attach considerable importance to the presence at the Burgundian court of Leonello's bastard son Francesco, from 1444 on; and to the trip of the chapel singer Gerard Leay to Burgundy in 1445.

5. *English Music and Musicians.* The very large number of English compositions in Mod B is more difficult to explain. The compiler of the manuscript knew what he was up to in this section particularly well: of fifty-two works (all by English composers, save Dufay's 'Fulgens iubar', isolated here from the great sections of Dufay's works elsewhere in the MS), as many as twenty are not known from any other sources. It also appears that the versions given in Mod B are unusually trustworthy in pitch content; they derive from authoritative originals, whatever those may have been.[34] In this section the extant concordances differ from those of earlier sections. We find

---

[32] Ibid., p. 22, n. 46, for the 1448 Ferrarese document on Benoit.

[33] These include the works in Mod B by Binchois on fols. 51ᵛ, 52, 52ᵛ, and 70–2; also by Dufay, fols. 74ᵛ–76.

[34] See Hamm and Scott, 101; and Hamm, ed., *Complete Works of Leonel Power*, i, p. xxi.

here many more pieces concordant with Aosta than elsewhere in the manuscript, as well as many found also in Trent 92, which is closely related to Aosta. From recent studies on Aosta, it appears that its earliest layers may also have stemmed from the Papal Chapel under Eugenius IV, particularly in the light of Eugenius's meeting in 1433 with the Emperor Sigismund, whose musicians play a major role in the later portions of Aosta.[35]

Yet the truly substantial number of English works and the presence of works by a flock of minor composers (Pyamour, Plummer, Stone, Benet, Forest and Sandley, some of whom seem never to have left England) suggest some more direct means of transmission. Ann Scott has amply reviewed the known evidence of diplomatic and other connections between Ferrara and England at this time; yet a few new points may be made.[36] First, there is no doubt, as Scott suggests, that the Council of 1438 may have been an occasion for much interchange that could have included music. Yet the evidence here is refractory: an English delegation to the Council at Ferrara was indeed prepared in May 1438, but further evidence not cited by Scott reveals that the expenses of this delegation, from York and Canterbury, were not voted by the clergy, and in fact there is no clear evidence that these emissaries ever left England.[37] Thus collapses any speculation about the possible presence of Leonel Power at the Council, along with Scott's hypothesis that Dufay and Leonel could have met at Ferrara and that Dufay's 'Seigneur Leon' might then have been written as a tribute to Leonel. The only prominent Englishmen who certainly were present at Ferrara during the Council were the King's resident Proctors at the papal court, especially Andrew Holes (in Italy 1429–44), a noted collector of books and benefactor of Wells Cathedral.[38] This is suggestive because the composer Forest, who has as many as four works in Mod B, was long attached to Wells Cathedral, as deacon and archdeacon, and in fact died there in 1446.[39]

From a Ferrarese standpoint, a more lasting and significant point of contact with Englishmen was through the university, where a distinctive group of English students was in residence precisely during these years. If we may extrapolate from evidence later in the century, there may well have been a natural association between foreign students at the university and their compatriot musicians who were either residents or visitors. In view of the prominence of several members of the 'English nation' of the university, this group may have formed a point of contact through which music was readily transmitted.

---

[35] Cobin, 'The Compilation of the Aosta Manuscript; a Working Hypothesis'.

[36] Scott, 'English Music in Modena Biblioteca Estense, Alpha X. 1. 11 and other Italian Manuscripts'.   [37] Gill, *Eugenius IV, Pope of Christian Union*, p. 114.

[38] On Holes see Bennett, 'Andres Holes: a Neglected Harbinger of the English Renaissance', Schirmer, *Der englische Frühhumanismus*, pp. 59 f.

[39] On Forest recent summaries are in Hughes and Bent, 'The Old Hall Manuscript – a Reappraisal and an Inventory', 112; and in Ford, 'Some Wills of English Musicians of the 15th and 16th Centuries', 82.

The concentration of English students at the university in the 1440s clearly reflects the aspirations of younger members of well-placed English families to gather in the fruits of the new learning from Guarino, whose reputation as scholar and teacher was by this time widely known.[40] One of the first is William Grey (*c.*1408–78), a member of a noble house and later Bishop of Ely. Grey had behind him university training at Oxford and Cologne when he arrived at Ferrara in 1447 with a substantial retinue, and his enthusiasm as a collector of manuscripts had won him the praise of Vespasiano da Bisticci. Another promising English student was Robert Flemmyng, later Dean of Lincoln. But the most prominent member of this group, locally and internationally, was Reynold Chichele, who came to Ferrara for classical studies by 1447, possibly as early as 1445, remaining until 1449. He was the son of John Chichele, 'citizen and chamberlain of London'. His great uncle was Henry Chichele, Archbishop of Canterbury and founder of All Souls' College at Oxford; another uncle, William, had taken a degree at Bologna in 1423 and was Archdeacon of Canterbury. On behalf of Reynold Chichele, letters were written to Leonello by both King Henry VI and his wife, Queen Margaret of Anjou, in which they thanked Leonello for the 'honourable and liberal treatment' accorded to Reynold at Ferrara; the Queen, as a token of thanks, sent Leonello a horse (an 'ambling hobby'). In 1449 Reynold was made rector of the university, a rare mark of recognition for a foreign student. He evidently broke his stay abroad with a return journey to England during these years, since the King's letter thanks Leonello for his benevolence to Reynold and also 'to other Englishmen travelling through his territory'. How much pride was felt in local humanistic circles over these English disciples of the Guarinian tradition is clear from Lodovico Carbone's funeral oration for Guarino (1460) in which he mentions five of them by name and praises the sage for having 'liberated' the English from their barbaric ways of speaking.

The ecclesiastical associations of several of these English students suggest other ways in which music by at least some of the English composers of Mod B may have found its way to Ferrara. We have already mentioned the attachment of Andrew Holes, the papal proctor, with Wells Cathedral, where the musician Forest was a high-ranking member of the chapter. It is equally conceivable that the Chichele family's close association with Canterbury Cathedral could have worked in favor of obtaining, for the Ferrarese chapel, music by Leonel Power, who had been attached to Canterbury since 1423, was certainly in service there in 1439–45, and died there in 1445.[41]

London and the Chapel Royal of Henry VI are more likely sources of

[40] On the English student population see especially Mitchell, 'English Students at Ferrara in the XV Century', 75–82; Schirmer, *Die englische frühumanismus*, and Scott, 'English Music'.

[41] On Chichele see Jacob, *Henry Chichele and the Ecclesiastical Politics of His Age*; and the same author's *The Register of Henry Chichele, Archbishop of Canterbury 1414–43*. For recent research on Leonel Power and the entire spectrum of choral institutions maintained by English churches and private patrons in the 15th century, see the excellent study by Bowers, 'Choral

music by John Plummer, who was a member from at least 1441 until 1447.[42] And the retinue of the Duke of Bedford seems an equally likely primary source for the means by which Leonello's chapel secured music by Dunstable as well as by Pyamour.[43] Works by Dunstable, Pyamour, Benet, Stone, and Sandley could readily have come to Ferrara either directly from England or through continental intermediaries, whether the Imperial Chapel of Sigismund or the court of Burgundy; for the present we have no way of choosing between these hypotheses. It is striking that so many works by Dunstable in Mod B are either *unica* or concord very frequently with the contemporary MSS Aosta, Trent 87, and Trent 92; nevertheless, Benet's pair of motets are both *unica*, and both seem certain to have been written for England, as they venerate St. Alban and St. Thomas of Hereford. Initially, a different hypothetical direction is suggested by the works of Stone and Plummer in Mod B, since compositions by both have recently turned up in the fragmentary manuscript discovered by Reinhard Strohm in the Archivio di Stato in Lucca.[44] Yet although this find provides firm evidence of the further copying of English polyphony into Italian sources, it is of no help for determining the potential origins of Mod B, since the Lucca codex was probably not made earlier than about 1471, the year of the arrival in Lucca of the English Carmelite monk, John Hothby, whose intimate knowledge of the music of just these English compatriots is evident from comments in his theoretical writings.[45]

The date assigned to the binding of Mod B on the basis of the archival entry mentioned earlier (p. 52) is 1448. If this is accurate for its binding and final redaction, it would agree with what the watermark reveals through concordance with archival registers, and it also corresponds to the first appearance at the court of one of the two English musicians named 'Johannes', briefly mentioned earlier. One of these, evidently a harpist and thus a secular musician, is called in the records 'Johannes ab arpa de anglia' and he is found in 1448, 1449, and 1450. In 1450 the lutenist-singer Niccolò Tedesco requests the court to help him recover money owed him by the English harpist, who is

Institutions within the English Church – Their Constitution and Development, 1430–1500'. I am indebted to Dr Bowers for a microfilm of his dissertation and for helpful correspondence. Documents in Appendix B, 6 of his dissertation show Leonel Power as Master of the Lady Chapel at Canterbury Cathedral from 1439 until his death on 6 June 1445.

[42] On Plummer see, most recently, Trowell, *Four Motets by John Plummer*, pp. 4–7, presenting new archival data on Plummer in the Chapel Royal.

[43] On Pyamour see *The New Oxford History of Music*, iii, p. 194.

[44] Strohm, 'Ein unbekanntes Chorbuch des 15. Jahrhunderts', 40–2. In 1973–4 I had occasion to study the fragments of this important MS firsthand, and profited also from a seminar report on it made in 1975 at Princeton University by Mr Jonathan Glixon.

[45] Hothby is known to have been inducted as 'Magiscolo' at San Martino in Lucca in 1471; he served in that capacity until 1486 when he was called back to England by the King; see Nerici, *Storia della musica in Lucca*, pp. 42 f., 92–7. Hothby in his *Dialogus Johannis Octobi Anglici in Arte Musica*, p. 65, refers to these English composers whose works appear in Mod B: Dunstable, Leonel, 'Plumere', Forest, and Stone ('Stane'), as well as a still larger group of continental composers, including two associated with Lucca (Peragulfus and Michelet) whose works appear in Florence, Biblioteca Nazionale Centrale, MSS Panciatichi 27 and Magliabechi XIX, 176.

called a 'famulus' of Leonello's.[46] In 1448 we have already found, thanks to Franceschini, a notice dated 1448 referring to a 'Johannes quondam alterius Johannes presbiter Londini'; this London priest is somewhat later found at Ferrara Cathedral in a teaching role,[47] and he too may have been one of the intermediaries through whom the more than fifty English compositions it contains came to the chapel.

For several reasons it seems likely that the scribe of Mod B was French, rather than English, and probably one of the French-trained singers of Leonello's chapel. Promising candidates include Gerard Leay or Jean Filibert; the latter procured singers for Leonello in France in 1446, and in 1447 he purchased the volume containing 'six new Masses'. The scribe of Mod B writes a careful and fine music hand, using delicate, pointed note-heads, thin stems, and clefs, all familiar characteristics of many French music manuscripts of the fifteenth century. Further, the scribe spells correctly and with remarkable consistency the names of all French composers in the manuscript (e.g. 'Dufay', 'Binchois', 'Benoit') without any of the spelling variants we often see in MSS of the period; he even spelled correctly the names of all the Burgundian singers who are named by Binchois in his celebration motet, 'Nove cantum melodie' (fols. 70ᵛ–72). The names of the English musicians are also spelled correctly and consistently (e.g. 'Dunstaple', 'Leonel', etc.) with the exception of Plummer; his name appears four times in the MS – three as 'Polumier', once as 'Polmier', perhaps inadvertently omitting the 'u'. This looks like a French variant of whatever spelling of 'Plummer' the scribe knew. Finally, although the musical material is of good quality, the Latin texts of many motets are corrupt and at times senseless, showing that the scribe did not know Latin well enough to know when he was going wrong. Many examples were cited by Bukofzer in the Critical Report to his edition of the works of Dunstable, for example, the phrase written as 'natum unicum quem' instead of the correct 'novum mirum que' (misreading Gothic script). This kind of error seems unlikely for the cathedral-trained English musicians of the type represented in the manuscript, and equally so for that English singer known to us as 'Johannes . . . presbiter Londini'; also very unlikely for the English students, all of whom were fluent Latinists.

To what extent does the large and varied repertoire of sacred music in Mod B show traces of Ferrarese liturgical practices and thus suggest they were specifically intended for Ferrara? Hamm and Scott, and Ward have taken an optimistic view of 'local' elements in the texts of several works, specifically Dufay's hymn for the festival of St. Francis as well as his antiphons for St. George and for St. Anthony of Padua.[48] I am inclined to doubt that these works can be specifically attributed in this way. Although St. George was indeed the patron of the city and titular saint of its cathedral, he was also

[46] ASM, *Mandati*, 1450, fol. 52ᵛ.
[47] For this reference I am indebted to Adriano Franceschini.
[48] Hamm and Scott, p. 111.

widely worshipped elsewhere, and on a grand scale; the same is true of St. Francis and St. Anthony of Padua.[49] Better candidates are the two antiphons by Fede for St. Dominic, because we know that Fede spent ten months in service under Leonello and it is true, as Hamm and Scott aver, that the two Dominican churches of the city were important ones. On the whole, the contents of Mod B seem to me more striking for the absence of well-defined local features than for their inclusion; thus, there is no composition specifically addressed to Leonello or any other member of the Estense dynasty; nor are other Ferrarese individuals or events commemorated, as we might well expect in a collection locally compiled and intended for local use. Among the saints omitted is St. Maurelius, the sixth-century bishop and martyr who was buried in Ferrara and who was the object of a particularly strong cult there in the earlier fifteenth century. Maurelius ranks with St. George as a major patron of the city and is depicted repeatedly in many local illuminated MSS of this time.[50]

To sum up, all this strongly suggests that the music assembled in Mod B was accumulated primarily from sources outside Ferrara, not written there, nor written specifically for Leonello's chapel. The accumulation of so much polyphonic material probably took place over a substantial period, no doubt extending well back into the 1430s, and was undoubtedly stimulated by the active intermingling of ecclesiastical patrons during the Council year of 1438. The bulk of the material was at hand when Layer I was made; Layer II probably represents a slightly later phase of redaction than Layer I. Distinctively set apart is the small group of pieces forming Layer III, which can be tied closely to the presence of Johannes Fede at the chapel during the ten months from July 1445 to April 1446. The MS as a whole was then evidently assembled and bound not later than 1448. The absence of local composers except Fede is symptomatic of the structure of Leonello's chapel altogether; most of its members were apparently skillful singers but not composers. The whole volume reflects careful and consistent collecting of works by composers associated with the musical establishments of the papacy (implying also Florence and Bologna as centers), the Imperial chapel of Sigismund, the chapel of Philip the Good of Burgundy, and the great wave of English musicians who were based at insular cathedrals and other foundations, as well as those who worked in the centers of English rule in France during the 1420s and 1430s, above all the chapel of the Duke of Bedford. The breadth of material reflects the same aspirations to European stature that were inherent in the very foundation of Leonello's chapel and its staffing by foreign singers. As a medium-sized choirbook, written with exceptional

[49] See *Bibliotheca Sanctorum*, vi, cols. 512–31 (St. George); ii, cols. 106–35 (St. Anthony); iv, cols. 691–734 (St. Dominic).

[50] On St. Maurelius see *Bibliotheca Sanctorum*, ix, cols. 173–183; for examples of his portrayal along with St. George in Ferrarese illuminated MSS, see, e.g. the illuminated choirbooks of the Duomo of Ferrara, e.g. Corale VI, fol. 2.

clarity and careful text-fitting, it would readily have functioned directly and efficiently as a performance source in Leonello's chapel, or as a source of further copies from which his singers could perform.[51] It shows that Leonello's musicians were collecting and performing works well marked by those features of full sonority and fauxbourdon that were spreading to many centers of polyphonic practice. These represent some of the strongest and most progressive features of current polyphonic style then being brought to maturity by Dunstable, and his lesser English compatriots, and by Dufay, Binchois, and their Franco-Flemish followers. The mobility of these musicians, and their readiness to seek careers under Italian patronage, were bringing the new musical developments swiftly to those few musical institutions in Italy that were endowed with the skill and experience to perform such music.

[51] On the dimensions of Mod B in comparison to other contemporary choirbooks see Besseler, 'Chorbuch', in *Die Musik in Geschichte und Gegenwart*, ii, cols. 1331–9, and his *Bourdon und Fauxbourdon*, p. 143.

7

Secular Music

IN turning to secular music under Leonello, we only partially revert to those aspects of his outlook and rule that are painted most vividly by his early biographers. They emphasize Leonello's polished Ciceronian eloquence, which is indeed reflected in his letters and his few known Latin writings, chiefly state documents; but they tell us nothing of his importance as patron and author of vernacular poetry, still less of secular music as a component of the social life around him.[1] Italian poetry as a local tradition had already been established at Ferrara in the time of Niccolò III. The poet Simone Forestani, 'il Saviozzo', had written a canzone for the death of Niccolò II in 1388 and remained at Ferrara in the early years of Niccolò III's rule. Saviozzo's *sirventesi* could well have been performed with musical accompaniment, and would have been sung to relatively simple melodic-rhythmic formulas capable of sustaining dozens of verses with the same metrical structure.[2] By the 1420s and 1430s literate court residents could hardly have been unaware of the widely circulating poetry of Leonardo Giustinian, the more so since this former pupil of Guarino's occupied a position of intellectual and political eminence at Venice and had contact with such humanists as Barbaro, Barzizza, and Traversari, whose role at the Ferrara Council in 1438 has already been noted. Traversari's praise of Giustinian's musicality is reinforced by the poet's own remark on his pleasure in music, 'to which I am drawn not by will but by nature itself, which guided me easily to the full possession of every type of music.'[3] Traversari ascribes to Giustinian's 'agile and resplendent imagination' his ability to produce the 'sweetest melodies'

[1] Two of Leonello's sonnets were first published in Baruffaldi, *Rime scelte de poeti ferraresi antichi e moderni*, vol. i, p. 21, with the editorial remark that they were selected from an entire manuscript of his poetry. One sonnet ('Lo amor . . .') was later published by Carducci, *La coltura estense*, vol. xiii, p. 163; the other ('Batte el Cavallo . . .') by Fatini, 'Le "Rime" di Ludovico Ariosto', 15. For evidence of the copying of a MS collection of Leonello's verse at court in 1437 see above, Chapter 6, n. 7.

[2] For Saviozzo's poetry see Ferraro, ed., *Alcune poesie inedite del Saviozzo e di altri autori*; more recently the edition of his *Rime*, ed. Pasquini. On the likelihood of improvised singing of Saviozzo's *sirventesi* see Pirrotta, 'Two Anglo-Italian Pieces in the Manuscript Porto 714', p. 259.

[3] Given in Italian translation by Rossi, *Il Quattrocento*, p. 215, from a letter of Giustinian's to his former master, Guarino, from Murano. See Sabbadini, ed., *Epistolario di Guarino Veronese*, i, pp. 292–7; also vol. iii, p. 120, for Sabbadini's remark that this letter, of 1420, is evidently the first in which Giustinian makes reference to music, although he must have been occupied with it long before. See also Sabbadini, 'Sugli studi volgari di Leonardo Giustiniani'.

(*arie suavissime*), reflecting the pleasure of the humanistically inclined observer in one man's ability to conceive his poetry and music as a single form of expression.

From Leonello's time are a group of sonnets by Francesco Accolti, who came as a lecturer to the university in 1442. The young Mantuan poet Giovan Francesco Suardi became a student in the university in 1445 and eked out a living as *lettore-scolare* there until 1452. We have several poems in the vernacular by Suardi, addressed to ranking members of the Este family, reflecting both a student's outlook and a more personal acquaintance with their family affairs.[4] Suardi's poems to Isotta d'Este, Leonello's sister, link him with Accolti and with the native Ferrarese Girolamo Nigrisoli, whose long strophic poem in honor of Isotta, written in 1444 or 1446, was the basis for two-voice polyphonic settings by a certain 'Galfridus de Anglia'. As Pirrotta observed, Galfridus set only two verses out of seventeen, and these were copied in reverse order in the Porto MS (stanzas 12 and 1 of the poem, in that order).[5]

In view of Leonello's serious preparation as an amateur musician, standards for secular music were probably higher at Ferrara than at many rival Italian courts of the time. We have seen that he could play the organ well enough to perform in his court chapel, that he played the lute as early as his student years and could probably sing to his own accompaniment, that he had treatises on the rudiments of music copied for him, and brought in musicians in numbers far beyond those hired by Niccolò or by most Italian princes. We can also assume that the principal contemporary categories of secular music were in use at the court: (1) secular monophonic song, certainly in Italian, as self-accompanied singing of strophic poetry, no doubt often improvised; (2) composed and notated secular polyphonic song, chiefly in French and, to the extent available, in Italian, performed by varied combinations of voices and instruments; (3) performance on 'soft' instruments (e.g. lute, harp, and portative organ) both as accompaniment to singing, and in ensemble and solo roles; (4) performance on 'loud' instruments (chiefly the *Alta* band of two shawms and trombone) for a variety of ceremonial and recreational purposes, and also to accompany the elegant art of court dance, which seems to have been well developed in Ferrara at this time.[6]

Inevitably, much of the music used for secular purposes was not only not written down but by its nature had no need to be, and we must account for it

---

[4] On Accolti see *Dizionario biografico degli Italiani*, i, pp. 104 f.; on Suardi and his poems to Leonello and Borso see Belloni, 'Un lirico del Quattrocento a torto inedito e dimenticato: Giovan Francesco Suardi', esp. 147–50; also Catalano, *Vita de Ludovico Ariosto*, i, pp. 98 f., for Suardi's poem to Leonello. On Suardi's and Accolti's poems to Isotta d'Este see Belloni, 'Un lirico', 157–9, and Pirrotta, 'Two Anglo-Italian Pieces', pp. 254–6.

[5] Pirrotta, 'Two Anglo-Italian Pieces', pp. 258–60.

[6] On possible and probable combinations of instruments and voices in this period see, most recently, Brown, 'Instruments and Voices in the 15th-Century Chanson', and Wright, 'Voices and Instruments'.

by way of imaginative hypothesis, by extrapolation from the known historical facts about performers and texts, and from a few later examples of
notated music which may have drawn upon unwritten repertoires.[7] This situation contrasts sharply, of course, with the formal and institutional music-
making characteristic of the court chapel, at which Leonello could hear Mass
and Vespers every morning and evening. Whether Leonello and his *famigliari*
were in the city or at a country villa, the musicians were expected to be at
hand and had to be ready to perform whatever was called for on short notice
or no notice at all. To do this, they clearly had to have at their disposal
memorized repertoires consisting in part of models for improvisation; of
carefully learned songs that could be sung with polyphonic accompaniment;
and of dance tenors around which they could weave suitable contrapuntal
textures. In short, they had to have a comprehensive repertoire of both *choses
faites*, that is, written-out compositions, and carefully prepared improvisational techniques.[8] To judge from the majority of pictorial scenes from the
period – which, whether or not we regard them as realistic, are bound to
present us with norms of procedure that were socially reasonable – from
these we can see that much music-making took place out of doors, in the
private gardens and walled enclosures of the palazzi, and was mingled at
times (perhaps quite frequently) with erotic courtly diversions and revels
for which texts of unrequited love would have been quite appropriate. Such
diversions were enlivened by music performed not from manuscript volumes
but from easily portable single sheets or scrolls, around which several
performers could cluster.[9] That such sheets contained only a few compositions does not mean that more music was not potentially available; but rather
that portability made good sense in view of the spontaneous uses to which
secular music must have been put. Although we have documentary references
to several 'libri de canto' that were made at Ferrara during Leonello's mature

[7] Most convincingly by Rubsamen, 'The Justiniane or Viniziane of the 15th Century',
172–83; see, on this point, Pirrotta, 'Ricercare e variazioni', 60, n. 5.

[8] On *choses faites*, meaning written compositions, as opposed to those improvised, see Ferand,
'What is *Res Facta?*'.

[9] The importance of scrolls was emphasized especially by Wright, 'Voices and Instruments'.
For an example from the period, see the frequently reproduced illustration from the astrological
treatise entitled *De Sphaera* (Modena, Bibl. Estense Alpha X. 2, 14 [Lat. 209]), in which a group
of bathers in a large fountain is entertained at one side by a four-man shawm band (typically,
with only three playing and one silent) playing the instruments of the *Alta* (two shawms and
trombone), and at the other side by three singers performing the chanson 'Mon seul plaisir' from
a scroll. As Brown, 'Instruments and Voices', pp. 93–5 and plate 2, has shown, the well-known
setting of this text by Bedyngham is not the one portrayed; more likely it is a fanciful composition, not a real one, and the point is to suggest humorously that the 'seul plaisir' enjoyed in this
scene by the fully-clothed musicians is the piece they are singing, i.e. music as a more sedate
diversion than nude bathing. Although the MS has been preserved in the Estense Library since
the 17th century, its provenance is clearly Milanese rather than Ferrarese, as it bears the arms of
Francesco Sforza and its illuminations are attributed to Cristoforo de Predis; however, more
recently a dating before 1466 and attribution to a predecessor of de Predis's has been suggested;
see Alexander, *Italian Renaissance Illumination*, p. 94 and plate 27. For a color reproduction
see Wangermée, *Flemish Music and Society in the 15th and 16th Centuries*, plate 84.

years, we cannot be sure that these were MSS of secular music.[10] Thus far, only one extant MS, Porto 714, has been traced in any convincing degree to Ferrara from the period prior to 1471, when Ercole I took power. But although it seems clear that some of the textual material in Porto 714 was written at the time of Leonello's rule, it also seems likely now that the MS itself was compiled between about 1454 and the early 1460s (cf. Chapter 11 below, pp. 109 ff.).

Groups of Secular Musicians

During Leonello's ten-year rule the main groups of secular musicians at the court were established, and, despite growth in the number and variety of special talents in later years, the groups remained essentially the same to the end of the century. By that time the patronage of instrumentalists had become virtually a specialty, as it did with Cardinal Ippolito I d'Este, but in the context of numerous rival patrons and of a much larger musical world. In Leonello's time the secular performers were divided into three main groups: (1) trumpeters; (2) *piffari*; (3) performers on 'soft' instruments, among whom we can count the lutenist-singers.

The trumpeters were kept to a minimum number by Leonello: but we must emphasize again that, as we do not have salary rolls before the 1450s, our conclusions are tentative. The *Mandati* from the early 1430s to 1450, when they mention trumpeters, give us a new name or two each year. From this we may conclude either that the total number was growing or that there was a rapid turnover. Only in 1440 and 1446 is the same name found twice, that of a certain Pierino; characteristically he is an Italian, as the trumpeters continued to be, in contrast to the other groups, throughout the century. The *trombetti* had to perform ceremonial and functional roles, rather than purely musical ones, and since, so far is known, the city did not have trumpets of its own, those of the court undertook civil duties as well.[11] They called the public together to hear a court proclamation; they preceded the Marquis in his travels and public appearances; they acted as messengers and political agents. Owing to the relative stability of Leonello's rule and his tastes for

[10] For references to the copying of 'libri de canto', for Leonello in 1433 and 1435 see my 'Dufay and Ferrara', p. 24, Docs. 1 and 2. The next certain references to the copying of music are more than a decade afterwards, from the later years of Leonello's rule: for the items of 1447 and 1448 see ibid., p. 10 and nn. 53, 54, 55. To these we can now add an item dated 16 May 1446, cited by Bertoni, 'Un copista del Marchese Leonello d'Este', 106, n. 1: a copyist named Simone da Pavia was paid for writing, illuminating, and binding a 'libro de canto'.

[11] Thus far, no Ferrarese historian has made reference to players employed by the city, which confirms in a small way the complete subservience of civic political institutions to the ruling Estense oligarchy. In sharp contrast were the long traditions of town *piffari* employed in Florence and Lucca, to name only the most obvious Tuscan examples (see Reese, *Music in the Renaissance*, p. 174). Similarly long established were the traditions of town players in Flanders and in Germany; on the former see Polk, 'Municipal Wind Music in Flanders in the Late Middle Ages', 3.

sophisticated pleasures rather than public display, a small group of trumpeters sufficed. By comparison, the contemporary Duke of Burgundy, Philip the
Good, maintained in these years a normal staff of from five to seven *trompet-
tes de guerre*, plus at least one *trompette de menestrels*, the latter meaning a
trumpeter who played with the wind band.[12] At Milan in 1450 the ducal staff
boasted twelve trumpeters; again, all but one of them were Italian, and not
only from Lombardy but from Rome and Siena. The city of Milan also
maintained its own corps of six trumpets for civic functions.[13]

The number of *piffari* is also uncertain for any year before the period of
Borso, but we can piece together some aspects of the development of this
group. Niccolò III kept two such players, as a rule; Leonello apparently
maintained two at first but by the mid-1440s there appear to be an average of
three. Among them we can single out one, known as Corrado *piffaro*, or
Corrado de Alemania, as one of the important figures in the court's musical
apparatus over many years. Corrado spent forty years in service, from 1441
to 1481, and was one of the most conspicuous performers of wind instruments in Italy. He was recruited in 1441 from the small court at Monferrato,
and was taken officially into Ferrarese service in March that year. In June
1441 he brought his wife from 'Alemania'; by 1445 he was sent on business
trips by Leonello, in 1449 to 'Alemania' specifically to recruit a fellow
piffaro. In 1447 he had received Ferrarese citizenship. He appears to have
remained firmly in local service, which means that he witnessed the entire
reigns of Leonello and Borso as well as ten years of that of Ercole.[14] Corrado
is evidently the leading figure in the *piffaro* group throughout this time at
court, and like him, the other wind players are brought in from 'Alemania' –
this probably means any German-speaking area to the north and it may also
mean the region of Basle or other parts of Switzerland.[15] The other *piffari* in

---

[12] See Marix, *Histoire*, p. 104 and the lists of *ménéstrels* for the years 1420–68, pp. 264–74.
These show one player called 'trompette des menestrels' in each year in which this category
appears. The only apparent exception is in 1456, in which Marix's use of ditto marks appears to
show that the number increased to four; but there may well be an error in the records or in her
published material, as in the remaining years (1459–68) the number in this category is again just
one player.   [13] Motta, 'Musici alla corte degli Sforza', 39–42.

[14] Data on Corrado *piffaro* is drawn from the following sources: ASM, *Mandati*, 1441–2,
fols. 21, 30^v, 186; *Mandati*, 1445–6, fols. 28, 219; Mandati, 1449, fol. 59^v. During the years
1456–81 he is found regularly in the *Bollette de' Salariati* that are preserved for these years, but
not thereafter in the registers listing musicians.

[15] That the importation of *piffari* from Germanic regions at this period was a normal pattern
is clear, but not entirely easy to explain. The shawm, their normal instrument, had become by
the 14th century, and perhaps earlier, the regular instrument used by watchmen in the walled
towns of northern Europe (e.g. the 'waits' of London). The construction of such instruments was
a prized Germanic speciality. German craftsmanship in manufacturing wooden wind instruments
remained famous for many centuries, while in Italy stringed-instrument manufacture took the
lead, though probably not before the 16th century. Particularly important for the
manufacture of trumpets and trombones, but also of wind instruments, was Nuremberg, from
where they were exported all over Western Europe; see Jahn, 'Die Nürnberger Trompeten- und
Posaunenmacher in 16. Jahrhundert', esp. 31, 37. For a very cursory survey of German
instrumentalists in Italy in the 15th century, see Salmen, *Der fahrende Musiker im europäischen
Mittelalter*, pp. 173–5.

Leonello's time included Clemente de Alemagna and Michele Tedesco. Gifts were made to the *piffari* from time to time to reward their participation in special events; e.g. to Corrado in 1446 for his appearance at the festival of St. George, always a lively public *festa* in Ferrara with popular celebrations and the running of a *palio*. On occasions needing massive sonorities, the *piffari* could join forces with the *trombetti* but for more domestic uses they evidently played alone, or at most with one trumpeter, to judge from contemporary evidence elsewhere.

The principal instrument played by the *piffari* was evidently the shawm, both discant shawm, and its tenor counterpart, often called bombard. To this pair were normally added, by around 1450, a brass instrument with single or double slide and alto range, for which the name 'trombone' was coming into general use. At Ferrara the records are admittedly incomplete for this period, and I can find no record of the regular use of the term 'trombone' prior to 1452. Yet it remains distinctly possible, and even likely, that such an instrument was in use there much earlier, perhaps by the 1430s and certainly in the 1440s.[16] The reason is that this instrument, playing the Contratenor part in a three-part wind ensemble that became known as the *Alta*, assumed the normal role of performing the tenors needed for court dance.

To the year 1441 and the very beginning of Leonello's rule also belongs the first appearance at court of Pietrobono, who ranks above Corrado or any other Ferrarese musician of the century in personal fame. As early as the first year of Leonello's rule, Pietrobono, then about twenty-three years old, was paid the considerable sum of twenty gold ducats, for unspecified reasons; this was exactly the amount paid to Dufay when he visited Ferrara in 1437, and again in 1443 at Bruges. In the mid-1440s more payments to Pietrobono and an increase in his salary confirm his local success; and in 1449 we find a *tenorista* named Zanetto mentioned in direct connection with Pietrobono. From then on, wherever the name of Pietrobono is found, we find nearby that of a *tenorista* who seems to be associated with him, apparently as a player on a tenor viol against which Pietrobono could improvise on his lute, and with whom he would probably also sing in polyphony, certainly in two parts and possibly in three.[17] Apart from Zanetto, the records of the 1440s do not reveal more than a few isolated names of players on other 'soft' instruments (Rodolfo dall'Arpa and Giovanni dal Chitarino in 1447), but of course the English harper named John must be reckoned typical of the class of traveling instrumentalists who probably visited the court and stayed on, without their names appearing in those formal registers of court payments from which we

[16] See Besseler, 'Die Entstehung der Posaune', also his *Bourdon und Fauxbourdon*, pp. 188 ff. Although the term 'trombone' does not appear in Ferrara before the 1450s, it is entirely conceivable that an Alto instrument of the trumpet family, soon to achieve an independent name as well as identity, was in use for the burgeoning performance of court dance by the 1430s. See Polk, 'Flemish Wind Bands in the Late Middle Ages', pp. 38 ff.

[17] For further details see below, pp. 98 ff. and my article, 'Pietrobono', 115–33.

must reconstruct the social organization. Similar in function to the lutenist-singers, though representing a coarser and more popular class of entertainment (undoubtedly received enthusiastically by the courtiers) were the self-accompanied improvisers who recited or sang to simple formulas Italian verse on any subjects, and who ranked somewhere between musicians and *buffoni*. They too have a long and solid history at this court, as at others, partly itinerant but partly as temporary residents when they were particularly successful: thus we know of a Lodovico da Padova 'facetissimo pronunciatore in lingua volgare' (1445) and of a Prando da Verona, for whom Leonello in 1450 paid six months' rent in Ferrara and added on a stipend of six LM per month.[18] Despite Leonello's wish to be associated with the restrained and austere world of learning, he encouraged livelier entertainments as well.

Court Dance under Leonello

To specialists, it is by now a commonplace that under Leonello and throughout the second half of the fifteenth century, Ferrara became a principal center for Italian court dance. Yet this development of dance has not been seen within the context of Ferrarese court culture or of the personal styles of successive Estense patrons. All of the best-known masters of the newly codified art of court dance in Italy, down to the 1480s, are closely linked to Ferrara, in some cases for long periods as members of the official entourage.[19] The founding figure in this tradition, Domenico da Piacenza, is also called in some sources Domenico da Ferrara, and his work on new dances for the court was surely in progress by the 1430s, perhaps earlier. Even though the date 1416 mentioned in the Paris MS of his only dance treatise is probably unreliable, we can assume that Ferrara was the main seat of his activity before his association with Milan in the 1450s, and I can add to this that his name crops up in isolated Ferrarese court registers as late as 1470.[20] About a generation younger is his colleague from Pesaro, Guglielmo Ebreo, who reports in his own treatise that he was present at Leonello's wedding to Maria d'Aragona in 1444, apparently as choreographer. Guglielmo shows the rapid spread of this new vogue when he claims that he 'continued this science and art, on behalf of which I have visited the most distinguished and noble courts and festivals of Italy.'[21] If it is true, as some specialists believe, that Guglielmo Ebreo is actually identical with the 'Giovanni Ambrosio da Pesaro'

[18] On these performers, see Bertoni, 'Il Cieco di Ferrara e altri improvisatori alla corte d'Este', 271–8.

[19] For what follows I am mainly indebted to the articles on Domenico da Piacenza and Guglielmo Ebreo by Tani in *Enciclopedia dello spettacolo*, vols. iv, 828 ff., and vi, 37 ff; also Michels, 'The Earliest Dance Manuals'.

[20] ASM, *Bolletta de' Salariati*, 1456, fol. 10 ('Domengo da Piacenza' is paid the substantial monthly salary of 20 LM); and ibid., Estratto, 1470: 'Domenigo de Piacenza' is listed (the Estratto gives no other information).

[21] Quoted by Tani, from Guglielmo's treatise, in *Enciclopedia dello spettacolo*, vi, 38.

to whom is ascribed one copy of the treatise otherwise attributed to Guglielmo Ebreo, then he was still active at Ferrara as late as 1481 as dance instructor to the six-year-old Isabella d'Este. The line that reaches into the period of Ercole and the training of his children then continues with other masters and in a rapidly widening context of interest in dance forms representing widely diverse European styles, as we know from ambassadors' descriptions of various court festivities.[22] The third master (or fourth, depending on the identity of Guglielmo and Giovan Ambrosio) is Antonio Cornazzano, much better known than the others for achievements apart from his early dance manual, which, while dedicated to a Milanese nobleman, Ippolito Sforza, in 1455, strengthens our view that Cornazzano contributed to the Ferrarese dance traditions when he lived there during the last five years of his life, until his death in 1484.[23]

To what extent the *bassadanze* and *balli* of Leonello's time were created by Domenico and his successors by modifying indigenous dance traditions, to what extent by borrowing French and Burgundian models, is unclear. By the 1430s the *basse dance* was well established at the French and Burgundian courts. No doubt it made a strong impression on Italian visitors, perhaps even on the Francophile Niccolò III, although it does not seem very likely that he moved with graceful and delicate physical gestures on the dance floor. We can be more confident about Leonello's participation, however, not only because of Guglielmo's prominence at his wedding but much more through the titles of several of the best-known *balli* of the period, for which the tenors, or basic tunes, are preserved. Three of the oldest, with choreography created by Domenico (the first of all the dancing masters ever to codify dance steps), are named *Belfiore*, *Belriguardo*, and *Leoncello*.[24] The Estense villa called Belfiore had been built at the end of the fourteenth century, and was already famous for its paintings and decorations in the mid-1430s, when work was begun on the great country villa near Voghiera, called Belriguardo, which was also to be sumptuously decorated by a succession of artists, and would remain a centrally important country seat. The name *Leoncello* suggests precisely the same fanciful association of Leonello with the lion, the symbol of courage and wisdom, that is used by Pisanello for his portrait of Leonello in the wedding medal of 1444. The dance was possibly created for

---

[22] For example, in an unpublished letter from the French court at Lyon (18 October 1501), the Ferrarese ambassador describes in great detail some 'representationi' performed during or just after a banquet in which not only were dances of various regions performed but each group of dancers was dressed in the native costume appropriate to the region from which the dance was derived; e.g. 'ala todescha', 'ala francesca', 'ala spagnola', 'ala lombarda', etc.

[23] On Cornazzano see Silvestri, 'Appunti di cronologia cornazzaniana'.

[24] For these dances and their tunes see Kinkeldey, 'Dance Tunes of the 15th Century', pp. 91, 92, and 115. The Ferrarese connotations of the titles *Belfiore*, *Belriguardo*, *Leoncello*, and perhaps *La Marchesana*, were pointed out by A. Cavicchi, 'Sacro e profano', 69–70. Cavicchi (70, n. 45) supplies the otherwise unknown fact that Domenico da Piacenza was 'for some time in Ferrara in 1435 for the wedding of Leonello d'Este and Margherita Gonzaga', though he does not give a source for this information.

the same occasion, and just as the medal shows the paradox of the lion singing, the *ballo* title symbolizes the same ruler as participant in the dance.
Another early *ballo*, entitled *La Marchesana*, may also have local connotations, as may also several other imaginative titles used by Domenico and
Guglielmo.

By Leonello's time the dance masters were aiming to establish not only the
general courtly character and decorum of the dance, but to reflect something
of the court atmosphere around Leonello. The *bassa danza*, as a slow, highly
stylized, ceremonious group- or couple-dance, remains an expression of
courtly restraint; the *balli*, on the other hand, are freer and more varied in the
tempo, choreography, and character of expression. In a recent book, Michael
Baxandall has been able to show that several of the essential aesthetic terms
used by the dance theorists – *aere, maniera, misura, misura de terreno*, and
memoria – were used by certain contemporary writers with reference to
painting, as when in 1442 at Urbino a poet used the terms *misura, aere*, and
maniera with reference to Pisanello.[25] This striking parallel not only reflects
the receptiveness of spectators to the visual patterns created by dancing
figures, but offers further parallels in music that are plainly obvious. The
word *misura*, which in Domenico's lexicon means the general control of
speed of movement, 'according to the music', is manifestly an essential musical term. *Aere* was a term much used in this period for characteristic types
of melodies as well as for the expressive qualities associated with them:
thus we have the *aere veneziane*, which grew up everywhere in imitation of
Giustinian's *canzonette*. In 1460 the Ferrarese court singer Niccolò Tedesco
recommends to Milan a certain 'Brith, excellent in singing "aere veneziane".'[26]
Baxandall's view is also strengthened by other historical evidence on which
he did not draw; namely, that Pisanello's use of gestures and bodily movements, suggested by the dance, makes especially good sense in the context of
the Ferrarese court, where he was active at just the time of the major
festivities of Leonello's earlier years, above all his marriage to Maria
d'Aragona. These *feste* were obviously occasions for brilliant choreographic
display.

That the dances were not mere stylized patterns, but were, as Baxandall
says, 'semi-dramatic', is not an exaggeration, if we examine the choreographies described by Domenico and Guglielmo; they not only formulate
steps but imply physical attitudes and gestures that are suggestive of dramatic
situations.[27] Similarly, the dance historian Gino Tani has observed that
Domenico's choreographies 'include elements of pantomime, especially in the
plots that reflect figures and customs of everyday social life.'[28] The variety of
situations and numbers of participants, from two up to ten in a single dance,

[25] Baxandall, *Painting and Experience in 15th-Century Italy*, pp. 77–81.
[26] Valdrighi, 'Cappelle, concerti e musiche', 442.
[27] See Baxandall, op. cit., p. 78.
[28] *Enciclopedia dello spettacolo*, iv, col. 830.

created a wide variety of effects. As in musical performance, the court members shifted and alternated roles, as dancers and as spectators. In such a context, the familiar distinction made by music historians, following Besseler, between 'participatory' and 'presentational' forms of music in this period, tends to break down, amid a general scene of art and play. We are at the very beginnings of the long tradition of court dance in Italy. The tradition was to remain vital to the social habits of the aristocracy, and when it was transplanted and exported through the widening international contacts of later decades, it would come to influence both the French ballet and the English court masque.[29] With regard to this large-scale development, the short reign of Leonello was brief but seminal.

[29] On aspects of the later history of the *bassadanza* and its influence, see introduction to Gombosi, *Compositione de messer Vicenzo Capirola*; and Heartz, 'The Basse Dance: its Evolution circa 1450 to 1550'.

8

Cathedral Music

ALTHOUGH the cathedral lagged behind the court chapel as a focus of polyphonic practice, some new evidence has recently emerged that sharpens our perspective on the two institutions. One such piece of evidence is a recently discovered set of small polyphonic fragments; another is formed by new biographical data on the music theorist, Ugolino di Orvieto, who was a member of the cathedral hierarchy during the years of Leonello's education and rule.

Polyphonic Fragments in a Cathedral Manuscript. Several years ago Professor Don Randel was kind enough to call to my attention an *Ordo* (liturgical service manual) of Ferrara Cathedral, preserved in the Cornell University Library, of which a number of leaves were repaired with small strips of parchment that contain fragments of polyphonic music.[1] The *Ordo* itself, a large vellum manuscript, appears to date from the second quarter of the fourteenth century. As Professor Randel has informed me, it evidently originated elsewhere and was brought to Ferrara and put to use in the cathedral.[2] This is clear from the *Incipit* of the manuscript (fol. 21) in which the words 'ferrariensis ecclesie' were clearly added by a later hand, replacing and obliterating the name of another church. At Ferrara a pair of gatherings was added (fols. 1–20ᵛ), in which we find all but one of the references to St. George (the local patron saint) in the entire manuscript. This section was obviously added to adapt the manuscript to local use, just as additions were made to the liturgical calendar for the same reason. The whole volume can be compared with a Ferrarese *Ordo* of the year 1400 that is preserved in the British Library (Additional MS 28025). This is clearly a locally produced MS from the start, in which St. George is prominent both in liturgical status and

---

[1] Cornell University Library, MSS Bd. Rare BX C36 0635 (formerly MS B. 31).

[2] In a private communication to me in 1972, Professor Randel informed me of the polyphonic fragments in this volume, which he was the first musicologist to discover; it is a pleasure to record my indebtedness to him. The fragments are briefly mentioned in a short description of the MS by Calkins, 'Medieval and Renaissance Illuminated MSS in the Cornell University Library', 47, No. 24.

[3] The MS Add. 28025 is briefly described in *British Museum, Catalogue of Additions to the Manuscripts*, 1854–75. It is a vellum MS dated 12 July 1400, of 259 fols., with the original rubric, 'Incipit ordo manualis ecclesie maioris ferrariensis secundum consuetudinem sacrosanctae romane curiae' (the rubric has neither erasures nor additions). On fol. 8 there is a central miniature of St. George killing the dragon and two more illuminations of the same scene for the festival of St. George (fol. 263).

in the illuminations in the MS.[3] That the Cornell *Ordo* came to Ferrara in the early fourteenth century is suggested by a rubric in the added section at the beginning; it reads 'Rubrica nova facta pro domino Johannem papam XXII . . .', and Pope John XXII ruled from 1316 to 1334.

For us the main items of interest are fifteen small slivers of parchment that were used at some time to repair dog-eared or torn leaves of the MS. Most of them contain fragments of polyphonic notation, yet they do not add up to as much as a complete voice-part of an entire composition.[4] They are thus smaller and less valuable than many other fragmentary strips containing polyphonic notation that have turned up in recent years as binding or repair materials in non-musical documents and MSS of the period. But several of these strips are sufficient to show that these fragments once belonged to a collection of polyphonic Latin motets. Most striking of all is that their notation corresponds in all essential details to that of the hand that wrote the first layer of Mod B.[5]

The two strips that have incomplete words of text enable us to associate the material even more clearly with Mod B; these fragments with text are shown in Figures 4(*a*) and 4(*b*); they are transcribed here as Examples 4(*a*) and 4(*b*).

Example 4(*a*) consists of two small portions of a single vocal part, probably a Discant part, with the fragmentary text '–to [?] ad col–'. Assuming that

Ex. 4(*a*). Cornell, University Library, MS Rare BX C36 0635, p. 70

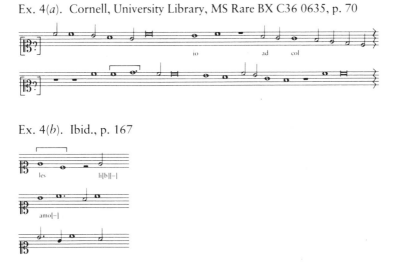

Ex. 4(*b*). Ibid., p. 167

[4] The strips occur on fols. 58, 64ᵛ, 66–66ᵛ, 70, 132, 166, 169, 172ᵛ, 177, 182ᵛ, 200ᵛ, 238ᵛ, 239ᵛ. All are in the same brownish ink and the same hand.

[5] Especially noteworthy are these: (1) narrow, lozenge-shaped note-heads with straight thin stems; (2) downward right-hand slant for ligatures descending, especially ligatures *cum opposita proprietate*; (3) clefs, for example the C clefs on fol. 167 of the *Ordo*, and F clef on fol. 166; the spacing, grouping, note-sizes, staff size and spacing, and text script.

the text is of Biblical origin, the standard concordances of the Vulgate help us to narrow down the origins of these syllables.[6] We find exactly ten instances in the Latin Bible in which the formulation 'ad col–' occurs, and judging by motets of the period, the most likely source is the Song of Songs, from which a good many Marian texts were then being drawn, following plainsong antecedents. Furthermore, it is precisely among those English composers who are represented in Mod B that settings of such texts abound. One promising possibility is a text especially favoured by English composers, 'Ibo michi ad montem mirre'; the first full line of text, adapted from the Song of Songs, 4:6 reads: 'Ibo michi ad montem mirre et *ad colles* libani . . .'. We have settings of 'Ibo michi' in Mod B by Leonel Power and by Stone, along with other motets based on texts from the Song of Songs. The music of the Cornell fragment, however, does not correspond to that of the Power or Stone settings, nor to another 'Ibo michi' setting, in Trent 90, that Ann Scott has attributed to the English composer Plummer.[7] But the 'Ibo michi' identification seems to be contradicted by the isolated final text-syllable of the word that comes just before 'ad': this may be read as either 'io', '-ro' or '-to', but it is surely not 'et', as in 'Ibo michi'. Nor does any other line in the Song of Songs contain this succession of syllables, and the only line in the Vulgate that does have them is from Leviticus, 1:15: 'Et retor*to ad col*lum capite' Yet this line, from God's words to Moses on how burnt offerings of fowls shall be made, seems most unlikely to be the one called for in a polyphonic setting of this time, and in fact is not used in plainsong or polyphony at any period. More likely, a variant of the Song of Songs text is the one in use in this composition, and quite possibly 'Ibo michi' itself.

This seems still more probable when we examine the second fragment with bits of text, example 4(*b*). Here only the syllables '–les lib–' remain from the original text; these too would fit the next portion of the same first line of 'Ibo michi', namely '. . . ad col*les lib*ani' We are on safe ground in this instance, since no concordance of the Vulgate records another combination of these syllables to end one word or begin another. Very likely, the word in the next staff below, almost certainly from the same voiced part, is in full form 'amica', of which only the first three letters remain. This familiar word occurs as many as nine times in the Song of Songs, all in texts well known from musical settings at this time. These include the settings of 'Tota pulchra es', of which there are three in Mod B alone, by Forest, Plummer, and Stone.[8] It seems likely, therefore, that these two fragments are both from Song of Songs texts, very likely 'Ibo michi' for the first, perhaps a setting of 'Tota pulchra es' for the second. They appear to be hitherto unknown.

[6] I have used principally *Concordantiarum SS. Scripturae Manuale*.

[7] ' "Ibo michi ad montem mirre": a New Motet by Plummer?'.

[8] In Mod B, the Forest setting begins on fol. 101ᵛ; those of Plummer and Stone on 104ᵛ and 106ᵛ; surrounding these at fols. 100ᵛ ff. and 107ᵛ ff. are the two 'Ibo michi' settings by Forest and Stone.

From wherever the cathedral's hierarchy obtained the music leaves of manuscript from which these fragments were taken, their clear relationship to Mod B in content, scribal characteristics, and apparent repertoire seems undeniable. Such material could well have been copied for the use of Leonello's singers of sacred music outside their services in the court chapel itself; for example, for their use on the occasions of their performing in the cathedral, as happened from time to time.[9] At a later period, when the notation, function, and contents of such works had become obsolete, the leaves were taken apart for simple use in mending a liturgical volume that had more enduring functional value. This may have happened as early as the end of the fifteenth century, by which time the musical traditions of the cathedral seem to have fallen even further behind those of the court chapel, then expanding greatly under Duke Ercole I; perhaps by then the cathedral had abandoned any pretensions to the use of polyphony. The contrast is obvious: Mod B, as a manuscript of the court chapel and thus a potentially valued part of its collection of service books, was carefully preserved through the period of Ercole, had additions made to it during the 1470s, and was kept intact through the vicissitudes and losses of later centuries as a treasured volume in the Estense library.

Ugolino di Orvieto: Scholastic and Humanistic Views of Music

Throughout the 1430s and 1440s the cathedral, its diocese, and the ecclesiastical hierarchy of city and countryside, underwent a substantial transformation. This was principally owing to the new leadership provided by a single strong individual, Bishop Giovanni Tavelli da Tossignano (1386–1446), appointed in 1431.[10] Tavelli counts as the most important figure in Ferrarese church history in the fifteenth century. From the beginning of his tenure he set about reforming discipline and observance in the city and diocese, and tightening control over the ecclesiastical political structure of his domain. His efforts to increase religiosity in civic and public life coincided with the example of private devotion provided by Leonello d'Este. Though difficulties inevitably arose between the Este and any powerful church figures in Ferrara over such matters as appointments to local benefices, Tavelli's leadership contributed to the growing climate of lay piety and public religious observance that characterized the city in the middle and later decades of the century.[11]

[9] Scalabrini, in Ferrara, Biblioteca Ariostea, MS Cl. I, 456, fol. 82, gives a document from Duomo sources now lost: '1448/Primo die ix mense februarij expendi in colacione cantori Ill. d. n. marchionis qui cantavit missam magnam in coro in die sancte Mariae purificationis . . . qui fuerint X cantores in malvatico in brasadellis *L.O.s.* XI *d. O.*'

[10] For what follows I am principally indebted to Ferraresi, *Il beato Giovanni Tavelli da Tossignano e la Riforma di Ferrara nel Quattrocento*. This is essentially an uncritical and apologetic biography, not a searching or critical one, but it contains a good deal of valuable source material on Tavelli and local church history of his time.

[11] On the episode of conflict between Tavelli and Niccolò III see Ferraresi, op. cit., i, pp. 383–94.

Tavelli had studied at Bologna and at Venice, where he had known the future Eugenius IV and probably the members of Guarino's school at Venice as well. At Ferrara in 1426, as head of the local branch of the order of the Gesuati, he witnessed a strong surge of public piety that rose in 1431, when San Bernardino da Siena preached to the Ferrarese public. In that year Eugenius IV launched Tavelli's career as bishop.

Tavelli installed as his vicar-general don Angelo Diotisalvi of Foligno, who remained his second-in-command throughout his career. Next in importance among his church dignitaries was don Ugolino di Orvieto, now known as a music theorist, but mainly active all his life as a church administrator, first at Forlì and then at Ferrara, where he served under Tavelli as archpriest of the cathedral chapter.[12] Because of Tavelli's many extended absences from the city, on pastoral visits to various parts of his diocese or at Council sessions in Basle (1433) or Florence (1439), both Diotisalvi and Ugolino frequently acted for him outside the cathedral itself. In 1432 Ugolino served as Tavelli's vicar and substituted for him on more than one occasion in such formalities as the conferral of university degrees, which were bestowed either at the cathedral altar or in the Palazzo Vescovile. That this was done by the bishop or his vicars symbolized the bishop's role as titular chancellor of the university.[13]

By the time of Ugolino's installation as archpriest of the cathedral in 1431, he had already behind him an extended career at Forlì that had begun at the latest in 1411. In the 1420s he had become archpriest of the Duomo and rector of a local Ospedale. He had made himself a reputation for his knowledge of canon law, philosophy, mathematics, and music, and he was also a respected orator. In 1415 he had attended the Council of Constance, and was already well beyond his student years. When he left Forlì in 1431 he was one of its most distinguished citizens. At Ferrara he became more prominent and more active, in touch with such contemporaries as Ambrogio Traversari, who described him in a letter of 1431 as 'my old and musically most learned friend.'[14] He must have been in contact too with other church intellectuals of the period, especially during the year of the Council at Ferrara; he would thus have been in Ferrara when Dufay visited it in 1437, and it is at least a possibility that they met on this occasion. Some indirect evidence of this seems to emerge from the fact that a lost treatise by Dufay

---

[12] On the biography of Ugolino see Seay, 'Ugolino of Orvieto, Theorist and Composer', and id., 'The *Declaratio Musice Discipline* of Ugolino of Orvieto: Addenda'. Also Haberl, 'Bio-bibliographische Notizen über Ugolino von Orvieto ', and Peverada, 'Ugolino da Orvieto'.

[13] Ferraresi, op. cit., i, pp. 211–213. According to Ferraresi, the Faculty of Laws was located in this period in the Monastery of San Francesco; that of Arts in the 'Crocette di San Domenico', that is, in buildings facing San Domenico.

[14] The text is given by Haberl, 'Bio-bibliographische Notizen', 43. Haberl also quotes an impressive comment on Ugolino by Flavio Biondo, who in 1430 or earlier knew Ugolino in Forlì and calls him one whose knowledge of music 'by far surpasses that of all musicians of our epoch . . .'.

reflected, so far as we can judge its contents second-hand, Ugolino's teachings.[15]

As archpriest at Ferrara he presided over a chapter of ten residential and two non-residential canons, along with eight mansioners (among whom in 1431 we find the organist, Gioacchino Cancellieri, successor to Bartolemeo da Bologna).[16] Ugolino's versatility is apparent in several ways during these years: as an orator in 1433 he attracted substantial crowds while making pastoral visits, and as a scholar his writings ranged through wide fields of learning, including a treatise on physics.[17] But by far his most famous work is the *Declaratio Musicae Disciplinae*, in five books, one of the most comprehensive music treatises of the fifteenth century, or indeed in music theory altogether, between Jacob of Liege and Zarlino. Before considering its contribution to the philosophy of music in Ferrarese and broader Italian circles in its period, it may be helpful to put it into the context of the little we now know of Ugolino's practical initiatives in music teaching at the cathedral.

Since the retirement of Bartolomeo da Bologna as organist, in 1427, no one of fully comparable quality had held the position; his successor, Cancellieri, is unknown as a composer, though he was evidently a capable organist. But under the new leadership of Bishop Tavelli, from 1431, changes that eventually extended to the teaching of music began to take place in the structure and spirit of the diocesan organization. Higher priority was given by Tavelli to reforming the general clerical situation, and only in 1443 do we find the first evidence of a plan to form a *schola cantorum* as a means of improving the quality of observance in the cathedral.[18] Similar initiatives had sprung up at other Italian cathedrals, deriving in turn from the reforming ambitions of Eugenius IV.[19] According to documents copied by Scalabrini, Tavelli in 1443 planned to increase and stabilize the singing forces provided by the cathedral clergy, by obtaining from Eugenius IV two new posts for *mansionarii*, to be supported by income from a local parish church.[20] Scalabrini further asserts, and we have no reason to doubt it, that Ugolino, as archpriest of the chapter, had a strong hand in this plan, and that a *schola*, near the cathedral, was actually founded.[21] It is striking that this plan coincides exactly with Leonello's

[15] On this see Gallo, 'Citazioni da un trattato di Dufay', 149–152. These traces of a lost treatise by Dufay are known only through citations given by Gafori in an autograph treatise of his own, and Gallo has noted that the form of the passage on the hexachords that Gafori quotes, from a lost original, is closer to a comparable passage by Ugolino than it is to any other contemporary treatise.

[16] On the size of the cathedral chapter in this period see Ferraresi, op. cit., i, pp. 254–61, where he also gives a full list of the chapter members in 1432, including Ugolino di Orvieto.

[17] Ferraresi, i, p. 255, n. 61.

[18] Information communicated to me by Adriano Franceschini. See also Ferraresi, i, p. 216, quoting Scalabrini, MS Cl. I, 125, fol. 117ᵛ. Some useful further documentation on the scuola at the cathedral, the organists after Bartolomeo, and the organ contract of 1465, is given by Peverada, 'Vita musicale', 9–30.   [19] See above, Chapter 3.

[20] Ferraresi, i, p. 216, from Scalabrini. The parish church in question is the Pieve di San Donato in Pedrurio.

[21] Ferraresi, i, p. 215, quoting Scalabrini, MS Cl. I, 26, fol. 121.

recruitment of French and Flemish musicians for his court chapel and also with his payment to Dufay in Bruges. The founding of an improved facility for clerical education also fits well with the principles announced by Ugolino in the preface to the first book of his enormous and wide-ranging treatise, which he claims is intended 'for entirely didactic purposes'.[22] If Ugolino did teach even the most basic material of his treatise to the clerics, they received an exceptionally thorough and fundamental grounding in the notation, tone-system, typology, and principles of both plainsong and mensural polyphony. In part, the treatise is an enormous expansion upon the time-honored teachings of Johannes de Muris, which are themselves incorporated into the *Declaratio* and which we also find copied in many other Italian MSS of the period, including at least one made in Ferrara for a secular patron.[23]

By the later 1440s there were closer links between Leonello's chapel and the cathedral. The death of Tavelli in July 1446 opened the way for Leonello to gain or perhaps regain control of several benefices in the cathedral itself, and a few foreign singers of Leonello's chapel obtained them, as we have seen. These were held by the singers Niccolò Philippo de Olandia and Ugolino of Brabant.[24] In February 1448 his singers performed at Purification in the great church, in their full complement of ten singers (the number is actually noted in the document, showing that this was an unusual occurrence).[25] In the same year the English cleric, 'Johannes quondam alterius Johannis presbiter Londini', was called a singer and held a benefice at the cathedral, and in the next year, 1449, the canons improved their provisions for music beyond what had already been done.[26]

In the years preceding Ugolino's death in 1457, the training of the Duomo clergy in plainsong and polyphony continued at the cathedral, though evidently not on a scale matching that of the Duomo of Milan, to which in 1459 the young Josquin Desprez became attached as *biscantor*. In 1452 a certain Giovanni dalle Chiove was appointed at Ferrara to teach the clerics singing, and he is again mentioned in a record of 1454.[27] It also appears that a chapel in the Duomo, that of San Giovanni Evangelista, was now regularly assigned to the singing master. In 1460 we find an important change in manning, for

---

[22] *Ugolini Urbevetanis, Declaratio Musicae Disciplinae*, ed. Seay, vol. i, Book I, Chapter III, p. 21: 'Hos igitur libros quinque ad Dei laudem et honorem ad discentium utilitatem . . .'.

[23] The *Libellus Cantus Mensurabilis* of Johannes de Muris (Coussemaker, *Scriptorum de Musica Medii Aevi*, iii, pp. 46–58) is, as a recent Muris scholar puts it, 'the most widely disseminated music treatise of the Middle Ages': Michels, *Die Musiktraktate des Johannes de Muris*, p. 27. Particularly relevant for Ferrara is a glossed version of the Libellus contained in the MS Porto 714, to be discussed below (Chapter 11).

[24] Informatio from Adriano Franceschini (see Chapter 6, n. 17). In 1447 Niccolò Philippo de Olandia, 'diocesi tragetense', had been nominated for the chapel of San Giovanni Evangelista, took possession of it, then renounced it in favor of another cathedral chapel. Ugolinus de Brabantia had been given the chapel of Santa Maria in Nive, in the cathedral, in the same year (1447), when this chapel was founded by the Estensi.   [25] See above, n. 9.

[26] On 'Johannes . . . presbiter Londini', see Chapter 6, n. 17.

[27] Scalabrini, MS Cl. I, 447, fol. 278ᵛ; quoted by Cavicchi, 'Sacro e profano', 64, n. 38*bis*.

this post is taken over by a certain Robertus de Anglia, evidently a musician of great versatility.[28] In 1467 we find Robertus at San Petronio in Bologna, as its first *maestro di canto*; thus he had transferred to Bologna despite the obvious improvement in musical equipment at Ferrara Cathedral – the installation of a magnificent new organ, later painted by Cosimo Tura.[29] After Robertus's departure, the cathedral remained a musical backwater for the rest of the century, maintaining a thinly supported tradition that probably consisted of no more than an organist and a singing master, and depending for any further musical resources on the Estense chapel. Only the personal and intellectual reputation of Ugolino di Orvieto survived strongly in these years. In 1466 an inventory of the cathedral included notice of a handsomely bound copy of his treatise on music, and in fact we know of at least two copies that were made in Ferrara in the mid- or late fifteenth century, both of which may be among the ten surviving copies of this major work.[30]

The systematic teachings of Ugolino's treatise seem remote from practical musical life and from the atmosphere of musical recreation characteristic of the courts. In its expanded treatment of details this book goes far beyond the rudiments that must have been taught in the cathedral schools. Yet we need to dwell briefly on the approach and content of the treatise to see what it reveals of Ugolino's larger purposes. Not only is the *Declaratio* one of the most ambitious and important efforts of the century to formulate knowledge of music comprehensively, but it is the only major work in music theory produced at Ferrara throughout the Middle Ages and the Renaissance.[31] Beyond this, if we do not misread certain allusions that are found in the five prefaces of the treatise, the treatise contains some suggestive and direct references to one component in the philosophical background that influenced the rise of music at the court during these years.

---

[28] The first information on Robertus de Anglia at Ferrara Cathedral in 1460 was communicated to me by Adriano Franceschini, based on notarial archival documents. On Roberto at San Petronio see Gaspari, 'Ricerche, documenti e memorie riguardanti la storia dell'arte musicale in Bologna', 50. At Bologna he received a five-year contract with a salary of six *lire* per month; we do not know what his payment at Ferrara had been, but it seems unlikely that it was competitive.

[29] On the organ see Cittadella, *Notizie*, i, p. 66; the new organ was contracted for in 1465 and finished in 1468; Tura painted its panels in 1469, fittingly with scenes from the life of St. George. These magnificent panels are still to be seen in the Museo del Duomo in Ferrara.

[30] Rome, Biblioteca Casanatense, MS 2151; and Biblioteca Vaticana, Rossiana MS 455 are the prime candidates for copies made in Ferrara between the middle and the end of the 15th century.

[31] On the dating of Ugolino's treatise we have only fragmentary evidence, yet enough to show that it was still in progress when Ugolino moved to Ferrara in 1431. Flavio Biondo, in his *Italia illustrata* of *c*.1430, says of Ugolino (calling him a resident of Forlì) not only that he excels his contemporaries as musician but that his work 'will put into the shade all others who have written on the subject'; from the use of the future tense we may infer, with Haberl, that the work had not yet been completed. In view of the many demands on Ugolino as archpriest and assistant to Tavelli in Ferrara during the 1430s and 1440s, the treatise may well have been completed only during these decades or even in the 1450s; the only certain terminal date is that of Ugolino's death in 1457.

The first three books, to some extent the first four, are laid out systematically. Book I presents the rudiments of musical structure, the tone-system and the hexachordal system, the intervals, and the modes. Ugolino's discussion of the eight-mode system is derived at long range from Boethius and at nearer range from Marchettus of Padua. Book II is a comprehensive account of simple counterpoint (called 'musica melodiata'). Book III expounds the mensural system and its notation, incorporating a glossed version of the *Libellus Cantus Mensurabilis* of Johannes de Muris and commenting extensively upon it. Book IV extends the mensural system in an abstract direction, furnishing a treatise on the proportions. In Book V, Ugolino returns to several themes raised in a more practical context in Book I, and concludes with a speculative summation on each of them; he deals here with the categories of music, the definition of sound, and the divisions of intervals by various means of measuring the monochord. The last offers room for commentary on the classical authorities in this controversial field, from Pythagoras and Aristoxenus to Ptolemy and Boethius.

Much in this broad array of material delicately modifies traditional concepts without substantially altering them, and the lucid framework is developed with exceptional thoroughnesss. Ugolino's *summa* is virtually the last attempt to encompass in one large book the whole range of musico-theoretical thinking familiar to the late Middle Ages, at a time when most theorists were turning to more specialized topics for single treatises.[32] His method is not deductive, but rather begins with what is generally known and relatively familiar, and proceeds to more abstract levels. Without subverting what were for him basic categories of thought about music, both 'speculativa' and 'activa', he is able to reorder certain traditional priorities. Thus, the time-honored view of the superiority of the speculative musician to the practical one is now shifted in perspective, so that the true musician is seen as one who commands both theory and practice.[33] He maintains the three-fold hierarchy of *musica mundana, humana,* and *instrumentalis*, but with further subdivisions of *instrumentalis* according to means of tone-production.[34] Most striking of all is the importance he attaches to polyphony, not only as a further development of musical means beyond plainsong, but as having value for its didactic benefit as a discipline and for its possession of the effective ethical powers characteristically attributed to the modes.[35]

In the main body of his treatise, Ugolino's references to earlier authors are mainly to music theorists and are not numerous apart from his large-scale indebtedness to Muris. But in the five *Proemia* spread out through the treatise

[32] Pietzsch, *Die Klassifikation der Musik von Boetius bis Ugolino von Orvieto*, p. 70.

[33] Book I, Chapter 2; cf. Pietzsch, op. cit., p. 121, and Seay, 'Ugolino of Orvieto', 147, citing the same passage.

[34] Book I, Chapter 1; cf. Pietzsch, p. 122; and Seay, 'Ugolino of Orvieto', 146. Both note Ugolino's postulate that there is a category called 'musica caelestis', which encompasses the three Boethian categories and is both the heavenly and natural basis of all that is music.

[35] Book II, Chapter 1; cf. Pietzsch, p. 123, n. 3.

he deals with the broad principles, and in them he has scope for the wider allusions to the philosophical background familiar in scholastic treatises. The emphasis becomes clear if we compare the references to Plato and Aristotle. To Plato there are only two quite general allusions in the five *Proemia*; to Aristotle there are twelve, citing as many as six specific writings. Of these the most frequently mentioned is the *Politics*.[36] The significance of this choice is clear. In the Middle Ages, not only was the *Politics* the main authority for the principles governing the organization of society, but its Book VIII contained the most important extant classical statement on music as *paideia*. Here Aristotle sets forth the value of music in the training of the young, the purposes for which music should be studied, and the nature of music as a practical exercise that, well understood, could lead men to virtue.[37] Particularly important for the diffusion of these doctrines to the aristocracy of the fifteenth century was the French translation of the *Politics* by Nicolas of Oresme, which we mentioned earlier in connection with Niccolò III and his journeys to France. Oresme's translation of several of Aristotle's works had been commissioned by King Charles V in the 1370s, explicitly for the purpose of spreading their doctrines to the apparently sizeable proportion of the nobility that knew no Latin. As we saw earlier, this glossed translation was copied extensively for French noble households of the fifteenth century, and not later than 1436 the Estense library owned the 'Politica, in francexe' – which is surely the *Politics* of Aristotle.[38] Ferrara's political dependence on France, as we have seen, became official in 1431 with the quartering of the Estense arms with those of France. In effect, the large-scale importation of manuscripts of French poetry, chronicles, and other writings is best understood as the literary counterpart to the political efforts of the Estensi to become, in effect, Italian members of the French nobility, protected by the spiritual and temporal power of the French crown. This is, in fact, the 'association' with the French nobility that is celebrated in the motets by Feragut and Dufay.[39] It is not that the French nobility, and those north Italian dynasties that sought to imitate them, needed the stimulus of an Aristotelian tract to motivate their use of music in the training of their children. It is rather that this most fundamental of intellectual authorities furnished in the

[36] In the *Proemia*, the following works by Aristotle are cited or quoted (the number of references is given in parenthesis): the *Posterior Analytics* (1): *Ethics* (2); *De Anima* (2); *De Rerum Natura* (1); *Physics* (1); *Politics* (5).

[37] See among other editions, the critical edition in four volumes, edited by Newman, *The Politics of Aristotle*. For a conveniently available excerpt, see Strunk, *Source Readings in Music History*, pp. 13–24.   [38] See above, Chapter 2, nn. 14 and 15.

[39] To the earlier evidence of French MSS copied for Niccolò III, we can add the list of French manuscripts similarly copied for Leonello, whose interests had, according to his humanist biographers, become entirely centered on classical antiquity. In Bertoni, 'Un copista del Marchese Leonello d'Este', 101 f., evidence is shown that in 1447 the following French MSS were copied for him: 'uno *Boecio* in franzexe'; a MS on 'Santa Gradaldo'; an 'Asperomonte'; a 'libro grande in franzexe'; a 'Gurone in franzese'; another 'libro in franzese'; a 'Cronicha nova in franzexe', and a 'Troiano'.

Politics, Book VIII, a means of justifying in late medieval aristocratic education what might otherwise have been seen as the indulgence of a useless
pastime. The need to justify musical training runs on in courtly literature to
the sixteenth century; even Castiglione, who is obviously a Platonist not an
Aristotelian, frames his discourse on the value of music as an answer to the
belief that skill in music is unworthy of a genuine courtier, 'who ought not
with such delicacies to womanish their mindes and bring them selves in that
sort to dread death.'[40] Ugolino's emphasis on the didactic purpose of his
treatise, and his numerous citations of the *Politics*, Book VIII, could readily
have been understood by contemporary readers as oblique allusions to current trends in the music education of the aristocracy, especially that of the
French nobility and its Italian emulators.

At the same time, we are well aware that Leonello and his peers were being
heavily indoctrinated in quite different values by the newly developed and
newly codified methods of humanistic training that stressed the acquisition of
elegant Latin writing, speech, and the command of knowledge not of the
scholastic disciplines (which had included music) but of classical literature
and its interpretation. Music in the system of Guarino was at best an innocent distraction from that concentration on classical texts from which wisdom could be derived; and if his teachings valued any category of music in
particular, it was certainly not mensural polyphony – with its complex and
abstruse components of interlocking pitch and mensural systems (tone-
system, intervals, hexachords, ligatures, rests, proportions, difficult elements
of notation) – but rather the ideal of well-sung poetry. This form of expression fitted classical legends of the power of music to express suitable texts,
when the words were clearly and effectively conveyed, typically by a single
voice suitably accompanied by an instrument, often self-accompanied.
Whether or not Guarino himself openly espoused such views, they are clear
enough in the writings of other humanists of the time, especially in the later
part of the century, and are realized effectively in his time by various
practitioners, most of all by Guarino's good friend and former pupil,
Leonardo Giustinian.

The coexistence in Ferrara of various diverse categories and styles of musical expression (music of the court, of the court chapel, of the cathedral) presents no more bewildering a pattern of diversity than do the flatly opposed
contemporary intellectual approaches of a scholastic commentator like
Ugolino and a humanist teacher like Guarino. Their utterly divergent percep-
tions of learning and teaching form polar extremes. Between them there

---

[40] Castiglione, *The Book of the Courtier*, p. 75. The condemnation of music is made by
Gaspar Pallavicino as an interruption to the praise of music put into the mouth of Count
Lodovico di Canossa. Among other contemporary defenses of music against the explicit charge
that it is potentially damaging to the courtier and is an incitement to lust, see the opening of the
long passage on music in Paolo Cortese's *De Cardinalatu Libri Tres*. For a penetrating commentary on this passage see Pirrotta, 'Music and Cultural Tendencies in 15th-Century Italy';
repr. in *Music and Culture*.

circulate vastly different forms of music and of applications of music to religious and secular uses, doubtless cultivated by contrasting groups of musicians and heard, judged, and evaluated as different forms of musical expression by their patrons. The task of eventually closing the gap between the principles of traditional music theory and the teachings of humanism could not even begin until practical musicians began to find ways, in the generation of Josquin and his disciples, of accommodating contrapuntal procedures to the task of reflecting words, both in declamation and in meaning.

∽∾∾

9

Borso as Ruler

IN his *Commentaries*, Pope Pius II had this to say of the Estensi and especially of Borso d'Este:

It is an extraordinary thing about that family that within our fathers' memory no legitimate heir has ever inherited the principate; the sons of their mistresses have been so much more successful than those of their wives. It is a circumstance contrary not only to Christian custom but to the law of almost all nations . . . Niccolò III had several sons, both legitimate and illegitimate. His legitimate children were prevented from succeeding him by their father's own decision. He designated as his successor his bastard son by a Sienese concubine, Leonello . . . who was succeeded by Borso, his brother by the same mother. Leonello's son was passed over either because he was legitimate or because he was absent and a minor.

Borso was a man of fine physique and more than average height with beautiful hair and a pleasing countenance. He was eloquent and garrulous and listened to himself talking as if he pleased himself more than his hearers. His talk was full of blandishments mingled with lies. He desired to seem, rather than to be, magnificent and generous . . . during his lifetime the people erected in the square a statue representing him seated, administering justice. It bore an inscription composed in flattery and adulation, for Borso loved nothing so much as praise. He bought as many precious stones as he could and never appeared in public without jewels.[1]

Although the second part of this passage has become famous, by far the best-known personal description of Borso by a contemporary, the first part is equally important. When Leonello died on 1 October 1450, leaving as legitimate heir his twelve-year-old son Niccolò by his first wife, Margherita Gonzaga, Borso succeeded to power not by legal right but through an act of benign usurpation.[2] As Pius observes, Niccolò di Leonello was then too young to take political control, an orphan without local allies. Borso, after an early military career, had been active on the local scene since 1443 as a faithful and capable political ally to Leonello. In 1450 Borso was thirty-seven, an attractive figure in full maturity and popular with the people. His force of

---

[1] *The Commentaries of Pius II*, Book II, transl. Gragg and Gabel, pp. 180–1.
[2] On the circumstances of Borso's succession see Pardi, 'Borso d'Este duca di Ferrara', 24.

personality must have contrasted sharply with the more reserved character of Leonello. On the latter's death, having ridden into the city from Belriguardo with his brother Meliaduse and a crowd of vassals from nearby satellite-states (Carpi, Fogliano, Correggio), Borso was immediately 'invited' by the head of the city's twelve *Savi*, Agostino Villa, to stand in a specious election, and we can hardly doubt the chronicler's report that he was 'elected' by acclamation.

Although the twenty years of his reign were later seen as a golden age of peace and prosperity, a close look at the sources shows that this view was above all that of reflective and pessimistic citizens who were looking back at Borso's era during the difficult and uncertain period of Ercole.[3] Nevertheless, an objective basis does exist for seeing Borso's rule as one of relative tranquility in external affairs and of a generally benevolent though strongly self-serving tyranny in local government, perhaps more oppressive than that of Leonello but less violent and brutal than that of Niccolò III.[4].

Since he stayed in power more than twice as long as Leonello, Borso had time to carry out several political projects that left lasting impressions on the history of Ferrara. In external affairs he followed the cautious and defensive line that was by now traditional for this state. With the temporary equilibrium in purely Italian rivalries brought on by the Peace of Lodi in 1454, he was able to keep on good terms with Venice and passable terms with Milan; he even managed to avoid trouble with the four Popes who took office during his years in power.[5] What problems he experienced came from external pressures, chiefly French, which caused him to abandon the Aragonese alliance forged by Leonello, and to support the Anjou claim to Naples then being pressed through diplomacy and invasion by Charles VII of France. As usual, the coin had its reverse: Borso could expect that his reaffirmation of allegiance to the French crown would be rewarded by support for his own territorial expansion, of which the most likely prize, in the event of the French actually taking power in Milan and Genoa as well as in Naples,

[3] This is the spirit in which Ariosto writes of Borso in the *Orlando furioso*, iii, 45: '. . . fama di sua età, l'inclito Borso/che siede in pace, e più trionfo adduce/di quanti in altrui terre abbino corso . . .' ('. . . lo! Borso great and kind!/First Duke of thy fair race, his realm's delight/Who reigns secure and shall more triumphs find/In peace, than warlike princes win in fight/ . . .'; after William Stewart Rose's translation). In Ercole's time the hardships of war, flood, and hunger gave rise to the popular expression, 'Non son più i tempi del duca Borso'; on this atmosphere see Venturi, 'L'arte ferrarese nel periodo d'Ercole I d'Este', 91–6; and Bacchelli, *La congiura di don Giulio d'Este*, p. 42.

[4] Borso's acts of repression were in part aimed at minor local dignitaries, most conspicuously his *cancelliere* Uguccione dell'Abbadia, who was beheaded in 1460 for failing to reveal a plot against Borso by a third party; or they were directed at powerful land-owning families. The most notorious case is that of the brothers Pio de Carpi. On the Pio affair see Chiappini, *Gli Estensi*, pp. 136–8.

[5] On Borso's dealings with foreign governments, both Italian and non-Italian, see Pardi, 'Borso d'Este', 171–203; 241–88. For a general portrait of the diplomatic situation at this time see Ilardi, 'The Italian League, Francesco Sforza, and Charles VII (1454–1461)', 129–66.

would be the acquisition of Parma as an Estense fief.[6] None of this happened; peace reigned in northern Italy; yet Borso did inevitably arouse the hostility of those Italian statesmen whose positions were threatened by these French claims, including Pius II, Francesco Sforza (after 1458), and Ferrante of Aragon. All of them foresaw that the support of French interests in Italy would not only threaten their own regimes but would eventually lead to the collapse of all Italian dreams of national unity and to French domination of the entire peninsula. Yet in Borso's time the threat of French invasion was far in the distance, and his policies served to increase rather than to lessen the security of his state.

On a more personal level, Borso's ambitions were centred on improving his rank and in enjoying the greater political prominence that would result. As early as 1452, he bought the dukedom of Modena and Reggio from the Emperor by showering gifts on the hard-pressed Frederick III, who made two visits to Ferrara in that year and conferred the title on Borso in a splendid ceremony.[7] To gain a similar honor for Ferrara took longer, as the Popes were more resistant, but in 1471, just before his death, Borso traveled to Rome to receive the title of Duke of Ferrara from Pope Paul II, taking with him an entourage of such size and opulence that he exhausted the local treasury to pay for it.[8]

Typically grand as these two ceremonies were, there were in fact few comparable occasions in the course of his twenty years in power. This suggests that for all of Borso's flamboyance he was prudent in allocating expenses for court entertainments, which were later to be more expansively and frequently carried out by his own successor, Ercole. Whether Borso was in fact somewhat restrained in spending for all court expenses we cannot be sure, in the absence of a thorough economic study of him or of any Este ruler of the period; but the chances are that Pius II was not being merely mischievous in saying that Borso desired 'to seem, rather than to be, magnificent and generous . . .'. It does seem clear that he preferred to spend lavishly on more lasting forms of celebration that would be preserved for posterity, and by means of which his name and image would be glorified – paintings, manuscripts, statues, and architectural achievements such as the Certosa, that contributed to civic improvement and also kept his memory alive.[9]

Another factor that tended to limit expenses for entertainment at court was that Borso had no immediate family. He never married, kept no mistresses,

---

[6] Ilardi, 'The Italian League', 158, reports on an embassy sent by the French court in 1460 to Venice and Ferrara, proposing an alliance against Milan and the raising of a Council that would act against both the Turks and Pius II.

[7] On the investiture of 1452 and its ceremonies see Pardi, 'Borso d'Este', 384–88; also *Diario ferrarese*, pp. 34–37.

[8] On the journey to Rome in 1471 see Pardi, 399–416.

[9] On the founding of the Certosa see Rosenberg, 'Art in Ferrara during the Reign of Borso d'Este: a Study in Court Patronage', pp. 90–118; and his ' "Per il bene di . . . nostra cipta": Borso d'Este and the *Certosa* of Ferrara'.

had neither legitimate nor illegitimate children, and thus bore none of the typical expenses of the paterfamilias who had to provide for the servants, entourage, clothes, the entertainment of his children, and the matrimonial expenses of his daughters.[10] There was no female element at court during these years, and only two of his sisters cost him dowries: Beatrice d'Este, who hsd been left a widow by Niccolò da Correggio, married Tristano Sforza in 1455; and Bianca Maria d'Este, who married Galeotto della Mirandola in 1468. Further, Borso's brothers and other male members of the household were all provided for with well-paid civil or ecclesiastical administrative positions.[11]

Borso as Patron of Art and Literature; Music in the Frescoes of the Palazzo Schifanoia

As an art patron, Borso, through good luck or sound advice, managed to foster two of the classic achievements not only of Ferrara but of the entire Italian Renaissance. In the domain of miniature painting and book production he commissioned a series of splendidly executed manuscripts, including the large choirbooks of the newly founded Certosa, and above all the magnificent illuminated Latin Bible that has become known as the Bible of Borso d'Este (made 1455–61).[12] In the domain of large-scale wall-painting he ordered, paid for, and was the subject of, the great fresco cycle of the *Sala dei mesi* in the Palazzo Schifanoia, carried out by a number of Ferrarese artists in the late 1460s and early 1470s.[13] In the Bible, over one thousand miniatures, spread across more than six hundred pages of text, portray a vast array of subjects both decorative and text-illustrative, ranging from fantastic flora and fauna to symbolic devices and scenes of fifteenth-century life, including music and dance. To some extent its miniatures evolve from the painters' sharp observation of the world of objects, forms, and people around them, and directly reflect that world; to some extent, of course, they emerge from the

[10] That Borso evidently had no dealings with women was noted, no doubt with surprise, by at least one chronicler, quoted by Pardi, 'Borso d'Este', 53, n. 1: 'Non uxava cum le done'. But from this no conclusions about Borso's sexual preferences are drawn by either Pardi or Chiappini, *Gli Estensi*, p. 139. Although overt references to homosexuality are not likely to be found in the documents, we might note that among the entertainments put on for him by the improvisers and *buffoni* who were rather numerous at his court, was one of 1465, when he paid ten ducats to 'two *bofoni* who came dressed as women to sing before His Lordship's table' ('dui bofoni li quali vennero travestiti come donna a cantare dinanzi a la tavola della Soa Signoria'), quoted by Bertoni, 'Il Cieco di Ferrara', 272.

[11] Ercole became governor of Modena in 1462; Sigismondo, governor of Reggio. The other two brothers were *commendatori* of the most venerable ecclesiastical establishments in the domain: Rinaldo Maria at Pomposa, and Gurone at Nonantola.

[12] For the Borso Bible see the complete facsimile edition, with introduction by Venturi, issued as *La Bibbia di Borso d'Este*. For a recent discussion and further bibliography see Rosenberg, 'Art in Ferrara', pp. 119–64, and Donati, *Bibliografia della miniatura*, vol. ii, pp. 1120–1.

[13] On the Schifanoia frescoes see, conveniently, D'Ancona, *I mesi di Schifanoia in Ferrara*, and for an extended recent discussion and further bibliography see Rosenberg, 'Art in Ferrara', pp. 165–226.

stylistic traditions of miniature painting that had been flourishing in northern Italy for several decades. These traditions had been taken up by the Estensi as early as the 1430s in the making of the magnificent French Bible of Niccolò III, which in turn appears to have served as a direct model for at least a few details in the Borso Bible.[14]

Much more of Ferrarese life in Borso's time is depicted in the Schifanoia frescoes, despite their incomplete preservation and need for further restoration. It is by now well known that in these extraordinary paintings, the largest surviving cycle of secular frescoes from Ferrara, complex astrological and mythological symbolism was combined with what appear to be 'realistic' earthly scenes of Borso and his court along with non-courtly members of the local Ferrarese world of his time. The program behind these frescoes, originally carried through the entire twelve months of the calendar year, was discussed by the art historian Aby Warburg. His attribution of the plan to the court historian and astrologer, Pellegrino Prisciani, still seems plausible, even if, as Charles Rosenberg has recently argued, other local experts on astrological matters may also have contributed.[15]

For our purposes, it now suffices merely to note that the threefold division of each 'month' of the cycle places the depiction of Borso and of local events and situations in the lowest, or 'earthly' zone, and shows Borso in what appear to be varied scenes of his daily life, generally applicable or suitable to each month in which they occur. Thus Borso is seen departing for the hunt; receiving a letter; presenting a gift to his fool, Scocola, and so on. In what is preserved of these lower zones we see depictions of civic festive entertainments, such as the annual running of races on the festival of St. George (24 April) and two scenes of jousts. But so far as is now known, scenes of music-making do not appear among these portrayals, in contrast to the earlier fresco cycle at Belfiore, a generation earlier, in which scenes from the Marquis Alberto d'Este's life had included banquets and the associated theme of music-making.[16] In the glorification of Borso in the Schifanoia frescoes, however, musical instruments, both played and unplayed, do appear prominently in the highest, or symbolic zone, above all in the months of April, May, and June, typically when the coming of spring and the renewal of outdoor life formed a time-honored basis for turning to poetry and music. In this mythological context, the role of music is evidently founded not on merely personal or social uses, but on associations of music with the tutelary deities who preside over each of the months, known through literary traditions.

[14] For evidence that the French Bible of Niccolò III was used as a model by Borso's miniatures in 1455, see Rosenberg, 'Art in Ferrara', p. 144.

[15] Warburg, 'Italienische Kunst und internationale Astrologie in Palazzo Schifanoia in Ferrara'. See Rosenberg, 'Art in Ferrara', pp. 192 ff., for other suggestions on possible participation by local experts in astrology; also Zorzi, *It teatro e la città*, pp. 5 ff.

[16] On the Belfiore cycle, now wholly lost with the palazzo itself, see the valuable description by Giovanni Sabadino degli Arienti, published in full by Gundersheimer, *Art and Life at the Court of Ercole I d'Este*, pp. 23 f., 68, 71 f.

Thus, in April, presided over by Venus, lutes and recorders are held, but not played, by a group of court ladies and gentlemen as they surround and watch an erotic scene enacted in the foreground by two women and a man, all of them surrounded by symbols of procreation (see figs. 5(*a*) and (*b*).[17] The whole scene appears to be a commentary on the theme of the garden of love, in which music always had a role to play and was regarded as an erotic stimulus, as in contemporary literary references; it is as if the usual business of music-making, a relatively sober and temperate form of social recreation, temporarily stops during the moment that is depicted, to increase the shock of the erotic scene.[18] In May, a female figure prominently plays a lute as part of the celebration of music and poetry that is suitable to the god Apollo, the foil to this and other ladies being a group of poets on the other side of the central dividing line. In June, under the god Mercury, who is surrounded by merchants and businessmen, the middle ground depicts a group of three wind-instrument players, almost identical to the shawm band of the time, but slightly different in the instruments portrayed. The normal *Alta*, as we have seen it grow up under Leonello, consisted of discant shawm, bombard, and alto trombone, playing three parts of different range. This group seems to consist of a discant recorder and two discant shawms, forming an ensemble of uniformly high register. It is thus less realistic than the exact portrait of an *Alta* that we find in the Borso Bible, accompanying a circle dance. In the June fresco we may also note that the figure of Mercury (only partly preserved) holds a flat-backed cittern-like string instrument in an out-thrust manner which is not that of actual performance.[19] The wind trio, which is shown performing, is not placed in direct relationship to any other figures, nor to dance or song, and we may interpret it as forming rather an attribute of Mercury. In all, then, the portrayal of music in the fresco cycle is more symbolic and literary than realistic; and if it is true, as it seems to be, that Borso himself is not depicted as a participant in music-making or even as one

---

[17] On the instruments in this scene see Winternitz, *Musical Instruments and their Symbolism in Western Art*, pp. 49 f. The panel has been frequently reproduced, conveniently in Meiss, *The Great Age of Fresco*, pp. 166–7. To my knowledge, earlier commentators have not observed the potential importance of the fact that the instruments are not being played.

[18] That music was commonly regarded as a potential incitement to lust, and accordingly as a form of expression to be handled with care and moderation, is a theme sounded frequently by humanistic writers of the period, in part relying on ancient authorities. Thus Paolo Cortese, *De Cardinalatu Libri Tres* (1510), begins his passage on music with the observation noted above (Chapter 8, n. 40). Almost a century later Shakespeare's Duke Orsino opens *Twelfth Night* with the well-known 'If music be the food of love, play on . . .'.

[19] That Apollo is the god associated with order and harmony leads in part to his association with music; in the *Iliad* (line 603 f.) Apollo is shown with his lyre, singing to the gods at a feast, and this image became the most familiar means of portraying him; see Wegner, 'Apollon', *Die Musik in Geschichte und Gegenwart*, i, cols. 563–7. The now more obscure association of Mercury with music was actually quite familiar in the Quattrocento: Seznec, *The Survival of the Pagan Gods*, p. 22, points out the tradition used by Jacopo de Bergamo, in his *Supplementum Chronicarum* to the effect that Mercury was the 'first musician'.

who is actively engaged in hearing the strains of music – if he is not shown, in short, as a music-loving ruler, as Leonello could have been – this would in general suit the reordering of priorities that we will find in Borso's musical patronage when we compare it to that of Leonello.

Virtually all of Borso's biographers have observed that as literary patron he cuts an entirely different figure from that of Leonello. That he knew no Latin is at times regarded as unusual for a ruler of his type and background, especially for one whose personal tutor had been the humanist Toscanelli.[20] What he cared for, instead, were French romances, and, even more, adulatory literary works composed in his honor. Borso's less than small Latin was a trait he shared with his father Niccolò and his half-brother Ercole, and it reinforces the quite exceptional position of Leonello among rulers of the time; on the other hand, stronger literary interests were probably possessed by Borso's older brother Meliaduse, and also by his younger brother Alberto (1415–1502), for whom several manuscripts were copied.[21] Yet Borso understood the need to have humanistic writers and speech-makers as members of his circle. His literary favorite was Lodovico Carbone, who was distinguished for his garrulous orations, his native use of anecdote in his collection of *Facezie*, and fawning praise of his master. A more elevated but similar approach is that of Tito Vespasiano Strozzi, who had been a member of Leonello's circle but who also wrote an unfinished epic in ten books entitled the *Borsiade*.[22] The period of Borso is that of the transition from Guarino Veronese (died 1460) to his son, Battista Guarino; of the middle years of Cornazzano, another member of Borso's claque; and, most important of all for the future of Ferrarese literature, of the early maturity of Matteo Maria Boiardo, though he remained somewhat outside the circle of Borso's admirers. Boiardo's distance from the court was not merely psychological but physical, at least during his years of residence at his family estate at Scandiano, near Reggio; and he seems to have been closer to Ercole than to Borso, visiting him frequently in Modena after Ercole's appointment there as governor in 1462.[23]

The flourishing of the vernacular under Borso, noted by Gundersheimer, represents not so much a drastic change from Leonello as a change of emphasis. Abandoned now was Leonello's searching interest in classical traditions, in favor of the use of humanistic language as rhetorical ornament to courtly life, suitable for official occasions of all kinds. A chief supporter of the local humanistic traditions at this period was Borso's *referendarius*, Lodovico Casella, who evidently served as his adviser in cultural as

---

[20] On Borso's education see Pardi, 'Borso d'Este', 113–116.

[21] The personal connection of Meliaduse to L. B. Alberti was mentioned earlier. Alberto's patronage of letters is indicated by several surviving manuscripts; see Bertoni, *La Biblioteca Estense*, p. 12, and Gundersheimer, *Ferrara*, pp. 166 f.

[22] See Carducci, *La gioventù di Lodovico Aristo*, pp. 239–45.

[23] On Boiardo's early years see Gardner, *Dukes and Poets*, 253 ff.

well as political affairs, and whose death in 1469 occasioned a state funeral.[24]

Festive Occasions in Borso's Time. We have seen that despite Borso's reputation for extravagance, major court entertainments in his time were actually limited in number. By far the most lavish were his two investitures: in 1452 as Duke of Modena and Reggio, in 1471 as Duke of Ferrara. The former entailed, as we have seen, two separate visits to the city by the Emperor Frederick III, in January and June (about which we are well informed by the anonymous author of the *Diario ferrarese* and other sources). They seem to have been elaborate affairs; for the second visit, there were banquets and *balli*, at which the Emperor Frederick and other German nobles joined in the dancing.[25] Thereafter we know of no other major effort before June of the following year (1453), when Borso made an official visit to Modena and Reggio so that the populace could rejoice in his new status as Duke; about this too we have a long contemporary description and a verse account by Cornazzano.[26] The two family-weddings of his sisters (in 1455 and 1468) were relatively lesser events, as sisters' weddings were bound to be; to judge from the chronicles, the only further major occasion for court display took place in 1459, when Pope Pius II paid a nine-day visit to Ferrara. Lesser celebrations worthy of special notice include: *June 1461*: ceremonies for the possession of the Certosa by the Carthusians; *August 1461*: the entertainment of Galeazzo Sforza and Lodovico Gonzaga at Ferrara, ostensibly on a hunting trip; *May 1462 and May 1464*: jousts in Ferrara, the second intended to encourage citizens to return to the city after an outbreak of plague; *May 1465*: Ippolita Sforza passed through Modena and Reggio on her way to marry a Neapolitan prince, and Borso greeted her and held festivities in her honor; *September 1467 and September 1468*: the running of a *palio* at Ferrara in honor of Filippo Maria Sforza, then visiting the court; *December 1468 and February 1469*: the third visit to Ferrara of the Emperor Frederick III.[27] Even if we add to these such annual events as the races for the festival of St. George and the celebrations at carnival time, the total impression is slight by comparison to those of the short reign of Leonello and the long one of Ercole. The absence of state weddings and the relatively small number of visits by foreign dignitaries, while not signs of austerity, reflect an era in which courtly entertainment was centered upon Borso and on monuments that reflected his glory.

Similarly, his household appears to have been of moderate size, though apparently larger than that of Leonello. The state of preservation of the source materials does not permit exact accounts of the size and composition

[24] On Casella and his role in Borso's regime, see especially Gundersheimer, *Ferrara*, pp. 146–51.

[25] On the visit of Frederick III in 1452, see Pardi, 'Borso d'Este', 384–87, and Gandini, 'Saggio degli usi', 149.   [26] See Pardi, 'Borso d'Este', 388–95.

[27] See Pardi, 377–83, and the relevant entries in the *Diario ferrarese*.

of his entourage over his entire reign, though we can be reasonably sure of both the size of certain groups (including the musicians) and of some comparative salary figures for at least one year (1452). Pardi made some effort to work out the relative priorities of Borso's general expenditures but arrived at only approximate results that are indicative of trends. One is that his maintenance of peace in foreign affairs held down military expenses. Further, the expanded diplomatic activity of Borso's reign, including the installation of resident ambassadors at Venice, Florence, Milan, and Rome, means some increase in salaries since Borso underpaid them as much as he could or paid them in confiscated goods.[28] Pardi is able to assert that the total salaries for the faculty of the Studio in the late 1450s and early 1460s averaged from 6,000 to 10,000 LM, but this figure means little unless we can find a basis for calculating the value of gifts given by Borso to large numbers of his favorites, ranging from counselors and judges down to grooms, barbers, and blacksmiths. Borso may well have been buying loyalty from the wealthier classes or insuring himself against trouble by doling out land and incomes to many of his followers, but it is hard to believe Caleffini's figures, in his rhymed chronicle, which show gifts worth many thousands of *lire* given to some thirty-five individuals, followed by a long list of only slightly smaller donations to eighty-four more (the second group ranging from 300 to 20,000 LM, according to the chronicle), all before 1462.[29] If we exclude civic appointees, such as the *podestà*, judges, and other administrators, and estimate the probable size of Borso's household, from his counselors down to pages and stableboys, it was probably a good deal smaller than the six hundred which has been estimated for Ercole's household in 1476, based on the later prose chronicle by the same Caleffini. Pardi produced a figure of one hundred men attached to Borso's staff for hunting alone, but this is surely far too large; Caleffini's rhymed chronicle lists ten, which is probably much closer to the mark. If moderation rather than opulence characterized the size of Borso's staff, it would help to explain his readiness to hire the more specialized artists and specialists needed to produce fresco paintings and illuminated manuscripts, and to procure his own elaborate regalia and jewels; yet to do all this without normally going into debt. And against the restricted size of his retinue as a whole, the number of musicians he maintained as regular employees stands out as a proportionately large group.

[28] On the financial aspects of Borso's reign, so far as presently known, see Pardi, 39–58 and 134–46.

[29] On Borso's gifts see the Caleffini rhymed chronicle, ed. A. Cappelli, in 'Notizie di Ugo Caleffini', 293–301.

10

Pietrobono and the
Improvisatory Tradition

Court Musicians under Borso

IN an earlier article on music under Ercole I, I referred to Borso's patronage as being largely confined to instrumentalists as regular court musicians.[1] It now seems clear to me that while this view is factually correct, it requires interpretation not as a decline but as a shift in taste, resulting from the severing of one of the musical traditions cultivated by Leonello and the reinforcement of the other. At Leonello's death Borso allowed most of the former chapel singers to leave Ferrara for other destinations, mainly the Papal Chapel, and at no time did he replace them with musicians of their own type.[2] The only singer who continued in the salary rolls was Niccolò Tedesco, who, significantly, was also an instrumentalist (*pulsator*) and had always been associated with the secular side of Leonello's musical forces, not with the singers recruited by Leonello for his chapel. The chapel itself, as a physical structure, seems to have remained intact, and Borso probably utilized it for devotional purposes, but for him the music of Mass and Vespers was doubtless plainsong not polyphony. His public support of religious observance, implicit in the founding of the Certosa and in the making of liturgical and devotional manuscripts (some of them in the vernacular for his own use), probably indicates nothing more than the normal awareness of a fifteenth-century Christian prince of the public piety required by his status and the personal piety needed for salvation.[3] There is nothing to show that Borso

[1] 'Music at Ferrara in the Period of Ercole I d'Este', 105–6. This chapter expands my earlier discussion of Pietrobono in 'Pietrobono and the Instrumental Tradition at Ferrara in the Fifteenth Century'.

[2] Within two months of Borso's accession to power (1 October 1450), four of Leonello's singers entered the Papal Chapel (Johannes Proposto, Golinus Madoche, Johannes del Monte, and Johannes Filibert – I follow Haberl's spellings of names, for the moment); in 1451 two more entered the papal ranks (Florentio Alexander and Benedictus Diroche or Sirede). See Haberl, *Bausteine für Musikgeschichte*, iii, pp. 38–9. I take it that the names 'Diroche' and 'Sirede' are not authentic alternative names but that one of them is a misreading; which one, I do not know.

[3] 'Zur Geschichte der Miniaturmalerei', 258, docs. 162 and 163, show evidence of payments for an expensively bound and illuminated Missal which is said to be 'fato novo per la capela de lo illustrissimo nostro signore'; both payments stem from 1454. On Borso's religiosity see Pardi, 'Borso d'Este', 52, and Rosenberg, 'Art in Ferrara', pp. 110–112.

shared the religious bent of Leonello that is so heavily stressed by the chroniclers, let alone the even more intense and virtually fanatic religiosity of his successor, Ercole.

Indicative of this shift away from the polyphonic side is the absence among Borso's commissions for illuminated manuscripts of any for polyphonic music, or indeed, for any music, so far as is known, unless we include the sumptuous but purely conventional chant manuscruipts that were provided for the newly founded Certosa.[4] Yet just as significant as Borso's acquiescence in the dispersion of the polyphonic group is his enlargement of the number and variety of the instrumentalists, a trend that indicates a continued cultivation of improvisational performance, of court dance, and probably of some kind of ensemble chamber music, perhaps entailing some use of notated compositions that were never brought together in collected volumes and that have thus not come down to us. The quality of these performers was apparently high enough to be noted by competitors: on more than one occasion, Borso's musicians, not merely the particularly famous Pietrobono, were sought after by the court of Milan, and in 1458 Niccolò Tedesco was regarded as sufficiently expert that his opinion was solicited at Mantua about the securing of a singer.[5]

Neither Borso's treatment of his performers nor their number and quality betray any austerity in musical matters. The lists of musicians are extant for only five of the twenty years of his reign but they are well distributed (1456, 1459, 1462, 1470, 1471).[6] For 1456 they show a group of fourteen instrumentalists, from among whom we can separate the five *trombetti*. This still leaves a substantial group of nine:

> *Trombone*. Agostino trombone
> *Piffari*. Corrado di Alemagna
> Zoanne de Alemagna

[4] A conspectus of the MSS produced under Borso can be made, at least in provisional outline, from the entries published by Hermann (see n. 3). They show, in addition to the massive collaborative effort required to produce the Borso Bible, at least the following important MSS: 1450–5: a St. Augustine MS for the Malatesta of Cesena; a Suetonius; a Psalter, *Oficiolo*, and Antiphoner; a Donatus; a Missal; a large Breviary for Borso (1455–7); several French books; in addition, books were acquired from the libraries of others, as from Aurispa in 1461, from whom MSS were procured for Borso's own study, for the Certosa, and for Tito Vespasiano Strozzi.

[5] For letters between Borso and Milan on the services of musicians, see Motta, 'Musici', 46 f. (declining to send his *piffari* in 1456 because they are 'absolutely necessary for the festival of St. George'); 53 f. (on Pietrobono; see below); 55 f. (on Niccolò Tedesco, Borso's singer); 285 f. (Borso in 1468 explains his having recalled Gaspare *organo* from Milan to Ferrara).

[6] These are the earliest preserved registers (some are merely 'extracts' (*estratti*), but contemporary ones) in the series *Bolletta de' Salariati* in the ASM, ASE, Camera (an 'estratto' provides an index of names from the register which it once accompanied, organized alphabetically and indicating the page in the register at which the full entry would have appeared; the 'estratto' provides no other information). Their exact state of preservation is as follows: *1456*: full register; *1457*: 'estratto' only; *1459*: 'estratto' only; *1462*: 'estratto' only. Also preserved in this group is a register of 1465–71, called 'Pacti de Laboratori et Altri Salariati de la Camera per lo Oficio de la Possessione' – this contains a single entry for Corrado *piffaro* (fol. 47) but no list of musicians.

Harp. Paolo Grillo

Lute. Pietrobono del Chitarino (and his *tenorista*, Malacise)[7]
   Blasio Montolino[8]

Keyboard Performer. Leonello Fiescho

Singer. Niccolò Tedesco

In 1462 the cast of characters is still the same. But by 1470 it has undergone some minor changes: added then is a certain Cornelio di Fiandra, a singer who is to remain until 1512, and is thus the first Franco-Flemish singer to reappear at the court in full-time service in twenty years; a certain Jacomo da Bologna *sonadore* (it is not clear what he played); and the two earliest members of the Della Viola clan, Andrea and Giampaolo, whose family were to be prominent in local musical life far into the sixteenth century. It is most significant that they appear as early as 1467 (as far as is now known), and in 1468 are called 'pulsatores lirae et familiares sue Excellentiae', suggesting that the instruments they then played were not plucked but bowed *lire da braccio*, perhaps in a polyphonic duet.[9] Throughout the entire period of Borso's reign the only musician explicitly paid as a singer is the same Niccolò Tedesco, who disappears from the rolls in 1470 and is probably replaced by Cornelio di Fiandra. The group thus remains essentially the same until 1471, when Borso dies. In 1471, a year in which Borso's hopes of the dukedom of Ferrara were being realized and were spurring him on to more lavish spending than before, the simultaneous presence of two viol players and two lutenists (Pietrobono and Rainaldo del Chitarino) plus the *tenorista*, may stir speculation about instrumental ensembles; with the harp and wind players at hand the combinations could have been remarkably varied. This would have been even more true if we take note of other instrumentalists, especially in the 1460s, mentioned by Venturi although without reference to his sources, who were evidently short-term or itinerant visitors, not long-established functionaries. They include the harpists Salamon dall'arpa (1455–60), Ruggiero da Venezia (1467) and Richardin dall'arpa (1465); other viol players included Matteo de la violetta (1465), Alessandro de Alemagna and his companion Antonio, *cantori e suonatori di viola* (1470), and Berniero de Salo from Naples, another violist (1470).[10] The presence of instrument-makers, especially of organ and keyboard instruments, and the acquisition of

---

[7] This *tenorista*, Malacise, had replaced the earlier one, named Zanetto, who had been put into the *Bolletta* as Pietrobono's own *tenorista* in 1449, and in 1452 had been called in one list 'Zanetto Barbiere'; Pardi, 'Borso d'Este', 47, n. 1.

[8] Called 'Citharista' in Milan, 1472; see Motta, 'Musici', 54.

[9] The reference to the brothers Della Viola in 1467 was published by Venturi, 'L'arte a Ferrara nel periodo di Borso d'Este', 748, n. 6, who in fact gives three names as a single group: "Giovanni, Paolo, Andrea, suonatori di viola". I assume, however, that 'Giovanni Paolo' or Zampaolo as he is called elsewhere, is one person and not two. The 1468 entry (Pardi, op. cit., p. 48, note) refers to the two brothers, Giampaolo and Andrea.

[10] Venturi, op. cit., 748, n. 6.

clavicembali and other instruments indicates a lively atmosphere of performance.[11] Venturi suggests that Borso himself may perhaps have played keyboard instruments, though there is no proof of this or of any genuine aptitude for music on his part. Following in Leonello's footsteps, however, was the young Niccolò di Leonello who in 1454 bought a *chitarrino* from Pietrobono.[12]

If there is a single figure who epitomizes the prevailing character and function of music under Borso it is Pietrobono, normally called Pietrobono del Chitarino. This is not merely because his full maturity coincided with Borso's reign but is owing to his extraordinary position in the courtly society of fifteenth-century Italy as singer and lutenist. Celebrated by contemporary poets and writers, chiefly non-musicians, but also by music theorists; depicted on portrait medals; raised to the rank of the nobility; treated courteously by heads of state anxious to add him to their retinues or to borrow his services, his prominence in the fifteenth-century world of improvisational singing and performance on plucked instruments is so great that if we are searching for a master of comparable fame in the polyphonic tradition we have to wait until the early years of the sixteenth century, when the name of Josquin Desprez begins to resound in both humanistic and music-theoretical circles.[13] To put it as briefly as possible: of Pietrobono not a note of written music is preserved, yet he is beyond doubt one of the most important figures in all of fifteenth-century music, certainly in Italy. Only the tendency of modern historiography to base its views entirely on written sources, rather than on these in relation to the larger landscape from which they emerge, could prevent our seeing Pietrobono, in his domain, as a figure comparable to the greatest polyphonic masters of the period. That he belongs to a sector of musical training and practice that is fundamentally different from that of the polyphonic schools is beyond question; yet between these distinctive orbits of musical life a few delicate points of contact can now be discerned.

Up to now, the main biographical facts about Pietrobono have been drawn mainly from Cittadella, to whose local data were added a few references by contemporary writers and poets, along with an autograph letter of 1488 that

---

[11] In the years 1464–6, the instrument maker Constantino Tantino brought instruments from Modena to Ferrara and bought instruments for Borso, probably keyboard instruments. We also find organ builders mentioned in connection with the cathedral, and indeed it is worth reaffirming that it was during Borso's reign that the great organ with shutters by Tura was made for the cathedral, as well as the large organ for the Convent of San Paolo: see Venturi, op. cit., 747 f. and Cittadella, *Notizie*, p. 66.

[12] Venturi, 748.

[13] Although it is safe to assume that Josquin's reputation was spreading through Italian courts as early as the 1470s, when he joined the Sforza chapel, and remained well established through the next two decades, we do not find written evidence of his international fame before the first decade of the 16th century; from this decade are the evaluations made privately by Gian Cantore and Girolamo da Sestola ('il Coglia'), and publicly by Paolo Cortese.

was cited by Canal and published by Bertolotti.[14] To summarize briefly: it is known that Pietrobono's surname was 'de Burzeris' or 'de Burzellis', that he was a native of Ferrara, the son of a certain Baptista and his wife Margherita, daughter of a certain Biagio *todesco*; that he was 'barbiere' to Borso in the 1450s, and was already well-to-do by that time; that he was subsequently praised as a masterly performer by a long line of humanist writers, including Aurelio Brandolino Lippi, Cornazzano, Battista Guarino, Filippo Beroaldo, Paolo Cortese, and Raffaello Maffei – and, among music theorists, Tinctoris.[15] It is also known that from the mid-1450s to the mid-1480s he was at various times a visitor or in service at other courts: at Milan in the 1450s with Duke Francesco Sforza; at Naples in 1473; at Mantua in 1482–3; and in 1487–8 in the service of Beatrice d'Aragona, Queen of Hungary.[16] The writers unanimously praise him as a 'rarissimo citharista', but from the long poem by Cornazzano describing him as a singer at a wedding feast for Francesco Sforza it is clear that he also excelled in the singing of narrative verse, accompanying himself on a stringed instrument, almost certainly the lute. We will also see concrete evidence to show, and we must assume in any case, that his repertoire included many well-known melodies set to Italian verse (perhaps also French?) to which he must have provided not only vocal ornamentation but appropriate instrumental accompaniment. Whatever his fame as a singer, he is more consistently praised as a great lutenist, and it may not be merely poetic license when Cornazzano writes

> chi vole passar di un mondo all'altro,
> odi *sonare* Pietrobono [italics mine]

('Whoever wishes to pass from one world to another, should hear Pietrobono's playing').

We have already seen his beginnings under Leonello, and the rewards given him as early as 1441, when Leonello took office; he was then not more than twenty-four, if the traditional birthdate of 1417 is correct.[17] Most significant is that he must have grown up and learned his trade in the environment of

[14] Cittadella, *Notizie*, vols. i and iii. Pietrobono's letter of 13 January 1488 is cited by Canal, 'Della musica in Mantova', 662; and the full text with facsimile of his signature is published by Bertolotti, *Musici alla corte dei Gonzaga in Mantova*, pp. 12–13. The letter shows Pietrobono as an experienced hand in flattery, much as we might expect from the nature of his career.

[15] For the texts in praise of Pietrobono by Brandolino Lippi, Beroaldo, and Maffei, see Haraszti, 'Pierre Bono, Luthiste de Mathias Corvino', 78–83; on those of Cornazzano and Cortese see Pirrotta, 'Music and Cultural Tendencies', 139–61, repr. in *Music and Culture*. The passage by Tinctoris is from his *De Inventione et Usu Musicae*, ed. Weinmann, p. 45.

[16] For evidence of his relations to Milan see the documents cited later in this chapter and Barblan, 'Vita musicale alla corte sforzesca', p. 803. On his trip to Naples see Pirrotta, 'Music and Cultural Tendencies', 141, n. 53. On his Hungarian period see *Monumenta Hungariae Historica*, iii p. 410; also Fökövi, 'Musik und musikalische Verhältnisse in Ungarn am Hofe des Matthias Corvinus' 14.

[17] The basis for the date (given by Haraszti in *Die Musik in Geschichte und Gegenwart*, ii, col. 117) is uncertain, but in view of Pietrobono's considerable reputation by the early 1440s, it is plausible.

music-making fostered in the last years of Niccolò III's regime and in the period of the education of Leonello. Leonardo del Chitarino, already at court in the 1420s, is a hypothetical choice as his teacher. By 1449, as we have seen, a certain Zanetto is put into the *Bolletta* as *tenorista* for Pietrobono, who is called *citharedo*.[18] This is the earliest reference to a second musician serving as *tenorista* for him, an assignment that is always filled by a performer given this designation, and whose name is always found in close proximity to that of Pietrobono even in payment records. Presumably they were regular companions. Perhaps this was a player of a tenor viol, whose role was to furnish a mid-range pattern comparable to that of the tenor in the three-part wind ensemble for the *bassadanza*; against such a tenor pattern we can hypothesize that Pietrobono played and sang, improvising a discant in a two- or possibly a three-part ensemble.[19] That Pietrobono played and also sang in a high register is suggested by more than one source, among them a curious phrase used by the chronicler Caleffini in his prose narrative, in which he calls him, in 1484, 'meiore maestro de sonare leuto de Christiani, vz de soprano . . .'. Although Caleffini may not have known much about music, he could probably tell a high part from a low one.[20]

Pietrobono's reputation spread in the 1450s as he gained personal contact with such patrons as Francesco Sforza, whose rise to power in Milan in 1450 opened the era of the Sforza regime, and who seems to have cultivated lutenists in particular.[21] On 18 December 1455, Duke Francesco writes a letter to Pietrobono at Ferrara to acknowledge what the latter had told him about a certain Stefano *sonatore*, who had clearly been sent by Francesco to study with Pietrobono. And on the same day the Duke writes to Stefano to tell him that, since Pietrobono must depart from Ferrara (*ad extranee parte*),

[18] See above, Chapter 7, p. 69.

[19] While he is normally called 'Pietrobono del Chitarino' in payment records and other documents, this may be no more than a general reference to his profession as player of a plucked instrument; a number of documents from the later part of his career make it clear that he was a lutenist (e.g. those cited in n. 4 above, and Caleffini's reference to him as 'maestro di leuto'). While it is possible that in earlier years he played on a 'cittern' or 'gittern' (a four-stringed instrument with a flat back) there is no specific evidence to that effect. Cornazzano speaks of a 'cetra' but may not mean so literally; similarly, the small instrument shown on the reverse of the portrait medal of 1457 may not be intended realistically. At times such references are too vague to be helpful; at other times, they indicate distinctions fairly precisely, as when Isabella's agent, Francesco Bagnacavallo, writes to her (1491), 'canta bene in uno liuto, una citara, una violla . . .'. (ASMN, AG, B. 1232, letter of 24 October 1491).

[20] Caleffini's text is: 'Et in dicto zorno venero pure lettere al dicto Signore como messer Pietrobono dal chitarino cavaliero meiore maestro de sonare leuto de Christiani, vz de soprano, in la citade de Mantua, ove per le guerra et per la peste de Ferrara se era reducto era morto de febre et li sepolto.' ('And on that day there came letters to the aforesaid Lord to the effect that Master Pietrobono del chitarino, gentleman, the best master of lute-playing in Christendom [that is, the playing of high parts] had died of fever and been buried at Mantua, where he had gone because of the war and the plague at Ferrara'). The report of his death is false, premature by thirteen years.

[21] On Francesco Sforza as ruler and patron see Santoro, *Gli Sforza*, pp. 14–71; on his musical patronage see Barblan, 'Vita musicale alla corte sforzesca', pp. 802 ff.

Stefano should come back to Milan.[22] Into this context fit two other letters to Duke Francesco, both dated 26 December 1455, one from Pietrobono, the other from Stefano. In the former letter, which is now in the collection of Mr Robert Spencer, and which was published in full by me in an earlier article, Pietrobono tells the Duke that he has urged Stefano, whom he calls 'il tedesco', to return to Milan, that he has taught him 'two advantageous things' (*due avantagiate cose*) in the past few days which the Duke should observe, and that Stefano is making good progress.[23] In the letter from Stefano we learn that the student was without money and implores the Duke to send him some so that he can stay 'for several months with Pietrobono, even though he is departing . . . I can very well go with him to study with him . . .'.[24] From this we see the respect in which Pietrobono was held as a teacher. Pietrobono's own presence in Milan is confirmed a year later, when Duke Francesco writes to Borso to say that he was glad to see Pietrobono 'for his abilities and above all in playing . . . in which we believe he has not an equal in the world'; the letter has the character of a polite note meant to reassure Borso that Pietrobono's visit does not threaten a change of allegiance.[25]

Possible rivalry for his services, real or imagined, would help to explain the great improvement in Pietrobono's financial status that seems to have occurred between the mid-1450s and the year 1462, when Caleffini's rhymed chronicle mentions his wealth. Caleffini goes out of his way to list not only Pietrobono's gifts from Borso but those of other local musicians. Even if the figures are inflated, this contrasts sharply with Borso's apparent stinginess in dealing with so capable an artist as Francesco del Cossa, whose pitiable letter to Borso pleading for better payment for his work on the Schifanoia frescoes has become famous.[26] In 1457 Francesco Sforza writes again to Pietrobono, asking him to trace a certain Gaspare (perhaps the Gaspar *sonatore de organi* who is known at the Este court from 1446 to 1465); again in 1461, in a letter

[22] The full texts of these letters from Francesco, to Pietrobono and to Stefano, are given by Barblan, op. cit., p. 803.

[23] The text of this letter was published for the first time in my 'Pietrobono', 124–5.

[24] This letter was published by Tiersot, *Lettres de musiciens écrites en francais du XVe au XXe siècle*, pp. 5–7. This letter, preserved at that time in the Bibliothèque du Conservatoire, and now in the Bibliothèque Nationale, was not known to me at the time of publication of my article listed in note 23. For calling my attention to it I am grateful to my colleagues Jessie Ann Owens and Dr Martin Staehelin.

[25] Text in Barblan, op. cit., p. 803.

[26] Caleffini's rhymed chronicle, not to be confused with his later one in prose, was published by Cappelli in 'Notizie di Ugo Caleffini'. The latter part of the verse chronicle is explicitly intended to celebrate Borso's generosity; at the very end, the author produces the list of gifts made by Borso to members of his court at all levels. The include gifts 'A misser Pietro Boni predetto suo barbiero per . . . 2000; A Corado suo pifaro . . . 2000; A Zohane de Trento suo mastro de stalla . . . 2000; A Cirlo suo falconiero . . .2000; A Bartolemeo Fiascho suo sonatore de organo . . . 300'.

For Cossa's letter to Borso, see Ruhmer, *Cosimo Tura*, pp. 27–34 (in Italian); English translation in Chambers, *Patrons and Artists in the Italian Renaissance*, pp. 162–4.

of introduction, he presents a young man named Antonio de Pavia, probably another aspiring lutenist.[27]

Pietrobono's strongest outside connection in the 1450s seems to be with Milan, yet in that decade he seems to have remained largely in Ferrara. This may well coincide with Borso's generosity in assigning to him the proceeds of a local tax on *facchini* (transport of goods), as Caleffini reports:

> A Pietro Bono dal chitarin,
> L'ha habuto più de mille florin;
> Tra de fachin et de suo sonare
> Ch'il non ha briga da sbarbirare.

('As for Pietrobono del Chitarino, he has gotten more than a thousand florins; between the *facchini* and his playing, he has no more troubles to straighten out.')

Sbarbirare is a pun on *barbiere*, Pietrobono's former speciality as valet to Borso before his rise to wealth and status.

A portrait medal of Pietrobono had been struck in 1447, and in Borso's time he became an increasingly prominent citizen, again celebrated by poets such as Cornazzano.[28] In 1459 Cornazzano had completed a long poem for Francesco Sforza, *La Sfortiade*, in the ninth book of which a section is entitled 'Laudes Petri boni cythariste'; it describes a banquet following the wedding of Francesco Sforza and Bianca Maria Visconti. The fictitious date is 1441, but the strongest probability, as Pirrotta has suggested in an extended commentary on the passage, is that the performance to which the poem refers took place during Pietrobono's visit to Milan in 1456. It describes his role as a singer at a banquet, intoning the praises of Francesco and his bride, and 'singing, in well-ordered verses, to the cythara, the love tales of modern people who are praised'. We do not know in what meter he is supposed to have sung, but as Pirrotta suggests, it would have been suitable to improvise in any of several narrative meters familiar to the period, such as the *terza rima*, the *sirventese*, or the *ottava rima*.[29] Cornazzano celebrates his skill in at least two other poems: in his *Capitoli* he describes the festivities of 1453 for Borso's reception at Modena and Reggio as newly invested Duke, and reports that Pietrobono sang on that occasion before the assembled populace (thereby assuming the role of a *cantimpancha* or *cantastorie* for the occasion); and in his later treatise, *De Excellentium Virorum Princibus*, of 1466, dedicated to Borso, he mentions Pietrobono in a passage on the misadventures of Venus.[30]

---

[27] Barblan, op. cit., p. 803.

[28] For the portrait medal by the Venetian Giovanni Boldù (one of several of Pietrobono) that was made at Ferrara, see 'Bono Pietro', *Die Musik in Geschichte und Gegenwart*, ii, col. 118; also Gruyer, *L'Art ferrarais*, i, pp. 611–12.

[29] See Pirrotta, 'Music and Cultural Tendencies', 146; repr. in *Music and Culture*.

[30] On the festivities for Borso's trip to Modena and Reggio in 1452 see Pardi, 'Borso d'Este', 388. On Cornazzano's *De Excellentium Virorum Principibus* see Pirrotta, 'Music and Cultural Tendencies', 141, n. 53.

Although his later career goes beyond the limits of Borso's life, we may follow it briefly here in order to complete the portrait of this master performer and to show that the essentially improvisational tradition which he represents continued into the last decades of the century; further, that his personal fortunes increased even beyond earlier triumphs and took him to new positions abroad. In 1471 he accompanied Borso on the famous trip to Rome for his ducal investiture; after Ercole's accession he remained on the salary rolls and in 1473 was sent to Naples in the *comitiva* dispatched to bring back Eleonora d'Aragona as bride of Ercole. This was all that was needed to establish his reputation at Naples, for in 1476 Diomede Carafa wrote to Ercole to say that the King of Naples would like to borrow Pietrobono 'vostro sonatore di liuto'.[31] If Tinctoris was in Naples as early as 1473, as has been suggested, he may well have heard Pietrobono then; if not, he could certainly have done so when he came to Ferrara for a visit in 1479.[32]

In the early 1480s the ageing lutenist retreated to Mantua to shelter from the war that broke out between Ferrara and Venice, and he had not yet returned in the early months of 1484, when Caleffini's prose chronicle mentions a rumor of his supposed death.[33] By 1486 he had certainly returned, however, when another diplomatic assignment forced him to leave again, this time to accompany the eight-year-old Ippolito d'Este, second son of Ercole, to Hungary, where this young bearer of the family's hopes for high church office had been appointed Archbishop of Esztergom. Ercole was evidently responding to a request from his sister-in-law, Beatrice of Hungary, who had left Naples for Hungary to become bride of King Matthias Corvina, and whose wish to surround herself with familiar cultural styles entailed the importation of musicians; she had asked Ercole to send her 'Pietrobono and his viols'.[34] After some delay, Ippolito actually left with a large retinue on 18 June 1487, while Pietrobono, with the poet and courtier Niccolò da Correggio, went by another road.[35] Although all other musicians sent with Ippolito returned to Ferrara as soon as possible, Pietrobono was induced by Beatrice to remain, as we see from a letter sent by Pietrobono to Francesco Gonzaga, written from Vienna on 13 January 1488, reminding Francesco of his gratitude for past favors at Mantua and recommending his grandson for

---

[31] The letter is in Moores, 'New Light on Diomede Carafa', 16–23 (with other correspondence): the relevant passage is given in the original in my 'Pietrobono', 127 f., n. 38.

[32] For the text showing Tinctoris's visit to Ferrara from 7 to 11 May 1479, see my 'Pietrobono', 128, n. 39; also my 'Aspects of the "L'Homme armé" Tradition', 111, n. 38.

[33] See n. 20 above.

[34] Fökövi, 'Musik und musikalische Verhältnisse', 14: 'Et Messer Pier nostro sonatore de leuto quale sta qui con me continuamente, me prega che scriva a V.S. I.l. in commendare della moglie et sua famiglia . . .' ('And Master Pietro[bono] our lutenist, who is with me regularly, asks me to write to Your Illustrious Lordship on behalf of his wife and his family . . .'). Pietrobono's reluctance to go to Hungary had been overruled by Duke Ercole, in a letter to his wife, Eleonora, of 5 October 1486; see my 'Pietrobono', 128, n. 41.

[35] Morselli, 'Ippolito d'Este e il suo primo viaggio in Ungheria', 216.

Francesco's service.[36] In the same vein is a letter of May 1488 from Beatrice to her sister Eleonora, who is asked to take Pietrobono's family at Ferrara under her protection, as he is to remain in Beatrice's service.[37] His eventual return to Italy did not coincide with that of Beatrice herself, who was forced to abandon Hungary in 1500, after the death of Matthias Corvina. We find Pietrobono once again in the Ferrarese salary rolls in 1493 and 1494, and in 1497 his death is recorded on the date 20 September, in the *Libro della Compagnia della Morte*.[38]

From the small change of biographical detail emerges a picture that confirms Pietrobono's significant role in music at the Ferrarese court over more than half a century. His entire active career is unusually long, not only among musicians but for any members of the court's hierarchy, outlasting by sixteen years that of Corrado *piffaro* (his closest local counterpart as a famous instrumentalist), and spanning the full range of local cultural transformations from 1441 to 1497. He must have witnessed, except during his years away in the 1480s, every major turn in the development of music at the court, and while he was clearly a prominent member of the group of instrumentalists, he was equally and essentially a special figure – renowned as performer, rewarded lavishly by his patrons, admired by local and distant orators and poets, and much in demand at rival courts.

As a performer he occupied a strategic middle ground at which three musical traditions converged: the tradition of lute playing, of improvisational singing of narrative verse in the vernacular, and of polyphonic song. Secular polyphonic song, chiefly but not exclusively to French texts, was only gradually being assimilated into the musical activities of Italian patrons, but it nevertheless became codified in a series of chansonniers that were copied at Italian courts or for private patrons from the 1460s on. While we have such manuscripts in surprising numbers from Naples and Florence between about 1460 and about 1490, it is striking that during Borso's reign, which coincides with the early phase of this development, there are neither comparable manuscripts nor records of the preparation of such manuscripts for the principal musicians of the court. The Porto MS 714, to be discussed shortly, almost certainly does stem from Ferrara but appears to be a manuscript produced outside the circles of Borso himself.[39] The assembling of such repertoires probably gained impetus in the period of Ercole; in the time of Borso the

[36] For the full text see Bertolotti, *Musici alla corte*, pp. 12–13. The name 'Bosio da Coreza', as given in the text by Bertolotti, is that of Borso da Correggio, a long-time Estense diplomat and courtier, who was at the head of Ippolito's party when he traveled to Hungary in June 1487, seven months before this letter was written.

[37] Fökövi, 'Musik und musikalische Verhältnisse', 14.

[38] Cittadella, *Notizie*, iii, p. 294.

[39] For a recent detailed survey of Florentine and Neapolitan Chansonniers of this period see Atlas, *The Cappella Giulia Chansonnier (Rome, Biblioteca Vaticana MS Cappella Giulia XIII, 27)*, i, pp. 258 ff.

emphasis was clearly on the improvisational side, and the court was especially open to the visiting *canterini*, or improvisers, whose traditions reached
back to the *giullari* and who were akin to the popular *cantastorie* who
entertained crowds in Florence and elsewhere.[40] Evidence of the growing
presence of this kind of entertainment at the court in the 1460s is provided in
documents published by Bertoni, and at least two of these performers remained
at Ferrara for many years – Francesco Cieco da Ferrara, and Giovanni
Orbo.[41] For a glimpse of their role in domestic life at court we can turn to
two letters, both written on the same summer day (22 August, 1468) by
Sforza Maria Sforza, then a visitor at Ferrara (writing from Belfiore):[42]

[To his mother:] Heri non andassimo in campagna ma al disnare havessimo diversi
piaceri, de clavicembali, de liuti, de buffoni et de Magistro Zohanne Orbo; quale dixe
maravigliosamente, piu de l'usato.

('Yesterday we did not go out into the countryside but, while we were dining, we had
various amusements – of playing of harpsichords and lutes, and by jesters and by
Master Giovanni Orbo, who recited in a marvelous manner, quite out of the
ordinary.')

[To his brother:] Havessimo diversi piaceri de sono de organetti, de liuti, de
clavicimboli, de bufoni, cioè del Scocola, et de Magistro Zohane Orbo, quale
veramente dixe cose maravigliose de improviso.

('We had various amusements, consisting of the playing of small organs, lutes, and
harpsichords, and entertainments by jesters, that is, Scocola and Master Giovanni
Orbo, who truly recited remarkable things extemporaneously.')

Such testimony helps us to grasp something of the role of music as a
reinforcement and component of informal communal diversion in the daily
life of the court. The description emphasizes not only the setting indoors but
also the use of music while eating, and the variety of entertainments provided.
Such informal and spontaneous situations must often have demanded sudden
use of the court's resources, and, as we have seen earlier, the musicians and
buffoni had learned to be ready to perform on short notice. To do so they
obviously needed a repertoire of memorized material, subject to renewal and
modification, both verbal and musical, and if their normal performances were
entirely without the use of notation, then the use of fixed formulas was
clearly essential.[43] Yet the formulas needed by keyboard players, lutenists,
and *canterini* could hardly have been the same. While the improvisers made
use of narrative verse-forms, the instrumentalists probably adapted to their
own technical needs some of the increasingly familiar standard tunes of the

[40] Levi, *I cantari leggendari del popolo italiano nei secoli XIV e VX*, and Becherini, 'Un canta
in panca fiorentino, Antonio di Guido', 243–4. That there was a long history of such singers at
the Ferrarese court stretching back into the 14th century and earlier can be assumed in any event,
but some specific evidence is provided by Levi, *Francesco da Vannozzo*, who shows that
Francesco was in Ferrara in 1376.
[41] Bertoni, 'Il Cieco di Ferrara e altri improvvisatori', 271–8.   [42] Motta, 'Musici', 283.
[43] See Pirrotta, 'Novelty and Renewal', 56; repr. in *Music and Culture*.

day, very likely drawing on such resources as the current *bassadanza* repertoires, and thus using in informal circumstances music gathered and codified for more formal purposes – the conceptual model is obviously akin to the practices of twentieth-century jazz musicians improvising on 'hit tunes'.[44] The growing numbers of chansonniers in Italy does not necessarily indicate a lessening of instrumental participation; quite the contrary, the characteristic paucity of texts in these manuscripts, often the complete absence of texts apart from titles – goes together with the expected and accepted participation of instruments in chanson performance. As we will see, in the case of the one surviving Ferrarese chansonnier of the period of Ercole, the Casanatense chansonnier, exclusively instrumental performance seems to be specifically intended.[45]

The presumed role of Pietrobono in this mixed and transitional era may have been as a kind of mediator between the world of the improvisers and that of the contrapuntally trained and cultivated performers of part-music. He was probably one of the few lutenists who could compete with ease (as the poets tell us) with the narrative improvisers and yet also combine with others in polyphonic ensembles. What such a *concentus* looked like at Ferrara in the 1490s, his very last years, is suggested by the well-known *Concerto* painted either by Lorenzo Costa or Ercole de' Roberti (cf. fig. 6).[46] Pietrobono is too old to be the lutenist-singer depicted in the painting, but it probably reflects quite faithfully a performing combination that the court then knew. His long-established practice as a teacher implies either purely ostensive instruction or the use of some kind of tablature notation long before the earliest extant examples preserved, which date from the very end of the fifteenth century.[47] And he also taught others from his melodic repertoire, as we learn from two remarkable documents.

The first is a contact drawn up in the year 1465 between Pietrobono and a certain Girolamo Bondi, Venetian by background but living in Ferrara and very likely a long-term resident. The agreement provides that in exchange for payment Pietrobono will teach Girolamo 'the art of music on the "cytharino" and will show him seven *cantilenas*, well and properly, and will go daily to the home of Girolamo in Ferrara to teach him.' In exchange for this

---

[44] This helps to explain the occasional written links that we find between the tenors of certain *basse dances* and written chansons of the period in MSS that are of Italian provenance, such as the Seville chansonnier; see Plamenac, 'The "Second" Chansonnier of the Biblioteca Riccardiana', 120, n. 2.

[45] See the later discussion of the Casanatense chansonnier in Chapter 26. This modifies what I said in the article 'Pietrobono', 132, n. 54; on the other hand, other MSS containing manifestly 'instrumental' compositions may not have been, and in most cases probably were not, as specifically intended for instrumental use as was the Casanatense MS.

[46] Frequently reproduced, e.g. by Einstein, *The Italian Madrigal*, i, facing p. 143. The painting is attributed to Roberti by Venturi and a few later scholars; more recently to Costa by Longhi, *Officina ferrarese*, pp. 54, 143. However, Longhi's acceptance of the so-called 'Bentivoglio' concert painting (Lugano, Thyssen Museum) as being by Costa, seems to me incomprehensible, and raises some questions about the strength of his attribution of the London *Concerto* as well.   [47] See Rubsamen, 'The Earliest French Lute Tablature'.

Girolamo promises to pay Pietrobono six yards of black cloth and one gold ducat.[48] It is clear that this was not to be a long-term period of instruction, but rather that when Girolamo had learned the seven songs and, presumably, the rudiments of lute-playing, Pietrobono's duties would be finished. There is no hint of learning to read musical notation, nor of solmization or other rudiments. The whole method was probably one of teaching the songs by rote, text and music, until the student had mastered them; this fits in exactly with the account of Galeazzo Maria Sforza, who in his youth is described as having learned 'eight French songs, and every day he is learning new ones.'[49] Other similar evidence should convince us that there were as many forms of musical instruction afoot in the fifteenth century as there were methods of musical performance.

The other document is a letter written from Ferrara to Mantua on 2 August 1494, by a certain Don Acteon.[50]

Illustrissimo signore mio: aviso ala vostra Signoria come messer petro bono me a insignato vivi leto e non temere l'ocelo dale rame doro, e solame la tua partita et tute due le sue scaramele e queste cose le imparai dal principio di luio per fino a vinti del dito et li soi tenori che sono molto boni el quelo di per sin qui non o imparato altro e questo e stato che messer petro bono e stato gravemente infermo et non semai levato di leto. Pur al presente sta asai meio et dise che per amore della Vostra Signoria mai se vedera straco a insignarme et chel me insignara cose per amore vostro che mai la voluto insignare a niuno e vole che da qui a qualche di venga a sonare quelo che o imparato ala vostra Illustrissima signoria . . . [continues on non-musical matters]

Most illustrious Lord: This is to inform Your Lordship that messer Pietrobono has taught me 'Vivi lieto e non temere l'ocelo dale rame doro', and 'Solame la tua partita', and both of his *Scaramella*'s and these pieces I learned from the beginning of July up to the twentieth of the month, and also his tenors, which are very good. From that day on I haven't learned anything else, and this is because messer Pietrobono has been gravely ill, and has not been out of bed. Now he is much better, and says that for love of Your Lordship he will never tire of teaching me, and that he will teach me things, for your sake, that he has never wanted to teach anyone; and he wishes that, in a short while, I come to play what I have learned for Your Lordship . . .

Of the pieces mentioned by Don Acteon we can trace at least two to these polyphonic repertoires in which these popular tunes and verses were taken up and used for more elaborate settings: 'Vivi lieto' is known as incipit of a setting in the MS Florence 27, and it has a sacred contrafactum in the lauda 'A Maria fonte d'amore'; no text is known beyond the first words, and no other source is known.[51] There is also a piece in Petrucci's Second Book of Frottole with the incipit 'Vivo lieto nel tormento', which might be related.

---

[48] The source for this contract is ASF, AN, Not. Mengo Dall'Armi, doc. of 4 May 1465; the full text was published for the first time by Peverada, 'Vita musicale', 6, n. 15.

[49] Quoted by Barblan, 'Vita musicale', p. 818.   [50] Source: ASMN, AG, B. 1233.

[51] Jeppesen, *La frottola*, ii, pp. 122, 161. The letter is also published and discussed by Prizer, 'The Frottola and the Unwritten Tradition'.

Whether 'l'ocelo dale rame doro' is part of the text 'Vivi lieto' or a separate composition cannot now be determined; the same applies to the piece 'Solame la tua partita' (probably using solmization puns for its first four syllables). But the mention of *Scaramella* brings us to one of the most famous Italian popular tunes in Italy of the later fifteenth century, with its verse about a certain scarecrow-figure of a soldier named *Scaramella*, who goes to war, either with lance and shield, or with boots and shoes, depending on the textual variant adopted.[52] Yet although Don Acteon learned two *Scaramella* melodies from Pietrobono we find only one employed by the various composers who used it for polyphonic settings, and no other is now known. The same was used by Loyset Compère and by Josquin Desprez for polyphonic settings, no doubt during their Italian periods. Compère's setting is found in Petrucci's Fourth Book of Frottole and in a later MS from the Alamire workshop (Florence 2439); while the Josquin setting is found copied into three Italian MSS of the later fifteenth century, all of which are evidently Florentine. The terminus for one of them, Florence 229, is 1491, as we know from Brown, and thus we know too that Josquin's setting must have been written before that date, therefore during his Milanese or Roman period; the Compère setting could well date from 1494, when we know that he accompanied the armies of Charles VIII of France on their invasion route into Italy and was approached for music by the Ferrarese court.[53] *Scaramella* forms one of the key points of contact between the great French polyphonic masters, Compère and Josquin, and Italian popular music of their time, and we may assume that it was also found in the repertoires of many lutenist-singers apart from Pietrobono. It furnishes a concrete example of a tune sufficiently simple and clear in structure to remain constant and recognizable under the many transformations that it must have received, either from the improvisatory rhapsodies of a Pietrobono on the one side, or from the polyphonic settings of Josquin and Compère on the other. And if we can legitimately hypothesize that, as a variant form of performance, Pietrobono could not only sing it to his lute but utilize it as part of a polyphonic instrumental-vocal ensemble, then a moment of *rapprochement* between the two worlds of music-making and musical practice might have been temporarily realized.

[52] Jeppesen, *La frottola*, ii, p. 251, lists the Scaramella settings by Josquin and Compère as well as an anonymous setting in Florence, Biblioteca Nazionale Centrale, MS Magl. xix, 164–7.

[53] The terminal date for Florence 229 of 1491 has been established by Howard Brown in the preface to his *A Florentine Chansonnier from the Time of Lorenzo the Magnificent*, pp. 25, 41. For the letter from Ferrante d'Este to his father Ercole, dated 7 October 1494, concerning Compère, see my 'Music at Ferrara in the Period of Ercole I d'Este', 115–16 and 129–30; also below, p. 200.

11

A Secular Manuscript of the Borso Period: The Porto MS and Rinaldo Maria d'Este

FROM Borso's era of 'sudden and unexpected music' as a primary form of household diversion, we have only one extant manuscript that contains secular polyphony and thus embodies a written tradition of contemporary music and poetry: Porto [Oporto], Biblioteca Pública Municipal, MS 714. Whether this MS belongs to the period of Leonello or to that of Borso has been uncertain up to now, but I believe that the question can be resolved with a fair degree of confidence. Yet the matter is delicate and requires a careful review. Although this manuscript has been known to scholars since the mid-1920s, and was discussed from different standpoints by Besseler and Bernhard Meier, its provenance and dating were neglected until Pirrotta raised these questions in 1970. He suggested for the first time that it probably originated in Ferrara in the middle of the fifteenth century.[1] Pirrotta's main arguments for Ferrarese provenance were based on these points: (1) the linguistic peculiarities of the Italian texts employed for six compositions in the MS; (2) his discovery that two of the Italian texts, both set for two voices by an otherwise unknown Englishman named 'Galfridus de Anglia', are actually stanzas from a long poem evidently written in 1444 for Leonello's younger sister, Isotta d'Este.[2] The poem was written by a Ferrarese poet, Girolamo Nigrisoli, and it laments the imminent departure of Isotta from the city. Isotta experienced two unhappy marriages in short succession: in 1444, aged nineteen, she married Oddantonio de Montefeltro, Count of Urbino, but was widowed only two months later when he was killed. In 1446 she married a Dalmation nobleman, but was so mistreated by him that she returned to Ferrara in 1449. As the poem does not mention her widowhood it seems

[1] 'Two Anglo-Italian Pieces in the Manuscript Porto 714'.

[2] These are the two two-voice pieces, 'Io zemo, suspiro', and 'Che farò io', which set inner strophes of the eighteen-strophe poem by Girolamo Nigrisoli published in Ferraro, ed., *Alcune poesie inedite del Saviozzo*. On other poems for Isotta see above, Chapter 7, p. 65. An earlier discussion on the Porto MS and this basis for its dating appeared in my 'Dufay and Ferrara', pp. 6–8, but is now superseded by the material presented here. The two pieces by Galfridus, and those in the MS by Robertus de Anglia, as well as the Nigrisoli poem, were published by Fallows, ed., *Galfridus and Robertus de Anglia, Four Italian Songs for 2 and 3 Voices*.

more likely that it refers to the earlier wedding in 1444, although either date, 1444 or 1446, may be plausible; these are accordingly the earliest possible dates for the manuscript. Pirrotta suggested that it be dated in the later 1440s, in some connection with Leonello's chapel, but since the staffing of the chapel was then entirely unknown, the matter rested there.[3]

Before considering further hypotheses, let us briefly survey the contents of the MS. It is a small MS of eighty-three parchment leaves, about 20 × 14 cm., consisting of two music-theoretical treatises followed by nineteen polyphonic compositions in black notation, on French and Italian texts.[4] The two treatises form a systematic pair: the first deals with the rudiments of plainsong, the second is an introduction to the mensural system. Superficially this is reminiscent of the 'pair of treatises' copied for Leonello in 1435, but, as will be seen, the treatises in Porto 714 can actually be traced to local traditions of music theory, specifically the work of the great resident theorist, Ugolino di Orvieto.

Fifteen of its nineteen compositions are attributed, but to only five composers: Dufay (with six works, the leading figure); Gilles Joye (one); and three English musicians: Johannes Bedyngham (two), Robertus de Anglia (two), and the Galfridus de Anglia (two) who set the verses for Isotta D'Este. None of these were regular members of Leonello's musical staff, let alone of Borso's, but two of them are found in connection with the court or elsewhere in the city. Dufay, as we know, visited the court in 1437, and was again paid by Leonello in Bruges in 1443. Further, it was recently discovered by Adriano Franceschini that Robertus de Anglia was made singing master at Ferrara Cathedral in 1460, as mentioned in a previous chapter (cf. Chapter 8, p. 81, n. 28). Although still more new evidence about Robertus has subsequently been found by Franceschini, these were the facts as known at the time of the preparation of an important recent contribution on the Porto MS and its history by David Fallows, to which we now turn.[5]

Concerning himself primarily with its English attributions, Fallows seeks to connect the MS closely with the Robertus de Anglia who is prominent in the collection and who is known only by this name. Fallows' view can be briefly summarized: (1) Robertus de Anglia is not to be associated with Robert Morton, as Besseler thought, but rather with the Robertus de Anglia who was at Ferrara Cathedral from 1460 to 1467, and at San Petronio in Bologna from 1467 to 1474. (2) The contemporary Bolognese poet, Cesare Nappi, mentions Robertus de Anglia as having set a poem of his to music;

---

[3] I must emphasize that the year 1444 concerns the dating of the *poem*, not necessarily of the musical setting by Galfridus or its copying into the Porto MS.

[4] For the full contents of the MS, a first extensive bibliographic description of it based on personal observation, and an extended discussion of its dating and provenance, see Fallows, 'Robertus de Anglia and the Oporto Song Collection'; some of Fallows' conclusions are embodied in the notes to his edition of the Galfridus and Robertus songs (see above, n. 2). For an earlier list of contents, see Meier, 'Die Handschrift Porto 714 als Quelle zur Tonartenlehre des 15. Jahrhunderts'.	[5] See n. 4.

the famous theorist, Bartolomeo Ramos, then at Bologna, cites Robertus in connection with a peculiar practice regarding mensuration signs, a practice that is reflected virtually without exception in Porto.[6] (3) The treatises in Porto are 'distillations' from material found in Ugolino's *Declaratio*. (4) The concordance of Porto 714 with other MSS show no connections with MSS of the 1430s or 1440s, (e.g. Oxford 213, Escorial V. iii. 24, or Trent 87) but do overlap in content substantially with MSS of the 1460s and 1470s, (e.g. Escorial IV. a. 24 and Berlin 78. C. 28, the only two MSS sharing as many as six compositions with Porto 714). (5) Fallows suggests 1467 as a plausible date, whether at Ferrara or Bologna; the MS would thus have been written in close connection with, or perhaps by, Robertus de Anglia while in his post at Ferrara or at San Petronio. We know, further, that in the year 1467 pieces by Dufay were brought from the north to Savoy, and they may have circulated further into Italy, including Bologna. According to Fallows, a date of 1467 for the pieces by Dufay in Porto would accord well with their style, and their possible late arrival would help to explain why the last part of the MS, in which they appear, lacks decorated capital letters.[7]

Of these arguments the first three are the strongest. The presence of Robertus de Anglia at Ferrara and Bologna gives us a firm basis for associating this MS with him, the more so in view of the prominence of his two compositions as the first and last in the collection. The testimony of Nappi and Ramos helps to clarify the importance of this English musician in Bolognese circles, hardly surprising in view of the central position of San Petronio in the city's life and culture. The further connection of the two treatises in Porto 714 to the *Declaratio* by Ugolino di Orvieto, not only sets the first part of the MS in the tradition of Ferrarese music teaching, as practiced by its most renowned musical savant, but could be thought to reflect the position of Robertus de Anglia as successor to Ugolino in the post

[6] The evidence regarding Nappi and Ramos was first brought forward by Fallows, 'Robertus de Anglia'. Nappi, a Bolognese poet of the late 15th century, published his poem, 'Iti caldi suspir', with a heading, 'super qua est cantus magistri Roberti Anglia'. See Frati, *Rimatori bolognesi del Quattrocento*, p. 255. On Robertus de Anglia at San Petronio, see Gaspari, 'Ricerche, documenti e memorie', reprinted in Gaspari, *Musica e musicisti a Bologna*, pp. 119–21. Ramos states that Robertus believed, ignorantly as Ramos claims, that when there is no mensuration sign for a voice part in polyphony, the music should be assumed to be in *tempus perfectum*. Fallows observes that this practice is followed in Porto in all twelve of the nineteen songs that are in perfect time, none of which has a mensuration sign. On the other hand, all the pieces in imperfect time have their mensuration signs, except the Contratenor of Dufay's 'Adieu m'amours'. Here its omission is an oversight, according to Fallows, since it was written very small in the margin where the illuminated letter, had it been completed, would have covered it.

[7] The initials for the songs are present except for the last gathering of the MS, ('9'), for which they are lacking. This suggests that this gathering failed to reach the illuminator in time to be completed, perhaps against a delivery deadline for the entire MS; similar evidence of haste in completion is found in other, later Ferrarese music MSS of the 15th century, as well as in MSS of other centers. Fallows shows that the song collection in the MS begins in the middle of the sixth fascicle (all quinterns up to this fascicle) but that the fascicles nos. 7 to 9, containing the bulk of the songs, are quaternions. As Fallows claims, this suggests that the treatises may have been prepared first and that then it was decided to add the song collection to them.

of *maestro di canto* at the cathedral, beginning only three years after Ugolino's death in 1457. As Fallows shows, the first treatise in the MS is a simple introduction to the solmization and modal system that presents in reduced form, but often verbatim, material from Ugolino's Book I; the second treatise is a version of the widely copied *Libellus de Cantus Mensurabilis* by Johannes de Muris that includes the introduction and glosses provided by Ugolino himself in the version of the *Libellus* that he included in Book III of his own large treatise.[8]

To all this we can now add new documentary material that sheds further light on both segments of the MS, on the biography of Robertus de Anglia, and on the extent of Estense musical patronage in Borso's time.

Robertus de Anglia and Rinaldo Maria d'Este. Recently Adriano Franceschini, to whom I am grateful for various items of documentation from Ferrarese notarial acts, was kind enough to send me a new discovery of his, namely evidence that in the summer of 1454 the musician Robertus de Anglia was in the service of Tinaldo Maria d'Este, *commendator* of the Abbey of Santa Maria di Pomposa.[9] This results from a notarial act of that year, dated 19 August 1454, recording the renewal of the Abbey's possession of certain lands, and having as one of its witnesses 'dominus Robertus Cantor . . . de Anglia', whose full name is now given for the first time: 'Venerabili vir domino Roberto cantore filio honorabilis viri Petri Suchar de Anglia, ad presens habitatore cum prefato Reverendissimo domino Commendatario.' From this we learn not only that Robertus was living in Ferrara in 1454, six years earlier than heretofore known, but we also learn his full name: 'Robertus, son of Peter Suchar' (very likely the notary is writing phonetically and the name may have been something more like 'Sugar' or 'Suger' or 'Sochar').[10] Equally revealing is that Robertus was then residing with Rinaldo Maria d'Este, holder *in commendam* (i.e. without duties) of the famous

---

[8] See Fallows, 'Robertus de Anglia', p. 125. Other Italian MSS of the period containing this much-copied treatise by Muris include British Library, Egerton MS 2954 and Berlin, Staatsbibliothek Preussischer Kulturbesitz, Mus. theor. ms. 1599. The latter contains an unidentified coat of arms, with the motto or inscription, 'APOMONI' (in Greek letters), and is probably a presentation MS for an unknown Italian recipient who possessed these arms. Significantly, the same motto is found on the most beautifully illuminated contemporary copy of the Ugolino *Declaratio*: Rome, Bibl. Vat., MS Rossiana 455; see A. Seay, ed., *Ugolino Urbevetanus, Declaratio Musicae Disciplinae*, i, Plate I. However, the texts of Muris presented in Porto 714 and in Berlin 1599 are not the same in all details, and differ sufficiently in wording and syntax to convince me that these redactions represent two different copyists' traditions for this treatise.

[9] On Pomposa see Salmi, *L'abbazia di Pomposa*, and *Atti del primo convegno internazionale di studi storici pomposiani*. The Estensi had signed an agreement in 1407 establishing their future jurisdiction over the *commenda* of Pomposa. An important document of Rinaldo Maria's years as titular head of Pomposa is the inventory of its books and possessions made in 1459 at his request and as part of an effort to reorganize and restore the monastery, which had fallen into disrepair. See Inguanez, 'Inventario di Pomposa del 1459'.

[10] From the document of 1460 (showing Robertus de Anglia in service at Ferrara Cathedral), it was already known that his father's name was Peter; see above, Chapter 8, n. 28. Perhaps

Abbey of Pomposa, located fifty kilometers east of the city of Ferrara and close to the Adriatic coast, where it still stands as one of the medieval glories of the region.

Rinaldo Maria d'Este was a younger bastard son of Niccolò III, born to Anna de' Roberti around 1430. The date is uncertain but it is known that this lady of good family was also the mother of Beatrice d'Este, who was born in 1427.[11] Rinaldo Maria lived a long and apparently comfortable life at court and in the territory, remaining an effective and useful vassal to Borso and Ercole until his death in the spring of 1503.[12] He seems to have been a lively and trusted member of the ducal entourage, employed for diplomatic purposes, good at jousts, faithful in time of political trouble, a helpful dependent. Early in his life, in 1451, he was given the substantial benefice, as *commendator*, of the Abbey of Pomposa. He maintained the income as his own until 1469, when he renounced it in favour of a ducal pension, and transferred the revenues from Pomposa to his own three bastard sons; by this convenient arrangement he probably added substantially to his own total income. In 1472, early in Ercole's reign, Rinaldo Maria married Lucrezia de Monferrato. He maintained an administrative hold on Codigoro and nearby Pomposa, and participated prominently in civic events.

In 1454 Rinaldo Maria d'Este could not have been more than about twenty years old, and the document cited above is the earliest now known about him as well as the first to indicate his musical interests. Since he enjoyed the income of one of the most venerable Benedictine monasteries of northern Italy, it seems altogether plausible that this young and entirely non-clerical member of the Estense clan should have been able to afford the presence in his house of an English friar, perhaps as his chaplain and also as music teacher.[13]

Robertus, while with Rinaldo Maria, acted as his curate; this role was apparently often taken by foreign students for wealthier local citizens, as a way of helping to finance their university studies. See the remarks of Mitchell on this practice, in *John Free*, p. 49.

[11] Rinaldo Maria's birthdate is as yet not determined. Valenti, in the Tavola II of the genealogical tables appended to his *Archivio di stato di Modena, Archivio segreto estense, sezione 'Casa e Stato', inventario*, gives '1435(?)'. Gardner, *Dukes and Poets*, Appendix, Table 'House of Este II', gives no date at all, but places Rinaldo Maria between Beatrice (born in 1427) and Margherita (no birthday given, but she died in 1452).

[12] Material on Rinaldo Maria is drawn from the major chronicles as well as from Gardner, *Dukes and Poets*; Catalano, *Vita di Lodovico Ariosto*; and Chiappini, *Eleonora d'Aragona*.

[13] In 1454 we also find in the service of Rinaldo Maria a 'Gaspare sonatore organorum filio Nicolai tubicine cive et habitatore Ferrarie in contrata Sancti Nicolai', mentioned in a notarial act of 7 December 1454 (communicated to me by Maestro Franceschini). This is clearly the same 'Gaspare sonatore de organi', son of Niccolò Trombeta, who was paid at the court as early as 1446, and was present thereafter in various years prior to his death in 1469; see Venturi, 'L'arte a Ferrara nel periodo di Borso d'Este', 747 f. That musicians 'belonging' to the court were also on various occasions and for certain periods hired or taken into the private service of members of the Este family, is to be assumed as having been a normal and fairly typical situation, whether or not officially sanctioned by the Duke. This probably became more frequent in Ercole's later years and became more formalized when his children acquired musicians of their own.

The first part of Porto 714 may have originally borne on its first page some heraldic or verbal indication of its intended recipient, as do other Italian MSS containing the same treatise by Muris or the various MSS of Ugolino's treatise; but since its first leaf is missing, we cannot really be certain of this.[14] What we can say, however, is that the prominence of Robertus de Anglia in the MS, and its combination of English, Burgundian, and Ferrarese contents makes it entirely plausible that the manuscript was made either by Robertus de Anglia himself or by a scribe who was copying from music in the possession of Robertus. Fallows' observation that Porto 714, in its notation, follows features ascribed by Ramos to Robertus himself, makes this still more plausible.[15]

The report of Robertus being in the service of Rinaldo Maria d'Este also makes sense in terms of the musical contents. The pieces by Dufay would presumably have been in circulation in Ferrara and may reflect Dufay's continuing connection with the court after his return to Cambrai in 1439; they may have been sent in 1443, when he was paid in Bruges, or over the years between that payment and the apparent copying of the MS.[16] The piece by Joye could have travelled by the same route, and represents the work of a Burgundian court musician, despite its Italian text. Alongside it we may place several of the unattributed French pieces in the collection, including No. 6, 'Mon seul plaisir', a very popular piece; No. 8, 'Helas', and No. 13 'Las ie ne plus', attributed in Trent 87 to Johannes Legrant. The Burgundian career of Gilles Joye covered the period 1462 to 1468, and later led him to important church positions, including a canonry at Saint Donatian de Bruges, where he remained until his death in 1484. He had a high reputation as a poet and theologian, more than as a musician. We have by Joye only five attributed works in all, of which one is textless, three are known only with French texts, and this single Italian piece.[17] However, one of the French pieces also shows a

[14] On several other Italian MSS of theoretical treatises containing arms of apparent recipients see above, n. 8. The list of course could be extended.

[15] If the treatises in Porto were copied as early as 1453 or 1454, and were given their illuminated capitals by Giraldi, he or a member of his workshop might have been responsible for further illuminated initials in the MS, made when the first polyphonic compositions were entered; it is at least plausible guesswork that this may have taken place at any time during the period between *c*.1454 to *c*.1460.

[16] Fallows, 'Robertus de Anglia', p. 103 ff., has advanced the view that the five Dufay songs at the end of the collection form a late group of Dufay compositions, only one of which is known from any other source. As we know that Dufay's music continued to be sent to Italy after his resettlement in Cambrai, and since we also know that in 1467 music by Dufay was brought to the court of Savoy by an emissary, Fallows supposes that these five chansons could have been among them and could have circulated further south to Bologna (where they could have been added to the MS by Robertus de Anglia). The dating for the MS put forward here, which conforms better to the Ferrarese, rather than to the Bolognese dialect elements in it, suggests a basis for its having been compiled in Ferrara between 1454 and 1460, and inevitably nullifies these arguments of Fallows. Perhaps still tenable is his view, expressed in 'Two More Dufay Songs Reconstructed', 358–60, that one of the Dufay chansons in Porto, 'En triumphant', is a lament for Binchois, who died in September 1460.

[17] On Gilles Joye see Marix, *Histoire de la musique*, especially p. 213 and 255–61.

link to Ferrara: his 'Non pas', well known in Northern circles, is found in the Casanatense chansonnier, and may have been in Ferrara for many years before that MS was copied, probably in 1480. The Italian piece in Porto suggests that Joye was at some point in Italy, or else that a text was transmitted to him through an intermediary; if the latter, a prime candidate would be Francesco d'Este, the bastard son of Leonello who spent virtually his entire life at the Burgundian court (1444–c.1480) and of whom we have the famous painting by Roger van der Weyden.[18]

The brings us to the English group of compositions, the most striking in the MS, which preserves one of the most interesting sets of secular compositions on Italian texts by English composers in any source of the period.[19] In view of the theory that Robertus de Anglia could himself have been the scribe, and is in any case to be seen as the compiler, his own compositions are easily accounted for. We might also assume a compatriot's interest in the works of Bedyngham, who is in any case well represented in Italian sources, and in the otherwise unknown Galfridus de Anglia.[20] As for Bedyngham, we might perhaps identify him with the 'Johannes de Anglia', also called 'Johannes de arpa de Anglia', who was at the court in 1449 and 1450; or with the 'Johannes quondam alterius Johannis presbiter Londini' who was at the cathedral in 1448.[21] But in the absence of positive identification of either of these with Bedyngham, we should be extremely cautious, especially in view of evidence, found by Fallows, that shows Bedyngham as a member of the London Guild of Parish Clerks in February 1449.[22] It appears that such membership did not necessarily entail constant residence, but we do not now have a strong case to make for Bedyngham's presence in Ferrara at this time.

Much more attractive hypotheses emerge from the prominent group of English students at the university, whom we have already encountered in Leonello's time and who continued in residence into that of Borso. Those who were scions of the wealthier classes were quite likely to have an active interest in music and poetry; and the traditional associations of polyphony with university life, certainly in France, are no doubt only the official side of a long and flourishing basis for music-making in university circles.[23] In the

[18] On Francesco d'Este and the portrait see Kantorowicz, 'The Este Portrait', 165–80; cf. above, Chapter 5, n. 3.

[19] This small group of compositions by English composers is more homogeneous than many comparable groups of English works in Italian MSS of this period. In immediately striking contrast is the very large mass of English compositions in Mod B, which form a discrete section of the MS but which have no discernible local (Ferrarese) associations.

[20] Of the various continental MSS of this period containing works by Bedyngham, Porto is one of the few in which his name is spelled correctly, reinforcing the theory that an Englishman had a hand in its compilation.

[21] See above, Chapter 8, n. 26.

[22] Communicated to me by Dr Fallows.

[23] For a preliminary survey of music at the universities see Carpenter, *Music in the Medieval and Renaissance Universities*; also Pietzsch, 'Zur Pflege der Musik an den deutschen Universitäten bis zur Mitte des 16. Jahrhunderts'. Although, as Kristeller showed in his 'Music and Learning in the Early Italian Renaissance', music teaching in the formal sense was cultivated

late 1440s we have seen the presence in Ferrara of the young Reynold Chichele, for whom letters of recommendation had been written by both the King and Queen of England. In the early 1450s, and down to the death of Guarino Veronese in 1460, the small but distinguished group of English students at the Studio continued to flourish. They included Robert Flemmyng (evidently in Ferrara from 1447 to 1451); Thomas Paslewe, who had taken a Bachelor's degree in Canon Law at Oxford before acquiring his doctorate at Ferrara in May 1452; and John Free, who had also been at Oxford for many years before his transfer to Ferrara to attend the school of Guarino in the years 1456–8. Later phases of the same distinguished tradition were represented by John Tiptoft, Earl of Worcester (at Ferrara in 1459 or '60) and John Gunthorp, who was in Ferrara when Tiptoft was there, that is, for some years prior to 1460.[24]

Pirrotta suggested that Galfridus de Anglia might be another English student at Ferrara. Indeed he may have been, although no records now known show it. The name itself is unusual; I entirely agree with Pirrotta's suggestion that it is unrelated to 'Walter' (Gualterus) and therefore has nothing to do with Walter Frye, of whom we have no record in Ferrarese documents or sources.[25] Rather, we find that the name is loosely related to the more common 'Geoffrey'. In fact the surviving records of Cambridge University in this period record only one student by this name: a certain 'Galfridus' who in April 1463 'incepted' a course of studies in the liberal arts (that is, he was admitted officially as a candidate for the degree of Master of Arts, having completed the Bachelor's degree).[26] It is at least conceivable that this 'Galfridus', who was an advanced student at Cambridge in 1463, might earlier have studied abroad, and perhaps accompanied one of the more wealthy and therefore better-known English students who attended the Ferrarese Studio in the early 1450s. Students often travelled in pairs, frequently as master and servant.[27] The possibility, at least, is attractive, and it would help to explain why a little-known Englishman, capable of writing two-part polyphony to recent poetry by a local versifier (cf. p. 109 above), should have had his two works included in a local collection. That the collection was compiled for Rinaldo Maria d'Este, by the way, would mean that the two pieces from Nigrisoli's poem for Isotta would have the character of personal album compositions concerning an older half-sister: Isotta, also a

rarely if at all in the Italian universities, we can hardly doubt that music-making was widely cultivated by members of university circles, including students, of course.

[24] On these students, see Mitchell, 'English Students at Ferrara', and her other studies on English students at continental universities, including the book, *John Free*.
[25] Suggested by Bukofzer in *The New Oxford History of Music*, iii, pp. 132–3; see also Pirrotta, 'Two Anglo-Italian Pieces', 257, n. 21.
[26] *Cambridge University, Grace Book A*, ed. Leathes, p. 35, and index, p. 248, cross-referring to 'Geoffrey'. See also *Alumni Cantabrigienses* compiled by J. Venn and J. A. Venn, pt. I, vol. ii, p. 189.
[27] Mitchell, *John Free*, p. 49.

natural child of Niccolò's, was born in 1425 and was thus only about five years older than Rinaldo Maria.

Two questions remain: the notation of the manuscript and its principal concordances. Although it is broadly true that black and red notation of its type disappears after the middle of the fifteenth century in continental sources, and is displaced by white notation, this development is manifestly not one to which an absolute chronological barrier can be raised. There are exceptions on both sides of the year 1450, and as more is learned about the notational habits and prejudices of individual scribes and particular manuscripts the borderline becomes more indistinct. To some degree, it depends on whether paper or parchment is in use for a given manuscript. Oxford 213, written in northern Italy in the 1420s and early 1430s, is mainly in white notation with only a few entries in black.[28] As Fallows points out, English manuscripts regularly continued to use black notation throughout the later fifteenth century and into the sixteenth century.[29] In view of the apparent connection between the peculiar use of mensuration signs advocated by Robertus de Anglia and found in Porto 714, Fallows seems to be right in suggesting that English MSS, e.g. the Fayrfax MS, form a better basis for comparison with the notation of Porto than do continental ones.

The main concordant MSS for Porto 714 are Escorial IV. a. 24 and Berlin 78. C. 28, both Italian chansonniers of the 1460s, and evidently both from Naples, though for Berlin 78. C. 28 the possibility of Florentine provenance cannot be completely ruled out.[30] Most of the other MSS sharing works with Porto 714 date from the 1470s or later, and are thus of no great help in determining its date or discovering the direction of flow of its material. Only one MS definitely earlier than 1450 shares a composition with Porto 714 – the Vatican MS 1411 of about 1440, containing the widely-traveled 'O rosa bella'. From such evidence, Fallows argued for a dating in the 1460s for Porto 714, not earlier. I am now inclined to agree that the entire collection can hardly be taken to represent a current repertoire of the 1440s, yet, just possibly, it may include many pieces that were circulating in the 1450s, at least in those Italian centers that were receptive to the music of Dufay – Ferrara, Florence, and the Papal Chapel chief among them. On the other hand, the English material in Porto seems to have no broad general framework of circulation, but to be peculiarly Ferrarese, written, so far as we can now tell, between the early 1450s and 1467, when Robertus left for Bologna. In view of the dates now attached to the earlier MSS of the Italian chansonnier tradition – those of Naples and the earlier Florentine group – it would appear that Porto 714 should be seen as one of the very earliest,

[28] Schoop, *Entstehung und Verwendung*, esp. pp. 44–5.
[29] Fallows, 'Robertus de Anglia'.
[30] Reidemeister, *Die Handschrift 78 C 28 des Berliner Kupferstichkabinetts*, argues for Florentine provenance; in favor of the Neapolitan thesis is Atlas, 'La provenienza del manoscritto Berlin 78 C. 28: Firenze o Napoli?'.

perhaps the earliest, MS of this phase of chanson importation into Italian centers – not as a late representative of the earlier period of chanson collecting in Italy that is represented by such MSS as Oxford 213, Escorial V. iii. 24, and Trent 87. It seems increasingly clear, then, that we can draw the following conclusions about Porto 714: (1) that it may well be of Ferrarese provenance; (2) that the likeliest dates of its compilation are between around 1454 and about 1460; (3) that it is, in its musical contents, the product of the conjunction of an English musician and a Ferrarese patron (Robertus de Anglia and Rinaldo Maria d'Este) – exactly the combination that its physical features, repertoire, and notation would seem to suggest.[31]

---

[31] In an earlier draft of this chapter, I had accepted as genuine a document published by Hermann, 'Zur Geschichte der Miniaturmalerei', 258, No. 161, which shows payment to Guglielmo de' Magri for illuminating 'uno libro . . . de ragione de canto et un altro, nominado Tibullo' for Rinaldo Maria d'Este, on 19 October 1453. This suggested that Rinaldo had a book of music theory prepared for him in that year. But as I learn from Dr Jessie Ann Owens, who checked the original for me in ASM, the registral volume quoted by Herrmann (*Debitori e Creditori*, P, 1453) is not available; and a corresponding entry in ASM, LCD 14 (1454), fol. 138, shows Magri paid for 'dui libri nominati uno drago de cento e l'altro Tibullo . . .'. The meaning of 'drago de cento', if it has any meaning, is unclear; but the view that it stood for 'ragione de canto' is now wholly uncertain. The importance of rechecking Herrmann's readings of documents can hardly be overstated.

PART TWO

MUSIC AT FERRARA UNDER
ERCOLE I D'ESTE (1471–1505)

❧

12

Ercole as Private and Public Figure

OF all the Estensi of the fifteenth century, only Ercole I has been known to music historians. Yet this knowledge has consisted of little more than awareness that his official title was used by Josquin Desprez for the Mass 'Hercules Dux Ferrarie', and that the pitches of its *soggetto cavato*, as Zarlino called it, were drawn from the successive syllables of his name. So far, general history has done little to sharpen the focus; the few existing biographical accounts of Ercole have been based essentially on contemporary chronicles, on early histories of the dynasty, and on limited archival research. His letters have not yet been collected or published.[1] Gundersheimer's recent account brought new insights into Ercole's patronage, especially of the visual arts, and his discussion paved the way for a more developed profile, but this has yet to be written. Accordingly, it is not at all surprising that Ercole's patronage of music, though it was probably even more important to him than his support of painters or poets, has remained entirely undocumented until now.

Unlike Leonello and Borso, Ercole was a legitimate son of Niccolò III, by his last wife, Rizzarda da Saluzzo. Born in 1431, he had been first raised in Ferrara, but in 1445 he was sent to live at the court of Naples, probably to remove him from the scene during Leonello's rule. Little enough is known of his early years under King Alfonso d'Aragona, but service at this royal enclave probably left lasting impressions and high ambitions. At Naples he was one of very few ranking Italian residents and was evidently well regarded at the court; in 1454 he was among those who witnessed the King's will.[2] And amid the colorful and multilingual life of the city, ruled by Spaniards but with resident groups from various Italian regions, Ercole must have experienced a mixture of cultural influences much richer than his native town could ever have provided.

---

[1] On Ercole and his times see, most recently, Gundersheimer, *Ferrara*, esp. pp. 173–228; also Gundersheimer's *Art and Life*; and his 'The Patronage of Ercole I d'Este'. Valuable too are the general accounts in Chiappini, *Gli Estensi*, Chapter 7; and Gardner, *Dukes and Poets*, Chapters 5–12.

[2] Ryder, *The Kingdom of Naples under Alfonso the Magnanimous*, p. 66.

Naples as a musical center in the Ars Nova had lagged far behind Florence and the north Italian cities, but several Italian musicians prominent in the earlier decades of the fifteenth century had originated there. Under the earlier Angevins, music had been much in evidence at the court.[3] But with the triumph of Alfonso and the Aragonese dynasty in 1442, southern Italy came under this proud and ostentatious Spanish regime. The kingdom, served by a massive bureaucracy as well as by a royal household, included a substantial *capella* staffed with singers. We saw earlier (Chapter 5, pp. 44 f.) that the household chapel of Alfonso had been regarded by Leonello (according to his chronicler) as a direct model for his own court chapel. And this fits well with Leonello's own political ambitions and familial ties with the Aragonese line and their kingdom – the 'reame', as it was called throughout the century – which he may have seen as a useful balance to his dependency on the French crown.

By 1444 Alfonso's chapel had fifteen musicians. By the 1450s it had grown to more than twenty singers and two organists. Most of them were Spaniards but there were also a few Italians.[4] Although the chapel undoubtedly had the function of training 'donzelli' (young nobles) for court life, it also provided the King and his nobles with daily and festive Mass and Vespers. Some of Alfonso's special observances may also have formed a model for Ercole in later years; most striking is the parallel observance during Holy Week, when Alfonso's rituals included his washing the feet of the poor on Maundy Thursday. At Ferrara thirty years later, this same act of public piety and charity became a fixed and distinctive annual event carried out by Ercole and by members of his family.[5]

Although the earliest preserved Neapolitan music manuscripts date from the mid-1460s, some of their material probably reflects court repertoires that go well back into the reign of Alfonso, as is becoming clear from the recent valuable research by Allan Atlas. As early as 1444, the principal singer and teacher of the boys was Giacomo Borbo, author of a surviving treatise. In the 1440s the chapel's ranks also included Pietro Oriola, of whom four pieces are preserved in the later manuscripts Montecassino 871 and Perugia 431, both Neapolitan but from later in the century.[6] That secular polyphony under Alfonso and, later, Ferrante d'Aragona, emphasized solo-singing to the lute and other instruments is amply documented, principally by the humanist Raffaello Brandolino Lippi, who coupled Alfonso and Borso d'Este as import-

---

[3] See Pirrotta, 'Scuole polifoniche italiane durante il secolo XIV; di una pretesa scuola napoletana'. For a survey see Anglès, 'La musica en la corte real de Aragon y de Napoles durante il reinado de Alfonso V el Magnanimo'.

[4] See Anglès, 'Las musica en la corte real', esp. 1019–22, based on lists published by Minieri Riccio, 'Alcuni fatti di Alfonso I di Aragona', 245, 411, 439.

[5] Ryder, *The Kingdom of Naples*, p. 86. On Ercole's custom, the primary early source is Sabadino; see Gundersheimer, *Art and Life*, pp. 90–2.

[6] For this information I am indebted to Allan Atlas.

ant patrons of music.[7] Neapolitan contacts with musicians and patrons elsewhere followed political avenues to Spain and to the north. The Ferrarese
link in the 1440s was mentioned earlier, and as partial evidence we cited
Leonello's gift to Alfonso of a wooden organ made in 1449 by the Modenese
organ-builder Constantino Tantino; we also know that in 1451 Tantino himself joined Neapolitan service. Contacts with Burgundy, well documented
in other fields, may have stimulated the relationship to Dufay and other
Burgundian court musicians that is evident in the Franco-Burgundian
chansons that dominate the earlier layer of Neapolitan manuscripts, before
the arrival of Tinctoris in the early 1470s. As early as 1454, Dufay in Geneva
had mentioned casually, in a letter to Piero and Giovanni de' Medici, that the
texts of his lamentations for the fall of Constantinople had been sent to him
from Naples. In addition to these Italian and transalpine connections, the
great port of Naples opened the way to Italy for Spanish singers, dancers, and
instrumentalists with their vocal repertoires and dances (including the
moresca), thus providing other Italian courts and their musicians with a new
set of transplanted and locally established performers and repertoires, and
bringing to Italian players new varieties of instruments, above all the guitar,
which, from then on, came to be seen as a Neapolitan specialty.

Alfonso's death in 1458 reopened the struggle between Aragonese and
French forces for control of the kingdom, and the traditionally pro-French
policies of Borso endangered Ercole's position at Naples. Afterwards when
Ercole went over to the French side, his position at court became untenable;
and by 1463, when Ferrante d'Aragona put down the French threat and took
power at Naples, it was time for Ercole to leave.[8] Borso then installed him as
Governor of Modena, a role he carried out faithfully until 1471. In turn,
Modena was a convenient base from which to strengthen his own eventual
bid for power at Ferrara; for seven years Ercole dutifully followed Borso's
orders, served as a military captain, and shored up political allies for the
future. His only serious rival was Leonello's surviving son Niccolò, who was
maintained at court by Borso but who lacked all the obvious qualities of
leadership.

When Borso died in August 1471, he had been Duke of Ferrara – the first
of the line to hold this title – for only three months. Thus Ercole, at forty,
entered into power as the first of the Estensi to succeed as Duke, the highest
title to which a member of the dynasty could aspire. Forty was then late
middle or early old age, and Ercole was viewed from the beginning of his rule
as an elderly man. Although he proceeded to father a substantial family and
to remain in office for the long span of thirty-four years, his career was not
regarded by contemporaries as one that realized in later life the ambitions of
youth, but was rather seen as a period of rule by an older man who could

---

[7] On Lippi's treatise see de la Fage, *Essais de dipthérographie musicale*; Kristeller, *Iter
Italicum*, ii, p. 99; and Perkins, ed., *The Mellon Chansonnier*, i, p. 34.
[8] On Ercole at Naples see Gardner, pp. 97–8, which cites earlier writings.

never fully adjust to the changing personal styles and customs of a younger generation, and who was unpredictably prone to periods of listless inattention to the daily demands of his office. In foreign affairs he won a reputation for being uncommonly astute and cautious, but in matters of civic life his rule was regarded by the populace as one of decline after that of the flamboyant Borso. His late-medieval and intensely religious mentality contrasted sharply with that of his ambitious and secularly-minded children.

Ercole's marriage to Eleonora d'Aragona in 1473 was a first step in renewing the Neapolitan alliance and ensuring the continuity of Estense rule. Eleonora's arrival at Ferrara re-established the Spanish element on the female side of the Ferrarese court that had been begun by Maria d'Aragona in the mid-1440s and which had lapsed after her death during Borso's twenty years as a bachelor ruler.[9] Eleonora was clearly not the beautiful princess depicted by later apologists, but she had much more solid virtues. She provided Ercole with excellent management of household affairs, reinforced his religious faith with her own piety and good works, and ably assumed the court's administration when he was away on one of his many journeys or on military campaigns.

Between 1474 and 1480 she gave birth to six children: first the two girls, Isabella (1474) and Beatrice (1475); then the hoped-for male heir, Alfonso (1476); then three more sons – Ferrante (1477), Ippolito (1479), and Sigismondo (1480). The larger clan also included two acknowledged bastards: Lucrezia (1473), later the wife of Annibale Bentivoglio; and Julio d'Este (1478), later the mainspring in the famous conspiracy of 1506, just after Ercole's death. Ercole's broad political ambitions were evident in the marriage plans he developed for the children. Isabella's early betrothal to Francesco Gonzaga (in 1480 when she was six, and he fourteen) assured stable relations with Mantua, the immediate neighbor to the north-west; and two Sforza-Este marriages were expected to do the same for Ferrara and Milan. This plan proved less enduring, for both Beatrice and Anna Maria Sforza died prematurely; and Lodovico il Moro then fell victim to his own misjudgements over the French invasions. Destined for the church was the third son, Ippolito, and through arrangements carefully contrived in the 1480s, with the help of the papal Vice-Chancellor, Ascanio Sforza, in 1486 Ippolito (aged eight) became Archbishop of Esztergom in Hungary. In 1495, when he had returned to Italy, he was made Cardinal at the age of sixteen, beginning one of the most profitable and powerful ecclesiastical careers of this admittedly flamboyant era. The other sons were less favorably treated. Ferrante was at first brought up in Naples (following a familiar pattern), and was later sent by Ercole to the court of France (1493–7), where he served as a minor courtier and secondary diplomatic agent for Ercole in dealings with the French monarchy during the period of invasions. Ferrante's letters reveal

[9] On Eleonora see, most recently, Gundersheimer, 'Women, Learning and Power: Eleonora of Aragon and the Court of Ferrara'.

the contrasts in Ercole's treatment of his children. He kept Ferrante perpetually short of money and ignored his complaints, yet saw to it that Ferrante fulfilled his role as a source of news about the royal court and as a helpful channel for court products, especially music. Important for music too in later years was the youngest son, Sigismondo, who eked out a limited existence until 1524. Intended at first for a career as a *condottiere*, he contracted venereal disease in his twenties, and was forced to spend the rest of his life as a semi-invalid in quiet residence in Ferrara.[10]

Ercole provided well for the education of his children and took an active interest in their response to it. Alfonso's first teacher was Lodovico Gualengo, replaced in 1490 by Jacomo Gallino, who also taught the other children.[11] Continuity with earlier phases of Ferrarese court education was provided by Battista Guarino, son of the famous Guarino Veronese, and the procedures were those of contemporary humanistic teaching, including Latin classics and a general literary education. That music played a fairly conspicuous role in education and in the daily domestic scene need not be vaguely inferred since it can be precisely demonstrated, for example in a letter written by the tutor Gallino in 1495 to Ferrante d'Este, his former pupil, then in France, about the current progress being made by his brothers Julio and Sigismondo:

> . . . Don Sigismondo has become very tall, so that if Your Lordship were to see him you wouldn't recognize him; and he is attending to his studies along with his brother don Julio. His studies are in letters and in music; and His Lordship your father takes great pleasure in hearing them and in singing along with them . . .[12]

Whatever the children of Ercole were learning in the school of practical politics that was provided by the court and by events abroad, Ercole maintained a paternal ideal of personal development that reflected contemporary aristocratic fashions. In 1494 he wrote to Ippolito, when the young archbishop had just returned from Hungary, telling Ippolito to study and 'make yourself learned, as your dignity requires', and not to spend so much time at the hunt. In later letters, he added:

> The more that we hear that you are devoting yourself to the study of letters, and also that you are conducting yourself in a way that will bring you praise and honor . . . the more pleased and contented we will be . . . [5 November 1494]

> . . . You will be covered with glory if every day you will attend to your studies and learn something of value, and some worthy lesson, and also if you practice and

---

[10] The literature on Alfonso and Ippolito is substantial; see Chiappini, *Gli Estensi*, for a preliminary survey and bibliography up to 1967; on Ferrante and don Julio there is very little apart from Bacchelli's brilliant interpretive essay, based on limited documentation, *La congiura di Don Giulio d'Este*; on Sigismondo, the least-known but among the most important of the brothers as music patron, see my study, 'Jean Mouton and Jean Michel'.

[11] On the teachers see Bertoni, 'I maestri degli Estensi al tempo del Duca Ercole I', 494–7.

[12] Ibid., 496 f.

become accomplished in speaking and writing elegantly in Latin . . . [12 August 1495][13]

Ercole's reign, from 1471 to 1505, was a long one by the standards of the time. As Gundersheimer puts it, '. . . the most Herculean thing about Ercole was his endurance.' Contemporary witnesses complained that he was lacking in firmness, foresight, and rigorous attention to affairs of state, preferring to travel and idle away his time in gaming and music. Yet in the long run, within the limits imposed by the small size of his state and his narrow financial and military resources, he succeeded in increasing the prestige of the family and the importance of his regime. As his children grew to maturity and developed their own interests and entanglements, he had to reckon with the development of the clan into a network of rivalries. But he held the reins firmly enough to wield considerable influence in both domestic and foreign affairs. To review the principal developments, very briefly, it will be simplest to divide his reign into three broad periods. The first extends from 1471 to the end of the war with Venice in 1484; the second period, from 1484 to 1494, closes with the death of Eleonora in 1493 and the French invasions of 1494. The third period spans the years from 1494 to Ercole's death in 1505.

In his first period Ercole took steps to consolidate his legitimacy and power, most dramatically in his suppression of the political threat posed by Niccolò di Leonello in 1476, but also in more positive and lasting ways. At first, he intended to celebrate his accession annually, with elaborate public processions on 20 August, but after a first anniversary celebration in 1472, the plan was apparently put aside, probably displaced in 1473 by ceremonies for his marriage to Eleonora d'Aragona.[14] He attended to problems of domestic architecture by rebuilding the ducal palace, its courtyard, and its gardens, providing it with a new *cortile* in 1473. He paved the *sala grande* of the palace so that it could be used for entertainments involving large numbers of people; and he built the new ducal chapel, called Santa Maria di Corte, which opened on to the new courtyard.[15] The chapel was not only needed for his private devotional use and that of the ducal *famiglia*, but was to be the symbolic and functional scene of his role as public religious leader in the civic sense; it also was to serve as the place of Ercole's earlier productions of religious drama.

Unless interrupted by floods or plague, traditional annual events for public diversion were continued: these were principally the *palio* on the festival of the city's patron saint, St. George (24 April); the first of May celebrations; and of course the major religious observances. Newly established by Ercole, and bearing a personal stamp, were his 'seeking of his fortune' at Epiphany

---

[13] The source for these letters is ASM, CTPE, B. 69/9; the letter of 5 November 1494 is No. 1652–XIV/11; that of 12 August 1495 is published in Gardner, pp. 450 and 552–4.

[14] On the ceremonies of 1472 see my 'Music at Ferrara', 109.

[15] On the reconstruction of the palace and the building of the new chapel see, most recently, Rosenberg, 'The Erculean Addition to Ferrara', 51 and n. 6, which cites Caleffini.

(his *ventura*, as it was called), and the massive cycle of rituals and acts of piety during Holy Week. In the first decade of his rule there were also numerous occasions for other celebrations, chiefly the births of his legitimate children, but also the visits of ranking foreign dignitaries.

In 1482 the outbreak of war with Venice brought Ferrara to its gravest political crisis of the period. For more than two years almost all normal diplomatic and civic functions were disrupted, and all projects and festivities were suspended. Only after the Peace of Bagnolo, signed in September 1484, did the slow recovery of civic morale begin. Ercole sought to promote a sense of return to normality by re-establishing traditional customs and institutions. Within a month after Bagnolo he had reopened the university, and by early 1485 he was permitting the wearing of masks at carnival time, a habit occasionally forbidden. Other local *feste* were held on schedule that year, and Ercole even accepted an invitation to attend one in Venice, a clear gesture of reconciliation. Early in 1486 he opened a new phase in public entertainment at Ferrara and in the entire Italian Renaissance by co-ordinating efforts to produce in the ducal courtyard the first performances of classic drama in the vernacular. This historic production of Plautus's *Menaechmi* was a resounding success: it and other plays were put on in Ferrara in the next year, 1487, and again in 1490, '91, '93, and then in every year from 1499 to 1503, culminating in the production of five dramas during the great festivities for the Este-Borgia wedding in February 1502.[16]

Ercole made diplomatic gains during the 1480s and early 1490s as well. In 1486 the eight-year-old Ippolito left for Hungary with a large contingent. His appointment as archbishop set the seal on a Ferrarese-Hungarian connection that had already begun indirectly ten years earlier when Beatrice d'Aragona (Eleonora's sister) married King Matthias Corvina. And in 1491 the Sforza marriages of Alfonso and Beatrice d'Este temporarily shored up the Milanese alliance, at least as long as the Sforza regime lasted. Yet the rising number and heavy costs of these entertainments strained the civic treasury, and in Ercole's later years his reputation as a miser grew, from a chronicler's complaints over bad harvests and taxation to the grumbling of minor courtiers such as the young Ariosto. Anticipating his later problems, Ariosto complains that he did not stay long in Ercole's service (to which he belonged from 1497 to 1500) 'after I had experienced the ingratitude of the prince.'[17] Since, at the

[16] Amid the copious literature on early drama at Ferrara see, most recently, Gundersheimer 'Popular Spectacle and the Theatre in Renaissance Ferrara', and Doglio, 'Una tragedia alla corte di Ferrara: "De captivitate ducis Jacobi" ', both in Lorch, ed., *Il teatro italiano del Rinascimento*; also Zorzi, 'Il teatro e la città: ricognizione del ciclo di Schifanoia', Venturi, 'Scena e giardino a Ferrara', and Bruscagli, 'La corte di scena: genesi politica della tragedia ferrarese', all in *Il Rinascimento nelle corti padane*; and especially, for documentation, Coppo, 'Spettacoli alla corte di Ercole I'.

[17] For Ariosto's complaint see Catalano, *Vita di Lodovico Ariosto*, i, p. 151, who quotes the early poem *De Diversis Amoribus*. On this situation, see also my 'Musicisti a Ferrara all'epoca di Ariosto'.

same time, Ercole's household staff included one of the largest and most energetically supported companies of musicians anywhere in Italy, it seems clear he continued in these years to base his cultural priorities on narrowly personal tastes and predilections, on family prestige, and on open rivalry with other courts, not on concern with local popular approval or consensus.

In his last ten years, from 1495 to 1505, Ercole, now over sixty, pursued foreign policy with his customary typical caution and prudence. The French invasions and the turmoil of Italian political reactions to them inflicted no particular hardship on him, since his French allegiance was as strong as ever. He made sure to encourage its continuation through courtesies shown to the invading Charles VIII, including the loan of several of his best instrumentalists. When Charles was succeeded by Louis XII in 1498, Ercole renewed his pledges of loyalty in meetings at Milan with the King, and, in addition to maintaining his son Ferrante as resident there, established a permanent ambassador at the French court. To cover his flanks in Italy, and to avoid being trapped between the perennial threat from Venice and new danger from papal ambitions in Romagna, he accepted a familial tie to Alexander VI by taking on Lucrezia Borgia as his daughter-in-law and by shrewdly exacting improved political terms as part of the arrangement.

As a patron of the arts, Ercole is even more ambitious in the 1490s than before, and on a broader scale. Just as his efforts at urban reconstruction and enlargement created work for laborers and builders, his renovation of several of the family's country estates created opportunities for new major works of decoration and embellishment. Of these the most important was the fresco cycle based on the myth of Psyche, now lost, which may have been among the major works of the painter Ercole de' Roberti, to whom it has recently been attributed by Werner Gundersheimer.[18] In 1492 the Duke began work on the extension of the city, called the *Addizione Erculea*, and from this year dates the transformation of Ferrara at the hands of the famous architect Biagio Rossetti. Planning for this important enlargement of civic space had actually begun, it seems, in the 1480s, and Ercole took a personal interest in some aspects of the preparation. Yet curiously enough, such long-range concern over civic and commercial affairs did not impress many of his contemporaries, for again he was accused by the chroniclers of lapses in attention to civic problems, except where they coincided with his personal hobbies. As one of them remarked of him in 1498, he 'remained in Ferrara . . . and rode every day, now to one church and now to another, to hear Mass sung, and let anyone go to war who wished to do so . . . and every day the duke looked after the construction of new buildings in Terranova [the new section of Ferrara] and in the various monasteries of the city . . . .'. The chronicler mentions too that Ercole kept in the palazzo a group of young boys, members of noble families, and had them instructed in 'deportment,

---

[18] For a recent summary on Ercole as art patron see Gundersheimer, 'The Patronage of Ercole I d'Este'.

letters, and singing'; and 'with these boys he amuses himself and is distracted from cares and boredom.'[19]

In the last years he also became even more deeply and openly religious than he had been before. He maintained good relations with Savonarola until the crisis between Florence and the papacy made that impossible; even more telling was his effort to institute some of Savnarola's reforms at Ferrara. Not only gifted religious orators but models of religious fervor were brought to the city, including the mystic Suor Lucia da Narni, who bore the stigmata, and for whom he built a convent. His increasing religious devotion in these last years is closely bound up with his intensified patronage of musicians for the court chapel, for which, above all, Masses were collected and composed. According to Teofilo Folengo, Josquin Desprez composed the 'Miserere' for Ercole at the Duke's express request. From the time of Alfonso's marriage to Lucrezia in 1502, the young heir assumed increasing influence and authority in local affairs, but the old man kept a tight grip on his power, closely attending to diplomacy and to the religious and musical functions of his court chapel. Far more devoted to religious practice than any of his sons, especially the ambitious Cardinal Ippolito, Ercole in his last years was virtually an anachronism among Italian princes, not only because of his late-medieval chivalric style, but probably also because of his tenacious belief in the efficacy of Christian practice.

[19] *Diario ferrarese . . . di autori incerti*, pp. 217 f.

13

Recruitment of Musicians in the 1470s

AWARENESS of music as a social art, as a means of intensifying poetic and religious expression, and as a mode of personal cultivation, spread through Italian literate circles in the later fifteenth century. The reasons were no doubt as complex as the results. The new patrons found in their squadrons of musicians a new way of competing for prestige with one another and with the great royal establishments, above all the French and the legendary Burgundian courts, which set a tone for European aristocratic culture. Such musical rivalries not only mirrored larger political intrigues but grew as the web of international relationships was spun wider and more finely, enmeshing them all. On the personal side, the growth of humanistic culture, with its emphasis on manners, refinement, and individual distinction, made patrons themselves more willing to cultivate music – with respect to the more manly traditions still a soft and effeminate art – as part of the search for a wider expression of personal values.

Nevertheless, the strength of Ercole's musical interests was exceptional for his time, perhaps rivaled only by the musicality of Charles the Bold, the last Burgundian Duke.[1] In carving out his own niche for posterity, Ercole apparently sought certain means that would compete effectively with his current peers but even more with those of Leonello and Borso before him. If the frescoes of Belriguardo offered a challenge to the glorification of Borso on the walls of the Palazzo Schifanoia, Ercole's intensive development of the court chapel as private oratory and as symbolic center of court worship, staffed by the best singers available in Europe, implicitly challenged the memory of one of Leonello's most celebrated earlier achievements.

Ercole was a practical musician of some ability. One chronicler says that even during the war with Venice, 'every day he sang and played' (*cantava et sonava*).[2] On his deathbed, in 1505, we are told by an eye-witness that

[1] On Charles the Bold as musician see Cartellieri, *Am Hofe der Herzöge von Burgund*, p. 167, which cites contemporary chroniclers. A thorough study of Charles the Bold as patron and musician is badly needed; the existing evidence that he was an occasional composer of chansons and of at least one motet, sung at Cambrai Cathedral in 1460, suffices to indicate that his musical abilities were of uncommon quality.

[2] Caleffini, *Croniche facte*, fol. 202: 'Et in questo tempo el Duca de Ferrara pocho se impazava del suo stato, ansi chi de quello ge parlava, el gli respondeva che andassero dal Duca di

towards evening he called for the keyboard player Vincenzo de Modena, and made him play for an hour on a harpsichord with pedals, 'from which his Lordship took great pleasure, continually beating time with his hand . . .'.[3] It is not mere flattery when his ambassador to Rome writes in 1487 that he recognizes Ercole's concern to have benefices reserved for Jacob Obrecht as a sign of Ercole's well-known interest in music. Arlotti refers not to passive appreciation but to 'your great inclination, skill, and pleasure in music as a liberal art, from the study and exercise of which you deservedly reap so much praise and glory; and also from your searching out and favoring men who excel in this profession . . .'.[4] Ercole, as we have seen, sang together with his sons; we shall later see that he also at times joined in singing with the professional *cantori* of his chapel.

Ercole succeeded Borso immediately after the latter's death, on 20 August 1471. By November he had brought in fra Johannes de Franza (= Johannes Brebis) as *cantadore*, and on 10 December 1471 he sent a letter to the Bishop of Constance announcing his plan to create an excellent court chapel. He writes, 'for the celebration of divine worship and the daily offices we are seeking most excellent musicians, whom we are looking for everywhere.' Although this letter was published almost a century ago by Valdrighi and was recently commented upon by Schuler, its true text has not been fully available up to now, and is presented in Appendix II (see also fig. 13(*a*)).[5] The main points of this important document can be summed up as follows: (1) Ercole explains that at the very beginning of his reign (less than four months earlier) he determined to establish an 'excellent court chapel' and is looking for singers everywhere. (2) He has heard that in Constance Cathedral there is a worthy priest named 'dominus Martinus de Alemania' who is highly skilled in music, and whom Ercole would like to bring to his chapel. (3) Ercole asks the bishop to permit Martinus to substitute someone else in his place at the cathedral, and to intercede with the canons and chapter of the cathedral in getting Martinus released. (4) Travel letters have already been prepared for Martinus and one companion or servant, and two horses are ready to travel to Constance and return to Ferrara.

Although it is not yet fully clear that this Martinus de Alemania was in fact

---

Calabria. Et ogni zorno como non havea che fare cantava et sonava.' The tone of restless disgruntlement over Ercole's tendency to amuse himself with music rather than attend to state business is frequently found in the chroniclers.

[3] For the full text, from a letter to Isabella d'Este of 24 January 1505, see my 'Music at Ferrara', n. 31.

[4] Full text and translation in ibid., 112 f. and 127 f.

[5] Schuler, 'Beziehungen zwischen der Kostanzer Domkantorei und der Hofkapelle des Herzogs Ercole I von Ferrara'. Although Schuler (16, n. 4) offers an improved version of the text of the letter by comparison to Valdrighi, his is also incomplete; the only surviving copy of this letter is a draft containing corrections and changes in wording, showing that Ercole framed it carefully. See Appendix II. None the less, Schuler has done good service in connecting this letter for the first time to the actual musical forces at the cathedral of Constance.

Johannes Martini, it seems likely that he was. It is true, as Schuler pointed out, that the name Johannes Martini (or a homonym) does not appear in the extant chapel list for 1472 (see Appendix V) but this may simply indicate an unexplained delay in actually assigning Martini to the salary rolls or perhaps a delay while this musician considered other posts. He might also have remained at Constance for some time before deciding to come permanently into Italian service. At all events, this identification seems the more likely when we find that on 27 January 1473, a 'Giovanni d'Alemagna' was officially installed as a member of Ercole's chapel. I assume that this entry also refers to Johannes Martini. In 1474, the very next year, we find that Martini left for a brief period of service at Milan, where he is mentioned in a famous list of Milanese court singers dated 15 July 1474 (together with Compère and Josquin).[6] An earlier Milanese list, compiled between 1472 and 1474, does not contain his name and Ferrarese records show that he returned to Ferrara not later than November 1474. Despite the uncertainties caused by variant spellings of names, the simplest and most plausible assumption is that the singer sought in Constance in December 1471 was indeed Johannes Martini, and that he was first in Ercole's service by January 1473; he made a brief appearance at the Milanese court in 1474, and then returned permanently to Ferrara, where he remained until his death in late 1497 or early 1498. This means that the most important contributor to the formation of repertoire and style in the first twenty-five years of Ercole's reign was a member of his chapel from its foundation.

How Ercole came to know of the 'dominus Martinus' at Constance is not clear, but Schuler has pointed out that several other musicians in Ferrarese employ in the 1470s had been members of the same cathedral chapel. They include Ulrich Pelczer (also called Udorigo de Constantia), who served Ercole from 1474 to 1488 (not 1481 as Schuler has it); also Johannes Bon *tedescho*, who was master of the boys for Ercole from 1473 to 1476 and either brought with him or recruited a group of German choirboys, one of them from Constance itself. Schuler discloses that Johannes Bon had been succentor at Constance Cathedral from 1457 to the summer of 1469, and in 1468–9 held a prebend and a canonry at Zurich. When Bon left Ferrara in 1476 and returned to Constance, Ercole sent the German choirboys home as well. Although Constance Cathedral was a large and celebrated one among the diocesan centers of southern Germany, its period of greatest musical prominence was not to come about until the turn of the sixteenth century, when its staff included Sebastian Virdung, Hans Buchner, and Sixt Dietrich, and its liturgy was made famous by Isaac's gigantic cycle of Proper settings called the *Choralis Constantinus*.[7] Yet already in Ercole's time its musical forces were

---

[6] See Motta, 'Musici', p. 85 of extract; Barblan, 'Vita musicale', ix. 830, which gives the earlier list (made between 1472 and 1474) on p. 826.

[7] See Schuler, 'Beziehungen', 19 f.; for a conspectus on music at the cathedral see his article 'Konstanz' in *The New Grove Dictionary of Music and Musicians*, x, 180 f.

comparatively strong, and once the link had been established to Ferrara, more of its musicians streamed into Ercole's service. The link to Constance shows that at the beginning of Ercole's rule he did not recruit musicians by means of diplomatic emissaries or special agents but relied on recommendations through hearsay. This means of obtaining singers must always have remained useful, although, inevitably, it is poorly documented.

Just as Ercole used music patronage in his first years to establish his presence in the cultural market-place, he also used it to compete directly with other and larger courts, especially Milan. It is no accident that Ercole's recruitment campaign coincides with similar efforts made by Duke Galeazzo Maria Sforza at Milan. Between 15 October 1471 and 29 January 1473, Galeazzo dispatched a series of letters announcing his plans to form a chapel, and he sent an emissary, Raynerio, as far as England in this effort. Galeazzo's plans were on a larger scale than Ercole's since he could draw not only on a much larger court and its resources, but also upon the well-established musical company of Milan Cathedral. The singers at the Duomo had included, since 1459, the young Josquin Desprez, and in 1472 Josquin was formally brought into the *cappella di corte*, remaining a member until 1479. The brief stay of Martini at Milan in 1474 suggests a direct rivalry for singers between Galeazzo and Ercole, but there is also more direct evidence of that. At least four other singers passed from Sforza to Este service, or vice versa, during the 1470s: don Antonio de Cambrai, Zorzo Brant, Cornelio, and Michele de Feys. And the whole situation is put in a nutshell by an elaborately polite letter sent by Galeazzo to Ercole on 24 July 1475 (cf. fig. 13(*b*)):[x]

Perche ne rendemo certi che la Signoria vostra non vorria ne comportaria che alchuno de li suoy Cantori ne desviasse alchuno de li nostri, como ne anche nuy comportaressimo a nostro podere, poy che siamo colligati et fratelli . . . Avisamo Vostra Signoria che [uno] Michele Feyt alias nostro chantore è partito da li nostri servitij . . . don Daniele de li nostri Cantori . . .

Because we are certain that your Lordship would neither wish nor permit that any of your singers should steal away any of ours, just as we would shun such behaviour, since we are brothers and comrades . . . we must advise your Lordship that a certain Michele Feyt, a singer of ours, has left our service [along with] a don Daniele, another of our singers . . .

Just at this time we find a 'Michele cantore' admitted to service at Ferrara, and in 1479 Ercole takes on a singer named Daniele. Luring away singers from a rival chapel was standard practice in the period, but at times it could be risky for the agent if he were caught. In later years, especially after Galeazzo's violent death in 1476, the Milanese chapel underwent drastic changes and ceased to be a keen competitor of the Ferrarese ducal chapel. But during the earlier 1470s the two strongholds were in immediate and direct competition for talent, and it is wholly possible that Johannes Martini was

---

[x] In ASM, Cancelleria, Estero, Carteggio di Principi e Signorie, Italia, Milano, Busta 1.

involved in contacts that may have brought some of the Milanese singers to Ferrara after 1474. Both chapels may also be taken as rivals of the Papal Chapel under Sixtus IV, also in process of formation as a musical center of European rank around then; and these three musical groups form at this time the most important centers for polyphony in Italy.[9]

Having begun by creating a musical staff of unusually large size, Ercole continued throughout the 1470s to keep up its numbers and even to increase them. By 1473 he had in formal service at least twelve singers plus a large group of 'garzoni todeschi'; and even after the German boys were dismissed in 1476, the chapel increased in size through the addition of more foreign mature singers, while the Germans were probably replaced by local boys who could also be trained for court duties. In 1476 the chapel had reached the extraordinary number of twenty-seven or twenty-eight members; in 1477 it had twenty-four; and by 1481, the year before the outbreak of the Venetian war, it again had twenty-seven members. The singers constituted the largest single group of professionals, and presented the most varied national, regional, and linguistic backgrounds, within the entire Ferrarese court establishment. If we add to this large nucleus of singers the two other groups of musical functionaries – the *trombetti* and the instrumentalists – then the musicians as a larger group comprised a substantial portion of all the court employees of any type. This remained true throughout Ercole's reign.

[9] For a recent appraisal of the Galeazzo-Ercole rivalry, citing earlier studies, see my 'Strategies of Music Patronage in the 15th Century: the Cappella of Ercole I d'Este'.

14

Organization and Functions
of the Court Musicians

ᙔᙡᙓ

The Cappella di Cantori

ERCOLE'S letter to Bishop Hermann of Constance had stressed the importance of a corps of singers for the 'celebration of divine worship and the daily offices.' Doubtless the maintenance of a regular staff of singers was conceived as a means of augmenting the quality and solemnity of Ercole's varied forms of religious observance, which ranged from his daily participation in Mass and Vespers to special devotional actions, such as processions. Staffing a choir went hand in hand with Ercole's construction of a new court chapel, Santa Maria di Corte, on which he expended great efforts in the 1470s, as we will shortly see. The combination of a newly built center of worship for the duke and his family, together with the permanent hiring of a crowd of singers, gave prominence to the religious side of his leadership and reinforced the image of his visible role as Christian prince, devoted not only to the leadership of his state but to the welfare of his people, to whom his intercession could bring solace and security. That Ercole, in the spirit of the Kings of France and other lesser rulers, actually conceived of himself as a minister to his people, capable of curing the sick and bringing about miraculous results through prayers for intercession, is evident from a manuscript treatise on the ducal chapel written by Francesco Pellegrino Ariosto, an older relative of Lodovico Ariosto. In this description Francesco Ariosto reports on a whole series of miracles supposedly achieved through Ercole's piety and observance.[1]

From the chroniclers and account books too, we see plentiful evidence of the varied ways in which Ercole utilized his singers. First, for sacred functions. Like other princes of the time, Ercole heard Mass every morning; unlike many, he also heard Vespers in the evening. He seems to have held to this regime beyond the endurance of many members of his court. The contemporary chronicler Ugo Caleffini says in 1475 that

La Celsitudine del Duca ogni matina audiva la sua messa da li suoi cantori in canto cum la sua fameglia et mai non manchò zorno non lo audisse, mo ad una chiesia mo

---

[1] Modena, Bibl. Estense, MS lat. 309 (W. 4,4); for a brief description see Bertoni, '*L'Orlando furioso*' *e la Rinascenza a Ferrara*, pp. 30, 272, 301; also Fava, *La Biblioteca Estense*, p. 120.

ad un altra, vz, ut plurimi in nostra dona de corte. Ala quale messa de raro che li fratelli de sua Signoria et zentilhomini stesseno perche durava assai la messa, et lo Signore molto tarde manzava.[2]

His Excellency the Duke heard Mass every morning, sung by his singers, with his retinue, and never did a day pass by when he did not hear it, now at one church and now at another, but more frequently at [his chapel of] Santa Maria di Corte. It was rare that his Lordship's brothers and court gentlemen were present [throughout] because the Mass lasted so long, and his Lordship [consequently] dined very late.

That Ercole's remarkable stamina in religious observance made a strong impression is clear from other references by Caleffini and contemporaries. At Christmas season of the same year, 1475, Caleffini again recorded that Ercole was hearing a *'messa in canto*, as he did every day'. And in the following year Caleffini noted (6 March 1476) that every day Ercole was hearing Mass and Vespers.[3] In an important letter written twenty years later, Isabella d'Este's agent Bernardo Prosperi describes Ercole's presence in the court chapel with his singers, on a Saturday in the Christmas season, standing before the altar while his singers, together with the organ, sang the prayers that he had recently had printed in a devotional volume entitled *Corona Beatae Mariae Virginis*.[4] And still another diplomatic dispatch sent back to Mantua, on 7 December 1481, describes even more vividly the Duke's habit of participating in singing together with his *cantori*; this letter is unusually important in that it refers to their singing from a book of Masses and using solmization syllables rather than text (for providing this document I am grateful to Dr William Prizer):

Scrivendo questa, gionse lo cavalaro cum littere de vostra Excellentia le quale intese, lassaj stare lo scrivere et transferendomi a la Celsitudine de questo Signore, lo quale trovai in mezo parechi cantori, et havendo cantato alquanto non canzone ma la sol fa suso libri de messa ad suo piacere, me trassi a la fenestra et intese da mi quanto vostra Excellentia me scrive . . . Datum Ferarie, 7 decembris 1481.[5]

While I was writing this, there arrived the messenger with letters from Your Excellency. On reading them, I dropped my own letter and went off to His Excellency the Duke. I found him together with some of his singers; and when they had sung for his pleasure quite a while, not a song but solmization syllables in a book of Masses, he drew me over to the window and learned from me what Your Excellency has written to me . . . Given at Ferrara, 7 December 1481.

Ercole's singers were probably not called upon to sing Mass and Vespers in elaborate or even simple polyphony every day, but rather on important festivals or occasions. Nevertheless, the chances are that polyphony in both Mass and Vespers in his ducal chapel was much more frequent than in many household chapels of about comparable stature, to judge by the remarks of

[2] Caleffini, *Croniche facte*, fol. 53ᵛ.   [3] Ibid., fol. 63ᵛ, 72ᵛ.
[4] See below, pp. 199 ff., on this letter and on the *Corona*.
[5] ASMN, AG, B. 1231, fols. 163–4; letter from Pietro Spagnolo to Federico I Gonzaga. This could very well have been one of the Mass MSS Mod D or Mod E (See Chapter 20 below).

the chroniclers, the size and character of the chapel, and the collecting and composition of music.

In addition to daily Mass and Vespers and the Saturday office of the Virgin, for which the prayers published in 1496 were evidently applied, there were many important festivals of the Common and the Proper at which polyphony was probably used in both Mass and Vespers. Some of these must have commemorated the important saints to whom local churches were dedicated, and Ercole probably took his singers with him as he celebrated each festival suitably in the appropriate church. Among these were the great festival of St. George in the Duomo itself, and the various celebrations for San Domenico, San Francesco, Sant'Andrea, San Paolo, and the annual *offerta di San Marco*, which had its importance for Ferrara's troubled political relationship to Venice. There must also have been special attention to polyphonic singing on the greater festivals of the liturgical year, and above all during the special observances made by Ercole at Epiphany and Holy Week. No special *Ordo* or other liturgical manual survives from the ducal chapel, and we have no basis for assuming that Ercole maintained a special liturgy or liturgical calendar different from that of the cathedral. On the other hand, his observance of certain major festivals, especially Epiphany, Holy Week, and Christmas, bore a highly personal stamp.

At Epiphany he went out among the people of the city to seek gifts of food and other donations of all kinds – the duke in the guise of a mendicant. Although the point has not been generally stressed by earlier historians, Ercole typically went on his annual civic mission accompanied by singers, who sang in the *carretta* as he went about the city receiving alms. And at Holy Week, as we will see, the singers of the chapel were strongly and regularly involved in all of the ducal processions and other ceremonies, including the singing of the *Mandatum* while Ercole washed the feet of the poor, and probably also the singing of prayers while he and his family served dinner to a large group of poor citizens.[6] The singers also had to be ready to perform in more elaborate ways when state visitors came to Ferrara, as they frequently did, or on occasions of public solemnity: thus, on 1 June 1483, Mass was attended in the Piazza Comunale by a host of notable visitors, and Caleffini reports that the Credo was sung by the ducal singers. They were also at times given special roles, both figuratively and literally, as when in 1481 Ercole gave the first of a series of *sacre rappresentazioni*. In this Passion drama, fourteen singers were concealed in the head of a mechanical serpent, whose jaws opened and closed; eventually the singers emerged singing praise to God. At least some of the singers undoubtedly accompanied Ercole in visits of state, as, for example, when he met the King of France in Milan.

From a later recruiting letter of 1502 from Girolamo de Sestola, 'il Coglia', we know that in judging singers Ercole looked for voices that could be

---

[6] Caleffini, fol. 26ᵛ, on the *ventura* of 5 January 1473: 'cum li Cantori che andavano cantando in careta.' Also Zambotti, *Diario ferrarese*, p. 74 (*Mandatum* of 1480), p. 87 (1481).

equally well adapted to use in informal vocal chamber music as well as in the chapel:

Io adviso vostra signoria como Io o gia paura de inspirtarme a oldire chantare quisti chantori e non vedo l'ora che vostra signoria vegna solo per che quela se li goldderà in tanta consolatione che nol potria dire et in chapela e in chamara e como vorrà quella . . .[7]

I must tell Your Lordship that I am already in fear of being bewitched by hearing the singing of these singers, and I can hardly wait for Your Lordship's arrival because you will derive such enjoyment and consolation from them, not only in the chapel but in the chamber as well, and in any use you like . . .

Coglia's reference to the role of the chapel singers 'in the chamber as well' confirms the obvious assumption, namely, that the singers found plenty of opportunity to perform secular music as part of the domestic life of the court.

The surviving Ferrarese music MSS of the period do not include any manuscripts of secular music with texts, either French or Italian, but are confined in the secular sphere to a single source (Casanatense 2856) that was evidently intended for performance by the court wind-players, as we shall see later (Chapter 26). Yet it is wholly unlikely that composers of French chansons, such as Agricola and Japart, who visited Ferrara in the 1470s or who were employed there, and whose music was clearly known at the court, should not have found opportunities to hear performances of their chansons, and to participate themselves in the performance of these works, at times with the French texts sung. In some Italian courts the performance of French texts may perhaps have been unusual or infrequent; at Ferrara, with its emphasis on French epic poetry, French manners, dress, and the influence of the French political alliance that made access to that culture easy for court members, it seems unlikely that the heavily imported chanson literature was known exclusively in instrumental performance. At the same time, we need not minimize the importance of the instrumentalists in the performance of secular polyphony of the more complex as well as simple varieties. Although no local MSS of French or Italian secular music survive, we can in fact be certain that by the mid-1490s these repertoires were known at the court in ample collections. An important worksheet for an inventory of the court library, probably made in 1494, lists three volumes that were clearly secular: (1) *Cantiones a la pifarescha* (secular music for the wind players, probably the Casanatense chansonnier); (2) *Cantiones francese*; (3) *Cantiones [i]taliane*.[8] We can certainly assume that the performance of secular music in these years took many forms, possibly springing up in impromptu combinations of voices and instruments that happened to be on hand and that suited the ranges of the works; but we should also assume that the vocal groups

[7] Letter of Girolamo da Sestola to Duke Ercole I, 14 August 1502. For the full text see my 'Josquin at Ferrara: New Documents and Letters', p. 130, doc. 14.
[8] The worksheet is in ASM, Fondo 'Biblioteca Estense'.

performed the basic secular music of their time, either independently or in suitable combinations with instrumentalists, as we see in depictions of performing groups during these years such as the London *Concerto* (cf. fig. 6).

The Instrumentalists

Trumpeters. Everywhere in late medieval Europe, trumpeters carried out activities that were only marginally musical but were very significant in their civic, festive, and invocative functions. Every Italian town, whether a republic or the seat of a despot, maintained some trumpeters, and every lord had to keep at least a few on his payroll if he were to pretend to any sort of respectability. In Florence the *comune* had a squad of six *tubatores* as early as 1297, and each quarter of the city had its own *banditore* whose function was to make official announcements to the public while riding through the city, dressed in red and green, holding a silver trumpet. By the mid-fifteenth century Perugia regularly employed eight trumpeters, who were given salary, horse, and uniform. Their principal task was to make known all the pronouncements of the government (*fare tucte ei bandemente*) at the city portals, 'in such a way that they are satisfactorily heard by all . . .', and they received special payment for announcing wills, donations, and other personal legal acts.[9]

Among the larger states Milan may serve as an example. The city itself maintained six trumpeters, in addition to those kept by the ruling lord. His group ranged from twelve (in 1450) to twenty (in 1466). For special festivities, as on New Year's Day 1468, a gathering at the Castello Sforzesco mustered at least thirty-four trumpeters by combining the small groups maintained by a number of attending lords.[10] The sound of massed trumpets helped create the spirit of a public event; thus Tristano Calcho, in his description of the wedding of Alfonso d'Este to Anna Maria Sforza at Milan in 1491, reports:

Giunti alla Basilica, e acclamata la Sposa, volgono verso la citta, dando la destra agli ospiti, mentre le trombe rompono l'aria con i loro squilli; sono quarantesei coppie di suonatori.[11]

Having arrived at the basilica, and having acclaimed the bride, they [the nobles who took part in the wedding procession] turn towards the city, shaking hands with the guests, while the trumpets rend the air with their shrill sounds – there are forty-six pairs of players.

The trumpet itself was in rapid process of development. By about 1400 it was no longer merely a straight tube, but was being made in 'S' form and in

---

[9] Cellesi, 'Documenti per la storia musicale di Firenze', 584–6.
[10] Barblan, 'Vita musicale', pp. 788 f., 793.
[11] Lopez and de Carlo, eds., *Nozze dei principi milanesi ed estensi di Tristano Calchi*, p. 120.

folded tubing that permitted a wider range without becoming unplayable. A sliding mouthpiece made it possible to complete the range offered by the natural notes of the air column. In compositions, the assimilation of the trumpet, or at least vocal imitations of trumpet sonorities, becomes a familiar cliché in part of the literature, including Dufay's 'Gloria ad modum tubae', and Pierre Fontaine's 'J'ayme bien', with its part marked 'Contratenor trompette'. Besseler has shown that just in this period, from about 1440 to 1470, there is growing evidence of the development of the slide trumpet into that rarer form of the instrument that become known as *trombone* in Italy, or *sacqueboute* in France.[12] In part this was a response to the need for greater range in the wind instruments. The rise of the *Alta* band – characteristically two shawms and a trombone – is part of this same development. For this reason we find that the trombone players at the Ferrarese court are often grouped with the *piffari* rather than with the trumpeters; the payment records in this way reflect the practical groupings of the players.

At Ferrara the squadron of trumpeters was smaller than at the Milanese court, in accordance with the proportions of the other musical forces. In 1471 Ercole found six trumpeters already in court service. By 1478 he had added four more, along with four new wind players and at least one trombonist. By 1484 he had increased the numbers to twelve trumpeters – perhaps taking advantage of the increased availability of players during the recent Venetian war. Unlike the singers and the other instrumentalists, the trumpeters at Ferrara (and also at Milan and elsewhere) were mainly or exclusively Italians, with a slight preponderance of Tuscans. The list for 1484 follows in Table 1, with an indication of the known duration of service for each trumpeter over the years; their service tended to be fairly continuous.[13]

Table 1.   Court Trumpeters under Ercole I d'Este in 1484

Name	Monthly Wages	Total Span of Service
Raganello	LM 21. 0.0	1471 to at least 1506
Bachio	18.13.4	1484–1500
Antonio de Thomaso	13. 6.8	1481; 1484–1503
Rossetto	18.13.4	1484–1503
Bernardino da Sisi (= Assisi)	13. 6.8	1484–1503
Francesco da Montepulziano	13. 6.8	1481; 1484–1503
Stefano da Montepulziano	13. 6.8	1484 to at least 1503
Lucido	18.13.4	1478; 1482; 1484–97
Zilio (da Ferrara)	13. 6.8	1478; 1482; 1484–97
Piedroantonio da Bologna	18.13.4	1478; 1481–2; 1484–1500
Domenego del Reame	18.13.4	1484–6

[12] 'Die Entstehung der Posaune'.
[13] The list is from ASM, Memoriale del Soldo, registers for 1484. I have read this important *fondo* from 1484, when it begins, to 1522, when it ceased to list musicians. Throughout this period, it is an important source of records for all court musicians; in 1522 it ceases to be so, evidently owing to a change in administrative methods.

Trumpeters probably stayed long in service because they earned relatively high wages. In 1503 the average salary of the *trombetti* was LM 183 per annum, outdone only by the most outstanding *piffari* but higher than the average of LM 145 for the chapel singers (in the year of Josquin's presence as leader). But the trumpeters did not count as musicians in the same sense as the wind players or singers; they could not make use of the leverage of benefices or move easily to other employers, as the singers did. Many of them were probably musically and verbally illiterate, and very likely from poorer backgrounds than many of the singers or even the wind players, who crop up in connection with such events as the annual ceremonies at the university, where they appear at times as witnesses for fellow countrymen taking degrees. Yet Ercole knew his trumpeters as individuals; a reference to two of them in a letter of 1486 to Eleonora, on arrangements for young Ippolito's trip to Hungary, is suggestive:

... A la parte de mandare dui trombiti come scrive Vostra Signoria siamo contenti che se mandino et poterasseli mandare Lucido e Antonio da Ferrara, ou vero quelli dui che solevano stare cum il predetto Illustrissimo nostro fratello messer Sigismondo ...[14]

As for sending those two trumpeters, as Your Ladyship writes, we are glad to have you send Lucido and Antonio of Ferrara, that is, those two who used to be with our most illustrious brother, Lord Sigismondo, mentioned above ...

The relative quality of the best of his trumpeters, Raganello, can be judged from his salary and reputation; in 1503 Raganello was paid LM 252 per annum, more than any singer in the chapel except Josquin, and more than any instrumentalist except his companion, Piero Trombone (paid LM 288). In 1494, Ercole lent his '*piffari* and *tromboni*' to the French king, Charles VIII, at Pisa. It is indicative of the quality of Ercole's brass players that Charles borrowed them, then auditioned and admired them, and paid special gifts of money to Raganello and Piero Trombone. In 1496, a year and a half later, he asked for Ercole's players again, through Ferrante d'Este, but this time Ercole found reasons for not sending them.[15]

The Wind, String, and Keyboard Players.   In the earlier discussion of music under Leonello and Borso d'Este, and especially of the celebrated lutenist-singer Pietrobono del Chitarino, it became clear that a firm tradition of instrumental music had already been well established in Ferrara before Ercole's accession. Although Ercole's personal ideals required the acquisition of singers and the enhanced importance of his court chapel as a center for polyphonic music, the drift of the times inevitably favored greater cultivation

[14] Letter of Duke Ercole I d'Este to Eleonora d'Aragona, Reggio, 6 October 1486, in ASM, CTPE.

[15] Letters of Ferrante d'Este to Duke Ercole I d'Este: 7 November (from Lucca), 23 November (Florence), 28 November (Florence), 18 December 1494 (Nepi), 9 January (Lyons), and 13 March 1496 (Paris); in ASM, CTPE, B. 133/10.

of secular music, both foreign and Italian. Inevitably, the instrumentalists took part in this development, and in Ercole's time the principal players divide into two groups, according to instrument and function.

Under Leonello the court had witnessed the formation of an excellent wind ensemble (shawms and trombone), led by Corrado de Alemagna, who served at the court from 1441 to 1481. Like other emigrant wind players from Germany who found lasting posts at Italian courts, Corrado helped to recruit other *pfeifer* to Italian courts. He also served as a teacher and mentor to players sent by other Italian patrons (thus in 1458 the Mantuan court sent *piffari* as his pupils). The Ferrarese wind players under his leadership maintained a high level of technical polish, not only for dance music and for improvisational skill, but also for the performance of secular polyphonic music, that is, chansons played by wind ensemble. Throughout the 1450s and 1460s, the Ferrarese *Alta* ensemble was evidently made up of Corrado and Zoanne de Alemagna (shawms), and Agostino, also called Pietro Agostino (trombone). The trombone as an instrument was just then emerging as a variant of the familiar trumpet; it was a small instrument furnished with a slide and provided the tenor in the three-part ensemble music performed by the *Alta* band. It may actually be these three players (it is certainly their type of ensemble) who are depicted on the magnificent illumination for *Ecclesiastes* in the Borso Bible produced between 1455 and 1461. We can surmise that Corrado played the soprano shawm, not only as the leading player but also because his replacement after his death, a certain Adam *piffaro*, is called in one document *soprano piffaro*; while Zoanne de Alemagna, Corrado's partner, is once designated *tenorista piffaro*. What Corrado meant to the court's reputation can be judged from an entry in Caleffini's chronicle for 1476. Describing a *ballo* at court, he writes that it was carried on 'to the sound of the ducal *piffari*, who are considered the best in Italy, and above all Corrado, his *piffaro* from Alemagna.'[16]

Over the years of Ercole's rule, the number of wind players on the rolls increased from an earlier average of two or three to four or five. This no doubt reflects the growing diversity and prominence of their type of ensemble music at the court, and the widening range of music that they performed. The archival entries of 1480 and *c*.1494 for 'Cantiones a la pifarescha' not only show that the wind players were furnished with their own collection of polyphonic works, and instrumentally conceived pieces and transcriptions of secular vocal pieces – these entries also imply that the wind players stood on the same footing as the singers and the players of stringed and keyboard instruments. Contrary to conventional wisdom and some recent scholarship, they could probably read music and readily understand the minimal complexities of contemporary notation of secular music, certainly including instructions for the performance of three-voice canons. The sole surviving monu-

---

[16] On Corrado, the extensive archival sources range from 1441 to 1481; for a brief reference, see my 'Pietrobono', 119, n. 14.

ment of Ferrarese secular polyphony from Ercole's time, the Casanatense chansonnier, was made *a la pifarescha*, and was therefore intended for these players. The date of the MS strongly suggests that it was specifically compiled for use by Corrado and his companions, perhaps as a tribute to their virtuosity, and also to give a special touch to the festivities for the betrothal of Isabella d'Este and Francesco Gonzaga in 1480. Although Mantua had no corps of polyphonic singers at this time, it did have a group of instrumentalists to rival the Ferrarese, and this unusual step of producing a manuscript for Ercole's wind players might reflect rivalry in the one musical front – instrumental music – in which the two courts were then in direct competition.

The later career of Pietrobono was summarized in Chapter 10, and we saw that after his rise to wealth and prominence in the years of Borso, he spent his later years partly at Ferrara and partly abroad.[17] We also suggested that the tradition he represented – that of formulaic narrative singing, accompanied by lute, along with rhapsodic improvisation on the instrument itself – must have slowly lost ground in Ercole's years to an increasing local emphasis on contemporary repertoires of polyphonic song performed by court musicians. This meant three- and sometimes four-part settings of vernacular poetry, often performed on instruments or with mixed ensembles. Other lutenists came on the scene to take over Pietrobono's role: from at least the late 1470s to 1499 the chief lutenist at court was a certain Raynaldo del Chitarino, and there were undoubtedly many more musicians in court circles who could play well enough to accompany singers. Determining the precise numbers and names of lutenists is not always easy, since we find from recent work by William Prizer on Mantuan sources that a number of prominent composers of Italian secular music were also lutenists – these include Marchetto Cara, Bartolomeo Tromboncino, and Michele Pesenti (the last two were also active at Ferrara, but after Ercole's time).[18] On the other hand, we know of ample evidence that for festive occasions of all sorts there were both lutes and lutenists in abundance in Ferrara. Thus, during the *intermedi* of the 1491 performance of the *Menaechmi*, Apollo sang with a *lira* but was supported by a choir of nine Muses 'who sang several songs with lutes.'[19] And in 1499, for another Plautus performance in Ferrara, the chronicler reports that 'five persons sang a sweet and charming song with lutes . . .'.[20] The London *Concerto* (cf. fig. 6) shows what such ensembles looked like in the 1490s, and the prominence of the lutenist reaffirms the constant recourse to the lute as the most flexible and developed instrument for both instrumental ensembles and for instruments with voices. On the other hand, it does not appear that, after Pietrobono's death, any single musician in Ferrara dominated the scene as he had once done. The major lutenists of the early

---

[17] On Pietrobono and later lutenists at the court, see my 'Pietrobono'.
[18] Prizer, 'Lutenists at the Court of Mantua in the Late 15th and Early 16th Centuries'.
[19] Cf. Ghinzoni, 'Nozze e commedie alla corte di Ferrara nel febbraio 1491'.
[20] Cf. Luzio and Renier, 'Commedie classiche a Ferrara nel 1499', 178.

sixteenth century all come from elsewhere (e.g. Alberto da Ripa, from Mantua, and Francesco da Milano). Although excellent lutenists were always in demand and streamed through Ferrarese circles, providing occasional musical evenings, the court did not sponsor the career of another as great as Pietrobono under Ercole's regime.

Instead, it supported the growth of a vitally important school, even a dynasty, of viol players, and Ferrara became a major center for the performance of music on bowed string instruments. If it is indeed true, as Ian Woodfield has recently argued, that the viol entered Italy from Spain, primarily in connection with the Borgia family, but secondarily by way of Naples and the Aragonese court, it is interesting to note once more that the Este ties to the house of Aragon were very close as early as the 1440s (Leonello's chapel and his marriage to Maria d'Aragona are only part of the evidence); further, Borso's mission to Naples and Ercole's long residence there provide other means by which new kinds of musical performance could have reached Ferrara in advance of most Italian cities at mid-century. As far back as 1467, we find at court Andrea Della Viola (originally from Parma), who is the founder of the family of musicians who bear this name, and whose most prominent members are the composers Alfonso and Francesco Della Viola, madrigalists of the period of Willaert. Andrea remained at court from at least 1471 to 1506, and was the brother of Zampaolo Della Viola (who was later better known as a maker of carnival masks but who also played); we also find in the records an Agostino Della Viola, who served from 1497 to 1522. There were certainly other players of bowed instruments as well, including Urbano da Genoa, who appears at court in the 1490s. Beyond this, written evidence indicates that some musicians could play both plucked and bowed instruments. Viols are shown in paintings by local masters, and although these might be genre subjects of the late Quattrocento, nevertheless their prominence fits in with the clear emphasis on the viol as a new means of sonority for polyphony, used both independently and with voices and lutes. That the viol family had already evolved large-sized instruments by the 1490s is evident from a particularly relevant source; Bernardo Prosperi, agent in Ferrara of Isabella d'Este for many years, reports to her in 1493 the arrival of viol players from Rome 'che suonano viole grande come me'. The young Alfonso d'Este himself learned to play the viol, and ensembles of up to six viols are mentioned in descriptions of festive events at court as early as 1502.[21]

Finally, there is the strong tradition of keyboard players at the court, in the period of the very beginnings of the Italian cultivation of the harpsichord by both professionals and amateurs. The organists had, of course, a special function to carry out as members of the *cappella*; and we find that Ercole maintained and even increased the number of organists as the chapel grew,

---

[21] On the early viol and its Spanish origins, see Woodfield, 'The Early History of the Viol', esp. 143 f.; also his article 'Viol' in *The New Grove*, xix, 793 ff.

keeping two regular organists on the rolls in his later years as part of his chapel staff. On the secular side, the keyboard players come into view especially in the 1490s, when we find Ippolito and Isabella both learning to play the instrument.[22] In October 1494, Ippolito thanks Ercole for sending him a *clavicembalo*. As early as 1460 the court instrument-maker, 'Sesto' Tantino of Modena, had been paid for an instrument called by this name. Evidently, the art of manufacturing keyboard instruments with a plucked mechanism was developing strongly at Ferrara, or in connection with its patrons, during Ercole's period. That it had reached a level of considerable refinement by 1505 could be assumed in any event, but is confirmed by the report of Ercole on his deathbed calling for the keyboard player Vincenzo da Modena, who played upon 'uno clavacembalo con li pedali'.

The Ferrarese musical development thus provides a substantial matrix for instrumental music alongside the chapel and chamber singers devoted to vocal polyphony. The main inheritor of this tradition is Cardinal Ippolito I, whose large musical staff, in the period from about 1497 to 1520, was not only heavily but primarily populated by instrumentalists. Indeed, Ippolito's patronage is so strong on the side of instrumental performance that it is almost surprising to find among his musicians in the second decade of the sixteenth century a small band of singers – a group that includes the young Adrian Willaert. Instrumental performance was certainly not the province of any one patron, and Alfonso, Lucrezia, and Sigismondo d'Este all contributed to its development. But Ippolito, more than any other local patron, is the sponsor of *suonatori*.

Where were instruments kept and maintained? The answer is again found in the records, which show that as early as 1481 there was a special room in the palace to house instruments. A letter to Federico Gonzaga from one of his agents in 1481 is instructive on this point:

la Illustrissima Madona Duchesa Eleonora d'Aragona doppoi disenare vene a la camera de la Illustrissima Madona Clara [Clara de Gonzaga] dove steteno a rasonare sin ale xx[ti] hore, doppoi le mene ala camera de la musica e monstrò gli diversi instrumenti da sonare . . .[23]

After dinner the Most Illustrious Duchess Eleonora of Aragon came to Madonna Clara's room where they talked until about one o'clock in the afternoon; thereafter she took her to the music room and showed her the various musical instruments . . .

This may be the earliest known reference to a 'music room' in the annals of domestic architecture and life in the Italian Renaissance. It is certainly thirty

---

[22] Isabella asked for Girolamo da Sestola when she moved to Mantua, as we know from letters to her from Alfonso dated 26 June 1491 (in which he promises to send Sestola to her); 24 October 1491 (in which he mentions Sestola 'whom you have up there to learn to play') – all in ASMN, AG, B. 1185. Ippolito in 1494 thanks Ercole for sending him a *clavicembalo*, ASM, CTPE, B. 135/10, letter of 25 October 1494.

[23] Letter of Franciscus Siccus de Aragonia to Federico Gonzaga, dated 4 May 1481, in ASMN, AG, B. 1229, p. 215.

years earlier than references to the *camerini* of Isabella at Mantua and of Ippolito and Alfonso at Ferrara. It shows that by no more than ten years after Ercole's entering into power, the growth of this branch of music-making and of the number of instruments required for it had advanced to the point at which special domestic arrangements were necessary for maintenance and storage. The room could also be used for instrumental performance in a part of the palazzo where their sounds would not interfere with other activities.

Music in Daily Life

In order to grasp even partially what the active presence of music and musicians meant in the daily life of the court, centered as it was on the Duke himself and on the obligatory and optional functions to which he had to attend, let us follow Ercole through a reasonably typical year midway through his first decade of rule – 1476. For this year we are well informed about his comings and goings by the two main chroniclers of this time, Caleffini and Zambotti; it lies far enough into his reign to represent an established pattern; and its special events include the first phase of Ercole's rebuilding of the court chapel, commemorated on 2 February (Purification) by a procession in which a painted image of the Virgin was brought to this new chapel dedicated to her.[24] The table on p. 147 shows some of the annually recurring and distinctive events of 1476 at the court.

The general calendar of state and liturgical observances could not vary, and it dictated the ceremonial sequence of the Duke's affairs to a high degree. From New Year's Day to San Giovanni (June 24) the chain of major events was indeed fixed. After Epiphany and the Duke's annual *ventura*, the period of carnival was a time of masking, revels, and general release from constraints, which occasionally burst out into pranks and crimes; the court and civic officials sometimes sought to hold the population in check by the banning of masks. Lent was always rigorously observed, and culminated in the great Holy Week rituals at which Ercole again played the role of servant to his people. In April a span of three days brought the festivals of the Offering to the Bishop, of St. George (the city's patron saint), and of St. Mark, this last in part an act of obeisance to Venice and the Venetian legal resident called the *Visdomino*. The second *palio*, held on St. John the Baptist's Day (24 June), divided the year and signaled the summer lull, when, during the hot months, the family would normally leave the city for one of their country estates, especially Belriguardo. In the autumn, the opening of the academic year at the university and the resumption of more active civic and rural life brought on a busier swing of events; as we see, in 1476 the infant Alfonso was born

---

[24] The painted Virgin was still standing at the left of the chapel altar in the early 17th century, as we know from Guarini, *Compendio historico*, p. 190. Guarini notes that the chapel was rebuilt during the reign of Alfonso II d'Este (ruled 1559–97).

Table 2.   Some Principal Events at the Ferrarese Court in 1476

Date	Event	Source
5 Jan.	Ercole goes on his *Ventura* (solicitation of gifts from the people)	Caleffini, 65ᵛ; Zambotti, 4
22 Jan.	Ercole reorganizes his household, giving meals and lodging to those from out of town	Caleffini, 64ᵛ; 66–70
2 Feb.	Image of the Madonna transported by procession to the new court chapel in the Cortile della Piazza	Zambotti, 5
9–22 Feb.	Eleonora makes trip to Venice	Caleffini, 72ᵛ; Zambotti, 5
6 Mar.	Ercole said by Caleffini to be attending Mass and Vespers every day; then goes on hunt	Caleffini, 73ʳ, 73ᵛ
11 Apr.	Maundy Thursday; Ercole washes the feet of the poor and serves them a banquet	Caleffini, 73ᵛ
23 Apr.	*Offerta al Vescovado* (Offering to the Episcopate): Ercole attends Vespers with his singers	Zambotti, 26; Caleffini, 74
24 Apr.	Festival of St. George; *Palio*	Zambotti, 26; Caleffini, 74
25 Apr.	Festival of St. Mark; Ercole and Venetian *Visdomino* go to church of St. Mark	Zambotti, 26; Caleffini, 74
29 Apr.	Festival of St. Peter	Zambotti 26; Caleffini, 74
6 June	Jousts held at Modena	Zambotti, 10
16 June	In piazza of Ferrara, *sacra rappresentazione* of St. James of Compostela	Zambotti, 10
24 June	*Palio* of San Giovanni	Caleffini 76ᵛ
21 July	Birth of Alfonso d'Este; local celebrations for ducal heir	Ibid., 77
4 Aug.	Arrival of Hungarian retinue on way to Naples for wedding of Matthias Corvina with Beatrice of Aragon, with the 'best trumpets ever heard'	Ibid., 77ᵛ
9 Aug.	Festival of San Romano	
24 Sept.	Beginning of re-walling of chapel of Santa Maria di Corte	Caleffini, 83
13 Oct.	Baptism of Alfonso	Caleffini, 84; Zambotti, 22 f
24 Nov.	Ducal proclamation says no one is permitted to claim a benefice in ducal lands without Ercole's permission	Zambotti, 26
25 Dec.	Christmas	
26 Dec.	News of the assassination of Duke Galeazzo Maria Sforza at Milan	

on 21 July but his baptism was not held officially until 13 October, no doubt to make a greater public show on behalf of the legitimate ducal heir.

In this mix of court and church events, the value of a well-staffed corps of musicians, both singers and instrumentalists, is clear. Every major occasion involved some form of music-making, and, for each, Ercole's musicians were capable and ready to supply not merely routine but highly skilled performances, if we judge from their professional experience and the quality of their repertoires. At morning Mass, at Vespers, and on other religious occasions (including the *ventura*, the processions and services of Holy Week, and the *sacre rappresentazioni*), Ercole's singers could provide polyphony that represented the most developed contemporary form of musical expression. At times, as in Mass settings based on popular secular tunes or pieces (e.g. Martini's *Missa 'Io ne tengo quanto te'* or his *Missa 'La Martinella'*), the mingling of the secular with the sacred implied not merely an abstract broadening of the mode of religious expression, but reinforced the latent connection between religious experience and the familiar streams of everyday life that surrounded and enclosed it. All this involved implicit and perhaps direct competition with the larger retinue of Galeazzo Maria Sforza at Milan (which then boasted a much larger chapel, of twenty-six singers, including Josquin Desprez and Compère); the Milanese rivalry must have seemed all the more pointed in this year, for Galeazzo was stabbed to death on Christmas Day 1476 in the church of Santo Stefano in the presence of a crowd of citizens and of his assembled singers. In Ferrara, secular music abounded, especially during carnival; in July, when Alfonso was born; in August, when a Hungarian delegation came through *en route* to Naples, with noteworthy trumpets accompanying them; and at the *palios* and other civic celebrations that brought the people to the piazzas for amusement and a sense of civic participation. Just as the calendar of the year governed the larger sense of the passage of time in recurring patterns of activity, so the highly developed work of these musicians infused many of the year's events with a degree of expressive content and an intensity of auditory color that enlivened perception, and gave participants at all social levels a sense that the political leadership was providing not only for the practical needs of the state but also for its spirit and its quality of daily experience. When Caleffini records that Corrado was an outstanding *piffaro* and that the Duke's players were considered the best in Italy, his feeling of local pride is clear; that it was natural in Ferrara to think of the ducal musicians as a source of civic reputation and a means of shoring up the sense of local accomplishment and distinction, shows the practical result of Ercole's recruitment on a truly broad scale.

15

Size and Structure of Ercole's Cappella di Cantori

As we have seen, from the beginning of his reign and his first efforts to establish a *cappella*, Ercole spent money and effort to make it not only a highly competent body of singers but a large one as well. The entire court was small. Gundersheimer gives an estimate of 600 court members in 1476, including all ranks from noblemen to stable-boys. When compared to the Milanese or the papal court in numbers, wealth, and power, its staff of singers loomed all the larger. As early as 1472, Ercole's first full year in office, he employed fifteen singers. And while the numbers of singers actually enrolled in the *Bolletta de' Salariati* rose or fell at times (or fluctuated owing to the appearance and disappearance of certain singers who were paid incidentally or for short periods of time and did not remain as full-fledged *salariati*) nevertheless we can make very close approximations of the numbers of singers kept on fixed salaries in the *cappella* over almost every year of Ercole's reign. And evidence in the form of diplomatic correspondence and official documents about singers confirms the evidence of the registers and salary rolls.

To make both the size and national composition of the *cappella* as clear as possible, I have combined these two factors in Table 3. Inevitably, the assignment of a singer to the category 'French' or 'Franco-Flemish' is in some cases rather arbitrary; and indeed, 'nationality' in this period meant something rather more local and regional than truly national. Nevertheless, the bonds of language, cultural background, and regional proximity surely counted.

This table yields some surprises. Of the five primary national groups in the chapel, the most important and largest over the years is not the group originally from France or other foreign territory, but is made up of native Italian singers. This strikingly contradicts the generally accepted view that in the mid- and late fifteenth century Italian-born and Italian-trained singers of chapel polyphony were extremely rare. Admittedly, some of these singers in the chapel were members of the secular or regular clergy and were called *cappellani*; as such, they were functionaries of the chapel whose main business was to oversee the correct observance of the services, and their role as *cappellani* is increasingly distinct in Ercole's later years as his religiosity grew to virtual fanaticism. Yet, as early as 1477, Ercole was able to assemble as

Table 3.   The Singers of the Ferrarese Court Chapel under Ercole I d'Este, Grouped by National Origin

Year	Flanders and Low Countries	France	Italy	German Towns and Cities	Spain	Other	
1472	1	6	4	4	–	–	
1473	2	3	4	3*	2	–	
1474	3	9	4	3	1	–	
1475	(Full information not preserved; probably the same as in 1474, with addition of one new French singer, Michele de Ipry)						
1476	5	10	9	1	1	–	
1477	5	8	10	1	1	–	
1478	4	8	4	1	1	–	
1479	(Full information not preserved; at least one new Italian singer added [don Alessandro] and organist don Guido Zoanne)						
1480	4	6	9	1	1	1	(Piero Greco)
1481	4	8	9	1	2	3	(P. Greco; Rigo Cantore; M. Janes)
1482–3: Chapel disbanded owing to war with Venice							
1484	1	3	1		1	1	(P. Greco)
1485	2	5	5	1	1	1	
1486	2	4	8	1	2	2	(P. Greco; Piedro, maestro de ragazzi)
1487	(Twenty singers' names known only from Indulto list of 1487)						
1488	2	4	9	–	1–2	1	
1489	2	4?	8–9	–	1–2	–	
1490	2	3	11	–	1	–	
1491	2	5	10	–	2	1	
1492	(Lists not completely preserved; added is Verbonnet = Johannes Ghiselin)						
1493	3	7	10	–	2	1	
1494	2	6	10	–	1	1	
1495	(Lists not preserved; probably same as in 1494)						
1496	(Lists not preserved)						
1497	2	8	6–?	–	2	–	
1498	(Lists not preserved)						
1499	2–3	15	13	–	2	–	
1500	4	9	9	–	2	1	(Roberto Inglese)
1501	3	8	10	–	1	1	
1502	(Lists not preserved)						
1503	4	7	20	–	1	3	
1504	5 (Incl. Obrecht) 10	18	–		1	2	
1505	4	7	13	–	1	–	

*   Plus 'garzoni todeschi'

many as ten chapel singers of Italian origin, of whom at least two were native Ferrarese, two were from Commachio, one was from Mantua, and one from Modena. One of them, Andrea de Mantova, left Ercole's service in 1477 after five years in Ferrara, and in 1481 wrote to Ercole from Rome, signing his letter 'Andreas de Mantua Sanctissimi domini nostri pape Cantore.'[1] In this letter Andrea sends Ercole some new compositions ('cosse nove') that have come into his hands, praises Ercole's musicality in the usual fulsome terms, and apologizes diplomatically to Ercole for having left his service:

Chusi se io mi parti da Vostra Excellentia non fu perche non mi piacesse el servir quella ma aceso dal desiderio fui constreto partirme . . .

Thus if I left the service of Your Excellency it wasn't because I didn't want to serve you but rather that, fired by ambition, I was compelled to leave you . . .

If we count the singers from the Low Countries and France as one large group, in the earlier years of Ercole's reign they equal or outnumber those on the Italian side. But in the mid-1480s and later, after the re-establishment of the chapel in the post-war years, the increasing proportion of Italian singers overshadows the Northern contingent, which remains as before, except in those few years in which an entire group of French singers suddenly entered the chapel (e.g. 1499 or 1504). Let us briefly review the principal national groups and their members over the course of Ercole's reign.

National Groups

1. *The Flemish Group.* Though never numerically large, this group seems always to have consisted of singers of distinction. It averaged four singers in the 1470s, and fell to two or three in later years. Based on present information, I include in it the long-serving chapel leader, Johannes Martini, who is frequently reported in the records as being from Brabant. On Martini and on two others of this group – Niccolò d'Olanda and Cornelio di Lorenzo of Antwerp – I shall shortly provide separate accounts, but this is the place for a brief mention of several other singers. Among the journeymen was Jacomo Gualterio 'de Ulandia', who served from 1474 to 1476 and who was formerly confused with Obrecht by some scholars, though there is no basis for the identification beyond the first name 'Jacomo'. Much more striking, though for reasons other than his musical proficiency, is the presence in the chapel in 1476–7 of a certain 'Rodolfo de Frisia', as the bookkeepers call him. This is none other than Rudolph Agricola of Groningen, in Frisia, then a student at the Ferrarese Studio but also active as an organist in the ducal chapel. In view of the importance of Rudolph Agricola for the later development of Renaissance philosophy and the spread of Italian humanism to northern Europe, it is interesting to realize that in his student days he could

[1] ASM, Musica e Musicisti, B. 2.

function as an organist in one of the best musical establishments in Europe. His gratitude for his post may partly explain Agricola's praise of Duke Ercole's musical abilities in his well-known inaugural address opening the academic year at the Studio in 1476.[2] In the last years of Ercole's rule the Flemish and Dutch contingent, having diminished for a few years (after the brief presence of Verbonnet, officially a singer only in 1492), picks up again with the appearance of three musicians: the singers Giam de Fiandra (not identical with Verbonnet) and Bartolomeo de Fiandra, the latter sent as an emissary to the Low Countries in 1503 to recruit singers while traveling home on personal business. The third and greatest member of this group is of course Jacob Obrecht, for many years sought by Ercole as a member of his chapel and at last brought in as chapel master in 1504 when Josquin departed. We will return to Obrecht in a later chapter.

2. *The French Group.* Consistently the largest of the foreign national groups, the French chapel singers came from far-flung sections of that kingdom and from a few outlying French-speaking areas including Picardy, Savoy, and Gascony. Particularly strong in numbers were natives of Picardy (including, in the banner year 1499, three singers called 'Picardo') and a steady influx from Cambrai.[3] The cathedral at Cambrai had, of course, through the century been a prime source of well-schooled musicians, thanks to the fame of its *maitrise* and to the reputation of Dufay and his many students and imitators.[4] In 1474 we find Rainaldo de Cambrai and Jachetto Cambrai; by 1478 there is an Antonio de Cambrai, who remains until 1481. In later years the rise of Savoy as a musical center makes it an attractive source of singers, and Ercole follows a familiar pattern in sending one of his agents – the later infamous Gian de Artiganova – to Savoy in 1502 to lure some singers to Ferrara, an adventure from which Gian barely managed to escape with his life, as he wrote to Ercole after his return.[5] Other singers of the French group hailed from Paris, Troyes, Ypres, Nantes, Chièvre, and no doubt from other towns near the cathedral schools in which most of them must have been trained. Despite the large and imposing number of French singers, few of them are known as composers. Brebis is a composer on a small scale, and Antonio de Picardy is very likely the composer of a single motet in the Montecassino MS 871, as will be seen. But of other French

---

[2] On Rudolph Agricola see especially von Bezold, 'Rudolf Agricola, ein deutscher Vertreter der italienischen Renaissance', Van der Velden, *Rudolphus Agricola*, pp. 81–7; also Agricola's letters as published by Hartfelder, 'Unedierte Briefe von Rudolf Agricola', and Allen, 'The Letters of Rudolph Agricola'. Agricola's inaugural address of 1476 is reprinted in *Deutsche Literatur in Entwicklungsreihen, Reihe Humanismus und Renaissance*, pp. 164–183; the passage on music is on p. 177. On 'Giam de Fiandra' and Verbonnet see my 'Josquin at Ferrara', p. 109, n. 19; the article 'Ghiselin' in *The New Grove* is incorrect.

[3] The Picard singers of 1499 included fra Andrea Picardo cantore (dismissed in November); messer Gilleto Picardo and Messer Piero Picardo (assumed on 26 November).

[4] For a recent study of Cambrai in the Dufay era see Wright, 'Dufay at Cambrai'.

[5] On the Savoyard singers see Bouquet, 'La cappella musicale dei duchi di Savoia, dal 1450 al 1500'; also, her article, 'La cappella musicale dei duchi di Savoia dal 1504 al 1550'.

singers who served for more than a brief stay, the only really prolific composer is Josquin. Even Longaval, who was in Alfonso d'Este's private service and was to some degree a chapel member in 1504, just before Ercole's death, is really known for only a small handful of pieces. Despite the abundance of talent from France, it appears that Johannes Martini held the primary role of composer for the chapel's Mass and Vespers repertoires as something of a monopoly until his death in 1498. The secular domain offered a freer field for contributions, to judge from the Casanatense chansonnier; it contains pieces by Japart, then a chapel member (and himself another Picard) and, of course, also by Josquin, who was probably in Ferrara at that time as well, in the retinue of the exiled Milanese cardinal, Ascanio Sforza.[6]

3. *The German Group.* Although the free city of Constance was Ercole's first source of singers and choirboys when he began to organize his chapel in 1471, his German contingent became depleted after 1474 and was represented for many years by only one singer – the tenor Ulderigo (= Ulrich) Pelczer de Constantia. But even he proved to be a part-time musician; during these years in the chapel, Pelczer was also a student of medicine at the university, and he left the chapel in 1488 when he took his medical degree.[7] Afterwards, there were, in fact, no definitely German singers in the chapel. At the same time, Ercole's instrumentalists continued to include Germans, indicating a difference in recruiting patterns and not national barriers. So long as he could procure excellent singers from France, the Low Countries, and, even more easily, from Italian towns, he had no need to seek them again in Germany.

4. *Spanish, Greek, and English Groups.* We can consider these small groups together. The Spanish group actually included only one long-term member, Bartolomeo Spagnolo; for some years he was joined by a singer called 'Pedros', or at times 'Pedrosso' or 'Petrosso', whom I also take to have been a Spaniard. The small number is surprising in view of the Spanish-Neapolitan background of the Duchess Eleonora and Ercole's own experience at the Aragonese court. A marginal Greek 'group' is represented by one singer – a certain Pietro de Candia Greco, often called simply 'Pietro Greco', who served from 1480 to 1494. The occasional but ultimately important appearances of English musicians in earlier phases of Ferrarese musical life, under Leonello and Borso, did not leave any mark upon Ercole's earlier years, but in 1500 a post was taken in the chapel by a 'Roberto Inglese', whose real name was Robert Frost.

The wanderings of many of these singers, from city to city and even from country to country, rendered their national origin only a partial determinant of language and cultural background, and we ought not to assume that a

[6] See my 'Josquin at Ferrara', p. 112 and docs. 7–9.

[7] See Pardi, *Titoli dottorali conferiti dallo Studio di Ferrara nei secoli XV e XVI*, p. 81. The degree was granted on 10 April 1488 to 'Ulricus Pilcer de Constantia cantor ducis Ferrarie', and two of the three witnesses were ducal singers.

singer's place of origin is a sufficient clue to his contribution to the life and character of the chapel. Johannes Martini, for example, was originally from Flanders, but was called 'cleric of Cambrai' in beneficial documents; and of course he had served in Constance before coming to Ferrara. Martini's personal connections to German musicians, above all Hofhaimer, form an important channel for the exchange of music. Like other foreigners, singers who devoted their lives to service at an Italian court often became citizens, raised families in their new surroundings, and became property-holders; like visitors and residents of later generations and later centuries, they became Italianate. Many of them learned to speak and write Italian fluently, as we see from at least some extant correspondence.

The *cappella di cantori* undoubtedly formed within the court a cluster of foreign and non-Ferrarese Italian specialists, comparable in a small way to the various 'nations' within the university, the only other nuclear center within the city that housed large numbers of foreigners. Indeed, there were direct personal links between the court singers and the foreign student population, as notarial documents readily show.

Rank and Hierarchy in the Chapel

Within the chapel we can distinguish several ranks and levels of importance, so far as the large but often impersonal factual evidence tells us something of the individual careers and personalities of the members. Their status depended in varying degrees on such factors as reputation, nationality, length of service, and loyalty to the Duke. The possession of lay or clerical status affected the individual's legal ability to hold benefices, but there is no indication that Ercole regarded such status in itself as affecting membership of the chapel. The Papal Chapel always employed a *magister cappellae* as its administrator (in the late fifteenth century this was always a bishop, and this post was filled by a musician for the first time when Carpentras was appointed to it by Leo X). But a court chapel like that of Ferrara had no need for such an ecclesiastical position. Since the chapel's functions were divided between the liturgical-ceremonial, on the one hand, and secular music on the other, no non-musician administrator seems ever to have been needed; instead, it was apparently managed directly by the Duke himself (or in his absence by the Duchess) with one chief singer who acted as the principal member of the chapel but who, in the early years, was not called *maestro di cappella*. We can distinguish five categories of members:

1. *Cantadore compositore.* The first singer hired for the chapel was Johannes Brebis, who entered service in November 1471, a mere three months after Ercole's accession. Brebis was called *cantor* (or *cantadore*). When Johannes Martini was hired, first in 1473 and then permanently, serving from November 1474 until his death in late 1497, he was always called *cantadore compositore*, a title given to no other member of the chapel. The

implication was clear: Martini was the leading member of the chapel both as singer and as composer. To the extent that new compositions were needed for the chapel, it was his job to produce them, and indeed Martini is the main, attributed composer, in collaboration with Brebis, of the large set of double-chorus music for Lent and Holy Week that is preserved in the choirbooks of the Biblioteca Estense, MSS Alpha M. 1. 11–12 (Latin 454–455), produced in the late 1470s (cf. fig. 9). Similarly, most of his Masses were probably written for the chapel, and were available for copying by not later than about 1480. Although the chapel under Martini was served for many years by a nucleus of faithful and competent singers, whose musical abilities were sufficient to uphold its high reputation, very few of these singers are known as composers, even of a single occasional piece. A rare exception is the 'Anthonius Piccardus' whose name appears in Montecassino 871. This is very likely to be the singer Antonio Baneston de Cambrai, who served at Ferrara from 1478 to 1481.[x]

2. *Cantori.* This is the occupational 'title' carried by most of the members of Ercole's chapel, and it was sufficient to denote an individual as '— *cantore*' to distinguish him from a namesake holding some other menial position at court. At times, of course, an individual singer was denoted by his voice range instead, such as 'Jacheto contratenore' or 'Girolamo soprano'; but normally this occurred only when the singer was being distinguished, as in correspondence, from another with the same given name, or when a book-keeper did not know the singer's full name, which must have happened often. To some extent, it seems clear that habits of naming, once established, were simply carried forward mechanically by scribes and secretaries over many years, so that certain singers were always called by their voice-ranges as a matter of course: e.g. 'Zoanne soprano' and 'Domenego contro basso'. But the basic occupational status was that of *cantore*, and this meant that the individual was hired primarily to serve in the *cappella di corte*, that he might find himself called upon to serve members of the household from time to time, but that his personal allegiance was to the Duke. Although he might also be given other tasks to perform, his main role was as singer – of Mass, Vespers, and other liturgical and devotional occasions, and in vocal chamber music.

3. *Maestro di cappella.* In Ercole's earlier years this title denoted the singer whose job it was to manage and teach the boys, whether the imported 'garzoni todeschi' or the local 'ragaci' who displaced them after about 1476. The first to hold this title was Brebis, in 1473 (when Martini appeared and took over the role of *cantadore*). Thereafter the position of 'master of the boys' is assigned to the singer from Constance called Giovanni Bon (at times spelled 'Gon'), who looked after the boys from Germany; later (1490–1502)

[x] See Pope and Kanazawa, *The Musical Manuscript Montecassino 871*, No. 65 and p. 598. This piece would have been suitable for a representation of Apollo, as in one of the *intermedi* of 1491.

it is given to an Italian named don Girardo, whose yearning for benefices is evident in three fulsome letters he wrote to the Duke in 1502.[9] In later years, after Martini's death, Ercole seems to have made the title of *maestro de cappella* a badge of leadership in the chapel itself; the first singer to be so named is Josquin Desprez when he arrives in 1503, and the new title is doubtless a mark of special honor to this most distinguished leader, whose coming Ercole had avidly awaited. Thereafter it is held also by Jacob Obrecht (1504–5) and by Antoine Brumel (1506–10), but following the temporary collapse of the chapel in 1510 and its reconstitution on a smaller scale in the years 1512–21, the title *maestro di cappella* is again abandoned.[10]

4. *Cappellani.* From the beginning of his reign, Ercole had more than one *cappellano* as a member of his personal retinue, to oversee and conduct the daily religious services and to supervise the maintenance and functioning of the court chapel. At times this functional title was combined with others, as when, in 1472, a singer referred to himself, in a letter to the Duke, as 'Nicolaus Cantor, Organista et Capellanus'.[11] But very few of the *cantori* in later years were also known as *cappellani*. By 1473 Ercole was striving to secure a benefice for fra Pietro Cariom, from the ducal town of Bondeno, who was to remain one of his *cappellani* all through his reign. Over the years, the number of *cappellani* and their apparent separation from the *cantori* becomes more noticeable. Among the singers there were generally a few, but not more, who were designated as members of the regular orders by the title 'fra' ('brother', e.g. 'fra Zoanne Brebis') while those of the singers who held more than merely minor orders but were secular clerics, were called 'don' (e.g. in 1477, of a total of twenty-six singers eleven were called 'don'). Throughout the 1490s, the *cappellani* tended to intermingle with the *cantori* in the lists of singers and their payment records; but beginning in 1503 (again, coinciding more or less with the arrival of Josquin) we find that even the bookkeepers distinguished sharply between a group of five *cappellani* and a larger assemblage of twenty-three *cantori*. Now four of the *cappellani* were called 'don', and one (Roberto da Ferrara) is called 'fra'. This distinction was meaningful in the registers since the *cappellani* were mostly paid far less than the singers. To what extent some of them made up the difference in income from benefices we shall consider later on.

5. *Visitors.* Ercole liked nothing better than to attract distinguished singers and composers to his court, who might take an interest in his musical forces, and perhaps think of remaining. In the 1470s we can be sure of the visits to Ferrara of Alexander Agricola (1474) and of Johannes Tinctoris (1479), the latter coming from Naples on a mission for his King and stopping

[9] ASM, Musica e Musicisti, B. 2 (all three letters are from the period May to August 1502 when recruiting for the chapel was especially intense and the conflict between Gian and Coglia was at its height).

[10] On the use of the term *maestro di cappella* at Ferrara much later in the 16th century, see Newcomb, *The Madrigal at Ferrara, 1579–1597*, i, p. 155.

[11] ASM, Musica e Musicisti, B. 2.

off at Ferrara just at the time when Ercole had had a new organ installed in his *cappella di corte.*[12] By 1480–1 we can be fairly confident that Josquin Desprez had visited the court, perhaps not long after his joining the Milanese ducal chapel in 1472. It seems likely that he was in Ferrara for a longer stay after his departure from Milan in 1479; in 1480–1 his devoted employer, Cardinal Ascanio Sforza, was in residence in Ferrara, exiled from Milan, and Josquin was probably with him. In 1487 we are sure of the visit of Jacob Obrecht, for whom Ercole tried vigorously but unsuccessfully to procure benefices from Rome. And we may well believe that in the years after Heinrich Isaac's appointment at Florence, beginning apparently in 1484, he made more than one visit to Ferrara. This would help explain the presence of the name 'Henricus de Alemania' on the list of singers for whom Ercole obtained his first Indult in 1487.[13] By putting down this name, Ercole may well have thought that he could lure Isaac from Florence to his own service, but then failed to do so. In 1502 we know that Isaac was indeed considering this very move. The visits of numerous distinguished diplomatic visitors must also have brought musicians to the court as members of their retinues. What is certain is that once the chapel had been so well and firmly established, it became a target of interest for musicians, many of whom remained free of long-term commitments as long as they could, frequently roving from one place of employment to another. Apparently recognizing their peripatetic tendencies, Ercole took great trouble to recruit his singers and make his terms of employment as attractive as possible. That he succeeded in attracting the loyalty of a substantial number of singers shows that for the most part he calculated wisely.

In the Eighth Book of his treatise in praise of Duke Ercole, written in 1497, Sabadino degli Arienti makes special mention of the musical chapel, its purpose, structure, and functions. He writes as follows:

. . . essendo tu creato Duca correndo li anni dela salute mille et quattrocento septanta uno et giorni vintiuno de augusto, e cresciuta la dignitate con le richeze, l'animo tuo sempre magnanimo con prudentia sancta crescette ad cose più alte de religione. Facesti duo chori in la musica de periti cantori: uno de vintequatro adoloscentuli e l'altro de magiori, de tanto numero, peritissimi, che insignavano ali minori. Et così ogni giorno dove la tua ducal Alteza si trovava, audivi in optimo canto messa celebrare et li festivi giorni quella con l'organo se cantava. Questo ordine diece anni servasti, sino che'l bellico furore delli principi venetiani la tua Excellentia et il tuo populo turbarono. Di che alhora il choro deli adoloscentuli deponesti, facendo de' duo musici chori uni, et così sino al presente giorno hai observato. Ma li giorni solemni non solo la messa, ma li vesperi solemni odi sempre in canto, genuflesso. Nè non intermitti, cantando li musici, lo officio che devotamente non legi e dici molte altre oratione, et in la messa sempre stando genuflesso legi officio et oratione, et con atentione grande, existendo

---

[12] For the document on Tinctoris see my 'Pietrobono', 128; the same item has recently been reprinted by Woodley, 'Iohannes Tinctoris: a Review of the Documentary Biographical Evidence', 243.   [13] On the Indult of 1487 see below, Chapter 18.

col capo scuperto, odi el sacro Evangelio. Et dimentre la consecratione se para, tu alquanto retrocedi e posto con ambe la genochie e con le junte mane, el salutare pietosamente adori.[14]

. . . having been created Duke in the year 1471, on 21 August, and with the growth of dignity along with riches, your always magnanimous soul with holy prudence grew towards higher matters of religion. You created two choirs for music, of excellent singers: one of twenty-four adolescents and the other of adult singers, to the same number, of the highest quality, who taught the younger ones. And thus every day, wherever your ducal Highness was, you heard mass celebrated in excellent singing and on festive days it was sung with organ. This arrangement you maintained for ten years, until the warlike fury of the Venetian princes disturbed your Excellency and your people. So that then you dispensed with the choir of boys, making of the double chorus only one, and this arrangement you have observed to this day. But on solemn days you hear not only the Mass but Solemn Vespers in music, while kneeling. Nor, while the musicians are singing, do you enter into the office but devoutly you read and say many other prayers; and in the Mass, always genuflected, you read the office and prayer, and with great attention, with head bared, you hear the holy Gospel. And while the consecration is prepared, you move farther back and with both knees and hands joined, you piously adore the salutation of the holy sacrament . . .

The general tenor of Sabadino's account rings true, even if his language is unctuous and his figures somewhat inflated. The registers confirm, in fact, that during the 1470s Ercole had a double chorus, and that he maintained a group of boys, as we have seen; furthermore, this arrangement is no longer listed in the documents after the war with Venice of 1482–4, so that the basic outline of Sabadino's story is indeed verified. However, in the 1470s Ercole did not have twenty-four boys and twenty-four male singers; he had about half as many. Nevertheless, even a chapel of twenty-four singers was, as we have seen, a very large one for this time, and no other rival chapel seems to have had a double-chorus arrangement as a fixed means of performance. The rest of Sabadino's account confirms that it was indeed Ercole's custom to have polyphony in use on festivals for Mass and for Vespers, and this is supported by the chronicles as well. Most of all, Sabadino emphasizes Ercole's constant personal attention to religious observance, his steady ritual observance, and his lengthy periods of prayer.

Apart from his unusual division of the chapel into a double chorus, Ercole, like any patron of singers, had to maintain a balance in his choir among voice-ranges. Although we cannot be sure of the range of a good many of the singers, enough of them are known so that approximations of the preferred balances can be made. We know, for instance, that, as in many other chapels of the time, the soprano singers were numerous in comparison to those of lower register, quite apart from the use of boy sopranos. In 1473, when the chapel altogether had fifteen adult singers, four were sopranos; and similar

---

[14] Sabadino's treatise is published in Gundersheimer, *Art and Life*, p. 89; and see my review in *Renaissance Quarterly*, xxxv (1973), 496.

proportions were apparently maintained in the years after the war with Venice. We could infer Ercole's concern for such matters but we can also demonstrate it. In May 1504, the young heir Alfonso was sent on a diplomatic mission to France and to England; in a ducal minute of 17 May 1504, Ercole told him:

Preterea perche havemo pur bisogno de Cantori per la capella nostra, et voluntieri voressimo uno bono Tenorista alto, dui contra alti boni, uno contrabasso bono, dui soprani boni . . .[15]

Moreover since we still have need of singers for our chapel, and we would gladly have a good high tenor, two good contraltos, a good contrabasso, and two good sopranos . . .

Ercole knew where to procure such singers, thanks to information supplied him by one of his chapel singers, Bartolomeo de Fiandra, who had searched for singers for him in Antwerp, in Therouanne, and in Bruges just a year earlier. As Frank D'Accone has indicated in an excellent conspectus of the known dispositions of various chapels of the period, soprano singers tended to be more numerous than singers of lower parts, perhaps owing to the weakness in volume of men's voices when singing falsetto. He also observes that the reinforcement of the soprano register could be related to the 'treble-dominated' style of mid-fifteenth-century polyphony, which could have profited from strengthening of the upper line.[16] In the Ferrarese chapel it seems entirely likely that in the singing of polyphony the organ was used regularly (perhaps, on occasion, two organs) so that reinforcement of the soprano register may have been even more advisable if the mid-range and lower voices were thickened by organ doubling.

[15] On the letter and Bartolomeo's mission to Flanders for singers, see my ' "Messer Gossino" and Josquin Desprez'.

[16] D'Accone, 'The Performance of Sacred Music in Italy during Josquin's Time, *c*.1475–1525', p. 613.

16

*Some Representative Singers
of Ercole's Chapel*

Johannes Brebis

EVIDENTLY a Frenchman, Brebis is first documented at Ferrara in November 1471, when he is listed as 'fra Zoane de Franza Cantadore', and is among the first singers hired by Ercole after his accession. In 1472 he is listed as 'fra Zoanne Biribis, maestro di cappella'. From documents published by Valdrighi it had been known that in 1472 he was in debt to the court and that in 1475 Ercole interceded to cancel a similar debt for him. Recent documents found by Franceschini show that in 1476 he was given a benefice in the town of Cesta; that by 1478 Ercole had made him archpriest of the parish church of Cocanile, in the Ferrarese *contado*; and that he had also been holder of a benefice in the church of Santa Giustina of Ferrara, which he himself assigned in 1478 to the ducal singer Daniele di Fiandra. A notarial document of 12 February 1479 reveals that Brebis died just shortly before that date. This document records the collation of the singer Antonio Baneston of Cambrai as holder of the benefice of the church in Cocanile, in place of the defunct Johannes Brebis, a 'most religious man . . . and singer of our celebrated and Illustrious Duke of Ferrara . . .'.[1]

Brebis served as singer, composer, and probably as coadjutor to Johannes Martini in the administration of the chapel in the 1470s. A motet of his was copied as a later addition into the MS Mod B (see above, Chapter 6) and celebrates the virtues of Duke Ercole; possibly it was written for Ercole's accession in 1471 or for the first anniversary of that event, in August of 1472. A few works in the large double-chorus MSS Modena, BE, MSS Lat. 454–455 (Mod C₁ and C₂) are attributed to Brebis, and a record of payment for these MSS shows that Brebis and Martini were its co-composers. The motet for Ercole is an artful polyphonic composition, whereas these double-chorus Psalms and Hymns correspond to the requirements of a simpler and

---

[1] The documentation of Brebis as ducal singer from 1471 to 1477 is in ASM, LCD 89 (1471), which lists 'fra Zoane de Franza cantadore' for November-December; LCD 96 (1472); Guardaroba (1473); LCD 103 (1474); LCD 114 (1476); LCD 118 (1477); Estratto Bolletta 1478 and LCD 120. The notarial document of 1478 and the document of 12 February 1479 referring to his death, were supplied to me by Adriano Franceschini; the source for the latter is ASF, AN, Not. G. Miliani, Matr. 179, Pacco 5s, fols. 186–7.

more declamatory style. They are among the earliest of all known double-chorus compositions in the north Italian tradition.[2]

Magister Nicolò d'Olanda

This well-regarded soprano singer was among the first musicians hired by Ercole in 1471, and he remained steadily in his service for a decade. He is known in every document referring to him as 'Nicolò d'Olanda', and was apparently a singer of exceptional merit. We know this not only because Ercole says so in a letter of 1478 giving him a house in Ferrara, but also because Ercole is warned, on 11 December 1476, by Carlo Manfredi of Faenza, that 'by way of Venice, I hear that someone is trying to lure away a Nicolò d'Olanda, your soprano singer . . .'. This Nicolò d'Olanda is not identical with the celebrated singer called Niccolò Tedesco who served under Leonello and Borso. Nor is he likely to be identical with the 'Magister Nicolaus Cantor Organista et Capellanus' who wrote Ercole a letter on 18 September 1472 from the Tyrolean town of Brixen (Bressanone); the latter 'magister Nicolaus' is probably Nikolaus Krombsdorfer, who was organist and principal singer under Duke Sigismond of Austria, to whom he refers in this letter as 'my dearest Lord'. The importance of the letter is that it shows another connection between Ferrara and the court at Innsbruck under Duke Sigismond (he ruled from 1446 to 1490). It thus adds to our knowledge of the channels by which music by Martini and Hofhaimer was transmitted between these centers.[3]

Cornelio di Lorenzo of Antwerp

Already a member of the musical staff of Borso in 1470, this soprano singer and agent, despite two periods of absence, was active in Estense service longer than any other musician of his time. By 1511, when the chapel was reconstituted by Alfonso after its temporary collapse in 1510, Cornelio had worked at the court for forty-one years, absent only for periods of service in Milan (1474–7), and in Florence (1482–4 and again 1488–90). Yet even while in Florence, he served Duke Ercole as an agent for the procurement of music and musicians. As D'Accone has discovered from Florentine documents, Cornelio, during the Ferrara-Venice war (1482–4) took refuge in Florence and joined the musical companies of two institutions there. On 5 July 1483 it was noted that Cornelio di Lorenzo, 'a soprano who is staying at the con-vent' (of the Annunziata), had become one of its singers, and he maintained

---

[2] On Brebis as a composer see below, Chapter 24.

[3] The letter is preserved in ASM, Musica e Musicisti, B. 2. The first payment to him is found in ASM, LASP, Ercole I, 1471–5, under the date 23 January 1472; thereafter he is listed in the basic court payment registers until 1480, always under the name 'Nicolò d'Olanda', and is some-times called 'soprano'. Vander Straeten, *La Musique aux Pays-Bas avant le XIXe siècle*, vol. vi, pp. 90–2, published the letters about him from 1476 and 1478.

contact there for some years, even after returning to Ercole's service in 1485. In September 1484 Cornelio turns up in the rolls of the Baptistry of San Giovanni, that is, the central civic and religious institution of Florence and its most prominent musical center. A group of letters sent by Ercole, by his Florentine ambassador, and by Cornelio, gives us insight into Ercole's acquisition of music in the 1480s. Although the texts of these letters were previously published by Bain Murray, they can be included here as well, since the earlier publication contains some slight misreadings and inconsistencies.

1. Letter of Duke Ercole I d'Este, Ferrara, 16 March 1484, to Antonio Montecatini, Ferrarese ambassador in Florence. ASM, Ambasciatori, Firenze, Minuti ducali, 1484.

. . . Preterea volemo che subito faciati trovare Cornelio che era nostro cantore il quale è li et che in nostro nome li dicati che subito il ne mandi la messa del homo armè de Philipon nova. Et quando bisognasse farla notare et pagare qualche cosa, facetilo et poi avisatime del tutto, pur che ce la mandiati presto . . .

We also wish you to have Cornelio, our former singer, found as quickly as possible, since he is there. And tell him in our name that he should quickly send us the new 'L'homme armé' Mass by Philippon. And if it should be necessary to have it copied and to pay something for that, do it and let me know all about it, so long as you send it to us quickly . . .

2. Letter of Antonio Montecatini, Florence, 27 March 1484 to Duke Ercole I d'Este. ASM, Amb. Firenze, B. 3 (not 'Minuti ducali', as indicated by Murray, 509).

. . . La Messa che adimandai a Cornelio da parte di vostra excellentia è fornita et notata: et per la presente cavalcata la mando a quella . . .

. . . the Mass which I requested from Cornelio on Your Excellency's behalf is ready and is copied; and I am sending it to you by means of the present courier . . .

3. Ducal minute of letter to Antonio Montecatini, 25 August 1484. ASM, Amb. Firenze, B. 3, Minuti ducali.

. . . La messa notata che mi ha mandato Cornelio mi è piaciuta . . .

. . . The Mass sent to me by Cornelio has pleased me . . .

Another letter (No. 4 below) was tentatively assigned by Cappelli to the year 1484, and in fact can now be definitely attributed to that year, since in it Ercole tells Cornelio that 'as yet we have not yet made a decision about the restoration of our chapel.' This can only refer to 1484, since Ercole reconstituted his chapel after the conclusion of the war with Venice in September of that year. Cappelli dates this (undated) minute 27 August 1484; he is certainly right about the year, whereas his estimations of the month and day are plausible but not certain.

4. Ducal minute of letter to Cornelio di Lorenzo Cantore, undated (but 1484). ASM, Musica e musicisti, B. 2.

Ad Corneliu[m] Laurenti Cantorem: . . . La messa de Jacob Obrecht che ni haveti mandata ne è stata grata, et accepta, et havemolo visto et recevuta molto volontiera, et di bona voglia et cussi vene regratiamo et commendiamo assai. Per anchora non havemo facta deliberatione alcuna del ritornare di la nostra capella: Siche non ni potemo respondere per quello soprano che diciti vi bastaria lo animo di menar qua . . .

To Cornelio di Lorenzo singer: . . . The Mass of Jacob Obrecht which you sent has been gratefully received, and we have seen and received it most willingly and thus we thank you for it and commend you. As yet we have not made any decision about restoring our chapel, and therefore we cannot give you any answer regarding that soprano, whom you say you would risk your soul to bring here . . .

As D'Accone observed, this letter is of value on several counts. It shows that Obrecht's Masses were known in Florence and Ferrara by the early 1480s; it reconfirms other evidence of competition among the court chapels, and it shows Cornelio acting as an agent for Ercole even before his own return to Ferrarese service and while serving in Florence at San Giovanni. Ercole's acquaintance with Obrecht ripened into a more personal one three years later, when he went to exceptional lengths to recruit Obrecht for the Ferrarese chapel, sending Cornelio on a mission to the Low Countries for this purpose. We know of this journey from several sources. On 5 September 1487 Ercole's ambassador in Milan, Giacomo Trotti, reports that Cornelio had just arrived there and was leaving that day on his travels.

5. Dispatch of Giacomo Trotti, Ferrarese ambassador in Milan, to Ercole, 5 September 1487. ASM, Amb. Milano, B. 5.

. . . Cornelio vostro Cantore fu qua. Il quale subito feci expedire ad vota, meglio di quella che'l domandava. Et hoggi se ne è andato al Camino suo . . .

. . . Your singer Cornelio was here, and I sent him at once to fulfil a vow better than the one he requested. And today he has gone on his way . . .

On 19 November the same ambassador, answering a request from Ercole, says that 'if Cornelio and that other singer [certainly Obrecht], whom he is bringing from France, arrive here, I will send him . . . to Mantua . . .' (where Ercole was about to go). Between September and November Cornelio had found his way to the cathedral of St. Donatian in Bruges, armed with letters that requested the canons to permit Obrecht to visit Ercole in Ferrara. The cathedral record of this visit mentions Cornelio (here called 'Cornelius de Lilloo', but undoubtedly the same Cornelio, as Ercole had only one singer by this name); along with him went the important Milanese singer Johannes Cordier. The canons indeed gave Obrecht a six-month leave of absence and made Johannes Rykelin his temporary successor as 'succentor'.

6. Acta cap. of Cathedral of Saint Donatian of Bruges, 2 October 1487 (published by A. C. de Schrevel, *Histoire du Seminaire de Bruges* (Bruges, 1895), vol. i, p. 160 f).

Exhibite fuerunt littere missive D. Herculis ducis Ferrarie . . . per quemdam Cornelium de Lilloo ejus cappelle cantorem, quibus capitulum regat quatenus permittere vellent quod Magister Jacobus succentor apud ipsum veniret per aliquot menses ibidem moraturus. DD. audito eodem Cornelio et etiam D. Johanne Cordier, qui retulit quod idem dux cum valde delectetur arte musica, et compositionem musicalem dicti

Magistri Jacobi preter ceteras compositiones magnipendat, dudum affectaverat ipsum videre, mox eundem Magistrum Jacobum in capitulo venientem et petitioni ipsius dicus acquiescentem, a festo S. Donatiani proximo ad sex menses se absentare permiserunt et licentiam concesserunt, dummodo tamen officio suo et choralibus ita interim provideat quod non sit defectus. Et nominato D. Johanne Rykelin capellano ad onus hujusmodi subveniendum, DD. fuerunt contenti, ordinantes litteras scribi ad D. ducem graciosas et presentantes prefato Cornelio duas cannas vini cum pane . . .

Letters from Ercole, Duke of Ferrara were shown to the chapter by a certain Cornelio de Lilloo, a singer of his chapel, which request the chapter to permit Magister Jacob the *succentor* to come to him for some months in the near future. The chapter members having heard this Cornelio and also Don Johannes Cordier, who affirmed that this Duke is strongly devoted to the art of music, and strongly favors the musical composition of Magister Jacob, over other compositions, and has for a long time wished to see him; presently, Magister Jacob, having come before the chapter and agreeing to the Duke's petition, the chapter members allowed him to absent himself for six months beginning on the next festival of Saint Donatian, provided that his office and the singing would be provided for in the interim period and not remain empty. And since Don Johannes Rykelin *cappellano* was hired for this position, the chapter members were content, and ordered favourable letters to be written to his lordship the Duke and the aforesaid Cornelio was presented with two casks of wine and with bread . . .

Obrecht then came to visit Ercole (who went to even greater lengths to obtain benefices for him), undoubtedly accompanied by Cornelio. Although we know of other cases of recruitment of Northern singers by Italian princes of the period through the use of agents. Ercole's dispatch of letters to the cathedral chapter in Bruges is indicative of his energetic patronage. It is possible that Cornelio was the link through which Ercole learned of Obrecht's presence in Bruges in 1487; if that were so, we could readily infer that the long-standing Medici connections with Bruges (above all through the Medici Bank, which had been used as a means of recruiting singers as far back as 1448) could be the key to Cornelio's knowledge, and that such information would have been more easily available in Florence than anywhere else.

Present once more in Florence in 1490, Cornelio again served as an agent for Ercole in procuring music, especially polyphonic Masses. Since we have every reason to assume that Cornelio knew the repertoires of the Ferrara chapel thoroughly, we can assume that the works he sent from Florence were new to Ferrara at that time:

7.   Letter of Cornelio di Lorenzo, Florence, 11 March 1490, to Duke Ercole I d'Este. ASM, Musica e Musicisti, B. 2 (published by Vander Straeten, vi, p. 81).

. . . Mando ala Excellentia Vostra una missa de Gasparo, facta sopra Princesse et amorette. Credo piacerà a quilla. Mando ancora una cansone che si cantò in quista terra il dì di Carnasale anche non dispiacerà ala Excellentia Vostra. Aviso ancora ala Signoria Vostra che yzac sia facto una missa supra Jay pris amours, et presto la mandarò ala Signoria Vostra.

Ulterius prego Vostra Signorij non si maravigli¡ si non son venuto ali servicij de quilla como era mia intencione al presente la causa è stata per essere messa in parto la dona mia de quatro giorni fanno, la quilla come sarà in termine de potere caminare, et como il tempo serà anche più disposto per potere comodamente condure la brigata mia, serò subito mosso et veromene a vivere sotto l'ombra de la Excellentia Vostra, como è stato sempre mio gran desiderio . . .

. . . I am sending to Your Excellency a Mass by Gaspar [Weerbecke] based upon 'Princesse et amorette'. I believe it will please you. I am also sending a song that was sung here on Carnival Day, which also will not displease you. And I am notifying Your Lordship that Isaac has composed a Mass upon 'J'ay pris amours', and soon I will send it to Your Lordship.

Finally I beg Your Lordship not to be surprised that I haven't yet come back to your service, as was my intention. At the moment the reason has been that my wife has been in labor for four days. When she is able to travel and when the weather is also more hospitable for traveling with my family, I will return immediately and will come to live under Your Excellency's protection, as has always been my great desire . . .

Exactly two months later Cornelio fulfils his promise:

8.   Letter of Cornelio di Lorenzo, Florence, 12 May 1490, to Duke Ercole I d'Este, from Florence, 12 May 1490. ASM, Musica e Musicisti, B. 2.

Mando a vostra excellentia una Missa nova sopra jay pris Amours credo piacirà a quilla. Non piglia admiracione la excellentia vostra del mio tanto tardare ali servitii de quella. Como ho statuito più tempo fa, per che il procede per ritrovarse la donna mia essere Inferma per esserse levata fresca dal parto. La quala como serà sanata subito me metterò a camino, che una ora pare mille che sia ali serviti de quella. Como è mio sommo desiderio . . .

I am sending to Your Excellency a new Mass on 'J'ay pris amours', which I believe will please you. Your Excellency should not be astonished that I have taken so long to come to your service. As I indicated some time ago, the reason is because my wife has been ill directly following her childbirth. As soon as she is better I will take to the road, since one hour seems to me a thousand when I am not in your service, which is my greatest desire . . .

In accepting Cornelio's return to his service, after a second absence, Ercole implicitly confirms his tolerance in dealing with his singers, as well as Cornelio's value to the chapel. Cornelio's status as family man is evident in 1503 when he is listed among the small group of 'laizi' in the chapel who did not hold any benefices.[4]

---

[4] In addition to the basic payment registers from 1470 to 1511 which list Cornelio (see Appendix V), material about him was published by Murray, 'New Light on Jacob Obrecht's Development – a Biographical Study'; and by D'Accone, 'The Singers of San Giovanni', 334, 341, 342, and 343, esp. note 170. Cf. also Cappelli, 'Lettere di Lorenzo de' Medici con notizie tratte dai carteggi diplomatici degli oratori estensi a Ferrara'. Adriano Franceschini has kindly supplied the documents of 1482 and of 1 September 1495 showing Cornelio as witness; the former is particularly important because it lists both a 'dom. mag. Cornelio de Florentiis de Zelandia' and a 'dom. Cornelius Laurentii de Lilloe . . . cantor domino nostri Ducis'; the second lists, along with 'Johannes Martini de Brabant', 'Cornelio Laurentii Hantwerpia'.

Jachetto de Marvilla

Almost as long and well documented as the career of Cornelio is that of the singer Jachetto de Marvilla. But the pattern is quite different, since Jachetto was apparently never used by Ercole as an emissary or agent. He is one of the more well-traveled musicians of the second half of the century, a highly representative figure among the numerous French chapel singers who forged their careers primarily under Italian patronage but are entirely unknown as composers. Variously called Jachetto from Marville, from Rouen, and from Lorraine, this singer first appears on the Italian scene in Naples, where he evidently served from 1455 to about 1468. The stages of his career are briefly as follows:

1455–*c*.1468	Naples, court chapel
1468	Siena, Cathedral
1469–71	Rome, Papal Chapel
1472–3	Ferrara, court chapel (called 'Jachetto Contratenore')
1474	Milan, Sforza court chapel
1476–99	Ferrara, court chapel
1500	released at Ferrara, tries to secure employment at Mantua
1501	re-hired at Ferrara and released again

Though Jachetto moved gradually across the Italian chess-board, he was not a pawn. His letters of 1466 and 1469 to Lorenzo de' Medici show him to be a singer of some initiative, capable of advertising his talents and offering to serve as an agent for his current patron. His 1466 letter to Lorenzo is revealing of a persistent sense of expatriation felt by singers from the North whose lives were spent entirely in Italy – he tells Lorenzo that although he has been in the chapels of two Kings of Naples and of the Pope, he has always wanted to live in Florence 'because I would be able to have news from home every day.' In 1500, dismissed by Ercole after twenty-nine years of service, he complains bitterly that he had 'never missed a day in my post in the chapel', and pleads with the Marquis Francesco Gonzaga to take him on. But Francesco was not much interested in chapel singers, and employed none at that time, so nothing came of it; Francesco may also have preferred not to be told by Jachetto that in 1483 he had been asked by Francesco's father, the Marquis Federico Gonzaga, to form a chapel at Mantua, but that the plan had been abandoned because of Federico's death. Jachetto, complaining about Ercole, neglects to mention that in 1474–5 he himself had abruptly left Estense service to go to Milan after auditioning with the Milanese ambassador at Bologna. As the ambassador put it to Duke Galeazzo, Jachetto wanted to go to Milan at that time as flies go to fruit – 'al mele va le mosche'. On the other hand, during his main years of service at Ferrara, Ercole went to some lengths to treat him well, to pay him a fair salary, and to help him to procure benefices. There is a nostalgic postscript to Jachetto's letter to Francesco

Gonzaga of 1500, in which the now aged singer, with a career in Italy of at least forty-five years behind him, takes pride in his profession:

Io non ho persa ne la voce nel cantare salvo lo falexeto che non havè may io cantorò fine ala morte per natura . . .

I have not lost any of my voice, except for the falsetto which I never had anyway; I am a singer by nature and will sing until the day I die . . .

Perhaps because Francesco declined to have him, Ercole re-hired him in 1501, probably in recognition of his long service (he was now called 'Messer Jachetto vecchio' in the records) but then released him again, after which he disappeared. He exemplifies the true professional court singer of the period, whose existence would never be revealed to us from the musical sources alone but who took part in virtually all of the most active Italian court chapels, and who must have known many of the most famous singer-composers of the time.[5]

Johannes Martini

By far the central figure in the chapel under Ercole was Johannes Martini, consistently called in the local records 'cantadore compositore'. In the recruiting and management of Ercole's musicians, in the formation of the chapel's repertoires and compiling of its manuscripts, in the performance and composition of new music, and in the teaching of music to Ercole's children and probably to other members of the court establishment, Martini played the leading role for nearly twenty-five years.

Except that he came originally from Brabant (he is regularly called in Ferrarese records 'Johannes Martini de Brabantia' or 'Barbante') nothing is documented on Martini's early years before his appearance in Ferrara, though some inferences seem plausible. If he can be identified with a 'Ioannes Martinus' mentioned in 1531 by the Flemish writer Jacques de Meyere, then we could assume that he came originally from Armentières, in northernmost France, and had two brothers named Thomas and Petrus, both singers.[6] Indeed, a motet by a Thomas Martini is preserved in a Ferrarese MS of about 1525 (the Paris-London-Modena partbooks, now dispersed).[7] As we saw earlier, the earliest dated document that appears to refer to Martini is Ercole's letter of 10 December 1471 to Bishop Hermann of Constance recruiting

---

[5] In addition to the payment registers (see Appendix V) listing Jachetto de Marvilla (= 'Jachetto contratenore'), material about him is drawn from Motta, 'Musici'; Bertolotti, *Musici alla corte dei Gonzaga a Mantova*; and D'Accone, 'The Singers of San Giovanni, 324, who publishes a letter of 1469 from Jachetto to Lorenzo de' Medici in which he calls himself a 'contratenore'. A letter of 7 March 1503 from B. Costabili to Ercole I refers to a benefice vacated by Jachetto's death (ASM, Amb. Roma, B. 14).

[6] Finscher, 'Martini', *Die Musik in Geschichte und Gegenwart*, viii, col. 1724, gives the text from de Meyere.

[7] The motet was based on the text 'Congaudentes exultemus', with second part 'O beate Nicolae'.

singers for the chapel. In this letter Ercole requests the services of a 'Don Martinus de Alemania', who was evidently in service at Constance.[8] That Martini had contacts with German musicians is clear from later evidence; this includes his attested friendship with the great organist Paul Hofhaimer, and the appearance of works by Martini in the MS Munich 3154, which originated at Innsbruck.[9] On the other hand, these German contacts could just as easily have been formed by Martini during travels from his post at Ferrara after 1473, for all we now know. Another suggestive reference is supplied by a papal document of 1486, which refers to Johannes Martini as 'clericus Cameracensis', that is, cleric of Cambrai.[10] We do not know when Martini secured a benefice at Cambrai, but in all probability it must pre-date his firm establishment at Ferrara in the early 1470s. If he had been present in Cambrai in the late 1460s or very early 1470s, this would have placed him there during the very last years of Guillaume Dufay, who died in 1474. This possibility may suggest that Martini's musical outlook was not merely subject to general and indirect contacts with the work of Dufay but that these could have been augmented by personal contacts. If so, it might help to explain the continued appearance of works by Dufay in Ferrarese sources compiled during the period of Martini's direction of the chapel, above all the *Missa 'Ave regina coelorum'* in the large volume of Masses put together about 1481 (Modena, BE, MS Alpha M. 1. 13 (Mod D); cf. fig. 10).

All that is certain, however, is that on 27 January 1473 a 'Giovanni d'Alemagna' was appointed to the Ferrarese chapel; as we saw, this probably refers to Martini, since no other singer named 'Giovanni' appears in these early years. This is the basis for associating Martini with Ferrara as early as the beginning of 1473; he then seems to have interrupted his Ferrarese service briefly in 1474 to enter the chapel of Galeazzo Maria Sforza.[11] The Milanese service may have lasted from February to October of that year; it could not have lasted longer, since in November 1474 Martini re-entered Ercole's service and remained at Ferrara for the rest of his career. The point is of some importance, because the appearance of Martini's name in a Milanese court

---

[8] See above, p. 131 f. Also Schuler, 'Beziehungen', 15–20. Schuler's insistence that Martini's name is properly 'Martinus' or even 'Martin' is factually correct but has little point. Although the bookkeepers and scribes who wrote the archival registers called him 'Martin', 'Martino', or 'Martinus', etc., he is specifically called 'Io. Martini' in several musical sources of the period, including those produced in Ferrara under his own direction (e.g. Modena, Bibl. Estense, MS Alpha M. 1. 13, and Rome, Bibl. Casanatense, MS 2856), and not all of these ascriptions can be construed in the genitive.

[9] See Noblitt, 'Das Chorbuch des Nikolaus Leopold (München, Staatsbibliothek, Mus. MS 3154)'; also his discussion of the dating of the same MS in 'Die Datierung der Handschrift Mus. MS 3154 der Staatsbibliothek München'.

[10] For this notice I am indebted to Jeremy Noble. The reference appears in Rome, Bibl. Vat., Archivio Segreto Vaticano, Reg. Vat. 719, fol. 353a, b, and concerns the bull appointing Johannes Martini to the benefice of the parish of Saint Ambrose of Rivalta.

[11] See Motta 'Musici', 526 f., and Barblan, 'Vita musicale', p. 830. The latter, p. 825, reproduces a Milanese passport of 28 February 1474 permitting Johannes Martini to travel to Mantua and return to Milan.

list of 15 July 1474, together with those of Compère and Josquin, has given rise to the wholly incorrect view that his principal seat of activity was Milan. In fact, his Milanese service is a short episode of nine or ten months in an Italian career that lasted about twenty-five years. Since the brief duration of Galeazzo's chapel ended with his murder on Christmas Day 1476 – while that of Ercole's chapel was maintained smoothly and successfully throughout his long reign, ending with his death in 1505 – the question of Martini's primary allegiance is of some importance for both his own development and for that of the chapel.

From the beginning Martini stood apart from his fellow singers in being recruited as a composer and as holding a position of leadership in the chapel. He received an above-average salary and was given a house in Ferrara. More important, he was among the first of Ercole's musicians to receive benefices producing additional income, an aspect of his career that has not heretofore been known or documented. As we shall see shortly in more detail, Ercole's distribution of local benefices began sporadically in the 1470s. As early as 1479, Johannes Martini received a minor benefice in the small town of Dogato.[12] By 1482 he had received the more impressive benefice of the chapel of Sant'Agostino in the Ferrarese Duomo.[13] But still greater advances in his beneficial career took place in the mid-1480s, when Ercole embarked in earnest on a program to widen and strengthen his control of benefices and thus the stability of the chapel. Accordingly, his Roman ambassadors began to work upon the complex bureaucracy that controlled benefices. One of the first of his cases, in 1485, was that of Martini's eligibility for a parish church benefice in Rivalta, a town near Reggio Emilia. On 10 December 1485 the ambassador, Niccolò Bendedei, wrote to Ercole:

. . . When I arrived here I spoke to messer Paolo Casella on the renunciation he promised Your Lordship to make in favor of don Zohane Martino, so that he should leave me a memorandum about it; and I have pressed strongly about the matter in the name of Your Excellency . . .[14]

Bendedei goes on to explain that the case may appear in a poor light in Rome because this Casella may be accused of acting for gain or of committing simony, but that, if it is clear that he is acting at Duke Ercole's request, then all might be well; further, that the renunciation might be made in favor of another benefice in Montechio. But the matter was still unsettled five months later, when Ercole wrote to his new resident ambassador in Rome, Bonfrancesco Arlotti:

We have learned with great pleasure that messer Paolo Casella has renounced the rights that he pretended to have in the *pieve* of Rivalta to don Zoane Martino, our singer, as you will see from the supplication that we send you herewith. It is signed

---

[12] Communication of A. Franceschini.
[13] Communication of A. Franceschini.
[14] ASM, Amb. Roma, B. 8. See Appendix II, doc. 2.

with the necessary solemnity. And in order to achieve the dispatch of what is needed for this renunciation, we want you to see to the expediting of the necessary bulls and seals (*usque ad plumbum*); then Don Zammartino will come down there. And for expenses at present, Beltrame de Cardano, our citizen and merchant here, is writing there to the bank of Gaddi for letters of exchange by which he will be reimbursed for the amount of money that he will need . . .[15]

But the case dragged on again for more than six months, and Martini finally made his trip to Rome in February 1487. On 15 February 1487 Arlotti reported to Ercole that Martini was in Rome and had collected the bulls for this benefice: '. . . don Zoanne Martini, your singer, has been here, and is returning with his bulls, well satisfied with his affairs, despite all the doubts and suspicions that he had had about messer Paolo Casella . . .'.[16] Yet, two days later, Arlotti reported that Martini, perhaps attracted by the sights and life of Rome, had not yet left the city. Arlotti explains that he had wanted to send an immediate dispatch to Ercole with current news, but

because I did not have a definite messenger, and did not want to incur expenses for you, I have waited for the departure of don Zoanne Martino; although he was sent for very early and requested every hour to come [to you], still I have not been able to send him on his way. These tribes of singers are a terrible thing; they never come to a conclusion. Today he is absent since he has gone on the pilgrimage of the Seven Stations. As soon as he has returned I will give him your letter. Your Lordship should be of good cheer, because the Pope feels very favorably disposed towards you, and I guarantee you that you have the love and grace of His Holiness . . .[17]

By the following year Martini was in line for a more important benefice; a canonry in the collegiate church of Reggio Emilia, where Arlotti himself was bishop. Again he traveled to Rome. Arlotti's dispatch of 2 November 1488 hints strongly that there was at least one other strong contender for this canonry:

. . . Yesterday there arrived here frate Zoanne your singer for the new provision and expediting of his case; and also don Zoanne Martino, whom I have seen and received very gladly; and I have set in motion the business of both of these cases according to Your Excellency's needs and the instructions that have been brought; and Your Lordship should not doubt that both missions will be helped on and expedited with good will. It is true that there is one who would wish to have the canonry of don Zoanne Martino, with the payment of a certain income . . .[18]

But Martini received the canonry, one of the most prized rewards that Ercole was able to bestow upon a singer. Martini's journeys to Rome in 1487 and 1488 may help to explain the presence of two of his Masses in early polyphonic choirbooks of the Cappella Sistina, the MSS 35 and 51. Similarly,

[15] Ibid., B. 7; letter of 4 May 1486. See Appendix II, doc. 3.
[16] Ibid., B. 5. See Appendix II, doc. 4.
[17] Ibid., B. 5; letter of 17 February 1487. See Appendix II, doc. 5.
[18] Ibid., B. 5. See Appendix II, doc. 6.

1. Pisanello, Portrait of Leonello d'Este (Bergamo, Accademia Carrara)

2. Pisanello, Portrait medal of
Leonello d'Este (Washington,
DC, National Gallery of Art,
Kress Collection)

3. Ferrara, Courtyard of
Palazzo Ducale (now Palazzo
Municipio), Portal of the
former ducal chapel of S. Maria
di Corte

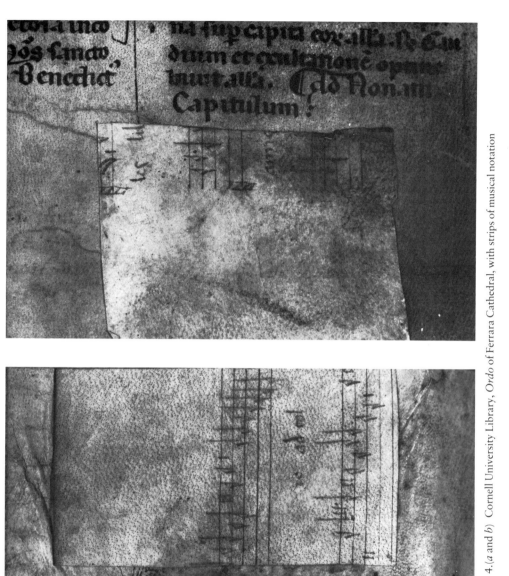

4. (*a* and *b*) Cornell University Library, *Ordo* of Ferrara Cathedral, with strips of musical notation

5.(b) Ferrara, Palazzo Schifanoia, Sala dei Mesi, April (detail)

5.(a) Ferrara, Palazzo Schifanoia, Sala dei Mesi, April

6. Lorenzo Costa or Ercole de' Roberti, *Concerto* (London, National Gallery. Reproduced by permission of the Trustees of the National Gallery)

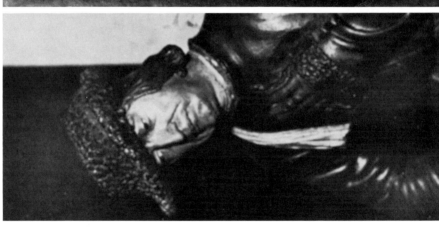

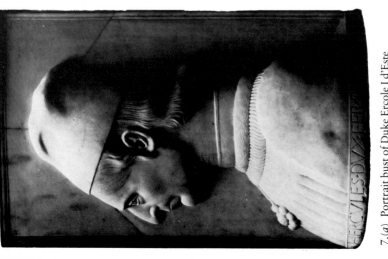

7.(*a*) Portrait bust of Duke Ercole I d'Este (London, Victoria and Albert Museum). (*b*) Guido Mazzoni, Sculptured figure of Duke Ercole I d'Este as Joseph of Arimathea (Ferrara, Chiesa del Gesù). (*c*) Dosso Dossi, Portrait of Duke Ercole I d'Este (Modena, Galleria Estense)

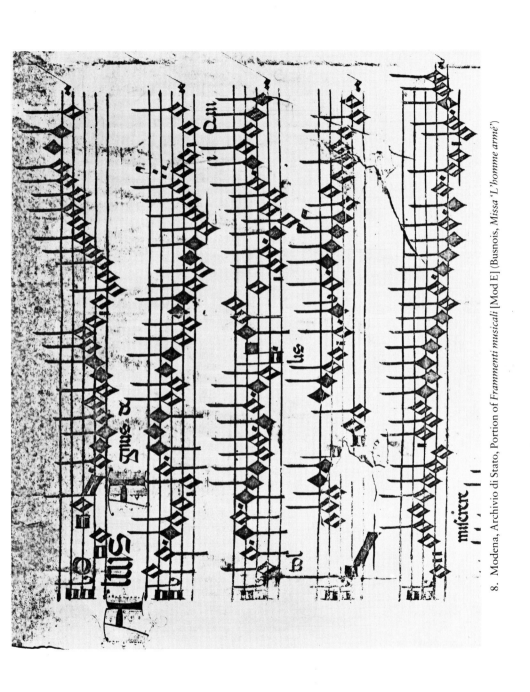

8. Modena, Archivio di Stato, Portion of *Frammenti musicali* [Mod E] (Busnois, *Missa 'L'homme armé'*)

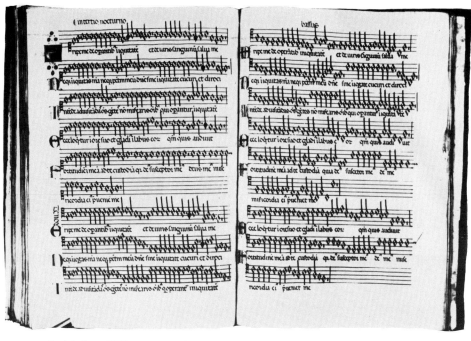

9. Modena, Biblioteca Estense, MS Alpha M. 1. 11–12 [Mod C₁ and C₂] (Portion of the psalm 'Eripe me' by Johannes Martini)

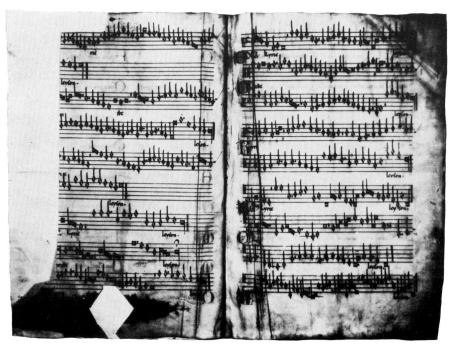

10. Modena, Biblioteca Estense, MS Alpha M. 1. 13 [Mod D], fols. 1ᵛ–2 (Portion of *Missa 'Orsus'* by Johannes Martini)

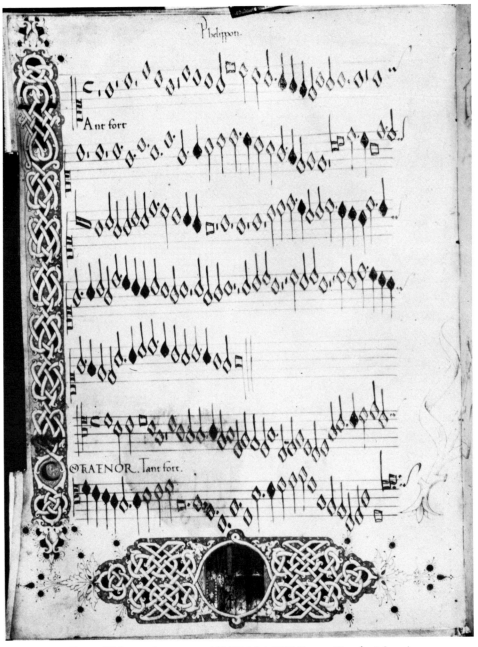

11. Rome, Biblioteca Casanatense, MS 2856, fol. 1ᵛ (Philippon, 'Tant fort', Superius and part of Contratenor)

12.(*a*) Josquin Desprez, *Missa 'Hercules Dux Ferrarie'*, Tenor: Kyrie, Gloria, Credo
(from O. Petrucci, publisher, *Missarum Josquin Liber Secundus*, Venice, 1505)

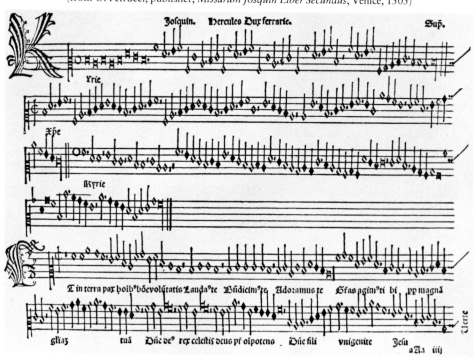

12.(*b*) Josquin Desprez, *Missa 'Hercules Dux Ferrarie'*, Superius: Kyrie and
beginning of Gloria

13. Modena, Archivio di Stato, Documents on musicians in the period of Duke Ercole I d'Este
13.(a) Draft of Duke Ercole's letter, 10 December 1471, to Bishop Hermann of Constance
(Appendix II, doc. 1)

13. (b) Letter of Duke Galeazzo Maria Sforza of Milan, 24 July 1475, to Duke Ercole, on singers defecting from the Milanese chapel

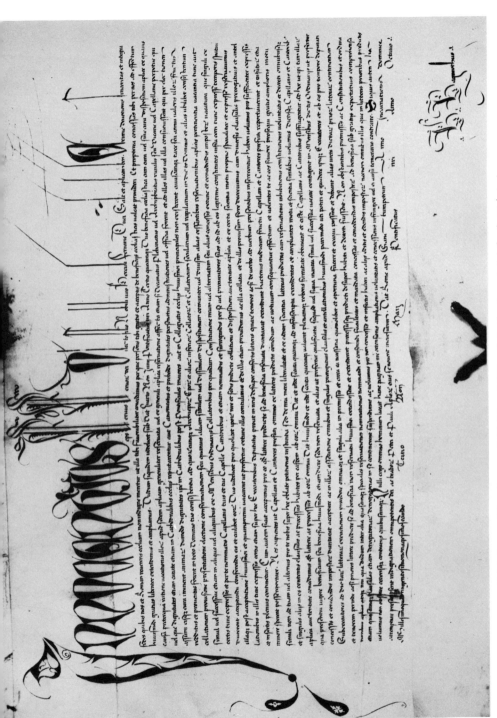

13. (c) Letter of Pope Innocent VIII, 2 June 1487, to Duke Ercole, on Indult for the Duke's singers

13. (d) Letter of Pope Alexander VI, 11 May 1493, to Duke Ercole, on Indult for singers of the Duke's chapel

13. (e) Letter of Girolamo da Sestola ('il Coglia'), 14 August 1502, to Duke Ercole, on Josquin Desprez

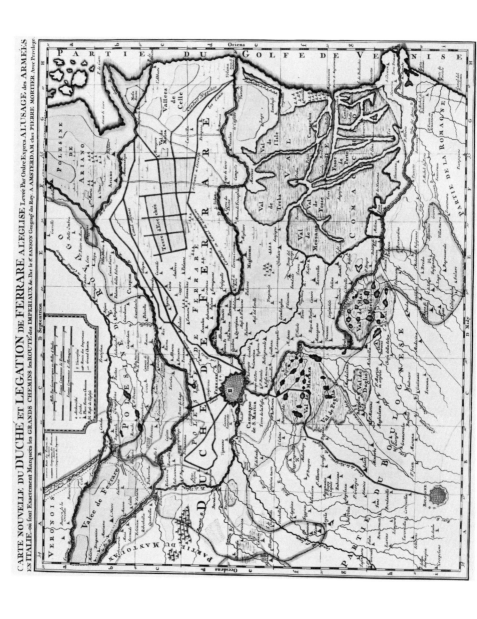

14. Map of the diocese of Ferrara and its churches (eighteenth century)

his earlier period in Milan, and his evident personal connections with Constance and with other musical strongholds of southern Germany, may well show us how compositions of his became readily available to copyists of manuscripts made in these centers.[19]

In Rome in February 1487, Martini could well have come into contact with several prominent musicians of the period. Josquin Desprez had apparently just left Rome then, but on hand in papal service were Gaspar Weerbecke, Marbriano de Orto, Bertrand Vaqueras, and Antonius Baneston (who had been in Ferrarese service from 1478 to 1481). In November 1488, Martini would have encountered the same group, with the addition of the papal singer Johannes Baldessaris, a recent arrival. Besides these putative Roman contacts, it is likely that his journey to Rome took him through Bologna and Florence, and visits to Florence in these years might well furnish partial explanation for the profusion of his secular works in Florentine MSS of the later 1480s and early 1490s.

Martini's travels took him far to the east as well. In 1486 Ercole insisted that he go with the eight-year-old Ippolito to Hungary for the child's investiture as Archbishop of Esztergom.[20] While there, Martini must have made a strong impression on the court of Matthias Corvina and Beatrice of Aragon, for three years later, in 1489, he was mentioned by Beatrice, in a letter to Ercole, as a potential emissary who might help to bring his friend Hofhaimer into her own service.[21] We can readily assume that among the musicians in Ercole's service in the 1470s — before the appearance on the scene of such international masters as Obrecht, Verbonnet, and Josquin — it is Martini who is likely to have established the connections with foreign composers that enriched the repertoires of the chapel.

His own compositions of the 1470s are closely related to the development of the chapel and to the religious proclivities of his patron. He collaborated with Brebis on the great collection of double-chorus music for Holy Week preserved in the paired MSS, Modena, Biblioteca Estense, MSS Alpha M. 1. 11–12 (cf. fig. 9). In other fields of sacred music, above all polyphonic Mass, Martini also contributed both as composer and, probably, as compiler. Of his eleven attributed Masses not less than nine are found in the large collection Alpha M. 1. 13, which was completed by 1481.[22] This important source gives every sign of having been assembled under Martini's supervision, as chapel director; and its textual variants, both in his own works and in those by others, when compared with readings found in manuscripts made at Trent, Milan, and Rome, may well reflect either his own revisions or modifications

---

[19] The sources include the important Milanese choirbook made at the Duomo under Franchino Gafori, the MS 2268 of the Duomo; also the MSS Trent 91, Verona 759, and Munich 3154.

[20] On the journey see Morselli, 'Ippolito I d'Este e il suo primo viaggio in Ungheria'. On Beatrice and Hofhaimer see *Monumenta Hungariae Historica*, iii and iv.

[21] Fökövi, 'Musik und musikalische Verhältnisse', 15.

[22] On the basis for dating see below, Chapter 20.

reflecting local performance practices under his direction. At every turn, his music mirrored the sacred and secular needs of the court he served.

In 1491 and 1492, following the wedding of Isabella d'Este to Francesco Gonzaga, Martini was in correspondence with Isabella on musical matters.[23] He sent her music, promised to look out for singers whose voices were suitable for singing *in camera*, and offered judgements on various prospective singers. The correspondence has a tone of respectful familiarity that suggests a teacher-pupil relationship. By staying in close touch with current patronage and music at Ferrara, Isabella was immediately seeking to establish the Mantuan court as an active musical center, a domain in which it had never before been notable.

Newly found documents clarify the date and circumstances of Martini's death. On 21 October 1497 Ercole wrote to Feltrino Manfredi:

At present don Zammartino our singer is so gravely ill that it is believed that he will die. He has a canonry in the church at Reggio, and the rights to another, in the diocese of Reggio. We want you to seek an audience at once with His Holiness, and ask him to reserve these benefices for me for one of our singers, as we hope he will do; it should be noted that among our singers none has been provided with any benefices, and those that had them have lost them . . .[24]

It now seems likely that Martini's death took place between late October and December 1497, rather than early in 1498. The point turns on the interpretation of the text of another letter, from Ercole to Cardinal Ippolito, dated 29 December 1497:

Before the benefices of Zoane Martino, our singer, fell vacant because of his death, we wrote to messer Ludovico de Carissimi [ambassador in Rome] to ask His Holiness to reserve these benefices; His Holiness was content to do so, and, in the event that they should fall vacant, agreed to give me the collation and provision of them to the person whom we would nominate . . .[25]

Ercole continues to say that he is thinking of nominating the brother of a faithful household servant of his, Francesco da Cesi, as a reward for Cesi's long service. And by May 1498 the ambassador Carissimi acknowledges receipt of Ercole's requests concerning the benefices 'that formerly belonged to Zoane Martino'.[26]

---

[23] His letters are in ASMN, AG, B. 1232. Although they were published by Davari, a new critical edition should be made.

[24] ASM, Minutario Cronologico, B. 4, 1497, Letter of 21 October 1497. See Appendix II, doc. 7.   [25] ASM, CTPE, B. 69. See Appendix II, doc. 8.

[26] ASM, Amb. Roma, B. 10, letter of 24 May 1497. In Ercole's letter to Ludovico Carissimi, on the same date as his letter to Ippolito, he refers to the 'benefices that *were*' in the hands of Martini ('per quelli benefici che furono di Zammartino nostro Cantore . . .'), implying that his death had already taken place. The strongest probability is that Martini died in November or December 1497, as I indicated in 'Music at Ferrara', 119, n. 50. Carissimi's letter to Ercole is in ASM, Amb. Roma, B. 10; see Appendix II, docs. 9a, b.

17

Social and Economic Status of the Musicians

IN the well-known preface to his *Proportionale* Tinctoris divides all of music history into three broad phases. The first is Antiquity. The second is the Christian Middle Ages (from the time of Jesus Christ, 'the greatest of musicians') to Jean de Muris. The last is Tinctoris's own time. Writing about 1476, and addressing himself to his royal Neapolitan patron, Ferrante d'Aragona, Tinctoris speaks of his own period not in terms of its regional and personal musical styles and qualities, but as one in which a new flowering of patronage has made possible a vast increase in the cultivation of music. He writes: '. . . the most Christian princes . . . desiring to augment the divine service, founded chapels after the manner of David, in which at extraordinary expense they appointed singers to sing . . . praise to our God with diverse (but not adverse) voices.' He then continues, not without a touch of irony: 'And since, if their masters are endowed with the liberality which makes men illustrious, the singers of princes are rewarded with honor, glory, and wealth, many are kindled with a most fervent zeal for this study.'[1]

This shrewd appraisal of the current scene by one of its leading thinkers and practitioners gives us a key in which to interpret some aspects of patronage in the later fifteenth century. Tinctoris's compliments mask his awareness of the intensely competitive atmosphere of the Italian courts, and the highly variable conditions faced by musicians in dealing with courtly patrons. He must also have been aware that the systems of rewards by which musicians were compensated for their services varied substantially with the musical interests and political energy of the patrons. In fact, the amounts spent on musicians by some of these patrons were not all so 'extraordinary', but were held closely in check and partially channeled to sources of income that would minimize the drain on funds from the court's own resources. For patrons like Ercole d'Este, Galeazzo Maria Sforza, Sixtus IV and his successors, the process of recruiting musicians entailed a narrow balance between creating conditions that would attract the needed musical talent, and, on the other hand, utilizing the system of church benefices as much as possible to augment the singers' incomes and bind them to court service. Thus, recruiting procedures

[1] Coussemaker, *Scriptorum de Medii Aevi Nova Series*, iv, p. 154; English translation in Strunk, *Source Readings*, pp. 194 f.

and the benefice system become the principal levers of patronage. Yet neither of these levers could be entirely manipulated by the court rulers and private patrons. The local financial outlay for music and musicians could be more or less controlled by the patron, so long as he reckoned with the more basic needs of his state and its financial underpinning. But the benefice system entailed a constant need to negotiate with the papacy, which in turn not only sought to control the enormous machinery of benefice distribution on a European scale, but was also itself, in the later fifteenth century, a direct competitor for the same musicians coveted by the princes of the greater and smaller states.

Inducements to Singers

In writing to the Bishop of Constance in 1471, Ercole had sought musical talent in a city in which he maintained no diplomatic agents and had no known political business. Probably, he had heard of singers at Constance through other musicians. But in his other recruiting in this period he made extensive use of the expanding network of diplomatic contacts created by his resident orators at the courts of France, Rome, Milan, and Florence, and by special agents, chiefly musicians, sent on particular missions.

In all this, as we saw earlier, he was at first in direct competition with other patrons, above all Galeazzo Maria Sforza, who used the same recruiting procedures for a chapel even larger than Ercole's. But as Ercole continued in the later 1470s to increase the size and quality of his chapel, he began to formalize his methods. Specific evidence is visible in two letters of 1479 and 1480. In the first of these he instructs his resident ambassador in Milan, Cesare Valentini, on how to proceed in the recruitment of three Milanese singers who had made known their interest in coming to Ferrara to join the chapel.

The first letter, dated 22 November 1479, is as follows:[2]

Messer Cesare: You will call in that messer Gasparo Gyletto, the singer, and you will explain to him that we have received his letter whereby we have understood the request made by him and by Zohanne and Ottinetto. And you will tell him on our behalf that we are glad to give them the ten ducats every month for twelve months a year, as they request, [and also] fifty ducats a year in benefices *senza cura* for each one, when they fall vacant in our dominions and which we can give them. Thus, we will not be lacking in providing for them, and if it should happen that they lose their voices then it will be understood that they will be allowed to exchange these benefices, but with our approval, as they may request. As for the two extra ducats a month that they request when they have to travel outside Ferrara, for expenses, I will not agree to give them these unless they are asked to accompany me outside my dominions and lands. Also, we are happy to give them ten ducats each to enable them to purchase a horse.

[2] ASM, Amb. Milano, B. 2. For the original text see Appendix II, doc. 10; also in my 'Strategies of Music Patronage', pp. 245–6.

But do not give them this in Milan because people up there would find out about the whole affair; when they arrive here we will immediately give the money to them. As for their horses, we are not going to pay for their expenses, either in our stables or elsewhere. We will give them clothing as we are accustomed to do. But they will have to find the housing that they ask for at their own expense. And this is the reply that we make to all the sections of their letters which you will communicate to them in our name.

And also you will reply to Torquin da p[er]si [= Victor Tarquin de Bruges] that we are willing to give him the horse to come here, and also the money for his expenses along the way, as he requests us in his letter. And if his companions do not want to come here at present, but rather to wait until Christmas to see how that matter will go up there, then let it be so in God's name. And so that Torquin may come you will have to buy him a horse for ten or twelve ducats and give it to him, and give him two ducats to spend for travel expenses, since that will be enough for his trip here. And you will inform me of what you have concluded with them. Ferrara, 22 November 1479

The second letter is written in January 1480, little more than six weeks later, and is addressed directly to the singer 'Tarquin', that is, Victor Tarquin of Bruges.[3]

Our honored and most cherished [friend]: Replying to your letter, we tell you that we are glad to have our Ambassador give you the ten ducats [that you need] to buy a horse to be able to come here, and another ten ducats for your removal with your possessions and for your expenses *en route*. And this twenty we give you out of our good will, as we have written to our Ambassador. And we will also be glad to have your payment begin on the first day of this month, and that you will receive ten ducats a month as payment; and each year, a suit of clothes such as our singers have. And also the rent will be paid to you on a house you can live in, and further we will provide you with benefices up to a hundred ducats; at present we can provide you with a part of that, perhaps about half of it, and it will be increased up to the full amount when a benefice falls vacant in our territory. But we cannot promise to give them to you before the festival of St. John the Baptist, because it might happen that between now and then no benefice would fall vacant that we could give you, but you will have one as soon as possible. And to clarify the matter for you all the more we have signed this letter with our own hand. . . . Have in mind that before you leave you should ask permission from Her Ladyship there, since if you do not have it we do not see how we can accept you in honor. Farewell. Ferrara, 12 January 1480.

These two letters, among the most illuminating documents of Italian patronage of the period, enable us to reconstruct the details of Ercole's recruiting habits. By comparing them with other evidence we can evaluate his offers against other court salaries.

After the violent death of Galeazzo Maria at Milan on Christmas Day 1476, Ercole had kept the portals of his chapel open to singers of the Milanese chapel, and during the tumultuous years in Milan that followed the

---

[3] ASM, Musica e Musicisti, B. 2, filed incorrectly under 'Borghi, Vittorio'. For the original text, see Appendix II, doc. 11; also in my 'Strategies of Music Patronage', pp. 247–8.

disappearance of Galeazzo – the period of the regency of Bona di Savoia and of the young Giangaleazzo Sforza – Ercole managed to take on new singers when he could. In 1477 it was decided at Milan not to dissolve the court chapel altogether but to maintain the best singers and let the others go. This resulted in dismissals of twelve singers, including Loyset Compère. Five of these singers made their way to Ferrara by the following year. They were: Antonio de Cambrai, Cornelio, Michele Feyt, Daniele Schak, and Johannes Japart.[4] Now, in 1479, three of the remaining singers – 'Gaspar Gyletto', a singer named Johannes, and another named 'Ottinetto' – made a joint request to come to Ferrara; and a fourth singer, Victor Tarquin of Bruges, had made a separate request on his own behalf. The singers asked for specific salaries; for at least approximate levels of income from benefices; for extra funds if they should have to travel outside Ferrara; for money to buy horses; and for housing in Ferrara. We can summarize Ercole's offer in the first letter as follows:

Salary:	10 ducats per month (= 32 LM per month = 384 LM per annum)
Benefices 'senza cura':	to value of 50 ducats per annum (= 160 LM) when they fall vacant; to be 'exchanged' if they lose their voices.
Travel supplement:	2 ducats per month (= 5.4.0 LM) but to be paid only when Duke Ercole orders them to accompany him outside his own lands.
Horse:	10 ducats each (= 32 LM)
Clothing:	agreed; amount not specified
Not included:	housing in Ferrara; stable expenses

The entire annual package that Ercole offered his singers in 1479 is therefore as follows:

Salary:	384 LM
Benefices:	160
Travel supplement:	76.8.0 LM (maximum, per annum; in reality much less, since not called for each month)
Horse:	32
Total:	652.8.0 (not including clothing allowances)

In his letter to Victor Tarquin of Bruges, Ercole offered essentially the same terms for salary and other items, but improved the conditions in two areas. Now the benefices were quoted at a value of 'up to a hundred ducats' per annum (of which half to be provided at once, the remainder when suitable benefices would fall vacant); he would also cover the cost of both a horse and of travel expenses to Ferrara; and Ercole was also offering a house in Ferrara,

---

[4] For the document of 1477, showing travel passes for a group of singers, including Compère, see Lowinsky, 'Ascanio Sforza's Life: a Key to Josquin's Biography and an Aid to the Chronology of His Works', pp. 40 f.

along with a clothing allowance ('a suit of clothes such as our singers have'). The figures were now as follows:

Salary:	384 LM
Benefices:	320
Horse and travel:	64 (single payment)
House Rental (estimated):	120 per annum (extrapolated from known payments to other singers for housing)
Total:	888 LM

Yet despite these improved inducements, Victor Tarquin did not join the chapel. His name does not appear in the lists for either 1480 or 1481.[5] Indeed, of this group only Egidio (= 'Gaspar'?) Giletto appears in the chapel, in 1481. But in 1482 the chapel collapsed altogether when the war with Venice broke out, and thereafter we hear nothing more of these singers in Ferrara.

Although benefices would soon play a vital role in Ercole's plans, their value as income inevitably varied considerably, and in the 1470s Ercole could not yet assign them with the freedom that he gained in the later 1480s. Accordingly, for the first period of the chapel's development, comparisons of the status of singers will be restricted to what we know of their salaries.

Salaries and Status

Although a wealth of information survives on salaries and other payments made to Ferrarese singers and instrumentalists in Ercole's period, what follows will be deliberately restricted to samplings from certain years of his rule and to some additional information. The information presented here is selected from comprehensive research on the social and economic status of the singers; but the absence of any comprehensive modern work on the financial structure of the court as a whole makes it impossible as yet to put this special study of the musicians into an accurate collective account of the court economy.[6] At the same time, I shall provide here some comparative figures on members of other court occupations, gathered along the way; and my hope is that this brief conspectus may stimulate historians interested in the economic history of a major Renaissance court to undertake the research that would provide the needed framework.

Musicians' Salaries under Borso (1456). From the period of Borso we have employment lists for various years, but salary figures only for the year 1456. The *Bolletta de' Salariati* preserved for 1456, the fifth year of his rule,

---

[5] The sources extant in ASM for singers in 1480 and 1481 are these: LCD 130; *Bolletta de' Salariati*; LCD 139; and *Memoriale eee*, 1480. For material from the last of these I am indebted especially to Dr Jessie Ann Owens.

[6] Still the only extensive account of the financial bureaucracy and economic structure of the court in Ercole's time is Sitta, 'Saggio sulle istituzioni finanziarie'.

contains an apparently full listing of Borso's musicians. His cadre of five trumpeters, two *piffari* and one trombone, five other instrumentalists, and one singer, appears to be representative in size for his twenty-year reign. In 1470 there was still only one singer and the group of instrumentalists was about the same in number.

For 1456 the monthly salaries for musicians are as follows:

Table 4.   Musicians' Salaries under Borso d'Este, 1456

	LM per month
Fiescho sonatore	12
Pietrobono dal Chitarino	8
Francesco Malacise (*tenorista*)	2
Niccolò Tedescho cantarino	24
Blasio Montolino	4
Paolo Grillo (harpist)	4
Corrado d'Alemagna piffaro	30
Zoanne d'Alemagna piffaro	8
Trumpeters (Tomaso de Faenza; Guasparo; Perino; Nicolo da Modena; Baptista da Norsa)	10 each
Agostino trombone	10

Of course these monthly salary figures do not include special payments and gifts, which Borso probably bestowed less lavishly than is claimed by the chronicler Ugo Caleffini. The odds are that by 1456 Pietrobono, as shown earlier, was far wealthier than his fellow musicians, thanks to his gifts, his special role, and his wide reputation. But if the salary figures for the others are representative, and at present we have no reason to think otherwise, they show a pattern. The outstanding German *piffaro*, Corrado, is the best paid of all the musicians; while the younger members of his *Alta* (Zoanne *piffaro* and Agostino *trombone*) are paid a third of his salary or less. Of the others, only the single *cantarino* of the group, Niccolò Tedescho, is truly well paid; the others, receiving salaries ranging from 4 to 12 LM, are at average levels. The trumpeters, however, all receive the same salary, 10 LM; this gave them financial status equivalent to that of such court functionaries as the *maestro al compto generale* and the *notaio a la camera*, and greater than that of the cooks. The trumpeters were liveried servants, but their treatment was not niggardly.

For the same year, 1456, here are some comparative figures for various other members of the court staff, carried in the *Bolletta*:

	LM per month
Domenico da Piacenza [dancing master]	20
Guarino da Verona [in his final years]	25
Michele de la Savonarola, phisico [physician]	40

Zoanne Bianchino, factore generale [chief financial officer]	20
Cristophoro a Constantino, maestro al compto generale [agent in charge of general court accounts]	10
Dulcino dai Dolcini, notaio a la Camera [notary for the court chamber]	10
Gulielmo cuogo [cook]	6
a group of 8 *occellatori* [bird-handlers]	4–13

Musicians' Salaries under Ercole (1476). From the vast array of registers and salary figures surviving from the thirty-four years of Ercole's rule, I select first those of the year 1476. This was the year whose calendar of events we looked at earlier and it is especially open to comparative observations on salary and status, because of the extensive list of court functionaries and their salaries included in the chronicle of Ugo Caleffini. On Caleffini's figures for the court as a whole, we have a recent discussion and analysis by Gundersheimer.[7] Quite apart from Caleffini's names and numbers, I made a comprehensive listing of the court musicians and their salaries from the *Zornale de Usita* for that year, compiled by the ducal treasurer Zohane de Ieson and now preserved as *Libri Camerali Diversi*, No. 114. This register regularly lists the principal court musicians, and gives their monthly stipends. It does the same, of course, for all the other court functionaries mentioned by Caleffini, and in fact it seems quite likely that this volume was itself Caleffini's source. It gives monthly payments of salary amounts to musicians on eleven dates spread out through the year, from 27 January to 24 December; and Caleffini's figures correspond exactly to the amounts paid to the musicians on one of two dates – either 30 April or 21 May. This shows us when he probably compiled the figures listed in his chronicle. LCD 114 helps to confirm the accuracy of his figures, which for the musicians are indeed correct. The full listing of musicians and their monthly salaries in LM for 1476 is as follows (the classification follows that of Caleffini, and corresponds to the typical division used in other court records); see Table 5.

Although these figures shed some light on the financial and social structure of the musical population, they can only be properly interpreted against what is known of the tradition of the court and of the age of individuals, duration, and type of service rendered. As Gundersheimer notes, the highest-paid musician is not a singer but is the leading *piffaro*, Corrado de Alemagna. But this is characteristic, since Ercole was always ready to pay instrumentalists more than singers, changing only in the case of Josquin Desprez, whose salary in 1503 was to be a matter of direct court controversy. In 1456, under Borso, Corrado had also been the highest-paid performer when there was only one singer on the court payroll. Indeed, in 1456 Corrado had been paid even more in comparison to his peers, receiving three times as much as the trumpeters and more than seven times as much as two of the regular wind

---

[7] Gundersheimer, *Ferrara*, Appendix I, pp.285 f.

Table 5. Musicians' Salaries in 1476

		LM *per month*
'Musici'	Pietrobono dal Chitarino	18
	Francesco Malacise, 'suo tenorista'	4
	Paolo Grillo	10
	Rodolfo de Frisia (= Rudolph Agricola, as chapel organist)	11.4
	Zampolo de la Viola	15
	Andrea de la Viola	15
	Rainaldo dal Chitarino	15
	Constantino Tantino maestro de fare organi in Modena	10
	Mathio Marian de Tomasi da Siena	10
'Trombeti'	Gasparo de alemagna	10
	Bazo	12
	Lucido da Norsa	10
	Marcho da Norsa	12
'Piffari'	Corado de Alemagna	26
	Stephano de Savoia	15
'Tromboni'	Pietro de Augustino	18
	Zoanne de Alemagna	12

Then follow in Caleffini's list groups of *sarti, stafieri, balestrieri, mulateri*, and *carateri*. These are followed by:

'Cappellani'	Don Bartolomeo da Luciano da Comachio	15
	Don Lorenzo da Modena	10
	Don Pietro de Luciano	10
	Don Zoanne de Bechari	10
'Cantaduri'	Frate Zoanne Brebis maistro de capella	16.13.0
	Don Andrea da Mantova tenorista	16.13.0
	Nicolo de Olandia	24.19.6
	Don Domenico controbasso	12.15.6
	Rainaldo de Cambrai	19.8.6
	Don Hieronymo soprano	8.6.6
	Iacheto de Cambrai	19.8.6
	Pietro soprano	13.17.6
	Bartolomeo Raimondo	13.17.6
	Piroto tenorista	19.8.6
	Zoanne Martino 'de Barbanti'	13.17.6
	Don Zoanne Pedrosso	19.8.6
	Mathio de Parixe	16.13.0
	Jacomo Gualtiero	19.8.6
	Don Zoanne Marescalcho	16.13.0
	Don Zoanne de Troia de Franza	11.2.0
	Alberto soprano	7.15.6
	Gulielmo de Flandria	19.8.6
	Michele de Ipri	19.8.6
	Udrigo tenorista	16.13.0

players. Now, twenty years later, when he was even more in demand than he had been under Borso, his 26 LM per month was higher than the salary of other players, but their averages had increased substantially. If we omit the miserably paid Malacise (*tenorista* of Pietrobono), the averages for the other players range from ten to eighteen LM per month. The lowness of Pietrobono's salary, a mere 18 LM, again suggests the need for great caution in using salary figures alone as an index of status; in 1476 Pietrobono was at a late stage of his career, and was famous throughout Italy and abroad. But, in his case, gifts, property, and other sources of income undoubtedly augmented what looks otherwise like a fairly low salary. In general, we should assume that the instrumentalists were treated as expert specialists, and that the demand for their services at court balls, festivities, receptions for noble visitors, and other special appearances, regularly lined their pockets beyond the bare salary figures. This was probably much less true for the chapel singers except for those who participated in secular music-making or teaching, as Martini undoubtedly did. We can assume that such opportunities were reasonably frequent for some of them, not so for all. We also find substantial evidence that visiting members of the nobility paid lavish tips to *piffari* and trumpeters belonging to their hosts and other nobles, but there is as yet no comparable evidence of special gifts to singers in court chapels, at least in northern Italy.[*] As for the objective value of these salaries, we can assume that they did not purchase much. The singers were often in debt before the end of the month, and borrowing from money-lenders was frequent.

As early as 1476, at least some of the singers were beginning to augment their salaries with the income from the benefices obtained for them by Ercole. In addition, many of the singers were given 10 LM per month for housing, as we see from Ercole's offer to the Milanese singers and to Victor Tarquin of Bruges in 1479. This subsidy was used to attract certain desirable singers and was provided for many already hired, but it was not offered initially to all potential recruits.

Among the twenty singers of 1476, several levels can be distinguished by means of salary. At the top is the long-established Niccolò d'Olanda, by now rounding out five years of court service. At the bottom were two apparently very young singers, Girolamo and Alberto, both sopranos, and both receiving between 8 and 9 LM per month. No other singers received less than 11 LM per month. Of the others, seven singers received 19.8.6 LM; five received 16.13.0 ; and three received 13.17.6. These groups cut across nationalities and other apparent qualities, so far as we know; and in 1476, only four years

[*] Evidence of the payment of tips to *piffari* is found in various sources, including Barblan, 'Vita musicale', p. 791. Although similar payments may have been made to singers long before specific records of them emerge, the first concrete evidence of this in Ferrarese records dates from October of 1515, when Alfonso visited Francis I at his encampment near Vigevano, and paid Mouton 25 gold ducats. Still, his principal tips were paid to as many as 14 groups of trumpeters, 4 groups of *piffari*, and some ranking French court members (not musicians). See my 'Jean Mouton and Jean Michel', 212 f.

after the establishment of the chapel, longevity could not have counted greatly. In many cases Ercole had to offer a salary that would induce the singers to come into his service; and in these years especially, competition with Milan would have raised the salaries of some of them. Finally, we note that the *cappellani* in 1476 are treated as a special group, and are more poorly paid than almost all the singers; three of them at 10 LM and one at 15. This small band of clerics doubtless saw to the functioning of the chapel, lived frugally, and were expected to accept poverty as virtue. Whether they did so or not, the *cappellani* were always badly paid. It is indicative of Ercole's competitive instinct that in 1479 he would offer the Milanese singers salaries as high as 32 LM per month, along with other inducements, when his highest-paid singers in that year, despite some salary increases since 1476, were getting less than 20 LM, and only one (Nicolò d'Olanda) was receiving 25.

In his summary and study of the long list of court employees for the year 1476, ranging from scions of ranking families down to stable-boys and scullions, Gundersheimer calculates that Ercole's entire staff totaled some 600 individuals, with an average stipend of about 15 LM per month. And, if one omits the inflated amounts paid to a few very high-ranking individuals, including Ercole's relatives, the average comes closer to 21 LM per month. As Gundersheimer puts it:

It is clear from the list that a man could live, though almost certainly very badly indeed, on less than 2 LM per month, though he would probably have had to do so without frequent recourse to the money economy, through bartering, handouts, and good luck. A stipend in excess of 25 LM was sufficient to keep an important gentleman in good style . . . anything in excess of 40 LM, ranging to 85 or 90, was reserved for the great grandees of the court, and for extremely talented specialists from without, such as the jurists of the *Consiglio di Giustizia*. The extremes of wealth and poverty must have been as striking toward the end of the century as Gandini found they were during the time of Niccolò III.[9]

Some comparative figures for musicians and other functionaries, from the years 1488 to 1491, are readily available in the *Memoriale del Soldo* for 1491, which contains extensive summary lists of the names and annual salaries of court members. In these registers, which are primarily those of the military service of the establishment, we may be surprised to find musicians; but in fact these are the principal sources listing the court musicians between 1482 and 1520.

For the years 1488 to 1491 we find the following salary figures, on an annual basis, for military men of various classes and for musicians;[10] see Table 6.

---

[9] Gundersheimer, *Ferrara*, p. 295.
[10] The source is ASM, Memoriale del Soldo, 1491 (Reg. No. 4895/97), fols. 147–70; this register contains a full summary of amounts paid in the years 1488–91.

Table 6.   Salaries of Some Military Men and of Musicians, 1488–91

	LM per annum
Military Figures	
Francesco de Ortona (military leader)	720.0.0
Valiadosso capo di squadra	408.18.0
Mathio de Ferrara homo d'arme	213.6.8
Zoanne Francesco da Cremona homo d'arme	177.0.0
(many other *homini d'arme* paid the same)	
Alberto da Riggio balestriero	120.0.0
(and 45 other crossbowmen paid the same)	
Bortello stafiero (= squire)	96.0.0
(and 10 others paid the same)	
Musicians	
Trumpeters	
Raganello	252.0.0
Pier Antonio	224.0.0
Bachio	224.0.0
Rosso	224.0.0
Lucido	224.0.0
Stefano de Montepulciano	192.0.0
Francesco de Montepulciano	192.0.0
Zilio	160.0.0
Antonio di Thomaso	160.0.0
Instrumentalists	
Andrea de la Viola	200.0.0
Zampollo de la Viola	200.0.0
Rainaldo dal Chitarino	200.0.0
Lodovigo da Bologna piffaro	120.0.0
Piero trombone	288.0.0
Zoanne trombone	201.12.0
Adam de Alemagna piffaro	201.12.0
Michele piffaro	240.0.0
Gregorio de Alemagna piffaro	201.12.0
Singers	
Mathias Cantore	72.0.0
Bartolomeo Spagnolo	72.0.0
Jacheto cantore	72.0.0
don Hieronimo cantore	72.0.0
Zoanne cantore	72.0.0
m. Gian cantore (= Giam de Troia)	72.0.0
don Christoforo de Modena	72.0.0
m. Pedros cantore	72.0.0
m. Zoanne Martin cantore	72.0.0
don Girardo cantore	72.0.0
don Zoane capellano	36.0.0
don Hieronymo cappellano	36.0.0
don Bernardin Colornio cappellano	36.0.0
don Piero Cariom	36.0.0

From these figures we see that the singers, as salaried employees, were in the lower echelons of the establishment, and that the *cappellani* stood even lower. In terms of salary alone, an experienced singer, and even a leading figure such as Johannes Martini, made less than the squire attending on a man-at-arms, and only slightly more than half of what was paid to the crossbowmen. Even more indicative is the difference in salary level between singers and their fellow musicians of other types: even the least of the trumpeters are paid more than twice as much as the singers, while the average is more like three times as much for trumpeters, an extraordinary difference. Even higher average salaries are regularly paid to the instrumentalists, as in earlier years. Although the famous Corrado *piffaro* had retired by this time, his place is filled by a Michele d'Alemagna *piffaro*, who makes 240 LM a year, and the *Alta* is underpinned by the principal trombone player, Piero, whose 288 LM makes him the single highest paid of all the musicians at the court. The singers' low salaries were increased by benefices, and by the late 1480s Ercole was able to assign these himself, to at least twenty singers. But even with supplementary payments for housing in Ferrara, for special travel when required, and additional seasonal gifts, it remains clear that Ercole could maintain this cadre of specialists at relatively moderate salaries, and that the large size of his chapel did not signify heavy financial burdens through salaries. Despite continuing competition with rivals, the assurance Ercole could give of security, of benefices, and of gifts, probably meant more to singers than salary, and enabled him to hold the chapel intact. Since it appears, from some fragmentary evidence at least, that Ercole was much in debt, especially to the Florentine banking family of the Gondi, the chances are that his extensive recruitment of musicians, on largely modest salaries augmented by benefices, represented a highly economical cultural investment at minimum cost.

18

Benefices

A principal instrument of patronage was the church benefice, and one of the most important and enduring of Ercole's strategies for securing musicians was his endeavor to obtain a Papal Indult that would give him the right to confer benefices on his singers within his own dominions. Singers were certainly not the only members of the court establishment eligible to hold benefices, but, as many of them were unmarried and held minor clerical status, they were peculiarly eligible for this means of support. The surviving documentation on Ercole's singers and their benefices is immense, and only a partial account can be given here, with references to many unpublished documents (see Appendix IV). But one can show that, over the years, Ercole's realization of his ambitious plans to create a chapel of European stature was bound up closely with his single-minded and fanatical pursuit of control over the dispensing of benefices to his singers. Since this placed him in perpetual confrontation with the papal bureaucracy, it became a major topic in his diplomatic dealings with the papacy over more than thirty years of his rule.

Let us begin by tracing the first steps that he took to procure benefices for his singers. We saw earlier that in 1473 he had sent a supplication to Rome, through his ambassador, for a benefice on behalf of one of his *cappellani*, fra Pietro Cariom.[1] But this remained an isolated case and throughout the 1470s he obtained only a handful of small local benefices for several singers. The business of conferring benefices in Ferrarese lands was in any case complicated by the inexact correlation between the political boundaries of the state and those of the diocesan and other ecclesiastical jurisdictions that governed its parishes, churches, and other religious institutions. Within the city itself, there were numerous churches whose chapels and canonries carried incomes of some substance. These included some of the endowed chapels and mansionary posts in the Duomo, and extended to the lesser churches in the various quarters of the city. The same mixture of chapel and peripheral posts was to be found in the other major cities, Modena and Reggio.[2] The countryside and its larger and smaller villages were dotted with minor parish churches whose lands produced annual incomes of some size; possession of any of these, especially if residence was not required, could add significantly

---

[1] ASM, Amb. Roma, B. 1, letter of B. Arlotti, Rome, 15 June 1473, to Ercole I d'Este.
[2] On the political and ecclesiastical situation see especially Prosperi, 'Le istituzioni ecclesiastiche e le idee religiose'.

to the modest salary of a chapel singer or other court functionary. Ferrara was then the seat of a bishop, but so were Modena and Reggio. Frequently, a parish or church in a border area was open to the conflicting claims of two ecclesiastical authorities.

To bring the situation within his control in early years, Ercole began in 1476 by issuing a *grida*, or proclamation, which declared that appointments to benefices in his own dominions were in his power, and which threatened fines to anyone who laid claim to a benefice without his permission.[3] But making proclamations was not the same as being able to confer a benefice, since most of these, even in rural parishes, were actually controlled on a grand scale by the papal bureaucracy that was set up to manage the process and to reap profits from it. As the reigning Pope throughout the later 1470s, Sixtus IV, was hostile to Ercole, it is not surprising that only minor local benefices were awarded.[4] Thanks to notarial material discovered by Adriano Franceschini, we find that a number of these were awarded to singers from 1476 to 1484, the year of the death of Sixtus. All of these are listed in Appendix IV.

The election of Innocent VIII opened up new opportunities, which Ercole sought to exploit as soon as the war with Venice ended in the summer of 1484. By November he had begun, through his Roman ambassador, to try to persuade the new Pope to give him an Indult that would allow him to distribute his own benefices to his singers. At first the Pope refused. He countered by offering Ercole only vague promises to respect his requests for appointments whenever benefices might fall vacant in his lands. The Duke's ambassador, Christoforo de' Bianchi, wrote to Ercole on 13 November 1484:

Then I asked His Holiness if he would agree to having Your Excellency distribute benefices to your singers, as I had already asked His Holiness on an earlier occasion the reason why he was of this opinion, and he said to me: 'Rather, Messer Christoforo, write to His Lordship the Duke and tell him to have a little patience until these acts of obedience have been given and our affairs are somewhat better settled, and then we will do it. I know that it annoys His Lordship in this and in larger matters; so when there may be some benefice vacant in his state let him write to us, and we will do all we can to serve him.[5]

This letter was soon followed by two more, of 26 and 29 November 1484, in which Bianchi assured Ercole that he was working on Innocent to grant this concession, but without hope of immediate success. Instructive too is his reference to an Indult that had been given earlier by Sixtus IV to 'His Majesty the King', which can only, in the Italian context, refer to King Ferdinand I of Naples. On 29 November Bianchi reported:

---

[3] Caleffini, fol. 86; Zambotti, p. 26.
[4] For a very brief overview on church benefices and papal reservations about conferring them, see Noble, 'New Light on Josquin's Benefices', pp. 78 f; and earlier studies cited there.
[5] ASM, Amb. Roma, B. 8, letter 35/13. See Appendix II, doc. 12.

I hope today to have a copy of that Bull that was given to His Majesty the King for his singers, and on the model of that I will have a supplication drawn up in Your Excellency's name; and then I will do all in my power to obtain what you desire . . .⁶

Thanks to information kindly supplied by Professor Jeremy Noble, we can determine the nature of the Indult that Sixtus had granted to Ferdinand I of Naples, Ercole's brother-in-law. On 1 September 1479, the Pope had issued a *motu proprio* in favor of forty unnamed members of Ferdinand's chapel, reserving to each of them benefices up to the value of 100 florins. But if the former Pope had conceded this much to the King of Naples, the new Pope did not yet feel pressed to do the same for the Duke of Ferrara, and when Ercole, in November 1484, continued to present his request for an Indult, Bianchi replied as follows:

. . . I was with His Holiness to press the cause of Your Excellency regarding the singers, and I used every bit of ingenuity and diligence that I could muster. At last His Holiness replied that he wishes Your Excellency to have patience for the present, for until the acts of obedience have been made to His Holiness he does not wish to grant favors of this kind, despite a general expectation that such courtesies are often made at Christmas time . . .⁷

Innocent carefully assured the ambassador that he was aware of Ercole's long-standing friendship, his religiosity, and his recent expenses resulting from the war with Venice. As soon as his status as Pope was more fully settled, he said, he would be glad to comply with Ercole's request. Moreover, he wanted Ercole to know that he had not yet confirmed the Indult for Naples which had been drawn up only in the previous year. (This must refer to Innocent's renewal of the Neapolitan Indult of 1479.)

For the next three years Ercole patiently pursued his diplomatic campaign. Meanwhile individual cases involving particular singers and benefices were being taken up on his behalf by several of his emissaries, chiefly his resident *oratore*, Bonfrancesco Arlotti, Bishop of Reggio. Late in 1485 and through half of 1486 the emissaries handled the complex case of Johannes Martini regarding the parish church of Rivalta in the Ferrarese *contado*, and early in 1487, as we saw earlier, Martini went south to Rome to settle the matter for himself.⁸ In 1486 and 1487 a similar problem came up concerning don Bartolomeo de l'Organo, who wished to renounce a benefice at the parish church of Santa Maria Maddalena oltra Po in favor of Jachetto de Marvilla. Similar problems affected the granting of a minor benefice to the court singer Pietro Greco.⁹ Although Ercole readily encouraged trading in benefices among his singers, asking one of them to give up a certain benefice in favor of another singer, in expectation of receiving a different benefice as a reward,

---

⁶ Ibid., letter 35/16. See Appendix II, doc. 13.
⁷ Ibid., letter 35/17. See Appendix II, doc. 14.
⁸ See above, p. 170 f.
⁹ ASM, Amb. Roma, B. 5 (B. Arlotti), and B. 7.

this exchange was not always easy to carry out, owing to the bureaucratic obstacles at Rome and the sense of impropriety attached to such transactions. We learn this from an ambassadorial dispatch of 10 December 1485 regarding Ercole's attempt to have Paolo Casella, a court secretary, renounce a benefice in favor of Johannes Martini:

> . . . he [Paolo Casella] replied to me that he had already written to you in good time about this and went on to indicate that the matter is difficult, saying that . . . these renunciations always bring a certain bad reputation to those who make them, for he is [considered to be] a seller of benefices . . .[10]

The first peak in the campaign came at last in June 1487, when the Indult was finally granted. To obtain it, Ercole had been forced not only to invoke the help of his old friend Ascanio Sforza, as Papal Vice-Chancellor, but had himself gone to Rome to see the Pope in early April 1487. At first he had planned to make a pilgrimage to Compostela, but for good political reasons changed his plans and traveled to Rome instead. This change of plans, whatever other purposes it served, enabled him to leave his entire body of singers behind in Ferrara, thus shielding them from excessive exposure to the inducements of Roman patrons (including the Pope himself) and also enabling him to claim, as he did, that he had come without them because his original plan had been to carry out a religious pilgrimage to a famous shrine, and 'it did not seem fitting to me to take them along'.

> . . . and now that we are coming there with this same retinue [i.e. to Rome] it did not seem fitting to have them join me; so, in order not to cause too much expense to His Holiness and to the other Lords who will do us honor, you will see that we are bringing with us no more than three trumpeters, even though we have ten in our service. And these three are being brought along only to wake up and call the entire company when it is time to mount their horses. And thus we are coming in as modest a fashion as if we were going on our journey to Santo Jacomo . . .[11]

Although the Indult of 1487 was the chief goal of Ercole's policy on benefices for his singers, its provisions turned out to be more limited than he might have hoped. On the positive side it did grant him the right to confer two benefices, within his lands and domains, to each of twenty singers of his chapel, and the names of all twenty singers are given in the document.[12] It also permitted the Duke, on the death or resignation of any of the named singers, to nominate another in his place for the same benefice. But its other provisions consisted mainly of limitations. First, the papacy withheld from the Indult many categories of benefices over which it held direct or indirect jurisdiction. It not only excluded from the Duke's power those benefices that were reserved to the Holy See; it also excluded the principal offices in

---

[10] ASM, Amb. Roma, B. 8. See Appendix II, doc. 15.
[11] ASM, Amb. Roma, B. 7. See Appendix II, doc. 16.
[12] The original Indult is in ASM, Canc., Roma, Papi, B. 9. A brief summary is given in Appendix III, No. 1.

collegiate churches; the greater offices in the cathedral churches after the pontifical ones; the benefices belonging to the familiars of the living Cardinals (a very significant provision); and those that might fall vacant in the See of Rome. It also provided that if the income from any of the singers' benefices should exceed an annual value of twenty-four gold ducats, they would have to seek new provisions from the papal court within three months and submit all the necessary documents, including letters of supplication, or stand to lose the benefice at the end of the three-month period. In 1491 Ercole tried to obtain an amendment to the Indult, and his Roman ambassador, Giovanni Antonio Boccaccio, commented ironically on the entire document. He spelled out its various limitations with regard to collegiate churches and other particulars, and concluded:

. . . one can also say that everything will remain at the disposition of the Pope: first, the non-reserved benefices that are not conceded in this Indult, and the aforesaid dignities of benefices in the court of Rome, and also those of the familiars of the Cardinals, which, in effect, are assigned by the Pope. Judge now, My Lord, what grace is conceded to you; in my opinion it is worth little or nothing. Therefore it is necessary that you write with all haste when benefices are to become vacant, because if you get there first the Pope will certainly comply with your requests continually, as he does for the Duke of Milan and other princes . . . and this will be the best and most ample Indult that one could have. For years and years might pass and perhaps an age before this Indult could have an effect regarding any benefice . . .[13]

Six months later Boccaccio reviewed the provisions once again, and after listing the exemptions held by the papacy, he vividly puts the case to the Duke: 'See and consider, Your Excellency, what fruits you can pluck with this Indult, and what fish you can catch with it . . .'.[14]

Some evidence exists to show that Ercole sought to use the Papal Indult not only as a means of getting benefices for his current corps of singers but also as a potential bargaining tool for attracting new ones. This seems the most likely explanation for a probable discrepancy between the list of singers named in the Indult of 1487 and the roll of singers who were actually in his employ in that year. Admittedly we lack an exact list from archival sources for that year, but we can readily and confidently fill it in by comparing the full lists that are extant from both the preceding year (1486), and the following year (1488). The Indult presents the following twenty names:

Singers named in the Indult of 1487	Comments
1. Marinus de Castelucio	'Don Marino Cappellano' was in Ercole's from 1473 to at least 1499.
2. Petrus Carione de Bondeno	In Ercole's service 1481–1504.
3. Ieronimus de Ferraria	In service 1483–94.

---

[13] ASM, Amb. Roma, B. 1. See Appendix II, doc. 17.
[14] ASM, Amb. Roma, B. 9, letter of 5 January 1492.

4.	Iohannes de Locha	In service 1486–1504.
5.	Petrus de Candia Grecus	In service 1480–94.
6.	Iohannes Martinus Flamengus	In service 1471–97.
7.	Mathias Gallicus	In service 1471–1500.
8.	Iohannes Gallicus	'Johannes de Troia' (= Troyes), in service 1474–1504.
9.	Petrus de Valentia	Identity not certain.
10.	Iachet Gallus	Jachetto de Marvilla, in service 1472–1501.
11.	Ieronimus de Finis de Ferraria	In service 1472–94.
12.	Cornelius Gallus	In service 1470–1511.
13.	Bartholomeus de Valentia	In service 1484–1503.
14.	Christoforus de Mutina	In service 1485–94.
15.	Uldericus Teutonicus	'Ulderico de Constantia', in service 1472–87.
16.	Johannes Gallicus professor ordinis fratrum minorum	This singer could perhaps be identical with Fra Zoanne Francesco da Lodi, who is called 'Johannes Franciscus ordinis fratrum minorum Cantore' in a document of 4 January 1494 (ASM, ARo, B. 9) but for the fact that singer did not begin service until 1491, continuing until 1511. It is also clear that Lodi is not a French locality, so that we would have to infer that 'Gallicus' is a mistake. More likely this refers to a Franciscan friar and singer of French origin, at present unidentified.
17.	Antonius Gallus	Perhaps identical to Antonio Baneston de Cambrai, in service 1478–81; but this singer was in papal service from 1483 to 1502 (Haberl, *Bausteine*, iii).
18.	Johannes Gallicus	Identity not certain (perhaps Jean Japart, who had been in service 1477–81).
19.	Henricus de Alemania	Identity not certain. No singer named 'Enricus' or 'Enrico' is ever known to have been in Ercole's service. Accordingly, it is possible that Ercole had in mind the possibility of attracting Heinrich Isaac to his service as early as 1487. Isaac had been in Florence since at latest July of 1485, perhaps earlier (see Staehelin, *Die Messen Heinrich Isaacs*, v. ii, p. 19).
20.	Antonius de Alemania	Identity not known. Certainly not the 'Antonio de Alemania piffaro' who was in service in 1506–11.

Six of these twenty names do not correspond to those of singers who were definitely in Ercole's employ in 1486 and 1488, and although one or two of them may have been hired in 1487 and dismissed in that same year, this does not seem likely for most of them and is not certain for any of them. Perhaps

Ercole inserted the last five names on the list in the hope that he could then attract these singers to his court, or recruit singers who happened to hold such common names as 'Johannes Gallicus' and 'Antonius de Alemania'.

The papacy under Innocent VIII continued to react in a comparatively favorable manner to Ercole's strategy on benefices. In March 1492 the Duke managed to obtain a new papal letter extending and amplifying the original Indult. But Innocent died the same year, and in 1493 Ercole had to renegotiate the whole affair with the new Pope, Alexander VI, who delayed as long as possible before issuing a letter of confirmation. He finally did so on 6 March 1493, confirming the Indult of 1487; then another papal letter, of May 1493, declared an earlier revocation invalid (see fig. 13(*d*); Appendix III).

In 1503 the brief papacy of Pius III and the subsequent election of the powerful Julius II again complicated the matter considerably, as did unexpected and bitter competition for a similar Indult on the part of Ercole's son, Cardinal Ippolito, acting in his capacity as Archbishop of Milan.

Ippolito's spectacular rise to power had picked up speed since his early and famous appointment as Archbishop of Esztergom in 1486. Since his return from Hungary in 1494 and his next major appointment, as Cardinal and as Archbishop of Milan, in 1497, he had become increasingly independent of family influence. Conflict was inevitable. Ercole expected Ippolito to act on behalf of the family dynasty and of Ferrarese interests; Ippolito was vigorously seeking to extend and consolidate his personal empire. The first indications of Ippolito's campaign for his own Indult came early in 1502, just as Ercole was about to seal his alliance with Alexander VI by accepting Lucrezia Borgia as the bride of Alfonso and future Duchess of Ferrara. On 22 January 1502, Costabili wrote from Rome to say that Ippolito was writing on his own behalf to Ercole 'that . . . the Pope will give him the rights on benefices up to several thousands of ducats, in the states of the Most Christian King, in Milan.'[15] Throughout the first half of 1502 Ercole was attempting, all at once, to settle a special question about the reservation of benefices for two of his singers (frate Francesco da Lodi and don Nicolo Fiorentino); to secure a new Indult for his singers (with better provisions); and to assist Ippolito in expediting his own Indult for Milan, no doubt anticipating that any increase in family leverage in this complex market would ultimately benefit them all. But he reckoned without Ippolito's implacable style and without the ability of both the Pope and Ippolito to achieve a mutual understanding that excluded him.

By December 1502 Ercole was still hearing from Costabili that Alexander was unwilling to give him a new Indult. The reasons included absurd pretexts:

. . . now the Datary gives me to understand that this supplication was examined in the Signature and that the *referendarii* were all against it, and that his Holiness wanted

---

[15] ASM, Amb. Roma, B. 13.

to confirm this Indult only for the singers who were named in the Indult of Pope Innocent [in 1487] for whom that Indult had not yet produced any good results . . .[16]

Of course, Costabili explained patiently that 'of the singers named in the Indult of Innocent very few are now around', and that Alexander did not have to deal with the matter in this highly formal way but also could handle it under his own power – but all this brought no results.

In September 1503 Alexander was succeeded by Pius III, whose term of office lasted only a month. But in November there swept into power the new Pope, Julius II, magnificently ambitious and politically much stronger than his recent predecessors.

On 26 November 1503, the very day of Julius's consecration, he confirmed Ippolito's Indult that allowed him to confer benefices on his familiars and singers in the territory of Milan and, in part, in his other jurisdictions, while Ercole had to suffer not only the embarrassment of further delay but also that of seeing his son receive so easily the same privileges to which he had been devoting twenty years of struggle.[17] Ippolito was even in a position to challenge Ercole's jurisdiction in his own territories; for, having added to his titles that of Bishop of Ferrara, he could readily do so if he dared. Julius then played son against father by demanding in April 1504 that Ippolito as Bishop of Ferrara furnish in writing his approval of any Indult given to Ercole that would apply to benefices in Ippolito's diocese of Ferrara. When Ippolito had the temerity to refuse to put any such assurances in writing, Ercole exploded in a letter to his Roman ambassador of 8 April 1504:

M. Zoanne Luca: You write us that in pressing our case with the Cardinal Alexandrino for our Indult, His Lordship told you that the Pope was content to concede this Indult but that he wanted a letter from the Cardinal, our son, as evidence that he is content that this Indult should pass through his diocese here. Since we have asked our son for this letter, it seems that he is being difficult in furnishing it, nor have we been able to advise you about it, and we tell you that still you should try, without the letter, to do the best that you can about this Indult, obtaining it freely for all the other dioceses; and for this one of the Cardinal you can obtain agreement that it will be valid when his consent is obtained; because it might be that he would later be willing, and if you can also obtain it freely for his diocese, without his writing another letter, he will be satisfied. But you must make sure that, when the benefices that are now held by the singers and chaplains of our chapel fall vacant, we can give them to other singers of ours, even if they happened to be in the diocese of the Cardinal our son, without our having to have his permission. Attend therefore to the expediting of this Indult . . .

Postscript: Seeing the obstinacy and tenacity that our son the Cardinal uses with us

[16] Ibid. Letter of B. Costabili to Ercole I d'Este, Rome, 20 Dec. 1502: 'Ma che hora el datario me facia intendere che epsa supplicatione pure, se hera examinata in signatura, et che li referendarij li herano stati tuti contro, et che la Santita Sua voleva confirmare dicto Indulto per li cantori nominati solum ne lo Indulto de Innocentio, per liquali dicto Indulto non havesse havuto anchora effecto . . .'.

[17] Julius's confirmation of Ippolito's Indult is dated 26 November 1503 and is in ASM, Principi Esteri, Roma, Papi, B. 11. See Appendix III.

about the Indult, and since we are extremely unhappy with such inconvenient terms, we have had him notified that he should take himself out of our dominions, and go to Rome or Milan, or wherever he likes, as long as he doesn't stay in our lands . . . because it doesn't seem to us proper that we should have with us a son who is so obstinate in dealing with our wishes, and so disobedient as he is. And let him not think to put up with our displeasure, for his obstinacy, if he is absent from here; nor, if we should see him here, but also if he leaves, that we would not molest the means of income that he has in these parts. And truly we would have believed that, if we had requested him to leave this Episcopate out of love for us, not just for a minor matter like this, he ought to have complied. It has seemed advisable to let you know about all of this, so that you would hear how we see the matter, and that if you should hear about the departure of the Cardinal you will know how things stand, and how this dispute proceeds, and you can justify our position where necessary; and if you find it advisable to speak of the matter with the Pope or others, without waiting for them to talk to you about it, that is up to you.[18]

Two months later, on 12 June 1504, Julius II at last gave Ercole assurance of his own Indult once more, renewing his right to confer two benefices on each of twenty singers and presenting an up-to-date list of the singers in Ercole's chapel, with the name of 'Joschinus francigena' (= Josquin Desprez) at the top of the list.[19] Within another half year Ercole was dead. The story of the court chapel and its Indult then continued when the new Duke, Alfonso, in November 1506, secured a papal letter confirming earlier provisions for his singers, and sent to Rome a new set of twenty names, once more bringing matters up to date. But thereafter the collapse of good relations between Alfonso and Pope Julius canceled any further steps in this direction, during the rest of Alfonso's rule, down to 1534. In this period, provisions for singers were made locally or through salary and gifts, as well as through occasional individual benefices; no longer did an official Indult issued by a Pope give, or even seem to give, the rights of benefice distribution to the Duke.

Benefices and the Strategy of Recruitment; the Case of don Philippo de Primis

Whether or not the Indult of 1487 was an effective instrument by which Ercole could actually manipulate benefices for his singers, both the Indult itself and the network of benefices that he seemed to control, or was reputed to control, increased Ercole's prestige as a patron. It doubtless attracted singers to join his service. When he secured a benefice for a singer, often enough through crafty and patient negotiating, and with the awareness of the constant danger of rival claims by other patrons, it was a matter of some importance not only for the singer, financially and as regards his reputation, but also for the Duke. Thus, in 1495 Ercole commented to the Cardinal of

---

[18] ASM, Amb. Roma, B. 20, Doc. 122–III 8. See Appendix II, doc. 18.
[19] The document is in ASM, Canc., Roma, Papi, B. 11. See Appendix III.

San Pietro in Vincoli that he did not want to take a benefice away from a certain singer 'who has been in possession of it for some time', because if it were taken away from him 'it would cause great scorn and embarrassment for us, and bring shame upon us . . .'.[20] The promise of benefices was a bargaining lever in Ercole's dealings with the more famous musicians of his time, beginning with Obrecht in 1487–8 and again with Josquin Desprez in 1502–3. And whether or not he could actually deliver on his promises, few other patrons were making any efforts that were even approximately comparable. In fact, his only major Italian rival after 1476 in this matter was the Pope himself, who possessed not only similar ambitions to create an international chapel but also had the power to upset Ercole's hopes on benefice appointments.

Most of Ercole's singers tended to remain with him for years, and it would seem that to be in his service was, by the standards of the time, a desirable situation. But on one occasion in 1491, we find the illuminating exception: a singer who defected to the Papal Chapel and bitterly resisted Ercole's efforts to get him back again. This was the case with the singer Philippo de Primis, who served in the Ferrarese chapel in 1491, but who had disappeared by October of that year. On 18 October Philippo wrote to Ercole from Rome to explain what had happened. Having taken leave, he explains, to go to his home in Fano, owing to the illness of a relative, he found that this relative had died and that he was threatened with being disinherited by certain relatives of his who had occupied the house. Thereafter, he continues, he had come to Rome to pursue his rights, and while there he had accepted an offer to join the Papal Chapel, of which he was now a member.[21]

But Ercole decided to put up a struggle this time, and at once instructed his ambassador to take steps to get Philippo released and returned to Ferrara. The further correspondence is illuminating and deserves to be quoted at some length, as it demonstrates the tendency of singers to use the patronage system to their own advantage, and the patron's limitations in enforcing control. On 2 November the ambassador wrote to Ercole as follows:[22]

With regard to that don Philippo, your singer: as soon as I had seen your letter, I rode to the palace to find out all about it, and found that he had already been accepted into the Papal Chapel by the chapel master a week before I received the letter. I quickly went to see the Cardinal of Benevento, and read him your letter, and without delay he sent for the chapel master, who is the Bishop of Cortona; but not finding him, he sent me off to the Pope, with whom, within the hour, I had an audience and I read him the letter. The Pope issued orders to the Bishop of Urbino, who was present, that he require the chapel master to dismiss this singer altogether. And thus it was ordered by the aforesaid Bishop and also by the Cardinal of Benevento – who, however, said that he did not want to obey the order, saying that this was the habit of all singers – to

[20] ASM, Amb. Roma, B. 9, copy of letter sent via the French ambassador in Rome (28 February 1495).   [21] ASM, Musica e Musicisti, B. 2.
[22] ASM, Amb. Roma, B. 9. See Appendix II, doc. 19a–c.

leave their posts, with and without permission – that anyone can excuse them, as they do it every day, and that the chapel had great need, since it was short of singers, and that His Holiness had placed the blame on him. He said that if His Holiness wants it that way, then he would leave the chapel and take no more trouble about it; he was angry with His Holiness about it, not to displease Your Excellency but on behalf of the honor of the chapel. The Pope, with an angry expression, replied, 'We do not want any such miserable creature in our chapel', and quickly dismissed him.

That evening, at our audience with the Pope in our presence, and in the presence of Monsignor Ascanio, he pretended not to know anything about the dismissal . . . I replied to him, 'Holy Father, please give us back our singer.' He replied to me, 'We have chased him away in great malice.' I replied, 'But there is still need of him, Holy Father.' He replied, 'What do you want?' [I replied] 'You should facilitate his return to us, because he will be treated better than ever, and will be held in esteem by my master, and he will provide him with benefices.' This commission was given to Monsignor Ascanio, who will see to it very willingly.

On 12 November 1491 the Estense ambassador wrote again to Duke Ercole I:

That singer don Philippo has been dismissed from the Papal Chapel, and yet the Bishop of Cortona, the chapel master, is holding on to him. The other day I spoke to His Reverence the Cardinal of Benevento about it, who was astonished and disturbed to hear it, and said, 'I know that the Pope doesn't want him to remain there at all, and has issued firm orders about it in my presence, that he should not only be packed right off but that he should be chased away like a miscreant'; and at length he told me to go 'and leave the business to me', that he will not remain.

He [don Philippo] was with me a few days ago, sent by the aforesaid Bishop, in order that I should write to Your Excellency on his behalf, a proposal to which I strongly objected. I encouraged him to return, and he finally said that he would. His Reverence Monsignor Ascanio did the same thing. And then, at last, he said, most impertinently, that he would rather go to Turkey. It is a year and more ago that someone was here to enter the Papal Chapel and was not accepted then, because no place was vacant. However, he was given hope that if any place should become free, it would be given to him. The aforesaid Monsignor Ascanio told me that don Philippo is being entirely excluded from the aforesaid chapel. I know that he will come back to me to gain my favor; for now it is necessary for him to come back to me.

And finally, on 15 November, Ercole replied to Boccaccio:

We have learned with pleasure that don Philippo the singer has been dismissed by His Holiness, and that His Holiness was so complimentary and courteous to you. For this you must thank him on our behalf. And also see if you can induce this singer with fine words to return to our service, for we will be very glad to have him back and will treat him extremely well.[23]

But Philippo did not come back. He remained in the Papal Chapel for the next ten years (1492–1502), as a lesser colleague of Josquin Desprez until 1494, and alongside the ex-Ferrarese chapel singer Antonio Baneston. This time Ercole's promises, including benefices, failed to persuade.

[23] Ibid.

19

The Last Years of Ercole's Patronage
(1497–1505)

TWO themes dominate the last years of Ercole d'Este – his deep religiosity and a studied prudential calculation in his dealings with men and affairs. The religious side was stressed by Gardner, who saw in Ercole, among the Italian princes of the late fifteenth century, a model of 'sincere but ineffectual mysticism'.[1] Recently, new evidence of Ercole's preoccupation with secular court painting, secular drama, literature, town architecture and planning has led Werner Gundersheimer to a new appraisal in which Ercole's secular and religious leanings are more nearly in balance.[2] Yet there remains the quality of detachment, pessimism, and aloofness in Ercole's personal style, which, in his patronage of music as of other forms of expression, calls for at least brief comment. Difficult as it is to read motivations at a distance of four centuries, my own study of Ercole's family correspondence and the unearthing of much new evidence about his interest in music and musicians suggests a partially new line of approach.

There seems no doubt that in the last ten or twelve years of his life this ageing Duke and paterfamilias became ever more deeply preoccupied with the fate of his soul and the expression of religious belief. The death of Eleonora d'Aragona in 1493 deprived him of her strong help in civic affairs, her advice, and her shrewd management; and he seems to have retreated further into his personal interests, especially religious and artistic ones. With the maturity of Alfonso as ducal heir, he could pass on some affairs of state by the early 1490s, and give him increasing responsibilities; when Alfonso succeeded him, in 1505, he was almost thirty. The *Addizione Erculea* not only provided new houses for some of the wealthy families of the city, but it also gave an opportunity for the building of new churches or the reconstruction of existing ones. Along with church improvements went Ercole's deliberate attempt to further intensify popular devotion by importing preachers and mystics said to possess powers of revelation.

Indicative, too, is his special effort to bring Suor Lucia da Narni to the city, and his sympathy for Savonarola.[3] In summing up his views on the character

---

[1] Gardner, *Dukes and Poets*, p. ix.
[2] Gundersheimer, *Ferrara*, pp. 185 ff., esp. p. 208.
[3] For a recent appraisal of Ercole's role as religious leader, see Zarri, 'Pietà e profezia alle corti padane: le pie consigliere dei principi'.

of Alexander VI, with whom he had forged his last major political affiliation, Ercole struggled to maintain a deeply-felt line of condemnation against his awareness that political constraints had driven him to come to terms with the territorial ambitions of the Borgia papacy in order to maintain the independence of his state. A letter quoted by Gregorovius and Gardner is highly revealing of the moral and political drives that pulled Ercole, the tension of which undoubtedly influenced his tendency to vacillate, to withdraw from public view, and to attend to seemingly narrow preoccupations. Although the letter is designed to placate his French political masters, it has the ring of sincerity:

To make clear our feeling about the question about which many are asking you, whether the death of the Pope grieves us, we assure you that it does not displease us in any way. On the contrary, for the honor of God and for the universal good of Christianity, we have often wished that divine goodness and providence would send a good and exemplary pastor and that the church would be relieved of so much scandal . . . Nor could our private interests make us wish otherwise, since the honor of God and the common weal will always count most with us. But we tell you too that there never was any Pope from whom we did not have more favor and gratification than from this one, even after the alliance contracted with him. All we had was what he was obliged to give us, and hardly that; so that we did not depend on his good faith in any way. But in nothing else, whether great, middling, or small, have we been gratified by him. This we attribute in great measure to the Duke of Romagna [Cesare Borgia], who, since he could not do what he wanted with us, was never close to us, nor revealed his movements to us; nor did we communicate with him. And finally, since he inclined to the Spaniards, and saw that we were good Frenchmen, we had nothing more to hope for from him or from the Pope. Therefore we are not sorry for the death of the Pope, and expect nothing but evil from the great Lord Duke . . .[4]

Attracted to the spiritual tenacity of a Savonarola, repelled by the shameless but effective politics of Alexander, Ercole nevertheless possessed only a fraction of their taste for power. To Machiavelli he remained a distant and steady figure who ruled well by virtue of his membership in a long unbroken dynasty, not by the exercise of that decisive pure will, untainted by moral scruples, for which Machiavelli's model was the same Prince of Romagna whom Ercole feared and whom he had to accept as his relative in order to restrain him.

Between the years 1490 and 1493, just before Eleonora's death, Ercole rapidly married off three of his children to important allies; Isabella to the Gonzagas and both Beatrice and Alfonso to Sforzas. In 1493 Ippolito became Cardinal. Yet by 1497 three women of the family had died: his wife Eleonora, his daughter Beatrice, and his daughter-in-law Anna Sforza. The year 1493 is also that of the cartoons drawn by the great court painter,

---

[4] Extract from letter of Duke Ercole I d'Este to G. G. Seregni, Ferrarese ambassador in Milan, 24 August 1503, ASM, Amb. Milano, B. 18. The original text is also in Gregorovius, *Lucrezia Borgia*, doc. 46; see also Gardner, *Dukes and Poets*, p. 433 f.

Ercole de' Roberti, which Gundersheimer has convincingly associated with the lost frescoes of the Sala di Psyche at Belriguardo.[5] To the 1490s, too, belongs the completion of the *Addizione Erculea* and of its greater buildings, especially the Palazzo dei Diamanti. Annual ceremonies and public diversions continued as before, with performances of classical plays in 1493, 1499, and also in 1502 for the wedding of Alfonso and Lucrezia. Amid these events, scarcely touched by any serious threat of disruption by war despite the French invasion, thanks to Ercole's steadfast role as a French ally, the court in the 1490s and the first years of the sixteenth century slowly shifted in cultural tone and perspective as the children of the dynasty matured. They separated into factions – on one side, the dominating sons, Alfonso and the implacable Ippolito; on the other, the weak and virtually ignored Ferrante, the profligate Sigismondo, and the bastard, don Julio. On the female side, the death of Beatrice in 1497 cut off an important Este influence at Milan, but Isabella was more than making up for that at Mantua, while she also kept a very sharp and cool eye on events at Ferrara. With the arrival of Lucrezia Borgia in 1502, still other cultural tides began to advance at the court. Lucrezia brought a Roman and Spanish entourage; there also appeared the new literary developments headed by Pietro Bembo and Ercole Strozzi, of which she was the apparent focus. We can also follow in this period the early maturity of the young Ariosto, who served Ercole in the late 1490s, perhaps as an actor as well as in other roles, but who saw in the old Duke little more than a stingy patron. If Ercole's attitude was felt as neglect of local talent in favor of foreign visitors and residents, when it came to musicians Ariosto's envy was at least seemingly justified, to judge from the size of the chapel and the importance of its singers to Ercole and his daily life.

Even if the Ferrarese people were taught to believe that they, like their princes, were true French allies, the French invasions of 1494–5 brought prophecies of doom and calamity. Boiardo's famous closing lines of his *Orlando innamorato* reflect the general feeling:

> Mentre che io canto, O dio Redentore,
> Vedo l'Italia tutta a fiamma e foco
> Per questi Galli . . .

But amid the continued political turmoil that followed the battle of Fornovo and the constant renewed threat of French invasions, Ercole by 1496 had reverted to his role of staunch defender of the faith and Christian prince, for whom 'the honor of God and the common weal will always count most . . .'. After a visiting preacher had told that the Blessed Virgin had appeared to the Pope presaging calamity, Ercole joined the populace in fasting and praying (putting aside any lingering doubt that Alexander VI was worthy of such a visitation). And in the same year, at Christmas time, he typically gave gifts to nine churches of the city to improve their means of observance. Most

---

[5] Gundersheimer, *Ferrara*, pp. 258–62; also his article, 'The Patronage of Ercole I d'Este'.

characteristically, he saw to the local publication of his religious booklet in honor of the Virgin, the *Corona Beatae Mariae Virginis*, issued by the Ferrarese printer Laurentius de Rubeus. Like his chapel itself, it followed northern European models in title and character; the *Corona* was also a perfect expression of Ercole's fervor.[6] It consists of a set of prayers based on the seven words of the imploration, 'Ave mater dei, ora eum pro me'. Thus, the first prayer, taking the word 'Ave', is the *Ave maris stella*; and the rest follow similarly. The great importance of this collection is shown by a letter from Bernardo Prosperi to Isabella d'Este Gonzaga, on 26 December 1496.[7]

El Signore ha facto cantare la sua Corona sabato passato a madona de Corte, et mentre che li Cantori la Cantorono cum l'Organo sua Signoria stete in mezo cum epsi In pedi nanti al Lenzalo. Et cussi intendo che ogni Sabato se haverà a Cantare a quella madonna. Credo che Vostra Signoria l'habii per che La Excellentia Sua ne mandete parecchie a questi di a Madona mia; se no piacendogli darme adviso ch'io ge no remetterò una per che sono facte a stampa . . .

My Lord had his *Corona* sung last Saturday at Santa Maria de Corte, and while the singers were singing it with organ, His Lordship stood among them on foot before the altar-cloth. And thus I understand that he plans to sing these prayers every Saturday at the chapel. I believe that Your Lordship has a copy because he has sent several to my Ladyship; if not, may it please you to let me know and I will send one, as they are printed . . .

Thus Ercole's daily observance was augmented through a special Saturday office for the Virgin Mary, for which he selected at least some of the prayers. This probably implied an expansion of the more traditional forms of sacred polyphony practiced in the court chapel – polyphonic Mass and Vespers settings – to include, in the 1490s, a larger number of antiphons and motets, especially settings of votive antiphons for the Virgin, such as the 'Ecce ancilla Domini'. In fact this text is prominent in the *Corona* collection, and not only were there well-known and fairly recent settings of Masses on the antiphon by Dufay and Ockeghem, but Ockeghem's Mass 'Ecce ancilla Domini' was copied into a Ferrarese Mass collection only a few years later.[8]

Throughout the 1490s and down to 1504, his last year in office, Ercole continued to build up the prestige and quality of his musical forces. His *cappella* was one of the largest of its time, ranking with the Papal Chapel or any European court. From 1491 to 1504 there were never less than nineteen or twenty singers in the chapel, and in some years there were almost thirty. In 1499 twenty-nine regular singers were on the roster for most of the year, and

[6] On the *Corona* print see Thurston and Bühler, *A Check List of Fifteenth-Century Printing in the Pierpont Morgan Library*, pp. 90 f. and No. 1038, which also cites other bibliographical references and descriptions. The Morgan Library copy is probably from the second edition, of 1497.   [7] ASMN, AG, B. 1234.

[8] Modena, BE, MS Alpha M. 1. 2.

in November six more were brought in, of whom five were non-Italians. In 1503 there were again twenty-nine singers; in 1504, thirty-one singers and three organists. After Ercole, Alfonso at first maintained similar numbers, but after the collapse of the chapel in 1510, he reconstituted it in 1512 with six, and kept thereafter an average of six to eight musicians on a permanent basis. So far as surviving records make it possible to be sure, other court chapels were not then generally on this scale. As Frank D'Accone states in a recent study, we know little or nothing of the exact size of the Milanese and Neapolitan court chapels in this period; and even the size of the company at St. Mark's in Venice is only partially certain after the early 1490s, when it had fifteen adult singers and twelve boys.[9] The Papal Chapel maintained only sixteen to twenty-one singers in the first decade of the sixteenth century and rose to thirty-one for the first time in 1521; the French Royal Chapel had twenty-three singers in 1515, on the occasion of the funeral services for Louis XII. Clearly, then, Ercole's musical forces were much larger than was normal for court establishments of comparable size.

With increasing numbers came greater internationalization, which went along with the growing expansion of Ferrarese diplomatic contacts in these years. In the 1470s Milan had been the main rival and source of musicians; in the later 1480s and thereafter, Ercole turned to Florence as a hunting ground, and also of course to Rome, which offered a swarm of patrons and informers who could help recruit musicians for his service. In the 1490s he began to import music increasingly from France, thus gaining continued access to the work of the most famous composers of the time. When the death of Johannes Martini brought a major opening in his chapel in 1498, he responded favorably to the idea of recruiting from the ranks of these masters themselves. After Charles VIII invaded Italy, Ercole's son Ferrante came down in his entourage, and on 7 October 1494 Ferrante wrote from Casale Monferrato, where Charles was encamped, to send a Mass to Ercole and to describe his efforts to get new music from Loyset Compère, who was also with the King's retinue. This letter is the first known evidence of Compère's return to Italy after his sojourn in Milan in the 1470s.[10]

The growing rivalry of Alfonso, Ippolito, and Isabella as patrons in the 1490s intensified the role of music in court politics. Agents emerged who were skilled in using the musical interests of the young patrons as levers for personal advancement, and it is hardly surprising that the two principal agents of this time were themselves musicians. Both were important for the recruitment of Josquin Desprez, and both cut important figures at the court: they were Gian de Artiganova, a court singer; and Girolamo da Sestola, alias 'il Coglia', a court agent of many talents.

In 1491 Gian Guascon, or Gian de Artiganova, appears for the first time in

[9] D'Accone, 'The Performance of Sacred Music', p. 606.
[10] For the original text of the letter see my 'Music at Ferrara', 129 f.

the *Bolletta de' Salariati* as a young male soprano.[11] In the course of a decade
this talented and venal figure became a confidant of the young Alfonso, and
also an agent available to other family members, especially Ippolito. At Milan
in 1498, Ippolito requested that Gian obtain some music from the ducal
library for his use. Gian replied to ask Ippolito to forgive him for having been
unable to do so, since Duke Ercole had explicitly forbidden any music of the
court to be sent out of the city; still, Gian had won the Duke's permission to
send Ippolito a single motet.[12] In 1500 Gian began to be called 'Gian Cantore
dito Chamerlengo', ('called the chamberlain') and by 1502 he was sent by
Ercole to obtain singers covertly from the court of Savoy. There, Gian was
caught and put into prison, and Ercole had to send a messenger to get him
out. On returning to Ferrara, he then began to play a sizeable role in the
negotiations that would lead to the recruitment of Josquin, and he is in fact
the author of the famous letter on Josquin and Isaac (cf. pp. 204 ff. below).
By 1506, however, it became clear that Gian had overplayed his hand, and
had fallen in with the disgruntled Estense brothers Ferrante and don Julio,
whose attempted *coup d'état* against Alfonso and Ippolito in that year
resulted in lifelong imprisonment for them and in the execution of Gian after
brutal torture.[13]

His principal rival and counterpart, Girolamo da Sestola, was more austere
and luckier. Known by the scurrilous nickname 'il Coglia', or simply 'Coglia',
as we will call him, this remarkable person was a man of many roles:
courtier, horseman, dancer, musician, spy, newsmonger, and emissary.[14]
Coming to Ferrara from the little town of Sestola in the Modenese
Appenines, in 1488 Coglia was an organist at San Paolo in Ferrara.[15] But he
quickly applied his talents at the court. As early as 1491, he was sent to
Isabella at Mantua as a music instructor, ostensibly to improve her keyboard
prowess, but perhaps as an agent for her as well. He undertook trips to
Flanders for Ercole, bringing back horses, tapestries, music, and musicians. In
1498 he and Gian together returned with a bundle of Masses for Ercole –
'about twenty of them', as he promised in a dispatch.[16] Similar journeys
continued over the years. Prior to 1505 Coglia worked at various times as
private agent for Duke Ercole, for Ippolito, and for Alfonso, and doubtless as
an informer for Isabella as well. As a dancer, he planned the 'maschere dele
torze', the torch-ballet, that was staged in 1502 at the wedding festivities;
and he continued to plan and execute the *intermedi* that were inserted
between the acts of the Ferrarese comedies, above all in 1508 for the first
performance of *La cassaria*, the early masterpiece by his good friend Ariosto.

[11] For a summary of the documentation on Gian see my 'Josquin at Ferrara', p. 111 and n. 28.
[12] ASM, Musica e Musicisti, B. 1.
[13] See Bacchelli, *La congiura di don Giulio D'Este, passim.*
[14] For a general picture of Coglia see my 'Josquin at Ferrara', pp. 110 f.
[15] Ferrara, Archivio Capitolare, Archivio di San Paolo de Ferrara, Mazzo 7 (1488), fol. 32:
'Gerolamo da Sestola fu Conduto a sonare l'organo nostro de sanpollo . . .' (1 June 1488).
[16] ASM, Amb. Germania, B. 1 (letter of 27 June 1498, from Antwerp).

(It is, in fact, from a letter of Coglia to Isabella, dated 7 July 1533, that we know with certainty the date of death of Ariosto.)[17] For the development of the chapel, however, Coglia's truly signal contribution was his direct aid in recruitment of Josquin Desprez.

Josquin Desprez at Ferrara (1503–4)

The enlargement of the singing forces in 1499 may reflect Ercole's hopes of finding a new leader to succeed Martini. And the increasing interest of Ippolito in forming his own base for musical patronage, now that he had attained the Archbishopric of Milan (1497), gave Ercole an additional reason to keep up the hunt energetically. Accordingly, in November 1499, while visiting King Louis XII in Milan, Ercole unsuccessfully tried to recruit Gaspar Weerbecke, long in Milanese service.[18] In 1501, his ambassador in France, the aged Bartolomeo de' Cavalieri, began to send music collected in France by Verbonnet for Ercole's use. Verbonnet had been in Ferrarese service in 1492 and had subsequently shifted his allegiance to Isabella, but continued to look out for Ercole's interests as well. On 21 July and 25 September 1501 Cavalieri sent music that had been given to him by Verbonnet, and on 13 December Cavalieri makes the remarkable statement that, while in Blois, he has met 'a singer named Josquin, whom Your Excellency had sent to Flanders to find singers.'[19] Although this implies that Josquin was already in ducal service by 1501, I can find no record of such service; further, it is curious that Cavalieri should speak here of 'a singer named Josquin', as if he had not heard the name before, even though three months earlier he had written 'Verbonnet is sending a new work which he says is by Josquin', showing that he had known the name before. Perhaps Josquin's apparent commission to look for singers for Ercole was made through another singer, conceivably Verbonnet himself. Or perhaps Cavalieri was mistaken in his recollection that the singer whom he met in Blois was Josquin himself. At all events, this is the earliest record of 1501 that indicates a personal connection between Josquin and Ercole; yet if my theory of Josquin's earlier stay in Ferrara is correct, they were now renewing a personal relationship that had been established as early as the 1470s, and that had already been fruitful during Ascanio Sforza's residence in 1480–1. At all events, the indications are that in 1501 and 1502, just before his acceptance of Ercole's offer to come to Ferrara, Josquin was in France; where, we do not know.

In May 1502 Alfonso had made a diplomatic journey to France, to visit Louis XII and probably to reassure him that his recent wedding to Lucrezia Borgia did not signal any weakening of Ferrarese allegiance.[20] His retinue

[17] Catalano, *Lodovico Ariosto*, i, p. 498.
[18] ASM, Memoriale del Soldo, 1499, fol. 45 (29 November 1499).
[19] ASM, Amb. Francia, B. 3; Osthoff, *Josquin Desprez*, i, p. 51. This section is largely drawn from my 'Josquin at Ferrara'.   [20] Zambotti, p. 339.

included the singer Girolamo Beltrandi, who had been a member of the choir of St. Peter's in 1492 at the same time that Josquin was in the Papal Chapel, and who probably knew Josquin.[21] With Alfonso too went the ubiquitous Coglia. On 30 May Coglia advised Ercole that Alfonso was about to send him to Paris. It was surely at Paris, by mingling with the French Royal Chapel, that the best chance lay of attracting a major musician to Ferrarese service, possibly of obtaining access to Josquin himself, who had some sort of connection with the French chapel.

In the meantime, by July 1502, Gian de Artiganova had gone to Savoy on his mission, and had attracted some new members to the Ferrarese court chapel. In early August, both Coglia and Gian were reporting to Ercole on the remarkable singers whom Gian had brought back from Savoy. Since the letters from Coglia to Ercole of August 1502 are a direct background to the recruitment of Josquin, we can quote them *in extenso:*[22]

> Don Alfonso . . . informs Your Lordship that Gian has arrived safe and sound, that the singers have at last arrived at Modena, and that by the grace of God they all look well, and I can only tell Your Lordship that the singers are truly perfect and Don Alfonso cannot wait for Your Lordship to come here for many reasons but all the more to hear these singers. And tell Tommaso that I want him to listen to them with fear and awe. To Your Lordship, His Lordship Don Alfonso sends his greetings and so do Il Socio and I and Gian, to whom I have said, on behalf of Your Lordship, that he is pardoned . . . [Coglia to Ercole, 4 Aug. 1502]

Three days later, on 7 August, Gian writes a letter to Ercole to tell him the same thing ('. . . I have arrived there safely and have brought with me three singers who are excellent in this art . . .'). Thus in the late summer of 1502, a rivalry sprang up between Coglia and Gian for the leading role in recruitment for the chapel, and this crystallized into a controversy over the question of recruiting Josquin or another leading musician. In 14 August 1502 Coglia once more praises the new singers and specifically recommends Josquin (cf. fig. 13(e)):

> I must tell Your Lordship that I am already in fear of being bewitched by . . . the singing of these singers, and I can hardly wait for Your Lordship's arrival, because you will derive such enjoyment and consolation from them . . . not only in the chapel but in the chamber as well, and in any use you like . . .
>
> The singer Bartolomeo [de Fiandra] requests Your Lordship's consent to give him a three months' leave to go home . . . Your Lordship is bound to let him go because he says that Your Lordship promised it to him . . .
>
> My Lord, I believe that there is neither lord nor king who will now have a better chapel than yours if Your Lordship sends for Josquin. Don Alfonso wishes to write

---

[21] That Beltrandi went with Alfonso is strongly suggested, at least, by Alfonso's letter to Ercole asking permission for him to do so (ASM, CTPE, B. 70); full text in my 'Josquin at Ferrara', p. 124 (doc. 5).

[22] These letters are in ASM, Particolari, 'Coia'. For complete transcriptions and facsimiles see 'Josquin at Ferrara', pp. 126 f., 129 f., facs. 8–10.

this to Your Lordship and so does the entire chapel; and by having Josquin in our chapel I want to place a crown upon this chapel of ours.

This letter shows that Josquin had already come up for active consideration, and that Coglia was strongly in favor of bringing him to Ferrara. He further claims that this is also the wish of Alfonso and the singers. Particularly striking is the reference to Josquin as the potential culminating figure in a chapel that is already strong, one who will raise it beyond that of any lord or king if he is brought to lead it. It must be remembered that Borso had obtained the title of 'Duke of Ferrara' in 1471, just a few months before his death, and Ercole had entered into power as the first real Duke of Ferrara. Legally, he was a vassal of the papacy and the Empire; politically, a vassal of France. The symbol of his rank was not a crown but a beret, as we see it in the famous portrait of him by Dosso Dossi (cf. fig. 7(c)). Josquin, then, is portrayed by Coglia as being metaphorically a crowning figure, and the implication is that, by hiring him, Ercole can aspire to higher status than most dukes can claim. A further implication is that the musician of great reputation can confer upon a patron the same measure of reflected glory that had traditionally been attributed to poets and painters.

The communication from Coglia also shows us for the first time how to interpret the well-known letter written by Gian. This is the letter, dated simply 2 September, the year of which has been a matter of contention for some time – indeed, ever since its first publication by Vander Straeten a century ago.[23] Thanks to new evidence, it can now be definitely assigned to the year 1502, and it fits exactly into this chain of events. It is the letter on Josquin and Isaac that contains the famous description of Isaac's recent trip to Ferrara, of his writing of a motet on the motif 'La mi la sol la mi' in only two days, and of the offer to Isaac to join the chapel. I quote its best-known passage:

To me he [Isaac] seems well suited to serve Your Lordship, more so than Josquin, because he is more good-natured and companionable, and he will compose new works more often. It is true that Josquin composes better, but he composes when he wants to, and not when one wants him to, and he is asking 200 ducats in salary while Isaac will come for 120 – but Your Lordship will decide.

There is a second part to this letter that has never been discussed since it was published by Vander Straeten, but which is crucial for fixing its date. It reads in part:

Don Alfonso has told me that Your Lordship has written to say that those two sopranos are to be dismissed. I must notify you that one is good and very suitable, and today another one named Coletta arrived from the Kingdom of Naples . . . We will try

    [23] For the original text of Gian's letters see Vander Straeten, *La Musique*, vi, p. 87, and Osthoff, *Josquin Desprez*, i, p. 211; a complete facsimile is in *Die Musik in Geschichte und Gegenwart*, vii, col. 194; see also my discussion of its date in 'Josquin at Ferrara', p. 113 f., and Staehelin, *Die Messen von Heinrich Isaac*, ii, pp. 156–9.

out this Coletta and one of the two singers mentioned before, and we beg Your Lordship to tell us what you want done. I believe news has reached Your Lordship that fra Giovanni, the soprano, is on his death-bed, and if the Lord takes him, it would be well to put one of these in his place . . .

The mortal illness of fra Giovanni and the arrival of Coletta are facts that can be exactly corroborated by other letters, written the day before and the day after the letter of Gian, which in turn is written less than three weeks after Coglia's letter in favor of Josquin.[24] So Coglia and Gian were opposed to each other. Gian was in favor of Isaac (or perhaps against Josquin), Coglia was in favor of Josquin. Within several more months it must have become clear that Josquin's services could be obtained, and the stage was set for Coglia himself to bring Josquin from Paris to Ferrara in April 1503.

In mid-April 1503 Josquin was established as 'maestro de cappella'. His entire tenure at Ferrara lasted from the end of April 1503 to April 1504, about a calendar year. His name was set at the head of the other singers in the payment registers, and if one examines the monthly payments made to him and the annual tabulations of payments, it becomes clear that his total salary was 200 ducats a year.[25] This is exactly the figure mentioned by Gian in his famous letter of the previous September; from this we see that Gian was well informed on Josquin's terms as well as on his character. Perhaps he had found out these things in Savoy.

Osthoff published the valuable list of benefices held by the court singers that is dated 17 October 1503; curiously, the list contains no benefices next to Josquin's name.[26] But even if Josquin had received no benefices, he left Ferrara in April of 1504 as the highest paid singer in the history of its chapel.

The evidence of his activity at Ferrara is limited, and comes largely from outside sources. No family correspondence between the Duke and his children mentions him. But we can be quite sure that word of his arrival at Ferrara spread quickly. In February 1504 the ducal ambassador in Venice sent a work to Ferrara by an unnamed composer 'to have it looked over by that singer of yours named messer Josquino, the most excellent composer, to

---

[24] The other letters are those of 1 September 1502 (Alfonso to Ercole) published in 'Josquin at Ferrara', p. 126 (doc. 10); and that of 3 September 1502 (Ferrante to Ercole) on Coletta soprano; its source is ASM, CTPE, B. 134.

[25] On Josquin Desprez's salary payments at Ferrara see 'Josquin at Ferrara', p. 137 (Table III).

[26] The Mantuan ambassador, Giacomo d'Adria, told Isabella on 12 April 1503 that Josquin had been promised benefices as well as other inducements to come to Ferrara; see Osthoff, *Josquin Desprez*, i, p. 53, as well as Vander Straeten, *La Musique*, viii, p. 527, and Davari 'La musica a Mantova'. There is no sign that Ercole tried to procure any benefices for him, though he names him in a list clearly intended to review the available benefices for his singers (Osthoff, i, pp. 212–215). Perhaps Josquin was unwilling to accept a benefice in northern Italy at this time if he was already contemplating the possibility of a provostship in his native city of Condé, which in fact he received as early as May 1504. On his benefices in general see Noble, 'New Light on Josquin's Benefices'; on the document showing for the first time that he was provost at Condé directly after leaving Ferrara, see Kellman, 'Josquin and the Courts of the Netherlands and France', p. 207.

see if it is praiseworthy'.[27] Three months later, the same ambassador sent more music, this time identifying the composer as a twenty-year-old Dominican friar named 'fra Iordano de Venezia'. This is none other than Giordano Paseto, who in 1520 became chapel master at the cathedral of Padua, and who is the scribe and compiler of the important motet manuscript A 17 of the Capitular Library in Padua, written in 1522.[28]

These letters from Venice support the inference that strong musical links existed between Ferrara and Venice at this period, the more so as Venice became increasingly the vital center of music printing. Josquin's stay at Ferrara falls just between Petrucci's publications of his first and second books of Masses, and it coincides with a period of increasing expansion and rapidity of output of new music from Petrucci's shop. It is at least a possibility that, during Josquin's residence in Ferrara, new music by him and new copies of older works may have come into Petrucci's hands more easily than in preceding years. And Ferrara may well have been an important source for Petrucci in other prints as well.[29] The Duke's preference for sacred music contrasted strongly with that of Alfonso and Ippolito for secular music and for the exchange of poetry, music, and musicians with Mantua. The sparse documentation suggests that Josquin furnished principally Masses and motets. The Duke was still receiving Mass settings from his agents abroad, including a Mass promised him by Louis XII and given his ambassador by Prioris, then master of the King's chapel. A copyist at Ferrara was paid for the copying of a Mass by Josquin in August 1504; unfortunately, the Mass is not named. In the years 1503 and 1504 sacred dramas were lavishly mounted. On 28 March 1504, for example, a representation of the life of St. Joseph was staged, which a chronicler describes as follows:

It was performed in the cathedral on great platforms, with scenery painted to depict castles; and on the roof of the cathedral, before the great altar, was constructed a heaven that opened and disclosed the glory of Paradise; and one saw and heard angels playing and singing various melodies, and these were the singers and players of our Duke . . .[30]

We may wonder whether Josquin was among the singers, or if the music performed could have been his, a point on which we can only speculate at present. Outside evidence enables us to attribute two motets to the Ferrarese period with considerable confidence: 'Miserere mei, Deus' and 'Virgo salutiferi'. Folengo tells us that the 'Miserere' was written at the express request of the Duke of Ferrara; this is further corroborated by an

[27] ASM, Amb. Venezia, B. 11; text in my 'Josquin at Ferrara', p. 134 (doc. 23).

[28] See, on this MS, Rubsamen, 'Music Research in Italian Libraries', 80–6.

[29] A possible link between Ferrara and Petrucci may be sought, first of all, in the Venetian patrician Girolamo Donati, whom Petrucci names in the preface to the *Odhecaton* as one of his patrons. Donati for many years was the Venetian *Visdomino*, residing in Ferrara. Of course, many other conduits also existed between Ferrarese musicians and musical life in Venice, for in Venice the Ferraresi bought such items as harpsichord strings; after 1501, of course, printed music as well.   [30] Zambotti, p. 357.

added sixth part written by the famous singer Bidon, who was among the singers Gian brought from Savoy and was a member of the chapel at Ferrara under Josquin.[31] Another work assignable to this stay is the five-voice 'Virgo salutiferi'. This text, until a few years ago, had been known only from a late sixteenth-century anthology of metric prayers, but Edward Lowinsky found that it is by the Ferrarese court poet Ercole Strozzi, and was published in 1513.[32] Ercole Strozzi was active at Ferrara both as literary man and as administrator during the whole year of Josquin's residence. Some scholars have assigned the 'Hercules' Mass to this period as well; even though it was probably composed much earlier, about 1480 or 1481, there is no doubt that when it was published by Petrucci in 1505, the very year of Ercole's death, it was seen publicly as a tribute by a great composer to a famous patron.

Josquin's departure from Ferrara could have been a purely prudent gesture. Chroniclers and letter writers tell us that in July 1503 plague broke out at Ferrara and lasted throughout the summer and autumn. By September, Ercole and his entire court were ensconced at Comacchio, on the coast; two-thirds of the citizens of Ferrara had fled the city, where many lay dying. Correspondence about the plague between Ercole Strozzi and the Duke was carried on until January 1504. After Josquin's departure, his place was taken by Obrecht, who in turn fell victim to the plague early in 1505. Josquin departed for Condé, his birthplace in northern France, where he was apparently to spend the last seventeen years of his life.[33]

Jacob Obrecht (1504–5)

The Duke liked being on good terms with famous composers: Isaac, Josquin, Obrecht lead the list. With Josquin's departure, he might have sought once again to obtain Isaac, from Florence, although he had passed him over in favor of Josquin in 1503. But instead he turned again to Obrecht, whose music he had been collecting since the early 1480s. We remember that he had brought Obrecht down from Bruges in 1487 by sending his own emissary, Cornelio, to the cathedral of St. Donatian; and he had then sought major benefices for him from Pope Innocent VIII. But Obrecht had returned to the north when the benefice strategy failed, and had held positions in Bergen op Zoom, Bruges, and Antwerp, restlessly moving between these familiar centers and maintaining a beneficial post at Antwerp all the while. In the years 1500–3 Obrecht was listed as holding a chaplaincy at Notre Dame, Antwerp, unpaid at first, since he was evidently absent. He may have come from Antwerp to Ferrara in late summer of 1504; this hypothesis would fit well

[31] On the 'Miserere' see my 'Josquin at Ferrara', p. 117; Osthoff, *Josquin Desprez*, ii, pp. 119 ff.; and below, pp. 261–5.
[32] 'Virgo salutiferi' in *Werken, Motetten*, Bundel vii, no. 35. Cf. Lowinsky, *The Medici Codex*, iii, esp. pp. 194 ff.
[33] Documents on Josquin's arrival in Condé and on other aspects of his last years were presented by Kellman, 'Josquin and the Courts', pp. 207–9.

with Alfonso's trip to the Low Countries in August, which extended also to England and France, before news of Ercole's illness brought him rushing back to Ferrara to protect his title and inheritance.[34] At all events, we find 'meser Ubreto' *compositore* listed at the head of the chapel roster, beginning in September 1504 and continuing until early in 1505. The last record of Obrecht in the payment records is dated 12 February; it shows the payment of a small debt of his to the Ferrarese bankers Jacomo and Baldissera Machiavelli. This falls exactly one week after the funeral services for Ercole himself, on 5 February, at which the singers had performed a Mass *in canto figurato*, an appropriate tribute to their master and protector over the years. Since the five months of Obrecht's tenure coincide with Ercole's own decline and death, we can hardly be surprised to find no references to him in the little surviving ducal correspondence of these months. It is probably to these months, however, that we can properly assign the compilation of the manuscript Alpha M. 1.2 of the Biblioteca Estense, which commemorates especially Obrecht but also Josquin, and Ercole as the patron of both. It contains, in order, six Masses by Obrecht, then two by Josquin, another by Obrecht, and finally the Mass by Ockeghem on 'Ecce ancilla Domini', the antiphon that figured prominently in Ercole's printed *Corona* of 1496. Furthermore, the two Josquin Masses are deliberately selected so as to make the most of comparison with those of Obrecht; the sequence, in the later part of the MS, is:

Obrecht	*Missa 'Fortuna desperata'*
Josquin	*Missa 'Fortuna desperata'*
Josquin	*Missa 'L'homme armé super voces musicales'*
Obrecht	*Missa 'L'homme armé'*
Ockeghem	*Missa 'Ecce ancilla Domini'*

Not only are we sure that in August 1504, after Josquin's departure, his Masses were still being copied at Ferrara, but further records of music copying from October show us more copying of Masses.[35]

   For whatever reasons, Alfonso, on succeeding Ercole in February 1505, did not keep Obrecht on as his chief musician, but let him go and chose to make a new appointment, eventually filled by Antoine Brumel a year later. Perhaps the wave of new secular music was rising too rapidly in Ferrara, and Mantua, with Alfonso, Ippolito, and Isabella as patrons, to suit Obrecht's primary role as a composer of Masses and motets. Although Obrecht wrote some secular music, none of it is written to Italian texts, and he was probably not very interested in the lighter vein of the frottola, then greatly cultivated in both Ferrara and Mantua. Perhaps other personal factors were involved as well. We do know that Obrecht died of plague in Ferrara sometime before 30 August

[34] Richard Sherr has found documents of the Papal Chapel, as yet unpublished, which show that Obrecht was under consideration in the reign of Julius II for possible membership in the chapel. Sherr assigns this to the period between November 1503 and September 1504.
[35] On the copying of Masses in Ferrara in October 1504 see ASM, LASP, Alfonso I, fol. 43ᵛ (9 October and 31 October).

1505; this is clear from a later document concerning his will and belongings. But from another, heretofore unpublished letter concerning Obrecht, dating from early May 1505, we can also be sure that Obrecht's departure from official chapel service in late January or early February had not come about through a total decline in his powers as a musician; and it also reveals the surprising fact that in May, three months after the last known reference to him in Ferrara, he was in Mantua, seeking an appointment under Francesco and Isabella Gonzaga. The new letter, presently the last dated document on Obrecht that is known, is a note of recommendation for him written by Ferrante d'Este to Marquis Francesco Gonzaga:[36]

Illustrissimo signor observandissimo: Messer Hobreth maestro già de la capella del signor mio padre bone memorie presente exhibitore vene alla excellentia vostra per presentarli alcune sue compositione quale benche sij de tale virtù singolare che sempre presso lei è, per esser racolto humanamente, come è suo costume et naturale verso ogni persona virtuosa: Nondimeno havendomi recerchato chio lo voglii con queste mie indriciare alla Excellentia vostra per essere persona che ultra la virtù per le optime sue conditione amo sumamente: Mi è parso a satisfactione sua dargline questo poco de noticia et recomandarlo alla excellentia vostra, alla quale io insieme me recommando: Que bene valeat: Ferrarie ij° Maij MDV
De Vostra Illustrissima
Servitor
Ferrante da Est

Most Illustrious and Honored Lord: Messer Obrecht, formerly master of the chapel of my late father, of blessed memory, the present bearer, is coming to Your Excellency to give you certain of his compositions. Even though he is possessed of such singular virtue that is always to be received warmly by you, as is your custom and habit towards every person of virtue, nevertheless, having requested of me that I might with these lines address myself to Your Excellency, as being a person whom I greatly love, beyond his merits, for his excellent character – it has seemed to me proper for his sake to give you this small notice of him and recommend him to Your Excellency, to whom I also commend myself; Farewell: Ferrara, 2 May 1505
Your Most Illustrious Lordship's
Servant
Ferrante d'Este

That the letter is written by Ferrante d'Este is very striking. Just at this time Ferrante was beginning to devise his plot against Alfonso and Ippolito, together with his equally disgruntled brother, don Julio, and aided by Gian de Artiganova. No doubt Obrecht had made a good impression on Ferrante, who knew music and musicians well, as we have seen from his correspondence with Ercole in 1502 and even earlier (1494, on Compère). And we may speculate as to whether Obrecht's removal from his post by Alfonso could have driven him for protection and support into the faction dominated by Ferrante;

---

[36] Letter of Ferrante d'Este, Ferrara, 2 May 1505, to Marquis Francesco Gonzaga; in ASMN, AG, B. 1189.

if so, we may imagine that Coglia, the Josquin supporter, and staunch defender of the Duke and Cardinal, remained aloof. At all events, Obrecht did not receive a position at Mantua, which remained without a *cappella de' cantori* altogether until the opportunities of 1510 gave Francesco a chance to build one, because of Alfonso's political misfortunes.

PART THREE

FERRARESE MUSICAL REPERTOIRES
AND STYLES IN THE LATE
FIFTEENTH CENTURY

⟨∿⟩

20

The Production of Music Manuscripts
under Ercole I

LONG before Ercole's ascent to power in 1471, Ferrara was an established center for the production of manuscripts.[1] Local workshops under Leonello had stressed the classics and humanistic subjects, and under Borso had shifted their focus to magnificent illuminated books, to translations, and to vernacular literature. Under Ercole they broadened still further. Following Leonello's model were handsomely illuminated MSS of classical and modern authors, on which abundant documentation was supplied by Bertoni and other scholars. Emulating the Borso Bible, Ercole ordered at least four splendidly illuminated Breviaries for his personal use. He also commissioned a series of magnificent choirbooks for the cathedral of Ferrara, thus matching Borso's well-known series for the Certosa. New directions under Ercole are visible in the manuscripts dealing with military narratives and chivalric tales, just as we should expect in the time of Boiardo and the young Ariosto; also in moral tracts and religious volumes. The growth of manuscript production also reflects the expanded interests of the court and its younger members – the restless, striving, younger Estensi and their new outlook on their times – and beyond this diversity, outside commissions were also accepted, to keep the scribes busy when local orders for new books fell off. Although printing in Ferrara was very limited, still there were a few sporadic printing ventures over these years.[2] But it was essentially as a focal point of scribal traditions that the

---

[1] Apart from studies of individual illuminators and a few special studies of scribes and individual MSS, the only broad accounts of Ferrarese manuscripts of the period are those of Hermann, 'Zur Geschichte der Miniaturmalerei', which includes a massive number of documents; also Bertoni, *La Biblioteca Estense*, and Fava, *La Biblioteca Estense*.

[2] On early printing at Ferrara see Procter, *Index to Early Printed Books in the British Museum*, i, pp. 381–4; he counts a total of only eight printers active in Ferrara before 1500, which is certainly indicative of the marginal role of the new technology there in Ercole I's time.

court supported its great literary development, maintaining some of the best workshops of the period.

The work of scribes and illuminators was concentrated under the supervision of a single leading figure. During Ercole's time this role was held by a certain Andrea dalle Vieze, who at various times was scribe, decorator, planner of MSS, and chief of the teams who produced the bulk of the Herculean MSS. Valuable documents on MSS produced under Andrea dalle Vieze were published as long ago as 1900 and 1903 by the art historian Hermann Julius Hermann and by the literary historian Giulio Bertoni, including documents directly relevant to the dating of our music MSS; but these documents have either passed unnoticed by music historians or have not been utilized until now.[3]

The role of Andrea dalle Vieze was that of a special court agent entrusted with the supervision of MS production; Ercole in a letter of 1479 called him 'nostro scriptore', and went to great pains to assure his welfare.[4] We do not know how priorities were set up for the commissioning of different types of MSS, but we do know that Andrea's responsibilities were to co-ordinate and pay each man or group of craftsmen involved in the production chain. The method of producing a manuscript was as follows. First, the paper or parchment needed was ordered from the *cartolaro*, a local merchant in the paper business. The *cartolaro* would prepare the raw material: he would scrape and smooth it, cut it to the specified size, and bind the leaves into fascicles (usually quinterns, to judge from the documents). From him it went to the copyist, who would write out the text, presumably one fascicle at a time, leaving space for the larger and smaller initials and for the marginal and border decorations to be inserted later by the illuminator. After copying and illuminating was completed the finished material went back to the *cartolaro* (often the same one who had supplied the paper or parchment) and he would have the MS bound, usually in leather or cloth-covered boards. If it were especially elegant, the last stop would be a metal shop for corners and jewels along with metal buckles. It was then ready for delivery, at times in a ceremony. Since a number of MSS were often worked on simultaneously, it appears that the process could easily stretch out over two years or more, for a larger MS.

How did the process work? As a first sample, we can look at a document

---

[3] According to Bertoni, *La Biblioteca Estense*, p. 26, Andrea was a member of a local family, and perhaps the founder of a small dynasty of experts on book production; his son Cesare became an important illuminator in the period of Alfonso and Isabella. Bertoni quoted in part from the surviving letters of Andrea dalle Vieze, all preserved in ASM, Fondo Biblioteca Estense; Bertoni also corrected Campori's view that Andrea was primarily an illuminator, interpreting his role correctly as 'scriptor' and agent in charge of MS production (p. 40 ff.). Hermann's documentation on Andrea is found in the study cited in n. 1, 266–8 (docs. 288–301).

[4] ASM, CTPE, B. 67; Ercole to Eleonora, 6 June 1479; Andrea had been physically injured in some way by a citizen of Modena, and Ercole had sent him back to Ferrara under escort, 'because we would not want our *scriptor* to be offended . . .'.

of 1481, in which Andrea dalle Vieze is paid for work on a Breviary for the Duke's personal use:[5]

[2 June 1481. Payment to]

Maestro Andrea, scriptore per sua mercede de havere scripto, aminiato
e ligato li infrascripti volumi ...

		L. s. d.
[1]	per scrivere et miniare uno martirologio, scripto in lettera minuta et posto in uno breviario de la excellentia del prefato nostro signore ..	11. 9.0
[2]	Item per scrivere de lettera paresina lo offitio de la Madona	5.12.0
[3]	Item per scriptura da quinterni quaranta septe de uno breviario, de forma picola et lettera minuta	117.10.0
[4]	Item per regadura de dicti quinterni quarantasepte	9. 8.0
[5]	Item per miniadura de lettere 3,213 grande d'oro, fiorite de azuro oltramare, a s. 1 d. 6 l'una	240. 0.0
[6]	Item per miniadura de lettere 12,028 picole ... a s. 10 al centenaro	60. 0.0
[7]	Item per miniadura de principi quatro, lavoradi intorno li marzeni et cum arme et divise et altri ornamenti, a l. 2 m. l'uno	8. 0.0
[8]	Item per miniadura de lettere 214 ... a s. 4 l'una	42.16.0
[9]	Item per ligadura del dicto breviario	4. 0.0
		498.10.0

It covers a total of nine items costing nearly 500 lire (exactly 498 *lire*, 10 *soldi*, and no *denari*). This is the equivalent, at the time, of a year's salary for a court functionary at the rank of ambassador.[6] It is about twice as much as the annual salary of the highest-paid singer of this period. The nine items can be sorted into groups that cover four procedures: (1) lining the paper or parchment; (2) copying the text; (3) decorating letters and borders; (4) binding. If we follow the items down the list we get a fair idea of relative costs. Item 1 is a payment of 11.9.0 for copying (and in this case also illuminating) a Martirology that is written in small characters. The Martirology is to be inserted into the Breviary, as is, also, the second item, an Office of our Lady, to be written 'in lettera paresina', which cost about half the previous item. Item 3 stipulates a total of 117.10.0 for the copying of the Breviary text on 47 quinterns in small format and in small letters, at the rate of 2.10.0 per quintern (almost certainly on parchment). The next item pays for the drawing of lines on the 47 quinterns for the insertion of the text; the cost of 9.8.0 averages to 5 *soldi* per quintern, which is about half the charge for the drawing of text lines that we find in other payments of this period; no doubt this is

[5] The document is in ASM, Memoriale *eee*, 1481, fol. 104; published also by Hermann, op. cit., doc. 297.

[6] For comparative figures from Caleffini see Gundersheimer, *Ferrara*, Appendix I, pp. 295 ff; and Chapter 17 above.

because the Breviary is in small format, intended for personal use and therefore to be portable. The next four entries show us how illuminators were paid at this period for decorating letters: the exact total number of letters was counted up and the illuminator was paid for the total on the basis of a fixed unit cost. So in item 5 we see him paid for 3,213 large letters, decorated in gold and 'flowered in ultramarine blue', at the rate of 1.6.0 per letter; these are large capitals for the opening of sections of the Breviary text. The unfortunate bookkeeper also had to count up all the small capitals in the Breviary, for which the total given is 12,028 'lettere piccole'. These are paid for at the rate of 10 *soldi* per 100 and the total comes to exactly one quarter the cost of the large gold letters in item 5. Then payment is made for the elaborate decoration of borders and margins of four 'opening pages' (*principi quatro*) in the MS, with one to have the ducal arms. Each of these cost 2 *lire* – that is, more than twenty times the cost of each gold letter. Finally, 214 illuminated letters are paid for at 4 *soldi* each. To sum up, we see that the decorating of the letters in these 47 quinterns, both ornate and simple, cost about 350 *lire*, while the copying of the text on the same number of leaves cost about 135. If this sample is reasonably representative, it means that the decorating of letters was much more costly than copying of text, just as we might expect, running here at about two and a half times the cost of the other. Binding, on the other hand, was very cheap; a mere 4 *lire* (again, this is a small MS). We can keep these proportions in mind as we turn to the music MSS produced by the same workshop at this period.

From the entire period of Ercole's reign (1471 to 1505) we have six extant polyphonic MSS – listed in Table 7 as Mod C_1, C_2, D, E, F, and Cas 2856.[7] Of these Mod E is a fragment consisting of only three leaves of a once large MS of Masses; its companion volume is Mod D. The five principal MSS fall into three groups: (1) large polyphonic choirbooks from the earlier period of Ercole's chapel, consisting of the paired MSS C_1 and C_2, along with the Mass volumes Mod D and Mod E; (2) a single secular MS, the chansonnier Casanatense 2856; and (3) the single Mass MS called here Mod F, with Masses by Obrecht and Josquin, no doubt from the last years of Ercole's reign.

The apparent emphasis on sacred music directly reflects Ercole's nurturing of the development of the chapel; yet we know of several secular MSS now lost. An approximate balance is shown in an inventory of the court library made about 1495, ten years before Ercole's death; it shows eleven music MSS, including one theory treatise, two volumes containing Masses, one of

---

[7] The music MSS surviving from Ferrara have been utilized for modern editions of various works they contain, but have never been studied as a group until now. A brief account of the contents of the MSS in the Biblioteca Estense is found in Lodi, *Catalogo delle opere musicali . . . R. Biblioteca Estense . . .*; other catalogues in the library itself may be consulted there, and are listed in the *Annuario delle biblioteche italiane*, Part I (A–M), pp. 438–40. Special studies of Mod C_1 and C_2 were made by Kanazawa, 'Polyphonic Music for Vespers', pp. 421–5. Other special studies will be mentioned in connection with each manuscript.

Table 7. Extant Polyphonic Music Manuscripts from Ferrara, Datable between c.1479 and 1505 (Period of Duke Ercole I d'Este)

Symbol	Location and Shelf-mark	Size (cm.)	Fols.	Material	Date	Contents
Mod C$_1$	Modena, Biblioteca Estense, Alpha M. 1. 11 (Lat. 454)	56.4 × 40.2	116	Parchment	1479–81	Music for Vespers of Lent and Matins of Holy Week (Psalms, Hymns, Magnificats, etc.) by Martini and Brebis (odd-numbered verses)
Mod C$_2$	Modena, Biblioteca Estense, Alpha M. 1. 12 (Lat. 455)	56.4 × 40.2	101	Parchment	1479–81	(Same as Mod C$_1$, with portions of two Passion settings on fols. 91v–101); has even-numbered verses of Psalms and Hymns; Mod C$_1$ and C$_2$ make up matching MSS for double chorus.
Mod D	Modena, Biblioteca Estense, Alpha M. 1. 13	56.5 × 38	224	Parchment	1481	18 Mass settings, all anon. in MS except the *Missa 'L'homme armé'* of Faugues, but identified through concordances; Martini (7); Faugues (2); Vincinet (1); Domarto (1); Caron (1); Dufay (1); Weerbecke (1); anon. (5).
Mod E	ASM Frammenti musicali	55 × 38	3	Parchment	1481	Incomplete portions of Agnus Dei of Busnois, *Missa 'L'homme armé'* and of Agricola, *Missa 'Je ne demande'* (identified by M. Staehelin and L. Lockwood, independently). The Busnois fragment has numeral 'XII' in upper r.h. corner; the Agricola fragment has numeral 'XIIII'; these are similar to numerals of Mod D and show that these fragments belonged to a large MS collection of Masses resembling Mod D.
Cas 2856	Rome, Biblioteca Casanatense, MS 2856	27 × 20	164	Parchment	1479–81 with some later additions	123 textless, secular compositions for 3 and 4 v.; principal composers are Martini (23); Agricola (19); Busnois (11); Hayne (9); Compère (6); Ockeghem (5); Josquin (4); Ghiselin-Verbonnet (3); Japart (3); Barbireau (2); Basin (2); 14 named composers with one each; 3 anon. On origins of MS 'a la pifaresca' see text, p. 226.
Mod F	Modena, Biblioteca Estense, M. 1. 2	55 × 39	173	Parchment	1504–5	Collection of ten polyphonic Masses, of which 8 are attributed and 2 (Nos. 1 and 4) are anon. in MS but have been ascribed to Obrecht; see Staehelin (1973), 85. Composers: Obrecht (5); Josquin (2); Ockeghem (1); perhaps two more are also by Obrecht.

'Tenori todeschi in canto' (that is, Tenors for instrumental improvisation), one volume of pieces set to Italian texts, and the rest all called simply 'Libri de canto'.

Table 8. Music Manuscripts Listed in Two Late Fifteenth-Century Inventories of Estense Libraries

---

I

Undated list of 'libri che se ritrovano in lo presente Studio', (this looks like a worksheet for a more formal inventory, most likely that of 1495). Source: ASM, Fondo 'Biblioteca Estense', B. 1.

p. 3:   Libri di Musicha

    Cantiones a la pifarescha
    Arte de musicha
    Arte de canto
    Tenori todeschi et altre cantiones
    Messe
    Messe et cantiones
    Moteti
    Cantiones francese
    Cantiones taliane

II

From inventory of ducal library, 1495 (published by Bertoni, *La Biblioteca Estense*, Appendix II[2]).

No.

24	Arte de musica coperto de brasilio stampato
80	Canzone in canto coperto de brasilio in cartone
283	Libro de canto comenzato coperto de carta pecorina
284	Libro de canto comenzato coperto de carta membrana
292	Libro de canto che fece do. Beltrame coperto de montanina morella
293	Libro de canto coperto de corame rosso
297	Libro de canto cum fondello de corame rosso
305	Libro de canto coperto de brasilio rosso stampato
338	Messe de canto coperte de montanina rossa
340	Messe et canzone de musiche in albe senza fundello
341	Musicha et canzone taliane coperto de veludo carmesino
472	Tenori todeschi in canto coperto de montanina verde

The list does not include the double-chorus MSS nor at least one of the Mass MSS, which by then were probably stored in the chapel itself. Furthermore, the records for this period do not disclose a large number of entries for polyphonic MSS that might later have been lost; on the contrary, for sacred polyphony especially, there remain extant, in part or whole, virtually all the MSS that we can be sure were then made.[x] On the secular side, one MS is

---

[x] A thorough search of court records from about 1430 to about 1520 has revealed more than 60 notices of payment for the copying of music by local scribes, whether into large MSS or on to small fascicles or sheets. The majority of these entries are as yet unknown even to specialists in Ferrarese MS traditions and to music historians.

extant and about six MSS are missing. We see from the records that when Ercole started his chapel in 1471 he began by commissioning new plainsong choirbooks for its use.[9] When these were finished, towards the end of his first decade, he turned to the codification of polyphonic music for the most important liturgical occasions, and especially also to Masses. In the period after Ercole, 1505–30, the situation changes; the number of references to the copying of music on separate small fascicles increases sharply, while the number of references to large MSS declines. We have a number of whole MSS from the later period, but, nevertheless, more is missing from the later period than from the earlier.

In 1481 we also find the first detailed entry for a polyphonic MS:

[8 August 1481. Source: ASM, Memoriale *eee*, 1481, fol. 142]
Maestro Andrea dale Vieze, scriptore . . . per sua mercede de havere
facto scrivere, miniare et fare a la prefata sua Signoria in l'anno
presente più e diversi libri.

[10 April 1481]
per uno libro de canto figurato, chiamato li Vesperi dela
quadragesima, ligato insieme cum li matutini de la septimana sancta,
videlicet:

	[L. s. d.]
a mastro Francesco d'Alzio, cartolaro, per rasadura, incoladura, et rigadura de quinterni 15 et carte 4	6. 4.0
per lo primo principio del dicto libro cum le arme et divise delo illustrissimo nostro signore	1.10.0
per un altro principio, zoè de li matutini dela septimana sancta, senza arma	1. 0.0
per lettere d'oro 77	11.11.0
per lettere de penna . . . 1,293	7.14.0
per vernise et inchiostro	0.12.0
per ligadura . . . a mastro Francesco d'Alzio	5.12.0
	34. 3.0

I believe that this entry corresponds to the MS designated here as C_1, the first of the two double-chorus MSS (cf. fig 9). It covers payment for all aspects of the MS except the actual copying of the music and text, which must have been handled elsewhere. If we follow the items in the document, we find the following: (1) what is being paid for is a book of polyphony called the 'Vespers of Quadragesima', bound together with the Matins of Holy Week; (2) a payment of 1.10.0 for decorating the first opening of the MS with the ducal arms; (3) the *cartolaro* is paid 6.4.0. for 'scraping, smoothing and lining' 15 quinterns and 4 leaves of parchment for this volume; (4) just 1 *lire*

---

[9] In the 1470s Ercole had various liturgical books made for the chapel; details will be given in the next chapter.

was paid for a similar decoration of the beginning of the Matins section of the MS, this time without the ducal coat of arms; (5) for 77 gold letters a total of 11.11.0 was paid; (6) 1,293 linked letters cost 7.14.0; (7) ink and paint went for a mere 12 *denari*; and (8) binding this volume cost a rather substantial 5.12.0, suggesting a handsome binding and confirming that this is a large MS.

Let us now compare these entries with Mod C_1 and C_2. First we find that the number of leaves prepared by the *cartolaro* is greater than in either MS in its present form. Mod C_1 now has 116 leaves and is incomplete; Mod C_2 has 101 leaves and is even more incomplete, breaking off in the middle of a Passion setting for Good Friday. The total mentioned is 15 quinterns and 4 leaves — that is, 75 double leaves plus four, equal to 154 single leaves; it seems rather unlikely that as many as 38 leaves could have been lost from C_1 or as many as 53 from C_2, though it is not impossible. Many large archival registers of the court from this period do contain large swatches of blank leaves, especially at the end of the volumes. To understand this we must not only use our document but think critically about its meaning. What the supplier is being paid for is not a finished MS but a specific number of leaves that were *intended* for it, leaves which he prepared and made ready for this source. Therefore, before the MS was actually copied, someone had to estimate how many quinterns would be needed for its material. For a MS of double-chorus Psalms and Hymns with alternating verses this might have been unusually difficult, in view of the unequal length of the Psalm texts and the absence of precedents for this type of responsorial polyphony. Presumably, the musician in charge of the repertoire explained what he wanted to the chief of MS production; we are on very safe ground in assuming that the musician was Johannes Martini and the MS chief was Andrea dalle Vieze. I would submit that the payment to the *cartolaro* represents the total number of fascicles that were *allocated* for the MS at an early stage, but that not all of the fascicles turned out to be needed. They could then be available for another MS of the same format, if one were wanted, and indeed, in this case, a matching MS was required (C_2). That the use of paper was handled in exactly this way is shown by another payment of the same year, in which a MS copy of Apuleius's *The Golden Ass* is recorded as being made up of twelve quinterns, with the remark that four of these were new but 'the other eight were the remainder from the *Deca* of Biondo' — a book by Flavio Biondo just finished in the same shop.[10]

Let us continue the comparison with Mod C_1. The payment covers the decoration of the first opening of the MS with the ducal arms; if we now look at the first opening of C_1 we see that indeed there were originally both border decorations and arms at the center bottom — until some later vandal cut them out. But we do find in the MS the *second* decorated opening, which begins the Matins section of the MS at folio 50^v. Just as the document says, the

---

[10] The payment for the Apuleius MS is in Hermann, 'Zur Geschichte', doc. 299c.

second opening has the border but not the arms. Finally, the gold and inked letters must be compared. The record calls for 77 gold letters. If we exclude the decorated opening folios, which are paid for separately, we find that Mod C$_1$ has 79 such letters (Mod C$_2$ has 73). Mod C$_1$ is slightly closer, yet there may have been a discrepancy in the paymaster's counting, or two letters may have been made by a later hand. Nor can we say anything of the folios missing at the end, except that in some other large MSS of this period letters were at times not fully entered in later folios, perhaps owing to haste in final preparation. As for the inked capital letters, the entry calls for payment for 1,293 of these. Again excluding folios 1 and 50 (the major openings), the total in the MS turns out to be a maddening 1,298 – differing from the payment record by a total of 5 out of almost 1,300. Again we can adduce a variety of reasons: (1) the MS supervisor may have miscounted; (2) I may have miscounted – but I can testify, at least, that I had the whole job checked by my research assistant and feel confident; (3) there may have been an error in the writing of the entry by the paymaster, four months later, or in the original register from which this was copied. Evidence of haste in the making of the small capitals turns up here and there. On folio 103^v of Mod C$_1$ we find the word 'velociter', but the capital that is inked in is not 'V' but 'A'. Did the paymaster notice this error and deduct accordingly? Whatever the reason, a difference of 3 to 5 inked capitals out of 1,298 is so small that it is totally unlikely that a different MS could possibly be implied on that ground alone, while the contents and other principal features fit perfectly.

I feel safe in assuming that this entry refers to Mod C$_1$, which tells us that this MS was completed by 1481, when its payments were made, or recorded, in full. Another entry, of 1479, which also seems to refer to this MS, gives us a probable starting point for it; possibly, its music and text were completed by 1479 but only finally illuminated two years later, which might explain why the copying of music and text is not included in the entry of 1481.[11] As for the second MS of the pair, Mod C$_2$, this seems certain to be the MS referred to in the entry No. 1 in Table 9 (see p. 223), which mentions a 'book of polyphonic music written and notated by Philippo de San Giorgio, called the responses of Vespers of Quadragesima, decorated in gold and ink with the ducal arms'. The 'responses of Vespers' is exactly what Mod C$_2$ contains. On the other hand, the date '1483' given for this entry is unlikely, for a number of reasons. One is that, by May 1483, Ercole was in the midst of war with Venice, and had temporarily suspended his chapel, which was not re-stored to full status until 1484. We also saw from documents and from Sabadino that, up until the war with Venice, Ercole maintained a double chorus but did not do so thereafter. So a more likely date altogether is 1480 or 1481, around the same time as its companion, Mod C$_1$. This evidence permits a major conclusion: it allows us to determine exactly when and under

---

[11] The entry of 1479 was first published by Hamm and Scott, 'A Study and Inventory', 110 (from what is actually a Guardaroba register of 1479).

what conditions the Vespers and Holy Week music of the ducal chapel was codified by Martini and Brebis (the only composers named in the MS) and established as a fixed repertoire in a simple polyphonic style. The MS is therefore not generically representative of what we should call 'late fifteenth-century style'; it is specifically the product of the particular conditions of the ducal chapel under Ercole in the period from about 1472 to about 1480, conditions no longer holding after 1482.[12]

Further references of the same period enable us to date the two major Mass collections Mod D and Mod E. An entry of 1481 is again promising:

[13 July 1481. Source: ASM, Memoriale *eee*, 1481, fols. 142–3.]

In uno libro da canto figurato, zoè da messe, che fece el fra de sancto Domenego et fo quinterni 29 et carte quatro, videlicet:

a maxtro Francesco d'Alzio, cartolaro, per rasare, incolare et rigare   [L. s. d.]
quinterni 29 et carte doe 10.14.0
et per ligare el dicto libro 5.12.0
per miniadura del primo principio cum le arme et devise del prefato
nostro signore 1.10.0
lettere d'oro 65 a soldi 3 . . . . 9.15.0
lettere de penna . . . 1,013 . . . . 6. 0.0

                                                                                         _____

                                                                                         33.11.0

It tells us of the completion of a large MS containing Masses, written by 'el fra de sancto Domenego', made up of twenty-nine quinterns and four leaves, decorated in the same way as the Vespers MSS, prepared and bound by the same *cartolaro* at the same cost, therefore approximately of the same format. Although, at first glance, Mod D fits this well, it turns out to have fairly wide discrepancies in matters of numbers of leaves, gold letters, and inked capitals (65 gold letters instead of 77; 1,013 inked capitals instead of 1,341). It seems much more likely that what the entry refers to is the MS I am calling Mod E – the three-folio fragment in the Archivio di Stato (cf. fig. 8). These contain fragments of a 'L'homme armé' Mass that Charles Hamm identified as being the one by Busnois (giving us another Italian source for that work). I have subsequently identified the second Mass as a fragment from Agricola's *Missa 'Je ne demande'* (incidentally, based on Busnois). Now, since the Busnois Mass has the original number 'XIIII' we can infer that this was a large MS, on the same scale as Mod D. The entry referring to Mod D, as I see it, is the one calling for a 'libro da messe de canto', put together by fra Philippo de San Giorgio (see Table 9, No. 4), which would have had 27 quinterns or 270 leaves, while the incomplete Mod D has 224; again the entry appears in a much later version that bears the date 1483, or appears to do so, but it

[12] This view entirely displaces the conclusion advanced by Bukofzer, in his 'The Beginnings of Choral Polyphony', regarding the supposedly broad historical importance of the 'huge choir-books at Modena' (*sic*) for 15th-century musical practice in general.

probably goes back to about 1481 as well. In other words, fra Philippo would have been working on the two Vespers MSS and one of the Mass MSS at the same time.

Table 9.   Some Further Payment Records for Ferrarese Polyphonic MSS

[From Modena, Bibl. Estense, MS Alpha H.1.13, an eighteenth-century compilation of payments for MSS, made from fifteenth-century sources now lost]

['15 September 1483'; order for payment to Andrea dalle Vieze for the following MSS:]

1. Uno libro da canto figurato che scrisse e notò fra Philippo da San Zorzo, chiamato lo respondente de li Vespri de la Quaresima lavorado d'oro et de pennello con l'arma ducale; di quinterni XVII de carta di capretto.

2. Un libro da messe fatto dal Fra de San Domenico . . . [see entry above under 13 July 1481, on p. 222]

3. Un libro da canto figurato, che scrisse e notò Don Alessandro Signorello a la pifaresca, con un principio miniato all'antica, con l'arma Ducale e con letere d'oro a l'antica.

4. Un libro de Messe da canto che ha fatto fra Philippo da San Zorzo di quinterni 27 di carta di capretto, con principio, arma, e lettere come sopra.

[From *Libro di Amministrazione di Alfonso I*, No. 35 (1503–5), fol. 9ᵛ:]

[4 April 1503]
E adi dito Lire uno soldi dixe de marchesane per sua Signoria a m. Girolamo Cartolaro da laquila per hauer ligato uno libro de canto grande notado de mese como una bale in una arma per sua signoria 1.10.0

[from ibid., No. 36 (1504–5), fol. 30ᵛ:]

[5 April 1505]
A sua Signoria Lire uno soldi quindexe de marchesane per tanti pagati per sua Signoria per fare rigare quinterni sette de carte reale data a zoanne michel cantore e zoanne maria Burseto per notare messe 1.15.0

Now it happens that this hypothesis, suggested by the payment records and by the format and contents of the MSS, is exactly confirmed in an unpublished letter written by Andrea dalle Vieze to Duke Ercole, telling him of the problem of funds needed for the preparation of MSS. It specifically refers to fra Philippo.[13]

Your Excellency said that you would speak to M. Bonifacio, and tell him to make a payment to my office each month, so that I will be able to take care of your books and not those of others. So I am asking you and reminding you kindly to write to him on my behalf. I must also remind Your Lordship that it would be good to establish the rule that I receive at least 5 lire every fortnight, for the miniaturists and the *cartolaro*, in order to have work done on these three music manuscripts (*questi tre libri de canto*)

---

[13] ASM, Fondo Biblioteca Estense, B. 1. The key passage in the original is '. . . Ricordo etiam a V. Exᵃ voglia metere qualche ordine che Io habia almancho Lire V. ogni quindexe dì per li miniaduri e cartolaro per far lavorare questi 3. libri de canto che Io ho di V. S. & anche per far conzare delle carte che fra philippo possa lavorare; el quale molto me solicita . . .'. Unfortunately the letter is undated. But it cannot well date from any other point in Ercole's reign.

that I have in hand for Your Excellency – and also to have the paper prepared, so that fra Philippo can proceed with his work, for he is constantly asking me about it . . .

I would therefore assign to this period, around 1481, the three matched MSS, Mod C,, C,, and Mod D, all by fra Philippo; and also the closely related MS Mod E, made by the 'fra de san Domenego'.

This leaves us with only two more MSS extant from the period of Ercole d'Este that are certainly Ferrarese: one is the famous chansonnier now in the Biblioteca Casanatense in Rome; the other is the MS, again a Mass collection, here called Mod F.

The Casanatense chansonnier is among the most interesting secular MSS of the later fifteenth century. It is a MS of medium format but substantial size, containing 123 chansons by as many as 27 composers. The leading figure, as in all of these local sources, is Johannes Martini, with 23 attributed compositions; then comes Agricola (19), Busnois (11), Hayne van Ghizeghem (9), Compère (6), Ockeghem (5), Josquin (4), Ghiselin and Japart, (3 each). Especially striking is the complete absence of texts – only incipits are given, and these often in a French that is execrable even for an Italian MS of this period. Not only the text incipits but the composers' names are often strangely spelled; for example, 'Morton' is given as 'Borton', 'Josquin' is given several times with a 'k' instead of 'qu', and it may also be he who is meant by the name given as 'Jossin' or 'Josfim'.

In 1965 Jose Llorens suggested that the MS was a wedding codex for Isabella d'Este, compiled in honor of her marriage in 1490 to Francesco Gonzaga.[14] He argued mainly from the combined coats of arms on the title page, showing the Este arms on the left, and those of the Gonzaga on the right. Although Llorens' hypothesis was plausible, it rests on no other evidence, and I would like to submit another view. To begin with, the Este and Gonzaga dynasties were allied by long-standing ties that considerably preceded the wedding of 1490. As early as 1435, Leonello had married a Gonzaga, Margherita, and the chronicles show constant social interchange and good political relations between these two neighboring small states. So it is not surprising to find that when Ercole began to plan politically advantageous marriages for his children, which he did as early as possible, he proceeded first to shore up his alliances with the Sforza of Milan and the Gonzaga of Mantua, by marrying his daughters Beatrice and Isabella into them. For this reason, the betrothal of Isabella took place a full ten years before her wedding, in early May of the year 1480, when she was only six years old; her fiancé was a more advanced but still tender fourteen-year-old. The betrothal was carried out in a full-dress ceremony, signed by the heads of both families, and arrangements were made for the bride's dowry. The

[14] Llorens, 'El codice Casanatense 2856 identificado como el Cancionero de Isabella d'Este (Ferrara) esposa de Francesco Gonzaga (Mantua)'. More complete and with much original discussion of the MS, though still relying on Bertoni for its presumed date, is Wolff, 'The Chansonnier Biblioteca Casanatense 2856; its History, Purpose, and Music'.

Gonzaga wanted Isabella to come to Mantua when she was only twelve, but her mother held out for thirteen; when the wedding was finally held, in 1490, she was sixteen.

In the payment records for polyphonic MSS, although now transmitted through a secondary source, we find this entry (Table 9, No. 3):

A book of polyphonic music, written and notated by don Alessandro Signorello, *a la pifaresca*, with a first page illuminated *all'antica* and with the ducal arms and with gold letters *all'antica*.

It seems more than likely that this entry refers to the Casanatense MS. The opening page (see fig. 11) shows us exactly what the entry calls for: the border of the page is handsomely adorned with an intricate white vine decoration, in several colors; the interwoven filigree is white on a blue background, the small filled-in spaces are red and green, in alternating patterns, and a few are in gold. Also in gold is the capital 'T' of the word 'Tant', the incipit of the chanson by Philippon, as is the 'C' of the word 'Contratenor'. Further, these letters are in the form and style of Roman capitals then called 'antiqua'. The decoration is very close to that of a Propertius MS of about 1475 from Ferrara. At the bottom is the coat of arms; admittedly the entry does not refer to *two* coats of arms, but we cannot exclude overpainting; and it is entirely plausible that the entry merely mentioned this feature without going into details about its content.

I have mentioned several times that the date of this archival entry poses a severe problem of interpretation. To start with, the date of this entry was given as '1485' when it was published by Giulio Bertoni in 1903, but this was a slip on Bertoni's part (which has led a number of scholars astray).[15] The document from which he was working is an eighteenth-century source in the Estense Library that was copied from fifteenth-century archival registers now lost; but when one looks at the eighteenth-century copy, one finds that the date given is not 1485 but rather 1483. Yet this too presents problems. As I mentioned earlier, by 1483 Ferrara had gone to war, and life in the city and court was in disruption. Some musicians, among many others, had fled the city, and a policy of austerity had set in. So a dating before May 1482 seems entirely plausible on external grounds.

To this we can now add, for the first time, an identification of its compiler, don Alessandro Signorello. For we find him as a singer in this very ducal chapel at precisely the time to which this hypothesis points; he is a new member of the chapel in 1479 and he remains in service up to 1481.[16] Thereafter the chapel breaks up but when it is re-established in 1484 he is no longer found. This would strongly confirm the view that the right dating is

[15] Bertoni, *La Biblioteca Estense*, p. 260; see also Wolff, op. cit., pp. 29 f. The source for this document, as given by Bertoni, is an 18th-century copy of Este payment records, probably made for Tiraboschi, the literary historian. It is the MS Alpha H. 1. 13 of the Biblioteca Estense.

[16] Signorelli is found in the lists of singers for just these years, mostly as 'Don Alexandro'. But in Memoriale *eee*, 1481, his full name is given. He is one of the two lowest-paid singers.

between 1479 and 1481, with the likeliest occasion centering on the betrothal of 1480. This dating would offer grounds for new conclusions. First, the MS represents in its basic repertoire the chansons by local and international masters accumulated at the court during the 1470s; and it enables us to date approximately half of the secular output of Johannes Martini as being not later than 1480. Second, this dating would fit perfectly with the presence in the MS of works by Japart, who had joined the chapel in 1477, and who was highly esteemed by Ercole. It also enables us to set a *terminus* of 1480 for the four works by Josquin that it contains, including the very strikingly entitled piece, 'Ile fantazies de Joskin'. There is conclusive evidence that Josquin's employer Ascanio Sforza was in Ferrara at just this period, for the local chronicler Caleffini tells us that Ascanio was present at the festivities for the betrothal, on 28 May 1480.[17] This would place the Casanatense MS a full ten years earlier than the big Florentine chansonnier Florence 229, with which it has the largest number of concordances. Howard Brown dates Florence 229 to about 1491. This means that if there is a flow of material between the two sources its direction is from Ferrara to Florence, not the other way.

The entry includes, additionally, the curious remark that the MS is written and notated *a la pifaresca*. This means 'in the *piffaro* style', and *piffaro* generally means wind player. Locally, in the rosters of musicians at Ferrara, this term means a wind player as opposed to the *cantori*. If we think of the MS as being intended primarily for the use of the well-known virtuoso performers of the court, especially the wind players, much about it becomes clear. It helps to explain why it is so carefully prepared in decoration and note-content but lacks texts altogether, and even why it treats the text-incipits in a cavalier fashion. It helps too, to explain the presence of pieces that smack of use for instrumental purposes, such as 'Ile fantazies de Josquin' or 'La Martinella'. The contrapuntal style of many of the three-part pieces seems to suggest very plausibly instrumental performance, as has in fact been suggested recently in several studies. I can now see no other plausible meaning for *a la pifaresca* than that it designates a volume destined for use by the *piffari*. That this was a term in general use is clear from the inventory work-sheet of *c.* 1494 (see above, Table 8, p. 218) which lists as a separate item, 'Cantiones a la pifarescha', referring to this MS or a similar one. It seems clear that music passed back and forth between Isabella and Ercole especially in the early 1490s, when she was first establishing herself at Mantua, and when the ageing Martini was occasionally visiting her there. In the work-sheet, furthermore, the term 'Cantiones a la pifarescha' stands in contra-distinction to 'Cantiones francese' and 'Cantiones taliane'. We will return to this repertoire and its instrumental character later on.[18]

Finally, we come to the last of the surviving MSS that belongs to this period, though to its very last years – the large MS Alpha M. 1. 2 of the

---

[17] Caleffini, *Croniche*, fol. 127ᵛ.
[18] This conclusion is anticipated by Wolff, op. cit., pp. 139 f.

Estense Library (Mod F). The contents show a special choice of material: it contains a total of ten Masses, of which five are attributed to Obrecht, while two are by Josquin, one by Ockeghem (the Mass 'Ecce ancilla'). The remaining two are anonymous but one is certainly by Obrecht, and Martin Staehelin has recently conjectured that the other is also by him. Interesting is the juxtaposition of paired works by Obrecht and Josquin – in order, Obrecht and Josquin's Masses on 'Fortuna desperata', followed by 'L'homme armé' Masses by both composers. The likely background for this would seem to be the successive service of Josquin and Obrecht at Ferrara, evidently the only center at which they both served. In 1505, after Obrecht's death, still more payments were made for the copying of Masses, and I believe that 1504–5 is the likely period of the origin of Mod F. The predominance of Obrecht's works suggest that Mod F may be a commemorative MS for him, somewhat comparable to the Chigi codex for Ockeghem (Chigi 234). The inclusion in it of Josquin Masses on the same subjects points up the successive presence of the two masters at the court. The Mass by Ockeghem may not be merely a space filler, for it is based on the Marian text, 'Ecce ancilla', which had been particularly preferred by Duke Ercole in his later years, and which had been given prominence in his *Corona* of 1496.

With this Obrecht memorial MS, as I interpret it, I can close this survey. The chronological scope is not large (only thirty-four years) and the number of extant sources is modest. A similar approach can be carried out, however, for both earlier and later periods, thanks to the rich documentation and the other MSS, especially from the first half of the sixteenth century. The large polyphonic choirbooks can be seen to have been produced for the direct use of the devotional activities of the ducal chapel; and they focus on the music needed to enhance the solemnity of its activity. Such choirbooks in turn reflect the importance of the large corps of singers, brought in to staff the chapel, who form a large proportion of the entire ducal entourage. These volumes implicitly replace and supplement traditional plainsong choirbooks, they formalize a modern repertoire for the chapel, and they make that repertoire available for future use. Seen from another angle, these codices constitute the musical segment of the growing library of the court, in a period in which the acquisition of handsomely decorated manuscripts is a conspicuous activity among rival Italian patrons. They embody what appear to be the nuclei of the earliest of all music libraries in a secular context. Similar assemblages of polyphonic choirbooks at this time were elsewhere found mainly in cathedral collections or religious establishments – for example the Duomo of Milan, San Petronio in Bologna, the cathedrals of Verona and Modena, not to mention the Sistine Chapel.

21

The Principal Repertoires in Ercole's Earlier Years

(1471–82)

TO trace the nature and development of a musical center over a limited time-span, as I have sought to do here, one must first assemble and interpret historical data that primarily concern musicians and their clients. Inevitably, the knowledge required in this project parallels research in other areas of cultural activity; the results we obtain deal mainly with the roles and functions of members of a social hierarchy rather than with their musical products. In turning now to problems of style, however, we need to invoke other criteria and trace quite different relationships. In the last segment of this study the focus shifts from musicians to music; to genres whose cultivation was much wider than the single center studied here, and whose history plays upon a national and international stage. Yet to bind the stylistic approach to the historical and social structure built thus far, we need to direct our attention to certain connected questions. Did the constellation of musicians working at Ferrara over the last third of the fifteenth century form an identifiable 'school', and participate in a development that produced not only distinctive repertoires but also locally definable traits of style? To what extent was the local musical development in the main an assimilation of musical methods and procedures imported from outside; to what extent did it owe its existence to indigenous creativity and continuity? Through questions about this narrow and local context and its creative products we can imply a wider range of answers; for the larger issue of the relationship between extrinsic aspects of an artistic context and the intrinsic aspects of the products of that context is surely among the most important questions with which all of music history must grapple. And the effort to provide answers, however incomplete, reinforces our awareness that, by posing these problems for a small and manageable slice of history, we reinforce our ability to answer them without having to fall back entirely on broad, abstract, and floating generalities.

Of the emerging patterns of musical life that typified Italian centers of the late fifteenth century, that of Ferrara is among the most centralized, continuous in patronage, and assimilative in character. Just as the unbroken line of its ruling family distinguished Ferrara sharply from the other Italian states of the period, so the central role of the court gave its musical life a special and strongly personal character. Similar in size, political continuity, and general cultural tone was Mantua, with its long period of domination by the Gonzaga. But the evident absence of musical interests or of energetic recruitment of musicians among the family members, until the very end of the century, left Mantua at best a musical dependency until the arrival of Isabella in 1490.[1] At Milan there was a strong development under the Sforza, as we have seen, but the political instability that set in after the murder of Galeazzo Maria Sforza in 1476 totally disrupted the continuity of musical activity at court. At the same time, music at Milan Cathedral received a strong impetus not only from local pride in perpetuating the Ambrosian liturgy but from the strong personal leadership of Franchino Gafori. From 1490 until his death in 1525, Gafori imposed a specific pattern of development on the Duomo of Milan as a center for the performance, collection, and composition of polyphonic church music drawing on both local and international repertoires suited to his aims. The role of a Gafori at Milan, like that of Giovanni Spataro at Bologna's San Petronio, stands in sharp distinction to that of any of the leading figures at Ferrara in this period, whether Martini as court composer or the famous *maestri di cappella* who followed him up to 1505.

Throughout the period of Ercole, despite the steady flow of musicians who passed through the court, no important or even minor theorist of music was hired for the chapel or remained in residence for any length of time. The only trifling exception seems to have been Tinctoris, whose short visit in 1479 coincided with the installation of a new organ in the court chapel; through the family links to Naples, Tinctoris may occasionally have exerted slight influence on musical matters, but certainly not more. The works of Ugolino di Orvieto (cf. Chapter 8 above) continued to be copied, almost forty years after his death. The absence of a theorist and pedagogue, and the reduced importance of Ferrara Cathedral as a musical center, help to explain why the axis of musical life lay with the court and its ceremonial and civic leadership, not with an accessible teaching institution that could furnish a strong tradition of musically educated and literate clerics or lay singers. An immediate contrast is struck with Verona, where the *Scuola degli Accoliti* attached to the cathedral contributed directly to the development of local musicians and thus also to the development of native Italian polyphonic genres, principally

---

[1] On Mantuan musicians of the late 15th and early 16th centuries, older and still useful studies are those of Canal, 'Della musica in Mantova'; Davari, 'La musica a Mantova'; and, much less reliable, Bertolotti, *Musici alla corte dei Gonzaga*. Apart from special studies on the cathedral or on individual musicians, the primary new archival work on Mantua in this period has recently been done by Dr William Prizer, whose articles include 'La cappella di Francesco II Gonzaga e la musica sacra a Mantova nel primo ventennio del Cinquecento'; and 'The Frottola and the Unwritten Tradition: Improvisors and Frottolists at North Italian Courts'; see also his *Courtly Pastimes: the Frottole of Marchetto Cara*.

the frottola.[2] At Ferrara, Johannes Martini remained for more than twenty-five years the leading figure in the chapel and in secular music as well – but despite his apparent prowess as music master to the younger patrons of the family, especially Isabella, we have no evidence that it was part of his function to give the court's musical forces a role in civic education. On the whole, Ferrara maintained a primarily aristocratic and politically closed musical life that was centered around the court, visible to the local public through pageant, procession, and religious spectacle, but lacking any other direct contact with the lower strata of city life and with education. Nor is this in any way discordant with the role of the court in other aspects of cultural expression. With the cathedral dormant, the only other epicenters in which music had any substantial role were several of the local monasteries, perhaps especially the Carmelite house of San Paolo. Nothing at Ferrara corresponds to the level of popular involvement in civic festivities or other forms of expression that was known at Florence through the participation of the guilds, the neighborhoods, and the discrete segments of Florence society.[3] In some ways, Medici patronage in this period was quite comparable to that of the Estensi; at Florence the leading figure from 1484 on was Isaac, who was, like Martini, a vastly productive Flemish composer, neither a theorist nor pedagogue, but a practitioner highly adaptable to local demands and requirements. That the two composers were in fact close rivals and thoroughly knowledgeable about one another's work is clear from the famous opening fascicle of the MS Florence 229, in which a whole series of secular works are set up so as to alternate their authorship.

To establish a court chapel meant not merely building a small church and locating it centrally in the palace environment; hiring singers and providing them a leader; and fitting out the chapel with the necessary liturgical tools. It meant too the assembling of the necessary service books for worship, including of course the Antiphoner and Gradual, but also other volumes of plainsong. During the 1470s, as we saw earlier, Ercole ordered just such volumes for the chapel, mainly from Florence. By the end of the decade, Martini, with some assistance from Brebis, had seen to the composition or compilation of several large books of sacred polyphony that reflected the special devotions of the chapel during Lent and Eastertide, in addition to daily and festal Mass and Vespers, as a personal and official obligation of the Duke.

When Ercole entered into power in 1471, the ducal library included a small

[2] On Verona and the *scuole*, the primary study is still that of Spagnolo, *Le scuole accolitali in Verona*, and later research by Turrini, partially published in his *La tradizione musicale a Verona*; for a brief account from a later historical vantage-point, see my *The Counter-Reformation and the Masses of Vincenzo Ruffo*, pp. 12–14. Cf. also Paganuzzi, 'Medioevo e Rinascimento'.

[3] For a recent review of Medici rule in Florence that stresses their long-range tendencies towards an oligarchy similar to that of the Estensi, see Hale, *Florence and the Medici*.

'libro de canto' (*uno libro de canto de forma picola*) otherwise unspecified, as well as two other 'libri de canto' and a large Gradual associated with the chapel of Leonello. In the next few years the pace of production of volumes of plainsong for the chapel picked up rapidly.[4]

1. 8 March 1473: Payment for binding and rebinding of *libri de canto*.

2. 1474: Payment for the inscribing, illuminating, lining, and binding of two Psalters (carried out by Andrea dalle Vieze).

3. 1474: Thirty quinterns given to Andrea dalle Vieze to write a Psalter (see preceding item) and to begin a Hymnary for the chapel of the Duke.

4. 1474: Payment to Andrea della Vieze for copying a Manual for the ducal chapter.

5. 1474: Payment to Andrea della Vieze for two Hymnaries and an Antiphoner ordered by Ercole.

6. 1476: Payment for 'a book of music on good paper, with cursive letters, illuminated, with brasil-covered boards . . . purchased by the Duke from maestro Johane de Francia' [= Brebis].

This volume of 1476 belonging to 'fra Zohane Brebis' was described in another entry of that year as 'as high as a hand's span' (*alto quasi uno palmo*). Another entry of the same year refers to 'a certain book of music' that had belonged to 'don Giovanni Bon Theotonici', 'formerly master of the boys', obtained by a certain Johannes Biscacia from Giovanni Bon when the latter departed in 1476.[5] Thus, by the middle of Ercole's first decade, he had provided the chapel with a whole series of plainsong service books that supplied material for the regular performance of the Hymns, Psalms, and Mass Propers needed for daily Mass and Vespers.

On the polyphonic side, the chapel had also inherited from the period of Leonello the substantial MS Mod B, and although its motets and more strictly liturgical compositions were thirty to forty years old by this time, it could still serve as a model, showing the collection of polyphony on a European scale by the local patron for use in Vespers and other services throughout the liturgical year. That it was actually in the chapel's possession in Ercole's first years is clear from the addition made to it of Brebis's celebration motet for Ercole I, 'Hercules omni memorandus aevo', presumably written in 1472; by adding this work, the old MS, inherited from Leonello, is made to serve the new tastes of his successor once-removed. The large body of English compositions in Mod B would no longer have reflected current trends in the 1470s, since in this group the composers represented most heavily were Dunstable and Power; there is no sign of the newer English generation of Morton, Frye, or Robertus de Anglia. On the continental side,

---

[4] The sources for these payments are as follows (all in ASM): (1) LASP, Ercole I, No. 21, fol. 26ᵛ.; (2) Guardaroba, 1474, fol. 28; (3) Ibid., fol. 274.; (4) Ibid.; (5) Ibid.; (6) Guardaroba, Ercole I, 1471–4, fol. 45.

[5] ASM, Mandati, 1476, fol. 96; previously published by Valdrighi, 'Cappelle, concerti e muische', doc. xlvii. This name is spelled as both 'Bon' and 'Gon' in contemporary sources.

however, the dominance of Dufay in the MS could well have reflected an awareness at Ferrara of his sustained influence and powerful reputation, although three decades had now passed since Dufay's return to residence at Cambrai. We know from recent research that despite his primary residence at Cambrai, broken by a period at Savoy in the 1450s, Dufay remained in touch with Italian patrons.[6] His music continued to be copied and circulated in Italian centers throughout the 1470s, his last decade, and in certain circles for some years thereafter. We have good reason to believe that at Ferrara his reputation remained especially vivid, not only through the collecting and copying of his music and its apparent stylistic influence on the music written there at this time, but through the steady appearance at Ferrara of musicians who had worked at the cathedral of Cambrai. Under Dufay's leadership, that great Northern liturgical center had become a vitally important European center of performance of sacred polyphony and a model to be emulated by other chapels everywhere.[7]

[6] See the fundamental study by D'Accone, 'The Singers of San Giovanni', 318 f.; and my 'Dufay and Ferrara'.

[7] The continental importance of Cambrai as a musical center has recently been reinforced, on the basis of much new and important evidence, by Wright, 'Dufay at Cambrai'.

22

Masses by Martini and Other Composers

MOD D and the fragmentary Mod E show us what the chapel's repertoire of polyphonic Masses looked like prior to 1481. At least seven Masses by Martini were composed by then, and possibly several of the three or four others ascribed to him in contemporary sources. His Masses fall into several distinct categories. They were probably written to exemplify these categories, to provide the Duke with polyphonic settings for diverse occasions, and to display a variety of melodic and polyphonic antecedents on which Masses could be based (see Table 10).

Table 10.   Masses by Johannes Martini

1. Masses based on polyphonic antecedents

	No. of voices	Sources	Antecedent	Composer
Missa 'Cela sans plus'	4	Sistina 51	chanson, 3v.	Colinet de Lannoy
Missa 'Coda de Pavon'	4	Milan 2268; Mod D	Dance-lied, 'Der pfoben Schwanz'	Barbingant
Missa 'La Martinella'	4	Sistina 35	chanson, 3v.	Martini
Missa 'Ma bouche rit'	4	Milan 2268; Mod D	chanson, 3v.	Ockeghem
Missa 'Or sus, or sus'		Mod D; Sistina 51	chanson, 3v.	
Missa 'Nos amis' (doubtful)	4	Mod D	chanson, 3v.	Basin

2. Masses based on arbitrary subjects

Missa 'Cucu'	4	Mod D; Trent 91

3. Masses based on plainsong antecedents

Missa de feria	4	Mod D; Sistina 35
Missa dominicalis	4	Mod D

4. Masses based on Italian secular songs, probably monophonic

Missa 'Dio te salvi Gotterello'	4	Mod D
Missa 'Io ne tengo quanto te'	4	Mod D; Milan 2268

Although a thorough study of Martini's Masses has yet to be written, it is possible to offer a few broad observations on his output and approach.[1] His ten attributed Masses make him a substantial contributor to the large and growing literature of the Mass Ordinary in the second half of the century, in the wake of Dufay's composition of a classic group of Masses that set a pattern for later composers. By about 1475, the concept of the unified Mass cycle was itself only about thirty years old. If we accept a dating of about 1450 for Dufay's great four-voice Tenor Masses on 'Se la face ay pale' and 'L'homme armé', then these major works, which extended the cantus firmus principle in the Mass for the first time to the domain of secular music, formed models only a generation older than the settings by Martini based on polyphonic songs. Assuming that Martini was born about 1440 or 1445, which seems plausible, he was younger than Ockeghem, about contemporary with Josquin, ten years older than Obrecht and Isaac. He seems to belong most securely with the composers whose work can be mainly assigned to the years from 1460 to 1490; that is to say, with the French generation dominated by Ockeghem and Busnois and with those pupils or emulators of Dufay associated with Cambrai, the Burgundian court, and the northern-oriented Italian centers. This includes Caron, Faugues, and Tinctoris; and Isaac, Obrecht, and Agricola in their earlier periods of activity. Indeed, Mod D and the fragment Mod E give us exactly the context in which to measure Martini's Masses. In both, the only figure who is definitely older is Dufay; the contemporaries included are Faugues, Caron, Vincinet (whose presence points to Naples), Domarto, Weerbecke, Busnois, and Agricola. In the period of Ockeghem the principal antecedent for Mass settings is the three-part chanson, and the most conservative and classical means of elaboration is that of utilizing the chanson tenor as tenor cantus firmus for a four-voice Mass cycle. In Ockeghem's own works the means of derivation were broadening. Of his fourteen Masses five are based on three-voice chansons; at times the original Superius is used as Tenor in the Mass, and sometimes parts of both Superius and Tenor are used, though not simultaneously. Ockeghem was also extending the range of antecedents to include special structural

---

[1] For a recent conspectus and bibliography see my article on Johannes Martini in *The New Grove*, xi. 726 f.

devices that could generate an entire Mass cycle, as in the *Missa Prolationum* and *Missa Cuiusvis toni*. His *Requiem*, in addition, furnished a model for a special tradition. In the Masses of Obrecht and Josquin, each of whom composed over twenty such works, the range of procedure is also extensive, and both base several Masses on chansons. But the larger pattern of their choices and procedures looks quite different from that of Martini, in several crucial respects. If we assume that Martini, in setting Masses based on three-voice chansons by Lannoy, Ockeghem, and perhaps by Basin, was following conventions well known in the 1470s, it is also clear that his other choices were exceptional. Thus his Mass based on the *basse dance* 'Der pfoben schwanz' by Barbingant may well be the earliest Mass on a dance composition (its only contemporary rival is Faugues's Mass *La Bassadanza*). Martini knew the music of Faugues, as we see from the Ferrarese chapel choirbooks. His Mass setting based on 'La Martinella', his own chanson, seems to have been modeled on a piece designed primarily for instrumental performance (as were many of his other 'chansons', as we shall see later). The *Missa 'Cucu'* also suggests Martini's strong attachment to the instrumental fantasia. On the other hand, his two Masses based on Italian-texted melodies may well be based on songs known to the Ferrarese court and could well reflect the popular melodies of their milieu. Thus 'Dio te salvi Gotterello' may have been a song about San Gottardo. For this work the Mass 'La mort de San Gothard', attributed by Besseler to Dufay but certainly by a later composer, may be a parellel type, since 'La Mort' is also based on a simple and memorable tune that remains undisguised in the Mass setting. As for 'Io ne tengo quanto te', we find in Mod D that its full first line is indicated as follows: 'Io ne tengo quanto te, deste frasche fronde'. Among the annual festivities of the Este court was the celebration of the first of May, the *Kalenda maia*. The usual procedure was for the entire court to go out into the countryside to cut green branches and bring them home to display at windows or doorways. Zambotti reports that this custom was still being observed in 1476, the year in which his chronicle begins, and we can assume that it was much older. He reports as follows for 1 May 1476:

. . . Our Duke, after Mass, went on horseback in armor and adorned as if it were the day of St. George [the city's patron saint] to cut the May branches [*a tuore le mai*] and greens, with the entire court; among them were . . . messer Sigismondo and messer Raynaldo da Este, fitted out entirely in armor but bare-headed; and then they galloped with pleasure and joy through the entire piazza, holding the green branches . . .[2]

We could hardly imagine a more suitable Mass setting for this day than Martini's *Missa 'Io ne tengo'*, assuming that its reference to *frasche fronde*, or 'fresh branches', means what it seems to say. Although Cesari and Disertori have attempted to reconstruct the original melody of 'Io ne tengo'

---

[2] Zambotti, *Diario Ferrarese*, p. 7 (1476).

from the Superius of the Mass, it is at least equally likely that the tune lies in the Tenor; if we set side by side the opening tenor portions of the surviving related movements ('Et in terra', 'Patrem', 'Sanctus'; and 'Qui tollis', 'Crucifixus', 'Osanna') we can propose the following form for the tune:

Ex. 5(*a*). J. Martini, *Missa 'Io ne tango quanto te'*, opening tenor segments of principal movements

Too few of Martini's Masses have yet been published to permit thorough comparison, but we can comment briefly on two of them – the *Missa 'La Martinella'* and the surviving movements of the *Missa 'Io ne tengo'* – which seem to offer diverse approaches to the genre. In the principal sections of the

Ex. 5(*b*). Ibid., opening tenor segments of secondary movements

Gloria and Credo of the *Missa 'Io ne tengo'*, the tenor is characteristically the last voice to enter in a four-voice texture in *tempus perfectum*, but in both movements is soon absorbed into a predominantly dense and rhythmically active contrapuntal texture. This entails constant use of all available voices (three voices in the introduction, four after the arrival of the tenor) rather than a technique using varied and alternative voice-groupings. In the contrasting sections of these principal movements, variety of sonority, a desideratum strongly advocated by Tinctoris, is achieved by forming central contrasts of two-voice rather than three-voice units, in varying voice-ranges. This brief table shows the difference in broad terms, by indicating the number of measures for two, three, and four voices in the four-voice sections of the Gloria and Credo:

	2v.	3v.	4v.
Et in terra	3.5	12.5	19
Qui tollis	15	3	53
Patrem	7.5	16.5	31
Crucifixus	17	33.5	46

In the *Missa 'Io ne tengo'* Martini employs a popular melody in various forms within a freely developing polyphonic and predominantly non-imitative texture. In the *Missa 'La Martinella'*, however, the disposition of the work proceeds not from a monophonic tune but from the closely organized and highly imitative structure of a three-part instrumental chanson from which he takes successive portions of the Tenor as the basis for the movement-cycles within the Mass. By this means, Martini avoids the customary symmetry by which the major movements ('Kyrie', 'Et in terra', 'Patrem', 'Sanctus', Agnus I) share not only opening counterpoint but the identical Tenor incipit. Here the Tenor openings form a successive pattern proceeding through the Mass, culminating in the Agnus I in which the Tenor replicates the Tenor of the chanson intact, with a few incidental changes of detail. The five openings do maintain essentially the same material in the other three voices, yet they also vary the contrapuntal disposition in each presentation. The result is a continuously developing form of the Tenor against a stable contrapuntal matrix that is presented in somewhat varied forms. Moreover, in the 'Et in terra' and 'Patrem' at least, and to some extent in the other movements as well, the Tenor remains apart from the highly animated rhythmic style of the other voices. The entire procedure contrasts sharply with the Tenor-integration of the *Missa 'Io ne tengo'*. So does the exceptionally active use, in the *Missa 'La Martinella'*, of imitative patterns that originate in the antecedent but for which Martini discovers in the material new combinative forms.

Martini's extensive use of secular cantus firmi for his Masses suggests a relaxed attitude toward the atmosphere of strong religious faith of the court under Ercole, at least at the abstract level of the choice of basic melody for a polyphonic Mass to be performed in his chapel. And the melodies selected for Mass might well have reflected some of the Duke's personal favorites. Beyond this, the possible reflection of family celebration in *Missa 'Io ne tengo'* might give it a relationship to personal tastes and interests that is otherwise visible in Josquin's works written for Ercole, above all his *Missa 'Hercules'*. If we compare Martini's choices with those of other composers favored in the chapel's collections of the late 1470s, we find that of eighteen Masses in Mod D only five are based on sacred material. Faugues has two Masses in Mod D, his settings of 'L'homme armé' and of 'Je suis en la mer'; and both his other known Masses are also secular in origin. So are two of the four known Masses of Caron. Further, it appears that the versions of a number of Masses in Mod D by Martini, Faugues, and Caron differ substantially from the versions found in contemporary MSS, copied at Trent, Verona, and Rome, although only an extended study of the textual traditions of Mod D and E can reveal the full extent of these differences. Pending the results of such a study, it appears entirely possible that the versions preserved in the Ferrarese sources are the products of considerable editorial supervision and revision, which we can provisionally ascribe to Martini.[3]

Linking the chapel's Mass repertoires equally to a well-known Burgundian and French Mass tradition are the 'L'homme armé' Masses by Faugues and Busnois, which may well have been joined at Ferrara by other settings from the complex of 'L'homme armé' Masses that are now lost to us. If indeed, as I have argued elsewhere, the 'L'homme armé' tradition originated in a Burgundian chanson that was first elaborated in Mass cycles by Dufay and his circle in the late 1450s and early 1460s, and which spread early to the French court under Ockeghem, then we should not be surprised to find numerous settings by composers at work in those Italian centers where Flemish and French musicians were principally active: Naples, Ferrara, and the Papal Chapel.[4] The Mellon chansonnier belongs to Naples around the year 1475, a dating that puts the manuscript squarely into Tinctoris's main period of activity there. Of about the same period is the Naples MS which contains a cycle of six 'L'homme armé' Masses and which presents a poem addressed to Beatrice of Aragon referring to the earlier enjoyment of these works by Charles, Count of Charolais (who became Duke of Burgundy, and was known as Charles the Bold, in 1467).[5] The Ferrara Mass sources of about 1480 contribute significantly to the body of evidence for an Italian courtly vogue of the 'L'homme armé'. To add to the Faugues and Busnois Masses there is the combinative chanson using the famous tune, by Jean Japart, who served in the chapel from 1477 to 1481. And most revealing is Ercole's letter to Montecatini, his ambassador at Florence, written on 16 March 1484, asking for 'the new "L'homme armé" Mass by Philippon' (= Basiron), which in fact is sent to him at once.[6] Whatever the original meaning of the 'L'homme armé' melody, and the hypothetical chanson that was its point of origin,

[3] A partial basis for such comparison is afforded by the two extant versions of the *Missa 'Cucu'*; one in Mod D and the other in Trent 91 (the latter published in *Denkmäler der Tonkunst in Österreich*, lxx, 1970).   [4] See my 'Aspects of the "L'Homme Armé" Tradition'.
    [5] See Cohen, *The Six Anonymous L'Homme Armé Masses in Naples, Biblioteca Nazionale MS VI E 40.*
    [6] For the letter, its background, and its original text, see my 'Aspects', 111, n. 40.

there seems little doubt that the soldier-rulers of the late fifteenth century could interpret the melody and its implied text as a reflection of their role as military leaders and defenders of the people and of the faith. Like Charles the Bold, though to a lesser degree, Ercole spent most of his active career as a military man; and the cultivation of the genre by various composers offered a means of associating himself with those Burgundian and French rulers – Dukes and even Kings – for whom Masses on this tune had been written by composers of great prominence.

I have also argued earlier that if there is a missing link in the chain of evidence for an Italian contribution to the 'L'homme armé' tradition, it is Milan. Here the ducal chapel under Galeazzo Maria had in the earlier 1470s included both Josquin and Compère, as well as singers from Cambrai and Burgundy. Although we know that Josquin was paid in 1475 for copying music for the Sforza court, we do not know just what he copied; but there is nothing in the *Missa 'L'homme armé' super voces musicales* that is incompatible with a dating in Milan in the 1470s, sometime prior to Josquin's departure in 1479. Yet it is also possible that it could have been written in Ferrara in 1480 or 1481, if Josquin, as I believe, accompanied Ascanio Sforza during his residence in the city in those years.

23

Josquin's Missa 'Hercules Dux Ferrarie'

AT what intersecting point in the careers of the composer and patron was the 'Hercules' Mass written? The boundary dates for the work are August 1471, when Ercole became Duke, and June 1505, when it was published by Petrucci in Josquin's Second Book of Masses. These are also about the only fixed points that can be established absolutely, despite a number of adventurous theories. Although dates as far apart as 1487 and 1503 have been suggested, the fact is that neither the musical sources nor the circumstantial evidence is really conclusive for any single date. There are a total of eleven known manuscript sources which contain part or all of the Mass, including Brussels 9126, Jena 3, and Vienna 4809 (all beautiful calligraphic products of the Habsburg-Burgundy court); also one of the Gafori MSS from Milan (Archivio del Duomo, MS 2267) and one of the Spataro MSS from San Petronio in Bologna. But although these and other sources testify to the wide dissemination of the work, none of them can be dated earlier than June 1505, and are thus of no help in finding a date of composition earlier than the Petrucci print. On the other hand, the delicate problem of evaluating various mixtures of external facts and internal evidence presents a special challenge in this case, and in itself may prove instructive. If we can carefully extract various sets of pertinent observations from its historical and theoretical backgrounds, its style, and its symbolic significance for Josquin's contemporaries, the resultant combinations may favor certain hypotheses as being considerably more persuasive than others.

The theoretical background of the Mass has rarely been subjected to close scrutiny. It will be useful to distinguish three levels of consideration: the systematic, the conventional, and the individual. By 'systematic' here I mean the basic tone-system of the period, as we find it expounded by the best-informed and most authoritive theorists of Josquin's time, especially Tinctoris. By 'conventional' I mean particularly those features of design it shares with other polyphonic Mass settings, or rather with certain branches of the Mass literature with which it has most in common. The individual features of the work stand out against these backgrounds.

I need scarcely say that, in broad terms, the tone-system underlying the work is still the familiar Guidonian gamut. Inherited from the Middle Ages and gradually modified to meet the needs of polyphonic music, the system in the fifteenth century was being subjected to expansion and to criticism. But it nevertheless remained in force as the basic framework of musical thought down to the end of the sixteenth century. Essential to it, of course, was the familiar system of seven overlapping hexachords on C, F, and G, which divide the total range into symmetrically functioning subsets. The hexachordal system extends to all voices of a polyphonic complex the same basis for the analysis of melodic behavior that was characteristic of the mono-phonic repertoires for which the whole system had originally been devised. The second dimension of theory that is vital for the background is, of course, the concept of mode, conceived as collocations of the available species of fifth and fourth, and thus also as primarily linear structures.[1] In the later fifteenth century, there emerges a new sense of the significance of these systematic concepts, particularly of mode as a means of integrating not merely the indi-vidual line but the large-scale polyphonic composition. This point of view receives its most important theoretical statement in Tinctoris's treatise on the modes, written in 1476 at Naples. And evidence of the practical application of these concepts is provided by the very titles of such works as Josquin's *Missa 'L'homme armé' super voces musicales* and *Missa 'L'homme armé' sexti toni.*

Whatever their true chronological order, it seems clear that Josquin's Masses exhibit an unprecedented variety of source material and of proce-dures, and their extraordinary diversity was commented upon by such con-temporaries as Glarean.[2] It is as if they represent a deliberately constructed *summa* of contemporary techniques for integrating the Mass cycle, using subjects in part conventional and in part totally original. Every known type is represented: the paraphrased plainsong ordinary in the *Missa de Beata Virgine*; the complete single plainsong in the Masses 'Gaudeamus', 'Ave maris stella', and 'Pange lingua'; the canonic cycle in the Mass *Ad fugam*; the pre-existent secular melody in the two 'L'homme armé' Masses, and the bor-rowing of cantus firmi from known or presumed polyphonic secular models in many of the others. But the group that stands most fully apart from the practices of immediate predecessors or contemporaries is made up of those that use ostinato subjects based on solmization syllables. Of these there are basically three: 'La sol fa re mi'; 'Faisant regretz' (with its ostinato subject *fa-re-mi-re*), and the 'Hercules'. Of these, only the 'Hercules' has a *soggetto cavato*, and it may well be the first of this kind.

---

[1] Recent noteworthy studies of mode in this period include Perkins, 'Mode and Structure in the Masses of Josquin'; Meier, *Die Tonarten der klassischen Vokalpolyphonie*; Powers, 'Mode', *The New Grove*.
[2] Glarean, *Dodekachordon*; on Josquin's Masses see especially Dahlhaus, 'Studien zu den Messen Josquins Desprez', and Osthoff, *Josquin Desprez*, vol. i, *passim*; also the articles by Haar, 'Some Remarks on the "Missa La Sol Fa Re Mi" ', and Lenaerts, 'Musical Structure and Performance Practice in Masses and Motets of Josquin and Obrecht', along with other material in that volume.

In the 'Hercules' Mass, even more than in the others of this group, the rigorous repetitions of the subject determine the structure not only of single movements but of the entire cycle. In laying out the Mass, Josquin proceeds on the assumption that the subject should always be stated as a complete entity and in notes of equal value (which is not at all common in this period); thus it remains almost wholly independent of the rhythms of the other voices. The eight-note cantus firmus is also used as a mathematical module for the entire Mass, since the expositions are virtually always alternated with silences identical in length to the expositions, whether these are in the normal breve-measures or in diminution by half, as in the last part of the Credo or in the Osanna. If we look closely at the Tenor part as it was published by Petrucci, the rigid character of its organization is graphically clear (cf. fig. 12(a)). The scheme is such that the entire cantus firmus consists not of each single statement but of three statements in rising order on D, A, and D, the final and confinal of the mode. This is confirmed by the fact that when the subject is stated in retrograde (as at the 'Et in spiritum') the order of the intervals is also reversed, descending from D to A to D. It is also very curious that on the Tenor part of the Mass Petrucci prints the word 'Resolutio'. This term is normally used for the full notational spelling-out of a theme given in abbreviated form with a verbal canon, such as is frequently found in use for proportional cantus firmi in the late fifteenth century. Well-known examples appear in works by Dufay, Busnois, Ockeghem, and Obrecht. Josquin himself uses fanciful canonic instructions in other works; these include the *soggetto cavato* of his *Missa 'Vive le Roy'*, to which I shall return later. He also uses them in other Masses, such as *'L'homme armé' super voces musicales*, *'Malheur me bat'*, and *De Beata Virgine*. It may not be entirely capricious to imagine that the 'Hercules' Tenor could originally have been written out only once for each movement, with canonic instructions telling the singer how to derive the subject from the name, how to alternate it with rests, and how to handle the diminutions. It may not be a complete coincidence that there are twelve complete threefold expositions of the subject in the Mass; the association of its name and this number might well have evoked the mythological Hercules with his twelve labors. If it did, it would have blended perfectly with the glorification of the figure of Hercules in literary and artistic products at Ferrara under Duke Ercole, who never tired of the comparison. A court historian of the mid-sixteenth century actually suggests that the origins of the Estense family line could be traced back to the French royal family and through them to a marriage between the original Hercules and a Celtic princess.[3]

The Duke's name yielded a subject with interesting intervallic properties and possibilities for elaboration. It begins and ends on the final of mode I, which is to be the tonality of the entire work; the subject therefore possesses

---

[3] Giraldi, *Commentario delle cose di Ferrara*.

inherent unity of mode and ends by step motion, which is useful for a Tenor voice moving below its Superius in contrary motion at cadences. This is also true when the subject is used later in retrograde form. Further, its eight tones clearly subdivide into two segments of four tones, each exhibiting different features of design:

Ex. 6. J. Desprez, *Missa 'Hercules Dux Ferrarie'*, basic form of subject

Thus, the repetition of the two-note figure in the first half brings this segment to a kind of *ouvert* ending on the tone below the final, while the second half has no repetition but again begins and then ends on the final. The first half has another inherent subdivision into units of two plus two, and thus mirrors the axial symmetry of the whole. And both levels of symmetry in the subject gave rise to repetitions and sequential figures in the other voices that reflect and articulate these components of the main subject. It is not merely that this segmentation is latent in the subject but that Josquin uses it to shape the phrase-structure of the larger composition.

A vital feature of the subject, and one that has not been discussed by earlier writers, is the extreme restriction of its intervallic motion. It contains nothing but step motion except for the rising minor third *re-fa*, which is the smallest possible expansion of diatonic step-motion in the system. Nor is this a matter of necessity owing to the ducal name; the vowel '*a*' of 'Ferrarie' can be sung on either *fa* or *la*, and therefore the closely-packed intervallic sequence is deliberate. Let us consider for a moment what the subject would have been like with *la* instead of *fa* as its sixth syllable, either a fifth above or a fourth below the final. It seems clear that there would be something awkward and exotic about it, in the context of the style of Josquin. For this I believe there are several reasons, not all of them so obvious. One lies in the extremely delicate balance in this style between the relationship of diatonic leap- and diatonic step-motion, between adjacent and disjunct members of the hexa-chord. In general, not only will a decisive motion in one direction in a given line be balanced by a motion in the other direction, as Jeppesen found for Palestrina; but a leap-motion will tend to be followed by step-motion and not by another leap, while a large leap will not be immediately followed by another leap but by step-motion, and not in the same but in the opposite direction. Nor could the fifth or even the fourth created by *la* have been anticipated by even so much as a minor third in the first half of the subject, so that a sudden disjunction between step-motion and leap-motion in the two halves of the subject would have been very apparent. Finally, there is another point that has large-scale consequences for the whole Mass. In its upper range above D the subject as it stands is not only completely within the basic pentachord of the D mode, but it remains well below the upper limit of that pentachord. The subject is to have its threefold repetition throughout the Mass, as we have seen, and, as a result of the restriction on its intervallic content, it is so designed that no single exposition anticipates the tone on which the next exposition is to begin. This helps to maintain the intervallic autonomy of the three expositions that form each complete statement of the subject.

Now, this limited intervallic content for the subject is not only characteristic of the 'Hercules' Mass, but is also found in the other two principal examples of the ostinato *soggetto* devised or used by Josquin, the 'La sol fa re mi', and *fa-re-mi-re* (of 'Faisant regretz'):

Ex. 7. J. Desprez, *Missa 'La sol fa re mi'* and *Missa 'Faisant regretz'*, subjects

Both of these, like the 'Hercules' subject, contain only one interval that is not a step motion, and in both cases the leap is the smallest possible – the minor third, *fa-re*. Indeed, the *fa-re-mi-re* figure may be interpreted as a permutation of the last four notes of the 'Hercules' subject, which reverses the order of the *re* and *fa* but maintains the cadential motion. The 'La sol fa re mi' differs both in its E-mode structure and in having no tone repetition, but it too maintains the small-interval principle; and when it is used in partial hexachordal transposition, as it is in portions of the Mass, the interval content of 'La sol fa re mi' is contracted to the same size as the 'Hercules' subject. It is instructive to compare the subject devised by Cipriano de Rore, about a half-century later, for one of his two Masses in honor of Duke Ercole II, the grandson of Josquin's patron. Here, the much longer subject does use a rising fourth and descending fifth in succession at 'se-cun-dus'; but Rore is clearly forced to do this in order to avoid the hopelessly monotonous threefold repetition of the syllable *ut*, at the words 'se-cun-dus dux', and he does so by shifting the hexachord for just one note. His figure for the word 'Ferrarie' is the same as that of Josquin.

This brings us to the relationship between the ostinato subject and the other voices of the complex. It is an established commonplace that the 'Hercules' Mass is exceptional for its strictness of organization and the rigidity of its treatment of the subject. Its avoidance of even partial transposition of its threefold statements of the subject differentiates it sharply from the other ostinato Masses. It is also exceptional for the virtually complete restriction of the material to the Tenor, which has no other function in the complex than to present the cantus firmus, while the other voices are designed in such a way that they avoid not only partial imitations of the subject but virtually any intervallic influence of it; there is one exception to which I shall return. This is not to say that the cantus firmus does not exert a strong influence on the contour and phrase-structure of the other voices – but it does so by virtue of its inflexible repetition of its own figures in equal durational units, and not by 'permeation' of its material to the other voices. The whole concept of 'permeation' is alien to the conception of this work. Thus, in the opening eight measures of Kyrie I, the Superius has the cantus firmus as an introduction, in order to permit the authentic cantus firmus in the Tenor to be the last voice to enter after its eight measures' rest:

Ex. 8. J. Desprez, *Missa 'Hercules Dux Ferrarie'*, Kyrie I

The first four-measure unit (divided as two plus two) is accompanied by a single two-measure phrase stated first in Alto (mm. 1–2) and then in Bass (mm. 3–4). At mm. 5–8, where the cantus firmus moves to its second segment, a new short motif is alternated between Alto and Bass. In mm. 9–16, during the first large Tenor exposition, the accompanying voices are segmented in the same way as the basic melody, which thus determines the articulation of the entire texture even though its motifs are not borrowed. In the Kyrie the closely-packed small-interval structure of the cantus firmus is restricted to the Tenor, while the other voices are characterized by wide-spanned phrase units, sometimes in close succession: see, for example, mm. 9–16 in Superius, Alto, and Bass. The Superius at 9–10 has the successive leap of octave, fifth, and third plus one passing tone and then third and fifth; similar patterns abound throughout the Mass.

What should the Tenor voice sing? It is obvious that the other voices can all sing the entire text of each movement, but that the Tenor cannot do so except in the Kyrie and Agnus Dei, since these have so little text but sufficient length. Smijers' edition shows the Tenor singing appropriate portions of the Mass text, but a familiar alternative is to have it performed by instruments. Perhaps the most suitable alternative is that the Tenor should sing the name and title 'Hercules Dux Ferrarie' throughout the work against the Mass text in the other voices, and even in the two retrograde expositions. If it did so, it would fit in with the later traditions by which Masses with explicit double text in the sixteenth century were typically celebration compositions for great personages: thus Morales' Mass for Pope Paul III and Palestrina's for Pope Julius III, Gombert's Mass for the Emperor Charles V, and others.

Certain symbolic aspects of early Renaissance music have been explored by scholars for a long time, and the subject has recently received renewed emphasis through the contributions of Willem Elders and Maria Rika Maniates.[4] It has long been recognized that musicians of the time sought to establish correlations between various graphic and structural properties of

---

[4] Elders, *Studien zur Symbolik in der Musik der alten Niederländer*; Maniates, 'Combinative Chansons in the Dijon Chansonnier'.

music – including its notation, its text, and details of musical structure – and that these relationships can be regarded as a type of symbolism. One such procedure is the use of special features of musical notation to indicate the special meaning of a text: thus Josquin's lamentation for the death of Ockeghem (the familiar 'Nymphes des bois') is written entirely in black notation in one early source. Similar texts referring to affective or pictorial concepts evoke symbolically appropriate notation from composers down to the end of the sixteenth century, and, indeed, down to the time of Bach. Broadly speaking, an expressive approach to text is one of the great accomplishments of all Renaissance music.

But the symbolism in the 'Hercules' Mass is not of this type. With the possible exception of one short passage, this work is not characterized by close rhetorical embellishment of its text. The single brief exception is the one passage in the Mass in which a partial segment of the cantus firmus *is* quoted in another voice without a full exposition of the entire melody. It is at the beginning of the Gloria, at the words 'Et in terra pax hominibus bonae voluntatis'.

Ex. 9. J. Desprez, *Missa 'Hercules Dux Ferrarie'*, Gloria, mm. 1–4, with plainsong intonation

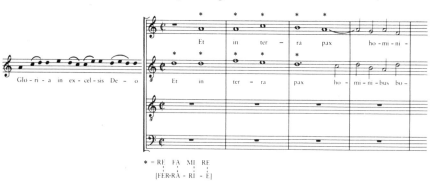

Here the upper two voices have a figure that literally uses the notes *re fa mi re* the order of vowels in 'Ferrarie'; cf. fig. 12(*b*). This brings in the name of the city at just the point where the Mass text refers to men on earth ('Et in terra'), having just referred to God in heaven in the preceding plainsong intonation ('Gloria in excelsis Deo'). But this is a totally isolated moment, not taken up elsewhere. And by and large it must be said that, although in the Mass as a whole the text is enunciated correctly and accurately, the work is not designed to make the music reflect the meaning of the words to any large degree.

This composition is symbolic in another sense, because of its unique combination of this unprecedented cantus firmus with the Mass itself. On the one hand, it provides a liturgically usable setting of the Ordinary; on the other, it is a new type of tribute to a contemporary ruler, whose name is made a part of the fabric of the Mass and becomes a counter-subject to the liturgical text.

There is ample evidence that the 'Hercules' Mass was recognized as being a distinctive type of glorification. When it was copied into manuscripts destined for the libraries and choirs of other princes, it received an appropriate change of title. Thus, in the MS Brussels 9126, intended for Archduke Philip, just crowned King of Castile, this Mass appears with the text *Missa 'Philippus Rex Castiliae'*. About twenty years later, it was copied for Duke Frederick the Wise, the friend of Luther, and here it was named *Missa 'Fredericus Dux Saxsonie'*. Of course the music remains unchanged, so that the new names do not fit, but unless its audience knew the original the risk was probably small that the subject would be traced to its solmization syllables. The political importance of the piece is shown by later Masses of the same type, which evolve new cantus firmi from the syllables of patrons' names: one is the Mass for the Emperor Charles V with the subject 'Carolus Imperator Romanorum Quintus', and at least three Masses that were written for the grandson of Ercole, Duke Ercole II d'Este. What had originally been a fusion of the Mass as liturgy and as political celebration had now become a tradition.

24

The Psalms, Hymns, and Other Vespers Music by Martini and Brebis

THE double-chorus manuscripts Mod C_1 and C_2 fully represent the types of polyphonic Office compositions produced for Ercole's chapel in the 1470s. Their style is closely constrained by the narrow limits imposed by genre and convention, and shows much use of fauxbourdon and chant paraphrase in a simple manner. Martini's effort to enrich the content of several of his Hymn and Magnificat settings through close imitation and canon belong to a phase of Vespers composition that is freer in approach than that of his predecessors.[1]

The foundations of the approach to liturgical polyphony for this genre had been established in Italy in the period of Dufay, above all by his own famous cycle of hymns, but also in other works, which used fauxbourdon, by him and his contemporaries. Whether or not Dufay himself was the 'inventor' of fauxbourdon – and it seems more than likely that his uses of the procedure fall back on improvisational techniques known to earlier generations of singers in Italy – he adapted it with striking effect in various works; and this means of using full consonant sonorities made great headway in the mid- and later fifteenth century. It formed an important component of the simpler levels of polyphonic liturgical music in the Italian princely chapels. At Ferrara the rich sonorities of note-against-note fauxbourdon had been well known in the chapel of Leonello – 'quanto piaceva li vespri con le Messe, wrote the chronicler – and among the main composers of Mod B are a number of the major representatives of the fauxbourdon style, all of them contemporaries of Dufay: Feragut, Fede, Binchois. The growth of Italian chapels, the increasing observance of the Vespers Office among their patrons, and the continued use of fauxbourdon in the late fifteenth century go hand in hand. In this development the material of Mod C_1 and C_2 forms a principal source for the 1470s.

We know that Ercole's double chorus, including his group of choirboys from Germany, lasted until 1482, when the war with Venice broke up the chapel. It is exactly in this period that the double-chorus Psalms, Hymns, and

---

[1] Brawley, 'The Magnificats, Hymns, Motets and Secular Music of Johannes Martini'; Kanazawa, 'Martini and Brebis at the Estense Chapel'.

other pieces of these paired in-folio choirbooks were composed. The basic contents of C₁ and C₂, as studied by Kanazawa, show us what Ercole's requirements were for the chapel for the Vespers of Lent and Matins of Holy Week.

The main contents of the two paired MSS are as follows (after Kanazawa):

Table 11.   Contents of MSS Mod C₁ and Mod C₂

Mod C₁		Mod C₂	
1ᵛ–34	35 ferial Vespers Psalms, odd-numbered verses; all but one written as 2-voice compositions, implying fauxbourdon; one composition has 3 written-out voices	1ᵛ–34	35 ferial Vespers Psalms, even-numbered verses; to alternate with those of C₁
34ᵛ–38ᵛ	8 Vespers hymns; odd verses only; 4 by Brebis, 3 by Martini	34ᵛ–38ᵛ	Even-numbered verses for first 6 of 8 hymns in C₁ (last 2 missing); all by Martini except one.
39–42ᵛ	4 Magnificats; odd verses only; 1 by Brebis, 1 by Martini		Corresponding even-numbered verses of these Magnificats missing in MS (14 fols. removed from C₂, only stubs remain)
43–46	blank		
47ᵛ–49	Tract 'Domine non secundum', 3 voices, by Martini		
49ᵛ–50	blank		
50ᵛ–114	33 Psalms for Matins or Lauds of Maundy Thursday, Good Friday and Holy Saturday, odd verses only; 22 in fauxbourdon; 11 are in 3 written-out voices	39–91	33 Psalms as in C₁ even-numbered verses only (first setting lacks opening)
114ᵛ–116ᵛ	fragment on 116 and 116ᵛ.	91ᵛ–97	A setting of the Passion
		97ᵛ–101	Passion

If we distinguish the stylistic constraints of the three main genres, the Hymns and Magnificats emerge as comparatively richer in procedure and invention than the Psalms, although all three categories show considerably less freedom of contrapuntal treatment than motets or Masses. The largely unattributed body of Psalms presents a problem of authorship, but, like the remainder of the MS, they may well be the joint work of Brebis and Martini. It is possible, however, that the MS was not yet fully finished in 1479 when Brebis died and that the final form of the collection was overseen by Martini, as would have been likely in any case.

The Hymns follow the broad tendencies of polyphonic hymn setting in Italy as established by Dufay in the 1430s and later developed by his younger contemporaries, including the Genoese composer Antonius Janue.[2] They form a partial cycle of hymns for the liturgical year, with three hymns for Lent and Easter, and five for the Common of the Saints (Apostles, Martyrs, Confessors, Virgins). Brebis wrote the odd-numbered stanzas for four of them (possibly five, one being unattributed) and Martini the corresponding even-numbered verses. All are for three voices, with a paraphrase of the plainsong in the Superius, and in the Tenor and Contratenor relatively simple counterpoint within the range of an octave below the highest voice. Kanazawa has distinguished the styles of hymn setting by Martini and Brebis:

> In general, Brebis prefers a simpler texture of music, often indulging in parallel motions among voices and in a more homorhythmic structure. Martini is the more sophisticated of the two, and particularly favors an extensive use of imitative writing.[3]

The examples transcribed by Kanazawa and Brawley make clear the different levels on which Martini and Brebis stand. Brebis, not much in evidence as a composer beyond these few works and one or two motets for Ercole, on the whole writes freely expanding contrapuntal material, well made and reasonably consistent, in phrases of limited span and with simple contrasts. Martini aims to intensify and to elaborate through imitation the contrapuntal possibilities inherent in a brief phrase, contrasting imitative phrases with non-imitative ones as a means of achieving large-scale formal organization.

In Martini's section of the hymn 'Deus tuorum militum', Kanazawa rightly calls attention to his tendency to set the Superius and Tenor as well-made vocal lines, maintaining small ranges and carefully formed linear contours, while the Contratenor, as in the three-voice chanson style familiar since Dufay, tends to use large skips, wide-spanning intervals, and sudden juxtapositions of high and low ranges.

Ex. 10(*a*). J. Brebis, 'Deus tuorum militum', stanza 1

[2] On the development of the hymn in the 15th century the most general study is that of Gerber, *Zur Geschichte des mehrstimmigen Hymnus*, esp. pp. 96–107; more recently, the subject has been re-examined by Ward, 'The Polyphonic Office Hymn from the Late Fourteenth Century to the Early Sixteenth Century'.   [3] Kanazawa, 'Martini and Brebis', 426.

Ex. 10(*b*). J. Martini, 'Deus tuorum militum', stanza 2

In view of the substantial size of Ercole's chapel, even in the 1470s, we may speculate as to whether the Contratenor part, which in the chapel was surely sung, not played on instruments, was performed by several singers on the same part. If so, in passages calling for sudden skips between widely separated tessituras, subgroups of the Contratenor section might easily have divided their part so that only one or two of them sang each phrase; one in low register, the other in high. If so, this would have formed a method of realizing in performance what Kanazawa calls 'self-imitation', that is, a quasi-imitative passage within the single vocal part. In a few other sections of these hymns that are either explicitly ascribed to Martini or can be attributed to him with some confidence, the range of technical procedure varies between segments of short canonic imitation, concluding with cadences (as in 'Audi benigne conditor', pointed out by Kanazawa), and simple successions of parallel consonant intervals, as in Martini's portion of 'Vexilla regis', the Easter hymn.

We can also mention here Martini's four-voice settings of the hymns 'Ave maris stella' and 'Festum nunc celebre', significantly not found in the Modena choirbooks but rather in the important Munich MS 3154, recently studied by Thomas Noblitt with a view to dating its component fascicles by means of watermarks and paper types. Noblitt assigns the copying of both settings to

1476, along with other works in that fascicle of the MS.[4] This date might fit in well with Martini's work for the Ferrara chapel; on the other hand, it seems much more likely that these independent, imitative four-voice motet-like settings of hymn texts fit in much better with the apparent development of balanced, imitative four-voice motet-style evidently cultivated at Milan in the years between *c.*1471 and 1476 by Weerbecke, Compère, and Josquin, the masterpiece of which is Josquin's metrical 'Ave Maria', likewise said by Noblitt to have been copied in Munich 3154 in 1476. So this type of hymn setting, a freely developed contrapuntal composition for four voices, might well date from 1474, the year of Martini's presence in Milan for nine months or more (see above p. 268 f.). The Milanese emphasis on four-voice motet settings, exploring the balances created by regular imitative procedures, pairing of voices, high-low repetitions of the same or similar passages – all this is in sharp contrast to the stress placed in Ercole's chapel on the strictly liturgical, simple paraphrase settings of hymns and other forms for three voices, with much use of declamatory fauxbourdon.

Noblitt has similarly dated at least one of Martini's Magnificats (the *Magnificat Octavi Toni*) to Milan, supposing that Martini was in Milan throughout 1474 and 1475; in fact he was there only in 1474. His assumption here is based on the use of the Ambrosian textual variant for Verse 5 of the Magnificat text. On the other hand, this variant might have been entered in a Milanese choirbook in order to conform to local use, and indeed the work appears in the indigenous Milan Codex 2269 as well as in Munich 3154. In the latter MS, which is liturgically neutral as regards Ambrosian and Roman textual variants, Noblitt finds that the Magnificats of Martini were copied about 1480–2, which fits in well with the date of completion of Mod C_1 and C_2. In his Magnificats Martini shows the same traditional use of the plainsong as a basis for cantus firmus or paraphrase as in his hymns; but here the extended form of the work gives rise to much greater use of sectional contrast involving imitative procedures that alternate with freer contrapuntal segments. The imitation sometimes extends to three voices rather than to the two that are more customary for him in the hymns; and the use of imitation at very close time- and pitch-intervals prevails. In the Magnificats, too, however, as in the hymns, we can distinguish a florid and expanded style as opposed to a simple and functional one; the latter style rules in the single attributed *Magnificat 3. Toni a fauxbourdon* that is found in Mod C_1 (missing from C_2), and of which the even-numbered verses were certainly originally in C_2 before these leaves were cut out; see Ex. 11. The difference in approach between the elaborated style of the big four-voice compositions, and the simple, austere setting for the Ferrarese choirbooks, reflects the special qualities of expression desired by Ercole for his chapel services.

---

[4] Noblitt, 'Die Datierung'.

Ex. 11. J. Martini, *Magnificat 3. Toni*, I

Finally, the Psalms of C_1 and C_2 deserve comment. Since the polyphonic setting of Psalm texts was to become a major form of composition in the work of the mature Josquin and his followers, developing into one of the foremost expressive categories of the sixteenth-century Latin motet, it is interesting to examine these double-chorus Psalms as potential harbingers of some aspects of the vastly expanded motet style of the next generation. Here we find the greatest possible austerity. Of the sixty-eight settings, more than fifty are in fauxbourdon, with the simplest presentation of the cantus firmus in the highest voice and with the lower voice moving almost always in complete rhythmic co-ordination with the upper line. Furthermore, as Kanazawa points out, the fauxbourdon dictates that the two notated voices will almost always be in parallel sixths.[5] In all, these are the most constrained

[5] Kanazawa, 'Martini and Brebis', 431.

of compositions. Historically, they do not anticipate the free Psalm-motet compositions of the elaborate type, but rather belong to the strictly liturgical Psalm tradition, of which the legitimate descendants are the double-chorus Psalms by Willaert and Jacquet of Mantua, published in 1550. Zarlino notes that Psalm compositions fall clearly into two general categories, the free and the liturgical Psalm, and these belong to the latter category. The absence of all contrapuntal ornament results in the clear declamation of text, doubtless suited to the recitative character of Psalm-recitation long familiar in the Offices. It makes possible polyphonic but fairly rapid and clear declamation of the texts, which intensifies the formulaic character and avoids any hint of the domination of the Psalm texts by the rich confusion of polyphony. Had there been any potential danger of accusation of too much indulgence in counterpoint in a liturgical situation, these works would have answered it. Although we do not find any concerted complaints of this sort at so early a date, nevertheless Savonarola was heard in the 1490s denouncing just this type of music in princely chapels on the grounds that the use of elaborate polyphony obscured the sacred texts:[6]

Egli hanno questi signori le cappelle de'cantori, che bene pare proprio un tumulto, perche vi sta la uno cantore con una voce grossa che pare uno vitello, et li altri cridano a torno come cani, et non s'intende cosa che dicino. Lasciate andare i canti figurati et cantate i canti fermi ordinati dalla chiesa . . .

These Lords have chapels of singers that seem like a great tumult, because there stands a singer with a big voice like that of a calf, and the others yell around him like dogs, and no one understands what they are singing. Leave aside figured music and sing the plainsongs ordained by the church . . .

The style of these Psalms, and, to a lesser extent, that of the hymns, Magnificats, and other music of C_1 and C_2, shows that as early as about 1476–80, a deliberate simplicity of style in the embellishment of plainsong was preferred in this chapel, thus introducing some eighty years *avant la lettre* a kind of 'intelligible music' of the type favored by the Counter-Reformation. Ercole's religious feeling and preferred mode of expression for the daily office are mirrored in the austerity of the Psalm settings.

[6] Quoted by Pirrotta, 'Italien, 14.–16. Jahrhundert', *Die Musik in Geschichte und Gegenwart*, vi, col. 1492; and in my 'Music and Popular Religious Spectacle at Ferrara under Ercole I d'Este', p. 580.

25

The Motet at Ferrara

IN later years, the development of wider musical and diplomatic contacts broadened the motet literature available to the chapel. So did the increasingly international character of the chapel itself, as it came under the leadership of musicians of the stature of Josquin and Obrecht. Among the handful of motets by Martini himself, we can distinguish several types. His wedding motet for Ercole and Eleonora, 'Perfunde coeli rore', doubtless composed in 1473, is a four-voice tenor motet with absorption of the cantus firmus into the active texture, which displays many of the familiar contrasts of Martini's more florid works: non-imitative vs. imitative sections, rambling and rhythmically asymmetrical activity in all voices, and little attempt to simplify by means familiar in the Milanese four-voice motet style of the same period.[1] In his later motets we find a variety of types: the three-voice 'Domine non secundum' (a Tract for Ash Wednesday) is found in Mod C_1 and thus probably served as an Office composition, despite its normal use in the Mass. The three-voice setting in the Segovia MS labeled 'O intemerata' may be a contrafactum, in view of its extreme simplicity of style. Between these extremes fall the few four-voice motets: 'Salve regina', 'Levate capita vestra', and 'O beate Sebastiane'. The 'Salve regina', published by Gerber, can probably be associated with the devastating war of 1482–4; it is a heart-felt cry for peace along with an appeal to the Virgin, combining with the Compline antiphon text the cantus firmus 'Da pacem', followed later in the motet by segments from famous plainsongs associated, respectively, with Passiontide, the Common of Apostles, Palm Sunday and Pentecost.[2] The overall layout of the motet is as shown on p. 259.

Another likely topical motet is Martini's 'O beate Sebastiane', which invokes the aid of the martyr against plague, and thus may well be from the 1480s, either during the war years or the middle years of the decade, when several outbreaks of plague occurred.

Ercole's agents later brought in increasing numbers of motets by foreign composers, chiefly from France. Thus, in 1501, Verbonnet sent a Responsory

---

[1] This motet, from Trent MS 91, was published by Disertori, ed., *Johannes Martini: Magnificat e Messe*, p. 89. The date '1471' given in *The New Grove*, xi, 727, is an editorial mistake; I had originally written '1473', as here.

[2] In *Das Chorwerk*, xlvi, ed. R. Gerber.

Section	Main Text	Second text as cantus firmus
1	Salve regina, misericordiae, dulcedo et spes nostra, salve.	Da pacem, Domine, in diebus nostris; quia non est alius qui pugnet pro nobis, nisi tu, Deus noster.
2	Ad te clamamus, exsules filii Evae.	O crux ave, spes unica, hoc passionis tempore
3	Ad te suspiramus, gementes et flentes in hac lacrimarum valle.	Auge piis iustitiam reisque dona veniam.
4	Eia ergo. (3-voice section)	——
5	Advocata nostra, illos tuos misericordes oculos, ad nos converte.	Vos amici mei estis, si feceritis, quae praecipio vobis, dicit Dominus.
6	Et Jesum, benedictum fructum ventris tui, nobis post hoc exsilium ostende.	Gloria, laus et honor, tibi sit, rex Christe, redemptor cui puerile decus prompsit Osanna pium.
7	O clemens,	O clemens,
8	O dulcis Maria.	Da tuis fidelibus in te confidentibus sacrum septenarium.

Ex. 12. J. Martini, 'Salve Regina', mm. 1–13

for Corpus Christi; and in 1502 the new works that were arriving at court included a 'Salve Regina' by Josquin.[3] We can assume that the Ferrarese repertoires kept up with the new devotional and liturgical motets then being produced by Josquin and his contemporaries, although no large Ferrarese motet manuscript of this period has been preserved. But from the period of Josquin's own tenure at Ferrara, we can now date two of his most characteristic motets: the 'Virgo salutiferi' and the 'Miserere mei, Deus', both of which were evidently written at court at this time and epitomize the motet-types favored by Ercole in his later years.

The motet 'Virgo salutiferi' is one of the largest and most fully developed of Josquin's Marian motets. Closely resembling the Sequence motet, 'Inviolata, integra et casta es', which is also a five-voice motet with two-voice canonic cantus firmus, the 'Virgo salutiferi' is found in at least one Roman MS, Sistina MS 42, in a segment that probably dates from about 1505–10; this anticipates by a decade or more its first published appearance, in Petrucci's Third Book of the *Motetti de la Corona*, 1519. For a long time it was simply accepted as an apparently non-liturgical motet, based on a text of unknown origin. But, as noted earlier, Edward Lowinsky has discovered that the author of the poem is the Ferrarese poet, Ercole Strozzi (*c*.1470–1508), son of the poet and humanist Tito Vespasiano Strozzi (1425–1503). It was published in the Aldine edition of poems by father and son – *Strozzi Poetae Pater et Filius* – which was dedicated to Lucrezia Borgia and which contains a poem lamenting Ercole Strozzi's violent death in 1508.[4] The three sections of the motet all make use of a canonic statement of the Marian antiphon, 'Ave Maria, gratia plena', on which Josquin had based a four-voice motet in a quite different style. The cantus firmus canon progressively telescopes in distance between the *dux* and *comes* as the work advances from its first to its third main

[3] See Gottwald, *Johannes Ghiselin–Johannes Verbonnet*, p. 14; and my 'Josquin at Ferrara', p. 122, Appendix I, item no. 4.
[4] See Lowinsky, *The Medici Codex*, iii, pp. 199 f.

section, and also makes some use of diminution of note-values in the second and third sections. The entire scheme is essentially the same one used in the 'Inviolata' motet, which, incidentally, also circulated in Ferrarese sources; we find it in one of the surviving partbooks of the London-Paris-Modena manuscript which dates from approximately 1530 and which is of unquestioned Ferrarese origin.

The great companion-piece to the Marian composition is Josquin's monumental motet, 'Miserere mei, Deus', his five-voice setting of the Penitential Psalm 50. Osthoff notes that the Psalm is traditionally used for funeral services; but to this we can add that among its other normal uses in the liturgy are not less than three occurrences of the entire Psalm text during Holy Week – at Lauds of Holy Thursday, Good Friday, and Holy Saturday. That the motet was written at the express request of Duke Ercole is claimed by the lively macaronic poet Teofilo Folengo, also known as Merlin Cocai, whose comments on musicians and especially on Josquin have become well known. In a laudatory passage on Josquin, whose music is fancifully portrayed as being sung by the chief musicians of Leo X (including several formerly at Ferrara), Folengo twice mentions the Duke of Ferrara, in connection with a list of famous works by Josquin.[5]

> O felix Bido, Carpentras, Silvaque, Broyer,
> Vosque leoninae cantorum squadra capellae:
> Josquini quoniam cantus frifolabitis illos,
> Quos Deus auscultans coelum monstrabit apertum:
> Missa 'super voces Musarum, lassaque farmi,
> Missa super sextum, fortunam, gaudeamusque
> Missaque de Domina, sine nomine, duxque Ferrarie':
> Partibus in senis cantabitur illa: 'Beata,
> Huc me sidereo, se congie, praeter' – et illud
> Compositum 'miserere' Duce rogitante Ferrara . . .

The colossal size and formidable structure of the 'Miserere' has attracted much favorable commentary – Lowinsky compares it to Michelangelo's Last Judgement and claims that 'we have here in music a work of a power, an intensity, a vision, a greatness of conception, and a religious fervor fully comparable to, and in some aspects perhaps exceeding, Michelangelo's work.'[6] Though this is a sweeping claim, its main point is correct in that it identifies Josquin's extraordinary concentration of means and effects in this motet with the religious intensity it is meant to express. Surprisingly, although Lowinsky notes that the work was composed 'between ca. 1503 and ca. 1505', he does

---

[5] Folengo, *Opus Merlini Cocai Poete Mantuani Macaronicorum . . .*, fol. 90; see my 'Josquin at Ferrara', p. 117, and Haar, 'Some Remarks', esp. p. 568.
[6] Lowinsky, *The Medici Codex*, iii, p. 196.

not mention Folengo's reference to its origins at the request of Ercole d'Este or that its manifest universality can also be interpreted as encompassing specific musical and observant practices that belonged to the traditions of Ercole's chapel.

The remarkable form and technique of the work require brief comment, however familiar they may be by now. Josquin divides the long Psalm text into three extensive parts of 169, 120, and 135 measures respectively. The whole is unified by means of an ostinato in one of the two Tenor voices, incessantly repeating the words 'Miserere mei, Deus', and descending by steps through an octave, then rising an octave in the second part, then descending a fifth in the third part. To this, the other voices add a varied tissue of material that etches out the text with great clarity, setting each Psalm verse with brief segments of carefully-formed, melodic-contrapuntal content that fit the words, while offering strongly contrasting relief from the powerful recurrent ostinato. Each time the ostinato occurs it brings with it the entire tutti complement that is heard nowhere else in the immense motet. Inevitably, the symbolic implication is clear: the five-voice ostinato, each time returning, in effect personifies the voice of the Psalm-singer, uttering in *voce plena* his cry for mercy. As Lowinsky points out, the use of the *pes ascendens* and *descendens* for the ostinato assures a variety of cadential steps for the piece, and thus a variety of harmonic positions for its successive cadeness. The expressivity of the whole is, indeed, unprecedented, and it is scarcely surprising that the 'Miserere' motif, and indeed the motet itself, became a classic of the sixteenth-century motet literature and a highly influential work.

What of its significance in local musical traditions? From what we have seen so far, the answers could hardly be clearer. Ercole's high expectations on the arrival of Josquin, the special importance of Josquin's position at the court, the submission of pieces from elsewhere to be judged by him; all these elements of evidence convince us of what we could in any case have assumed – that Ercole saw in Josquin a true 'crown for this chapel of ours', as Coglia had put it directly to him. Presumably, in the first half-year or more of Josquin's stay at the court, Ercole asked him to compose a work that would be suitable for the Holy Week services of 1504 and that would be in keeping with the solemn and striking observances that Ercole had carried out for years. These included his washing of the feet of the poor; his banquet for the poor; the ducal processions and prayers; the special performances of the Passion and other sacred dramas. At Passiontide Ercole focused all civic attention upon the drama of the agony and resurrection of Christ, and upon his own unrelenting personal quest for redemption through intense observance and piety.

Of course, the Psalms had been a vital component of the court chapel's Offices of Vespers, Matins, and Lauds for Lent and Holy Week for many

Ex. 13. J. Desprez, 'Miserere mei, Deus', mm. 1–24

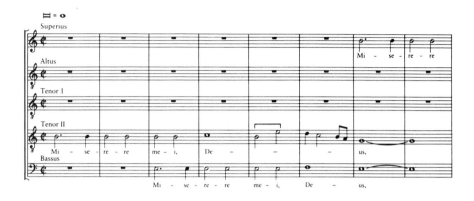

years. As we have seen, a strict declamatory style of performance of these long and expressive texts had been a fixed and essential aspect of the services since the 1480s. This is also the case with the Passions Ercole had had performed, both the fragmentary ones in the 1480 double-chorus MSS and some of the more complete Passion settings known to us, including that of Longaval or of other Ferrarese composers of later vintage, including Maistre Jhan.[7] In this local tradition, Josquin's immense 'Miserere' forms a first culmination and synthesis. It uses the declamatory style of the earlier Psalm tradition but raises it to a higher level of expressivity by much greater and more varied means of structural articulation. It reflects, in its use of ostinato and the stepwise motion of the ostinato figure, something of the same architectural strictness and symmetry that Josquin had employed for this same patron in his *Missa 'Hercules'*, where the rising threefold statement of the figure extends its function over longer sections in much the same way as the octave and fifth spans of the ostinato do here. It employs the collective, polyphonic medium as a symbol of Ercole's personal devotion, placing him figuratively in the role of the Psalm singer. That all this was accomplished by Josquin with a sense of writing for one of the great chapels of singers then in existence, is also to be assumed; but we can also sense the recognition of his work in the attempt by one of the virtuoso singers of the court – Antonius Collebaudi alias Bidon – to write an added voice for the work, preserved in the MS St. Gall 463.

Recently, Mr Patrick Macey has made the remarkable observation that this Josquin motet may well have been linked not only to Ercole's personal piety but to Savonarola's well-known meditation on Psalm 50, which was published at Ferrara earlier than it was elsewhere, and in which the Psalm's opening words, 'Miserere mei, Deus', are printed in bold capitals every time they appear in the text.[8] Macey suggests, quite plausibly, that Savonarola's meditation might not only have played a role in Ercole's apparent commission to Josquin to write this setting (and to emphasize the opening refrain) but that it also reflects Ercole's well-established sympathy for the martyred Savonarola. Josquin might have had the text of the meditation in mind in composing the work. Macey's views on the 'Miserere' are strengthened by his further discovery that the settings of the text 'Infelix ego', by Williaert, Rore, Vicentino, and others, also take their origin from Savonarola's medi-

---

[7] Longaval was in Alfonso's service in the ten months from December 1503 to September 1504; therefore his residence at Ferrara overlapped that of Josquin Desprez for five months (December 1503 to April 1504); see Lockwood, 'Jean Mouton and Jean Michel', 204, n. 31. His Passion, long misattributed to Obrecht, is in the important motet MS Florence, Biblioteca Nazionale Centrale, Fondo nazionale II.1.232, on which see Cummings, 'A Florentine Sacred Repertory from the Medici Restoration'.

[8] Macey, 'Savonarola and the Sixteenth-Century Motet'.

tation on Psalm 50, while another motet by Clemens non Papa derives from his meditation on Psalm 30. This shows that the later Ferrarese tradition of motets using the 'Miserere' refrain involves not only the 'authority' of Josquin but the continued veneration of Savonarola, especially in the 1530s and 1540s.

26

Secular Music at the Court: Chanson and Instrumental Music

SECULAR polyphony in the Renaissance is inevitably less well documented than is sacred music. Chroniclers have generally little to say about secular compositions beyond brief references to the presence of music at festivities of all kinds. Further, the loss of sources is greater than for sacred music, since manuscripts often depended for survival on their preservation by private collectors, or eventually found their way into libraries far from their places of origin. Yet enough music and documentation remains to justify the claim that Ferrara had a role in secular music equal to its importance for sacred music, even in Ercole's period.

It is now clear that around 1470 the creation of new court chapels had important consequences apart from the sacred genres their singers were hired to perform. With the arrival of foreign singers, the French chanson – long an international body of music – came in abundance to the Italian courts and became the model of polyphonic secular style. For this development Dufay is still the patriarchal figure, as late as the 1460s and probably even in the 1470s, but by the end of Ercole's first decade of rule and into the 1480s, chansons in numbers by the next generation of composers – Ockeghem, Busnois, Agricola, Caron, Hayne, and many others – were being copied into Italian MSS and were being performed by the newly appointed musicians of the chapels, perhaps by skillful amateurs as well. Beginning about 1460, and throughout the decades that lead to the rise of the frottola, we must envisage in Italy the absorption of currently composed and highly varied repertoires of foreign polyphonic song, principally French but including, to a lesser degree, some English, Flemish, and purely instrumental pieces. It is doubtful whether the newly imported repertoires in any way displaced the Italian popular-song and narrative formulas that were familiar at the courts; rather, they co-existed with them. However, they probably did provide Italian musicians and patrons with a new awareness of the resources of expression and technique then available to the French courtly tradition, and they formed an analogue in music for the volumes of French romance and other literature that many Italian patrons, including the Ferrarese, were avidly importing as well. Furthermore, although at some centers, above all Mantua, the rise of Italian semi-polyphonic or fully polyphonic settings of vernacular poetry can in part be felt as a reaction against the impact of French poetry and music in Italy, Ferrara, for reasons by now made amply clear, was particularly receptive to French music and poetry, and continued to be so through the first decades of the sixteenth century. It did so despite the rise of printing at Venice, which sharpened awareness of the poetic and stylistic distance that divided the frottola literature from the chanson.

If we restrict our account to the surviving MSS of secular music, we find that beginning around 1460, and continuing into the next two decades, a series of MSS of secular music is produced in several Italian centers – Naples, Florence, and Ferrara.[1] From Naples alone we have at least six, possibly seven, polyphonic sources that were copied between about 1460 and the late 1480s (1487 is the explicit date of the diminutive manuscript Bologna Q 16, which appears to be the last of the Neapolitan group). From Florence we have at least two separate periods of secular MS production – one from the 1470s and early 1480s, the other from the 1490s. The two groups differ in repertoire, and reflect different phases of local activity. Only in the later group do we see music by composers who were primarily active at Florence and whose work had by the 1490s reached sufficient prominence and circulation to attract the attention of collectors. Individual patrons played a large role as collectors of secular music and a number of the MSS that we attribute to courts may really have belonged to such collectors. Accordingly, although we have not yet identified surviving chansonniers of this period that belonged to patrons or households in Rome, Venice, Milan, Urbino, Siena, or many other centers, we can assume that such MSS existed. Some may simply be concealed by the broad and generic term 'Libro de canto' found in many library inventories of the period.

At Ferrara the French vogue gained in force during the 1490s, as we see from Ercole's contacts with Charles VIII, his loan of instrumentalists to Charles during the French invasion, and his interest in obtaining music from Compère in 1494. At Mantua, with the newly arrived and ambitious Isabella dominating the cultural scene, the frottola was becoming fashionable through the work of a new generation of Italian-born composers – principally Cara, Tromboncino, and Michele Pesenti; yet the powerful musical stronghold at Ferrara did not challenge Mantuan leadership in this sector, though Ferrara was much stronger in its musical manpower and traditions. It appears that, at Ferrara, musicians of the new type – well-trained Italian-born lutenists and singers with some degree of prowess in melodic and contrapuntal techniques – were not then much established. Yet the younger Ferrarese patrons, especially Isabella's brothers, Ippolito, Alfonso, Ferrante, and don Julio – were certainly in touch with the new Mantuan activity being encountered and manipulated by Isabella, partly through correspondence and partly through intermediaries, including the inevitable Coglia. But at Ferrara the frottola

---

[1] For a recent survey of the chansonniers produced in Italy in the late 15th century, see Atlas, *The Cappella Giulia Chansonnier* i, p. 258.

grows in close competition to the chanson literature, which is steadily pursued by locally established musicians from France, by the brilliant groups of instrumentalists, and is fed by the copyists and collectors of *chanterie*. By 1501 the *Odhecaton*, in all respects a North Italian chansonnier, makes it possible to purchase a collection of this type.

At Ferrara we know that the musical holdings of the court library had grown from a few MSS in the early 1470s – of which one or two at most may have contained secular works – to at least twelve such manuscripts in 1495. Of these at least four and perhaps as many as nine contained secular works. From Table 8 (see p. 218 above) we saw that, in the undated worksheet that precedes the 1495 inventory, there were at least four types of secular manuscripts, carefully differentiated even in the library list:

> Cantiones a la pifarescha
> Tenori todeschi et altre cantiones
> Cantiones francese
> Cantiones taliane

The first of these is clearly for the *piffari* – and may well refer, as I assume, to the Casanatense chansonnier. Presumably also for the instrumentalists is the set of 'Tenori todeschi', obviously dance tenors for use by the players for improvisation. Striking, then, is the pair of manuscripts evidently intended for the singers, one of which was 'francese', the other 'taliane'. These labels tell us that the court scribes and librarians, as well as the musicians, could readily distinguish collections of French and Italian polyphonic pieces – and the obvious assumption is that they could do so because the pieces had not only titles (as does also the Casanatense) but also some amount of text. If the 'Cantiones francese' was a collection of chansons, and the Italian volume a collection of frottole, as seems likely, then the distinction implied a stylistic difference as well, in keeping with the two linguistic and musical developments. And this in turn implies that, at this court at least, the performance of texted secular polyphonic music was not exclusively a matter of instrumental rendition, but that local performers could sing the texts if they wished to do so, and that the words were probably entered into the MSS accordingly. This runs counter to a current view that at Italian courts in this period French chansons were in a typical sense not sung, but played on instruments; a view that arises quite plausibly from a look at the surviving Italian chansonniers themselves, but not from archival evidence.[2] The Ferrara inventory and its context strongly suggests that at this court the conditions for performance were a good deal more varied than that. Whether they were also more varied elsewhere remains to be seen as the historical evidence emerges more fully.

Ercole had other sources of secular music at his disposal. One was a set of 'Tre libri in carta de capretto da canto figurato per Sua Excellentia da portare

---

[2] See, most recently, Litterick, 'Performing Franco-Netherlandish Secular Music of the Late 15th Century'.

in Villa'; these three books are now lost, but almost certainly contained secular compositions.[3] They would also have been among the earliest known sets of partbooks, a distinction now assigned to the Glogauer Liederbuch, made about 1480.

The Casanatense Chansonnier

We saw earlier that this sole surviving Ferrarese chansonnier of Ercole's time originated not in 1490 but about 1480, in close connection with the betrothal of Isabella d'Este and Francesco Gonzaga. We saw too that it can be linked to an archival entry that reports the compilation of a volume of 'Cantiones a la pifarescha'. Now it is time to look closely at the collection itself.

The original contents of the MS consisted of one hundred three-voice pieces, entered on fols. 1 to 131 and numbered consecutively. The main scribe – don Alessandro Signorello – left a gap equal to two gatherings (fols. 131–46) and then entered ten four-voice compositions, which he properly numbered '102' to '111' on fols. 147ᵛ–64. All of these pieces were then supplied with attributions, voice-rubrics, and text incipits, and the MS was given its index and elaborate opening decorative first page, with capital letters *all'antiqua*, with the coat of arms at the bottom of the page, and with the elaborate white vine lattice-work in the left and lower margins of the first page (cf. fig. 11). At a later stage (scholars agree that this probably took place about 1492) another scribe entered ten more three-voice pieces on the folios that had been left blank (131–46). This later section includes several pieces by Martini, and the three pieces by Ghiselin that the MS contains (Nos. 105–6, 108). Since Ghiselin-Verbonnet is found at the Ferrara court for the first time in July 1491 and is listed as a chapel singer in Ferrara in 1492, before his departure for Florence in October of that year, it seems plausible that Ghiselin-Verbonnet may himself have entered this later section some time between mid-1491 and the autumn of 1492. Or this section may have been added shortly after that period by another scribe who had access to his music.

The manuscript is laid out in the format typical of chansonniers of the period, and when one sees the book it seems clear that it was well suited to serve a group of performers playing directly from its pages. Despite its small-medium format (27 × 21 cm.) it has seven staves per page and a staff-size that is relatively widely spaced, so that the note-shapes are well formed, large, and clear. The use of gilt paint for the voice-rubrics throughout assures that the part-names are visible from several feet away; this visibility

---

[3] The document is quoted by Bertoni, *La Biblioteca Estense*, p. 261, and by Hermann, 'Zur Geschichte', doc. 300. Its only source is the later MS (early 18th century) of the Biblioteca Estense, Alpha H. 1. 13, from which Bertoni drew the entry for Signorello as the scribe of the MS containing 'Cantiones a la pifarescha' (Casanatense 2856). The original from which this 18th-century compilation was derived is lost. See above, p. 225.

is augmented by the imaginative decorative pointers that carry over the Contratenor part in three-part pieces from the lower left-hand to the lower right-
hand page of each opening.

Besides the archival entry, other aspects of the MS also point clearly
to instrumental usage. Some of the compositions are adjusted in their
extremes of tessitura, both high and low, in such a way that they can accommodate the known ranges of the instruments of the *Alta* – the shawms and
trombone.[4] Samples are shown in Ex. 14.

Ex. 14. MS Casanatense 2856, examples of adjustment of range

RANGES OF INSTRUMENTS OF THE *ALTA* (From Agricola, *Musica Instrumentalis Deudsch*, 1529)

Not transposing   Transposing

DISCANT SHAWM

BOMBARD

TROMBONE

TEXTUAL VARIANTS APPARENTLY REFLECTING INSTRUMENTAL RANGES

1. J. Martini, 'Vive, vive', mm. 18–25

(a) Seville/Paris, fols. 28ᵛ–29; Florence 229, fols. 44ᵛ-45

(b) Casanatense 2856, no. 25

---

[4] For a valuable contribution to this interpretation of the MS I am indebted to Mr Michael
Long.

2. A. Agricola, 'Vostre hault bruit', Tenor, mm. 12–13

(a) Florence 229; Florence 178; Verona 757

(b) Casanatense 2856

3. A. Agricola, 'Dictes moy', Contratenor, mm. 15–16, 20–1

(a) Six sources

(b) Casanatense 2856

(a) Six sources

(b) Casanatense 2856

At the same time, the ranges of these instruments were wide enough to accommodate the most contemporary pieces, while other wind instruments such as the crumhorns, where not. The MS contains no text for any of its works; and whereas this is also true for many other chansonniers compiled in Italy, only this one, so far, has been shown to have a distinctively instrumental function. Furthermore, it includes a number of pieces that bear titles denoting them as instrumental works. Among these are a group of canonic pieces inserted on single pages of the MS. They include Busnois's 'Trinitas in unitate' (No. 4); Johannes Martini's 'Fuga' (No. 39); Obrecht's 'Fuga' (No. 72); Josquin's 'Ile fantazies de Joskin' (No. 88); another piece by Martini bearing the term 'Fuga' (No. 79); Martini's two pieces called 'La Martinella' (Nos. 48 and 69); Morton's 'La Perontina' (No. 73); and others. Throughout much of the MS we also find that pieces have been grouped together on the basis of criteria that suggest an abstract principle of ordering, and thus a basis other than that of texts for setting up the MS. Many pieces are paired by composer; some by title; and some in the mensural sequence ¢–O, which looks like a prototype of the pairing of instrumental dance-movements familiar from sixteenth-century collections of instrumental music.

The distribution of works by composer reflects the leadership of Martini in the musical establishment, and he may also have had a strong hand in the selection, ordering, and editing of the works, just as in the large MSS of sacred polyphony. But the distribution may well reflect more than merely random preference for certain composers, or the haphazard acquisition of their music. We can assign the best represented composers to at least these groups, around 1480; see Table 12.

Table 12.   Composers Represented in the MS Casanatense 2856

---

1. Composers active at Ferrara
    Martini (23)
    Japart (3) (at Ferrara 1477–81)
    ———
    Ghiselin (3) (later layer; at Ferrara definitely Jan.–Oct. 1492, and again in 1493)

2. Visitors to Ferrara
    Agricola (visited Ferrarese court in 1474)

3. Milanese group (*c.* 1470–81)
    Josquin Desprez (4) (probably at Ferrara 1480–1)
    Agricola (19) (1471–4)
    Compère (6) (1474–7)
    Colinet (1) (left Milan 1477)
    Japart (at Milan 1473–7; at Ferrara 1477–81)

4. Burgundian group
    Busnois (11)
    Hayne (9)
    Morton (1)
    Joye (1)
    Molinet (1)
    Basin (2)

5. Cambrai group
    Caron (7)
    Dusart (1)
    Obrecht (?) (2)

6. French Royal Chapel group
    Ockeghem (5)

7. French group
    Brumel (1)
    Philippon (Basiron) (1)
    Tourant (1)

8. Antwerp
    Barbireau (2)

9. Uncertain identity
    Malcort (1)
    'Bolkim' (1)
    'Bossrin' (1)
    'Sonspison' (1)

Martini's Secular Music

As the principal singer in the establishment and as the leading composer, Martini can be taken as the representative Ferrarese musician of the time, and accordingly as the key figure in secular as well as in sacred repertoire development. He is the leading composer in the Casanatense MS, and the twenty-three pieces by him constitute more than half of all the secular pieces attributed to him in contemporary sources. These pieces give us a sure sense of the aesthetic, technical, and practical criteria by which secular music developed at the court in this period.[5]

Martini's secular works can be divided into several groups, according to their titles and their potential origins as pieces with French or other texts. But it is at least as significant that, of the entire body of Martini's secular output, only a handful (at most five, of which at least one is probably not authentic) are preserved with any text at all. Two of these ('Fortuna desperata' and 'Fortuna d'un gran tempo') are based on a famous Italian popular song, known in many settings, while another ('Cela sans plus') merely consists of Martini's *si placet* voice to a three-part voice piece by Colinet. A fourth, 'J'ay pris amours', is a piece written in competition with his colleague, Jean Japart. The overwhelming majority of Martini's secular works are preserved with no text in any source; several of them exist with both French incipits and with Latin or Italian incipits (that is, as contrafacta in Italian sources), and a number of them bear titles that seem scarcely likely to have been part of poetic texts but rather seem to denote instrumental pieces having either a special function or a solmization basis for their titles. The Martini secular pieces with explicit or instrumental function, interpreted on this basis, are as follows:

No. (after Evans)

5	'Der newe pawir schwantcz'
11	'Fuga ad quatuor'
12	'Fuge la morie'
22	'La Martinella'
23	'La Martinella pittzulo'
27	'Non per la'
28	'Non seul uno'
37	'Vive, vive' (called 'Martinella' in Florence 229 and 'Gardes vous' in Seville-Paris)
38–44	Preserved without any texts or text-incipits

To these fifteen compositions, which seem likely candidates for pieces intended to have instrumental use or perhaps only instrumental performance, we can add several others that are at least probable candidates for instrumental status and, so far as we know, never had poetic texts. They exhibit a dense imitative and often partially canonic means of composition, with much rapid rhythmic motion, repetition of short figures, and little breathing space for a sung text. We can take as a sample of the style the famous three-part 'La Martinella', used as basis for his four-part Mass discussed earlier.

---

[5] Recently, a first attempt has been made at a complete edition of the secular works of Martini: E. Evans, ed., *Johannes Martini, Secular Pieces*. Other studies of Martini's secular music include the dissertation by Brawley, 'The Magnificats'; Wolff's dissertation on the Casanatense MS, 'The Chansonnier'; and Karp, 'The Secular Works of Johannes Martini'.

Ex. 15. J. Martini, 'La Martinella', mm. 1–40

The bipartite structure of 'La Martinella' is fairly common among the secular pieces by Martini and some other composers of the period: in such pieces, as in rondeaux, the first section ends on a medial cadence on the confinal of the mode, that bears a fermata. Yet the resemblance to the French rondeau, or to any other of the traditional *formes fixes*, is wholly superficial and probably coincidental. Since there is no reason to suppose that most of Martini's secular pieces of this type ever had texts, let alone French texts, it is not surprising that the piece differs from the classical rondeau not only in layout (apart from the two-section plan) but in contrapuntal style. The title probably refers to Martini's own name; this would link it to several other contemporary instances in which instrumental compositions were named for individuals – Ghiselin's 'La Alfonsina' and Josquin's 'La Bernardina' are two famous cases, but there are others. Most important and characteristic for the piece is its inner layout in a series of phrases of varying length and delicately contrasting style, each beginning as a brief canonic duo (with or without a third accompanying voice) and then moving to a strong cadential finish for three voices, followed by the next contrapuntal point. The basic idea is to concatenate canonic segments that contrast with one another in the choice and shape of the motivic figures and in the time-interval of the canon. The larger layout can be shown as follows:

Table 13. Johannes Martini, 'La Martinella'; Segmentation

Segment	Measures	Texture	Pitch-Interval	Time-Interval of Canon
Part 1				
A₁	1–12	Canonic	Octave	2 breves
A₂	13–17	Non-canonic	–	–
B	17–24	Canonic	Octave	1 breve
C	25–9	Canonic	Octave	2 breves
D	29–34	Canonic	Octave	2½ breves
Coda	35–40	Non-canonic	–	–
Part 2				
E	41–7	Canonic	Octave	1 breve
F	48–55	Non-canonic	–	–
G	56–66	Canonic	Octave	1 breve
H	68–73	Canonic	Octave	2 breves
I	74–9	Canonic	Octave	1 breve
Coda	79–89	Non-canonic	–	–

The number of distinctive contrapuntal and canonic points within the piece is impressive, and 'La Martinella' may be taken as the prototype of the canonic large form of the instrumental chanson in Martini's output. We may compare it readily to Josquin's 'Ile fantazies de Joskin', also in the Casanatense MS, which is set up on a smaller scale, is non-canonic, and is even more definitely instrumental in purpose than 'La Martinella'. Slightly more than half as long as 'La Martinella', 'Ile fantazies' is set up in five segments, all contrapuntal and non-canonic, standing in contrast to one another in subtle ways that mirror the high degree of intervallic control and motivic ingenuity that are natural to Josquin.

Ex. 16. J. Desprez, 'Ile fantazies de Joskin', mm. 1–22

The formal outline is as follows:

Table 14.   Josquin Desprez, 'Ile Fantazies de Joskin'; Segmentation

Segment	Measures (mm.)	Tonal motion of phrase
A	1–12	a/a/e—g
B	12/2–17	d/g/d—g
C	17–24	g/d—B♭
D	25–35	B♭—d
E	35–50	d/g—g

In this piece we can focus well on the means of contrast available even within so small a time-scale and texture. *Segment A*: the first motif is completely in step-motion, in a small span from A to G; the second motif is a falling sequence, descending steadily from B♭ to G a tenth below and back to G an octave above that; the pairing after mm. 1–3 is Superius and Tenor against Bassus. *Segment B*: here the Bassus has an independent, animated transition figure at mm. 13–14; Superius and Tenor again pair in slower imitation; once more there is a step-motion figure, in small span, its direction in contrast to that of A. *Segment C*: Superius and Tenor again imitate in minimal space, the leap at m. 20 in the Superius is the first leap in that entire part except the octave at m. 10. *Segment D*: a new point; Superius and Tenor at distance of 1½ measures (formerly the time-interval was 2/1/1). *Segment E*: integrates features of earlier segments; the Superius at 36–8 brings figures associated with earlier material (cf. m. 6 ff); and at m. 44 the rhythmic figure recalls the animated transition figure from the Bassus at m. 13; this echo permits the piece to end with the same distinctive figure that had ended the short but well-formed exposition of this miniature work.

These works represent an 'advanced' style for 1480. As autonomous instrumental compositions, they form a genre separate from the text-bearing chansons of the French tradition, and in their strong imitative continuity within a miniature time-scale, they show the adaptation of the imitative principle to a non-syntactic musical form. We see here that, although in the motets of the 1470s and 1480s the rise of imitation is indeed closely linked to the importance of text-declamation and text-expression taken phrase by phrase (the classic model is Josquin's 'Ave Maria'), in these small works the same procedures are transferred to the instrumental domain. In effect, they demonstrate the achievement of an independent body of instrumental ensemble music that anticipates the *canzon francese* in Italy almost three generations before the rise of that repertoire. And the establishment of such works as fixed types by the time of the compilation of the Casanatense chansonnier shows that Ferrara and its players were able to set a pattern for other centers in this period in this domain as well. The writing of such pieces is clearly picked up in Florence in the later 1480s, especially by Isaac, and we find samples in the principal Florentine collections, especially Florence 229.[6] For Isaac, the writing of a fantasia in 1502 was remarked on by the agent Gian as being merely indicative of his facility in composition and perhaps of his imagination as a composer; but it may now be seen also as a tribute by Isaac to a court in which the instrumental fantasia had indeed been well rooted since the 1470s, when Josquin's 'Ile fantaizies' and other works of this type had already been collected, played, and valued as new forms of musical expression.

---

[6] On the instrumental ensemble repertoires of the period see Kämper, *Studien zur instrumentalen Ensemblemusik des 16. Jahrhunderts*, 39–85. For a recent discussion of Martini's 'La Martinella' in relationship to several other, related settings, see Brown, 'Emulation, Competition, and Homage: Imitation and Theories of Imitation in the Renaissance', 29–35.

27

Music for Court Festivities
and Theater

THE rise of theater, spectacle, and public show is one of the permanently important features of the late Quattrocento, and for this development Ferrara is the acknowledged springboard. Ercole's sponsorship of translations of classical comedies effectively inaugurated the Italian theater of the later Renaissance, and established a precedent from which vast developments emerged. Whatever the local antecedents of Ercole's theatrical patronage, especially under Leonello, it remains clear that theater focused a variety of interests that most strikingly characterized his court – festivity, spectacle, the humanistic aspirations of local literary circles, and the maintenance of his prestige as a cultural patron. All these were implicitly interwoven into the staged presentations that were put on in the courtyard of the palazzo from 1486 onward.[1] And to the secular plays, which have captured most attention from modern scholars and writers, we must also add the many sacred representations that preceded the first secular plays and were then revived at intervals over the three-and-a-half decades of his rule.[2] In all of these events music played at least some role, whether as song or as instrumental prelude or accompaniment to the brilliant *intermedi* that began as decorative inter-ludes and gradually became important components of the entire spectacle. Although we can reconstruct the music used in the secular and sacred dramas only very partially and with some degree of speculation, the present brief survey may help to focus current knowledge.

[1] From the large literature on Ferrarese theater under Ercole I we can cite here only a few primary studies. These include the chroniclers Caleffini, Zambotti, and the anonymous *Diario ferrarese*; the further documentary material published by D'Ancona, *Origini del teatro italiano*; the article 'Ferrara', by Povoledo, *Enciclopedia dello spettacolo*, v, cols. 173–85; Luzio and Renier, 'Commedie classiche a Ferrara nel 1499'; and most recently, Coppo, 'Spettacoli alla corte di Ercole I', with important documentation and a good review of the earlier literature; finally, Gundersheimer, *Ferrara*, pp. 209 ff., offers stimulating and provocative ideas, as does also his essay 'Popular Spectacle'.

[2] The sacred representations have received less attention than the secular, but much basic material was published by D'Ancona, op. cit.; see also my 'Music and Popular Religious Spectacle', pp. 571-82.

Music for Public Festivals, Jousts, and Special Events

Musicians were on hand to enliven every kind of public social event and festivity. Yet we have little, if any, written record of the actual music then performed by the court musicians, and for many we must assume that it ranged from improvisatory flourishes by the trumpeters to extended contrapuntal glosses on tenors by the *piffari*, and to well-chosen and carefully rehearsed polyphonic pieces performed by the instrumentalists and the court singers. It is safe to assume that types of music were specifically stratified according to the types of festivities, following the conventions common to the time. Thus the use of the *trombetti*, for calling up the public and for the jousts and races of the *palio*, was part of the vivid color of these civic sporting events; and we must fall back on occasional glimpses of what such music may have been like that are provided by remarks in the chronicles or partial preservation of fanfare pieces in the written polyphonic repertoires. The courtly celebration of the first of May, described earlier in connection with Martini's Mass on 'Io ne tengo quanto te', is a vivid example of the blending of courtly ritual and popular seasonal festivity.

To celebrate family weddings, baptisms, and other events, Ercole often gave *balli* in the *sala grande* to which he invited not only nobles but also townspeople of both sexes; at these and other *feste*, such as the public games and matches of carnival time, or the festival of St. George, the secular musicians were kept busy.[3] Even before the inauguration of public theater in the vernacular, in 1486, there were certain public events which specifically entailed the use of secular music. One of the least-known and yet most interesting is the *Giostra dell'Amore*, of June 1478, repeated in 1480. In this remarkable *festa* – a moral fable combining joust, myth, and spectacle – enacted for the public in the Piazza Comunale, a tribunal was set up in the main square, with a gallows. Cupid, on a triumphal carriage, played by a boy with bow and arrows, was put on trial. Pleading for his life was 'Madame Venus', his mother. Prosecuting him were two courtiers (Ercole's brother Rinaldo Maria, and Jacopuzo, seneschal of his brother Sigismondo), declaring that he was a traitor. Also present were about thirty-three *giostraduri* who claimed that he did not deserve to be hanged and should be freed. Then the joust took place, and the winning side would determine if Cupid lived or died. Finally the opponents of Cupid won the joust, and he was about to be hanged despite the implorations of Venus. But at the last minute, the Duchess, Eleonora, herself cried out, 'gratia, gratia', and was joined by the whole populace; so Cupid was set free. The chronicler tells us of 'some other children (besides Cupid) who were dressed as cherubs and

---

[3] Examples of *balli* in the palazzo mentioned by chroniclers include those of 17 January 1473 (Caleffini, p. 14; *Diario ferrarese* p. 85); 5-6 July 1473, for Ercole's marriage to Eleonora (Caleffini, p. 19); and many more; see Pardi's index to his edition of Caleffini, ii, p. 455, under 'Feste di ballo'. See also Zambotti, Index, p. 402, same heading.

sang very well, both early in the action and later, when Venus wept for her son; 'and when he descended (from the gallows) the putti sang with joy.'[4]

Though what the putti sang is not reported by the chronicler, the idea of a moral fable in which Cupid is put on trial is strongly reminiscent of other court spectacles of the period, especially one given at Urbino in 1474, in which Cupid was accused of treachery by six legendary female figures from antiquity – Biblide, Canace, Mirra, Nictimene, Semiramis, and Cleopatra – and judged by six 'holy and wise blessed women' and by Modesty personified.[5] At Urbino a danced scene was added to the trial, in which twelve nymphs took part and in which a trio of singers sang 'una laude intonata nel canto de Je pris Amor.' As Wolfgang Osthoff has pointed out, 'J'ay pris amours' is one of the most familiar and most frequently arranged songs of the period, and one of its best-known settings is by Jean Japart, while another three-voice setting is carved into one of the famous intarsias of the Studiolo in the Ducal Palace in Urbino. Especially interesting for us is that Japart himself was at Ferrara in the same year in which this *Giostra dell'Amore* was first presented. The Casanatense MS does not include 'J'ay pris amours' among its Japart selection, but it does include the fricassee by him on the texts 'Amours fait mont'/'Amour'/'Il est e bon heure né'/'Tant que nostre argent dure'.[6] And we also find, in the MSS Florence 229 and Segovia, respectively, two settings of 'J'ay pris amours' by Martini, which artfully rework material from what appears to be the primary setting, that in Dijon 517. Either the Japart chanson or one of many other contemporary settings of chansons on the theme of *Amor* could well have been sung on this occasion.

Music for the Intermedi of Secular Drama

On 25 January 1486, an estimated ten thousand spectators crowded into the palace courtyard to witness a performance of Plautus's comedy *The Menaechmus Brothers (Menaechmi)*, with scenery painted to represent a city with its houses and with the parts taken by masked actors who 'declaimed in Italian verse'. This apparently means that they intoned all the verses of the comedy ('the masked men, who, singing in verse in the vernacular, declaimed all the verses of the aforesaid play', as the chronicler Caleffini writes)[7]. We may assume that the expression 'in canto' means simply that they declaimed the verses with some degree of pitch-inflection. In this momentous event, which opens the history of Italian theater in the modern era, music had no

---

[4] For the *Giostra dell'Amore*, of 1478, the primary source is Caleffini, p. 114; a briefer description is in Zambotti, p. 51 f.; both also describe the performance of this *festa* that took place in 1480 (Caleffini, p. 128; Zambotti, p. 79).

[5] See Osthoff, *Theatergesang und darstellende Musik in der italienischen Renaissance*, pp. 33 f.

[6] Rome, Bibl. Casanatense, MS 2856, No. 121.

[7] Caleffini, p. 245 f.: 'li homeni in mascara che in rima vulgariter in canto disseno tuti li versi de la dicta comedia'; see also Zambotti, p. 171 f.

vital role to play. The opening of the four-hour production was marked by flourishes from the 'trombeti e pifare et altri soni', as another chronicler tells us; but in this first production there were neither interludes with music nor occasions for songs within the play.[8] To rouse the spectators and keep their attention, accordingly, a fireworks display was put on at the end. That this was well advised is inferable from the remarks of the most learned of the chroniclers, Zambotti, who notes that the horde of spectators watched the play itself 'con taciturnità'.[9]

In the following year's play, the *Cefalo* of Niccolò da Corregio, interludes were inserted between the acts and instrumental music was used to enliven them, a point especially noted by Zambotti; yet his fellow chronicler Caleffini reports that this comedy 'did not much please the people who witnessed it'.[10] Later in that same winter season there followed the *Amphitryon* of Plautus, again with *intermedi* which probably included music, and at its second performance the musical side came even more into its own than before. Now Zambotti reports that the backdrop consisted of a 'heaven . . . with lanterns that shone against the background of black curtains and glistened like stars, and with little boys dressed in white to represent the planets.'[11] At the second performance, on 5 February 1487, this striking scenery was used again, and the total effect was now enhanced with singing. The point was evidently to 'represent' the legendary music of the spheres: '. . . there was heard enchanting singing and playing, by marvelous singers, and they had Jove come down from heaven . . .'.[12] This display of the Duke's excellent musicians was then followed by a symbolic display of his own mythological lineage, with a representation of the Labors of Hercules.

Elaborate costumes and scenery were certainly used for the later performances of classical comedies in the 1490s and continued to be employed down to the crowning festivities of 1502, for the celebration of Alfonso's marriage to Lucrezia Borgia. For several of them we have descriptions of the *intermedi* which regularly included pantomime by actors in exotic costumes and roles, at times with music that was more than mere rhythmic accompaniment to the dances and *moresche*. Thus the performance of Terence's *Andria* on 14 February 1491 included *intermedi* involving nymphs and savages, and the Plautus performance the next day repeated in the *intermedi* the 'angelic songs and sounds of the planets' along with other effects.[13] To make sure of the quality of music for these productions, Ercole went to his usual pains. In 1499 he asked Francesco Gonzaga to be sure to send back the first-rate player

---

[8] On the trumpeters and *piffari* the source is the chronicler Ferrarini, quoted by Coppo, 'Spettacoli alla corte di Ercole I', 45.   [9] Zambotti, p. 172.

[10] Caleffini, p. 250: 'che non piacque troppo al populo vedere'.

[11] Zambotti, p. 179: 'l'era construito uno celo . . . con lampade che ardevano a li lochi debiti de drio de tele negre subtile e radiavano in modo de stelle; e ge herano fanzuli picoli vestiti di bianco in forma de li planeti . . .'.

[12] Zambotti, p. 180: 'nel quale si senti cantare e sonare suavemente da cantori perfectissimi, e feceno venire Jove da celo.'   [13] Zambotti, p. 221.

called Michele *piffaro* to Ferrara so that he would be on hand for carnival time.[14] Shortly thereafter, the Ferrara audiences were offered at least nine public performances of classical comedies, all through February, replete with *moresche* of great variety for which nearly 200 costumes had to be made, as the agent Prosperi reported to Isabella.

At one of the 1499 performances (that of 9 February) there were four *moresche* as *intermedi*, and afterwards, in the *sala grande* of the palazzo, all the costumes made for the production were put on display. The *moresche* were rendered as diverse as possible, but all of them had twelve performers, at times in episodes in which singing as well as instrumental dance music was prominent. Prosperi describes them:[15]

Lo terzo fo cinque damiselle vestite multo galante de biancho et erano seguitate da cinque cum dolci canti et queste hora fugendo et abscondendossi et questi seguendole cum suoi canti et soni voltorono el tribunale quattro fiate . . .

The third had five damsels dressed very handsomely in white, and they were followed by five [men] singing sweet songs, and the girls would try to flee and hide themselves, but the men followed them with their singing and playing; and they made the rounds of the platform four times . . .

And again:

la quarta comedia forono pure XII giovani vestiti gallanti che al tempo del sono de uno passo et mezo . . . ferno un'altra moresca . . .

the fourth episode also had twelve young men dressed as gallants who danced another *moresca* to the sound of the rhythm of the *pass'e mezo* . . .

Too elaborate and complex for full description here are the festivities for the great wedding of 1502, at which five Plautus comedies were given within nine days, all in Italian and with *intermedi* of the most varied types, including one using 'musiche Mantuane' led by Bartolomeo Tromboncino. For the edification and pleasure of the assembled diplomatic and patrician audiences, elaborate and fantastic representations were put on, including many with songs and music, in honor of the *spoxi* and probably also in praise of Duke Ercole, as well as on other themes. The first set of five *moresche* included one in which a horse was disguised as a unicorn and for which four singers and a lutenist stood on a carriage hidden by foliage, singing four 'canzone belissime'. Still another included a group of fourteen satyrs, one of whom had in hand a silvered ass's head that concealed a wind instrument called a *fistula*; together with another, who held a Turkish drum and a *zuffolo*, they made a farewell exit, one by one, playing their instruments.[16] It is undoubtedly for this

---

[14] Letter of Francesco Gonzaga, 24 January 1499, to Ercole I d'Este, in ASM, Principi Esteri, Mantova.

[15] Letters of Bernardo Prosperi to Isabella d'Este, Ferrara, 3 and 8 February 1499, in ASMN, AG, B. 1094; original texts of both letters are given by Coppo, op. cit., pp. 53-4.

[16] The longest and most vivid description of these details is the one written by Niccolò Cagnolo of Parma, which was included in full in the chronicle of Zambotti, pp. 318-33. Written

occasion that a four-voice polyphonic song in praise of Ercole was set to music by a composer known to us only by his initials ('G. L.', perhaps Giorgio Luppato), preserved in a manuscript written later in the year (1502):[17]

Ex. 17. 'G. L.', 'O triumphale diamante', mm. 1–20

at the end of February 1502, directly after the events themselves, it is a fresh account of the festivities by an eye-witness.

[17] Paris, Bibliothèque Nationale, MS Res Vm⁷ 676, No. 67. See Bridgman, 'Un Manuscrit italien du debut du XVIᵉ siècle', 181, 231.

From the growing number of references to music at these festivities, and the remarkable variety of instrumental and vocal styles and combinations that quite clearly were employed, we can see that these moments of dazzling public display were also special occasions for the presentation of the Duke's musicians, especially the instrumentalists. They were for the players and secular singers quite as important as the religious occasions and ceremonies were for the demonstration of his chapel of singers. Just as the repeated need for new themes for *moresche* and *intermedi* led to the elaboration of ever more fantastic and experimental ideas, so the music needed to accompany these must have sought to match the dancing and dramatic episodes in its variety of modes of expression. The basic forms of contemporary dance music were maintained for the *moresche*. To these were added the songs, *canzoni*, and special background music, like that of the planets of 1487. All this suggests that the later development of richly elaborated music for the Italian theater, in all its massive growth, from pastoral to ballet and proto-opera, could look far back to an already complex stage of development well before the turn of the sixteenth century.

Music for Religious Spectacles

The *cappella di corte* and the piazza of the ducal palace were also the original locations for the first religious spectacles under Ercole that utilize dramatic content. As these dramatic productions continued to be given in later years, they grew in complexity and size, and were aimed at increasingly larger segments of the public; accordingly their places of production shifted to larger spaces. We are certain of six occasions between 1476 and 1504 when Ercole staged sacred spectacles of various kinds. The first two, in 1476 and 1481, apparently coincided with his first completion of the court chapel and its remodeling and improvement. These sacred dramas were thus the first steps Ercole took towards public drama of any kind and antedated the revivals of Plautus by five and ten years, respectively; and the dates of all his productions up to 1486 suggest that at first he may have considered this type of spectacle an exceptional event that should be given about every five years. Later, the novelty and success of the classical comedies may have prompted more frequent sacred productions to balance the two sides of Ercole's public image as patron.

In 1476 the major production was a sacred play on the theme of St. James of Compostela, to whose shrine Ercole later planned to make a pilgrimage. Significantly, this first attempt was carried out not by local talent but by a Florentine entrepreneur, who built a stage in the piazza near the bishop's residence.[18] Ferrarini's chronicle tells us the argument of the play and that it lasted for two hours; lacking the text, we can only assume that it represented

---

[18] On the 1476 play of St. James, see Coppo, op. cit., p. 43, quoting Ferrarini.

a temporary importation into Ferrara of the established type of Florentine *sacra rappresentazione*, for which the popular religious *lauda* had by now become a long-established musical component.

By 1481 Ercole's ambitions for sacred drama had grown considerably. On Good Friday of that year he produced in the court chapel a dramatization of the Passion that was remarkable not only by local standards but is noteworthy even in the established tradition of Passion performances in the fifteenth century. The machinery was spectacular. Inside the chapel the Duke had installed a large wooden head of a serpent, which opened and closed, and inside of which was the Limbo of the Holy Fathers. First, various characters appeared: Maria Magdalena, St. John, and the Virgin Mary; then an actor playing the role of Christ, who went up to the head of the serpent, saying 'Atollite portas.' At this the head opened, and fourteen men came out of it, dressed in white, singing and praising God, while within the head were heard devils rattling chains and shooting off flames that reached the chapel's ceiling. All this is vividly described by the chroniclers, who also tell us that the crowd at the portal to the chapel was so great that it blocked the passage entirely.[19] The fourteen liberated men were of course the Duke's own singers, members of his large musical company. Whatever the antecedents of this spectacle in other civic productions or religious dramas, the magical emergence of the singers is also reminiscent of certain sensational and extravagant moments in secular court festivities, especially the well-known Banquet of the Oath of the Pheasant at Lille, in 1454. There, the Burgundian court singers were concealed in various model structures – a church and fortress – placed upon the banqueting tables, and other singers entered the banqueting room on a horse and on a stag.[20]

The Passion of 1481 reflects a new trend in Ercole's projection of his spiritual leadership. It not only furnishes an intensification of the usual Holy Week ceremonies, but is also a powerful conclusion to the cycle of devotional actions that he undertook in Holy Week, especially on Maundy Thursday. We have seen already that it was his practice, each Maundy Thursday, to wash the feet of selected citizens from among the poor of the city, to the accompaniment of singing by his court choir. Often, other members of his immediate family participated in the ceremony, which seems also to have lasted beyond his death, even into the time of Alfonso and Ippolito (despite their very different attitudes to religious practice).[21] The washing of the feet took place after the Duke, his nobles, and family members, carrying large candles that were kept burning until next day, had made procession to and from Mass in the

---

[19] Especially Zambotti, p. 87 f.

[20] For the most recent account of this sensational entertainment see Gallo, *Il Medioevo II*, pp. 100-5. A brief recent account also in Vaughan, *Philip the Good*, pp. 143-5.

[21] An entry in the account books of Cardinal Ippolito I shows his purchase of perfume for the foot-washing ceremony.

ducal chapel. Another essential part of the ceremonies was the elaborate meal that was served to the poor by Ercole and his relatives at a large table in the *sala grande* of the palace. The important role of music in all this can be inferred from the nature of the services, and from the chronicler's reports: the singers sang the Mandatum, they sang during the meal, and they sang during all the processions and services.[22] The chronicler Sabadino also mentions that Ercole gave away money generously at this time to various groups – to the poor, to mendicant friars, and even to needy musicians, when he was pleased by their singing ('questa elymosina fai quanto de la scientia musicale prendi dilecto, essendo in epsa perito.'). In view of Ercole's general reputation for stinginess, this may just possibly be a touch of irony in Sabadino's normally fulsome style.[23]

In later years a Passion drama like that of 1481 was given at least three times – in 1489, 1490, and 1503. In 1489 it was given again but the action was not divided between the chapel and the piazza; it took place entirely in the piazza, and was given not in Latin but in Italian. Again, the enactment concluded the Duke's own personal devotions and foot-washing, and now, instead of the fantastic machinery of a serpent's head concealing singers, the actions had a fully liturgical character, put on, however, in the open air and in the public square. Zambotti describes the Passion drama that was held 'in mezo la Piaza, denanzi al pallazo del Podesta', that is, in the Piazza del Duomo: 'it lasted until three in the night, with lighting provided.' The next day, Zambotti continues, there was a sermon by Baptista Paneto of the Carmelite Order, a reformer of the time.[24] The cross was displayed before the multitude and the souls of the holy were taken out of Purgatory, 'with the singers singing and praising God and with great devotion by the people.' In this remarkable scene, we note the use of the ducal singers as performers in the public square, attracting and intensifying the fervor of the crowd. This is one of the few authenticated instances in the period in which the professional singers of a princely chapel are employed for a mass religious demonstration.

We can briefly review the later dramatic spectacles. In the next year, 1490, the Passion was given again and now was added a play on the Assumption of the Virgin. In 1494 a Passion drama was given in San Francesco, and in 1502 three performances of the Passion were put on during Holy Week in the bishop's residence; these last may perhaps have been aimed at reinforcing Ercole's allegiance to religious observance in the wake of his alliance with the Borgia family in that year. And in 1503, when five plays by Plautus were again put on in carnival time, they were again followed by three sacred dramas: one a Passion play, one on the Annunciation, and another on the Adoration of the Magi. They were held in the Duomo, and the Annunciation

---

[22] Cf. on the processions Sabadino degli Arienti, 'De Triumphis Religionis' in Gundersheimer, *Art and Life*, p. 91: 'In questo mezo che tanto sacramento è portato et reposto nel'ornato sepolcro; li cantori, con solemne voce, oratione et prophetie non cessano de cantare'.

[23] Ibid., p. 95.   [24] Zambotti, p. 205; also Caleffini, p. 266.

nvolved a striking scenic effect when the heavens opened and revealed God the Father and his angels. In 1504, Ercole's last year of life, the play on St. Joseph was given in the Duomo. As we saw earlier, it was given on a platform, with scenery painted to depict castles; on the ceiling of the cathedral was constructed a heaven that opened and showed the glory of Paradise, with angels playing and singing. Of course, the angels were the Duke's singers. I have already suggested that the music sung could have included a motet by Josquin Desprez, who was then concluding his year of service at the court.[25]

Of the precise uses of music for the plays themselves we know little or nothing; the verbal portions of the sacred dramas were probably without any sung or played music, so far as we know; or were at most occasionally colored by brief musical interludes. What suggests such a possibility, for example for the play of 1489, is the preservation of a short piece, evidently for three instruments, by Johannes Martini or Loyset Compère, under the title 'Cayphas' in a contemporary MS.[26] The Biblical Caiphas indeed appeared in the 1489 drama, and we may wonder whether this short composition could have 'introduced' him. Admittedly, however, this is pure speculation. Beyond this, we may speculate on the potential use of motets and other sacred pieces that would have been well within the repertoire of the ducal singers, in those instances for which we are sure that the singers were present. Music clearly played an essential role in the ritual elements of the Holy Week ceremonies, and not only plainsong as prescribed by fixed usage but also polyphony, as we have in fact already seen.

[25] Zambotti, p. 357.
[26] Johannes Martini, *Secular Pieces*, No. 2. The piece is known only from the Segovia MS where it is ascribed 'loysete compere Zohannes Martini'. This may indicate that the scribe was uncertain which of these two was the true composer; or possibly that a setting originally by Compère was reworked by Martini, as happened with 'J'ay pris amours'.

Epilogue

THE basic term of this book is 'development'. Its aim has been to trace and interpret the main stages of a complex process that changed the nature of music over several generations in the history of an Italian city-state in the fifteenth century. Narrowly perceived, this story seems merely to deal with an obscure slice of history – a single phase in the local annals of a politically minor but culturally important unit in the network of Italy in the period. Perceived more broadly and more imaginatively, it presents a detailed account of some of the operative factors in both music and in patronage that contribute to much larger patterns of change. It deals with the transformation of an established culture from a condition we can call 'pre-musical' to one in which art-music had achieved the status of a major cultural resource, and in which those engaged with music, as professionals or amateurs, could participate in a strongly rooted and consistently active cultural life. Formerly an occasional pastime, secular music had become a wide-ranging form of expression comprising a plurality of styles and means of performance; and sacred music had become under Ercole a true expression of his role as Christian prince, living in a local ambience of intensified piety and enriching many of the major liturgical and devotional occasions of his life with polyphony in the widest variety of styles then available. In its full maturity, the spectrum of music under Ercole ranged from simple and easily communicated forms of popular music, of the city and countryside, to the most sophisticated and refined modes of musical structure and expression known to the time.

Any case-history has larger implications. In this one they lie principally in the grey area that separates the domain of musical thought and style from the conditions imposed by the society supporting these activities. To what extent was this musical growth a product of essentially musical developments, the result of what musicians, not patrons, thought and did? To what extent did the rivalries and ambitions of patrons spur musicians to reshape their compositional procedures and make them amenable to current tastes? To what degree was this development at Ferrara a product of peculiarly local conditions and to what extent did it reflect changes that were sweeping across all of Italy at this period, however differently expressed in the various regimes that crowded the peninsula?

I hope that the detailed factual and interpretative discussions in earlier chapters have given a sense of the complexity of these issues and show how closely intertwined were the interests of patrons and musicians. The nature of this development depended on the specific ambitions of the major individual patrons, in this case the successive Este rulers. Brief answers to such questions would only distort and oversimplify. Accordingly, it now remains to try to put the story into perspective in another way – by distinguishing, in music and patronage, some of the forces of continuity from the forces of change.

On the patronage side the forces of continuity are especially clear. First among them is the state itself, which plays so large a symbolic role in the cultural products of the period, from the frescoes of Tura and Roberti to the poems of Ariosto; I mean the state not simply as a political entity, but as a fabric of communal consciousness possessing a strong sense of identity and common traditions, habits, dialects, and customs, at all levels of society. Second, there is the ruling family, repressive but responsive to the class pyramid that supported it; conscious of its role as the longest-established and most continuous of the dynasties that ruled the Italian states of its type. Each of the Este leaders of our period knew not only his place in contemporary events but his place in the family line. He knew as well what struggles and manipulations had brought him to power and given him a chance to make his mark in history. From this followed inevitably the strong impulse of each not simply to strengthen the state but to strengthen it distinctively; to find new ways to govern and to increase his status at the same time; above all, to give these efforts a personal stamp that would carve out his niche for posterity. In this sense Ercole's civic and architectural changes, most of all in the *Addizione Erculea*, were the most striking of the century; in the same vein his construction of the Palazzo dei Diamanti, manifesting in stone his emblem of rule, is the architectural counterpart of the Josquin *Missa 'Hercules Dux Ferrarie'*, which, in musical structure and sonority, symbolizes his official title.

Further elements of continuity are not hard to find. The basic institutional and personal roles of both patrons and musicians remained essentially fixed, whether or not the individual patron himself participated in musical events or was merely a passive witness. The obligatory patterns of religious observance and of recurrent or similar recreational functions formed a fixed category, differing only in intensity or in degree of opulence. Another element of continuity was the rivalry with other courts; despite the differing levels of competition that the Estensi felt with other dynastic patrons, there remained intact the continuity of the larger cultural system of all Italy, of which Ferrara itself was only a small but strategic component.

Against these factors worked the forces of change. In patterns of government the successive rulers of this period were strongly individual, as every historian of Ferrara has emphasized. And if the impulse to create a new form of patronage was inevitably present in any comparable ruler, normally inheriting the state from a father or father-figure, it was almost certainly much more pronounced in the lives of these three Este dynasty members, all of whom were half-brothers and sons of a common father – the earthy and powerful Niccolò III. The strong sense of individuality that the Italian Renaissance so strongly implanted as a personal aim – the realization of the concept of *virtù* – was inevitably defined against a background of inherited family status. For music, important changes occurred as each ruler came to power and sought to develop his own pattern of patronage – Leonello most of all in literature and the classics; Borso in self-glorifying frescoes, magnificent manuscripts, and chivalric epics. Ercole picks up both of these trends from his predecessors, amplifies them, and adds to them many other achievements in new areas that neither of his predecessors had been able to cultivate.

Other aspects of change came from outside the state. One was the widening political and diplomatic framework within which Ferrara was embedded. It opened new channels by which music could be imported, musicians could be recruited, and news of the rising importance of music at this court could be spread abroad. Improvement in the preservation of music was part of the same development, and as more music became available, more of it was collected and copied for local patrons; thus the building of repertoires for local use became an important ancillary activity. To some extent of course, similar tendencies were present in rival states, especially France and the larger Italian centers, including Rome, Milan, and Florence.

In both continuity and change the entire development must certainly be seen in relationship to the most important cultural development of the period – the rise of humanism as a primary intellectual and aesthetic outlook. Guarino's training of Leonello had set a pattern for Ferrarese humanism; in turn Leonello's piety and musicality set a standard that Borso could ignore but which Ercole could revive, emulate, and surpass. And whereas music in earlier phases of humanistic thought had been relegated to the status of a minor pastime, in the late fifteenth century and during the period of Ercole, changes in the role of music were emerging. One was the recruitment of significant numbers of skilled foreign musicians in Italy, alongside the traditional improvisers, lutenist-singers, and occasional composer-singers who had been known for generations. The appearance in numbers of new types of singers, also specialists in the more complex forms of musical notation and performance, went hand in hand with the formation of professional chapels and the support of these chapels by the princes, as Tinctoris noted.

With this came an increasing recognition of the new modes of relationship between music and the verbal rhetoric that the humanists prized above all – the idea of eloquence as an element in the achievement of personal virtue. In the motets of Josquin and his contemporaries there begins to emerge a new relationship between polyphonic music and text – a relationship in which the music and text are placed on an equal footing, and in which the claims of both are satisfied to a degree formerly unknown. What was emerging in both sacred music, and, to the extent it was cultivated in Italy as a sung form, the French chanson, was a formal balance between these elements that could satisfy the demands of both clarity and expression. What Helmuth Osthoff called 'the breakthrough to musical humanism' was being carried out, chiefly in the work of Josquin but also in that of his younger contemporaries, including Compère, Obrecht, Isaac, Agricola, and others. Ferrara was of course only one of the seats of this development, but it was an important one. And one consequence of this change, not to be overlooked, is that the new relationship between text and music inevitably brought about a new way of hearing music; one in which the reflection in a composition of one element upon another, of text and polyphonic fabric as equal components in a musical whole, must have given listeners the sense of a new form of musical experience, in which the mind could alternate its focus of attention and of perception between textual and musical components, as a composition itself adjusted flexibly to both.

In this sense, we must recognize that the domain of patronage and the domain of music were themselves balanced elements in a reciprocal relationship, in which musicians subtly moved their methods closer to the modes of understanding that were implicitly or even directly required by the dominating intellectual forces of the time, and in which patrons felt that they were entering into a new mode of musical perception, one that was potentially reconcilable with the tenets of humanism. The long-range consequences of these developments lay far in the future, but the first peak stands in the last quarter of the fifteenth century.

Precisely this increased sensitivity to musical expression, and awareness of it as a new dimension of personal enrichment, distinguishes the period of Ercole from that of his predecessors, distinguishes him personally as a patron, and reinforces the view that one of the main results of this increased 'musicalization' of Ferrarese culture is that it provided a significant expansion of aesthetic experience. That this is not an exaggeration is surely clear, as regards Ercole, from all the evidence of his intense concern with music. He is an early prototype of the music-intoxicated Italian prince, anticipating by more than a century Shakespeare's portrayal of Duke Orsino in *Twelfth Night*. That he is not a total exception in his time is evident from other signs of concern among musicians, at least the learned ones, to question, and reflect upon, the very nature of music itself, above all in terms of its 'effects'. This is precisely what Tinctoris does in his important treatise *Complexus Effectuum Musices*, in which, amid a traditional compilation of anecdotes and observations on the variety of music and its means of production, the theorist also reflects upon the multiplicity of effects that music can produce. Among them is its ability to drive out melancholy, to increase reflective piety, and to arouse a listener to ectasy. To men of the earlier fifteenth century one justification for interest in music had lain in its use as an aid to 'spiritual consolation'. Now, in a more expanded cultural environment, this remains only one of the many values in music that the changing conditions of musical life were bringing to the surface.

APPENDIX I

Sources in the Archivio di Stato, Modena

NO substantial part of this archive is presently described in detail in a published inventory other than the segment 'Casa e Stato' (see item 2 below). The following are the best available current guides to the general organization of the materials in the Este court section of the archive. Of the numerous repositories listed below, those marked with an asterisk (*) were especially important for this project.

1. *Gli Archivi di Stato Italiani* (Bologna, 1944). Issued by the Ministero dell'Interno, has descriptive chapters on 24 of the major Italian state archives, with broad accounts of their main holdings; also brief accounts of the 20 other lesser archives in southern Italy and Sicily. Section on Modena, pp. 183–207.

2. F. Valenti, *Archivio di Stato di Modena, Archivio Segreto Estense, Sezione 'Casa e Stato', Inventario*, Ministero dell' Interno, Pubblicazioni degli Archivi di Stato, xiii (Rome, 1953). First of a projected three-volume inventory of major portions of the Estense archive (other volumes not published). They were to include inventories of the 'Cancelleria', both Interno and Esterno, and the 'Archivi Particolari'. The 'Archivi della Camera' were not intended to be included in this series; Valenti asserts in his preface (p. v) that 'they are undoubtedly of lesser interest to scholarship.' The published volume is a fully detailed inventory of the following Estense material:

I. *Casa e Stato*
 (a) Official acts, diplomas, investitures, treaties
 *(b) Genealogies and histories of the Este household
 *(c) Letters between members of the Este family, various branches (reigning and non-reigning), 14th to 18th C.
 *(d) Documents concerning Este princes (wills, contracts, bulls, papers, from 1202 onwards; includes, e.g. entire small *fondo* on Lucrezia Borgia)
 *(e) *Corte*: small *fondo* on court ceremonies in various periods
 (f) Acquisitions of territory
 (g) State trials
 (h) State controversies (e.g. on restitution of Modena and Reggio in 1530–1)
(concludes with valuable genealogical tables of family from 11th to 19th C.)

3. F. Valenti, *Panorama dell'Archivio di Stato di Modena* (Modena, 1963). Pamphlet of 34 pp., nevertheless the most complete description of the archive yet published, except for the section 'Casa e Stato' fully inventoried in item 2. What follows here is principally taken from the *Panorama* and is thereafter described in more detail for those segments of value to music history.
 (1) *Casa e Stato* (summarizes material of item 2).

(2) *Cancelleria, sezione generale Registri:* * $\left. \begin{array}{l} \textit{Epistolarum} \\ \textit{Officiorum Publicorum} \\ \textit{Decretorum} \end{array} \right|$ 47 vols., 1463–1792

> *Minute sciolte*   28 *buste*, 1403–1795
> *Copialettere*   18th C. only

> Three series of *Minute* of
>> *Cancelleria* of Cardinal Luigi (1538–86)
>> *Cancelleria* del Cardinal Alessandro (1568–1624)
>> *Cancelleria* del Cardinal Rinaldo (1617–72)

> * *Carteggi di consiglieri segreti e cancellieri* (1400–   )
> *Consiglie giunte consulte e reggenze*
> *Segretaria di gabinetto* (1773–96)
> *Supremo ministro* (1784–96)
> *Carteggi di ufficiali camerali*
> *Decreti e chirografi sciolti* (1382–1796)
> *Chirografi ducali* (1749–85)
> *Gride* (separate or in volumes) (1350–1786)
> *Statuti capitoli e grazie*
> *Esenzioni e privilegi* (1417–   )
> *Atti dell'archivio segreto estense* (= Archive of archive; old inventories and letters, 1467–   )

(3) *Cancelleria, Estero*
> *Carteggi con principi esteri*
>> $\left. \begin{array}{l} \textit{Italia} \\ \textit{Fuori d'Italia} \end{array} \right\}$ c.650 *buste*
>> (E.g. subseries 'Roma' has collection of papal bulls and large correspondence with individual cardinals.)
> *Carteggi con rettori di stati e città estere*
> *Carteggi di oratori e agenti presso le corti* (= *Carteggi ambasciatori*)
> Total of 1,699 *buste*; 937 *buste*, *Italia*, as follows:

*Bologna	1436–1796
*Firenze	1413–1792
Genova	1449–1794
Guastalla	1602–1762
Lucca	1479–1658
*Mantova	1454–1771
Marche	1481–1744
Massa	1621–1779
*Milano	1440–1796
Mirandola	1468–1696
Monferrato	1483–1533
*Napoli	1448–1775
Parma	1527–1792
*Roma	1376–1794
Romagna	1468–1721
Saluzzo	1485–1533

Torino	1496–1793
*Venezia	1406–1795

762 *buste, Fuori d'Italia*, as follows:

*Francia	1470–1796
*Germania	1482–1793 (incl. Fiandra, Austria, Trento)
*Inghilterra	1470–1799
Levante	1505–1732
Malta	1583–1658
Polonia	1520–1712
Spagna	1468–1771
Svizzera	1531–1714
Trieste	1519–1793
Tunis	1464–1573
*Ungheria	1479–1739

Also in this section:

Avvisi dell'estero (130 *buste* and 14 vols., 1468–   )
Confini dello stato
Convenzioni e trattamenti
Documenti di stati esteri (196 *buste*)

(4) *Cancelleria, carteggi diversi*
   Carteggi di regolari (religious orders; arranged alphabetically by name of sender)
   **Carteggio e documenti di Particolari*: miscellaneous letters, arranged alphabetically by names of senders, preceded by a series of *pergamene* beginning in 1337
   = Total of 1,190 *filze*

(5) *Cancelleria, interno*
   Carteggi dei rettori dello stato

(6) *Archivi per materie* (these rubrics have been changed from time to time as material was reorganized).
   Main rubrics examined:

   **Biblioteca Estense*
   **Letterati e letterature* (see Kristeller, *Iter*)
   *Miniatori
   **Musica e musicisti* (4 *buste* and Supplement)

   Manoscritti della Biblioteca. (This consists of the manuscripts preserved in the archive, including a folder of leaves from plainsong manuscripts and three leaves of a once large codex of polyphonic Masses of the late 15th C.; for the latter, see above, Part Three, Chapter 20.)

(7) *Archivi militari*

(8) *Catastri delle investiture*: 45 registers, parchment (plus 5 of indexes), xii–xvii; notarial acts for distribution of real property. Presumably supplements enormous Archivio Notarile Ferrarese, preserved in Ferrara, Archivio di Stato.

(9) *Archivio della camera marchionale poi ducale*
  (a) *Amministrazione della casa e dei principi*
         * *Guardaroba* (begins with year 1440; 301 registers)
         Arazzi e tapezzerie
         Castalderie e possessioni
         Bestiame
         Cucina
         Cantina
         Granai
         Spenderia
         Spezeria
         Armeria
         Stalle e scuderie
         Goielli
         Paggeria
         Navi
         Funzioni sacre (has nothing earlier than 17th C.)
         * *Biblioteca Estense*

  also:

     * *Registri d'amministrazione dei singoli principi, regnanti e non regnanti* (important)
     Fabbriche e villeggiature (important for history of art, Villa d'Este, palazzi)
     Agenti in Ferrara (on goods in Ferrara belonging to Estensi after their departure in 1598)

  (b) *Camera vera e propria* (Valenti divides into three main sections)
   (i) *Archivio della Cancelleria della Camera*
   (ii) *Archivio della Computisteria*
      * *Mandati* (1422–   )
      * *Memoriali* (Series began in 1438 but earliest preserved is from 1447)
      * *Conto generale* (several preserved from period 1440–50 and from late 16th C.)
      * *Libri Camerali Diversi* (period 1423–1505, 211 registers)
      * *Memoriale del Soldo* (1482–1546; 28 vols. between 1482 and 1506)
      * *Bolletta de' Salariati* (1456–   )
   (iii) *Investiture di Feudi e livelli* (original *atti*, 1117 onward)
      Zecca e monete
      Ferma e fermieri

APPENDIX II

Documents

DOC. 1. Letter of Duke Ercole I d'Este to Hermann, Bishop of Constance, 10 December 1471, on the recruitment of singers. Source: ASM, Epist. reg. 1471–5, p. 87. (The surviving text is not that of the final version of the letter but is rather a corrected draft. The corrections are shown below in brackets; cf. fig. 13 (*a*).)

Ad D. hermanum Episcopum Constantienum. Reverendus in Christo pater et domine pater noster dilectissime. – Inter ceteras provisiones quas facere cupimus [*originally* 'decrevimus'] in principio nostre assumptionis ad hunc nostrum ducatum, statuimus pro nostra spirituali recreatione, Instituere Capellam celeberrimam, in qua ad divinum cultum et officia celebranda habeamus Cantores Musicos prestantissimos, quos undique perquirimus. Qua de re cum ad noticiam nostram pervenerit [*originally* 'pervenisset'] de sufficientia, integritate, ac vite honestate venerabilis domini Martini de Alemania, Sacerdotis in ecclesia cathedrali V. D. et habita per nos informatione quod in arte Musica, plurimum valet, ipsum in cantorem capelle nostre predicte delegimus atque conduximus [*after this word the two words* 'et acceptat' *are deleted*]. Quapropter vestram R. P. ex corde rogamus ut eadem velit intuitu et amore nostro acquiescere et contentari ut ipse D. Martinus Loco sui ponere et subrogare possit alium idoneum qui curam habeat celebrandi et Gubernandi beneficium suum quod habeat in ecclesia maiori Constantiense nec non velit ipsa D. Vestra se interponere cum Capitulo et venerabilibus illis Canonicis ecclesie predicte, ut et ipsi huic voto nostro libenter annuantur. Quum id a vestra Rev. P. et a suis Reverentiis loco singularis beneficij acceptabimus, offerentes nos quoque [*crossed out:* 'et Statum nostram'] ad quicunque vel similia vel etiam multo maiora beneplacita vestra in omne tempus paratissimos. Bene valete semper etc. Datum in civitate nostra Ferrarie Die x° Decembris anni Mcccclxxi.

Item predicto D. Martino facte fuerunt littere passus pro se et uno sotio vel famulo et cum duobus equis pro eundo constantiam et redeundo.

DOC. 2. Extract from letter of Niccolo Bendedei to Duke Ercole I d'Este, Rome, 10 December 1485. Source: ASM, Amb. Roma, B. 8, Doc. 37/9.

. . . Quando giunsi qua io parlai a messer Polo Casella de la renuncia il promesse a Vostra Signoria de fare cum favore de don Zohane Martino poichè lui me ne lassete uno ricordo: et ho strinse assai in nome de Vostra Excellentia . . .

DOC. 3. Extract of letter of Duke Ercole I d'Este to Bonfrancesco Arlotti at Rome, 4 May 1486. Source: ASM, Amb. Roma, B. 7, Doc. 30–xviii/21.

Cum nostro singulare piacere et contento habiamo inteso come messer Polo Casella ha renuntiato. . . . le ragione sue che 'l pretendeva havere ne la Pieve de Rivalta a don Zoane Martino nostro cantore come per la supplicatione che qui inclusa vi mandiamo vedereti. La quale è signata cum la solemnità necessarie; et aciò che 'l si venga ala expeditione di quanto se ha ad fare circa questa renuntia volemo che faciati expedire le bolle necessarie usque ad plumbum poichè di poi Don Zammartino venirà laoltra: et per quanto bisognarà al presente expende per questo effecto Beltramio da Cardano nostro citadino et mercadante qui scrive laoltra al bancho de Gaddi per sue Littere de cambio che 'l sia exbursàto sino ala quantità de li dinari ch'el bisognarà . . .

DOC. 4. Extract from letter of Bonfrancesco Arlotti to Duke Ercole I d'Este, Rome, 15 February 1487. Source: ASM, Amb. Roma, B. 5, Doc. 30–vii/17, p. 3.

El venne don Zoanne Martino vostro Cantore, el quale ritorna cum le sue bolle, et ben satisfacto nel facto suo per ogni dubio et suspitione l'havesse havuto de messer Paulo Casella . . .

DOC. 5. Extract from letter of Bonfrancesco Arlotti to Duke Ercole I d'Este, Rome, 17 February 1487. Source: ASM, Amb. Roma, B. 5, Doc. 30–vii/20.

. . . perchè non havendo certo messo, et non volendomi farvi spesa ho expectato la partita de don Zoanne Martino, el qual benche presto fù ben expedito, et sollecitato da me ogni hora al venire, pur non l'ho potuto spingere via, che queste compagnie de cantori sonno una terribile cosa Maij non se finiscono. Hogi lo è absente, che lo è andato alle septe chiese. Tornato che 'l sia li consignarò la vostra lettera, como se sia la Excellentia vostra ha ad stare de bona voglia, perchè il Papa vi compiace molto voluntiera, et certificovi che haveti lo amore et gratia de sua Santità . . .

DOC. 6. Extract from letter of Bonfrancesco Arlotti to Duke Ercole I d'Este, Rome, 2 November 1488. Source: ASM, Amb. Roma, B. 5, Doc. 30–viii/42, p. 4.

El giunse qui heri frate Zoanne vostro Cantore per la nova provisione et expeditione per el facto suo, et don Zammartino lo visto et receptato de bona voglia et dato principio ad Indrizare l'una et l'altra cosa secundo la comissione de vostra Excellentia bisogno suo et instructione che l'a portato. Et non dubita Vostra Signoria che 'l facto de l'uno et l'altro serà aiutato et expedito con bona animadversione, lo è vero che 'l ce che haveria voluto el Canonicato de Don Zammartino con Responsione de certa pensione . . .

DOC. 7. Extract from letter of Duke Ercole I d'Este to Feltrino Manfredi, Rome, 21 October 1497, on illness of Johannes Martini. Source: ASM, Minutario Cronologico, B. 4 (1497).

Preterea il se retrova si gravementè infermo don Zammartino nostro Cantore che 'l se tiene che le morirà. Lui ha uno Canonicato in la Chiesia de Reggio, et la prove de un'altra posta in la diocesi de distreto de Reggio. Volemo che incontinente vi ritrovati al conspecto de la Santità de nostro Signore; et la supplicati che la voglia riservarmi li benefici per uno delli cantori nostri come volemo sperare la debba fare attento che de epsi nostri Cantori, non è stato provisto de alcuno, et quelli che haveano hanno perso . . .

DOC. 8. Extract from letter of Duke Ercole I d'Este to Cardinal Ippolito I d'Este (at Rome), dated Medelane, 29 December 1497, on death of Johannes Martini. Source: ASM, ASE, CTPE, B. 69/9, Doc. 1652–xiv/54.

Inanti che vacasseno li beneficij de Zoanne Martino nostro cantore per la morte soa, scrivessimo a messer Ludovico di Carissimi, che suplicasse ala Santità de nostro Signore per una reserva de dicti beneficij. La predicta Santità fo contenta de farla, et in caso, che già dicti beneficij vacasseno assentì di farmi collatione, et provisione adicto die a chi noi nominassimo . . .

DOC. 9a. Extract from letter of Lodovico Carissimi to Duke Ercole I d'Este, Rome, 24 May 1498. Source: ASM, Amb. Roma, B. 10, Doc. 77–i/50.

Ho receputo etiam una altra de Vostra Illustrissima Signore de viii del dicto sopra le beneficij furno de don Zoane Martino . . .

b. Extract from letter of Duke Ercole I d'Este to Lodovico Carissimi, Medelane, 29 December 1497. Source: ASM, Minutario Cronologico, B. 4 (1497).

Messer Lodovico: havemo scripto al Reverendissimo Cardinale nostro figliolo la intentione nostra per quelli benefici che furono de Zammartino nostro Cantore . . . .

DOC. 10. Letter of Duke Ercole I d'Este to Cesare Valentino, Ferrarese ambassador in Milan, Ferrara, 22 November 1479. Source: ASM, Amb. Milan, B.2.

Ad eundem [*follows another ducal minute of the same date on the same page*]: Messer Cesare: Voi fareti chiamare quello messer Gasparo Gyletto Cantore et gli fareti intendere como havemo riceuuto la sua per laquale havemo inteso la dimanda ni fano lui et zohane et ottinetto. Et che per parte nostra vui gli haveti arispondere come siamo contenti didarli li X. ducate ogni mese arasone de paga XII l'ano segondo che ni richedono. [*Item*] ducato 50 l'ano de beneficij senza cura per cadauno quando accaderano vacare nel dominio nostro che geli potiamo dare et per questo non gli mancharemo dela provisione. Et che quando caso venisse che perdessino la voce che li sia licito lassereli permutare epsi beneficij ben cum nostra voluntà segondo che loro domandono et che do li dui ducati che dimandano il mese quando gli accadèra astare fuora de Ferrara per le spexe. Il non mi pare de dargeli senon quando gli accadesse venire cum nui fuora del dominio et terre nostre. Et che siamo contenti di darli ducati X per cadauno de loro per potersi comprare uno cavallo. Ma che in Milano non ni pare defargeli dare perchè si veniria adiscoprire la cosa laoltra. Et giunti qui incontinente geli faremo dare. Et che ali Cavalli soi non li volemo far le spexe ne ala stalla nostra ne altrove. Et cussi li faremo dare et li vestimenti segondo il nostro costume. Ma la casa che ni dimandano per habitatione se la haverano a trovare loro a sue spexe. Et questa è la risposta che facemo a tute le parte dele sue lettere liquali gli fareti intendere in nostro nome.

Et haveriti etiam arispondere a Torquin da p[er]si [*sic*] [= Victor Tarquin of Bruges] che nui siamo contenti dedarli il Cavallo per venire qua et cussi li dinari per le spexe et per la via segondo il ni richede per la sua scripta. Et se li compagni non voleno venire al presente, ma expectare anadale [= a Natale] per intendere come passarano quella cosa de la sia col nome de Dio. Et acio che epso Torquin possi venire auraiti de comprarli un Cavallo da X in XII ducati et dargelo et dargeli dui ducati daspendere per la via perche li bastarano dinanzo per il venire fin qui. Et advisaritimi de quello che haveriti conclusi cum loro. Ferrariae xxij Novembre 1479.

DOC.11. Letter of Duke Ercole I d'Este to the singer Victor Tarquin of Bruges, Ferrara, 12 January 1480. Source: ASM, Archivio per materie, Musica e musicisti, B. 2.

Venerabilis nobis dilectissime. Respondendo ala vostra lettera dicemo che siamo contenti di farui dare [d]al nostro Ambassatore lie ducati dieci da comprarvi uno cavallo da potere venire qua. Et altri ducati dieci per levarvi cum le vostre cosse et per farvi le spexe per via. Et questi vinte vi donaremo de bona voglia: et cussi a scripto e dicto nostro Ambassatore. Et restaremo etiam contenti che la vostra provisione cominci a Kalende de zenaro presente, et che habiati ogni mese ducati dieci de provisione. Et ogni anno una veste come hanno li nostri cantori: Et cussi che vi sia pagato la pisone de una casa per vostra habitatione: Et anchora vi provederemo da beneficij per cento ducati, et al presente gli serà modo da darvene parte, forsi per la mitade o circa, et comperassi fin ala dicta summa, quando lo accaderà che vachino de li benefitij sul nostro dominio. Ma non volemo obligarsi de haverveli dati de qui ala festa de Sancto Zoanne baptista, perche el potria essere che fra questo tempo non vi vaccaria da potervene dare . . . a li haverete quanto più presto si potria. Et per più vostra chiareza havemo sotto scripto questa lettera de nostra propria mano . . . habiate a mente Inanti che vi partiati de havere bon licentia da quella Illustrissima Madona perchè non havendo non vedemo come vi potessemo acceptare cum nostro honore. Bene valeat. Ferrarie xij Januarij 1480.

DOC. 12. Extract from letter of Christoforo de' Bianchi to Duke Ercole I d'Este, Rome, 13 November 1484. Source: ASM, Amb. Roma, B. 8, Doc. 35/13.

. . . Poy pregay la Santità sua che fusse contenta, che la Excellentia Vostra potesse beneficiare li soy Cantori, como già un'altra volta havea dicto a Sua Santità e lie . . . de le raxone perche la Santità Sua haveva di questo compiacere. La Excellentia de la Santità Sua me disse queste formule purche, Messer Christophoro, scriviti al signor Duca, che habia uno pocho de pacientia per fin che 'l sia prestate queste obedientie, et che siano uno pocho meglio assetate le cose nostre che faremo poy. So che noia sua Signoria et inquesto et in mazore cosa, et questo quando lo rende ad vachare niuno beneficio nel stato suo che 'l vi scriva che tuti li daremo ache voia luy.

DOC. 13. Extract from letter of Christoforo de' Bianchi to Duke Ercole I d'Este, Rome, 29 November 1484. Source: ASM, Amb. Roma, B. 8, Doc. 35/16.

Io spero hozi havere una copia de quella bolla havè la Maestà del Re per li soy Cantori, et sopra di quello farò formare uno suplico in nome di vostra Excellentia, et poy farò ogni Instantia per obtenere quello desidera quella . . .

DOC. 14. Extract from letter of Christoforo de' Bianchi to Duke Ercole I d'Este, Rome, 5 December 1484. Source: ASM, Amb. Roma, B. 8, Doc. 35/17.

. . . Io sono stato cum la Santità del Nostro Signore per expedire el facto deli Cantori de vostra Excellentia, et ho usato sopra de ciò ogni inzegno et diligentia che ad mi sia stato possibile. Finche la Santità Sua vole che la Excellentia vostra habia patientia per adesso, poi che per fin che 'l non sia prestate le obedientie ad sua Santità la non vole fare simile gratie, non pur una expectatione che communiter se soleno fare a natale . . .

DOC. 15. Extract from letter of Niccolo Bendedei to Duke Ercole I d'Este, Rome, 10 December 1485. Source: ASM, Amb. Roma B. 8, Doc. 37/9.

. . . il mi respose che 'l havea scripto circo ciò opportunamente a quella, et andome difficultando la cosa mostrando che . . . queste renuncie se stima sempre siano qualche mal guardato chi si faci et che 'l sii . . . uno venditore beneficij . . .

DOC. 16. Extract from letter of Duke Ercole I d'Este to Bonfrancesco Arlotti, Gonzaga (nr. Mantua), 6 May 1487 (on question of his bringing his singers with him on his proposed trip to Rome). Source: ASM, Amb. Roma, B. 7, Doc. 30-xix/24.

Vero che li haressimo potuto mettere li Cantori de la capella nostra, ma poi che eravamo in peregrinagio de andare a Santo Jacomo non mi parse de menarli, et venendo mo in la cum questa comitiva medema, non mi è parso giongerli ni menarli altramente, et per non dare tanta spexa ala Santità de Nostro Signore et ad altri signori che ne fanno honore. Vederiti anche che non menemo piu che tri Trombiti, se bene ne havemo Dece, liquali tri menemo solamente per suegiare et chiamare la brigata quando se ha ad montare a cavallo. Et se ne veniremo pur cussi ala domestica, come se trovavamo andare al viaggio de Santo Jacomo . . .

DOC. 17. Extract from letter of G. A. Boccaccio to Duke Ercole I d'Este, Rome, 19 July 1491 (on limitations of the Papal Indult for Ercole's singers). Source: ASM, Amb. Roma, B. 1.

. . . se po etiam dire che tuti restariano a disposicione del Papa, et primo li non reservati che non se concedeno in dicto Indulto et le prefate dignitade beneficij in corte de Roma et cossi quilli deli familiari de Cardinali et per consequenza del Papa. Zudica mo vostro Illustrissimo signore che gratia gli'è concessa, judicio mio parva vel nulla; bisogna aduncha com il scrivere ogni celerità quando vacarano beneficij perchè essendo lei prima certamente il Papa la compiacerà continuamente come La fa etiam al Duca de Milano, et altri principi . . . et questo serà il megliore et piu amplo Indulto che la poterà havere. Poteriavi passare anni et anni et quodammo una eta mane che dicto Indulto potesse havere effecto in alcun beneficij . . .

DOC. 18. Letter of Duke Ercole I d'Este to Giovanni Luca Pozzi (in Rome), Ferrara, 8 April 1505. Source: ASM, Amb. Roma, B. 20, Doc. 122-III/8.

Messer Zoanne Luca. Voi ne scrivesti che Instando cum il Reverendissimo Cardinale Alexandrino per lo Indulto nostro, Sua Signoria vi dixe che la Santità de Nostro Signore era contenta concederne epso Indulto, ma che la voleva una lettera del Reverendissimo Cardinale nostro figliolo per fede che sua Signoria fusse contenta che dicto Indulto passasse per la diocese sua qui. Et perche havendo Noi facto Instantia cum dicto nostro figliolo per dicta lettera, pare che il se renda difficile ad farla, ni è parso darvene adviso, et dicemovi che pur debiati vedere senza dicta lettera de fare al meglio che poteti, circa dicto Indulto, obtenendolo libero per tute le altre diocese. Et per questa del Cardinale el poteriti obtenire che l'habia loco accadendoli il consentimento suo, perchè poteria essere che poi el seria contento, et se poteti etiam obtenirlo libero per la sua diocese, senza che lui altramente scriva, el ni piacera; Maisi haveti advertire che li beneficij che hora tengono li Capellani et Cantori nostri, quando vaccano, li potiamo dare ad altri nostri Cantori, etiam se fussero de la Diocese del dicto Cardinale, senza che in questo ge habia ad essere il consentimento suo, attendeti mo ad sollicitare per la expeditione de dicto Indulto . . . Ferrarie viii Aprile 1504.

Postscriptum. Vedendo noi la dureza et obstinatione, che usa cum Noi il Cardinale nostro figliolo, circa dicto Indulto despiacendoni ultramodo simili termini desconvenienti, gli havemo facto notificare et commettere, che il deba levarse del dominio nostro, et andare a Roma overo a Milano, overo dove li piace, pur che 'l non stia in le terre et lochi nostre. Perche non ni pare conveniente, che habiamo presso Noi uno figliolo che sia retrogrado a le voglie nostre, et verso noi desobediente, come lo è Lui. Et non parera de supportare più facilmente il despiacere, che havemo preso, per questa sua obstinatione, se'l sia absente de qua, che se lo vedessimo stare qua maisi se ben el se parte, non li molestaremo però le intrate sue, che lo ha qua. Et veramente haveressemo creduto, non che de una cosa minima come era questa, Ma che se lo havessemo rechiesto ad lassare questo Episcopato per amore nostro, il ne dovesse havere conpiaciute. Ni è parso del tuto darvi adviso, Aciò che se sentisti come vedemo, che sentireti, che 'l se parlasse laultra de la partita de qui del Cardinale sapiati come passa la cosa et dove procede tale partita, et che poteti justificarmi dove bisognava. Et se 'l vi paresse de parlar de questa cosa cum la Santità de nostro Signore overo cum altri, senza expectare, che ne sia parlato a vui, se ne remettemo a vui.

DOC. 19a. Extract from letter of G. A. Boccaccio to Duke Ercole I d'Este, Rome, 2 November 1491 (on the singer Don Philippo de Primis). Source: ASM, Amb. Roma, B. 9, Doc. 54-i/27.

. . . Ala parte de quello Don Philippo suo Cantore, subito visto la lettera de vostra Illustrissima Signoria cav[a]lcai a palazo per intendere el tuto; io trovai che già in capella era stato acceptato per il mestro de quella de octi giorni avanti io recevesse dicta lettera; che continente me transferì al dicto Cardinale de Benevento e li lessi la dicta litera el qual sine mora mandò per el dicto Maestro de Capella che è el Vescovo de Cortona et non trovatossi el me remesse al Papa al qual eadem hora io ebe adito et lecta essa litera. El comandò expressamente al Vescovo de Urbino che li se trovava che 'l comandasse per parte sua al dicto Maestro de Capella che licensasse el dicto

Cantore ornamente et cosi li fù comandato per dicto Vescovo et anche per esso Cardinale de Benevento el qual per niente voleva obedire, dicendo che questo era costume de tuti li cantori partirse cum licentia et senza, et che ad ogni homo era licito scusarli come si faceva ogni dì et che la capella n'haveva gran necessità per esser senza cantori, et che soa Beatitudine me portava gram biasmo cum dire che se pur soa Santità vorà cosi io abandonarò la capella et non mi ni impazarò più in colera fu com soa Beatitudine sopra de ciò non già veramente per dispiacere a Vostra Illustrissima signoria ma per honore de la capella. El Papa turbata facie li replicò, non volemo per niente questo tristo in la capella nostra et subito licentialo. In questa sira che fù la nostra audientia in presentia del dicto Monsignor Ascanio finse non intendere dicta licentia . . . Io disse, padre Santa restituiscere el nostro Cantore; il me respuose, Havemo facto caciare vituperosamente; replicavi, pur c'è bisogna, padre Santa; respuose, che volete [?] che faciate confortare el ritornare per che il serà el meglio visto che mai et carissimo al signore mio et li provederà de beneficij. Questa commissione fu data al dicto Monsignor Ascanio el qual farà l'officio molto voluntiera . . .

b. Extract from letter of G. A. Boccaccio to Duke Ercole I d'Este, Rome, 12 November 1491. Source: ASM, Amb. Roma, B. 9, Doc. 54–i/34.

Fu data licentia de capella del Papa a quello don Filippo Cantore et pur il Vescovo de Cortona maestro de la capella ge'l retiene. Ne parlai l'altro heri col Reverendissimo Cardinale de Benevento, se ne maravigliò e turbo pur assai com dire, io so che 'l Papa non vuol per niente che 'l vi stia et in mia presentia et turbatamente ge ha commesso che nedum lo licentia ma lo cacia come uno tristo et demum me disse andati e lassati questo caricho a mi, che 'l non vi starà. Il fu com mi a questi giorni mandato pur dal dicto Vescovo ad ciò ch'io scrivesse a Vostra Excellenza in suo favore, recusavi penitus, et com molte ragione lo confortai a ritornare et tanto lo persuasse che 'l me deti intentione de farlo; questa medesima opera fece el Reverendissimo Monsignore Ascanio; dopoi ha respuosto et pertinazamente che più presto l'andaria in Turchia; lo è già uno anno et più che 'l fu chi per entrare in dicta capella non fu acceptato per non esserli loco. Tamen li fu data speranza, che vacando qualche loco li serrà dato. Il dicto Monsignore Ascanio me ha dicto, come il sia excluso in tuto de la dicta capella; io so che 'l ritorna da mi per favore, alhora bisognarà che 'l ritorna . . .

c. Extract from letter of Duke Ercole I d'Este to G. A. Boccaccio, Belriguardo, 22 November 1491. Source: ASM, Amb. Roma, B. 9, Doc. 54-vii/5.

. . . De quello haveti operato de don Philippo nostro Cantore accio che 'l ritorni a Nui, . . . vi comendemo grandemente.

APPENDIX III

A *Précis of Papal Letters to Duke Ercole I and Duke Alfonso I d'Este on Provisions for the Singers of the Ferrarese Court, 1487–1506*

Source: ASM, ASE, Can., Carteggio di Principi Esteri, Roma, Papi. The following *buste* contain the entire mass of Papal Bulls and Letters to the Ferrarese court that survives from the period 1471–1513: B. 8 (Letters from Pope Sixtus IV, 1471–83); B. 9 (Letters from Pope Innocent VIII, 1484–92); B. 10 (Letters from Pope Alexander VI, 1492–1502); B. 11 (Letters from Pope Alexander VI, 1502–3; from Pope Pius III, 1503; and from Julius II, 1503-6); B. 12 (Letters from Pope Julius II, 1507–13; from Leo X, 1513–14); B. 13 (Letters from Leo X, 1515–21).

1. Bull of 2 June 1487 (Papacy of Innocent VIII) conferring on Duke Ercole I d'Este the right to confer two benefices on each of twenty singers of his chapel, with various limitations on the types of benefices that he may confer. Singers named in the document: Marinus de Castelucio; Petrus Carione de Bondeno; Ieronimus de Ferraria; Iohannes de Locha; Petrus de Candia Grecus; Iohannes Martinus Flamingus; Mathias Gallicus; Iohannes Gallicus; Petrus de Valentia; Iachet Gallus; Ieronimus de Finis de Ferraria; Cornelius Gallus; Bartholomeus de Valentia; Christoforo de Mutina; Uldaricus Teutonicus; Iohannes Gallicus professor ordinis fratrum minorum; Antonius Gallus; Iohannes Gallicus; Henricus de Alamania; Antonius de Alamania. See p. 188 above and fig. 13(*c*).

2. Papal Bull of 5 March 1492 (Papacy of Innocent VIII), extending and amplifying the Indult of 1487 on benefices for Duke Ercole's singers.

3. Papal letter of 6 March 1493 (Papacy of Alexander VI), confirming the earlier Indult of Pope Innocent VIII for benefices for the singers of Duke Ercole's chapel.

4. Papal letter of 11 May 1493 (Papacy of Alexander VI), declaring an earlier papal revocation of Ercole's Indult for benefices for his singers to be invalid, and confirming the Indult (cf. fig. 13(*d*)).

5. Papal letter of 26 November 1503 (Papacy of Julius II) to Cardinal Ippolito I d'Este, giving him an Indult to confer benefices within his diocese as Archbishop of Milan.

6. Papal Bull of 12 June 1504 (Papacy of Julius II), giving Duke Ercole I d'Este the right to confer two benefices on each of twenty singers of his chapel. The singers named in the Indult are the following: Joschinus francigena; Johannes de Troia; Bartholomeus Ispanus; Nicolaus Florentini; Frater Franciscus de Laude; Frater Johannes Franciscus de Padua; Antonius de Venetiis; Jeronimus de Verona; Frater

Felix de Nolla; Michael de Luca; Thomas dictus Misinus; Johannes de Flandria; Ludovicus de Modena; Rossus Sopranus; Giannes de Artiganova; Gervasius Gallus; Bernardino de Scandiano; Jannes de Scotia; Joannes Michael de Sabaudia; Pedemontanus de Pedemontium. (See the roster of singers for the year 1504 in Appendix V.)

7. Papal Bull of 14 June 1505 (Papacy of Julius II) to Duke Alfonso I d'Este, giving him the right to confer two benefices on each of twenty singers of his chapel. The singers named in the Indult are the following: Frate Johannes Franciscus de Padua; Nicolaus Florentinus; Frater Johannes Franciscus de Laude; Michael de Luca; Bartholomeus Ispanus; Johannes Vivasius; Jeronimus de Verona; Johannes Ansaut; Antonius Colobaudi; Thomas Lupus; Johannes de Flandria; Frater Felix de Nolla; Petrus Som de Milleville; Illarius; Johannes de Artiganova; Antonius Organista; Jacobus Galinus; Johannes Maria cl[er]icus Capelle; Johannes de Praia; Bartholomeus de Saxolo. (See roster of singers for the year 1505 in Appendix V.)

8. Papal letter of 7 November 1506 (Papacy of Julius II) confirming the earlier agreement on benefices for the singers of the ducal chapel.

APPENDIX IV

A Chronology of the Correspondence between Duke Ercole I d'Este and Ferrarese Ambassadors at Rome and elsewhere, on Benefices

Appendix IV occupies pages 305–313

Appendix IV

Year	Date	Source	Writer	Recipient	Main Content
1473	15 June	ASM, ARo B.1	B. Arlotti	Ercole	Supplication being submitted for fra Pietro Cariom
(1474)					
(1475)					
1476		ASF, AN	Notary		don Bartolomeo *organista* made deacon
		"	"		Pedros de Valentia, ducal singer, receives benefice of chapel of SS Fabian and Sebastian in Duomo
		"	"		Johannes Brebis receives benefice of San Michele in Cesta; had been archpriest of Cocanile
		"	"		Zoanne Troia (= Zoanne Salico) receives benefice of church in Crespino
		"	"		Peroto *cantore* receives benefice of church of SS Giacomo and Filippo
	Nov.	Chronicles	Caleffini, 84; Zambotti, 22 f.		Ercole issues *grida* claiming his right to confer benefices in his dominions
(1477)					
1478		ASF, AN	Notary		Brebis transfers benefice of S. Giustina to Daniele *cantore*
1479		"	"		Johannes Martini receives benefice in Dogato
		"	"		Matteo de Parise receives benefice
		"	"		Antonio de Cambrai receives benefice of Cocanile on death of Brebis
		"	"		Johannes Martini receives benefice at 'Villae ducati'
		"	"		Bartolomeo Spagnolo receives benefice of S. Maria a Nive
1482		"	"		Johannes Martini receives benefice of S. Agostino in Duomo
		"	"		Matteo de Parise
1483		"	"		Jachetto Marvilla receives benefice of S. Jacob oltra Po
		"	"		Laurentio de Cambio rents benefice to Daniele *cantore*
1484	13 Nov.	ASM, ARo B. 8	C. Bianchi	Ercole	Bianchi asked Pope to allow Ercole to distribute benefice to singers; Pope delays; Ercole wants Indult

Year	Date	Source	Writer	Recipient	Main Content
1484	26 Nov.	ASM, ARo B. 8	C. Bianchi	Ercole	Ercole wants Indult like that which Pope Sixtus IV gave to King (of Naples)
	29 Nov.	"	"	"	Bianchi trying to obtain Neapolitan Indult, will have supplication drawn up on model of that one
	5 Dec.	"	"	"	Pope asks Ercole to have patience and wait for Indult
1485		ASF, AN	Notary		Jachetto de Marvilla ordained rector of S. Giacomo oltra Po
	23 Nov.	ASM, ARo B. 8	Ercole	N. de Bendedei	On renunciation to be made by Paolo Casella of benefice of Rivalta in favor of Johannes Martini
	10 Dec.	"	N. de Bendedei	Ercole	Bendedei says Casella is reluctant to make this renunciation because renunciations create a bad impression
1486	4 May	" B. 6	Ercole	Arlotti	Johannes Martini is coming to Rome about benefice of Rivalta
	27 June	" B. 5	Arlotti	Ercole	Official documents are being drawn up for Johannes Martini's benefice at Rivalta
	27 Aug.	" B. 6	Ercole	Arlotti	Bartolomeo de l'Organo is to renounce benefice of S. Maria Maddalena oltra Po in favor of Jachetto da Marvilla
	18 Oct.	" B. 5	Arlotti	Ercole	On Bartolomeo de l'Organo and renunciation of benefice
	20 Nov.	"	"	"	More on Bartolomeo de l'Organo and Jachetto da Marvilla
1487	11 Jan.	"	"	"	More on Bartolomeo de l'Organo and Jachetto da Marvilla
	15 Feb.	"	"	"	Johannes Martini has been in Rome and will now be returning with the official documents for his benefice
	15 Feb.	"	"	"	Bartolomeo de l'Organo is trying to go ahead with his renunciation in favor of Jachetto
	17 Feb.	"	"	"	Johannes Martini has still not left Rome; today he went to carry out the rite of the Seven Churches (of Rome)
	2 June	" B. 9	"	"	INDULT for singers of Ercole's chapel
	30 July	" B. 7	Ercole	Arlotti	Ercole believes Bartolomeo de l'Organo will have benefice of San Marco of Fossalta, disputed with Mathia cantore; by now Bartolomeo should have renounced benefice of Santa Maria Maddalena in favor of Jachetto
	14 Sept.	" B. 5	Arlotti	Ercole	Bartolomeo has renounced benefice and Jachetto can have it

	25 Oct.	,,		,,	More on Jachetto and benefice
	12 Dec.	,,		,,	Arlotti acknowledges Ercole's request to secure a canonry for Jacob Obrecht and praises Ercole's strong interest in music (published in my 'Music at Ferrara', 127)
1488	3 Jan.	,,		,,	More on request to Pope for benefice for Obrecht (published in Murray, 'New Light', 512 ff.)
	17 Jan.	Arlotti	B. 7	Ercole	On benefice for Obrecht (published ivi, 514 f.)
	21 Feb.	Ercole	B. 5	Arlotti	Pope has agreed to give one of two benefices to Obrecht at Ercole's request if it becomes vacant; further on procedures (published in my 'Music at Ferrara', 128)
	12 May	,,		,,	New provision has been made for Mathia cantore for benefice at Campiolo
	23 May	Arlotti	B. 7	Ercole	Ercole pleased with plan for Campiolo benefice for Mathia, wants to know how much bulls for it will cost
	25 May	Ercole	B. 5	Arlotti	Arlotti sends copy of supplication for Campiolo and reports his expenses for it
	7 June	Arlotti	B. 7	Ercole	Ercole acknowledges supplication copy and will reimburse Arlotti
	16 June	Ercole	B. 5	Arlotti	On benefice for Pietro Greco cantore
	12 July	,,		,,	As for 16 June
	25 July	,,		,,	As for 16 June
	30 July	,,		,,	On benefices for don Mathia
	2 Nov.	,,		,,	Yesterday there arrived frate Zoanne cantore and Zoanne Martino; on benefice for Pietro Greco
	12 Nov.	Arlotti	B. 7	Ercole	Urges Arlotti to continue good work for frate Zoanne and for Martino
	22 Nov.	Ercole	B. 5	Arlotti	Frate Zoanne and Zoanne Martino left yesterday; latter has documents with him, all in good order
	11 Dec.	,,		,,	On renunciation made by frate Zoanne
1489	26 Mar.	,,		,,	Has received Duke's letter on Zoanne Martino
	28 Mar.	,,		,,	On case of Zoanne Martino, Arlotti appends a letter addressed to 'my archdeacon of Reggio'
	26 April	,,		,,	On don Gerardo di Gerardi, who wants a dispensation
	11 Sept.	,,		,,	Supplication of don Gerardo has been signed by Pope

Year	Date	Source	Writer	Recipient	Main Content
1489	12 Oct.	ASM, ARo B. 5	Arlotti	Ercole	On aspects of Indult
	16 Oct.	,,	,,	,,	On expenses for supplication of don Gerardo
1490	5 May	,,	,,	,,	On benefice for don Zoanne de Locha
	19 June	,,	,,	J. N. Corregio, ducal sec.	On benefice of Campiolo for don Mathia and procedures to be followed
	6 July	,, B. 7	Eleonora d'Aragona	Arlotti	don Girolamo Cantore, *mansionario* in cathedral of Ferrara, writes to renounce benefice at Vigoenza, as he is ill
	17 July	,, B. 5	Arlotti	Ercole	Cardinal of Benevento willing to accommodate Pietro Greco regarding benefice
	16 Aug.	,, B. 7	Eleonora	Arlotti	Acknowledges his efforts regarding benefice at Vigoenza, being renounced by don Girolamo in favor of Taddeo de'Lardi; Ercole is content with this arrangement, even though it is under his Indult
	24 Aug.	,,	Ercole	,,	Ercole wants to send Pietro Greco to Rome but he must go to Milan instead with Beatrice d'Este; Arlotti should take care of benefice procedures for him
	8 Nov.	,, B. 5	Arlotti	Ercole	Pietro Greco's expenses for benefice
1491	5 Jan.	,, B. 1	G. A. Boccaccio	,,	On benefice sought for don Mathia *cantore*
	29 Mar.	,, B. 5	Arlotti	,,	Acknowledges Ercole's request for new provision for benefice for don Cristoforo *cantore*
	5 May	,,	,,	,,	On benefice of Albaretto da Modena accepted by don Cristoforo da Modena under the Indult
	1 June	,,	,,	,,	Has obtained signature on supplication for don Cristoforo
	17 July	,, B. 1	Boccaccio	,,	On benefice of Thoano; Pope's view of limitations of Indult and his promise of this benefice to a favorite
	19 July	,,	,,	,,	On the limits of Ercole's Indult
	2 Nov.	,, B. 9	,,	,,	On defection of don Philippo de Primis to Papal Chapel and Boccaccio's attempt to retrieve him
	12 Nov.	,,	,,	,,	Further on don Philippo, who doesn't wish to return to Ercole's service
	15 Nov.	,,	Ercole	Boccaccio	Pleased that don Philippo has been dismissed by Pope; Ercole wants him back in his own chapel

Subject	Ercole	G. L. da Pontremoli	Source	Date
On Indult held by 'his Majesty the King' (of Naples)	Ercole	Boccaccio	,, B. 10	19 Dec.
On limitations of Ercole's Indult	,,	,,	,, B. 9	5 Jan. 1492
Bishop of Cortona indicates that he will return don Philippo *cantore* to Ercole	,,	,,	,,	14 Feb.
Papal letter extending and amplifying Indult of 1487	—	—	ASM, Princ. Esteri, Roma, Papi	5 Mar.
Difficulties presented by members of Apostolic Chamber over new letter on Indult	,,	,,	ASM, ARo B. 9	19 May
On occasion of Alfonso d'Este's visit to Rome, Pope reconfirmed all privileges, including Indult for singers	,,	,,	,,	2 Dec.
Papal letter issued by Alexander VI confirming Indult granted by Pope Innocent for 20 singers	—	—	ASM, Princ. Est., Roma	6 Mar. 1493
Boccaccio had minute of papal letter changed three times; if he hadn't, Indult would have been effectively nullified	Ercole	Boccaccio	ASM, ARo B. 9	11 Mar.
Boccaccio reports that on 12 March 1493 the papal letter on Indult was sent to Ferrara, in proper form and content	,,	,,	,,	13 Mar.
Ducal minute on benefice of Felina, which Ercole wants to bestow on an unnamed singer	Boccaccio	Ercole	,,	25 Apr.
Boccaccio sends Ercole a copy of Pope's assurance of Indult, declaring earlier revocation to be invalid	Ercole	Boccaccio	,,	6 July
Pope is willing to give a vacant benefice to frate Zoanne Francesco (Franciscan) *cantore* of Ercole's chapel; it is rare to see two benefices given to members of that order	,,	,,	,,	4 Jan. 1494
On need for dispensation from rule *ad duo incompatibilia* for Giovanni Francesco da Lodi	,,	,,	,,	16 Feb.
Ercole wants a benefice for his bastard son Julio; canonry in Vigoenza is held by a singer of Ercole's, and to take it away from him would be embarrassing for Ercole	Card. of San Pietro in Vinculi	Ercole	,,	28 Feb. 1495

Year	Date	Source	Writer	Recipient	Main Content
1497	31 Oct.	ASM, ARo B. 10	Ercole	D. Aretino	Duke wants Felino Sandeo to renounce benefice of San Lorenzo near Ferrara in favor of don Girolomo 'nostro cappellano' and will recompense Sandeo with greater rewards; mentions benefice of 'Porcile' in diocese of Modena, which had been conferred on don Zoanne de Locha but is contested by Cardinal Orsino; Ercole wants Aretino to discuss this with Orsino
1498	10 May	,, B. 8	G. B. Ferrari	Ercole	Will make up supplication for ducal singer for benefices formerly held by Johannes Martini; Pope was very difficult on the matter in days past
	24 May	,, B. 10	L. Carissimi	,,	Acknowledges Ercole's letter of 8 May on benefices formerly held by Johannes Martini
(1499)					
1500	18 Feb.	,, B. 11	S. Pinzoni	Card. Ippolito	On dispensations made for 'Rizardeto your musician'
1501	25 Apr.	,,	Ercole	G. Sacrati	Mathia *cantore* is dead; his benefices; Ercole wants his benefice of Santa Martino de Ruberti to go to Nicolo Fiorentino
	7 Oct.	,,	G. Sacrati	Ercole	Sacrati has asked Cardinal of Modena for renunciation of benefice desired by Ercole for don Nicola Fiorentino
	30 Oct.	,,	Ercole	G. Sacrati	Ercole has learned that Cardinal of Monreale cannot dissuade his *cappellano* from opposing claims of don Nicola Fiorentino and Zanfrancesco to the benefices
	19 Oct.	,, B. 12	G. Saraceni and E. Bellingieri	,,	Ercole wants chapel of *Tri magi* reserved for Thomaso da Milano his singer
	10 Nov.	,, B. 11	G. Sacrati	,,	Sacrati concerned that someone might be acting secretly against benefice claims of don Nicola Fiorentino and Giovanni Francesco; has found it is true, and agent is Rainaldo, *cappellano* of Cardinal of Monreale
	23 Nov.	,, B. 12	G. Saraceni	,,	Has seen Cardinal of Monreale who asks Ercole to release two chapels held by Jachetto *cantore*; one is San Jacomo, the other of Santa Maddalena
	24 Nov.	,,	,,	,,	Answering Ercole's request on behalf of frate Pietro Rosello *cantore* for a benefice
	24 Nov.	,,	,,	,,	On benefice of Santa Maria de Udriola, under Abbey of Frassinoro, held by Jachetto *cantore*

Year	Busta	Date	Sender	Recipient	Summary
		11 Dec.	Ercole	G. Saraceni	On dispensation asked for by frate Pietro Rosello, chapel singer
1502		4 Jan.	G. L. da Pontremoli	Ercole	Pope has assured that Indult of Ercole has not been renounced
	B. 13	20 Jan.	B. Costabili	,,	Among other benefices, that of frate Pietro Rosello has been sent out
		22 Jan.	,,	,,	Card. Ippolito is writing to Ercole to say that the Pope will give him the right to confer benefices in the lands of the King of France in Milan worth up to several thousand ducats
		1 Mar.	,,	,,	On difficulties caused by Cardinal Ippolito regarding Ercole's claims on benefices
		6 Apr.	,,	,,	On problems caused by Rainaldo Landola concerning benefice of frate Francesco da Lodi and don Nicolo Fiorentino
		25 June	,,	,,	Girolomo da Verona, singer, has fallen into dispute over benefice of San Jacomo Philippo of Reggio with Cardinal of Sanseverino
		4 July	,,	,,	Costabili has been to see Sanseverino
		9 July	,,	,,	Costabili acknowledges orders to see Sanseverino about benefices of Girolamo da Verona and Piero cantore
		21 July	,,	,,	On Costabili's discussions with Sanseverino
		3 Aug.	,,	,,	The Indult with extension for the singers is still not registered in Camera
		3 Aug.	,,	,,	Further on Sanseverino and benefice of Girolamo da Verona and frate Francesco
		24 Sept.	,,	,,	Will speak to Cardinal of Monreale and notes that Ercole is conferring benefice of Dosentola on don Antonio Scatolaro, singer
		28 Sept.	,,	,,	More on benefices of Dosentola and problems with Cardinal Monreale
		6 Oct.	,,	,,	Pope wished second part of Indult explained to him again, and declined to guarantee when he would sign it
		11 Oct.	,,	,,	More on benefice of Dosentola and Indult
		12 Nov.	,,	,,	On problem of date of Indult
		14 Dec.	,,	,,	Delays by Pope on Indult; he doesn't want to concede confirmation except for those singers named in Indult of 1487
		20 Dec.	,,	,,	Further on Pope's doubts about the Indult and Costabili's refutation of his arguments

Year	Date	Source	Writer	Recipient	Main Content
1502	24 Dec.	ASM, ARo B. 13	Costabili	Ercole	Datary has said that supplication for Indult has been proposed several times for signature but isn't yet signed.
1503	27 Dec.	,,	,,	,,	Pope refused yesterday to hear anything about the Indult
	4 Jan.	B. 14	,,	,,	Pope puts off discussion of Indult to another time
	19 Jan.		,,	,,	Benefices of Antonio Scatolaro still in doubt since supplication of Indult not yet signed; Pope constantly puts off the issue
	27 Jan.		,,	,,	Pope denies delay is due to ill will towards Ercole; says willing to expedite matter
	10 Feb.		,,	,,	Costabili had read portions of Indult to Pope, who gave him 'the usual answer', that he is very busy
	21 Feb.		,,	,,	Has had supplication of Michele de Lucca, singer, done in proper form
	23 Feb.		,,	,,	Pope says he had never conceded such an Indult except to King of Spain
	7 Mar.		,,	,,	Supplication of Michele da Lucca has been signed, also letter on benefices vacated by death of Jachetto; on delays caused by Datary on Indult
	15 Mar.		,,	,,	Further complications about singers named in Indult; Costabili has disputed it with Datary in presence of Pope
	21 Mar.		,,	,,	Supplications of Michele da Lucca and Tomaso Lupi are being expedited
	26 Mar.		,,	,,	Costabili has told Girolamo da Verona to return to Ferrara; 'he hasn't failed with regard to whom he was supposed to lure away here, from what he told me . . .'
	29 Mar.		,,	,,	Supplication of Indult is signed; now date is to be set
	30 Mar.		,,	,,	Costabili negotiating with Pope about date on Indult
	9 Apr.		,,	,,	About date on Indult; and benefice for Girolamo da Verona
	23 May		,,	,,	Pope says won't grant any more favors regarding benefices and if Costabili asks for any more he won't see him
	14 June		,,	,,	Date of Indult still in doubt
	17 June		,,	,,	Cannot induce Datary to assign date as Ercole wishes it
	2 July		,,	,,	Date of Indult still not settled
	1 Aug.		,,	,,	Supplication for Felice da Nola, singer, is signed

26 Aug.	,,	,,	,,	On archpriesthood of Adria for don Nicolo Fiorentino
13 Oct.	,,	,,	,,	In first audience with new Pope Costabili brought up Indult
3 Nov.	,,	,,	,,	Card. Ippolito has spoken with Pope about Ercole's Indult
12 Nov.	,,	,,	,,	Pope noted it would please Ippolito if he signed confirmation of Indult without reviewing it
21 Nov.	,,	,,	,,	Costabili told Ippolito that Ercole wants Indult to be unrestricted; Ippolito says Pope will not prejudice Indults of Cardinals
25 Nov.	,,	,,	,,	Datary told Costabili that it would be difficult to get Pope to sign Indult confirmation
26 Nov.	,,	,,	,,	*Bull gives Ippolito Indult to confer benefices*
9 Dec.	B. 20	G. L. Pozzi		Ippolito wants to provide benefices in Ferrarese lands up to one third of the singers, none in the Modenese, and will offer to divide remaining benefices for singers with Ercole
11 Dec.	,,	,,		Suggests what Ercole might tell Ippolito about benefice distribution
17 Dec.	,,	Ercole	Pozzi	Pozzi still working on Indult; only problem lies with the interests of Ippolito
23 Dec.	,,	Pozzi	Ercole	On benefice of Gervase *cantore*
1504				
22 Mar.	,,	,,		Words in Indult slightly changed but substance remains
1 May	,,	,,		Pope has signed mandate for expedition of Indult; other difficulties and costs to bureaucracy
8 Apr.	,,	Ercole	Pozzi	Ercole's anger towards Ippolito on benefice distribution
12 June	ASM, Princ. Est., Roma	Ercole		*Bull gives singers of Ercole right to retain two benefices each*
30 Sept.	ASM, ARo, B. 14	Costabili		On dispensation for frate Felice da Nola
29 Oct.	,,	,,		Costabili will refer supplication of Felice da Nola to Referendarius

APPENDIX V

A Chronological List of Musicians Active at Ferrara, 1377–1505

The following lists give the names of trumpeters, instrumentalists, and singers who were active at Ferrara, chiefly at the court, but occasionally at the cathedral, during the period indicated. When no other annotation is given, evidence is based on one or more archival records from the ASM, usually payment records of one sort or another; the sources are indicated as clearly as possible, and when no other source is indicated next to an individual's name, it means that the primary source listed at the top of the given year continues in effect. For some singers a few further details are given here, but these lists are not intended to supply biographical details about individuals, rather simply to list the rosters of those who were in service in a given year.

The following additional abbreviations are used in Appendix V:

BCA	Biblioteca Communale Ariostea (Ferrara)
Cath.	Cathedral
Franceschini	Archival source discovered by Maestro Adriano Franceschini and communicated to me
Guard.	Guardaroba
Inv.	Inventario
Mand.	Mandati
Scalabrini	All of these references (with MS number added) refer to individual MSS in the BCA, Ferrara, compiled by G. A. Scalabrini in the eighteenth century, consisting of documents on the Cathedral of Ferrara copied from older sources, many of them no longer accessible. Of the 40-odd autograph compilations by Scalabrini preserved in the BCA, the following are of value for their material on the history of the cathedral: MS C1. I, 125; 241; 389; 430; 431; 447; 450; 456; 459; 460; 468; 507. In what follows, references to individual MSS include the relevant shelf mark.

Note. The lists of musicians supplied for each year follow as closely as possible the order in which they are named in the primary archival sources that I have consulted. In those years for which more than one alphabetical group appears, divided by one or two horizontal lines, the order adopted (again following the sources) is as follows. Where there are three groups the order is, (1) *Trumpeters*; (2) *Instrumentalists* (apart from trumpeters); (3) *Singers*. Where only two groups appear, the order is: (1) *Instrumentalists*; (2) *Singers*. In each year having only two groups (as happens more frequently in the period 1487–1505) a special note indicates that the list of

Trumpeters for that year has been omitted. For the court musicians, these lists include those who were officially in service in a given year. A very few musicians, either listed as being attached to the Duchess Eleonora d'Este, or Ercole's son and heir don Alfonso d'Este, or mentioned only in correspondence, have not been included. The spelling of names follows the original sources.

1377
Enzellino piffaro   ASM, Inv., Perg.

1394
Enzellino piffaro   ASM, Inv., Perg.

1401
Filippo da Padua piffaro   Cittadella, 710 f.

1405
Bartolomeo da Bologna (Cath.)   Scalabrini, Ferrara, BCA, MS, C1.I, 456, fol 4ᵛ

1407
Bartolomeo da Bologna (Cath.)   Cittadella, 67

1416
Francesco da Bologna   ASM, Princ. Est., Napoli
Giovanni di Sicilia
Leonardo Tedesco

1419
Boemo piffaro   ASM, Nicc. III Off. Publ. Reg. 1415– 22. fol. 163

1422
Giovanni trombeta   ASM, Nicc. III Off. Publ. Reg. 1415–22
Passalaqua trombeta
Boemo piffaro
Marco d'Alemagna piffaro
Rodolfo dall' Arpa

1423
Anechino trombeta   ASM, Mand. 1422–24
Janes trombeta
Pietro dell' Arpa

1424
Giovanni d'Avignon piffaro   ASM, Mand. 1422–24
Leonardo dal Chìtarino
Marcolino piffaro
Zorzo piffaro

1426
Johannes de Aranda (Cath.)   Franceschini

1428
Hennequin Coppetrippe, trompette de guerre of Burgundian court, sent to service of Niccolò III d'Este   Marix, pp. 56, 66, 93 f.

1430
Ugolino di Orvieto comes to Ferrara from Forlì (Cath.)   Seay (1955), 117

1431
Payment 'pro collacione cantori domine Bertrandi et aliorum cantorum domini Marchionis qui cantaverunt in coro die dominico . . .' (Cath.)   Scalabrini, Ferrara, BCA, MS C1. I, 456, fol. 35ᵛ
(For related documents from Scalabrini's copies of older sources, on singing by 'singers of the Marquis' in cathedral in 1431, see Peverada, 5)

1432
Ludovico trombeta (has benefice of chapel of San Giovanni Evangelista in Duomo)   Franceschini
Gerardo de Leo [= Leay?] rector Sancto Marino   Scalabrini, Ferrara, BCA, MS C1. I, 450

1434
Santo trombeta   ASM, Mand., 1434–5
Tommaso trombeta

1435
Zanino dall'arpa   ASM, Mand., 1434–5
Payment to piffari of Marquis 'qui pulsarunt quando offerebatur pro parte sacristie.'   Peverada, 5
Payment to six singers who sang in the Cathedral at Mass, 'eo quia interfuit dominus Leonelus Estensis,' Ibid.

1436
Francesco Sbardelati trombeta   ASM, Mand., 1436–8
Nicolaus de Beccaria cantore
Niccolo Tedesco cantor et pulsator

1437
Gaspare de Alemagna trombeta   ASM, Mand., 1436–8
Clemente d'Alemagna piffaro
Giorgio piffaro
Giovanni d'Avignon piffaro
Niccolo Tedesco cantor et pulsator
Guillaume Dufay   Nic. III et Leonelli epist. reg., 1436–8, fol. 158; Valdrighi, 437; correct reading given by Besseler (1952), 166.

1438
Hieronymo trombeta   ASM, Mand., 1436–8
Pierino trombeta

1439
Gaspare de Alemagna trombeta   ASM, Mand.,
    1439–40
Clemente d'Alemagna piffaro

1440
Filippo trombeta   ASM, Mand., 1439–40
Pierino trombeta
Clemente d'Alemagna piffaro
Giorgio piffaro
Niccolo Tedesco cantor et pulsator

1441
Corrado d'Alemagna piffaro   ASM, Mand., 1441–2
Pietrobono dal Chitarino
Niccolo Tedesco cantor et pulsator

1442
Giovanni detto Vignocio piffaro   Franceschini

1443
Girardo tenorista   ASM, Guard., Calzamento, 1443
Gulino cantador
Zuliano Glus (= Claus?) cantadore
Zuliano de Monte cantadore

1444
Gerardo Leay paid for trip 'ad partes Burgundie de
    anno presente pro negociis prefato domini'
    (= Leonello)   ASM, Mand., 1445–6
Giovanni f.q. Ghilmare de Groninghen cantore
    (receives doctorate in arts at University of
    Ferrara)   Pardi (1900)

1445
Tommaso trombeta   ASM, Mand., 1445–6; see my
    'Dufay and Ferrara', *passim* and n. 31
Corrado d'Alemagna piffaro
Michiele Tedesco piffaro
Pietrobono dal Chitarino

Alberto chierico
Andrea chierico
Claus tenorista
Gerardo Leay
Giovanni chierico
Giovanni di Filiberto cantore
Johannes Fede
Niccolo Tedesco cantor et pulsator
Ugolino de Brabantia cantore

1446
Nicolo da Modena trombeta   ASM, Mand., 1445–6

Pierino trombeta
Corrado d'Alemagna piffaro
Pietrobono dal Chitarino
Rodolfo di Giovanni d'Alemagna piffaro

Gerardo Leay
Giovanni di Filiberto cantore
Giovanni Zopo cantore
Johannes Fede
Nicolo de Basilea
Nicolo d'Olanda
Niccolo Tedesco cantor et pulsator
Ugolino de Brabantia cantore

1447
Giovanni dell Chitarino   ASM, Mand., 1447; Guard.
    Deb. e Cred., 'G', 1447
Rodolfo dall'arpa (musician?)

Alberto Burbulius
Claus tenorista
Gerardo Leay
Giovanni cantore
Giovanni di Filiberto cantore
Giovanni Gobert   (listed by Haberl (1887), 37, 39–42
    as 'Jo. de Rems', in Papal Chapel 1448–68)
Giovanni dal Monte cantore
Johannes cantore capellano
Nicolaus cantore
Nicolo capelano
Ugolino de Brabantia cantore
Zohane Tedesco chierego de la chapela
Zuliano chierego de la chapela de corte

1448
Giovanni detto Vignocio piffaro   ASM, Guard.,
    Calzamento, 1448
Alberto dito Barbiero cantadore della capella
Benedetto de Zohane dito Benoit cantadore
Johannes cantor f. q. Johannes, presbyter
    Londini   Franceschini
Nicolo d'Olanda
Niccolo Tedesco cantor et pulsator
Zohane de Pire cantadore
Zohane Tedesco chierego de la chapela
Ugolino di Orvieto (Cath.)   Franceschini

1449
Corrado d'Alemagna piffaro   ASM, Guard.,
    Calzamento, 1449; Mand., 1449
Giovanni d'Alemagna piffaro
Pietrobono dal Chitarino
Zanino di Francia sonatore di arpa e tympano
Alberto Burbulius
Andrea da l'organo
Benedetto de Zohane dito Benoit cantadore

Fiorenzo d'Alessandro
Gerardo Leay
Giovanni di Filiberto cantore
Giovanni d'Inghilterra cantore
Giovanni Prepositus
Niccolo Tedesco cantor et pulsator
Zanetto tenorista
Zohane Tedesco chierego de la chapela
Costantino Tantino (instrument maker)

1450
Pierino trombeta   ASM, Mand., 1450; Guard.,
   Calzamento, 1450
Agostino del fu Urbano dal Chitarino
Giovanni dall'arpa Inglese
Pietrobono dal Chitarino

Agnolo chierego de Messer Ugolino
Alberto de 'Bologlia'
Frate Andrea dell'Ordine de San Francesco (= Fra
   Andrea dall' organo)
Barbauis cantor (identity uncertain)
Benedetto de Zohane dito Benoit cantadore
Giovanni di Filiberto cantore
Giovanni de Leodio
Giovanni dal Monte cantore
Giovanni Prepositus
Niccolo Tedesco cantor et pulsator
Ugolino de Brabantia cantore
Zohane Fonti
Zohane Tedesco chierego de la chapela
Zovelino dito Fiorenzo (= Florentius Alexander)
Enrico da Lira f. q. Giovanni cantore Vescovile
   (Cath.)   Franceschini
Iohannis de Albania (Cath.)   Franceschini
Iohannis de Durachio (Cath.)   Franceschini

1452
Giovanni delle Chioare (Cath.)   Franceschini

1456
Baptista da Norsa trombeta   ASM, Bolletta, 1456
Guasparo trombeta
Nicolo da Modena trombeta
Pierino trombeta
Tomaso de Faenza trombeta
Augustino trombone
Blasio Montolino
Corrado d'Alemagna piffaro
Francesco Malacise tenorista
Paulo Grillo
Pietrobono dal Chitarino   Franceschini
Zoanne d'Alemagna piffaro
Fiascho sonatore
Giovanni da Bologna
Niccolo Tedesco cantor et pulsator
Giovanni delle Chioare (Cath.)   Franceschini

1457
Guasparo trombeta
Niccolo Tedesco cantor et pulsator
Giovanni Albanese f. q. Petri a Sonis (given
   benefice)   Franceschini

1459
Guasparo trombeta   ASM, Bolletta, Estratto, 1459
Nicolo da Modena trombeta
Pierino trombeta
Corrado d'Alemagna piffaro
Francesco Malacise tenorista
Paulo Grillo
Pietrobono dal Chitarino
Zoanne d'Alemagna piffaro
Fiascho sonatore
Niccolo Tedesco cantor et pulsator

1460
Domenico cantore cappellano (Cath.)   Franceschini
Roberto Inglese (Cath.)   Franceschini

1461
Constantino Tantino   ASM, Inv.

1462
Baptista da Norsa trombeta   ASM, Bolletta, Estratto,
   1462
Guasparo trombeta
Nicolo da Modena trombeta
Pierino trombeta
Tomaso de Faenza trombeta
Augustino trombone
Blasio Montolino
Corrado d'Alemagna piffaro
Luca piffaro
Paulo Grillo
Pietrobono dal Chitarino
Zoanne d'Alemagna piffaro
Fiascho sonatore
Giovanni de Mercatello organista   Peverada, 28 ff.
Niccolo Tedesco cantor et pulsator
Antonio da Genova (Cath.)
Jacobo a Turri cantore (Cath.)

1463
Corrado d'Alemagna piffaro   ASM, Inv.

1464
Corrado d'Alemagna piffaro   ASM, Inv.
Constantino Tantino

1465
Corrado d'Alemagna piffaro   ASM, Camera, Pacti de
   Laboratori, 1466–71
Anna cantarina Anglica   Franceschini
(Contract for new organ at cathedral   Peverada,
   22 ff.)

1466
Giovanni da Faenza suonatore di trombetta   ASM,
  various registers
Guasparo trombeta
Luzido trombeta
Tommaso trombeta
Andrea della Viola
Augustino trombone
Francesco Malacise tenorista
Pietrobono dal Chitarino
Salvatore de Bonfioli maestro de chitarrino
Zampaulo della Viola
Guaspar del organo
Niccolo Tedesco cantor et pulsator
Constantino Tantino
Domenico cantore f. q. Jacobo d'Argenta (Cath.)
Giovanni d'Alemagna cantore
Giovanni de Mercatello organista (Cath.)

1468
Andrea della Viola
Corrado d'Alemagna piffaro
Zampaulo della Viola

1469
Francesco Malacise tenorista   Valdrighi, 443; ASM,
  Inv.
Pietrobono dal Chitarino
Zampaulo della Viola
Fiascho sonatore
Guaspar del organo

1470
Guasparo trombeta   ASM, Bolletta, Estratto, 1470
Marco d'Arezzo trombeta
Raynoldo trombeta
Andrea della Viola
Augustino trombone
Berniero di Sale Napoletano suonatore di viola   ASM,
  Inv.
Biagio Montolino
Corrado d'Alemagna piffaro
Francesco Malacise tenorista
Jacomo de Bologna sonadore
Paulo Grillo
Pietrobono dal Chitarino
Alessandro d'Alemagna   ASM, Inv.
Cornelio de Fiandra
Fiascho sonatore
Costantino Tantino
Mathio de Paxino

1471
Biagio trombeta   ASM, LCD 86, 1471
Daniele trombeta
Guasparo trombeta
Marco d'Arezzo trombeta

Raganello trombeta
Ruzido trombeta

Andrea della Viola
Augustino trombone
Biagio Montelino
Corrado d'Alemagna piffaro
Paulo Grillo
Pietrobono dal Chitarino
Rainaldo dal Chitarino
Stefano da Savoia piffaro
Zampaulo della Viola
Zoanne d'Alemagna piffaro

Cornelio cantore
Jaches cantore
Zoanne Brebis   ASM, LCD 89

1472
Andrea trombeta   ASM, LCD 96 (1472); LASP Ercole
  I, 1471–5
Bazo d'Arezzo trombeta
Daniele trombeta
Guasparo trombeta
Luzido trombeta
Marco d'Arezzo trombeta
Raganello trombeta
Zilio trombeta

Andrea della Viola
Corrado d'Alemagna piffaro
Francesco Malacise tenorista
Jacomo dell'arpa sonadore
Piedro de Augustino trombone
Pietrobono dal Chitarino
Stefano da Savoia piffaro
Zampaulo della Viola
Zanino de Polo da Venezia piffaro
Zoanne d'Alemagna piffaro

Andrea da Mantova cantore tenorista
Carles
Costantino Tantino
Domenico contrabasso
Girolimo soprano
Jaches cantore
Jacheto chievre
Jacheto contratenore
Jacheto de Nemport cantore
Marino cappellano
Nicolo d'Olanda
Piedre
Udorigo tenorista
Zoanne Brebis

Zoanne Gon maestro de' putti
Zoanne Polster
Zorzo Prando

1473
Guasparo trombeta   ASM, Guard., 1473
Luzido trombeta
Marco fratello de Bari trombeta
Marco fratello di Luzido trombeta
Rizo trombeta
Zilio trombeta
___ de Toscana trombeta

Bernardo sonadore
Piedro de Augustino trombone
Stefano da Savoia piffaro
Zanino de Polo da Venezia piffaro
Zoanne Todesco trombone
Bartolomeo Cattelana
Corado de San Michele garzon todesco
Domenico contrabasso
Florentio de Fiandra garzon todesco
Girolamo da Ferrara soprano
Guasparo garzon todesco
Jacheto
Ludovico tenorista
Marino cappellano
Melchiore garzon todesco
Nicolo d'Olanda
Pedros contra alto
Piedro de Nantes de Bretagna soprano
Pirotto tenore
Udoricho garzon todesco
Zoanne de Bechari de Ferrara
Zoanne Brebis
Zoanne Gon
Zoanne Martini
Zohane Bavaro garzon todesco
Zohane de Costantia garzon todesco
Zohane grande purchusen garzon todesco
Zohane Nispli garzon todesco
Zohane picolo garzon todesco
Zohane piffaro garzon todesco
Zohane de Preda garzon todesco
Zorzo Picoli garzon todesco
Zorzo de Saltipurgo garzon todesco

1474
Daniele trombeta   ASM, LCD 103 (1474)
Piero Antonio da Bologna trombeta
Raganello trombeta
Rizo trombeta

Andrea da Mantova cantore tenorista
Andrea della Viola
Nardo tamburino

Piedro de Augustino trombone
Rainaldo dal Chitarino
Zoanne d'Alemagna piffaro
Zoanne de Alemagna trombone

Alberto soprano
Bartolomeo Raimondo de Valenza
Bartolomeo de San Gallo
Bernardo Tedescho
Corrado Ghislin garzon todesco
Corado da Tridento garzon todesco cantadore
Domenico contrabasso
Florentio de Fiandra garzon todesco
Girolimo soprano
Jachetto Cambrai
Jacomo de Bechari
Jacomo Gualtiero de Ulandia
Jacopo de Morpach
Janes de Alemagna
Matio de Paris
Melchiore garzon todesco
Nicolo d'Olanda
Pedros contra alto
Piero soprano
Pirotto tenore
Rainaldetto Cambrai
Rodolfo Manin garzon todesco cantadore
Udorigo tenorista
Zoanne de Bechari de Ferrara
Zoanne Brebis
Zoanne Gon
Zoanne Marescalco
Zoanne Martini
Zoanne de Troia
Zohane Aman de Brugge garzon todesco
Zohane de Constantia garzon todesco
Zohane grande purchusen garzon todesco
Zohane grande de Valessia garzon todesco
Zorzo garzon todesco

1475 (Trumpeters not listed)
Andrea della Viola   ASM, various registers; Valdrighi,
    450–4
Francesco Malacise tenorista
Jacomo dell'arpa sonadore
Paulo Grillo
Rainaldo dal Chitarino
Zampaulo della Viola
Zanino de Polo da Venezia piffaro

Alberto soprano
Andrea de Mantova cantore tenorista
Bartolomeo Raimondo de Valenza
Domenico contrabasso
Fiascho sonatore
Giordano d'Olanda cantadore

Girolamo da Ferrara soprano
Guglielmo de Fiandra
Jachetto Cambrai
Jacomo Gualtiero de Ulandia
Janes de Alemagna
Jeronimo de Bruno musico
Matio de Paris
Michiele cantore soprano
Michiele Feyt
Michiele de Ipris cantore
Nicolo d'Olanda
Pedros contra alto
Piero soprano
Pirotto tenore
Rainaldetto Cambrai
Rodolfo de Frisia organista
Udorigo tenorista
Zoanne Brebis
Zoanne Gon
Zoanne Marescalco
Zoanne Martini
Zoanne de Troia

1476

Bazo d'Arezzo trombeta   ASM, LCD 114 (1476);
    Valdrighi, 455–7
Bernardino da Sisi trombeta
Daniele trombeta
Guasparo trombeta
Luzido trombeta
Marco da Norsa trombeta
Raganello trombeta

Andrea della Viola
Corrado d'Alemagna piffaro
Giovanni tenorista
Piedro de Augustino trombone
Rainaldo dal Chitarino
Stefano da Savoia piffaro
Zampaulo della Viola

Alberto soprano
Andrea da Mantova cantore tenorista
Bartolomeo da Luziano
Bartolomeo Raimondo de Valenza
Domenico contrabasso
Gerardo de Flandria
Girolamo da Ferrara soprano
Guglielmo de Fiandra
Jachetto Cambrai
Jachetto de Marvilla
Jacomo Gualtiero de Ulandia
Lorenzo da Modena
Marco de Paris
Marino cappellano
Matio de Paris

Michiele de Ipris cantore
Nicolo d'Olanda
Pedros contra alto
Piedro da Luziano
Piero soprano
Pirotto tenore
Rainaldetto Cambrai
Rodolfo de Frisia organista
Udorigo tenorista
Zoanne de Bechari de Ferrara
Zoanne Brebis
Zoanne Gon
Zoanne Marescalco
Zoanne Martini
Zoanne de Troia

1477 (Trumpeters not listed)

Andrea da Mantova cantore tenorista   ASM, LCD
    118 (1477)
Antonio da Hosta
Bartolomeo da Luziano
Bartolomeo Raimondo de Valenza
Cornelio de Fiandra
Costantino Tantino
Daniele
Domenico contrabasso
Girolamo da Ferrara soprano
Guglielmo de Fiandra
Jachetto de Marvilla
Lorenzo da Modena
Marino cappellano
Matio de Paris
Michiele de Ipris cantore
Nicolo d'Olanda
Pedros contra alto
Piedro da Luziano
Pirotto tenore
Rodolfo de Frisia organista
Udorigo tenorista
Zoanne de Bechari de Ferrara
Zoanne Brebis
Zoanne Japarth
Zoanne Martini
Zoanne de Troia

1478

Bazo d'Arezzo trombeta   ASM, Bolletta, Estratto;
    LCD 120 (1478)
Bragantino trombeta
Domenico da Vizenza trombeta
Guasparo trombeta
Luzido trombeta
Paulo trombeta de Castello
Piero Antonio da Bologna trombeta
Raganello trombeta
Zilio trombeta
Zoanne Maria trombeta

Andrea della Viola
Anzelino piffaro portonaro
Corrado d'Alemagna piffaro
Francesco Malacise tenorista
Nardo tamburino
Paulo Grillo
Piedro de Augustino trombone
Pietrobono dal Chitarino
Rainaldo dal Chitarino
Stefano de Piamonte tamburino
Stefano da Savoia piffaro
Zampaulo della Viola
Zampietro de Trani tamburino
Zoanne d'Alemagna piffaro

Antonio da Cambrai cantadore
Bartolomeo Raimondo de Valenza
Cornelio cantore
Costantino Tantino
Daniele
Domenico contrabasso
Girolamo da Ferrara soprano
Guglielmo de Fiandra
Jachetto de Marvilla
Matio de Paris
Nicolo d'Olanda
Pedros contra alto
Pirotto tenore
Udorigo tenorista
Zoanne de Bechari de Ferrara
Zoanne Brebis
Zoanne Japarth
Zoanne Martini
Zoanne de Troia
Zuliano capelano in Fossadalbero

1479 (Trumpeters not listed)
Andrea della Viola   ASM, LCD 126 (1479)
Corrado d'Alemagna piffaro
Gentile tamburino
Michiele Tedesco piffaro
Piedro de Augustino trombone
Rainaldo dal Chitarino
Zampaulo della Viola
Zoanne d'Alemagna piffaro
Zoanne garzon da Piedro trombone

Alessandro [Signorello]
Antonio da Cambrai cantadore
Bartolomeo Raimondo de Valenza
Cornelio cantore
Daniele
Franco Orbo da Fiorenza
Gasparo Gyletto
Girolamo da Ferrara soprano
Guglielmo de Fiandra

Guido Zohane
Jachetto de Marvilla
Jannes
Matio de Paris
Nicolo d'Olanda
Pedros contra alto
Udorigo tenorista
Zoanne Japarth
Zoanne Martini
Zoanne de Troia

1480 (Trumpeters not listed)
Corrado d'Alemagna piffaro   ASM, LCD 130
  (1480)
Nicolo de l'arpa
Pietrobono dal Chitarino
Rainaldo dal Chitarino
Stefano de Savoia piffaro
Zampaulo della Viola
Zoanne d'Alemagna piffaro

Alessandro Signorello
Antonio da Cambrai cantadore
Bartolomeo da Luziano
Bartolomeo Raimondo de Valenza
Cornelio de Fiandra
Daniele
Girolamo da Ferrara soprano
Guglielmo da Lege
Guido Zohane
Jachetto de Marvilla
Ludovico cantarino
Marino cappellano
Matio de Paris
Nicolo d'Olanda
Pedros contra alto
Piedro da Luziano
Piero Cariom
Piero Griego
Udorigo tenorista
Zoanne Japarth
Zoanne Martini
Zoanne de Troia

1481
Antonio trombeta   ASM, LCD 139 (1481); Bolletta,
  1481; Memoriale *eee*, 1481
Francesco trombetino
Piero Antonio da Bologna trombeta
Raganello trombeta

Andrea dalla Viola
Anzelino pifaro portonaro
Bernardino trombone cugnado de Piero
Corrado d'Alemagna piffaro
Francesco de la Gata tenorista

Michiele Tedesco piffaro
Nardo tamburino
Piedro de Augustino trombone
Rainaldo dal Chitarino
Roma ( ) piffaro
Stefano da Savoia piffaro
Zampaulo dalla Viola
Zoanne d'Alemagna piffaro

Alessandro Signorello, don
Alvaro dal Castello
Antonio da Cambrai cantadore
Bartolomeo da Luziano
Bartolomeo Raimondo de Valenza
Cornelio de Fiandra
Daniele
Egidio Giletto
Fiascho sonatore
Girolimo del Brum
Girolamo da Ferrara sporano
Guglielmo da Lege
Guido Zohane
Jachetto de Marvilla
Jannes
Ludovico da Domenico
Marino cappellano
Matio de Paris
Nicolo d'Olanda
Pedros contra alto
Piedro da Luziano
Piero Cariom
Piero Griego
Rigo cantore
Rinaldo da Forli
Udorigo tenorista
Zoanne Japarth
Zoanne Martini
Zoanne de Troia

1482
(No other data on musicians presently known; chapel probably dissolved owing to war with Venice)
Luzido trombeta   ASM, Mem. del Soldo (1482)
Marco da Norsa trombeta
Piero Antonio da Bologna trombeta
Zilio trombeta

1484
Antonio trombeta   ASM, Bolletta, Estratto (1484); Mem. del Soldo (1484)
Bazo d'Arezzo trombeta
Bernardino da Sisi trombeta
Domenica del Reame trombetta
Francesco da Montepulziano trombeta
Luzido trombeta
Piero Antonio da Bologna trombeta
Raganello trombeta

Rossetto de Thomaso trombetta
Sebastiano trombeta
Stiefano da Montepulziano trombeta
Zilio trombeta

Adam piffaro
Andrea della Viola
Francesco Malacise tenorista
Francesco de Orthona tamburino
Jacomo dell'arpa sonadore
Nardo tamburino
Paulo Grillo
Piedro de Augustino trombone
Pietrobono dal Chitarino
Rainaldo dal Chitarino
Stefano de Piamonte tamburino
Zampaulo della Viola
Zampietro da Trani tamburino
Zoanne d'Alemagna piffaro
Zoanne da Padova trombone

Bartolomeo Spagnolo cantore
Cornelio de Fiandra
Costantino Tantino
Jachetto de Marvilla
Marino cappellano
Matio de Paris
Piero Griego
Zoanne Martini
Zoanne de Troia

1485
Antonio trombeta   ASM, Bolletta, Estratto (1485)
Bazo d'Arezzo trombeta
Bernardino da Sisi trombeta
Domenico del Reame trombetta
Francesco da Montepulziano trombeta
Luzido trombeta
Nardo trombeta
Piero Antonio da Bologna trombeta
Raganello trombeta
Rossetto de Thomaso trombeta
Sebastiano trombeta
Stiefano da Montepulziano trombeta
Zilio trombeta

Adam piffaro
Andrea della Viola
Anzelino pifaro portonaro
Gregorio soprano piffaro
Jacomo dell'arpa sonadore
Ludovico da Bologna piffaro
Ludovico tenorista
Michiele Tedesco piffaro
Nardo tamburino

Paulo Grillo
Piedro de Augustino trombone
Rainaldo dal Chitarino
Stefano de Piamonte tamburino
Zampaulo della Viola
Zampietro da Trani tamburino
Zoanne da Padova trombone

Aluisio cantore
Bartolomeo Raimondo de Valenza
Bartolomeo Spagnolo cantore
Christoforo de Modena cantore
Cornelio de Fiandra
Girolamo da Ferrara soprano
Guido Zohane
Marino cappellano
Matio de Paris
Pedros contra alto
Rosso de Meniato organista
Udorigo tenorista
Zoanne Martini
Zoanne de Troia

1486
Antonio trombeta   ASM, LCD 153 (1486); Mem.
   del Soldo, (1486)
Bazo d'Arezzo trombeta
Bernardino da Sisi trombeta
Domenico del Reame trombetta
Francesco da Montepulziano trombeta
Luzido trombeta
Piero Antonio da Bologna trombeta
Raganello trombeta
Rossetto de Thomaso trombetta
Stiefano da Montepulziano trombeta
Zilio trombeta

Adam piffaro
Andrea della Viola
Francesco de la Gata tenorista
Francesco de Orthona tamburino
Gregorio soprano piffaro
Ludovico da Bologna piffaro
Michiele Tedesco piffaro
Nardo tamburino
Piedro de Augustino trombone
Pietrobono dal Chitarino
Rainaldo dal Chitarino
Stefano de Piamonte tamburino
Zampaulo della Viola
Zampietro da Trani tamburino
Zoanne d'Alemagna piffaro
Zoanne de Padova trombone

Bartolomeo da l'organo

Bartolomeo Raimondo de Valenza
Bartolomeo Spagnolo cantore
Bernardo da Colornio
Christoforo de Modena cantore
Cornelio de Fiandra
Girolamo da Ferrara soprano
Guido Zohane
Jachetto de Marvilla
Marino cappellano
Matio de Paris
Pedros contra alto
Piedro che insigna i ragazzi
Piero Griego
Rosso de Meniato organista
Udorigo tenorista
Zoanne de Locha
Zoanne Martini
Zoanne de Troia

1487 (Trumpeters not listed)
Andrea della Viola   ASM, Mem. del Soldo (1487);
   LCD 161
Biagio Montelmo
Ludovico dall'arpa
Michiele Tedesco piffaro
Nicolo de Carmielli dall'arpa
Rainaldo dal Chitarino
Zampaulo della Viola

Antonius de Alemania*
Antonio da Cambrai cantadore
Bartolomeo Raimondo de Valenza
Bernardo da Colornio
Christoforo de Modena cantore*
Cornelio de Fiandra*
Girolamo de Ferrara soprano*
Henricus de Alemania*
Jachetto de Marvilla*
Johannes Gallicus*
Johannis Gallicus professor ordinis fratrum
   Minorum*
Marino cappellano*
Matio de Paris
Petrus de Valentia*
Piero Cariom*
Piero Griego*
Udorigo tenorista*
Zoanne de Locha*
Zoanne Martini*

1488 (Trumpeters not listed)
Adam piffaro   ASM, Bolletta (1488); LCD 162
   (1488)
Dioda buffone
Francesco de la Gata tenorista

*listed by name in Papal Indult of 1487

Gregorio soprano piffaro
Ludovico da Bologna piffaro
Michiele Tedesco piffaro
Nardo tamburino
Piedro de Augustino trombone
Pietrobono dal Chitarino
Stefano de Piamonti tamburino
Zampietro da Trani tamburino
Zoanne da Padova trombone

Bartolomeo Raimondo de Valenza
Bernardo da Colornio
Christoforo de Modena cantore
Cornelio de Fiandra
Girolamo Albanexe capelano
Girolamo da Ferrara soprano
Guido Zohane
Jachetto de Marvilla
Matio de Paris
Pedros contra alto
Piero Cariom
Piero Griego
Rosso de Meniato organista
Udorigo tenorista
Zoanne de Locha
Zoanne Martini
Zoanne Raimondino cantore et organista
Zoanne de Troia

1489
Antonio trombeta   ASM, Mem. del Soldo (1489)
Bazo d'Arezzo trombeta
Bernardino da Sisi trombeta
Francesco da Montepulziano trombeta
Luzido trombeta
Piero Antonio da Bologna trombeta
Raganello trombeta
Rossetto de Thomaso trombeta
Stiefano da Montepulziano trombeta
Zilio trombeta

Adam piffaro
Andrea della Viola
Francesco de Orthona tamburino
Giovanni suonatore
Gregorio soprano piffaro
Guglielmo tamburino
Ludovico da Bologna piffaro
Michiele Tedesco piffaro
Piedro de Augustino trombone
Rainaldo dal Chitarino
Zampaulo della Viola
Zoanne d'Alemagna piffaro

Bartolomeo Spagnolo cantore

Bernardo da Colornio
Christoforo de Modena cantore
Girardo cantore
Girolamo da Ferrara soprano
Hieronymo capelano
Jachetto de Marvilla
Matio de Paris
Pedros contra alto
Piero Cariom
Zoanne cantore
Zoanne capelano
Zoanne Martini
Zoanne de Troia

1490 (Trumpeters not listed)
Andrea della Viola   ASM, Mem. del Soldo, Estratto
    (1490); some material for 1490 added from Mem.
    del Soldo, Estratto of 1491
Jacomo dell'arpa sonadore
Michiele Tedesco piffaro
Rainaldo dal Chitarino
Zampaulo della Viola

Bartolomeo Spagnolo cantore
Bernardo da Colornio
Christoforo de Modena cantore
Cornelio de Fiandra
Gian cantore
Giovanni Marco cantore
Girardo cantore
Girolamo da Ferrara soprano
Girolamo de la Frassina capelano
Guido Zohane
Jachetto de Marvilla
Matio de Paris
Michiele da Fiorenza cantore
Pedros contra alto
Piero Cariom
Piero Griego
Zoanne cantore
Zoanne capelano
Zoanne Martini

1491 (Trumpeters not listed)
Adam piffaro   ASM, Mem. del Soldo (1491)
Andrea della Viola
Gregorio soprano piffaro
Guglielmo tamburino
Ludovico da Bologna piffaro
Michiele Tedesco piffaro
Rainaldo dal Chitarino
Zampaulo della Viola
Zenovese tenorista

Bartolomeo Spagnolo cantore
Bernardo da Colornio

Christoforo de Modena cantore
Cornelio de Fiandra
Philippo de Primis de Fano cantore
Gian cantore
Girardo cantore
Girolamo de la Frassina capelano
Guido Zohane
Jachetto de Marvilla
Matio de Paris
Pedros contra alto
Piero Cariom
Piero Griego
Zoanne cantore
Zoanne Francesco da Lodi cantore
Zoanne Martini
Zoanne da Modena cappellano
Zoanne de Troia

1492 (Trumpeters not listed)
Andrea della Viola   ASM, LASP Ercole I, No. 25
 (1492)
Carlo da Bologna piffaro
Gregorio soprano piffaro
Ludovico da Bologna piffaro
Rainaldo dal Chitarino
Zampaulo della Viola
Zenovese tenorista

Bartolomeo Spagnolo cantore
Cornelio de Fiandra
Domenico organista
Gian cantore
Jachetto de Marvilla
Jacomo d'Alba
Matio de Paris
Pedros contra alto
Piero Cariom
Piero Griego
Zoanne cantore
Zoanne Francesco da Lodi cantore
Zoanne Martini

1493
Antonio trombeta   ASM, Mem. del Soldo, Estratto
 (1493)
Bazo d'Arezzo trombeta
Bernardino da Sisi trombeta
Francesco da Montepulziano trombeta
Luzido trombeta
Piero Antonio da Bologna trombeta
Raganello trombeta
Rossetto de Thomaso trombeta
Stiefano da Montepulziano trombeta
Zilio trombeta

Andrea della Viola

Carlo da Bologna piffaro
Francesco de Orthona tamburino
Gregorio soprano piffaro
Guglielmo tamburino
Jacomo dell'arpa sonadore
Ludovico da Bologna piffaro
Michiele Tedesco piffaro
Nicolo de l'arpa
Piedro de Augustino trombone
Pietrobono dal Chitarino
Rainaldo dal Chitarino
Zampaulo della Viola
Zenovese tenorista
Zoanne da Padova trombone

Bartolomeo Spagnolo cantore
Bernardo da Colornio
Christoforo de Modena cantore
Cornelio de Fiandra
Domenico organista
Gian cantore
Gian Francese cantore
Girardo cantore
Girolamo de la Frassina capelano
Guaspar del organo
Jachetto de Marvilla
Jacomo d'Alba
Jacomo capelano dela illustrissima madama
Ludovico da Modena
Marino cappellano
Matio de Paris
Pedros contra alto
Piero Cariom
Piero Griego
priette Turoso capelano
Zoanne cantore
Zoanne Francesco da Lodi cantore
Zoanne Martini
Zoanne da Modena capellano
Zoanne de Troia
Zoanne Vivas cantore

1494 (Trumpeters not listed, except Raganello)
Raganello trombeta   ASM, Bolletta (1494); Mem.
 del Soldo (1494)
Adam piffaro
Andrea della Viola
Francesco de la Gata tenorista
Gregorio soprano piffaro
Jacomo dell'arpa sonadore
Ludovico da Bologna piffaro
Michiele Tedesco piffaro
Nardo tamburino
Piedro de Augustino trombone
Piedro da Ragona maestro di clavicembalo
Pietrobono dal Chitarino
Rainaldo dal Chitarino

Zampaulo della Viola
Zampietro da Trani tamburino
Zenovese tenorista

Bernardo da Colornio
Christoforo de Modena cantore
Cornelio de Fiandra
Domenico organista
Girardo cantore
Girolamo da Ferrara soprano
Guido Zohane
Jachetto de Marvilla
Jacomo d'Alba
Jacomo cantore
Jacotin cantore
Matio de Paris
Michiele da Fiorenza cantore
Pedros contra alto
Piero Griego
Rosso de Meniato organista
Zoanne cantore
Zoanne Francesco da Lodi cantore
Zoanne Martini
Zoanne Raimondino cantore et organista
Zoanne de Troia
Zoanne Vivas cantore

1496 (Information for this year drastically
   incomplete)
Zenovese tenorista   ASM, various registers
Giam Francese cantore
Jacomo d'Alba (mentioned in letter of Ascanio Sforza
   to Ercole I, 14 May)

1497 (Trumpeters not listed; list of instrumentalists
   largely incomplete)
Agostino della Viola   ASM, Mem. del Soldo (1497)
Andrea della Viola
Bartolomeo Spagnolo cantore
Bernardo da Colornio
Bernardo da Scandiano cantore
Cordiere cantore
Cornelio de Fiandra
Domenico organista
Giam Francese cantore
Girardo cantore
Girolamo da Ferrara soprano
Jachetto de Marvilla
Jacomo d'Alba
Jacomo del Ponte cantore
Jacotin cantore
Johanne a Senesino musico
Matio de Paris
Michiele da Fiorenza cantore
Pedros contra alto
Piero Cariom
Pollo dalle Conchele

Zoanne Francesco da Lodi cantore
Zoanne de Locha
Zoanne Martini
Zoanne de Troia
Zoanne Vivas cantore

1498 (Information drastically incomplete)
Michiele Tedesco piffaro
Bartolomeo Spagnolo cantore
Piero Cariom
Roberto Ferrarese

1499 (Trumpeters not listed)
Adam piffaro   ASM, Bolletta, Estratto (1499); Mem.
   del Soldo (1499)
Agostino della Viola
Andrea della Viola
Gregorio soprano piffaro
Jacomo dell'arpa sonadore
Jacomo della Viola
Michiele Tedesco piffaro
Nardo tamburino
Rainaldo dal Chitarino
Zampaulo della Viola

Andrea Picardo cantore
Antonii cappellano
Bartolomeo cappellano
Bartolomeo de Fiandra cantore
Bartolomeo Spagnolo cantore
Bernardo da Colornio
Cornelio de Fiandra
Domenico organista
Egidio cantore
Gian cantore
Giletto Picardo cantore
Girardo cantore
Girolamo de la Frassina capelano
Guido Zohane
Jachetto de Marvilla
Jacomo del Ponte cantore
Jacotin cantore
Jani contrabasso
Ludovigo da Fulgano cantore
Marino capellano
Matio cantore
Matio de Paris
Nicolo Fiorentino cantore
Pedros contra alto
Piero Cariom
Piero Franzese cantore
Piero Picardo cantore
Pietro Rossello cantore
Pollo dalle Conchele
Roberto Inglese
Thomaso da Parixe
Zoanne cantore

Zoanne Francesco da Lodi cantore
Zoanne da Modena cappellano
Zoanne de Troia
Zoanne Vivas cantore

1500 (Trumpeters not listed; list of instrumentalists
certainly incomplete)
Andrea della Viola   ASM, Bolletta, Estratto (1500);
Mem. del Soldo (1500)
Jacomo dell'arpa sonadore
Nardo tamburino
Zenovese tenorista

Bartolomeo de Fiandra cantore
Bartolomeo Spagnolo cantore
Bernardo da Colornio
Cornelio cantore
Domenico organista
Egidio cantore
Giam Francese cantore
Giletto Picardo cantore
Hieronymo de la Frassina
Jacomo d'Alba
Jacomo Liti cantore
Jacomo del Ponte cantore
Ludovigo da Fulgano cantore
Matio Fiamingo
Matio de Paris
Nicolo Fiorentino cantore
Pedros contra alto
Piero Cariom
Piero Franzese cantore
Piero Picardo cantore
Roberto Inglese
Thomaso Fiamingo contrabasso
Thomaso da Parixe
Zoanne cantore
Zoanne Francesco da Lodi cantore
Zoanne da Modena cappellano
Zoanne de Troia
Zoanne Vivas cantore
Zohane de Argentina organista

1501 (Trumpeters not listed; list of instrumentalists
incomplete)
Piedro de Augustino trombone   ASM, Mem. del
Soldo (1501)
Pozato pifaro
Rizardeto

Bartolomeo de Fiandra cantore
Bartolomeo Spagnolo cantore
Bernardo da Colornio
Cornelio cantore
Domenico organista
Egidio cantore

Girolamo Albanexe capelano
Hieronymo de la Frassina
Jachetto de Marvilla
Jacomo d'Alba
Jacomo del Ponte cantore
Ludovigo da Fulgano cantore
Matio Fiamingo
Michiele da Lucca
Nicolo Fiorentino cantore
Piero Franzese cantore
Petro Rosello cantore
Roberto Inglese
Thomaso Fiamingo contrabasso
Zoanne cantore
Zoanne Francesco da Lodi cantore
Zoanne Francesco da Padova
Zoanne de Troia
Zoanne Vivas cantore

1502 (No lists of musicians available; see source note
below)
Rizardeto   ASM, Estratto della Bolletta (M. Gian
Cantore only); all others known from numerous
letters from and about musicians from this year
(see my 'Josquin at Ferrara').
Antonio Colobaudi dicto Bidon
Antonio Scatolaro
Baldessare cantore
Bartolomeo de Fiandra cantore
Coletta soprano
Gebia ala musica
Gerardo
Gian cantore
Girolamo
Girolamo Beltrandi
Girolamo da Sestola
Girolamo da Verona cantore
Jacomo da Sansegondo cantore
Nicolo Fiorentino cantore
Petro Rosello cantore
Zoanne cantore
Zoanne Francesco da Lodi cantore

1503 (Trumpeters not listed; list of instrumentalists
drastically incomplete)
Augustino trombone   ASM, Mem. del Soldo (1503)
Agostino della Viola
Antonio Colobaudi dicto Bidon
Antonio de don Guido
Antonio da Venezia
Bartolomeo de Fiandra cantore
Bartolomeo Spagnolo cantore
Bernardo da Colornio
Bernardo da Scandiano cantore
Carlo de Fiandra compositore de chantj
Cornelio de Fiandra
Domenico organista
Felice da Nola

Gebia ala musica
Gian de Fiandra
Girolamo Beltrandi
Girolamo de la Frassina capelano
Jacomo d'Alba
Jannes Pezenin
Juschino cantore
Ludovico da Modena
Massino
Michiele da Lucca
Nicolo Fiorentino cantore
Piero Cariom
Roberto Ferrarese
Roberto Inglese
Rosso de Meniato organista
Vincenzo Lusignano
Zoanne Francesco da Lodi cantore
Zoanne Michiele
Zoanne da Modena cappellano
Zoanne de Troia
Zoanne Vivas cantore

1504 (Trumpeters and instrumentalists not listed)
Andrea Picardo cantore   ASM, Mem. del Soldo
   (1504)
Antonio Colobaudi dicto Bidon
Antonio de don Guido
Antoine de Longueval
Antonio da Venezia*
Bartolomeo de Fiandra cantore
Bartolomeo Spagnolo cantore*
Benedetto da Como
Bernardo da Colornio
Bernardo da Scandiano cantore*
Cornelio de Fiandra
Domenico organista
Felice da Nola*
Gian de Fiandra*
Girolamo Beltrandi*
Girolamo de la Frassina capelano
Ilario Turluron
Jacomo d'Alba
Jannes Pezenin
Juschino cantore*
Ludovico da Modena*
Massino*
Michiele da Lucca*

Nicolo Fiorentino cantore*
Piero Cariom
Piedro Som de Milleville
Roberto Ferrarese
Rosso de Meniato organista*
Ubreto cantore
Vincenzo Lusignano
Zoanne Francesco da Lodi cantore*
Zoanne Francesco da Padova*
Zoanne de Locha
Zoanne de Troia*
Zoanne Vivas cantore*

1505 (Trumpeters and instrumentalists not listed)
Antonio Colobaudi dicto Bidon†   ASM, Mem. del
   Soldo (1505)
Antonio de don Guido†
Bartolomeo cappellano†
Bartolomeo de Fiandra cantore
Bartolomeo Spagnolo cantore†
Bernardo da Scandiano cantore
Cornelio de Fiandra
Domenico organista
Felice da Nola†
Gian de Fiandra†
Girolamo Beltrandi†
Girolamo de la Frassina capelano
Ilario Turluron†
Jannes Pezenin
Massino†
Michiele da Lucca†
Nicolo Fiorentino cantore†
Piero Cariom
Piedro Som de Milleville†
Ubreto cantore
Vincenzo Lusignano
Zoanne Francesco da Lodi cantore†
Zoanne Francesco da Padova†
Zoanne Guascon†
Zoanne de Locha
Zoanne Michiele
Zoanne Vivas cantore†

*listed by name in Papal Bull of 12 June 1504
†listed by name in Papal Indult of 14 June 1505

Bibliography

Abbreviations

AfMw	*Archiv für Musikwissenschaft*
AM	*Annales Musicologiques*
AMP	*Atti e memorie delle reali deputazioni di storia patria per le provincie modenesi e parmensi*
AR	*Atti e memorie della reale deputazione di storia patria per le provincie di Romagna*
GSLI	*Giornale storico della letteratura italiana*
JAMS	*Journal of the American Musicological Society*
MD	*Musica Disciplina*
RIM	*Rivista italiana di musicologia*
RMI	*Rivista musicale italiana*

WORKS PRINTED BEFORE 1800

Baruffaldi, G., *Rime scelti de poeti ferraresi antichi e moderni* (Ferrara, 1713)

Bergamo, J. de, *Supplementum Chronicarum* (Venice, 1483)

Corona Beatae Mariae Virginis . . . Super Septem Sequentibus Verbis: Ave Mater Dei Ora Eum Pro Me (Ferrara: Laurentius de Rubeis, 1496)

Cortese, P., *De Cardinalatu Libri Tres* (Castel Cortesiano, 1510)

Decembrio, A., *Politeia Litterariae Angeli Decembrii Mediolanensis* (Augsburg, 1540)

Folengo, T. (= Merlin Cocai), *Opus Merlini Cocai Poete Mantuani Macaronicorum* [Tusculanum, 1521]; modern reprint, incomplete, as *Merlin Cocai, Le Maccheronee*, ed. A. Luzio (Bari, 1928)

Giraldi, G. B., *Commentario delle cose di Ferrara* (Venice, 1597)

Glarean, H., *Dodekachordon* (Basle, 1547) [English translation by C. A. Miller, American Institute of Musicology, Musicological Studies and Documents, vi (Rome, 1965)]

Guarini, M. A., *Compendio historico dell'origine, accrescimento e prerogative delle chiese di Ferrara* (Ferrara, 1621)

Muratori, L. A., *Delle antichità estensi ed italiane* (2 vols., Modena, 1717–40)

Pigna, G. B., *Historia de' Principi d'Este* (Ferrara, 1570)

Sardi, G., *Libro delle historie ferraresi* (Ferrara, 1556)

Scalabrini, G. A., *Memorie storiche delle chiese di Ferrara* (Ferrara, 1773)

WORKS PRINTED AFTER 1800

Alexander, J. J. G., *Italian Renaissance Illumination* (New York, 1977)

Allen, P. S., 'The Letters of Rudolph Agricola', *English Historical Review*, xxi (1906), 302–17

Alumni Cantabrigienses, compiled by J. Venn and J. A. Venn (Cambridge, 1922–54)

Anglès, H., 'La musica en la corte real de Aragon y de Napoles durante il reinado de Alfonso V el Magnanimo', *Cuadernos de trabajos de la Escuela Española de Historia y Arquelogia en Roma*, xi (1930); repr. in Anglès, *Scripta Musicologica*, ii (Rome, 1975), 913–1028

Annuario delle biblioteche italiane (Rome, 1956–59)

Archivi di stato italiani, Gli (Bologna, 1944)

Archivio di Stato de Modena, Archivio Segreto Estense, Sezione 'Casa e Stato', Inventario, compiled by F. Valenti (Rome, 1953)

Ariosto, L., *Orlando furioso* (original edition, Ferrara, 1516); ed. G. Innamorati (Bologna, 1967); English translation by W. S. Rose, 1823–31, ed. A. Baker and A. Bartlett Giamatti (New York, 1968)

Atlas, A. ed., *Dufay Quincentenary Conference, Papers* (Brooklyn, 1976)

——, 'La provenienza del manoscritto Berlin 78 C. 28: Firenze o Napoli?', *RIM*, xiii (1978), 10–29

——, *The Cappella Giulia Chansonnier (Rome, Biblioteca Vaticana, MS Cappella Giulia XIII, 27)*, (2 vols., Brooklyn, 1975–6)

Atti del primo convegno internazionale di studi storici pomposiani: Deputazione provinciale ferrarese di storia patria: atti e memorie, n. s., xxix (1964)

Bacchelli, R., *La congiura di don Giulio d'Este*, 2nd edn. (Verona, 1958)

Barblan, G., 'Vita musicale alla corte sforzesca', *Storia di Milano*, ix (Milan, 1961), pp. 787–852

Baxandall, M., *Painting and Experience in Fifteenth-Century Italy* (Oxford, 1974)

Becherini, B., *Catalogo dei manoscritti musicali della Biblioteca Nazionale di Firenze* (Kassel, 1959)

——, 'Un canta in panca fiorentino, Antonio di Guido', *RMI*, 1 (1948), 243–4

Belloni, A., 'Un lirico del Quattrocento a torto inedito e dimenticato: Giovan Francesco Suardi', *GSLI*, li (1903), 147–206

Bennett, J. W., 'Andrew Holes: a Neglected Harbinger of the English Renaissance', *Speculum*, xix (1944), 314–35

Bent, I., ed., *Source Materials and the Interpretation of Music: a Memorial Volume to Thurston Dart* (London, 1982)

Bernich, E., 'Statue e frammenti architettonici della prima epoca aragonese', *Napoli nobilissima*, xv (1906), 8

Bertolotti, A., *Musici alla corte dei Gonzaga in Mantova* (Milan, [1890])

Bertoni, G., 'Il Cieco di Ferrara e altri improvvisatori alla corte d'Este', *GSLI*, xciv (1928) 271–8

——, 'I maestri degli Estensi a tempo del Duca Ercole I', *Archivium Romanicum*, i (1917), 494–7

——, *La Biblioteca Estense e la coltura ferrarese ai tempi del Duca Ercole I* (Turin, 1903)

——, *L'Orlando furioso e la Rinascenza a Ferrara* (Modena, 1919)

——, 'Un copista del Marchese Leonello d'Este (Biagio Bosoni da Cremona)', *GSLI*, lxxii (1918), 96–106

Besseler, H., *Bourdon und Fauxbourdon* (Leipzig, 1950)

——, 'Chorbuch', *Die Musik in Geschichte und Gegenwart*, ii, cols. 1331–9

——, 'Die Entstehung der Posaune', *Acta Musicologica*, xxii (1950), 8–35

——, 'Neue Dokumente zum Leben und Schaffen Dufays', *AfMW*, ix (1952), 159–76

Bezold, F. von, 'Rudolf Agricola, ein deutscher Vertreter der italienischen Renaissance', *Festrede zur Vorfeier des allerhöchsten Geburts- und Namensfestes Seiner Majestät des Königs Ludwigs II . . .* (Munich, 1884), 1–20

Bibliotheca Sanctorum (Rome, 1961–71)

Bouquet, M. T., 'La cappella musicale dei duchi di Savoia, dal 1450 al 1500', *RIM*, iii (1968), 233–85

——, 'La cappella musicale dei duchi di Savoia', *RIM*, v (1970), 3–36

Bowers, R., 'Choral Institutions within the English Church – Their Constitution and Development, 1430–1500' (Ph.D diss., University of East Anglia, 1975)

Brawley, J. G., 'The Magnificats, Hymns, Motets and Secular Music of Johannes Martini' (Ph.D diss., Yale University, 1968)

Bridgman, N., 'Un Manuscrit italien du debut du xvie siècle', *AM*, i (1953), 167–267

Briquet, C. M., *Les Filigranes*, Jubilee edition, ed. A. Stevenson (Amsterdam, 1968)

British Museum, Catalogue of Additions to the Manuscripts, 1854–75

Brown, H. M., ed., *A Florentine Chansonnier from the Time of Lorenzo the Magnificent*, Monuments of Renaissance Music, vii (Chicago, 1983)

——, 'Emulation, Competition, and Homage: Imitation and Theories of Imitation in the Renaissance', *JAMS*, xxxv (1982), 1–48

——, 'Instruments and Voices in the Fifteenth-Century Chanson', in J. Grubbs, ed., *Current Thought in Musicology* (Austin, 1976), pp. 89–138

Bruscagli, R., 'La corte di scena: genesi politica della tragedia ferrarese', in M. Lorch, ed., *Il teatro italiano del Rinascimento* (Milan, 1980), pp. 569–96

Bukofzer, M., 'The Beginnings of Choral Polyphony', in *Studies in Medieval and Renaissance Music* (New York, 1950), pp. 176–89

Caleffini, Ugo, *Diario di Ugo Caleffini (1471–1494)*, a cura di G. Pardi; in *R. deputazione di storia patria per l'Emilia e la Romagna, sezione di Ferrara. Serie: Monumenti* (2 vols., Ferrara, 1938–40). [Pardi's edition is an incomplete paraphrase of Caleffini's text, which I have consulted in the original (Rome, Biblioteca Vaticana MS Chigiani I. I. 4, 'Croniche facte et scripte per Ugo Caleffino notaio ferrarese . . .')]

——, *Notizie di Ugo Caleffini . . . con la sua cronaca in rima di casa d'Este*, ed. A. Cappelli, *AMP*, 1st Ser., ii (1864), 267–312

Calkins, R. G., 'Medieval and Renaissance Illuminated Manuscripts in the Cornell University Library', *The Cornell Library Journal*, xiii (1972), 95 pp.

Cambridge University, Grace Book A, Containing the Proctors' Accounts and Other Records of the University of Cambridge for the Years 1454–1488, ed. S. M. Leathes (Cambridge, 1897)

Canal, P., 'Della musica in Mantova', *Memorie del R. Istituto Veneto di Scienze, Lettere ed Arti*, xxi (1879), 655–774 (repr. Bologna, 1977)

Cappelli, Adriano, 'La Biblioteca Estense nella prima metà del secolo xv', *GSLI*, xiv (1889), 1–30

Cappelli, Antonio, 'Lettere di Lorenzo de' Medici con notizie tratte dai carteggi diplomatici degli oratori estensi a Ferrara', *AMP*, 1st Ser., i (1863), 231–320

Capra, L. 'Gli epitaphi per Niccolò III d'Este, *Italia medioevale e umanistica*, xvi (1973), 197–226

Carducci, G., 'La coltura estense', in his *Opere (Edizione nazionale)*, xiii (Bologna, 1936), pp. 10–19

——, 'La gioventù di Lodovico Ariosto', in ibid, pp. 115–374

Carpenter, N. C., *Music in the Medieval and Renaissance Universities* (Norman, 1958)

Cartellieri, O., *Am Hofe der Herzöge von Burgund* (Basle, 1926)

Casimiri, R., 'Musica e musicisti nella cattedrale di Padova nei secoli XIV, XV, XVI', *Note d'archivio*, xviii (1941), 1–31, 101–214

Castiglione, B., *Il libro del cortegiano*, ed. V. Cian, 4th revised edition (Florence, 1947); English translation by Sir Thomas Hoby as *The Book of the Courtier* (1561) (London, 1928)

Catalano, M., *Vita di Ludovico Ariosto* (2 vols., Geneva, 1931)

Catalogo della esposizione della pittura ferrarese del Rinascimento (Ferrara, 1933)

Cavicchi, A., 'Sacro e profano: documenti e note su Bartolomeo da Bologna e gli organisti della cattedrale di Ferrara nel primo Quattrocento,' *RIM*, x (1975), 46–71

——, 'Altri documenti per Bartolomeo da Bologna', *RIM*, xi (1976), 178–80

Cellesi, L., 'Documenti per la storia musicale di Firenze', *RMI*, xxxiv (1927), 584–99; xxxv (1928), 556–82

Chambers, D. S., *Patrons and Artists in the Italian Renaissance* (London, 1971)

Chiappini, L., *Eleonora d'Aragona, prima duchessa di Ferrara* (Rovigo, 1956)

——, *Gli Estensi* (Varese, 1967)

——, *Indagini attorno a cronache e storie ferraresi del secolo xv* (Rovigo, 1954)

Chiarelli, R., ed., *L'opera completa del Pisanello* (Milan, 1972)

Cittadella, L. N., *Notizie relative a Ferrara per la maggior parte inedite* (Ferrara, 1864–8)

Cobin, M., 'The Compilation of the Aosta Manuscript; a Working Hypothesis', in A. Atlas, ed., *Dufay Quincentenary Conference*, pp. 76–101

Cohen, J., *The Six Anonymous L'Homme Armé Masses in Naples, Biblioteca Nazionale MS VI.E.40* (Rome, 1968)

Collingwood, R. C., *The Idea of History* (Oxford, 1946)

Concordantiarum SS. Scripturae Manuale (Barcelona, 1958)

Coppo, A. M., 'Spettacoli alla corte di Ercole I', in *Contributi dell'Istituto di Filologia Moderna*, Serie Storia del Teatro, i (Milan, 1968), pp. 30–59

Coussemaker, C. E. H., *Scriptorum de Musica Medii Aevi Nova Series* (4 vols. Paris, 1864–76)

Cummings, A., 'A Florentine Sacred Repertory from the Medici Restoration' (Ph.D. diss., Princeton University, 1980)

D'Accone, F., 'The Performance of Sacred Music in Italy during Josquin's Time c.1475–1525', in E. Lowinsky, ed., *Josquin Desprez*, pp. 601–18.

——, 'The Singers of San Giovanni in Florence during the Fifteenth Century', *JAMS*, xiv (1961), 307–58

Dahlhaus, C., 'Studien zu den Messen Josquins Desprez' (Diss., University of Göttingen, 1953)

D'Alessi, G., *La cappella musicale del Duomo di Treviso* (Vedelago, 1954)

Dallari, U., 'Carteggio tra i Bentivoglio e gli Estensi dal 1401 al 1542 esistente nell'Archivio di Stato in Modena', *AR*, 3rd Ser. xviii (1900), 1–88, 285–332; xix (1901), 245–372

——, 'Inventario sommario dei documenti della Cancelleria ducale estense, nel R. Archivio di Stato di Modena', *Atti e memorie della deputazione di storia patria per le provincie modenesi*, 7th Ser. iv (1927), 157–275.

D'Ancona, A., *Origini del teatro italiano* (Turin, 1891)

D'Ancona, P., *I mesi di Schifanoia in Ferrara* (Milan, 1954)

Davari, S., 'La Musica a Mantova', *Rivista storica mantovana*, i (1884), 53–71 (repr. Mantua, 1975)

Deutsche Literatur in Entwicklungsreihen, Reihe Humanismus und Renaissance, ii, ed. H. Rupprich (Leipzig, 1935) [contains Rudolph Agricola's inaugural address for the Ferrarese Studio in 1476 (pp. 164–83)]

Diario ferrarese dall'anno 1409 sino al 1502 di autori incerti, ed. G. Pardi; *Rerum Italicarum Scriptores*, ed. L. A. Muratori; new edition, ed. G. Carducci, V. Fiorini, P. Fedele, vol. xxiv, part vii (Bologna, 1928)

Dictionaire d'histoire et de géographie ecclesiastique (Paris, 1912–)

Disertori, B., ed., *Johannes Martini: Magnificat e Messe*, Archivium Musices Metropolitanum Mediolanense, xii (Milan, 1964)

Dizionario biografico degli italiani (Istituto della enciclopedia italiana, Rome, 1960–)

Doglio, F., 'Una tragedia alla corte di Ferrara: "De captivitate ducis Jacobi" ', in M. Lorch, ed., *Il teatro italiano del Rinascimento*, pp. 241–60

Donati, L., *Bibliografia della miniatura* (Firenze, 1972)

Dorfmüller, K., *Studien zur Lautenmusik in der ersten Hälfte des 16. Jahrhunderts* (Tutzing, 1967)

Einstein, A., *The Italian Madrigal* (3 vols., Princeton, 1949; repr. 1971)

Elders, W., *Studien zur Symbolik in der Musik der alten Niederländer* (Utrecht, 1968)

Enciclopedia dello spettacolo (9 vols., Rome, 1954–62)

Evans, E., ed., *Johannes Martini, Secular Pieces* (Madison, 1975)

Fallows, D., *Dufay* (London, 1982)

——, ed., *Galfridus and Robertus de Anglia, Four Italian Songs for Two and Three Voices* (London, 1977)

——, 'Robertus de Anglia and the Oporto Song Collection', in I. Bent, ed., *Source Materials and the Interpretation of Music: a Memorial Volume to Thurston Dart* (London, 1982), pp. 99–128

——, 'Two More Dufay Songs Reconstructed', *Early Music*, iii (1975) 358–60; iv (1976), 99

Fano, F., *La cappella musicale del Duomo di Milano* (Milan, 1956)

Fatini, G., 'Le "Rime" di Ludovico Ariosto', *GSLI*, Suppl. 25 (1934)

Fava, D., *La Biblioteca Estense nel suo sviluppo storico* (Modena, 1925)

Fenlon, I., ed., *Music in Medieval and Early Modern Europe; Patronage, Sources and Texts* (Cambridge, 1981)

Ferand, E., 'What is *Res Facta*?', *JAMS*, x (1957), 141–50

Ferraresi, G., *Il Beato Giovanni Tavelli da Tossignano e la riforma di Ferrara nel Quattrocento* (4 vols., Brescia, 1969)

Ferraro, G., *Alcune poesie inedite del Saviozzo e di altri autori* (Bologna, 1879)

Finscher, L., 'Martini, Johannes', *Die Musik in Geschichte und Gegenwart*, viii, cols. 1724–26

Fischer, K. von, 'Kontrafakturen und Parodie in italienischer Werke des Trecento und frühen Quattrocento', *AM*, v (1958), 43–59

——, 'The Manuscript Paris, Bibliothèque Nationale Nouv. acq. Frc. 6771 (Codex Reina = PR)', *MD*, xi (1957), 38–78

Fökövi, L., 'Musik und musikalische Verhältnisse in Ungarn am Hofe des Matthias Corvinus', *Kirchenmusikalisches Jahrbuch*, xv (1900), 1–16

Ford, W. K., 'Some Wills of English Musicians of the Fifteenth and Sixteenth Centuries', *Royal Musical Association Research Chronicle*, v (1965), 80–4

Foucard, C. 'Fonti di storia napoletana nell'Archivio di Stato di Modena; descrizione della città di Napoli e statistica del Regno nel 1444,' *Archivio storico per le provincie napoletane*, ii (1877), 725–57; iv (1879), 689–803

Frati, L., *Rimatori bolognesi del Quattrocento* (Bologna, 1908)

Frizzi, A., *Memorie per la storia di Ferrara raccolte da A. Frizzi*, 2nd edn. (Ferrara, 1847–8)

Gallo, A., '*Cantus planus binatim*; polifonia primitiva in fonti tardive', *Quadrivium*, vii (1966), 79–90

——, 'Citazioni da un trattato di Dufay', *Collectanea Historiae Musicae*, iv (1966), 149–52

——, *Il Medioevo II*, Storia della musica a cura della Società Italiana di Musicologia (Turin, 1977)

——, and Mantese, G., *Ricerche sulle origini della cappella musicale del Duomo di Vicenza* (Vicenza, 1964)

Gandini, L., 'Saggio degli usi e delle costumanze della corte di Ferrara al tempo di Niccolò III (1393–1441)', *AR*, 3rd Ser. ix (1891), 148–69

Gardner, E. G., *Dukes and Poets in Ferrara: a Study of the Poetry, Religion and Politics of the Fifteenth and Early Sixteenth Centuries* (London, 1904)

Garin, E., 'Guarino Veronese e la cultura a Ferrara', in E. Garin, *Ritratti di umanisti* (Florence, 1967), pp. 69–106

Gaspari, G., 'Ricerche, documenti e memorie riguardanti la storia dell'arte musicale in Bologna', *AR*, i (1868), 21–60; repr. in *Musica e musicisti a Bologna* (Bologna, 1970)

Gerber, R., *Zur Geschichte des mehrstimmigen Hymnus* (Kassel, 1965)

Ghinassi, G., ed., *Viaggio a Gerusalemme di Nicolò da Este descritto da Luchino del Campo*, Collezione di opere inedite e rare dei primi tre secoli della lingua, i (Torino, 1861)

Ghinzoni, P., 'Nozze e commedie alla corte di Ferrara nel febbraio 1491', *Archivio storico lombardo*, 2nd Ser. ii (1884), 749–53

Gill, J., *Eugenius IV, Pope of Christian Union* (London, 1961)

——, *The Council of Florence* (Cambridge, 1959)

Gombosi, O., ed., *Compositione de messer Vicenzo Capirola* (Paris, 1955)

Gottwald, C., *Johannes Ghiselin – Johannes Verbonnet* (Wiesbaden, 1962)

Gregorovius, F., *Lucrezia Borgia* (Florence, 1883)

Gruyer, G., *L'Art ferrarais à l'époque des princes d'Este* (Paris, 1897)

Gundersheimer, W., ed., *Art and Life at the Court of Ercole I d'Este: the 'De triumphis religionis' of Giovanni Sabadino degli Arienti* (Geneva, 1972)

——, *Ferrara: the Style of a Renaissance Despotism* (Princeton, 1973)

——, 'The Patronage of Ercole I d'Este', *Journal of Medieval and Renaissance Studies*, vi (1976), 1–18

——, 'Popular Spectacle and the Theater in Renaissance Ferrara', in M. Lorch, ed., *Il teatro italiano del Rinascimento*, pp. 25–34

——, 'Women, Learning and Power: Eleonora of Aragon and the Court of Ferrara', in P. Labalme, ed., *Beyond Their Sex: Learned Women of the European Past* (New York, 1980), pp. 43–65

Günther, U., 'Das Manuskript Modena, Biblioteca Estense Alpha M. 5, 24', *MD*, xxiv (1970), 17–67

Haar, J., 'Some Remarks on the "Missa La Sol Fa Re Mi" ', in E. Lowinsky, ed., *Josquin Desprez*, pp. 564–88

Haberl, F. X., 'Bio-bibliographische Notizen über Ugolino von Orvieto', *Kirchenmusickalisches Jahrbuch*, x (1895), 40–49

——, 'Die römische "Schola Cantorum" und die päpstlichen Kapellsänger bis zur Mitte des 16. Jahrhunderts', *Vierteljahrsschrift für Musikwissenschaft*, iii (1887); also as *Bausteine für Musikgeschichte*, iii (Leipzig, 1888)

Hale, J. R., *Florence and the Medici* (London, 1977)

Hamm, C., ed., *The Complete Works of Leonel Power*, Corpus Mensurabilis Musicae, 1 (Rome, 1969)

Hamm, C. and Scott, A., 'A Study and Inventory of the Manuscript Modena, Biblioteca Estense Alpha X.1.11', *MD*, xxvi (1972) 101–43

Haraszti, E., 'Bono, Pietro' [*sic*], *Die Musik in Geschichte und Gegenwart*, ii, cols. 117–19

——, 'Les Musiciens de Mathias Corvin et de Béatrice d'Aragon', in J. Jacquot, ed., *La Musique instrumentale de la Renaissance* (Paris, 1955), pp. 35–59

——, 'Pierre Bono, Luthiste de Mathias Corvino', *Revue de Musicologie*, xxxi (1949), 73–85

Hartfelder, K., 'Unedierte Briefe von Rudolf Agricola', *Festschrift der Badischen Gymnasium* (Karlsruhe, 1886), pp. 1–36

Harvard Dictionary of Music, The, 2nd edn. (Cambridge, Mass., 1969)

Hay, D., *Europe in the Fourteenth and Fifteenth Centuries* (London, 1966)

Heartz, D., 'The Basse Dance: its Evolution circa 1450 to 1550', *AM*, vi (1958–63), 287–340

Hermann, H. J., 'Zur Geschichte der Miniaturmalerei zum Hofe der Este in Ferrara', in *Jahrbuch der Kunsthistorischen Sammlungen des Allerhöchsten Kaisershauses*, xxi (1900), 117–271

Hersey, G., *The Aragonese Arch at Naples, 1443–1475* (New Haven, 1973)

Hill, G. F., *A Corpus of Italian Medals of the Italian Renaissance before Cellini* (London, 1930)

——, *Pisanello* (London, 1905)

Hofmann, G., ed., *Acta Camerae Apostolicae . . . de Concilio Florentino* (Rome, 1950–)

——, 'Die Konzilsarbeit in Ferrara', *Orientalia Christiana Periodica*, iii (1937), 110–40, 403–55

Hughes, A., and Bent, M., 'The Old Hall Manuscript – a Reappraisal and an Inventory', *MD*, xxi (1967), 97–129

Ilardi, V., 'Fifteenth-Century Diplomatic Documents in Western European Archives and Libraries (1450–1494)', *Studies in the Renaissance*, ix (1962), 64–122

——, 'The Italian League, Francesco Sforza, and Charles VII (1454–1461)', *Studies in the Renaissance*, vi (1959), 129–66

Inguanez, M., 'Inventario di Pomposa del 1459', *Bollettino del bibliofilo*, ii (1920), 173–84

Jacob, E. F., *Henry Chichele and the Ecclesiastical Politics of his Age* (London, 1952)

——, *The Register of Henry Chichele, Archbishop of Canterbury, 1414–43*, (4 vols., Oxford, 1938–47)

Jahn, F., 'Die Nürnberger Trompeten- und Posaunenmacher in 16. Jahrhunder', *AfMW*, vii (1925), 23–52

Jeppesen, K., *La frottola* (3 vols., Copenhagen, 1968–70)

Johannes Ferrariensis, *Excerpta ex Annalium Libris Illustris Familiae Marchionum Estensium, 1409–1454*, in L. A. Muratori, ed., *Rerum Italicarum Scriptores*, rev. edn., vol. xx

Kämper, D., *Studien zur instrumentalen Ensemblemusik des 16. Jahrhunderts* [= *Analecta Musicologica*, x (1970)]

Kallenberg, P., *Fontes Liturgiae Carmelitanae* (Rome, 1962)

Kanazawa, M., 'Polyphonic Music for Vespers in the Fifteenth Century' (Ph.D. diss., Harvard University, 1966)

——, 'Martini and Brebis at the Estense Chapel', in *Essays Presented to Myron Gilmore*, ed. S. Bertelli and G. Ramakus (Florence, 1978), pp. 421–36

Kantorowicz, 'The Este Portrait by Roger van der Weyden', *Journal of the Warburg and Courtauld Institutes*, iii (1939–40), 165–80

Karp, T., 'The Secular Works of Johannes Martini', in J. La Rue ed., *Aspects of Medieval and Renaissance Music: a Birthday Offering to Gustave Reese* (New York, 1966), pp. 455–73

Kellman, H., 'Josquin and the Courts of the Netherlands and France: the evidence of the Sources', in E. Lowinsky, ed., *Josquin Desprez*, pp. 181–216

Kinkeldey, O., 'Dance Tunes of the Fifteenth Century', in D. Hughes, ed., *Instrumental Music* (Cambridge, 1959), pp. 3–30

Kristeller, P. O., *Iter Italicum* (Leiden, 1965–   )

——, 'Music and Learning in the Early Italian Renaissance', *Journal of Renaissance and Baroque Music*, i (1947), 255–74; repr. in his *Renaissance Thought*, vol. ii (New York, 1965), pp. 142–62

La Fage, A. de, *Essais de diptbérographie musicale* (Paris, 1864)

Laurent, V., ed., *Les 'Memoires' du Grand Ecclesiastique de l'Église de Constantinople Sylvestre Syropoulos sur le Concile de Florence (1438–1439)*, Concilium Florentinum Documenta et Scriptores, Ser. B, ix (Rome, 1971)

Lazzari, A., 'Il Signor di Ferrara ai tempi del concilio del 1438–39: Niccolò III d'Este', *La Rinascita*, ii (1939), 672–702

Lenaerts, R. B., 'Musical Structure and Performance Practice in Masses and Motets of Josquin and Obrecht', in E. Lowinsky, ed., *Josquin Desprez*, pp. 619–26

Levi, E., *Francesco da Vannozzo* (Florence, 1908)

——, *I cantari leggendari del popolo italiano nei secoli XIV e XV*, GSLI, Suppl. xvi (1914)

Litterick, L., 'Performing Franco-Netherlandish Secular Music of the Late Fifteenth Century', *Early Music*, viii (1980), 474–87

Llorens, J., 'El codice Casanatense 2856 identificado como el Cancionero de Isabella d'Este (Ferrara) esposa de Francesco Gonzaga (Mantua)', *Anuario Musical*, xx (1965), 161–78

Lockwood, L., *The Counter-Reformation and the Masses of Vincenzo Ruffo* (Venice, 1970)

——, 'Aspects of the "L'homme armé" Tradition', *Proceedings of the Royal Musical Association*, c (1973–4), 97–122

——, 'Dufay and Ferrara', in A. Atlas, ed., *Dufay Quincentenary Conference*, pp. 1–25

——, ' "Messer Gossino" and Josquin Desprez', in R. Marshall, ed., *Studies in Renaissance and Baroque Music in Honor of Arthur Mendel* (Kassel and Hackensack, 1974), pp. 15–24

——, 'Jean Mouton and Jean Michel: New Evidence on French Music and Musicians in Italy, 1505–1520', *JAMS*, xxxii (1979), 191–246

——, 'Josquin at Ferrara: New Documents and Letters', in E. Lowinsky, ed., *Josquin Desprez*, pp. 103–36

——, 'Music at Ferrara in the Period of Ercole I d'Este', *Studi musicali*, i (1972), 101–31

——, 'Martini, Johannes', *The New Grove Dictionary of Music and Musicians*, ii, pp. 726–7

——, 'Music and Popular Religious Spectacle at Ferrara under Ercole I d'Este', in M. Lorch, ed., *Il teatro italiano del Rinascimento*, pp. 571–82

——, 'Musicisti a Ferrara all'epoca di Ariosto', *Quaderni della Rivista Italiana di Musicologia*, v (1981), 7–29

——, 'Pietrobono and the Instrumental Tradition at Ferrara in the Fifteenth Century', *RIM*, x (1975), 115–33

——, 'Strategies of Music Patronage in the Fifteenth Century: the Cappella of Ercole I d'Este', in I. Fenlon, ed., *Music in Medieval and Early Modern Europe* (Cambridge, 1981), pp. 227–48

Lodi, P., *Catalogo delle opere musicali teoriche et pratiche . . . Città di Modena R. Biblioteca Estense*, Bollettino dell'Associazione dei Musicologi Italiani, 8th Ser. (Parma, 1917)

Longhi, R., *Officina ferrarese*, 2nd edn. (Firenze, 1956)

Lopez, G., and de Carlo, V., eds., *Nozze dei principi milanesi ed estensi di Tristano Calchi* (Milan, 1976)

Lorch, M. de Panizza, ed., *Il teatro italiano del Rinascimento* (Milan, 1980)

Lorch, M. and Fink, W., eds., *Zilioli Ferrariensis Comediola Michaelida* (Munich, 1975)

Lowinsky, E., 'Ascanio Sforza's Life: a Key to Josquin's Biography and an Aid to the Chronology of his Works', in E. Lowinsky, ed., *Josquin Desprez*, pp. 31–75

——, *Josquin Desprez: Proceedings of the International Josquin Festival-Conference . . . New York, 21–25 June 1975* (Oxford, 1976)

——, 'Music of the Renaissance as Viewed by Renaissance Musicians', in B. O'Kelly, ed., *The Renaissance Image of Man and the World* (Columbus, 1966), pp. 129–77

——, *The Medici Codex of 1518: a Choirbook of Motets Dedicated to Lorenzo de' Medici, Duke of Urbino*, Monuments of Renaissance Music, iii–v (3 vols., Chicago, 1968)

Luzio, A., and Renier, R., 'Commedie classiche a Ferrara nel 1499', *GSLI*, xi (1888), 177–89

Macey, P., 'Savonarola and the Sixteenth-Century Motet', *JAMS*, xxxvi (1983), 422–52

Malvezzi, N., 'Alessandro V, papa, a Bologna', *AR*, 3rd Ser. ix (1891), 362–79; x (1892), 39–55

Maniates, M., 'Combinative Chansons in the Dijon Chansonnier', *JAMS*, xxiii (1972), 228–81

Marix, J., *Histoire de la musique et des musiciens de la cour de Bourgogne* (Strasburg, 1939)

Martinez, M. L., *Die Musik des frühen Trecento* (Tutzing, 1963)

Meier, B., 'Die Handschrift Porto 714 als Quelle zur Tonartenlehre des 15. Jahrhunderts', *MD*, vii (1953), 175–97

——, *Die Tonarten der klassischen Vokalpolyphonie* (Utrecht, 1974)

Meiss, M., *The Great Age of Fresco* (New York, 1970)

Menut, A. D., ed., *Maistre Nicole Oresme, Le livre de Politiques d'Aristote*; *Transactions of the American Philosophical Society*, n.s., lx, pt. 6 (1970)

Michels, A., 'The Earliest Dance Manuals', *Medievalia et Humanistica*, iii (1945), 117–33

Michels, U., *Die Musiktraktate des Johannes de Muris* (Wiesbaden, 1970)

Minieri Riccio, C., 'Alcuni fatti di Alfonso I di Aragona', *Archivio storico per le provincie napoletane*, vi (1888), 1–36, 231–58, 411–61

Mitchell, R. J., 'English Students at Ferrara in the XV Century', *Italian Studies*, i (1937), 75–82

——, *John Free* (London, 1955)

Mommsen, T. F., *Petrarch's Testament* (Ithaca, 1957)

Monstrelet, Enguerran de, *La Chronique d'Enguerran de Monstrelet . . . 1400–1444*, ed. L. Douet-D'Arcq (Paris, 1858)

Monumenta Hungariae Historica, iii (Budapest, 1878)

Moores, J. D., 'New Light on Diomede Carafa', *Italian Studies*, xxvi (1971), 16–23

Morselli, A., 'Ippolito d'Este e il suo primo viaggio in Ungheria', *Atti e memorie dell'accademia di scienze, lettere ed arti di Modena*, 5th Ser. xv (1957), 196–251

Motta, E., 'Musici alla corte degli Sforza', *Archivio storico lombardo*, xiv (1887), 29–64, 278–340, 514–61

Muratori, L. A., ed., *Rerum Italicarum Scriptores . . .*, (25 vols., Milan, 1723–51) new edn., ed. G. Carducci, V. Fiorini, P. Fedele (Bologna, 1900–)

Murray, B., 'New Light on Jacob Obrecht's Development – a Biographical Study,' *The Musical Quarterly*, xlii (1957), 500–16

Musik in Geschichte und Gegenwart, Die, ed. F. Blume (16 vols., Kassel, 1949–79)

Nerici, L., *Storia della musica in Lucca* (Lucca, 1879)

New Grove Dictionary of Music and Musicians, The, ed. S. Sadie (20 vols., London, 1980)

New Oxford History of Music, The, vol. iii (*Ars Nova and the Renaissance, 1300–1540*), ed. A. Hughes and G. Abraham (London, 1960)

Newcomb, A., *The Madrigal at Ferrara, 1579–1597* (2 vols., Princeton, 1980)

Newman, W. L., ed., *The Politics of Aristotle* (Oxford, 1902)

Noble, J., 'New Light on Josquin's Benefices', in E. Lowinsky, ed., *Josquin Desprez*, pp. 76–102

Noblitt, T., 'Das Chorbuch des Nikolaus Leopold (München, Staatsbibliothek Mus. MS 3154)', *AfMW*, xxvi (1969), 169–208

——, 'Die Datierung der Handschrift Mus. MS 3154 der Staatsbibliothek München', *Die Musikforschung*, xxvii (1974), 36–56

Novati, F., 'Donato degli Albanzani alla corte Estense', *Archivio storico italiano*, 5th Ser. vi (1890), 365–85

Olivi, L., 'Delle nozze di Ercole I con Eleonora d'Aragona', *Memorie della R. Accademia di scienze, lettere ed arti di Modena*, 2nd Ser. v (1887), 15–48

Osthoff, H., *Josquin Desprez* (2 vols., Tutzing, 1962–5)

Osthoff, W., *Theatergesang und darstellende Musik in der italienischen Renaissance*, (2 vols., Tutzing, 1969)

Paganuzzi, E., 'Medioevo e Rinascimento', in *La musica a Verona* (Verona, 1976), pp. 9 ff.

Panofsky, E., *Early Netherlandish Painting*, 2nd edn. (New York, 1971)

Pardi, G., 'Borso d'Este duca di Ferrara', in *Studi storici*, xv (1906), 3–58, 134–204, 241–88, 377–416; xvi (1907), 113–70

——, *Leonello d'Este* (Bologna, 1904)

——, *Titoli dottorali conferiti dallo Studio di Ferrara nei secoli xv e xvi* (Lucca, 1900)

Pasquini, E., ed. *Saviozzo, Rime* (Bologna, 1965)

Perkins, L., Mode and Structure in the Masses of Josquin', *JAMS*, xxvi (1973), 189–229

——, L., and Garey, H., eds., *The Mellon Chansonnier*, (2 vols., New Haven, 1979)

Petrobelli, P., 'Some Dates for Bartolino da Padova', in H. Powers, ed., *Studies in Music History: Essays for Oliver Strunk* (Princeton, 1966), pp. 85–112

——, ' "Un leggiadretto velo" ed altre cose petrarchesche', *RIM*, x (1975), 32–45

Peverada, E., 'Vita musicale alla cattedrale di Ferrara nel Quattrocento: note e documenti', *RIM*, xv (1980), 3–30

——, 'Ugolino da Orvieto nella erudizione scalabriniana e alla luce di nuovi documenti', in *Giuseppe Antenore Scalabrini e l'erudizione ferrarese nel '700*, Atti dell'Accademia delle Scienze di Ferrara, lv (1977–8), 489–506

Pietzsch, G., *Die Klassifikation der Musik von Boetius bis Ugolino von Orvieto* (Halle, 1929)

——, 'Zur Pflege der Musik an den deutschen Universitäten bis zur Mitte des 16. Jahrhunderts', *Archiv für Musikforschung*, i (1936), pp. 257–92, 424–51; repr. Hildesheim, 1971

Pirro, A., *La Musique à Paris sous le regne de Charles VI (1380–1422)* (Strasburg, 1930)

Pirrotta, N., 'Ars nova e stil novo', *RIM*, i (1966), 3–19

——, 'Il codice estense lat. 568 e la musica francese in Italia al principio del '400', *Atti della Reale Accademia di scienze, lettere ed arti di Palermo*, 4th Ser. v, pt. 2 (1944–5) 101–54

——, 'Italien, 14.–16. Jahrhundert', in *Die Musik in Geschichte und Gegenwart*, vi, cols. 1476–1500

——, 'Music and cultural tendencies in Fifteenth-Century Italy', *JAMS*, xix (1966), 127–61

——, *Music and Culture in Italy from the Middle Ages to the Baroque* (Cambridge, Mass., 1984)

——, *Music and Theatre from Poliziano to Monteverdi* (Cambridge, 1982)

——, 'Novelty and Renewal in Italy: 1300–1600', in H. Eggebrecht and M. Lutolff, eds., *Studien zur Tradition in der Musik* (München, 1973), pp. 49–63

——, 'Ricercare e variazioni su "O rosa bella" ', *Studi musicali*, i (1972), 59–78

——, 'Scuole polifoniche italiane durante il secolo XIV; di una pretesa scuola napoletana', *Collectanea Historiae Musicae*, i (1953), 11–18

——, 'Two Anglo-Italian Pieces in the Manuscript Porto 714', in *Speculum Musicae*

Artis: Festgabe für Heinrich Husmann zum 60. Geburtstag, ed. H. Becker and R. Gerlach (Munich, 1970), pp. 253–61

——, 'Zacharus musicus', *Quadrivium* (Memorie e Contributi alla Musica dal medioevo all'età moderna offerti a Federico Ghisi) xii (1971), 153–75

Pius II (Aeneas Sylvius Piccolomini), *The Commentaries of Pius II*, translated by F. A. Gragg and L. C. Gabel, *Smith College Studies in History*, xxii, Nos. 1–2 (1936–7)

Plamenac, D., 'The "Second" Chansonnier of the Biblioteca Riccardiana (Codex 2356)', *AM*, ii (1954), 105–88

——, 'An Unknown Composition by Dufay?', *The Musical Quarterly*, xl (1954), 190–200

Planchart, A., 'Guillaume Dufay's Masses: a View of the Manuscript Traditions', in A. Atlas, ed., *Dufay Quincentenary Conference*, pp. 26–60

Polk, K., 'Ensemble Performance in Dufay's Time', in A. Atlas, ed., *Dufay Quincentenary Conference*, pp. 61–75

——, 'Flemish Wind Bands in the Late Middle Ages' (Ph.D. diss., University of California, Berkeley, 1968)

——, 'Municipal Wind Music in Flanders in the Late Middle Ages', *Brass and Woodwind Quarterly*, ii (1969), 1–15

Pope, I., and Kanazawa, M., *The Musical Manuscript Montecassino 871* (Oxford, 1978)

Povoledo, E., 'Ferrara', in *Enciclopedia dello spettacolo*, v, cols. 173–85

Powers, H., 'Mode', in *The New Grove Dictionary of Music and Musicians*, xii, pp. 399–412

Prizer, W., 'The Frottola and the Unwritten Tradition: Improvisors and Frottolists at North Italian Courts', Paper read at the annual meeting of the American Musicological Society, Denver, 1980

——, *Courtly Pastimes: the Frottole of Marchetto Cara* (2 vols., Ann Arbor, 1980)

——, 'Lutenists at the Court of Mantua in the Late Fifteenth and Early Sixteenth Centuries', *Journal of the Lute Society of America*, xiii (1980), 5–34

——, 'La cappella di Francesco II Gonzaga e la musica sacra a Mantova nel primo ventennio del Cinquecento', in *Mantova e i Gonzaga nella civiltà del Rinascimento* (Mantua, 1974), pp. 267–76

Procter, R., *Index to Early Printed Books in the British Museum* (London, 1898)

Prosperi, A., 'Le istituzioni ecclesiastiche e le idee religiose', in *Il Rinascimento nelle corti padane* (Bari, 1977), pp. 125–64

Rajna, P., 'Ricordi di codici francesi posseduti degli Estensi nel secolo xv', *Romania*, ii (1873), 49–58

Reaney, G., 'The Manuscript Oxford, Bodleian Library, Canonici Misc. 213', *MD*, ix (1955), 73–104

——, 'The Italian Contribution to the Manuscript Oxford, Bodleian Library, Canonici Misc. 213', in *L'Ars Nova italiana del Trecento*, iii (Certaldo, 1970), pp. 443–64

Reese, G., *Music in the Renaissance* (New York, 1954)

Reidemeister, P., *Die Handschrift 78 C. 28 des Berliner Kupferstichkabinetts* (Munich, 1973)

Renzi, R., ed., *Ferrara* (Bologna, 1969)

Richental, U. von, 'Chronicle', published as *Das Konzil zu Konstanz*, ed. O. Feger (Constance, 1954)

Rinascimento nelle corti padane, Il, introduction by Paolo Rossi (Bari, 1977)

Rosenberg, C., 'Art in Ferrara during the Reign of Borso d'Este (1450–1471): a Study in Court Patronage' (Ph.D diss., University of Michigan, 1974)

——, ' "Per il bene di . . . nostra cipta": Borso d'Este and the *Certosa* of Ferrara', *Renaissance Quarterly*, xxix (1976), 329–40

——, 'The Erculean Addition to Ferrara . . .', *The Early Renaissance, Acta*, ed. A. S. Bernardo, v (1978), pp. 49–67

Rossi, V., *Il Quattrocento*, Storia letteraria d'Italia, 8th edn. (Milan, 1964)

Rubsamen, W., 'The Earliest French Lute Tablature', *JAMS*, xxi (1968), 286–99

——, 'The Justiniane or Viniziane of the Fifteenth Century', *Acta Musicologica*, xxix (1957), 172–83

——, 'Music Research in Italian Libraries, *Notes*, 2nd Ser. vi (1948–9), 220–33, 543–69; viii (1950–1), 70–99

Ruhmer, E., *Cosimo Tura* (London, 1958)

Ryder, A., *The Kingdom of Naples under Alfonso the Magnanimous* (Oxford, 1976)

Sabadino degli Arienti, Giovanni (see Gundersheimer, *Art and Life at the Court of Ercole I d'Este*)

Sabbadini, R., ed., *Epistolario di Guarino Veronese*, in *Miscellanea di storia veneta*, 3rd Ser. viii (1915), 1–704; xiv (1916), 1–577

——, 'Sugli studi volgari di Leonardo Giustiniani', *GSLI*, x (1887), 363–71

Salmen, W., *Der fahrende Musiker in europäischen Mittelalter* (Kassel, 1960)

Salmi, M., *L'abbazia di Pomposa* (Rome, 1935)

Santoro, C., *Gli Sforza* (Varese, 1968)

Sartori, C., 'Matteo de Perugia e Bertrand Feragut, i due primi maestri di cappella del Duomo di Milano', *Acta Musicologica*, xxviii (1956), 12–27

Schirmer, W. F., *Der englische Frühhumanismus*, 2nd rev. edn. (Tübingen, 1963)

Schoop, H., *Entstehung und Verwendung der Handschrift Oxford, Bodleian Library, Canonici misc. 213* (Berne, 1971)

Schrade, L., 'Renaissance: the Historical Conception of an Epoch', in *Société Internationale de Musicologie, Cinquième Congrès, Utrecht, 1952 Compte-Rendu* (Amsterdam, 1953), pp. 19–32

Schuler, M., 'Beziehungen zwischen der Kostanzer Domkantorei und der Hofkapelle des Herzogs Ercole I von Ferrara', *Analecta Musicologica*, xv (1975), 15–20

——, 'Konstanz', in *The New Grove Dictionary of Music and Musicians*, x, pp. 180–1

Scott, A. B., 'English Music in Modena, Biblioteca Estense, Alpha X. 1, 11 and Other Italian Manuscripts', *MD*, xxvi (1972), 145–60

——, ' "Ibo michi ad montem mirre": a New Motet by Plummer?', *The Musical Quarterly*, lviii (1972), 543–56

Seay, A, ed., *Tres Tractatuli Contra Bartholomeum Ramum*, Corpus Scriptorum de Musica, x, (Rome, 1964)

——, ed., *Ugolini Urbevetanus, Declaratio Musicae Disciplinae* (Rome, 1959)

——, 'Ugolino of Orvieto, Theorist and Composer', *MD*, ix (1955), 111–66

——, 'The *Declaratio Musice Discipline* of Ugolino of Orvieto; Addenda', *MD*, xi (1957), 126–33

Seznec, J., *The Survival of the Pagan Gods* (New York, 1953)

Silvestri, M., 'Appunti di cronologia cornazzaniana', in *Miscellanea di storia, letteratura e arte piacentina* (Piacenza, 1915), pp. 130–71

Simeoni, L., *Le signorie* (Milan, 1950)

Sitta, P., 'Saggio sulle istituzioni finanziarie del ducato estense', *Atti e memorie della deputazione ferrarese di storia patria*, iii (1891), pp. 89–254

Spagnolo, A., *Le scuole accolitali in Verona* (Verona, 1908)

Staehelin, M., *Die Messen von Heinrich Isaac* (Bern, 1977)

——, 'Möglichkeiten und praktische Anwendung der Verfasserbestimmung an anonym überlieferten Kompositionen der Josquin-Zeit', *Tijdschrift van de Vereniging voor Nederlandse Muziekgeschiedenis*, xxiii (1973), 71–91

——, 'Obrechtiana', *Tijdschrift van de Vereniging voor Nederlandse Muziekgeschiedenis*, xxv (1975), pp. 1–37; xxvi (1976), 41–2

Strohm, R., 'Ein unbekanntes Chorbuch des 15. Jahrhunderts', *Die Musikforschung*, xxi (1968), 40–2

Strunk, O., *Source Readings in Music History* (New York, 1950)

Thibault, G., 'Emblems et devises des Visconti dans les oeuvres musicales du Trecento', *L'ars nova italiana del Trecento*, iii (Certaldo, 1970), pp. 131–60

Thurston, A., and Bühler, C., *A Check-List of Fifteenth-Century Printing in the Pierpont Morgan Library* (New York, 1939)

Tiersot, J., *Lettres de musiciens écrites en francais du xve au xxe siècle* (Turin, 1924)

Trowell, B., ed., *Four Motets by John Plummer* (London, 1968)

Turrini, G., *La tradizione musicale a Verona* (Verona, 1953)

Valdrighi, L. F., 'Cappelle, concerti e musiche di casa d'Este dal secolo XV al XVIII', *AMP*, 3rd Ser. ii (1883), 415–65

Valenti, F., *Panorama dell'Archivio di Stato di Modena* (Modena, 1963)

Valois, N., *La France et la grande schisme d'occident* (4 vols., Paris, 1902)

Van den Borren, C., ed., *Polyphonia Sacra* (Burnham, 1932)

Vander Straeten, E., *La Musique aux Pays-Bas avant le XIXe siècle* (8 vols., Brussels, 1867–88)

Van der Velden, H. E. J. M., *Rudolphus Agricola* (Leiden, 1911)

Vaughan, R., *John the Fearless* (London, 1966)

——, *Philip the Good* (London, 1970)

Venturi, A., 'I primordi del Rinascimento artistico a Ferrara', *Rivista storica italiana*, i (1884), 591–631

——, 'L'arte a Ferrara nel periodo di Borso d'Este', *Rivista storica italiana*, ii (1885), 689–749

——, 'L'arte ferrarese nel periodo d'Ercole I d'Este', *AR*, 3rd Ser. vi (1888), 350–422; vii (1889), 368–412

——, ed., *La Bibbia di Borso d'Este* (facsimile edn., Milan, 1937)

Venturi, G., 'Scena e giardini a Ferrara', *Il Rinascimento nelle corti padane*, pp. 553–68

Wangermée, R., *Flemish Music and Society in the Fifteenth and Sixteenth Centuries* (New York, 1968)

Warburg, A., 'Italienische Kunst und internationale Astrologie in Palazzo Schifanoia in Ferrara', *Atti del X Congresso di storia dell'arte in Roma* (Rome, 1922), pp. 179–93; repr. in G. Bing, ed., *Aby Warburg, Gesammelte Schriften* (Leipzig, 1969)

Ward, T., 'The Polyphonic Office Hymn from the Late Fourteenth Century to the Early Sixteenth Century' (Ph.D. diss., University of Pittsburgh, 1969)

——, 'The Polyphonic Office Hymn and the Liturgy of Fifteenth-Century Italy', *MD*, xxvi (1972), 161–88

Wegner, M., 'Apollon', *Die Musik in Geschichte und Gegenwart*, i, cols. 563–7

Wilkins, E. H., *Petrarch's Later Years* (Cambridge, 1959)

Winternitz, E., *Musical Instruments and their Symbolism in Western Art*, 2nd edn. (New Haven, 1979)

Wolff, A. S., 'The Chansonnier Biblioteca Casanatense 2856: its History, Purpose, and Music' (Ph.D. diss., North Texas State University, 1970)

Woodfield, I., 'The Early History of the Viol', *Proceedings of the Royal Musical Association*, ciii (1976–7), 141–57

——, 'Viol', in *The New Grove Dictionary*, xx, pp. 791–98

Woodley, R., 'Johannes Tinctoris: a Review of the Documentary Biographical Evidence', *JAMS*, (1981), 217–48

Woodward, W. H., *Studies in Education during the Age of the Renaissance* (New York, 1906)

Wright, C., 'Dufay at Cambrai; Discoveries and Revisions', *JAMS*, xxviii (1975), 175–229

——, 'Voices and Instruments in the Art Music of Northern France during the Fifteenth Century: a Conspectus', in *Report of the Twelfth Congress of the International Musicological Society, Berkeley 1977* (Kassel, 1981), pp. 643–9

Zambotti, B., [Chronicle:] *Diario ferrarese dall'anno 1476 sino al 1504* (by Bernardino Zambotti, doctor of civil laws) ed. G. Pardi, *Rerum Italicarum Scriptores*, rev. edn., vol. xxiv, part vii (Bologna, 1928)

Zarri, G., 'Pietà e profezia alle corti padane: le pie consiglieri dei principi', in *Il Rinascimento nelle corti padane*, pp. 201–21

Zevi, B., *Biagio Rossetti, architetto ferrarese, il primo urbanista moderno europeo* (Turin, 1960)

Zorzi, L., 'Il teatro e la città: ricognizione del ciclo di Schifanoia', in *Il Rinascimento nelle corti padane*, pp. 531–52

——, *Il teatro e la città* (Turin, 1977)

Index

⟲✵⟳

Note: Appendices I to V are not indexed.

Accolti, Francesco, 42, 65
Acteon, Don, 107–8
Adam *piffaro*, 142, 183
Agostino, trombone, 96, 142, 178
Agricola, Alexander, 138, 156, 222, 224, 234, 266, 272, 291; Missa 'Je ne demande,' 217
Agricola, Rudolph, 49n., 151–2, 180
Alamire, Petrus, 108
Albanzani, Donato degli, 11
Alberti, Leone Battista, 17, 29, 92n
Alberto soprano, 180–1
Alessandro, don (see Signorello)
Alessandro da Alemagna, 97
Alexander, Florentio, 95n
Alexander, J. J. G., 66n
Alexander V, Pope, 16n, 18–20, 24
Alexander VI, Pope, 128, 191–2, 197–8
Allen, P. S., 152n
Alta (shawm band), 16, 65, 66n, 69, 91, 140, 142, 184, 270
Ambrosian liturgy, 229, 255
Ambrosio da Pesaro, Giovanni, 71
Andrea da Mantova, don, 151, 180
Andrea Picardo, fra, 152n
Anglés, Higinio, 122n
Antonio (instrumentalist), 97
Antonio, trumpeter, 141
Antonio de Pavia, lutenist, 102
Antonio de Cambrai (see Baneston)
Antonius de Alemagna, 191
Apollo, 215n
Apuleius, 220
Aragona, Alfonso d', 41, 45, 121–3
Aragona, Beatrice d', 99, 103–4, 127, 147, 171, 239
Aragona, Eleonora d', 41, 103–4, 124, 126, 141, 145, 147, 153, 196–7, 214n, 258, 279
Aragona, Ferdinand I d', (also called 'Ferrante'), 88, 122–3, 173, 186–7
Aragona, Maria d' (second wife of Leonello d'Este), 39, 41, 70, 72, 124, 144
Aranda, Johannes de, 26
Ariosto, Francesco Pellegrino da, 135
Ariosto, Lodovico, 10, 87n, 127, 135, 198, 201–2, 213, 289

Aristotle, 14, 83–4
Aristoxenus, 82
Arlotti, Bonfrancesco, 131, 169–70, 187
Arpa, Rodolfo dall', 69
Atlas, Allan, viii, 104n, 117n, 122, 267n
Aurispa, Giovanni, 11, 29, 96n
Avignon, papacy at, 18–20

Bacchelli, Riccardo, 87n, 125, 201n
Bach, J. S., 248
Bachio, trumpeter, 140, 183
Bagnacavallo, Francesco, 100n
Bagnolo, peace of, 127
Baldessaris, Johannes, 171
ballo, 71–2
Baneston, Antonio (Antonio de Cambrai), 133, 152, 155, 160, 171, 176, 195
Banquet of the Oath of the Pheasant, Lille, 285
Baptista da Norsa, trumpeter, 178
Barbaro, Ermolao, 64
Barbingant, 233, 235
Barbireau, Jacobus, 217, 272
Barblan, Guglielmo, 99n, 100n, 101n, 102n, 107n, 132n, 139n, 168n, 181n
Bartolomeo da Bologna, 17–27; 'Arte psalentes', 20–22; 'Que pena major', 23; 'Vince con lena', 23; 'Et in terra', 24; 'Patrem', 24
Bartolomeo da Luciano da Commachio, 180
Bartolomeo de l'Organo, 187
Bartolomeo de Fiandra, 152, 159, 203
Bartolomeo Spagnolo, 153
Baruffaldi, Girolamo, 64n
Barzizza, Gasparino, 64
Basle, Council of, 30–1, 47, 68, 78
Basin, Adrien, 217, 233, 235, 272
Basinio da Parma, 42
bassadanza, 71–3, 106, 235
Baxandall, Michael, 72
Bazo (= Bachio) trumpeter, 180
Becherini, Bianca, 56n
Bedford, Duke of, 60, 62
Bedyngham, Johannes, 66n, 110, 115
Belfiore, villa, 71, 90 (fresco cycle at)

Bellini, Jacopo, 29
Belriguardo, villa, 43, 71, 87, 130, 146, 198
    (frescoes of the Sala di Psyche)
Beltrandi, Girolamo, 203
Bembo, Pietro, 198
Benedict XIII, Pope, 20
Bendedei, Niccolo, 169
Benet, John, 53, 58, 60
Bennett, Josephine W., 58n
Benoit (Benedetto di Giovanni dito Benoit),
    53–4, 57, 61
Bent, Margaret, 58n
Bentivoglio, Annibale, 124
Benzi, Ugo, 29
Bergamo, Jacopo de, 91n
Bernardino da Sisi (= Assisi), trumpeter, 140
Berne, treaty with Fribourg, 1438, 56
Berniero da Salò, instrumentalist, 97
Beroaldo, Filippo, 99
Bertolotti, Antonio, 99, 104, 167n, 229n
Bertoni, Giulio, 15, 42, 67, 70n, 83n, 89n, 92n,
    105, 125n, 135n, 213–14, 218, 224n, 225,
    269n
Besseler, Heinrich, 36, 38–9, 56n, 63n, 69n, 73,
    109–110, 140, 235
Bianchi, Christoforo de', 186–7
Bidon (Antonio Collebaudi dicto) 207, 265
Binchois, Gilles, 53, 56, 57, 61, 63, 114n, 250
Biondo, Flavio, 78n, 81n, 220
Biscacia, Johannes, 231
Boccaccio, Giovanni, 11
Boccaccio, Giovanni Antonio (ambassador),
    189, 195
Boethius, 82
Boiardo, Matteo Maria, 10, 92, 198, 213
Boldù, Giovanni, 102n
'Bolkim', 272
Bologna, 19–20, 39, 62, 81, 111, 229
Bombasi, Tommaso, 8n
Bon, Johannes (also spelled 'Gon'), 132, 155,
    231
Bona di Savoia, 176
Boniface IX, Pope, 19
Bonifacio, Messer, 223
Bondi, Girolamo, 106–7
Borbo, Giacomo, 122
Borgia family, alliance with Este family, 286
Borgia, Cesare, 197
Borgia, Lucrezia, 124–5, 128–9, 145, 191, 198,
    202, 260, 281
Bosoni, Biagio, 42
'Bossrin', 272
Bouquet, Marie Therese, 152n
Bowers, Roger, 59–60n
Brawley, John, 250n, 273n
Brebis, Johannes, 131, 152, 154–6, 160–1,
    171, 180, 217, 222, 230, 251; 'Hercules
    omni memorandus aevo', 55, 231; 'Deus
    tuorum', 252–3

Bridgman, Nanie, 283n
Briquet, Charles, 54n
Brown, Howard M., 65n, 66n, 108, 226, 277n
Bruges, 114, 163–4, 207
Brumel Antoine, 156, 208, 272
Bruscagli, Riccardo, 127n
Buchner, Hans, 132
Bühler, Curt, 199n
Bukofzer, Manfred, 61, 116n, 222n
Burgundy, court of, 3, 14, 32, 57, 60, 123
Busnois, Antoine, 217, 222, 224, 234, 239, 243,
    266, 271–2

Caesar, Julius, 29, 43
Cagnolo, Niccolo, 282
Calcho, Tristano, 139
Caleffini, Ugo, 25n, 44n, 50, 94, 100–3, 126n,
    130n, 135–7, 142, 146–8, 178–9, 186n,
    215n, 226, 278n
Calkins, R. G., 74n
Cambrai, 152, 168, 232
Cambridge University, 116n
Campori, Giuseppe, 214n
Canal, Pietro, 99, 229n
Cancellieri, Gioacchino, 18, 79
Canossa, Count Lodovico da, 84n
Canterbury Cathedral, 59
Cantus planus binatim, 13, 22, 49
Cappelli, Adriano, 14n
Cappelli, Antonio, 94n, 101n, 162, 165n
Capra, Luciano, viii, 12n, 38n
Cara, Marchetto, 143, 267
Carafa, Diomede, 103
Carbone, Lodovico, 29, 59, 92
Cardano, Beltrame de, 170
Carducci, Giosuè, 9n, 64n, 92n
Cariom, don Piero, 156, 183, 185
Carissimi, Lodovico, 172
Caron, Philippe, 217, 234, 239, 266, 272
Carpenter, Nan C., 115n
Carpentras, 154
Carrara, dynasty, 8
Cartellieri, Otto, 130n
Casella, Lodovico, 52n, 92
Casella, Paolo, 169, 188
Casimiri, Raffaello, 26n, 27n
Castiglione, Baldassare, 84
Catalano, Michele, 65n, 113n, 127n, 202n
Cavalieri, Bartolomeo de', 202
Cavicchi, Adriano, viii, 17–18, 23n, 24, 25n,
    26n, 51n, 71n, 80n
Cazeaux, Isabelle, viii
Cellesi, L., 139n
Cesari, Gaetano, 235
Cesi, Francesco da, 172
Chambers, D. S., 101n
Charles V, Emperor, 247, 249
Charles V, King of France, 14, 83

Charles VI, King of France, 13–14
Charles VII, King of France, 15, 35, 87, 267
Charles VIII, King of France, 108, 128, 141, 200
Charles the Bold, Duke of Burgundy, 42n, 130, 239–40
Chiappini, Luciano, viii, 87n, 89n, 113n, 121n, 125n
Chiarelli, Alessandra, viii
Chichele, John, 59
Chichele, Henry, 59
Chichele, Reynold, 59, 116
Chiove, Giovanni dalle, 80
Christoforo da Modena, 183
Cicero, 29
Ciconia, Johannes, 25
Cieco, Francesco, da Ferrara, 105
Cirlo falconiero, 101n
Cittadella, Luigi Napoleone, 16n, 42n, 81n, 98, 99n, 104n
Cividale, Council of, 24
Clemens non Papa, 245
Clemente de Alemagna, *piffaro*, 69
Cobin, Marian, 58
Codigoro, 113
Cohen, Judith, 239n
Coletta, 204–5
Colinet (see Lannoy)
Collingwood, R. C., 1
Colonna, Oddo (see Martin V, Pope)
Colornio, Bernardin, 183
Compère, Loyset, 108, 132, 148, 169, 176, 200, 209, 217, 224, 240, 255
Consandolo, 44
Constance, Council of, 19–20, 78; Bishop of, 131, 135, 167, 174; musicians, 153; and Martini, 131–2
Contrari, Uguccione de', 19
Coppo, Anna Maria, 127n, 278n, 281n, 282n, 284n
Cordier, Johannes, 163–4
Cornazzano, Antonio, 71, 92–93, 99, 100n
Cornelio di Lorenzo of Antwerp (= Cornelio di Fiandra), 97, 133, 151, 161–5, 176, 207
Cornelio de Florentiis de Zelandia, 165n
Corona Beatae Mariae Virginis (Ferrara, 1496), 136, 199, 200, 227
Corrado de Alemania, *piffaro*, 47n, 68–9, 96, 101n, 104, 142–3, 148, 178–9, 180, 184
Correggio, Borso da, 104n
Correggio, Niccolo da, 88, 103, 281
Cortese, Paolo, 84n, 91n, 98n, 99
Corvina, Matthias, 103–4, 127, 147, 171
Cossa, Cardinal Baldassare (see John XXIII, Pope)
Cossa, Francesco, 101
Costa, Lorenzo, 106
Costabili, Beltrame, 167n, 191–2
Coussemaker, Edmond, 80n, 173n
Cristoforo de Predis, 66n

Cummings, Anthony, 264n
Cupid, in *Giostra dell' Amore*, 279–80

D'Adria, Giacomo, 205n
Dahlhaus, Carl, 242n
D'Alessi, Giovanni, 49n
D'Alzio, Francesco, 219, 222
D'Ancona, Alessandro, 278n
D'Ancona, Paolo, 89n
Daniele, singer, 133, 160
Davari, Stefano, 172n, 205n, 229n
De la Fage, A., 123n
Decembrio, Angelo Camillo, 28n, 29, 44, 46
Dell'Abbadia, Uguccione, 87n
Della Viola, family, 97; Agostino, 144; Alfonso, 144; Andrea, 144, 180, 183; Francesco, 144; Zampolo, 144, 180, 183
Desprez, Josquin, vii, 1, 80, 85, 98, 132–3, 141, 148, 152–3, 156–7, 169, 171, 179, 193–5, 200–1, 208, 216–17, 224, 234–5, 256, 258, 264, 272, 287, 290–1; at Ferrara, 202–7; 'Scaramella', 108; *Missa 'Hercules dux ferrarie'*, 121, 207, 238, 241–49, 264, 289; 'Miserere', 129, 206–7, 261–5; 'Virgo salutiferi', 206–7; 'Ile fantazies de Joskin', 226, 271, 276–7; *Missa 'Fortuna desperata'*, 227; *Missa 'L'homme armé super voces musicales'*, 227, 240, 243; other works, 242–3
Diario ferrarese (DF), 19n, 25n, 42n, 93, 129, 278n, 279n
Dietrich, Sixt, 132
Diotisalvi, don Angelo,
Disertori, Benedetto, 235, 258n
Doglio, Federico, 127n
Domarto, 217, 234
Domenico da Piacenza, 70–2, 178
Domenico controbasso, 180
Domenico de Ferraria, 23
Donati, Girolamo, 206n
Donatus, 96n
Dossi, Dosso, 204
Dufay, Guillaume, 1, 2, 23, 31, 34–40, 43n, 48, 52–7, 61, 63, 69, 78, 79n, 80, 83, 110–11, 114, 117, 123, 140, 152, 168, 199, 217, 232, 234–5, 239, 243, 250, 252, 266; 'C'est bien raison', 12, 34, 36–8, 47; 'Seigneur Leon' (attributed), 58
Dunstable, John, 52–3, 60–1, 63, 231
Dusart, 272

Einstein, Alfred, 106n
Elders, Willem, 247
England, connection with Ferrara, 58ff; as source of singers, 153
English composers, 52–3; music and musicians, 57

Enzellino *piffaro*, 8n
Este family, mythical link to French royal line,
    10; formal link to French crown, 34;
    opinion of Pius II, 86; and Gonzagas, 224;
    alliance with Borgias, 286
Este, Alberto d', 11, 19, 90
Este, Alberto d' (younger brother of Borso), 92
Este, Alfonso I d', 15, 38, 124–5, 127, 129, 139,
    144–6, 147,–8, 153, 159, 161, 181n, 191,
    193, 196–7, 198, 200, 201–4, 205n, 206,
    208, 210, 214n, 267, 281, 285
Este, Alfonso II d', 147n
Este, Azzo VI d', 9
Este, Beatrice d', 89, 113, 124, 127, 197, 198,
    224
Este, Bianca Maria d', 89
Este, Borso d', 3, 29, 35n, 41–2, 68, 86–94, 95,
    101–4, 109–10, 112, 115, 121–2, 123–4,
    130–1, 141, 143, 144, 153, 161, 177–9,
    181, 204, 213, 290
Este, Ercole I d', vii, 15, 41, 44n, 49n, 55, 67, 68,
    71, 77, 87, 89n, 92–5, 104, 108n, 113,
    121–9, 130–7, 140–2, 144–8, 149,
    151–5, 156–76, 179–84, 185–210,
    213–14, 216, 219, 221–4, 226–7,
    229–31, 238–41, 243, 251, 254–5,
    257–8, 260–2, 264–9, 278–9, 281–91
Este, Ercole II d', 15, 88, 96, 103, 245, 249
Este, Ferrante d', 108n, 124, 125, 129, 141,
    198, 200–1, 205n, 209, 267
Este, Francesco d', 42n, 57, 115
Este, Ginevra d', 15, 29, 30n
Este, Gurone d', 15, 42, 89n
Este, Ippolito I d', 67, 103–4, 124–5, 129, 141,
    145–6, 171–2, 191–2, 197, 198, 200–2,
    206, 208, 267, 285
Este, Isabella d', 71, 100n, 124, 131n, 143–6,
    172, 197–9, 200, 201–2, 205n, 208,
    214n, 224–6, 229–30, 267, 269, 282
Este, Isotta d', 15, 65, 109, 110, 116–17
Este, Jacopino d', 279
Este, don Giulio (Julio) d', 124–5, 198, 201,
    208, 267
Este, Leonello d', 3, 15, 27–33, 34, 39, 40,
    41–5, 46–50, 52, 55–7, 59, 61–2, 64–5,
    67–9, 70–1, 77, 79–80, 83n, 84n, 86–7,
    91, 92–3, 95–6, 98–100, 109–10, 115,
    121–2, 123, 130, 141–2, 144, 153, 161,
    213, 224, 231, 250, 278, 290
Este, Lucia d', 30n
Este, Lucrezia Borgia d' (see Borgia, Lucrezia)
Este, Margherita d', 113n
Este, Meliaduse d', 15, 29, 42, 87, 92
Este, Niccolò II d', 8n
Este, Niccolò III d', 3, 11–27, 28, 30–44, 57,
    64–5, 68, 71, 83, 86–7, 89, 92, 100, 113,
    117, 121, 182, 290
Este, Niccolò di Leonello d', 86, 98, 123, 126
Este, Parisina Malatesta d', 11, 16

Este, Rinaldo Maria d', 15, 89n, 112–18, 235,
    279
Este, Sigismondo d' (brother of Ercole), 41, 89n,
    141, 235, 279
Este, Sigismondo d' (son of Ercole), 124–5, 145,
    198
Este, Ugo d', 8n, 11, 18, 25
Eugenius IV, Pope, 13n, 30–2, 39, 45, 49, 56–8,
    78
Evans, Edward, 273n

Fallows, David, 36, 39, 110–12
Fano, Fabio, 35n
Fatini, Giuseppe, 64n
Faugues, 217, 234–5, 239
Fava, Domenico, 15, 42n, 135n, 213n
Fede, Johannes, 48–9, 53–4, 62, 250
Feragut, Bertrand, 26n, 34–40, 83, 250
Ferand, Ernst, 66n
Ferrara, connections with Burgundy, 57;
    interchange with Florence, 57; connections
    with England, 58ff; connections with
    France, 83, 128; connections with
    Hungary, 127; liturgical practice, 61;
    instrumentalists at, 140–5
  book production at, 42–3, 46–7, 89, 96, 104,
    213–27, 230–1
  Castello Vecchio, 17
  Cathedral, 16, 17, 24–7, 31, 49, 51, 74f, 79,
    80, 98n, 213, 286–7
  Certosa, 88–9, 93, 95, 96, 213
  Chapel of Santa Maria di Corte, 44–5, 48,
    50–1, 77, 80, 126, 135–6, 146, 147,
    154–9, 284
  confraternities, 9, 51
  Convent of San Paolo, 98
  Council of, 30–3, 34, 48, 57–8, 78
  humanists at, 28–9, 84, 92–3, 290
  court library, 29, 42, 268
  Palazzo Schifanoia, 89, 90, 101, 130
  Palazzo Vescovile, 78, 198, 289
  patronage of studio painters, 43
  peace treaty, 30
  Piazza Comunale, 127, 279
  plague at, 93, 207
  university, 11, 29, 42, 49n, 51, 65, 78, 115,
    127, 141, 146, 151–2
  theater and sacred spectacle, 137, 143,
    147–8, 206, 278–87
Ferraresi, Giuseppe, 77n, 78n, 79n
Ferrarini, G. M., chronicler, 281n, 284
Feyt, Michele, 133, 176
Fiesco, Bartolomeo, 101n, 178
Fiesco, Leonello, 97
Filargo, Pietro (see Alexander V)
Filiberto, Giovanni (Filibert, Jean), 48–9, 52,
    61, 95n
Filippo da Padova, *piffaro*, 16

Finscher, Ludwig, 167n
Fischer, Kurt von, 20n, 24n
Flanders, 48, 150–2
Flemmyng, Robert, 59, 116
Florence, compared to Ferrara, 7; Council at, 31–3; Baptistry of San Giovanni, 49, 56–7, 62; other aspects, 139, 161f, 230, 267, 277, 285
Fökövi, Ladislas, 99n, 103n, 104n, 171n
Folengo, Teofilo, 129, 206, 262
Fontaine, Pierre, 140
Ford, Wyn K., 58n
Forest, 53, 58–9, 76
Forestani, Simone, 64
Forlì, 78
Fornovo, battle of, 198
Foucard, C., 41n
Fra de san Domenego, el, 222–4
France, alliance with Estensi, 34; and Ferrara, 83, 128; relations with Borso, 87–8; French singers, 150, 152–3; invasion of Italy, 197–8; chanson in Italy, 266f
Franceschini, Adriano, viii, 26n, 49, 50n, 51n, 61, 79n, 80, 81n, 110, 112, 113n, 160, 165n, 169n, 186
Francesco da Lodi, 190
Francis I, King of France, 181n
Frederick III, Emperor, 35n, 88, 93
Frederick the Wise, Duke, 249
Free, John, 116
Fribourg, 56
Frye, Walter, 116, 231
Frizzi, Antonio, 35n
Frost, Robert (= Roberto Inglese), 153

'G. L.' (= Giorgio Luppato?), 283
Gafori, Franchino, 79n, 171n, 229, 241
Galfridus de Anglia, 65, 109, 109n, 110, 115–16
Gallicus, Johannes, 46n
Gallino, Jacomo, 125
Gallo, Alberto, viii, 9n, 35n, 36n, 79n, 285n
Gandini, L. A., 16n, 93n, 182
Gardner, Edmund G., 12n, 28n, 29n, 92n, 113n, 121n, 123n, 126n, 196–7
Garin, Eugenio, 28n, 29n
Gaspare organo, 96n, 113n
Gaspari, Gaetano, 81n, 111n
Gasparo de Alemagna, trumpeter, 180
Gaza, Teodoro, 42
Gerber, Rudolf, 252, 258
Gesuati, order of, 78
Ghinzoni, P., 143n
Gian de Artiganova (= Gian; Gian Cantore), 98n, 152, 200–1, 203–5, 207, 209, 277
Giam de Fiandra, 152
Gill, Joseph, 30n, 31n, 58n
Gilleto Picardo (Gaspar Gyletto), 152n, 176–7
Giorgio de Allemagna, 42

Giostra dell'Amore, 279–80
Giovanni de Avignon, *piffaro*, 17
Giovanni da Francia, 26
Giovanni dal Chitarino, 69
Giovanni dal Monte, 49n, 95n
Giovanni de Groningen, 49n
Giraldi, G. B., 114n
Girardo, don, 156, 183
Girolamo cartolaro, 223
Girolamo soprano, 181
Giustinian, Leonardo, 2, 64, 72, 84
Glarean, Heinrich, 242
Glixon, Jonathan, 60n
Gobert, Giovanni, 49n
Gombert, Nikolaus, 247
Gombosi, Otto, 73n
Gondi, banking firm, 184
Gonzaga, family, 224, 229; Carlo di Francesco, 30n; Margherita, 30, 41, 86, 224; Francesco, 103, 124, 143, 166, 172, 209–10, 224, 269, 281, 282n; Lodovico, 93; Federico, 136n, 145, 166; Clara, 145; Isabella, 209
Gottwald, Clytus, 260n
Gregorio de Alemagna, *piffaro*, 183
Gregorovius, Ferdinand, 197
Gregory XII, Pope, 18, 24
Grillo, Polo, 97, 178, 180
Grossin, 53
Grey, William, 59
Gruyer, G., 43n, 102n
Gualengo, Lodovico, 125
Guarini, Marc'Antonio, 17n, 146n
Guarino, Battista, 92, 99, 125
Guarino of Verona, 11, 28–9, 31–2, 42, 46, 57, 59, 64, 84, 92, 116, 125, 178, 290
Guglielmo Ebreo, 70–2
Guido cantore, 150
Guidonian gamut, 241–2
Gulielmo de Flandria, 180
Gundersheimer, Werner, viii, 9, 12n, 28n, 29n, 31n, 42n, 43n, 90, 92n, 93n, 121, 122n, 124n, 126, 127n, 128, 149, 158n, 179, 181, 196, 198, 215n, 278n
Günther, Ursula, 13n, 20, 21n
Gunthorp, John, 116

Haar, James, 242n, 261n
Haberl, Franz Xaver, 81n, 95n
Hale, John R., 230n
Hamm, Charles, 47n, 52, 54–5, 57n, 61–2, 221n
Haraszti, Emile, 99
Hartfelder, Karl, 152n
Hay, Denis, 18n
Hayne van Ghizeghem, 217, 224, 266, 272
Heartz, Daniel, 73n
Hennequin Coppetrippe, trumpeter, 17

Henry VI, King of England, 59
Hercules, meaning at Ferrara, 243; labors of, 281
Hermann, Hermann Julius, 42n, 118n, 213n, 214, 215n, 220n, 269n
Hersey, George, 45n
Hieronimo cappellano, don, 183
Hill, George F., 43n
Hofhaimer, Paul, 154, 161, 168, 171
Hofmann, Georg, 31n, 32n
Holes, Andrew, 58–9
Hothby, John, 60
Hughes, Andrew, 58n

Ilardi, Vincent, viii, 88n
Innocent VIII, Pope, 186–7, 191–2, 207
Innsbruck, connection with Ferrara, 161
Isaac, Heinrich, 1, 132, 157, 165, 201, 204–5, 207, 230, 234, 277, 291

Jachetto de Cambrai, 152, 180
Jachetto de Marvilla (Jachetto cantore), 166–7, 183, 187
Jacob, E. F., 59n
Jacomo Gualterio 'de Ulandia', 151, 180
Jacomo de Bologna, 97
Jacopo da Bologna, 8n
Jaquet of Mantua, 257
Jahn, F., 68n
Janes, M., 150
Janue, Antonius, 252
Japart, Jean, 138, 153, 176, 217, 224, 226, 239, 272–3, 280
Jeppesen, Knud, 107n, 108n, 244
Jhan, Maistre, 264
Johannes ab arpa de Anglia, 60, 115
Johannes Gallicus . . . ordinis fratrum minorum, 190–1
Johannes presbyter Londini, 49, 50n, 61, 80, 115
Johannes Ferrariensis, chronicler, 28, 42n, 44, 50
John XXII, Pope, 75
John XXIII, Pope, 13, 19, 24, 201
Josquin (see Desprez)
Joye, Gilles, 110, 114, 115, 272
Julius II, Pope, 191–5, 208n

Kämper, Dietrich, 277n
Kallenberg, P., 9n
Kanazawa, Masakata, 56n, 155n, 216n, 250n, 251–2, 254, 256
Kantorowicz, Ernst, 42n, 115n
Karp, Theodore, 273n
Kellman, Herbert, viii, 205n, 207n
Kinkeldey, Otto, 71n
Kirsch, Edith, 35n

Kristeller, Paul Oskar, 115n, 123n
Krombsdorfer, Nikolaus, 161

Landini, Francesco, 2
Lannoy, Colinet de, 233, 235, 272
Laurent, V., 32n
Lazzari, Antonio, 11n, 12n, 38n
Leay, Gerard de, 47n, 48, 49n, 57, 61
Legrant, Johannes, 114
Lenaerts, Rene, 242n
Leo X, Pope, 154, 261
Leonard of Chios, Archbishop, 39
Leonardo dal chitarrino, lutenist, 16, 100
Levi, Eugenia, 105n
Lippi, Raffaelo Brandolino, 99, 122, 123n
Litterick, Louise, 268n
Llorens, Jose, 224
Lodi, Signor, viii
Lodi, peace of, 87
Lodovico da Padova, 70
Lodovico da Bologna, *piffaro*, 183
Long, Michael, viii, 270n
Longaval, Antonio, 153, 264
Longhi, Roberto, 106n
Lorch, Maristella, 12n, 127n
Lorenzo da Modena, don, 180
Louis XII, King of France, 128, 200, 202, 206
Lowinsky, Edward, 46n, 176n, 206n, 207n, 260–2
Luchino da Campo, 13n
Lucia da Narni, Suor, 129, 196
Lucido, trumpeter, 140–1, 180, 183
Luther, Martin, 249
Luzio, Antonio, 143n, 278n
Lymburgia, Johannes de, 55

Macey, Patrick, 264
Machiavelli, Jacomo and Baldassare, 208
Madoche, Golinus, 95n
Maffei, Rafaello, 99
Magri, Guglielmo de', 118n
Malacise, tenorista, 97, 178, 180–1
Malatesta, Carlo, 21; Pandolfo, 13n; Sigismondo Pandolfo, 30n
Malcort, 272
Malvezzi, N., 19n
Manfredi, Carlo, 161
Manfredi, Feltrino, 172
Maniates, Rika, 247
Mantua, 96, 229, 266–7
Manuscripts
  Aosta, Bibl. del Seminario, 55, 58, 60
  Berlin, Deutsche Staatsbibliothek, MS 40098 ('Glogauer Liederbuch'), 269
  Berlin 78.C.28, 111, 117
  Berlin, Deutsche Staatsbibl., Mus. theor. MS 1599, 112n

Bologna Q 15, 24, 55–6
Bologna Q 16, 267
Brussels, 9126, 241, 249
Cividale, Museo Archeologico, MSS LXIII, XCVIII, 24
Dijon 517, 280
Escorial IV.a.24, 111, 118
Escorial V.III.24, 111, 117
Florence 229, 108, 226, 230, 273, 277, 280
Florence 112*bis*, 56
Florence, Bibl. Naz. Centrale, MS Magl XIX, 164–7, 108n
Florence, Bibl. Naz. Centrale, MS Magl XIX, 176, 60n
Florence 27, 60n, 107
Florence 2439, 108
Florence, Bibl. Naz. Centrale, MS II.1. 232, 264n
Ithaca, Cornell Univ. Library, MSS Bd. Rare BX C36 0635, 74–7
Jena 3, 241
London, British Library, Add 5465, 117
London-Paris-Modena partbooks (see List of MSS), 261
London, British Library, Add 28025, 74
London, British Library, Egerton 2954, 112n
Lucca, Archivio di Stato ('Codice Strohm'), 60
Milan 2267, 241
Milan 2269, 255
Milan 2268, 171n
Modena, Biblioteca Estense, MS V.G. 12 (Latin 429) (Bible of Borso d'Este), 89–91, 96n, 142, 213
Modena, Biblioteca Estense, MS Alpha X.2.14 (Latin 209), 66n
Modena, Biblioteca Estense, Mod A, 20–1, 24
Modena, Biblioteca Estense, Mod B, 48, 51–63, 75–7, 115n, 160, 231–2, 250
Modena, Biblioteca Estense, Mod C_1, C_2, 155, 160, 171, 216–17, 219–22, 224, 250, 251–2
Modena, Biblioteca Estense, Mod D, 136, 168, 216–17, 222, 224, 233–5, 239
Modena, Archivio di Stato, polyphonic fragments (Mod E), 136, 216–17, 222, 224, 233, 234, 239
Modena, Biblioteca Estense, Mod F, 199n, 208, 216, 217, 224, 226–7
Modena, Biblioteca Estense, MS Alpha H. 1, 13, 225n, 269n
Montecassino 871, 122, 152
Munich 3154, 168, 171n, 254–5
Naples, Bibl. Nazionale, MS VI.E.40, 239
Oxford 213, 20, 23, 36, 111, 117–18
Padua, Biblioteca Capitolare, MS A. 17, 206
Paris, Bibl. Nationale, MS Nouv. acq. f. frc. 6771 ('Reina'), 20n

Paris, Bibl. Nationale, MS Res. Vm⁷ 676, 283n
Porto 714, 65, 67, 80m, 104, 109–118
Rome, Biblioteca Casanatense, MS 2151, 81n
Rome, Biblioteca Casanatense, MS 2856, 106, 115, 138, 143, 153, 168n, 216, 217, 224–5, 226, 268, 269–71, 280
Segovia, Catedral, MS s.s., 258, 280, 287n
Seville-Paris MS (see List of MSS), 106n, 273 106n, 273
Trent 90, 56, 76
Trent 87, 60, 111, 114, 118
Trent 92: 58, 60
Vatican, Biblioteca Apostolica Vaticana, MS Barb. lat. 613 (Bible of Niccolò III), 35
Vatican, Biblioteca Apostolica Vaticana, Cap. Sistina 15, 56
Vatican, Biblioteca Apostolica Vaticana, Cap. Sistina 35 and 51: 170
Vatican, Biblioteca Apostolica Vaticana, MS Rossiana 455, 81n, 112n
Vatican 1411 (see List of MSS), 117
Vienna 4809 (see List of MSS), 241
Verona 759 (see List of MSS), 171n
Marchettus of Padua, 2, 82
Marcho da Norsa, trumpeter, 180
Marescalcho, Zoanne, 180
Marix, Jeanne, 16n, 17n, 68n, 114n
Martin V, Pope, 3, 19
Martinella, La, 226, 235, 271, 273–6
Martinez, Marie Louise, 25n
Martini, Johannes, 131–2, 133, 148, 151, 153–6, 160–1, 165n, 167–72, 181, 184, 187, 188, 200, 202, 217, 222, 224, 226, 229–30, 233–9, 250–8, 269–71, 273, 279–80, 287
Martini, Thomas, 167
Martini, Petrus, 167
Mathio de Parixe (Mathias Cantore), 180, 183
Matteo de la violetta, 97
Medici, 163, 230; Cosimo de', 33; Lorenzo de', 166, 167n; Piero and Giovanni, 123
Meier, Bernhard, 109, 110n, 242n
Meiss, Millard, 91n
Menut, A. D., 14n
Mercury, 90
Meyere, Jacques de, 167
Michelangelo, 261
Michele *piffaro*, 183, 282
Michele tedesco *piffaro* (in Leonello's time), 69
Michele de Ipry, 150, 180
Michelet, 60n
Michels, A., 70n
Michels, U., 80n
Milan, 3, 8, 20, 26, 68, 80, 96, 133, 139, 148, 169, 175–6, 229, 240, 255
Milano, Francesco da, 144
Minieri Riccio, C., 122n
Mirandola, Galeotto della, 89

Mitchell, R. J., 59n, 113n, 116n
Modena, 12, 88
Molinet, 272
Mommsen, T. F., 8n
Monferrato, Lucrezia, 113
Monstrelet, Enguerrand de, 16n, 19n, 20–1
Montecatini, Antonio, 162, 239
Montefeltro, Oddantonio de, 109
Montepulziano, Francesco da, 140; Stefano da, 140, 183
Montolino, Blasio, 97, 178
Moores, J. D., 103n
Morales, Cristóbal de, 247
Morselli, A., 103n, 171n
Morton, Robert, 110, 224, 231, 271, 272
Motta, Emilio, 68n, 96n, 97n, 105n, 132n, 167n
Mouton, Jean, 38, 181n
Muratori, Lodovico Antonio, 12n, 15n, 31n, 35n
Muris, Johannes de, 80, 82, 112, 114, 173
Murray, Bain, 162, 165n

Naples, 16, 41, 45, 122–3, 239, 267
Nappi, Cesare, 110–11
Nerici, L., 60n
Newcomb, Anthony, viii, 156n
Niccolo Fiorentino, don, 191
Niccolò Philippo de Olanda, 47, 50, 80
Niccolò d'Olanda, 151, 161, 180–2
Niccolò de Beccariis, 47
Niccolò Tedesco, 27n, 47, 50, 60, 72, 95–7, 161, 178
Niccolo, trumpeter, 113n
Nicolo da Modena, trumpeter, 178
Nigrisoli, Girolamo, 65, 109, 116
Noble, Jeremy, viii, 168n, 186n, 187, 205n
Noblitt, Thomas, 168n, 254–5
Novati, Francesco, 11n
Nuremberg, 68n

Obrecht, Jacob, 131, 151–2, 156–7, 162–4, 171, 194, 207–10, 216, 227, 234–5, 243, 258, 264n, 271–2, 291
Ockeghem, Johannes, 199, 208, 217, 224, 227, 233, 234–5, 239, 243, 248, 266, 272
Odhecaton, 268
Orbo, Giovanni, 105
Oriola, Pietro, 122
Oresme, Nicolas of, 14, 83
Orto, Marbriano de, 171
Osthoff, Helmuth, vii, 202n, 204n, 205, 207n, 242n, 261, 280, 291
Ottinetto, 174, 176
Owens, Jessie Ann, viii, 101n, 118n, 177n

Padua, 3, 7, 8, 25, 27
Paganuzzi, Enrico, 8n, 230n
Palestrina, Giovanni Pierluigi da, 244, 247
Pallavicino, Gaspar, 84n
Paneto, Baptista, 286
Panofsky, Erwin, 42n
Pardi, Giuseppe, 28n, 30n, 32, 39, 41n, 42n, 44n, 45, 46n, 47n, 86n, 88n, 89n, 92n, 93n, 94, 95n, 97n, 102n, 153n, 279n
Parma, 25
Paseto, Giordano, 206
Paslewe, Thomas, 116
Paul III, Pope, 247
Pedros, 153, 180, 183
Pelczer, Ulrich (see Udorigo de Constantia)
Pellegrino, Ser, 16
Peragulfus, 60n
Perino, trumpeter, 178
Perkins, Leeman, 123, 242n
Perugia, 139
Perugia, Matteo da, 20, 26
Pesenti, Michele, 143, 267
Pessano, Ambrogio da, 26
Petrarch, 8, 11
Petrobelli, Pierluigi, 8n
Petrucci, Ottaviano, dei, 107–8, 206–7, 241, 243, 260
Peverada, Enrico, 24, 27n, 79n, 151n
Philip the Fair, King of Castile, 249
Philip the Good, Duke of Burgundy, 17, 57, 62, 68
Philippo de Primis, 193–5
Philippo de San Zorzo, copyist, 221, 222, 223–4
Philippon (Basiron), 162, 225, 239, 272
Piedro, maestro de ragazzi, 150
Piedrantonio de Bologna, trumpeter, 140, 183
Pierino, trumpeter, 67
Piero de Augustino, trombone, 180, 183–4
Piero Picardo, 152n
Pietro de Luciano, 180
Pietro Greco (= Pietro da Candia Greco), 150, 153, 187
Pietro soprano, 180
Pietrobono dal Chitarrino, 2, 16, 46, 69, 96–108, 141, 143, 178, 181
Pietzch, G., 82n, 115n
Pio de Carpi, family, 87n
Piroto, 180
Pirro, Andre, 14n, 34
Pirrotta, Nino, vii, 2, 9, 20, 24n, 32, 64n, 65, 66n, 84n, 99n, 102, 105, 109–110, 116, 122n, 257n
Pisa, 18–19, 24
Pisanello, 29–30, 39, 43, 71–2
Pistoia, Corrado da, 21
Pius II, Pope, 12, 29n, 86, 88
Pius III, Pope, 191–2
Plamenac, Dragan, 39, 106

Planchart, Alejandro, 35, 39
Plato, 83
Plautus, 127, 143, 280–1, 282, 284, 286
Plummer, John, 53, 58, 60–1, 76
Plutarch, 29
Polk, Keith, viii, 16n, 67, 69n
Pomposa, Abbey of, 112–13
Pope, Isabel, 155n
Pound, Ezra, 12n
Povoledo, Elena, 278n
Power, Leonel, 53, 58–9, 61, 76, 231
Powers, Harold, 242n
Prando da Verona, 70
Prato, Antonio Monti da, 26
Prioris, Johannes, 206
Prisciani, Pellegrino, 90
Prizer, Wiliam, viii, 107n, 136, 143, 229n
Procter, R., 213n
Preposto, Johannes, 95n
Prosperi, Adriano, 185n
Prosperi, Bernardino, 136, 144, 199, 282
Ptolemy, 82
Pyamour, 53, 58, 60
Pythagoras, 82

Raganello, trumpeter, 140–1, 183
Rajna, P., 9n, 15n
Raimondo, Bartolomeo, 180
Rainaldo de Cambrai, 152, 180
Rainaldo del Chitarrino, 97, 143, 180, 183
Ramos, Bartolomeo, 111, 114
Randel, Don, 74
Raynerio, 133
Reame, Domenego del, 140
Reaney, Gilbert, 20n, 23n, 36n
Reese, Gustave, 67n
Reggio, 12, 88
Rehm, Wolfgang, 48n
Reidemeister, P., 117n
René d'Anjou, 36
Renée of France, Princess, 15
Reynolds, Christopher, viii
Richardin dall'arpa, 97
Richental, Ulrich von, 19n
Ripa, Alberto da, 144
Roberti, Anna de', 113
Roberti, Ercole de', 106, 128, 198, 289
Roberto da Ferrara, 156
Roberto Inglese, singer *c*. 1500, 150, 153
Robertus de Anglia, 81, 109n, 110–118, 231
Rome, 154; Papal Chapel, 49, 57, 58, 95, 134; and Johannes Martini, 169–70
Rore, Cipriano, 245, 265
Rosenberg, Charles, viii, 88n, 89n, 90, 95n, 126n
Rossetti, Biagio, 128
Rossetto, trumpeter, 140
Rossi, Vittorio, 64n

Rosso, trumpeter, 183
Rubeis, Laurentius de, 199
Rubsamen, Walter, 106n, 206n
Ruggiero da Venezia, 97
Rühmer, E., 101n
Ryder, Alan, 121n, 122n
Rykelin, Johannes, 163–4

Sabadino degli Arienti, Giovanni, 90n, 122n, 157–8, 221, 286
Sabbadini, R., 64n
St Alban, 60
St Antoine de Vienne, 13–14
St Anthony of Padua, 61–2
St Dominic, 62
St Francis, 61–2
St George, 25, 61–2, 69, 74, 81n, 90, 93, 96n, 126, 137, 146–7, 279
St James of Compostela, 147
St John the Baptist, 146–7
St Marco, 146–7
St Maurelius, 25, 62
St Peter, 147
St Thomas of Hereford, 60
Salamon dall'arpa, 97
Salmen, Walter, 69n
Salmi, Mario, 112n
Saluzzo, Rizzarda da, 12, 30, 121
San Bernardino of Siena, 78
San Domenico, church of, 137
San Francesco, church of, 137
San Gotthardo, 235
San Marco, offerta di, 137
San Michele de Medicina, monastery of, 35
San Niccolo of Ferrara, monastery of, 18
San Paolo, Carmelite monastery, 9, 51
San Romano, church of, 147
Sandley, 53, 58, 60
Santoro, Caterina, 100n
Sardi, Giuseppe, 44n
Sartori, Claudio, 26n, 35n, 36n
Savonarola, Girolamo, 129, 196–7, 257, 265
Savonarola, Michele, 29, 178
Savoy, 31–2, 152
Scalabrini, Giuseppe, 17n, 18, 25n, 27n, 35, 77n, 79, 80n
Scaligeri, dynasty, 8
Scaramella, La, 108
Schirmer, W. F., 58n, 59n
Schoop, Hans, 20n, 23, 117n
Schrade, Leo, 46n
Schrevel, A. C. de, 163
Schuler, Manfred, 131–2, 168n
Scocola, 90, 105
Scott, Ann Besser, 47n, 52, 54, 55, 57n, 58, 59n, 61–2, 76, 221n
Seay, Albert, 78n, 80n, 82n, 112n
Secular music, Italian, 64f., 65, 104, 138, 266–77

Selmi, Dr, viii
Seregni, G. G., 197n
Sestola, Girolamo da, 'il Coglia', 98, 138, 145n, 200–5, 210, 264, 267
Seznec, Jean, 91n
Sforza, rule, 98n, 224, 229
Sforza, Anna Maria, 124, 139, 197
Sforza, Ascanio, 124, 153, 157, 188, 195, 202, 226, 240
Sforza, Filippo Maria, 93
Sforza, Francesco, 66n, 88, 99, 100–2
Sforza, Giangaleazzo, 176
Sforza, Ippolita, 93
Sforza, Lodovico, 124
Sforza, Sforza Maria, 105
Sforza, Tristano, 89
Shakespeare, William, 91n, 291
Sherr, Richard, viii, 208n
Sigismund, Emperor, 30, 58, 60, 62
Signorello, Alessandro, 150, 223, 225–6, 269
Simeoni, L., 13n, 15n
Simone de Pavia, 67n
Sitta, P., 31n, 47n, 177n
Sixtus IV, Pope, 134, 173, 186, 187
Smijers, Albert, 247
'Sonspison', 232
Spaggiari, Angelo, viii
Spagnolo, A., 49n, 230
Spagnolo, Bartolomeo, 183
Spagnolo, Pietro, 136n
Spain, 150, 153
Spataro, Giovanni, 229, 241
Spencer, Robert, 101
Staehelin, Martin, 101n, 204n, 217n, 227
Stefano sonadore, 100–1
Stephano da Savoia, *piffaro*, 180
Stone, 53, 58, 60, 76
Strohm, Reinhard, 60
Strozzi, Ercole, 198, 207, 260
Strozzi, Tito Vespasiano, 92, 96n, 260
Strunk, Oliver, 83n, 173n
Suardi, G. F., 65
Suchar, Peter, 112
Suetonius, 96n
Syropoulos, Sylvester, 32n

Tani, Gino, 70n, 72
Tantino, Costantino, 45, 98n, 123, 145, 180
Tarquin de Bruges, Victor, 175–7, 181
Tavelli, Bishop Giovanni, 27, 49, 77–80, 81n
Terence, 281
Thibault, Genevieve, 8n
Thomaso, Antonio di, trumpeter, 140, 183
Tinctoris, Johannes, 99, 103, 123, 156, 173, 229, 234, 238, 239, 241–2, 290–1
Tiptoft, John, 116
Tiraboschi, Girolamo, 225n
Tomasi da Siena, Mathio Marian, 180

Tomaso da Faenza, trumpeter, 178
Toscanelli, Paolo, 11, 29, 92
Touront, 272
Traversari, Ambrogio, 32, 64, 78
Trecento, musical life in, 2, 3, 7–10
Tromboncino, Bartolomeo, 143, 267, 282
Trombone, Piero, 141
Trotti, Giacomo, 163
Troubadours, 9
Trowell, Brian, 60n
Tura, Cosimo, 25, 81, 98n, 289
Turrini, Giuseppe, 230n

Udorigo da Constantia, 132, 153, 180
Ugolino di Orvieto, 51, 74, 77–85, 110–12, 114, 229
Ugolinus de Brabant, 48, 49, 50n, 80
Urbano de Genoa, 144
Urbino, 280

Valdrighi, L. F., 38n, 72n, 131, 160, 231n
Valenti, Filippo, viii, 113n
Valentini, Cesare, 174
Valois, Noel, 18n, 24n
Van den Borren, Charles, 34, 35
Vander Straeten, Edmond, 161, 204, 205n
Van der Velde, H. E. J. M., 152n
Vaqueras, Bertrand, 171
Vaughan, Richard, 285n
Venice, 25, 27, 30, 38, 186–7, 196, 206
Venturi, Adolfo, 43n, 87n, 89n, 97, 98, 106n, 113n
Venus, 91, 279–80
Verbonnet (= Ghiselin), Jean, 150, 152, 171, 202, 217, 224, 258, 269, 272, 275
Verona, 7, 8, 229, 230n
Vespasiano da Bisticci, 59
Vespasiano da Bisticci, 59
Vicentino, Nicola, 265
Vieze, Andrea dalle, 214–15, 219–20, 223, 231
Vieze, Cesare dalle, 214n
Villa, Agostino, 87
Vincinet, 217, 234
Vincenza da Modena (= Vincenzo Lusignano), 131, 145
Virdung, Sebastian, 132
Virgil, 29
Visconti, family, 8, 14, 30, 38, 102
Visdomino, in Ferrara, 146, 147, 206n
Vittorino da Feltre, 46

Wangermée, Robert, 66n
Warburg, Aby, 90
Ward, Tom, 56n, 61, 252n
Weerbecke, Gaspar, 164–5, 171, 202, 217, 234, 255

Weinmann, Karl, 99n
Wells Cathedral, 58
Weyden, Roger van der, 42n, 115
Wilkins, Ernest H., 8n
Willaert, Adrian, 144, 145, 257, 265
Winternitz, Emanuel, 91n
Wolff, Arthur S., 224n, 225n, 273n
Woodfield, Ian, 144
Woodley, Ronald, 157n
Woodward, W. H., 28n, 46n
Wright, Craig, 14n, 36n, 39, 65n, 66n, 152n, 232n

Zachara da Teramo, Antonio, 24

Zambotti, Bernardino, 25n, 44n, 137n, 146–7, 186n, 202n, 206n, 235, 278n, 279n, 280n, 281, 282n, 285n, 286, 287n
Zanetto tenorista, 69, 97n, 100
Zarlino, Gioseffo, 79, 121, 257
Zarri, G., 196n
Zilio da Ferrara, trumpeter, 140, 183
Zilioli, Giacomo and Zilio, 12
Zoanne de Alemagna, 96, 142, 178, 180
Zoanne, frate, 170
Zoanne, Guido, 150
Zoanne de Troia de Franza, 180
Zoanne trombone, 183
Zohane de Trento, 101n
Zorzi, Luigi, 127n

.

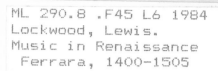